THE GLOBAL SOCIAL POLICY READER

THE GLOBAL SOCIAL POLICY READER

Edited by Nicola Yeates and Chris Holden

This edition published in Great Britain in 2009 by

The Policy Press
University of Bristol
Fourth Floor
Beacon House
Queen's Road
Bristol BS8 1QU
UK

Tel +44 (0)117 331 4054
Fax +44 (0)117 331 4093
e-mail tpp-info@bristol.ac.uk
www.policypress.org.uk

North American office:
The Policy Press
c/o International Specialized Books Services (ISBS)
920 NE 58th Avenue, Suite 300
Portland, OR 97213-3786, USA
Tel +1 503 287 3093
Fax +1 503 280 8832
e-mail info@isbs.com

British Library Cataloguing in Publication Data
A catalogue record for this book is available from the British Library.

Library of Congress Cataloging-in-Publication Data
A catalog record for this book has been requested.

ISBN 978 1 84742 377 1 paperback
ISBN 978 1 84742 378 8 hardcover

Cover design by Qube Design Associates, Bristol
Front cover: image kindly supplied by Getty Images
Printed and bound in Great Britain by Hobbs the Printers, Southampton

Contents

Contents

Sources of extracts

List of figures and tables

Figures

Tables

Acronyms and abbreviations

ALBA	Bolivarian Alternative for the People of Our Americas
APEC	Asia-Pacific Economic Cooperation
ASEAN	Association of Southeast Asian Nations
BNI	Basic Needs Index
BWI	Bretton Woods institution
CTT	currency transactions tax
ECHP	European Community Household Panel
ECOSOC	(United Nations) Economic and Social Council
ETI	Ethical Trade Initiative
EU	European Union
FCTC	Framework Convention on Tobacco Control
FSI	Food Security Index
FTAA	Free Trade Area of the Americas
GATT	General Agreement on Tariffs and Trade
GDI	gross domestic income
GDP	gross domestic product
GHG	global health governance
GIN	global issues network
GNP	gross national product
GPPN	global public policy network
GPPP	global public–private partnership
GSDF	Global Sustainable Development Fund
GSP	global social policy
HBS	household balance sheet
HDI	Human Development Index
HIPCs	heavily indebted poor countries
HPI	Human Poverty Index
ICC	International Criminal Court
ICESCR	International Covenant on Economic, Social and Cultural Rights
ICJ	International Court of Justice
IDA	International Development Association
IFAD	International Fund for Agricultural Development
IFC	International Finance Corporation
IFI	international financial institution
IGO	inter-governmental organisation
ILO	International Labour Organisation
IMF	International Monetary Fund
INGO	international non-governmental organisation
IO	international organisation

IPI	Integrated Poverty Index
ISA	intersectoral action
KWS	Keynesian welfare state
LAS	League of Arab States
LSMS	living standard measurement survey
MASS	Multilateral Agreement on Social Standards
MDG	Millennium Development Goal
MEO	multilateral economic organisation
MERCOSUR	Mercado Común del Sur (Southern Core Common Market)
NAFTA	North American Free Trade Agreement
NEPAD	New Partnership for Africa's Development
NGO	non-governmental organisation
ODA	overseas development assistance
OECD	Organisation for Economic Cooperation and Development
PPP	purchasing power parity or public–private partnership
PRSP	Poverty Reduction Strategy Paper
PWC	Post-Washington Consensus
RWI	Relative Welfare Index
SAARC	South Asian Association for Regional Cooperation
SADC	Southern Africa Development Community
TNC	transnational corporation
TRIMS	trade-related investment measures
TRIPS	trade-related aspects of intellectual property rights
TTC	transnational tobacco company
UN	United Nations
UNDP	United Nations Development Programme
UNHCR	United Nations High Commissioner for Refugees
UNICEF	United Nations Children's Fund
USAID	United States Agency for International Development
WC	Washington Consensus
WHO	World Health Organisation
WSF	World Social Forum
WTO	World Trade Organisation

Acknowledgements

We would like to thank everyone at The Policy Press for their hard work and patience during the process of compiling *The Global Social Policy Reader*. In particular, we would like to thank Leila Ebrahimi, Jo Morton, Emily Watt and Dave Worth, as well as Alan Halfpenny and Margaret Vaudrey. We would also like to thank the original publishers of each of the readings included here for granting us permission to use them.

Introduction

With a clear focus on the global and transnational dimensions of social policy and practice, *The global social policy reader* brings together for the first time in a single volume a range of key texts published since the mid 1990s that elucidate different approaches, themes, issues and debates in this diverse and dynamic area. The last decade has seen global social policy (GSP) becoming integrated into core educational and research programmes in the UK and internationally. As scholars researching and teaching in the field, we were acutely aware that global social policy did not benefit from a reader (or companion) in ways that other core areas of social policy or, for that matter, globalisation studies, do. This Reader aims to bridge the gap. *The global social policy reader* aims to be a resource that will be of interest and use to students throughout their studies, as well as to scholars in global social policy and related areas seeking a single volume that covers key readings and policy texts in the field.

The Reader is designed as a companion text to *Understanding global social policy* (Yeates, 2008a). That volume addressed key global social policy issues across a range of sectors (labour/employment, health, pensions, housing and urban development) and cross-cutting fields (migration, trade, population, and global governance). *Understanding global social policy* and *The global social policy reader* are complementary in a number of senses. First, both volumes focus on the *global* dimensions of social policy, governance and practice; they emphasise the transnational structures, institutions and policy processes that are integral to understanding contemporary social organisation, social welfare and well-being. Second, *The global social policy reader* includes extended extracts of readings, both contextualising and elaborating upon the contemporary debates and issues addressed in *Understanding global social policy*.

In the remainder of this Introduction, we offer an overview of the contextual, thematic and organisational basis of the Reader as a whole. We begin by surveying briefly the broad context of this Reader, looking in particular at the scope of global social policy and its distinctiveness as a field of study and then proceed to outline the structure and organisation of the reader, in which we contextualise the themes and issues covered in each of its sections.

Context

Since the 1990s, global social policy has emerged as a dynamic and expanding field of academic study and research. In the introductory chapter to *Understanding global social policy*, Nicola Yeates (2008b) outlined the main axes of discussion and scholarship shaping the development of this field. There, she clearly delineated the field of global social policy as focusing on the multiple and diverse activities, interactions and ties, and forms of social organisation that link the welfare of people and places across the borders of nation-states around the world. She emphasised the core concerns of GSP as (i) the content and processes of social policy formation in cross-border spheres of governance – be these spheres multilateral, governmental or non-governmental; and (ii) the effects and impacts of cross-border flows of people, goods, services, ideas and finance on the provision, finance and regulation of social welfare. This definition captures the ways in which GSP as a subject of academic research and analysis has come to widen its focus, broadening out from an early initial focus on the practices of an elite set of institutions and policy actors to embrace a more embedded notion of transnationalism which, in addition to those elite practices and organisations, also includes both a wide range of policy dialogues taking place around the world in national, subnational and transnational fora, together with the wide-ranging social forces and processes that both accompany and are formative of 'globalisation' processes.

Thus, GSP still retains at its core the 'practice[s] of supranational actors [embodying] global social redistribution, global social regulation, and global social provision and/or empowerment, and […] the ways in which supranational organisations shape national social policy' (Deacon, Hulse and Stubbs, 1997: 195). But in addition to the focus on the policies and practices of international governmental organisations (IGOs) such as the Bretton Woods institutions (the International Monetary Fund [IMF] and the World Bank) and the United Nations system, international non-governmental organisations (INGOs) such as Oxfam and Save the Children, and private actors such as private consultancy companies and the largest transnational corporations (TNCs), GSP now also embraces the imaginaries, activities and actions of non-elite actors and movements. It also encompasses social policies at national and subnational levels to the extent that they are 'co-determined by global policy actors and are transnational in scope' (Orenstein, 2005: 177-8). This embrace of embedded transnationalism has in turn opened up understandings of the 'globality' of social policy as not just being about 'vertically stacked' levels of government but about relationality – between people and places and an understanding of the world as made up of a dense network of interconnections. It has also opened up for analysis a much wider range of policy actors and institutions involved in global policy formation together with a variety of sites and scales of collective action. As one of us has argued elsewhere (Yeates, 2008b), while the core focus on international organisations remains, there is now also 'increasing focus on the *multiple socio-spatial sites and scales* across which social policy formation occurs, the wider range of global policy actors and the "everyday" transnationalisation of social welfare provision and policy-making'. This attention to a wider range of transnational entities involved in social policy-making has had a number of implications: it has led to a focus on sub-global transnational formations (e.g. regional groupings of countries), the role of non-elite transnational policy actors and their campaigning networks, and a wide range of ways in which transnational social regulation, financing and provision takes place.

Initially confined to social protection and health, global social policy has also expanded to examine a wider range of sectors and policy fields, including social care, labour/employment/livelihoods, education, housing, population and fertility, and utilities (water, energy) and food. Over this time, analysis of and debates about the social welfare impacts of (public and private) policy formation relating to areas such as international trade and corporate governance, development aid financing, debt alleviation and global governance reform have also developed.

The relatively recent emergence and development of GSP as an *academic* subject of study and research in many ways belies its much longer lineage as a *political practice*. The transnational institutions and practices that are often dated back only to the post-Second World War period with the establishment of the General Agreement on Tariffs and Trade (GATT) and the Bretton Woods institutions can in fact be seen in earlier centuries. For example, institutions and practices established as part of colonial rule are earlier forms of global social policy that underpinned the systematic accumulation, extraction and transfer of wealth from colonies to colonisers (Sexton et al, 2008; Yeates, 2008b). And during the 19th and 20th centuries, the world order was characterised by extensive international trade, international migration, transnational corporations and developed international monetary and exchange rate regimes. The political processes and normative values associated with GSP can also be found in examples dating back two centuries of political mobilisation that were international and extended beyond Europe, as can INGO activity in respect of humanitarian aid and relief, care and education. Early 20th-century examples of IGO fora in relation to social security and labour, and attempts at policy cooperation and learning across national borders, abound (Yeates, 2008b). In effect, not only do international cooperation and action on social policy issues long predate what is a relatively recent (circa early 1990s onwards) concern with 'globalisation', but there are numerous historical examples of transnational policy-making fora predating the emergence of post-Second World War global social policy institutions.

Nevertheless, most of the organisations which currently govern social policy at the global level were created following the Second World War, and were shaped by the particular imperatives of, and power relations between, the victorious states in that conflict. Some of these organisations, particularly the international financial institutions of the World Bank and the IMF, have since seen significant developments in the scope and nature of their activities as the world political economy has developed over time and they have sought to adapt to this changing environment. Such extensions and adaptations of function and influence have also been shaped by the dominant power relations of the post-war global political economy. Much of the debate within current global social policy analysis has thus been concerned with the problems of utilising, reforming, resisting or attempting to find alternatives to these organisations, which often function in a manner that is problematic for the development of effective responses to the social challenges of a globalising world.

The multiplicity of these organisations, their overlapping functions, and the differing degrees of power they have over national governments creates great complexity. Even the terminology can be confusing, with authors often using terms such as international 'institution', 'organisation' or 'agency' interchangeably when referring to the same entities. Some of these entities, such as the IMF, the World Bank and the World Trade Organisation (WTO), are perhaps best described as 'institutions', in the sense that they operate on the basis of a clear set of norms, have rule-creating and supervisory functions, and are relatively resistant to change (O'Brien discusses some of these issues in Chapter 3.1, although he chooses to use the term 'organisation' where others might use 'institution'). We have tended to use the term 'international organisation' as a generic term, but also refer to 'institutions' where this seems best suited to the specific context, and readers should be aware of the common practice of authors using multiple terms interchangeably to refer to the same entities.

The various readings in *The global social policy reader* both reflect and expand on the broad developments and themes discussed above. In the next part of this general introduction we outline how the Reader is organised and introduce the key themes of each of the five sections.

Structure and organisation

The first section, 'Rethinking social policy in a globalising world', provides a general introduction to the ways in which globalisation processes are impacting on the ways in which social policy and welfare formations are understood. The readings cover issues of how different understandings and processes of globalisation affect how we think about the making and remaking of social policy, including the rise of supranational and transnational policy organisations and processes. The section also includes extracts that argue in favour of strengthening the role of these organisations in social policy formulation. Overall, this section contains a range of readings expounding on the conceptual, theoretical and methodological aspects of the kinds of rethinking that have developed in recent years in academic social policy.

These issues are picked up in further detail in Section 2, 'Global poverty and inequality'. As this section title suggests, the thematic focus is oriented towards what a global analysis means for the study of and research into poverty and social inequality. A major theme here is the need for common international agreement on definitions and measurements of poverty, although whether this agreement should extend to the construction of data sets that are truly global is debated. Here, too, the gender aspects of global social policy come to the foreground, with a discussion of how current poverty measurements which take little account of the unequal distribution of social resources within households are doomed to failure as a basis for effective policy interventions. These 'technical' issues, of course, are far from being simply that: they are highly political. They are of the utmost significance for global (and national) policy formulation, as they shape what the problems to be addressed are perceived to be and what measures are developed in response.

In Section 3, 'Global policy actors, institutions and processes', the focus turns to major themes and issues in global social policy as a political practice and to the problems and complexities of collective action at the global level. With an emphasis thus on actual global social policy developments and debates, the readings elucidate in particular major manifestations of global social policies and governance mechanisms, such as global public–private partnerships, together with debates about global social regulation through, inter alia, codes of conduct. A major theme in global social policy is the participation of non-state actors, in particular the commercial business sector in the global policy-making process, and a number of the readings reflect this.

The question as to how best to understand the restructuring of social policy in a globalising world is the subject of Section 4, 'Globalisations and welfare transformations'. This is a two-part section, which provides an overview of overarching debates about the impacts of globalisation processes on welfare formations and outcomes. The first is concerned with the disputed impacts of economic globalisation processes upon national welfare states, while the second addresses debates around the political influence of the 'Washington Consensus' on social policy, both nationally and globally. Together, these readings point to a re-evaluation of the role of the state as well as the importance of socio-political conflict and struggle in the making of social policy.

In the final section, 'Global social policy futures', the readings cover contemporary debates about the reform, indeed transformation, of global social policy. Here, the point of departure is what should succeed the Washington Consensus that has dominated scholarly global social policy debate. These questions are not just about social policy content and approaches but about the system of global governance more broadly. The readings offer differing perspectives on what kinds of reforms are needed and on what actions and measures are appropriate. Here, the discussion ranges from democratising existing global organisations to dismantling them, from strengthening the regulation of international competition and economic actors to de-globalising the economy, from instituting the proper financing of global redistribution, through measures such as debt reduction and global levies, to the multilateralisation of global social regulation. As such debates are vibrant in the political community of global policy makers as well as in academic spheres, we have also included extracts from recent Global Commissions.

Each section of the Reader opens with a short editorial introduction to the key themes and debates covered in it, and each chapter is followed by its bibliography. The Reader contains a comprehensive combined author and subject index for ease of reference.

Incorporating 38 readings, we have aimed to be comprehensive in the range of perspectives to include, and to this end we have drawn from academic, policy, and activist sources; radical, progressive/reformist and conservative positions; from the Global South as well as the Global North. Reflecting to a large degree the actual formation of GSP, we have brought together key work in the area from diverse fields of academic study (e.g. social policy, health studies, political science, international political economy), policy texts from international organisations (IOs) and from the quarters of political activism.

The breadth of the field and the wide range of issues and problems across diverse geographical, social, economic and political contexts mean that we have necessarily had to be selective. As regards policy texts, we have confined ourselves to the 'classic' texts of IOs – Declarations etc – that are important in illustrating the general principles shaping GSP, and to key texts of recent Global Commissions. We have not attempted to cover either particular sectors or countries, focusing on drawing out the general issues instead; where particular country or sectoral experiences are addressed, this is by way of illustration of more general themes and issues.

Finally, global social policy, like national social policy, is a dynamic and fast-changing field. To keep abreast of the world of policy debate and analysis we commend *Global Social Policy: An interdisciplinary journal of public policy and social development* (Sage). This journal contains the best available source of up-to-date information in the field. It has a range of full-length academic articles and shorter policy-oriented contributions covering various aspects and dimensions of global social policy, together with review articles and digest sections.

General note

Throughout the Reader, where a reference is given to an author's name without a corresponding year of publication, the reference is to a chapter in the original volume.

References

Deacon, B. with Hulse, M. and Stubbs, P. (1997) *Global social policy: International organisations and the future of welfare*, London: Sage.

Orenstein, M. (2005) 'The new pension reform as global policy', *Global Social Policy*, vol 5, no 2, pp 175-202.

Sexton, S. et al (2008) 'Global population policy', in N. Yeates (ed) *Understanding global social policy*, Bristol: The Policy Press.

Yeates, N. (ed) (2008a) *Understanding global social policy*, Bristol: The Policy Press.

Yeates, N. (2008b) 'The idea of global social policy', in N. Yeates (ed) *Understanding global social policy*, Bristol: The Policy Press.

Section 1

Rethinking social policy in a globalising world

This opening section focuses on the ways in which globalising processes are recasting social policy, as a field of academic study, research and analysis and as a political practice. Since the 1990s 'globalisation' has generated a dynamic and productive debate across the social sciences about the characteristics of contemporary social life. Questions about the nature of globalisation, its onset, causes and effects, are regularly the subject of academic debate, with such debates also informing social and political practices of governmental and non-governmental entities worldwide. Whether or not one fully accepts all the tenets of the globalisation thesis – the general idea that contemporary social life is predominantly characterised by dense, extensive, time-space compressing networks of interconnections and interdependencies routinely transcending nation state borders – it is now established within and outside academia that truly *global* analyses are needed to comprehend the dynamics of social policy formation and its effects. In the academic domain, this entails deconstructing the methodological nationalism of social (policy) analyses that revolve around a conception of society as coterminous with state borders. It is now accepted that the determinants of social organisation, positioning, identities and outcomes in any one country do not solely reside within it, and that links, ties and activities that transcend national borders and that interact with those occurring within them generate the need for intellectual innovation to develop appropriate conceptual, theoretical and methodological frameworks. The readings in this section cover different aspects of this imperative to 'change gear' from methodologically nationalist analyses and practices of social policy to methodologically transnationalist (global) ones.

The first reading, by Bob Deacon, Michelle Hulse and Paul Stubbs, sets out the case for rethinking social policy in a global(isation) context. Deacon et al argue that social policy needs to move from analyses of cross-national comparisons of welfare states to focus on the global context and dynamics of social policy formation, and that seemingly 'local' and 'national' social issues cannot be properly understood without reference to their wider global dimensions. They also argue for the need to differentiate between different kinds of globalisation processes involved in the remaking of social policy. For example, international economic competition, the globalisation of welfare markets or global migrations are implicated in social policy transformations in different ways. It is perhaps their argument that globalisation brings new

1

actors into social policy formation, with the making of social policy being an established transnational practice of international governmental and non-governmental agencies, that has taken particular hold in the analysis of globalisation and social policy. Drawing attention to a distinct *global* institutional arena of social politics and policy, they underline the need to focus on the implicit and explicit social policies of global governmental and non-state actors that influence national social policy formation. These actors are not just part of the context of social policy formation: they are key social policy actors in their own right. In Deacon et al's account, welfare states in any one country need to be regarded less as the products of national politics and policies of that country alone than as the outcomes of co-determined processes involving a variety of national and supranational agencies.

Social science is not only about understanding society but also shaping it. So too in global social policy. A notable feature of global social policy analysis is its combination of a particular analytical stance with a set of normative arguments; namely, that alongside the need to analyse social policy as a transnational practice is the need to develop greater transnationalism in actual social policies. Here, Deacon et al's arguments about the need for a coherent analysis of global social policy find particular force in their insistence on a stronger and more effective global social policy based on social democratic principles. They bring the normative basis of global social policy to the fore in also addressing its political dimensions. For example, they argue that the challenges of theorising non-territorially-based, cosmopolitan citizenship encounter the political problem of forging global social policy constructed around universal rights that are not only transnational but have common, worldwide purchase. And the analytical necessity of recasting social and economic equity from a global framework is matched by the political challenges of forging a socio-institutional basis for transnational social solidarity as well as of forging international cross-class alliances in support of comprehensive social policy.

Any student or scholar of social policy will know that the practice of analysis in the service of social reform has a venerable history, and the second reading, by Vic George and Paul Wilding, is also illustrative of that tradition. Setting out ten arguments for a developed global social policy – from the realities of greater global interdependence to supporting global human rights to states' need for global policies to secure their legitimacy – they summarise well the case for better policy coordination between governments including the need to embed global economic policy within a vision of global society and to connect economic and social policy at whatever level of government or policy scale. These debates are subsequently explored further across the volume and especially in Section 5 'Global Social Policy Futures'.

As the Deacon et al reading testifies, an enduring theme in global social policy concerns the processes and dynamics of policy co-determination; in particular the balance of power between the various actors involved across the policy process which is crucial to the nature of proposed policy reforms and the relative success (or failure) in implementing them. The third and fourth readings, by Nicola Yeates and Mitchell Orenstein, address these concerns. Yeates warns against 'linear' accounts of the globalisation–social policy nexus that envisage the convergence of national welfare states around narrow policy goals, and against elitist accounts of global social policy development that privilege the role of selected political and institutional actors over others. Emphasising a wider conception of global social policy and governance, that looks beyond the bureaux and boardrooms of elite agencies (e.g. international organisations) and actors (e.g. government officials, NGOs, policy experts), Yeates proposes a conception and politics of global social policy situated in the context of a political and policy process spanning multiple sites and spheres. She emphasises the wider political process shaping global social policy development, including the 'local' as a site of global social policy formation as much as organisations like the World Bank, IMF, the WTO and the UN. That reading also emphasises the necessity of an *embedded transnationalism* that takes account of the ways in which globalising forces 'in and down here' as well as 'out and up there' are enmeshed.

Global social policy operates within a methodological transnationalist framework, but what is involved in researching global social policy? The final reading in this section, extracted from a study into the 'new' pension reforms by Mitchell Orenstein, addresses key theoretical, conceptual and methodological aspects of global social policy research and analysis. Orenstein's study focuses on the role of transnational actors in shaping domestic pension policy reforms, and he discusses the conceptual and methodological issues arising. These include how to identify and distinguish transnational actors from national ones (i.e. who and what is a transnational actor?), and how to disentangle the policy influences of transnational actors from those of domestic actors. This latter question is made more complex by virtue of the fact that transnational actors often operate as 'proposal actors', shaping the preferences of domestic actors which then adopt policy proposals (in this case, 'new' pension reforms) as their own. We do not include the details of Orenstein's research findings (these are summarised in his chapter in *Understanding Global Social Policy*), but it is worth noting that his results indicate variation in the nature and extent of the influence of transnational actors such as the World Bank in shaping domestic pension policy reforms around the world. Thus, his findings indicate unevenness and multiplicity in the globalisation–social policy relationship generally, and in the effects of global policy actors in social policy reforms in particular that Nicola Yeates' reading highlights.

Collectively, these readings variously argue for and attest to the importance of focusing on the transnational and global dimensions of social politics and policies, and the need to treat them less as optional add-ons than as integral to social policy formation. The readings in subsequent sections explore further the implications of globalising social policy across different issues and areas.

Chapter 1.1

Globalism and the study of social policy

Bob Deacon, Michelle Hulse and Paul Stubbs

The globalization of social policy and the socialization of global politics

Traditionally social policy has been the subject concerned with those state and non-governmental activities within one country that are designed to intervene in the operations of the free market in the interests of social protection and social welfare. Central to social policy has been the income transfer mechanisms whereby the employed support those excluded from work through age, infirmity, family responsibilities and the failures of the market.

In the present phase of world economic development however social policy activities traditionally analysed within and undertaken within one country now take on a supranational and transnational character. This is so for several reasons. Economic competition between countries may be leading them to shed the economic costs of social protection in order to be more competitive (social dumping) unless there are supranational or global regulations in place that discourage this (Kosonen, 1995). International migratory pressures generate the political logic that there could be income transfers between nations to stave off the political consequences of mass migration (Castles, 1993). Similarly common markets in capital and labour between countries give rise to the possibility of a supranational authority providing at a supranational level the social citizenship rights denied or threatened at national level (Baubock, 1994).

[...]

The relative decline of the power of national governments in the face of globally mobile capital challenges the traditional frameworks of social policy analysis in a number of ways.

First, it suggests that the *supranational and global actors* need to be given more attention in explanations of changing social policy. Because frameworks have derived from work on economically privileged North and West welfare states they have tended to downplay the importance of background institutions like the IMF and the World Bank. Now that social policy analysis (Esping-Andersen, 1996) is encompassing less economically privileged South and East welfare states, and because the sustainability of the welfare states of Europe is questioned by global economic competition, this relative neglect of these institutions is no longer justified. [...] They are now important influences on national social policy.

Secondly it introduces a new field of enquiry into the subject. This field encompasses what we call the supranationalization or globalization of social policy instruments, policy and provision. This supranationalization of social policy takes three (at least) forms. These are supranational regulation, supranational redistribution and supranational provision.

The first form embraces those mechanisms, instruments and policies at a supranational and global level that seek to regulate the terms of trade and the operation of firms in the interests of social protection and welfare objectives. At a global level such instruments and policies are at a primitive stage of development. The key issue here is whether the social regulation of capitalism practised by the European Union can and will be elevated to the global playing field. It is argued by some (Lang and Hines, 1996) that the General Agreement on Tariffs and Trade and the new World Trade Organization should embrace social and environmental concerns. These concerns are, of course, the stock-in-trade of development studies. It is scholars working in that field who have argued the case for the shift from free market structural adjustment to a socially regulated adjustment with a human face (Cornia et al., 1987). Our point is that with [...] the increasingly intense nature of global economic competition, these issues traditionally associated with development studies and poor countries should become also the concern of analysts of developed welfare states. The obverse argument, that development studies should emerge from its ghetto and address the implications of its analysis for global processes, has been made recently by Foster-Carter (1993) and echoed by Duffield (1996).

The second form that supranational social policy can take is that of redistribution between countries. At a subglobal level this operates effectively already within the European Union through the structural and associated funds that ensure a degree of support for poorer regions by richer ones. Once again the overlap with development studies and those scholars concerned with the emergence of global governance is obvious. The valued United Nations *Human Development Report* suggested that 'Human society is increasingly taking on a global dimension. Sooner or later it will have to develop the global institutions to match ... a system of progressive income tax [from rich to poor nations] ... a strengthened UN' (UNDP, 1992: 78).

The third form of supranational and global social policy is that of social welfare provision at a level above that of national government. This refers to the embryonic measures so far almost exclusively developed only at the subglobal, especially European, level whereby people gain an entitlement to a service or are empowered in the field of social citizenship rights by an agency acting at a supranational level. The United Nations High Commission for Refugees acts in the welfare interests of stateless persons and refugees. The Council of Europe empowers the citizens of member states to take their governments to the Strasbourg Court of Human Rights if they believe their rights have been circumscribed. Weale (1994) has argued that the EU could develop a European safety net social assistance policy that applies in all countries, to counter the xenophobic concerns with 'welfare tourism'.

The other side of the coin of the globalization of social policy is the socialization of global politics. In other words the major agenda issues at intergovernmental meetings are, now in essence social (and environmental) questions. The G7 summit in June 1996, with the Presidents of the IMF, World Bank and World Trade Organization and the UN Secretary-General in attendance, resolved, for example, to discuss the relationship between free trade and the 'internationally recognized core labour standards' at their Singapore meeting in the autumn of 1996. [...] In the example of UN preventive intervention in Macedonia (Deacon et al, 1996) a focus of concern is to find social policy mechanisms that increase co-operation across ethnic divides. [...] Figure 1.1.1 captures this shift in the content of global politics.

Figure 1.1.1: The globalization of social policy and the socialization of global politics

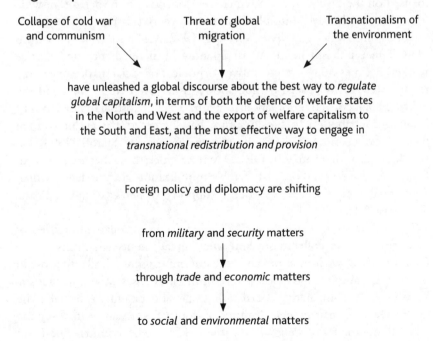

Collapse of cold war and communism

Threat of global migration

Transnationalism of the environment

have unleashed a global discourse about the best way to *regulate global capitalism*, in terms of both the defence of welfare states in the North and West and the export of welfare capitalism to the South and East, and the most effective way to engage in *transnational redistribution and provision*

Foreign policy and diplomacy are shifting

from *military* and *security* matters

through *trade* and *economic* matters

to *social* and *environmental* matters

With the collapse of the cold war, the rise of international migratory pressures, and the human suffering arising from social instability in many parts of the globe, the security that faces world leaders is, in effect, social security. Cancellation of debts arising from the ill-informed period of structural adjustment, transnational humanitarian aid to create global political security, and the 'threat' to economic competitiveness posed by the 'social protectionism' of European welfare states, are today's top agenda items. The 1995 UN World Summit on Social Development merely echoed this.

[...]

Globalism, the social sciences and social policy

[...]

Social policy as an academic discipline or field of study has [...] been rather slower to wake up to the impact of the new world (dis)order on its subject matter than some economists, political scientists, international relations students and sociologists. On the other hand, because of its commitment to welfare and the concern of its practitioners to not only analyse existing policy but prescribe better ways in which human needs might be articulated and met, its potential contribution to the new global politics is immense. The subject did break out of its Fabian reformism and national ghetto some years ago with the development of comparative analysis. Studies that have focused on the diverse ways in which developed western societies provide for social needs have multiplied in recent years (Castles and Mitchell, 1990; Esping-Andersen, 1990; Ginsburg, 1992; Mishra, 1990). The worlds of welfare capitalism in the West can now be divided into liberal (free market) regimes (USA), conservative corporatist or social market economy regimes (Germany), social democratic regimes (Sweden, as was), and the hybrid liberal collectivist or labourite regimes (UK, Australia). The feminist inspired contribution to the literature has suggested criteria of women friendliness against which to compare welfare states. Siaroff (1994) has concluded that there are four OECD regime types: three that are similar to Esping-Andersen's and one, 'late female mobilization welfare states', which neither encourages women's work nor supports women's caring (e.g. Spain, Switzerland, Japan). [...]

To these western regimes must be added the now collapsed regimes of state bureaucratic collectivism and their replacements which elsewhere (Deacon, 1992) we have argued include not only regimes similar to those in Western Europe, but also a new post-communist conservative corporatism. Very recently comparative social policy has also begun to describe the distinctive state management features of South East Asian welfare regime types (Goodman and Peng, 1996; Jones, 1993). The countries of Latin

America have been shown to offer a choice between neo-liberal and social democratic models (Huber, 1996).

Within the European context it is now being recognized that the future of welfare state diversity within the European Community will be affected by the supranational social policies of the Commission. The levelling down and up towards a social market economy regime type (rather than liberal or social democratic) is suggested together with an appreciation that redistribution of resources for meeting needs is now taking place between member states. Offe (1991) has argued that changing patterns of work within Europe suggest the need for the social policy of the Community as a whole to break from a work based entitlement to a citizenship entitlement of basic income or social dividend. A similar case has been put to encourage a flexible labour market in the former USSR (Standing, 1991).

Despite these useful excursions into *comparative* and European analysis, social policy writers have had little to say about the globalization phenomenon. George (1988) did begin to address the issue of wealth, poverty and starvation on an international scale and MacPherson and Midgley (1987) addressed issues of social policy in the Third World. Some time ago Deutsch addressed the idea that we should move from national welfare states to an international welfare system and concluded optimistically that the trends 'moving towards . . . [an] international welfare system are larger and stronger than the forces moving in the opposite direction' (1981: 437). Townsend (1993) has more recently contributed to the analysis of poverty on an international basis. In a subsequent paper with Donkor he concluded rather polemically that

> Far from scrapping the institutions and services which have become known as the 'welfare state' or targeting them in ways currently recommended by monetarists they should be improved and modernised, and the most vital parts of the basic infrastructure extended by stages to the poorest countries . . . The problems of the industrial revolution and exploitative forms of capitalism led in the late nineteenth century to the establishment of the welfare state in one country after another. The problems in the late twentieth century of the international market and the replacement of sovereignty and empire by international hierarchical power will demand the establishment of forms of an international welfare state. (1995: 20)

There has not yet been a sustained intellectual political project in this area. It is our argument that the collapse of the cold war, the consequent proliferation of little states, and the consequential increase in the importance of supranational, regional and global economic and political processes lead now to the need for social policy analysis to change gear from a focus solely on national and comparative social policy to a focus that gives equal weight to supranational and global social policy.

To embark on the study of the globalization of social policy the intellectual resources of social policy analysis need to join forces with those active in development studies in order to further the analysis of the obstacles to and the prospects for the better meeting of the human needs of everyone. The work of Doyal and Gough (1991) represents potentially the meeting point of comparative social policy with development studies upon which the further development of the study of the globalization of the social policy could be based. Their elaboration, within the subject of social policy, of the concept of basic human needs as being constituted of the twin elements of health and autonomy parallels the emergence within the United Nations Human Development Project of a human development index constituted of the three elements of income, longevity and literacy (UNDP, 1990). Although there is still controversy over the ways of defining and measuring human needs we do have useful frameworks for both measuring and comparing how good different types of welfare regimes are at enabling those needs to be met. In principle, therefore, we should be able to work, through appropriate mechanisms of transnational redistribution, regulation and provision, to increase the number of good welfare regimes in the world.

In another sense the tools of the subject of development studies need now to be used by social policy analysts if the discipline is to embrace the globalization process. The social policy of a country or locality is no longer wholly shaped (if it ever was) by the politics of the national government. It is increasingly shaped, as was suggested earlier, by the implicit and explicit social policies of numerous supranational agencies, ranging from global institutions like the World Bank and the International Monetary Fund, through supranational bodies such as the OECD and the European Commission, to supranational non-government agencies like OXFAM. These agencies [...] work in contradictory directions and are [...] increasingly the locus of the future ideological and political struggles for better global and national social policies. The lessons learned from the African and Latin American experience of structural adjustment policies need to be appreciated by analysts of the social policy of developed economies.

The discipline or academic activity of social policy has made a considerable contribution to the understanding of the processes that have hitherto shaped national social policy. In turn these analyses have contributed to effective political action either through institutional processes or through engagement in social movement activity. The discipline, in association with development studies specialists, should now embark on an analytical and political project focused on the globalization of social policy. The project should embrace, as we have already suggested, both the emergence of a global social policy between nations (transnational redistribution, regulation and provision) and the intervention in national social policy of global supranational agencies. [...]

The terrain of global social policy analysis

We have argued in the previous section that the focus of the discipline of social policy should shift from *comparative* to *supranational* or *global* social policy. In doing this it should combine its intellectual resources with those of the discipline of development studies. Together this could lead to a more effective intervention by experts within these disciplines within the supranational and global forums where issues of social policy are increasingly decided. Together they could better act as interpreters of need between social movements and supragovernmental agencies. The thrust of this argument is that the better focus of the (flawed) universal class of intellectuals is no longer the nation state but global institutions.

This section sets out in a little more detail the terrain of global social policy analysis. A systematic analysis of the phenomenon of global social policy could be constructed by proceeding through the following six steps:

1 *Pressures for globalization* and supranationalism and the consequent reduction of national sovereignty in the shaping of social policy could be investigated and analysed.
2 Traditional practical and analytical *issues* within the practice and study of social policy such as those of social justice could be reconceptualized at a global level.
3 A *typology* of supranational and global social policy *mechanisms* could be constructed for analytical purposes.
4 Possible *goals for global reformists* wishing to increase global justice might be formulated.
5 The *obstacles* to both the processes of globalization and the realization of a global social reformist project could be delineated.
6 The alternative *political strategies* available to global actors shaping global social policy could be distinguished.

All of these empirical, analytical, theoretical and political endeavours in the new terrain of global social policy would have implications for the analysis of national and comparative social policy. This new intellectual activity should enable hypotheses to be constructed and tested regarding not only the emergence of transnational social policy but also the possible futures of diverse welfare regimes. [...]

Pressures towards the globalization of social policy

Pressures leading to the globalization of social policy [... include] the end of the cold war, increased global economic competition, and the challenge now posed to global capitalism to regulate itself in the interests of human need. Also of importance is the dissolving frontiers phenomenon analysed elsewhere by Vobruba (1994). He points to the pressures for economic migration and the emergence of common transborder environmental threats leading to the necessity of formulating transnational social policy. As we have seen, however, these pressures do not lead automatically to the adoption of supranational or global solutions. National and regional self-interest and protectionism are alternative strategies available to governments. Supranationalization can be resisted. There might not be any global political actors of vision to seize the opportunity. [...]

Social policy issues in a global context

Standard texts within the subject of social policy not only describe and analyse particular social services such as medical care, housing and income maintenance and the social problems within these fields, but also address at a higher level of abstraction a number of social policy issues. The way these issues have been formulated and the exact nuances given to their analysis vary according to the theoretical framework of the policy analyst. Nevertheless, cutting through and across the liberal, social democratic, Marxist, feminist, anti-racist and post-structuralist perspectives on the 'welfare state' are a number of issues about which all the perspectives have something to say. These may be listed as:

Social justice What is meant by this concept and how might governments and other political and social actors best secure it? Trade-offs between social justice and economic competitiveness are a central concern here. Processes and mechanisms of rationing also feature.

Citizenship What is meant by, especially, the social elements of citizenship rights and entitlements and what are the processes of inclusion and exclusion at work?

Universality and diversity How might social justice and social citizenship be secured for all universally while, at the same time, acknowledging and meeting the very diverse needs of different social groups? Issues of discrimination and equal opportunities arise here.

Autonomy and guarantees To what extent do economic, political and social arrangements facilitate the autonomous articulation and meeting of social needs by individuals and groups from below and at a local level, and how might this autonomy trade off against social guarantees through social provision from above? Issues of subsidiarity and regionalism arise here.

Agency of provision Should the state, the market, the organizations of civil society, the family provide for the welfare needs of the population, and in what mix? The vexed questions of the level of public expenditure and the proportion of GNP devoted to the welfare effort feature here.

Public and private A subtheme of this concerns the extent to which the business of care is and should be a private matter (more often than not undertaken by women for men) or a public matter (within which the gendered division of care becomes a matter of political debate). There is often an ethnic dimension to this analysis too.

Different social policy analysts might organize the list slightly differently but there would be a fair measure of agreement that these issues are the stock-in-trade of our field of study and our political concern.

If the state is withering in importance, if the power of supranational agencies is increasing, if, through migration and global economic inter-connectedness, the world is becoming one place how then should we reconceptualize these issues at a supranational and global level? Let's take each in turn.

Justice between states

At one level this provides no major conceptual problems. Social policy analysis, thinking globally, would simply join forces with development studies specialists and analyse the extent to which the world was a 'fair' place. Data concerning social inequalities within and between nations are now much more accessible [... enabling scholars] to describe the extent to which the welfare needs of the world's population are increasingly being met but also the extent to which they are being met inequitably.

At another level, however, the issue of transnational justice raises difficult analytical and political questions. The Rawlsian conception of justice appropriate to a capitalist state (whereby that inequality is justified that raises the level of the poorest) becomes problematic at a global level. Attempts have been made to reformulate this principle between states (O'Neill, 1991). Equally the political processes of democratic class struggle within small relatively homogeneous states in parts of the North and West that have secured a degree of social justice are not easily replicable on a global terrain, and moreover competition between such relatively just states and those not 'burdened' with the same degree of social justice is, as we have seen, in danger of undermining the local social justice achievements of parts of the North and West.

Put simply, how can an alliance be constructed between the poor of the South and the better-off poor of the North that struggles to achieve an improvement in the conditions of the poor of the South without unacceptably undermining the relatively better-off poor of the North and in ways which are economically and ecologically sustainable? How, in other words, will the social commitments of European social and economic policy not only, as they are doing, secure a greater degree of justice within the territory of the EU but also secure this commitment in other parts of the globe? By what social and political processes will the uncertain global alliances from below translate into the construction of global political institutions that seek to secure an acceptable measure of global justice? Daunting as this prospect might seem, [...] we are already witnessing this process [...]. The World Bank is beginning to be concerned to secure a fairer world. The discourse between the Commission of the EU and the Directorate of the World Trade Organization is about regulating capitalism globally to prevent social dumping, to minimize global economic migration and to secure, therefore, greater global political security. [...]

Supranational citizenship

Thinking about the concept of citizenship in a globalizing world only serves to highlight the double-sidedness of the concept. On the one hand citizenship within the context of democratic capitalist society is about securing rights and entitlements for all within a state. On the other hand it is about excluding from the benefits of citizenship those outside the state. In the last years of the twentieth century we have seen a simultaneous deepening and strengthening of citizenship rights and entitlements within some states and tightening of restrictions on migrants seeking access to the citizenship rights of many of those same northern and western countries. Overlaying this development has been the emergence of supranational citizenship rights and entitlements within subglobal regions, notably Europe (Meehan, 1993). At the same time such subglobal regions act in an exclusionary way towards complete outsiders (Sivanandan, 1993).

To begin the process of reconceptualizing citizenship at a supranational level it is useful to return to Marshall's division of the concept into the components of political rights (the right to vote), civil rights (the right to equal treatment before the law) and social rights (the right to a fair share of the nation's resources). While these rights and associated duties were developed historically in capitalist societies within one state, the globalization process is generating the emergence of supranational citizenship entitlements of all three kinds. This process has developed furthest in the European context. The 30-odd member states of the Council of Europe provide for their citizens the right to equal treatment before the Court of Human Rights in Strasbourg with regard to human rights issues. No supranational political and social rights are guaranteed for the citizens of the member states of the Council of Europe but states are encouraged to ratify (and most have ratified) the Council of Europe's Social Charter which lays down a range of minimum social rights and entitlements [...]. For the smaller number of states of the EU a plethora of political, civil and social rights now exists and is enshrined in the supranational law of the community (Meehan, 1993). Sceptics of the supranationalization of social citizenship rights at a European level point however to the impossibility of a supranational body declaring such rights without it also at the same time having the power to direct and redirect economic resources to secure those declared social rights in reality (Closa, 1995).

At a global level the UN Declaration of Human Rights embraces social questions but as yet there is no legal enforcement of these rights in member states of the UN and no individual rights of petition. The International Court of Justice at The Hague serves so far only to regulate disputes between states and not between individuals and their state.

There are other ways in which the social aspects of citizenship are, in a piecemeal way, developing an international dimension. Numerous bilateral agreements exist between states regarding the reciprocal recognition of social security and other social rights [...]. At a global level the United Nations High Commission for Refugees assumes responsibility for the livelihood of stateless persons. At the same time as this process of the supranationalization and globalization of social citizenship rights gathers pace there are many examples of the tightening of access to national citizenship. Within the process of the emergence of new states in Eastern Europe and the former Soviet Union there are several examples (Estonia, the Czech Republic, the former Yugoslavia, etc.) where citizenship laws have been drawn up to exclude either former colonizing citizens (Russians in Estonia) or oppressed minorities (Romany population in the Czech Republic) from access to some of the benefits of citizenship. [...]

These issues flowing from the reconceptualization of social citizenship at a supranational level [... enable us to observe] that two parallel processes are taking place. Within the realm of insurance based social rights and entitlements an internationalization is taking place to accommodate a globally mobile skilled workforce, whereas in the realm of means tested social assistance a Poor Law localizing process is taking place where not only supranational bodies but states are shedding responsibility onto impoverished localities.

Global universality and diversity

Within the context of the analysis of social policy within one country the contemporary problematic was expressed recently as 'how to facilitate the universal meeting of diverse human needs' (Williams, 1994). This cogently captures the tension between the continued commitment to a morality of universalism typical of social policy analysts and the new sensitivity to diversity and difference that critical and postmodern social policy analysis has emphasized.

Projected onto a supranational and even global scale the problematic is further complicated. In the first place we can't readily assume a global commitment to the values of universalism which policy makers might use to guide their thinking in the context of diversity. Gellner (1994) has suggested that three competing world views presently vie for ascendancy. First is ethical relativism, very much a reflection of the collapse of the certainties of the socialist project. Second is fundamentalism of various kinds where place and reward are largely prescribed. Third, and only one among the three, is liberalism which still seeks after some notion of truth and within which paradigm the rationale discourse concerning justice, equality and universalism can take place.

While the search for rational truth and the assertion of fundamentalism do seem implacably opposed as world views, there is a dialogue between relativists and rational truth seekers. Within this context Bauman (1993) has recently argued that the new epoch of postmodernism creates a new space for moral discourse. Modernism of the capitalist and state socialist kind had dispensed with moral judgements and discourse. The best order would follow inexorably from the pursuit of one of these mirror image modernist projects. With the crisis in both projects the moral purpose of policy reasserts itself. Policy making, the regulation of capitalism globally, is called upon to justify itself against ethical concerns.

If this is so it explains the re-emergence, after a silence of decades, of scholarly and political interest in the charters of human rights. Regardless of the dispute between relativists, fundamentalists and rational truth seekers, the fact is that the emerging supranationalism of the current period is rationalist and is concerned to inject a morality of universalism into supranational and global policy making. The UN Charter of Human Rights and the much expanded Council of Europe's Charter of Human Rights are now taking on a character against which capitalism East and West, North and South, should be judged. Member states must pass these tests for full world membership.

Taking this one step further it can be argued that social rights are now on the supranational agenda. Where once the capitalist West could focus only on political and civil (legal) rights in its challenge to the 'communist' East which discounted these rights in favour of social rights, now, with the collapse of the 'communist' project, global capitalism is being called upon to be judged by its capacity to secure legal, political *and* social rights universally (albeit in diverse ways). [...] [T]he development of social rights [is] an issue being addressed by supranational agencies. This is not to suggest the project is plain sailing. Clearly the phenomenon of ethnic cleansing and the rise of xenophobia pull in the opposite direction [...]. At the same time this makes even more urgent the need to secure the power of international regulatory authority to intervene when political, civil and social rights are denied because of ethnic or cultural difference.

Subsidiarity and supranationalism: autonomy and guarantees

Before the collapse of 'communism', standard texts comparing western capitalism and state socialism (Davis and Scase, 1985) used to point to the apparent trade-off between individual autonomy, that is the right to articulate social needs from below, on the one hand (a feature of capitalism), and social guarantees, that is the universal commitment of the often paternalistic state to provide for social needs from above, on the other (a feature of communism). Projected onto a transnational terrain the same dichotomy might be observed. The more states have the autonomy to determine what and how social needs might be met within the country, the less there is the guarantee of their meeting those needs, and vice versa. Within the context of European supranationalism the debate is currently expressed in terms of the concept of subsidiarity. Subsidiarity, a principle now enshrined in the post-Maastricht policy making process, provides for decisions to be taken above a particular local, regional or national level only if they can better be made above that level. Conversely decisions (and often provision) should be as local as possible.

The principle of subsidiarity only serves, however, to beg the question as to which bits of social policy making *are* best determined supranationally. The choice between a policy of providing transnationally the means by which states can guarantee certain social rights, and a policy whereby states have the autonomy to make their own policy and provision, exemplifies the point. Any policy which provides for transnational redistribution and for the cross-national regulation of the rules of capitalist competition *must* be better taken *above* the level of the state if guarantees of subsidy to impoverished areas and guarantees against social dumping are to be secured. Moreover it should be possible to construct decision making processes to connect the local (articulation of need) to the supranational (provision of resources and rules) which aim at simultaneously guaranteeing provision and facilitating autonomy.

This process of the erosion of the autonomous power of states to determine policy in favour of the guarantees of supranational intervention and regulation is taking place not only within the region of Europe but also [...] at a global level. The recent questioning by UN bodies of the previously hallowed right of sovereignty is but one expression of this. [...]

Global welfare mix (agency of provision)

In the preceding sections we have tried to show how the policy issues with which social policy analysts are concerned take on interestingly different dimensions when transposed from the national to the supranational and global terrain. Social justice becomes transnational redistribution, citizenship issues become a matter of social exclusion, the search for universalism in the context of diversity turns into a global codification of human and social rights, the guaranteeing of social rights becomes an issue of supranational regulation against social dumping. Does the policy issue of the agency mix in social provision take on a new dimension when examined in a supranational context?

This brings us back to the question of global competition between kinds of welfare states. One paradigm that still has purchase on policy makers is that economic competitiveness and welfare state expenditure are trade-offs. The more economic competition takes place in an unregulated way, therefore, the less state welfare expenditure there might be. This paradigm seems especially to connect to policy debates about the level of taxation on firms and the costly regulations under which they have to work. If this paradigm prevails as a result of increased global competition then the development of supranational regulation will be slow and the welfare mix is likely to shift away from the state. There is evidence, as we noted earlier, that a competing paradigm might replace the previous one. This argues that certain kinds of state expenditure are beneficial to capital either in terms of investment in education, or in terms of the multiplier effect of the consumption of social security recipients, or in terms of securing political stability. This would lead to greater government intervention. [... To what extent is] this paradigm shift [...] taking place within and between global agencies such as the IMF, the World Bank and the OECD[?] One conclusion from this debate will be that welfare state expenditure might be affordable if consumers and not firms pay for it (Scharpf, 1995). This either leaves each country to its own devices in terms of whether it agrees to trade wages for welfare or, alternatively, suggests that a welfare orientated global regulation that did not want to damage the competitiveness of firms is likely to focus on the level of public not enterprise taxation.

The process of globalization is also likely to support the tendency away from national provision to local and regional. We have already explained this pincer movement of global and local eroding the state. Within this process there might be a case for the social policy obligations of states and firms to be carried out by the locality. Greater moves to federalism are a likely consequence of this process. The erosion of state and workplace welfare might also lead to the strengthening of civil society. More non-governmental organization activity seems to be a consequence of the process of the erosion of the state. [...]

Who services whom globally

[...] The globalization process is leading to the further widening of the gender, class and racial division of caring. In the USA (an example of a liberal regime towards which the world might be being impelled) white middle class professional men and women have their caring duties undertaken by black migrant (often illegally migrant) women from the poorer South. The analysis would apply equally for the public (and regulated private) institutions that provide for the care of dependants. The other side of the coin of this phenomenon of mobile, usually black, labour meeting the welfare needs of white people in privileged countries is the remittances returned to the South (and East) by these mobile workers. The remittances can contribute a significant percentage of the GNP of labour exporting countries. Families likely to be in receipt of such remittances may well be debarred from receipt of local social assistance.

This brief exposition serves to show how complex the question of caring relationships becomes once transposed onto a global terrain. The question is posed as to how, if it is desired, might regulations, transnational redistributions, or other policies be fashioned to lessen these global inequities in caring.

In this section we have reviewed the ways in which the policy issues of interest to social policy analysts might need to be reconceptualized in the light of the globalization process. Certain policy prescriptions at transnational level have been hinted at. In the next section we conceptualize three kinds of global social policy response.

Global social redistribution, regulations and provision

A very simple *typology of global social policy responses and mechanisms* would first separate out global intervention in *national* social policy and secondly distinguish three forms of global social policy, namely transnational *redistribution*, supranational *regulation* and global or supranational *provision*. All three types of supranational activity already take place but often these are confined within one regional economic trading bloc such as the European Union. Elements of all three are, however, to be found at a global level. The economic assistance from the West to the East may fall short of a Marshall

Plan but it is motivated in part by the wish to secure social stability in the former Soviet Union. Concern to prevent social dumping by multinational capital does now appear on the agenda of the World Bank. The United Nations High Commission for Refugees does operate an elementary system of global citizenship entitlements for stateless persons. Within this intellectual map the scholarly work presently being undertaken on the emerging social policy of the European Union could be a special case and exemplar of a future global social policy analysis and practice. Recent work by Kleinman and Piachaud (1993) discussing the issues of subsidiarity, citizenship rights and democracy in the emerging supranational European social policy can be transposed onto a global terrain. The same concerns apply: at what level can policy best be formulated; how can national citizenship be reconciled with supranational mobility; and how can national democratic constituencies be recast to ensure meaningful accountability at supranational level?

Fleshing out this initial conceptualization requires us to analyse which supranational and global agencies are actors in the emerging processes of influencing national policy and engaging in transnational *redistribution*, supranational *regulation* and supranational and global *provision*. *Coupled* with this we need an analysis of the *instruments* with which agencies and organizations acting above the level of the state can redistribute resources, influence and regulate national social policy and international competition, and contribute to supranational and global policy and provision. A moment's reflection on this topic leads to the appreciation that the subject matter is extraordinarily complex and that it is in a very rapid process of evolution. There are a very large number of agencies using a variety of instruments to push and pull country social policy and practice in often very different directions and seeking to impose very different degrees of regulation on international competition.

Table 1.1.1, which focuses on global intervention in national policy, captures the idea of the web of interconnectedness that, say, an East European country wishing to join Europe finds itself within in the sphere of income maintenance policy. This clearly demonstrates the contending influences of say the IMF, concerned to balance the state budget, with say the ILO concerned to seek the adoption of decent social security conventions. The tension between the budget balancing requirements of the IMF and the expenditure requirements of the Social Charter of the Council of Europe is another example. [...]

Table 1.1.1: Some contending influences on national income maintenance policy in the European region

Agency	Type of influence
All countries	
International Monetary Fund	Public expenditure limitations as loan conditions affect income maintenance budget
World Bank	Advice on social 'safety net' policy and social security expenditure; loans on condition of social reform
International Labour Office	Conventions on social security systems; advice on tripartite forms of government
Countries within the Council of Europe	
Council of Europe	Obligatory Charter of Human Rights; subject to Strasbourg Court of Human Rights Optional Social Charter; subject to independent expert judgements Optional conventions on social security
Countries within the EU	
EU	Obligatory Social Chapter; subject to Luxembourg Court of Justice Participation in Social Exclusion Project Net loser/winner in redistribution of Structural Funds

Table 1.1.2: Supranational and global redistribution and regulation

Agency	Instrument					
	Raise revenue from citizens or business	Raise revenue from states[1]	Expend money on some basis of social need	Lend money on non-market terms	Capacity to influence national social policy	Social regulation of trade
UN[2]	✗ (not yet)	✓	✓	✗	✓	✗ (not yet)
World Bank	✗	✓	✓	✓	✓	✗ (not yet)
IMF	✗	✓	✗	✗	✓	✗
OECD	✗	✗	✗	✗	✓	✗
WTO	✗	✗	✗	✗	✗ (not yet)	✗ (not yet)
EU	✗	✓	✓	?	✓	✓
NAFTA	✗	✗	✗	✗	✗	✗
ILO	✗	✗	✗	✗	✓	✓ (aspires to)

Notes: [1] By this is meant revenue over and above that needed just to fund the running of the organization.

[2] At this stage the UN is taken to be an umbrella body for all its social and other agencies, unless indicated separately. [...] The most important agencies through which the UN redistributes resources for social welfare purposes are UNICEF, UNDP, UNFAO World Food Programme and UNHCR.

Table 1.1.2 focuses on the global social policy mechanisms of redistribution and regulation and provides an initial indication of the most important global and regional agencies engaged in those aspects of supranational policy and the instruments with which they either facilitate redistribution or regulate activity. An important contrast is shown up here between the EU, where between-country redistribution accompanies free trade, and the North American Free Trade Association, which while freeing trade doesn't engage in compensatory social redistribution (or even significant social regulation) (Grinspin and Cameron, 1993). Of note also in this table is the lack of power the World Trade Organization has in the social redistribution or social regulation field. The comments in the table indicate where current international debate and discussion on the issue of developing global social regulatory mechanisms have reached. [...]

An important complexity arises if we turn to the *social provision* afforded by supranational and global authorities and agencies. Little direct provision of services yet operates at supranational level although the work of the UNHCR is an exception. We can however speak of the *empowerment* of citizens that some supranational bodies facilitate. One of the supranational instruments, identified in Figure 1.1.2, operates through the rights conferred on individual citizens by legal authorities existing at supranational level. Government policy and practice within the European region, for example in the spheres of social security, the right to social assistance, the equal treatment of men and women as well as human rights generally, has now to take account of the legal judgements of both the European Court of Justice in Luxembourg and the Council of Europe's Court of Human Rights in Strasbourg. Elizabeth Meehan (1993) has documented the impact of the Luxembourg Court on aspects of the social rights of citizens of the European Union. Davidson (1993) has recently reviewed some of the judgments with human rights implications of the Strasbourg Court. As yet individual citizens globally do not have recourse to the UN International Court of Justice in The Hague. This is reserved for disputes of a territorial kind between states or for war crime tribunals. In principle, however, and not just as a utopian vision, such a court could in due course adjudicate on aspects of human and social rights of global citizens. Figure 1.1.2 captures this evolving situation.

Supranational and global agencies already, therefore, contribute to the shaping of national policy and the terms of international competition by laying down social policy conditions on governments for the receipt of financial assistance, or by redistributing resources between governments, or by establishing conventions and offering technical advice and assistance as a step towards legal social regulation. Also as individual citizens are empowered to appeal to an authority above the state, a world within which universal

Figure 1.1.2: The emergence of supranational citizenship in the sphere of human and social rights

European Court of Justice[1,2] (Luxembourg)	Court of Human Rights[2] (Strasbourg)	International Court of Justice[2] (The Hague)
↓	↓	↓
EU member state governments	Council of Europe member state governments	United Nations member state governments
Citizens of EU member states	Citizens of Council of Europe member states	Countries of the UN member states

Notes: [1] Competencies in the social rights sphere
[2] Competencies in the human rights sphere

human and social rights are recognized and reinforced is in principle already possible. [...]

The argument [...] recapitulated

[...] [G]lobalization (a) sets welfare states in competition with each other, (b) raises social policy issues to a supranational level, and (c) generates a global discourse on the best way to regulate capitalism in the interests of social welfare East and West, North and South.

Global social policy as a practice of supranational actors embodies global social redistribution, global social regulation, and global social provision and/or empowerment, and includes the ways in which supranational organizations shape national social policy.

The classical concerns of social policy analysts with social needs and social citizenship rights become in a globalized context the quest for supranational citizenship. The classical concern with equality, rights and justice between individuals becomes the quest for justice between states. The dilemma about efficiency, effectiveness and choice becomes a discussion about how far to socially regulate free trade. The social policy preoccupations with altruism, reciprocity and the extent of social obligations are put to the test in the global context. To what extent are social obligations to the other transnational?

The entry of the former 'socialist' economies into the global capitalist arena has coincided with a period of intensified global economic competition which has contributed to the flexibilization of labour which, in turn, has challenged the viability of the traditional work based European social security and income maintenance systems.

[...]

Within this context and in the absence of any adequate formal global forum for the articulation and contestation of alternative social policy programmes, a hidden global discourse has emerged within and between the human resources divisions of these global organizations. The future for welfare not only in the East but by implication elsewhere is being resolved in the interplay between these global actors and the constrained decisions of national governments. [...]

Bibliography

Baubock, R. (1994) *Transnational Citizenship*, Cheltenham: Edward Elgar.

Bauman, Z. (1993) *Postmodern Ethics*, Oxford: Blackwell.

Castles, F. (1993) *Families of Nations*, Aldershot: Dartmouth.

Castles, F. and Mitchell, D. (1990) *Three Worlds of Welfare Capitalism or Four? Public Policy Discussion Paper no 21*, Canberra: Australia National University.

Closa, C. (1995) 'Some sceptical remarks on the solidarity dimension of the citizenship of the EU', Paper presented to Conference, 'A New Social Contract?' Robert Schuman Centre, European University Institute, 5–6 October.

Cornia, G., Jolly, R. and Stewart, F. (1987) *Adjustment with a Human Face*, Oxford: Clarendon Press.

Davidson, S. (1993) 'The European system for protecting human rights', in S. Davidson (ed) *Human Rights*, Oxford: Oxford University Press with Open University Press.

Davis, H. and Scase, R. (1985) *Communist Political Systems*, New York: St Martin's.

Deacon, B. (1992) *The New Eastern Europe: Social Policy – Past, Present and Future*, London: Sage.

Deacon, B. et al (1996) 'Action for social change: a new facet of preventative peace keeping', Report for UNPREDEP, Helsinki: National Research and Development Centre for Welfare and Health, STAKES.

Deutsch, K.W. (1981) 'From the national welfare state to the international welfare system', in W.J. Mommsen (ed) *The Emergemce of the Welfare State in Britain and Germany*, London: Croom Helm.

Doyal, L. and Gough, I. (1991) *A Theory of Human Need*, London: Macmillan.

Duffield, M. (1996) 'The globalisation of public policy', mimeo, University of Brimingham, Centre for Urban and Regional Studies.

Esping-Andersen, G. (1990) *The Three Worlds of Welfare Capitalism*, Cambridge: Polity.

Foster-Carter, A. (1993) 'Development', in M. Haralambos (ed) *Developments in Sociology*, vol 9, Ormskirk: Causeway Press.

Gellner, E. (1994) *Conditions of Liberty: Civil Society and its Rivals*, London: Hamish Hamilton.

George, S. (1988) *A Fate Worse than Debt*, Harmondsworth: Penguin.

Ginsburg, N. (1992) *Divisions of Welfare*, London: Sage.

Goodman, P. and Peng, I. (1996) 'The East Asian welfare states peripatetic learning, adaptive change and nation building', in G. Esping-Andersen (ed) *Welfare States in Transition*, London: Sage.

Grinspin, C. and Cameron, M.A. (eds) (1993) *The Political Economy of North American Free Trade*, London: Macmillan.

Huber, E. (1993) 'Options for social policy in Latin America: neoliberal versus social democratic models' in G. Esping-Anderson (ed) *Welfare States in Transition*, London: Sage.

Jones, C. (1993) 'The Pacific challenge: the Confucian welfare states', in C. Jones (ed) *New Perspectives on the Welfare State in Europe*, London: Routledge.

Kleinman, M. and Piachaud, D. (1993) 'European social policy: conceptions and choices', *Journal of European Studies*, 3(1): 1–19.

Kosonen, P. (1995) 'Competitiveness, welfare systems and the debate on social competition', Paper contributed to ISA RC19 Conference on Comparative Research on Welfare State Reforms, University of Pavia, Italy, 14–17 September.

Lang, T. and Hines, C. (1996) 'The "new protectionist" position', *New Political Economy*, 1(1).

Leibfried, S. (1994) 'The social dimensions of the EU: en route to positively joint sovereignty', *Journal of European Social Policy*, 4(4).

MacPherson, S. and Midgley, J. (1987) *Comparative Social Policy and the Third World*, Brighton: Wheatsheaf.

Meehan, E. (1993) *Citizenship and the European Community*, London: Sage.

Mishra, R. (1990) *The Welfare State in Capitalist Society: Policies of Retrenchment and Maintenance in Europe, North America and Australia*, Hemel Hempstead: Harvester Wheatsheaf.

Offe, C. (1991) 'Capitalism by democratic design? Democratic theory facing the triple transition in eastern Central Europe', *Social Research*, 4.

O'Neill, O. (1991) 'Transitional justice', in D. Held (ed) *Political Theory Today*, Cambridge: Polity.

Scharpf, F.W. (1995) 'Negative and positive integration in the political economy of European welfare states', paper presented to Conference, A New Social Contract?, Robert Schuman Centre, European University Institute, October 5–6.

Siaroff, A. (1994) 'Work, women and gender equality: a new typology', in D. Sainsbury (ed) *Gendering Welfare States*, London: Sage.

Sivanandan, A. (1993) 'European commentary – racism: the road from Germany', *Race and Class*, 34(3).

Standing, G. (1991) *In Search of Flexibility: The New Soviet Labour Market*, Geneva: ILO.

Townsend, P. (1993) *An International Analysis of Poverty*, Hemel Hempstead: Harvester Wheatsheaf.

Townsend, P. with Donkor, K. (1995) 'Global restructuring and social policy: an alternative strategy: establishing an international welfare state', Draft paper presented to ISA RC19 Conference on Comparative Research on Welfare State Reforms, University of Pavia, Italy, 14-17 September.

UNDP (1990) *Human Development Report 1990*, New York: Oxford University Press.

UNDP (1992) *Human Development Report 1992*, New York: Oxford University Press.

Vobruba, G. (1994) 'Transnational social policy in processess of transformation', in A. de Swann (ed) *Social Policy Beyond Borders: The Social Question in Transnational Perspective*, Amsterdam: Amsterdam University Press.

Weale, A. (1994) 'Social Policy and the EU', *Social Policy and Administration*, 28(1): 5–19.

Williams, F. (1994) 'Social relations, welfare and the post-Fordism debate', in R. Burrows and B. Loader (eds) *Towards a Post-Fordist Welfare State*, London: Routledge.

Chapter 1.2

Globalization and human welfare: why is there a need for a global social policy?

Vic George and Paul Wilding

We summarize the case under ten headings.

Greater global interdependence

Globalization compresses time and space and creates a keener sense of the world as one and so of interdependence. Scholte, for example, writes of 'a continued growth of global consciousness' since the 1960s (Scholte, 2000, p 85) and of a mind set encouraging supra territoriality. The Commission on Global Governance called its report 'Our Global Neighbourhood' (Oxford University Press, 1998). Giddens argues that 'humankind in some respects becomes a "we" facing problems and opportunities where there are no "others"' (quoted in Scholte, 2000, p 179).

Globalization fosters a more global discourse about welfare fed by reports from, for example, the World Bank on old age (World Bank, 1994), the OECD on the future of welfare provision (OECD, 1999) and the EU on the possibilities of European social policy (EU, 1994). An emerging global consciousness creates a sense of problems as global – for example the concept of 'the global commons' – which is both fed by, and feeds, the growth of global networks of, for example, environmental organizations. This, in turn, strengthens the sense of global consciousness and momentum for an attempt at global solutions.

The conceptualization of issues as global depends to a large degree on a sense of global consciousness emerging to complement a sense of national belonging, a sense of the world as one that feeds and legitimates the search for global solutions to problems redefined as global.

Global social problems

A global approach is needed to deal with problems which are global in character. In 1997 the OECD spoke of 'a growing internationalisation of many policy issues which were previously more domestic in nature'

(OECD, 1997, p 36). More and more issues are global in their impact and implications and they can be solved only by concerted international action – as, for example, was the eradication of smallpox or in current efforts to safeguard the ozone layer.

Crime and drugs have become genuinely global problems in their scale, nature and impact. Weiner writes of 'the growing global crisis in international population movements' (Weiner, 1995, p 155). Water supply and use is rapidly emerging as a major global issue. World consumption of fresh water quadrupled between the 1950s and the 1990s and continues to increase rapidly. Elliott reports over eighty countries, with 49 per cent of the world's population, facing water shortages with twenty six countries officially designated as water scarce (Elliott, 1998, p 2). The problem is global in its scale and in its implications and in the fact that global solutions are needed to complement national efforts.

AIDS is another example of a global problem only amenable to containment or solution on a global scale. As the World Health Organization Global Programme on AIDS put it 'AIDS cannot be stopped in any single country unless it is stopped in all countries' (quoted in Johnson and Soderholm, 1996, p 122). In October 1987, AIDS was discussed by the UN General Assembly, the first time a specific disease had ever been discussed in the Assembly – an illustration of the global acceptance of its global nature and of the perceived limitations of the nation state in AIDS policy-making.

The emergence and acceptance of a range of social problems as genuinely global stimulates pressures for the development of global social policies.

Mitigation of the effects of global competition

Global action in social policy is required to prevent a race to the neoliberal bottom. The neoliberal ideology of globalization puts pressure on national welfare states in the way it fuels demands for cuts in public expenditure, reductions in social welfare provision and the easing of labour and environmental regulation. These pressures grow out of particular notions of how economic efficiency and global competitiveness are to be achieved.

There is nothing new about competition. What is new, however, is its intensity, the overriding importance given to it by governments and the dominance of neoliberal notions of how it can best be promoted. The impact of these changes on states is highly significant. Cerny suggests that such pressures problematize the capacity of the state to embody communal solidarity so threatening its legitimacy and so reducing its capacity under globalization's pressures (Cerny, 2000, p 118). This is why there is a need for action at the global level.

Mishra suggests one answer to these down-driving pressures on nation state welfare – that standards of social protection must not become part of a competitive game but must be part of the rules of the game. That, he argues, requires a global social policy to compensate for the limitations which globalization imposes on national welfare states and to sustain the levels of social provision seen as necessary for civilised life at the national – and by extension – at the global level. The only way to head off pressure for a race to the bottom is for states to stand together and collaborate with supranational bodies to develop a raft of global social policies (Mishra, 1998, p 490).

Support for the idea of global human rights

Global social policy is an appropriate expression of emerging ideas of global citizenship and global human rights. One aspect of the development of global consciousness is the evolution of the concept of global citizenship and global civil society. Such ideas lead to a tentative extension of national aspirations to the global level. They foster ideas of global justice, of global minimum standards in health, education and income, of a concept of human rights at a global level. McCarthy sees the most successful transnational concept-building effort in recent years as the creation of a global concept of human rights (McCarthy, 1997, p 245). The concept is developed and promoted by several UN bodies, NGOs and international social movements.

The UNDP argues that the potential benefits of globalization will only be realised via stronger governance based on a principled globalization which is guided and governed by respect for human rights, a concern for equity, an emphasis on inclusion, a commitment to reduction of poverty and insecurity, a concern for a sustainable future (UNDP, 1999, p 2). What UNDP is arguing for, essentially, is globalization based on ideas of global citizenship. The World Bank's *World Development Report 2000-2001* argues along similar lines (World Bank, 2000).

The huge expansion in the number, size, resources and prominence of international NGOs and global social movements is both an expression of an emerging global citizenship and a force for its further development. At the Rio Earth Summit in 1992, for example, there were 20,000 participants from 9,000 NGOs from 171 countries. There have been similar manifestations of a new notion of global citizenship in other areas. O'Brien et al, for example, speak of the four UN Conferences on Women in 1975, 1980, 1985 and 1995 as having acted 'as great catalysts to the development of women's organisations and movements nationally and internationally' and of a global consciousness of gender rights and issues (O'Brien et al, 2000, p 34).

Complementing global economic policy

Global social policy is a corollary of a global(izing) economy. The symbiotic relationship between economic and social policy and between trade and social policy is now part of conventional wisdom. Globalization is partially economically driven but that does not mean it can sensibly be seen simply in economic terms. As *Our Global Neighbourhood* put it, 'Stability requires a carefully crafted balance between the freedom of markets and the provision of public goods' (Oxford University Press, 1998, p 135). If stability requires the provision of public goods, so too does economic integration if it is to be sustained (Leibfried and Pierson, 1994, p 43).

Development today is seen as meaning more than simply economic growth. It must be sustainable in the sense of not mortgaging the future for the sake of the present. It must raise all boats not just Olympic racing craft. The quest for sustainability raises major questions about the distribution of wealth, power and opportunity between rich and poor countries and within nation states. These questions suggest an important role for social policy – in UNDP's words 'to make globalization work for human development' (UNDP, 1999, p 9) or as the World Bank puts it 'global forces need to be harnessed for poor people' in a wide ranging set of strategies (World Bank, 2000, p 12).

Social policy has also become a more significant element in the globalization process as confidence in fundamentalist free market liberalism has ebbed. Informed opinion has moved away from a faith in unregulated markets to a belief in a socially regulated, socially embedded capitalism – and that means a global capitalism smoothed, sanded and sustained by social policies. Efficiency and competitiveness are important but so too are safety nets and human welfare.

The interdependence of economic and social policies is nicely illustrated by the way in which the World Bank and the IMF have come to give much more attention to social policy and the social dimensions of economic policy – and the pressure on the WTO to move towards 'conditional trade policies' – using trade agreements as a way to bring pressure to bear on countries to adopt desired policies in relation, for example, to core labour standards and environmental protection.

This is not to say that social democracy rules the hearts and minds of the big beasts of global economic policy-making. Rather it is to argue that social policy has now edged back into the frame of reference of economic policy-makers after two decades in the wilderness. Traditional economic thinking still dominates, but there is some acceptance of the need to develop social policies as a corollary of global economic development.

Strategy for a global social policy

A strategy for a global social policy would formalize existing trends and developments. Deacon boldly asserts that 'There is now a global social policy' made up of global redistribution mechanisms, global regulatory mechanisms, elements of global social policy provision and a global discourse about the future of national social policy (Deacon et al, 1997, p 213). Certainly there is a patina of incremental social policy superimposed on the globalizing economic system. The World Bank and the IMF have both come to take the social implications of globalization more seriouly (Deacon, 2001, pp 60-63). There is the varied pattern of activity of the UN's social policy divisions – WHO, UNICEF, ILO, UNHCR, for example – and the work of a wide range of specialist elements ranging from the Commission on Sustainable Development to the Global Programme on AIDS and the Global Environmental Facility. The WTO is constantly being pressed to add a concern for labour and environmental policy to its brief.

What exists is a plethora of very different organizations nibbling at a social policy agenda but in an essentially ad hoc and reactive fashion. There is – perhaps inevitably at this stage of development – no overall social policy strategy to match the grand liberalizing economic project which has been the primary, and uniting, preoccupation of the big economic players.

What is clearly needed is some rationalization of what is happening, some standing back from the here and now, some consideration of aims and objectives, strategies and choices and some attempt to coordinate the rather ragged looking rag tag and bobtail of policies which has emerged from such a disparate set of bodies. There need to be discussions about the overall shape, possibilities and limitations of global social policy – and a move on from what is essentially and hopefully a pre-figurative stage of development.

To avoid a backlash against globalization

Global social policy is essential to avoid a backlash against globalization. Globalization may be a powerful force for economic development but it is increasingly recognized that it has social costs. There is strong evidence that globalization – as it has developed in the past thirty years – has increased inequality, injustice and insecurity in some countries and has fragmented societies (eg, Scholte, 2000, chs 9 and 10). As the *Human Development Report 1999* put it 'Globalization is creating new threats to human security – in rich countries and poor' (UNDP, 1999, p 3). 'The volatility of markets', the Report concluded, 'is creating new vulnerabilities' (ibid, p 84). Globalization also increases knowledge of the nature and scale of deprivation and inequality and of the impact of disasters connected to the decline of market confidence and the resulting capital flight and of trends such as global warming.

The more perceptive analysts of globalization, Rodrik for example, see the need for policies designed to secure popular acceptance of globalization (Rodrik, 1997). That means policies to compensate losers, moderate inequalities and redress the more provocative inequities. If such pre-emptive measures are not put in place, there is the very real risk of a backlash as was first expressed to all the world in the television coverage of the demonstrations at WTO meetings in Seattle in November 1999 and at subsequent meetings of the WTO and the G8 – most notably in Genoa in July 2001.

On its own, the national state cannot guarantee to provide what is needed – because of the pressures of the new competitiveness and because of the nature of the problems which are at issue. What is needed, is action at a regional and a global level to protect and preserve the achievements of national welfare states and to display an acceptable face of globalization. The case can be made on grounds of economic and political rationality as well as justice because high rates of inequality, whether national or global, do not promote economic growth or political stability.

Expectations created by globalization

Globalization makes a global social policy (more) possible. Globalization creates the possibility of a global social policy. It helps create the economic resources which are a necessary, if not a sufficient, condition of global action. It stimulates aspirations on both sides as the poor see how the rich live and the rich are vividly confronted with the stark realities of abject poverty and unmet basic human needs. It creates a fragile consensus that some things should not be, for example high infant mortality rates, because they do not need to be. There is an emerging consensus about some issues of human rights – of workers, of women, of ethnic minorities and of children – and a feeling that basic human rights should be universally guaranteed. These elements are necessary preconditions of social policy development at the global level.

Crucial, too, has been the development of global networks of NGOs – most obviously in relation to the environment but also in relation to human rights. Globalization has been the midwife of that development and the emergence of a global network has transformed the debate in these areas. It has made it impossible for national governments to ignore environmental concerns and it has pushed them towards globally coordinated action because this is the way in which NGOs have successfully framed the debate.

There has also been the necessary institutional development. Supranational institutions have matured and consolidated their position and come to a broader view of their role and responsibilities, for example, the ILO, the WHO, the World Bank and the IMF. There has been a huge proliferation of treaties, committees, commissions, programmes and protocols. Globalization has also fostered the development of an issue-based social politics which transcends state boundaries and erodes the position of the state as the pre-eminent site of social policy making. If key issues are global – the rights of women, the rights of poor people, the rights of ethnic minorities, the protection of the biosphere – then the focus and canvas for social policy making must be global too.

Neoliberal ideology is not necessary

A global social policy is a corollary of the sense that the future is (at least partially) open. The development of a global social policy depends on the conviction that the outcomes of the particular model of globalization – neoliberal globalization – which has been dominant for the last thirty years do not simply have to be accepted as inevitable. As Michie put it, 'the fact that the economy is becoming internationalised does not dictate the form that this process is taking' (Michie, 1999, p 6). The process and the outcomes are open. There is scope for Scholte's 'ambitious reformism' (Scholte, 2000, p 39), Deacon's 'socialisation of global politics' (Deacon, 1995, p 56) or Radice's 'progressive internationalism' (Radice, 2000, p 16). This belief in possibilities is crucial to any attempt at social engineering. The decline of confidence in neoliberalism has opened the door to the reconsideration of the possibilities and potential of governance at a global level. Recent World Development Reports from the World Bank are edging towards this position.

States need global social policy

State social policies need the complementary and parallel support of global social policies because of the key role which social policy plays in securing and maintaining state authority and legitimacy. Social policy has been central to the maintenance of the legitimacy of the modern state – as has state legitimacy to the development of social policy. The modern state cannot be seen to be failing in what have come to be defined as among its central responsibilities without suffering serious damage. Globalization makes it more difficult for the national state, acting on its own, successfully to fulfil these responsibilities. The development of policies at a global level to protect the environment, to combat AIDS, crime and drug trafficking, to secure core labour rights, to reduce unemployment, for example, can help bolster state legitimacy which is essential both to successful economic globalization and to securing the welfare of citizens.

References

Cerny, P.G. (2000) 'Restructuring the Political Arena: Globalization and the Paradoxes of the Competition State', in R.D. Germain (ed.) *Globalization and its Critics* (Basingstoke, Macmillan).

Deacon, B. (1995) 'The Globalisation of Social Policy and the Socialisation of Global Politics', in J. Baldock and M. May (eds) *Social Policy Review* 7 (Canterbury, Social Policy Association).

Deacon, B. (2001) 'International Organizations, the EU and Global Social Policy', in R. Sykes, B. Palier and P.M. Prior (eds) *Globalization and European Welfare States*, (Basingstoke, Palgrave).

Deacon, B. with Hulse, M. and Stubbs, P. (1997) *Global Social Policy*, (London, Sage).

Elliott, L. (1998) *The Global Politics of the Environment* (Basingstoke, Macmillan).

EU (European Union) (1994) *European Social Policy – A Way Forward for the Union, A White Paper* (Brussels, Commission of the European Communities).

Johnson, C. and Soderholm, P. (1996) 'IGO and NGO Relations and HIV/AIDS: Innovation and Stalemate', in T.G. Weiss and L. Gordenker (eds) *The UN and Global Governance* (London, Lynne Reinner).

Leibfried, S. and Pierson, P. (1994) 'Semi-Sovereign Welfare States: Social Policy in a Multi-tiered Europe', in S. Leibfried and P. Pierson (eds) *European Social Policy* (Washington, Brookings Institute).

McCarthy, J.D. (1997) 'The Globalization of Social Movement Theory', in J. Smith, C. Chatfield and R. Pagnuccio (eds) *Transnational Movements and Social Rights* (New York, Syracuse University Press).

Michie, J. (1999) 'Introduction', in J. Michie and J. Grieve Smith (eds) *Global Instability* (London, Routledge).

Mishra, R. (1998) 'Beyond the Nation State: Social Policy in an Age of Globalization', *Social Policy and Administration*, 32 (5), 481-500.

O'Brien, R., Goetz, A.M., Scholte, J.A. and Williams, M. (2000) *Contesting Global Governance* (Cambridge, Cambridge University Press).

OECD (1997) *Towards A New Global Age* (Paris, OECD).

OECD (1999) *A Caring World: the New Social Policy Agenda* (Paris, OECD).

Radice, H. (2000) 'Responses to Globalisation: A Critique of Progressive Nationalism', *New Political Economy*, 5 (1), 5-19.

Rodrik, D. (1997) *Has Globalization Gone too Far?* (Washington, DC, Institute for International Economics)

Scholte, J.A. (2000) *Globalization: A Critical Introduction* (Basingstoke, Palgrave).

UNDP (United Nations Development Programme) (1999) *Human Development Report 1999* (New York, Oxford University Press).

Weiner, M. (1995) *The Global Migration Crisis* (New York, Harper Collins).

World Bank (1994) *World Development Report 1994: Averting the Old Age Crisis* (Washington, DC, World Bank).

World Bank (2000) *World Development Report 2000/2001: Attacking Poverty* (New York, Oxford University Press).

Chapter 1.3

Social politics and policy in an era of globalization: critical reflections

Nicola Yeates

Introduction

This paper critically examines the debate on the relationship between 'globalization', social politics and social policy. Globalization, by some accounts, represents a paradigmatic shift in the dynamics of welfare state development. Global capital and international institutions possess an unprecedented amount of political power and are instrumental in eroding national policy autonomy and shaping, even determining, the content of national social policies. The prospects for welfare states and for social and economic justice are said to be bleak, and a restricted range of strategically possible policy options, the retrenchment, residualization and marketization of welfare states and the lowering of social standards are forecast.

In this discussion, I argue that the emerging debate on globalization and welfare states shares many of the flaws that can be found in globalization theory, notably with respect to the exaggeration of the strength and degree of unity of capital interests, the underestimation of the powers of the state and of both countervailing changes and oppositional political forces to globalization more generally [...]. I suggest that the enduring power of 'local' factors to impact on and mediate globalization suggests that national institutional, cultural and political differences are likely to prevail rather than be eliminated under the weight of global, 'external' forces [...].

[... A] number of social dialogues and political strategies, of quite different types, are taking place with global capital [...]. Overall, the paper emphasizes a nuanced account of the dynamics of the relationship between globalization and social policy which recognizes the role of ideology and politics, the dialectical relationship between global and local, and the enduring resilience of local political forces.

Globalization: global capital against national states?

[...]

At the heart of what may be termed 'globalization studies' lies the problematic nature, status and powers of the national state in the contemporary world political and economic order. A number of related questions stand out. One set of questions has focused on whether, and the extent to which, the balance of power between states and capital has shifted to the benefit of capital – and global capital in particular. Another set has focused on how significant the national state is as a sphere of social activity and how effective governments can be in economic management. States are locked into an unprecedented scale and depth of both interdependence and competitiveness, but their capacity to effectively manage both the global, 'borderless' economy and their own 'national' economies is said to be diminished. A third set of questions has focused on whether the state is being hollowed out, is withering away, or is 'in retreat'. Few predict the actual demise of the state, and the debate has focused more on the retreat of the state *relative* to other forms of authority in the global political economy and the extent that this will cause it to undergo transformation and adaptation.

One's position on the issue of the consequences of globalization for the state and for the welfare state is likely to hinge on the acceptance of a qualitative shift from the 'old' international order based on inter-national relations primarily between nation states, to a 'new', globalized order characterized by 'global relations between organized capitals' under which relations between national states are subsumed (Teeple 1995). At its crudest, globalization theory views the world economy as dominated by uncontrollable global economic forces where the principal actors are transnational corporations which owe no allegiance to any state and (re)locate wherever market advantage exists (i.e. where profits can be maximized). Thus, Robinson argues that 'transnational capital [is] being liberated from any constraint on its global activity' (1996: 13-14), while Meiksins-Wood argues that globalization is 'another step in the geographical extension of economic rationality and its emancipation from political jurisdiction' (1997: 553). Closely associated with the supposed 'uncontrollable' powers of transnational corporations is the notion that globalization represents a new stage in the development of capitalism:

> The history of capitalism has ceased to be defined by and limited to national boundaries. It would be wrong to draw the conclusion that the world has entered a post-capitalist era. The ownership of capital still matters and it still remains the dominant factor of economic and sociopolitical power in the world. The great change that is occurring is not between a capitalist and post-capitalist society,

nor between a 'good' capitalism (the social market economy) and a 'bad capitalism' (the jungle, or 'casino' market economy). Rather, it is between a weakening of all aspects of a society founded on national capitalism and the growing power and dynamic of global capitalism. (Petrella 1996: 68)

Overall, 'strong' globalization theories stress the primacy of global forces over national or 'local' ones, and the primacy of economic forces over political ones. National states are deemed to have become instruments of global capital: international trade and investment bear a disproportionate amount of influence over the direction and content of national policy, so much so that governments are as sensitive or 'accountable' to the requirements of international capital as to their electorates. It is important to note that those who advance claims of 'strong' globalization come from both the right and left, politically; the former celebrate what the latter condemn.

A number of welcome counter-arguments have been made against 'strong' globalization theory which cast doubt on predictions about the diminished capacities of the state as a 'logical', inevitable outcome of the globalization process. 'Strong' globalization theory is deemed to be wildly overstated, speculative and ahistorical, which is problematic in terms of its validity, accuracy and the degree of generalization from short-term, cyclical or local changes involved. A principal criticism has focused on the way in which 'globalization' is depicted as something 'new' and uncontrollable. Gray argues that 'much current debate confuses globalization, an historical process that has been underway for centuries, with the ephemeral political project of a worldwide free market' (1998: 215). Indeed, much of the discussion on the contemporary world economy has 'emphasized the complete 'globalization' of economic relations, so much so that there is sometimes an unquestioning certainty about the existence of a truly global economy' (Axford 1995: 94). Hirst and Thompson (1996) show that current levels of trade and investment are actually little higher than at the beginning of the twentieth century, that much of what is passed off as 'globalization' amounts to no more than the intensification of existing exchanges between distinct national entities, and that capital flows have firmly remained within the Triad of Western Europe, North America and East Asia.

A further failing of 'strong' globalization theory is its assumption of a predetermined economic 'logic'. This renders it vulnerable to accusations of being a totalizing theory and a crude form of economic determinism, particularly the representation of globalization as a homogeneous and unitary process (Hirst and Thompson 1996; Patel and Pavitt 1991; Green 1997). 'Strong' globalization portrays capital as a unified force, whereas capital is as fragmented and fractured as the forces it faces globally. For example, foreign direct investment in a productive plant in a peripheral country has very different interests than speculative capital that flows into real estate and currency speculation. Domestic and global capital also have different interests; domestic capital has often been at the forefront of arguments for greater, not less, protectionism.

Furthermore, the economic determinism of strong globalization underestimates the continued importance of politics in the globalization process. The depiction of the huge resources of capital and its ability to leave the 'bargaining table' and set up elsewhere has been exaggerated. Most 'global' corporations are still decidedly national in their location and make-up (Ruigrok and Van Tulder 1995; De Angelis 1997). States continue to have strong regulatory powers over capital (Pitelis 1991; Pooley 1991). As Gordon argues, 'it is not at all clear that they [multinationals] have already achieved new global structures of coordination and control which will *necessarily* enhance their power' (1987: 25), because the relationship between multinationals and governments is 'both cooperative and competing, both supportive and conflictual. They operate in a fully dialectical relationship . . . neither the one nor the other partner is clearly or completely able to dominate' (1987: 61; Gray 1998). Capital is dependent on states to perform a range of functions that secure the conditions in which it can operate: the enforcement of property rights and the provision of infrastructure, education, training and the maintenance of social stability. Anyone who is in doubt of the powers of states need only look to their role in the downfall of the Multilateral Agreement on Investment (MAI). The MAI, if successful, would have significantly strengthened the powers of capital over states by allowing 'investment rights' even where it was against national or broader social interests (Sanger 1998).

A related point about the importance of the state in shaping globalization, rather than merely 'receiving' it, is the idea that much of the literature on globalization has focused on unifying economic and technological processes as evidence of greater global interdependence. In so doing, it has neglected the more fragmented political and social spheres which point to more moderate claims about the nature of 'globalization' as well as offering importance evidence of resistance to it. Although recent economic trends may be correctly identified, it is not clear how these relate to long-term structural changes, or how they are moderated by counterchanges or opposing forces. On this point, Green argues that 'the dialectic of history is missing . . . globalization theory has a strong tendency towards economism, reading the political off unproblematically from what it takes to be inevitable economic trends' (1997: 157). The neglect of these countervailing forces and counterchanges obscures decisive 'local' factors and fragmentation that are associated with globalization:

the conventional notion of globalization as an advancing force bulldozing the world around it is clearly at odds with the multiplicity of forms encountered or engendered in diverse contexts. Confusion occurs when one overlooks the way that centralizing elements of globalization fuse with distinctive local and regional conditions. (Mittelman 1996: 232)

Global economic forces, then, should not automatically be elevated above, or assumed to steamroll over, 'local' factors and forces which are internal to states and which can restrict *both* the state's *and* capital's margin of operation. These 'local' forces include the nature and strength of ideologies, social movements and traditions within countries which may resist or oppose 'investment' by global capital and the implementation of the policies of international institutions. Neither have been unopposed, and inhabitants of affected countries have responded with civil and political unrest, with the result that 'the new uprisings of the world's poor have altered the international political economy' (Walton 1987: 384).

Overall, globalization is not hegemonic or uncontested, nor does it steamroll over all areas of social life or trample over states as 'strong' versions have portrayed. International economic processes are refracted through national institutions and mediated by local conditions. States and governments are far from being 'victims' of globalization (even if they like to portray themselves as such), and although many have more than enthusiastically embraced the integration of their economies into the international economy they still possess substantial regulatory powers, both individually and collectively, over global capital. [...]

The impact of globalization on the welfare state

[...] The emerging debate on globalization and social policy has been predominantly framed in terms of the *impact* of globalization on welfare states (Teeple 1995; Mishra 1996, 1999a, 1999b; Rhodes 1996; Perraton *et al.* 1997; Wilding 1997; Garrett 1998; Pierson 1998; Stryker 1998). This approach has emphasized the constraints that economic globalization places on states, public policy and welfare states. [...]

International economic forces are said to have eroded the 'domestic' economic (and political) basis and conditions that have historically underpinned the welfare state. The relocation of corporations from 'high-cost' to 'low-cost' countries impacts on the employment structure in the exited country, leaving behind unemployment and a fiscal deficit, while the transnational nature of economic activity makes its control and taxation much more difficult (Perraton et al, 1997). Stryker (1998) identifies a number of ways in which the structure and operation of the global economy may shape national social policy. First, financial globalization exacerbates the structural dependence of the state on all forms of capital (domestic and foreign). Second, globalized financial and productive capital increase the perceived risk, or the credibility of the threat, of capital flight. Third, financial integration reduces the possibilities for national states to pursue expansionary economic policies to cushion unemployment and encourages them to pursue fiscal austerity. Fourth, the global economy has severed the link between domestic economic growth and full employment in First World countries – the concerns for private profit do not sit easily alongside national economic and employment health (witness record profits alongside redundancies). The fifth factor that Stryker identifies is an ideological one, and is possibly the most important of all – the transnational diffusion of neoliberalism. This stresses the 'complete impotence or perversity of national level economic and social policy making', and encourages governments to believe they cannot change the structure, operation or outcomes of the global economy and must therefore conform with the requirements of international competitiveness (reduce or remove barriers to trade, reduce the size and cost of the state, taxation and welfare) (Stryker 1998: 8–9).

Contemporary globalization, it is argued, alters the internal dynamics of welfare state development and heralds the decline of social democratic reformist politics and projects upon which the welfare state was built (Teeple 1995; Rhodes 1996). The balance of 'external', global influences to 'internal', national ones (e.g. demography, labour markets, the balance of political forces) is held to have altered in favour of the former. As Ash Amin argues, 'state policy *is* becoming more and more driven by external forces' (1997: 129, original italics). The range of 'structurally viable' policy options has not only been narrowed by economic forces but state policy will be primarily oriented to supporting market forces and promoting economic competitiveness. Governments will increasingly stay clear of radical programmes of redistribution, renationalization or other forms of intervention that capital does not 'approve' of. The outcome will be 'the retrenchment of national state intervention in spheres of social reproduction' (Teeple 1995: 5). Those that stray too far from these parameters will be punished electorally and economically due to loss of investment and employment and will leave themselves vulnerable to lower credit ratings, higher interest rates on borrowing, as well as currency speculation by international financial markets (Andrews 1994; Goodman and Pauly 1993; Stewart 1984). The force of these 'external' economic forces is such that it is said to impose a single model of development on countries: national welfare states will converge – they will all be 'driven in the same direction by the imperatives of international competition' (Taylor-Gooby 1997; Wilding 1997; Mishra 1996). Geyer (1998: 77) summarizes the convergence thesis well:

[D]espite varying national contexts and the policies of differing political parties, the welfare states of the advanced industrial countries should become increasingly similar as the forces of globalization squeeze them into a market-oriented welfare-state model. In essence it does not matter whether the national institutional contexts are conservative or social democratic, if the welfare state is conservative, liberal or social democratic; or if a leftist or rightist party is in power, the constraints have become so extreme that only market-conforming welfare-state structures will be allowed.

A major problem with these predictions about the power of the global economic forces, in particular global capital, to force a particular course of action is that they share many of the assumptions of 'strong' globalization theories in so far as they regard globalization as an 'external', naturalistic phenomenon; assume that capital interests are unified; assign a determinant degree of power to (global) economic forces over the course of (national) political action; and assume that globalization is a force primarily of unification. The criticisms levied against 'strong' globalization theories [...] suggest that the political and economic resources of global capital to directly determine individual states' public policies have been exaggerated and that globalization is not homogeneous or unitary in process or effect, either within or across states. Indeed, the issue is far more complex than one of simple causality for the reasons I have just described, as well as for the reasons outlined below.

Of prime importance, first of all, is ideology. As Rhodes argues, 'the nature of the contemporary welfare state dilemma ... is difficult to disentangle from ideology' (1996: 307). Ideology is of particular importance here because it has been central to the advancement of globalization as a political project – through the diffusion of neo-liberalism (Stryker 1998). Neo-liberal ideology emphasizes the limited influence and effect that governments can exert over national economic performance or in subverting the 'natural' outcomes of global markets, while stressing the costs of certain courses of political action: economic success (and prosperity) or failure (and hardship) in an interdependent and competitive global economy is seen as depending on maintaining a competitive advantage. From here it is but a short step to making explicit links between the extent and nature of state provision and delivery of welfare and national economic competitiveness. Stryker (1998: 11) argues that the impact of globalization on welfare states occurs *primarily* through ideological shifts *which in turn* cause national expenditure reductions, privatization and marketization in some social welfare programmes. However, even here, he asserts that the evidence over the past twenty years of left governments slowing welfare expansion and/or embarking on austerity programmes 'does not prove the idea that financial globalization and global diffusion of market-oriented cultural ideals facilitate welfare state retrenchment. But it is consistent with these ideas' (1998: 11). On a similar line, Jordan (1998) also notes the consistency between the 'new politics of welfare' of the British and American governments which put the wage-relation at the centre of welfare reform, and globalization which also hinges on the wage-relation. Ultimately, it seems, at best we may be able to demonstrate consistency rather than causality.

Ideology, rather than crude economic determinism, is important, therefore, in any explanation of the impact of globalization on welfare states. Policy-makers' beliefs, values and assumptions about the global economy are shaped by ideology: they may believe that particular interventions will prompt speculation on the national currency, mass capital flight abroad, or a downturn in investment by foreign firms. Moran and Wood (1996) refer to this framing of social policy by ideas and beliefs about national competitiveness in the global economy as 'contextual internationalization'. The contemporary welfare state 'dilemma' can be attributed to the political power of economic ideas, in particular neo-liberal ideas, which have shaped perceptions of global economic 'logics' and foreclosed 'the parameters of the politically possible' (Hay 1998: 529). Jordan similarly argues that 'the idea of a global market is probably even more powerful than global forces themselves; governments believe that they are competing for prizes in budgetary rectitude before a panel of international financial institutions, and this affects their actions' (1998: 9).

The second reason why it is not possible to establish causality is that states have other functions than economic ones and governments have to respond to a wider range of constituencies than just the international business community. These 'local' factors are decisive rather than incidental in determining the content of public and social policy and how sweeping any reforms may be. These 'local' factors include the political and institutional constellation of national welfare states, historical and cultural traditions, social structures, electoral politics, the partisan nature of government, the presence of strong 'veto players', and the internal structure of the state (Esping-Andersen 1996; Rhodes 1996; Hallerberg and Basinger 1998; Garrett 1998). Other 'local' factors mediating the way in which globalization is 'received' also include the degree of integration of the national economy into the international economy and the particular species of capitalism that has developed nationally.

The emphasis on welfare retrenchment, residualization and marketization as an *inevitable* and *direct* outcome of globalization may also be somewhat misplaced for the reason that the attention to unifying forces of economic change masks counterchanges. Cerny (1997) argues that although states may indeed become oriented towards maintaining economic competitiveness

– indeed, he predicts the rise of 'competition states' – they may become more, not less, interventionist in certain spheres. They may become more authoritarian in policing the consequences of economic globalization – poverty, marginalization and crime. In fact, far from overriding pressures for the state to reduce its welfare effort, a range of pressures to expand the scope of public policy intervention may be placed on governments to counteract marginalization and promote social integration, equality and justice. Public (social) expenditure may increase as a direct consequence of policies that pursue economic competitiveness (Garrett and Mitchell 1996, cited in Wilding 1997), while social protection programmes may be extended to cushion individuals, households and communities against increased economic risk. It is not evident that the predominant theme, or the only way forward, is marketization, as the recent nationalization of care insurance in Germany has illustrated.

While the issue of whether the 'embedded liberalism' of the international political economy imposes limits on redistributive justice (Rhodes 1996; Jordan 1998) is a pertinent one, economic globalization constitutes less of an objective constraint than it is often believed to be, while the convergence thesis is certainly exaggerated. The 'constraints' arising from the global economy are to a large extent 'imposed' by the political power of ideas about the logics and dynamics of the global economy. These constrain states and governments because they narrow the margins of what is believed to be possible and orientate them to the needs and exigencies of international competitiveness. Within these parameters, though, choices are still possible (Rhodes 1996: 309) and it is important to affirm that these choices have significant consequences for the distribution of resources, the quality, extent, and form of welfare provision, and the social rights of the population.

Global governance and social policy

Although arguments that the state has been emasculated by international economic forces should be treated with a good deal of caution, it is equally clear that states operate in a markedly different economic and political environment than they did, say, forty years ago. Social policy making, implementation and provision takes place in a context in which states are no longer the exclusive subject of international politics, the sole mediators of domestic politics, or even the principal representative of their populations. Political globalization and associated institutional and organizational changes in the way that territories, trade and populations are governed means that 'politics is becoming more polycentric' and that states are 'merely one level in a complex system of overlapping and often competing agencies of governance' (Hirst and Thompson 1996: 183). This framework of 'global governance', and the political processes associated with it, has implications for states' sovereignty and policy autonomy.

Gordenker and Weiss define global governance as 'efforts to bring more orderly and reliable responses to social and political issues that go beyond capacities of states to address individually' (1996: 17). Global governance is predominantly associated with 'the development of international organizations and global institutions which attempt to address such issues' (Bretherton 1996: 8). Governments collaborate with each other through cooperative arrangements in conjunction with, and through, international governmental organizations; they operate within a complex legal and political framework of international agreements, treaties, regulations and accords regulating economic exchange and accumulation between countries (Townsend and Donkor 1996). States have to take account of the international context in which they are embedded: they have to be increasingly 'other-regarding', of other states and of the policies and actions of international agencies and transnational corporations which extol the virtues and efficiency of 'free' markets (Mittelman 1996: 231).

International economic and trade institutions – notably the International Monetary Fund, the World Bank and GATT/WTO – have exerted a more tangible influence on states and national policies than has global capital. Government policies are legally bound to comply with the principles and regulations of international governmental organizations, international and supranational organizations (World Bank, IMF, UN system, EU, WTO). These institutions possess substantial financial and legal powers to regulate the international economy; they underwrite the conditions and patterns of international economic investment, production and exchange, set the parameters of national macroeconomic policy and, through this, largely determine the terms and conditions of social development (Townsend and Donkor 1996). They may override nation states' juridical sovereignty by, for example, legally obliging legislation of signatory states to conform with international principles. The economic and foreign-trade policies of states signed up to multilateral trade agreements are subject to enforceable WTO rules on 'free trade'. WTO rules restrict the range of policies that can be pursued nationally, even forbidding certain policies and courses of action if they present a barrier to the 'free' trade of foreign capital locally (e.g. subsidies, social and environmental legislation) (Nader and Wallach 1996).

There is, of course, nothing new about international governmental institutions, which have been in existence for over a century and have coexisted with major periods of welfare-state-building in the advanced industrialized countries. What appears to differ now is that one species of capitalism – global 'free trade' – is being sponsored by international institutions to compete with other species of capitalism (e.g. socially-regulated capitalism) that have historically developed at national level

(Gray 1998). One notable example of this is the conditions attached to the receipt of economic aid from the World Bank and IMF. These include the implementation of economic and social reform ('structural adjustment'), common elements of which are the reduction of public sector debt, expenditure and subsidies, deregulation, and the reduction of public service provision. The policy autonomy of governments in such countries has been undermined by the imposition of a particular model of social and economic development which prohibits them from acting to protect the social cohesion of their societies.

Although global governance is predominantly associated with the institutional framework of national states and international bureaucracies, a far wider range of actors participate in global governance. In its broadest sense, global governance refers to *all* non-state sources of 'authority' which have the power to allocate values and influence the distribution of resources: outlaw business organizations (such as drug cartels, the mafia); professional associations; transnational authorities in sports, art, music; transnational social, political and religious movements (Strange 1996). The Commission on Global Governance (1995: 3) also includes as actors in global governance non-governmental organizations, citizens' movements, multinational organizations, the global capital market and even the global mass media. Non-governmental organizations, for example, are increasingly seeking legitimacy, and justification for their rights claims, from the global as well as the national arena. They have helped raise the profile of social issues on international agendas (notably, social development, the environment, equality, poverty and population), and generally shape international responses to global problems. They also have formal channels of influence, working through bodies such as the UN Commission on Human Rights and the Commission on the Status of Women (Holton 1998; Gordenker and Weiss 1996). Whether or not NGOs' participation in global governance can be considered evidence of the existence of a 'global civil society', it is certainly evidence of the globalization of political and social action.

The field of population and fertility illustrates these structures and processes of global governance. From the outset – the 1950s – 'overpopulation' has been defined as a global issue requiring a global solution. The delivery of population control has involved a combination of both state and private-sector actors at the international, national, and local levels. The major push for this policy has been at the international level, and all the major international institutions have developed population policies: the UN and its various agencies, including WHO, UNICEF and even the ILO; and the World Bank. Also strongly involved in population control discourse has been that oldest of international institutions – the Catholic Church – as well as other, often fundamentalist, international religions and their institutions. At the level of policy implementation, global population control can be characterized as a hierarchy: the donor countries of the North at the apex and the women of the South as its base. Between these is an intermediate layer of international organizations (NGOs, UN agencies, development banks and private foundations), below which are the states of the South. On the national level are the government, the private (commercial) sector, the media (for 'social marketing') and national NGOs; at subnational level are the hospitals, clinics and family planning providers and motivators, including local NGOs, that implement the policy (Bandarage 1997; Koivusalo and Ollila 1997).

The European Union is another example of the ways that the changing institutional and political processes affect social policy. The European Union has been characterized as a system of multitiered governance (Pierson and Leibfried 1995). Although its institutional architecture is predominantly intergovernmental, states are only one, if an important, player amongst other non-state authorities, such as the EU administrative, political and legal institutions, business organizations, trades unions and non-governmental organizations. Political action is 'now having to be carried out through a web of common institutions, states, regional and local authorities and voluntary associations on the domestic front and simultaneously, in national and/or transnational alliances at the common level' (Meehan 1992: 159). Such alliances may consist of domestic interests, that may be antagonistic at times, against another state, or they may be bound by a 'shared interest among civil associations in promoting a common policy against the wishes of their respective governments' (1992: 159; Streeck 1996). The consequences of European political integration are that social policy (agenda-setting, consultation, policy-making, policy implementation and delivery) is no longer confined and controlled within the national sphere. Transnational alliances and formalized channels of influence over the content and direction of supranational social policy have introduced new dynamics into social policy development nationally (Streeck 1995). 'Sovereign' welfare states have been transformed into 'semi-sovereign' welfare states, or parts of multitiered systems of social policy (Leibfried and Pierson 1995, 1996) through:

> 'positive' social policy initiatives to construct areas of competence for uniform social standards at EU level (e.g. gender equality, health and safety); 'negative' social policy reform via the imposition of market compatibility requirements (labour mobility and coordination, freedom of services, regional and sectoral subsidies); and indirect (*de facto*) pressures of integration that force adaptation of national welfare states (social dumping, tax harmonization, stages of EMU). (1996: 187)

Global social dialogues and the social regulation of globalization

[...] Just as global governance has predominantly been characterized in institutional terms, so is 'global social policy':

> Global social policy as a practice of supranational actors embodies global social redistribution, global social regulation, and global social provision and/or empowerment, and includes the ways in which supranational organizations shape national social policy. (Deacon et al, 1997: 195)

[...]

Deacon, Stubbs and Hulse argue that national social policy and social development are increasingly decided by international institutions [...]. However, even here, they acknowledge that [policy outcomes are] still contingent on local factors. In the countries of Central and Eastern Europe, for example, international institutions have been instrumental in restructuring post-communist social policy, but the social policy prescriptions of the IMF have been accepted and implemented because they are consistent with the interests of national bureaucratic and political elites. In short, the national sphere is still a decisive site of struggle, and 'external' forces – be they capital or international institutions – are dependent on the 'ideological integration' of local political elites into the international economy.

Deacon's work on the social dialogue at the global level has been extremely useful in mapping the dominant political and ideological positions of different international institutions in the debate on how globalization should be socially regulated. [...] However, of notable importance in the context of the present discussion is that their work has showed that the 'socialization of global politics' in no way signals the emergence of a unitary view about the role of welfare states or about their future development (see Table 1.3.1).

Competing discourses emerge from within the same institution, while institutional prescriptions vary according to the world-region in which they are embedded. Thus the prescriptions of the EU and ILO reflect their continental European origins, while those of the IMF reflect its US origins (Deacon et al, 1997). This very diversity warns us against apocalyptic interpretations of globalization as 'the end of politics', or as a unifying, hegemonic force. However, Deacon et al's research also confirms that the range of welfare alternatives backed by these institutions is confined to variants of social liberalism, and there is a marked absence of any institution arguing a social democratic or redistributive welfare agenda.

The work of Deacon and his colleagues on the social policies of international institutions has been pioneering. Their focus can be explained

Table 1.3.1: Global social policy discourse

Orientation	Welfare world	Agency promulgating
Existing welfare as:		
Burden	Liberalism	International Monetary Fund, Organisation for Economic Co-operation and Development
Social cohesion	Conservative, Corporatist	European Union, International Labour Organization, World Bank
Investment	(Southeast Asia)	Organisation for Economic Co-operation and Development, World Bank
Redistributive commitment	Social Democracy	–
Emerging welfare as:		
Safety net	Social Liberalism	World Bank, European Union
Workfare	Social Liberalism	International Monetary Fund
Citizenship entitlement	Futuristic	International Labour Organization, Council of Europe
Redistribution	–	–

Source: Deacon and Hulse (1996: 52)

by the fact that it is at this level that the most obvious attempt is being made to formulate global social policy; but it is also a result of the institutionalist tendency in social policy analysis itself. However, this approach must be supplemented to explain the complexity of levels at which global social policy occurs and operates as well as the dialectical relationship between these levels. The focus on social politics and policy at the level of international institutions draws attention to the more visible actors, but in its emphasis on the forces and initiatives to modify 'globalization from above' the forces against 'globalization from below' are neglected (Falk 1997). It confines our view only to the social dialogue that takes place at international level and excludes other 'social dialogues' taking place at different levels and in various locations outside the boardrooms and bureaux of international institutions. A similar type of 'global social dialogue' has been going on between social movements in the shadow congresses that now accompany meetings of the G8, such as the Other Economy summit. Nor is this dialogue purely reactive; the International Encounter against Neoliberalism, for example, was brought together in response to calls from Zapatistas and social and political activists from a wide variety of countries. Another type of global social dialogue has been facilitated by the development of the internet; this technological factor makes global dialogue easier for highly disparate and isolated groups, many of whom cannot afford international travel.

In fact, a range of strategies and initiatives to regulate globalization can be identified, examples of which are presented in Table 1.3.2 below. Some of these seek not to oppose globalization but instead seek negotiated reform, working with and through international institutions and/or corporations. The Trades Union Advisory Committee to the OECD has argued for more effective global social governance by strengthening the 'social dimension' of globalization (Evans n.d.). Social clauses have been central to these attempts to strengthen the social regulation of global capital. They attempt to link trade agreements with minimum labour standards within the institutions and agreements that control international trade (Shaw 1996; Lee 1997). Shaw points out that a consensus exists amongst most participating parties in this debate that 'free trade is to be welcomed and protectionism is undesirable' (1996: 3), but positions on social clauses are locally and politically rooted. While trades unions are generally in favour of social clauses, non-governmental organizations have ranged from qualified acceptance to outright opposition on the issue. Similarly, some governments of the South, as well as of the North, oppose social clauses on the grounds that they are a form of protectionism. Overall, attempts to seek to regulate the global economy by working with international institutions have not so far been phenomenally successful, particularly when compared with the scale, pace and social effects of international trade and investment agreements.

Table 1.3.2: Strategies and proposals to regulate globalization

Sphere	Social	Economic
Political-institutional (top-down)	Social (labour) clauses; human rights (Council of Europe, UN Declaration of Human Rights)	International Financial Commission (TUAC); Global tax Authority; Tobin Tax*
Market (bottom-up)	Fair (ethical) trade; social labelling; consumer campaigns; trade and labour boycotts.	Corporate codes of conduct; Ethical investement

Note: * The Tobin Tax, proposed in 1974, is a tax levied on currency transactions.

Other strategies which engage in a 'social dialogue' with global capital take the form of direct action, often through the market mechanism. Market-based strategies include international campaigns by consumer groups and NGOs to bring about improved standards for groups of workers in particular industries by mobilizing consumers to redirect their spending power away from offending companies' products. Consumer, trade and labour boycotts and the social labelling of products have brought about corporate codes of conduct being adopted in global industries, such as in the baby foods market, pharmaceutical drugs industry and the textiles, garments and shoewear industries (Shaw 1996; Vander Stichele and Pennartz 1996). It is important to emphasize, though, that initiatives in the 'market' and 'political' spheres are not mutually exclusive forms of action. International institutions may be called on to back up local opposition: a labour union (OCAW) recently lodged a complaint against the German chemical company BASF with the OECD.

Global social politics also includes strategies of outright opposition and disruptive action at the local level, for example against local branches of transnational corporations. Numerous examples of such action can be cited, for example, of various tribal and indigenous groups and NGOs which have taken their concerns to the AGMs of transnational companies such as RTZ (Rio Tinto Zinc), Shell, BP and Monsanto. With genetic engineering, for example, which can be expected to have far-reaching social, economic and environmental effects, the introduction of new technology by capital on a global scale, often aided by permissive state regulation of this technology, has encountered a range of popular opposition strategies. Just as globalization prompts a variety of national responses, so a variety of national opposition strategies have arisen in relation to genetically modified foods. Here, the types of resistance vary geographically: in England, consumer boycotts and activist attacks on test crops have been the principal forms of resistance; in Asia and Europe, opposition has developed on an ideological level, often with a religious basis; in India resistance has taken the form of attacks on companies by mass farmers' organizations.

Global issues are often fought out on a local level, and over what at first appear to be 'local' issues. Local counter-struggles are fought by a range of groups and organizations: trades unions, women's groups, environmental groups, tribal and indigenous groups, consumer groups, civil liberties groups and anti-nuclear groups. Many of these struggles can be regarded as resistance to globalization in so far as they 'have a cooperative element and a degree of social and political consciousness' (Teeple 1995: 149). In countries across the world, neo-liberal, deregulatory policies have prompted mass and public resistance in the form of demonstrations, strikes and riots. The 1995 strike protest by public sector workers in France in response to proposed cuts to income maintenance policies, specifically pensions, shows how the fate of globalization is often decided locally rather than globally, is mediated by class struggle and is dependent on the national balance of power. Thus, despite the fact that one in every twelve French workers was unemployed and one in every five was in a part-time or temporary job, a major popular mobilization prevented proposed pension reforms (Jefferys 1996; Bonoli 1997).

Demands and movements for local economic autonomy, self-sufficiency and economic nationalism may also be regarded as forms of resistance and opposition to globalization. At the local level, self-help and community groups, cooperative movements have mobilized to fill in the gaps left by the failure of capitalism to provide employment. In both the First and Third Worlds alike new forms of local economic organization and cooperation have emerged amongst the poor (Rowbotham and Mitter 1994; Norberg-Hodge 1996). Local exchange trading systems (LETS) and local currency schemes which strive to relocalize the economy can be regarded as a symbolic and practical 'response to the local social and economic consequences of globalization', namely 'the economic and political marginalization of people and places marginal or unnecessary to the capitalist development process' (Paccione 1997: 1179–80; Meeker-Lowry 1996). The globalization process is a dialectical one in which 'local' events will impact globally and will inform global political responses. The costs, for example, of the latest financial crisis – in Asia in 1997–98 – were experienced both locally and globally (i.e. in the West) and prompted calls for reform to the IMF and World Bank and stricter regulation over international financial markets (although the eventual reforms have shied away from regulation in favour of the provision of emergency funds). In the same way, locally-expressed populist social dialogues have impacted on the more 'elitist' social politics and policies of international institutions. The push for a change in World Bank policy to take better account of poverty came from local and national factors. It was forced to take account of the destabilizing effects of its policies by local food riots and the threat of local social unrest and disruption.

The World Bank's strategic response to criticisms by international and national non-governmental organizations of the local social effects of structural adjustment programmes has been to include them in the policy process. Consultation with these organizations serves the useful purpose for the World Bank of testing the local social and political foundations before structural adjustment programmes are implemented; involving them directly in the implementation of social development programmes makes use of their grassroots links with 'hard to reach' populations and with other local movements (Deacon et al, 1997).

Conclusions

This paper has examined how the relationship between globalization and social policy has been approached within the academic literature. I have argued that this literature shares some of the assumptions – and the flaws – of 'strong' globalization theory in so far as globalization is conceived of as a top-down, 'external', naturalistic and unifying force. Consequently, some of the claims surrounding the process and impact of globalization on states, social policy and welfare states are simplistic and exaggerated. The 'constraints' that are placed on social policy development are primarily ideological and thus susceptible to political manipulation. I have also highlighted the decisive role of the state and politics in shaping globalization and in mediating its effect on welfare states. [...] Social policy now develops in a pluralistic and multi-levelled institutional framework of global governance which has altered the political dynamics of social policy. Social policy has been (partially) decoupled from the national sphere as a consequence of the greater involvement by supranational and international institutions in the political management of globalization. However, I have emphasized the decisive importance of 'local' factors in shaping globalization [...]. It is at this local level that non-geographically located global forces must 'touch down' and be expressed. When they attempt to do so, they often meet with a range of mediating, regulatory and oppositional forces. These forces may be as instrumental in shaping the political management of globalization as the formal social policies and discourses of international institutions.

This recognition of the importance of local factors tempers the more apocalyptic accounts of the prospects for welfare states under contemporary globalization and elevates the importance of politics, rather than economics, as the driving force of national social policy reform. Consequently, it allows a re-evaluation of 'traditional' factors such as class, ethnicity, race and gender politics in shaping social policy. From this perspective, 'globalization' in the sense of international economic forces is just one factor amongst others that influence welfare state development. Ultimately, while it is necessary to recognize the global context of social policy development, global economic forces are contested and mediated by states whose political responses are conditioned by local, internal factors, such as historical and institutional arrangements, cultural and religious values and traditions, political and social forces and the balance of political power.

References

Amin, A. (1997), Placing globalization, *Theory, Culture & Society*, 14, 2: 123–37.

Andrews, D. (1994), Capital mobility and state autonomy: toward a structural theory of international monetary relations, *International Studies Quarterly*, 38.

Axford, B. (1995), *The Global System: Economics, Politics and Culture*, Cambridge: Polity Press.

Bandarage, A. (1997), *Women, Population and Global Crisis: A Political-economic analysis*, London: Zed Books.

Bonoli, G. (1997), Pension politics in France: patterns of co-operation and conflict in two recent reforms, *West European Politics*, 20, 4: 111–24.

Bretherton, C. (1996), Introduction: global politics in the 1990s. In C. Bretherton and G. Ponton (eds), *Global Politics: An Introduction*, Oxford: Blackwell.

Cerny, P. (1997), Paradoxes of the competition state: the dynamics of political globalization, *Government and Opposition*, 32, 2: 251–74.

Commission on Global Governance (1995), *Our Global Neighbourhood*, Oxford: Oxford University Press.

De Angelis, M. (1997), The autonomy of the economy and globalization, *Common Sense*, 21: 41–59.

Deacon, B. (1999), *Towards a Socially Responsible Globalization: International Actors and Discourses*, GASPP Occasional Papers, STAKES: Finland.

Deacon, B., and Hulse, M. (1996), *The Globalization of Social Policy*, Leeds: Leeds Metropolitan University.

Deacon, B., with Stubbs, P., and Hulse, M. (1997), *Global Social Policy: International Organizations and the Future of Welfare*, London: Sage.

Esping-Andersen, G. (ed.) (1996), *Welfare States in Transition: National Adaptations in Global Economies*, London: Sage.

Evans, J. (n.d.), *Economic Globalization: the Need for a Social Dimension*, discussion paper, TUAC, Paris.

Falk, R. (1997), Resisting 'Globalization-from-above' Through 'Globalization-from-Below', *New Political Economy*, 2, 1: 17–24.

Garrett, G. (1998), *Partizan Politics in the Global Economy*, Cambridge: Cambridge University Press.

Geyer, R. (1998), Globalization and the (non-)defence of the welfare state, *West European Politics*, 21, 3: 77–102.

Goodman, J., and Pauly, L. (1993), The obsolescence of capital controls? Economic management in an age of global markets, *World Politics*, 46.

Gordenker, L., and Weiss, T. G. (1996), Pluralizing global governance: analytical approaches and dimensions. In T. G. Weiss and L. Gordenker (eds), *NGOS, the UN, and Global Governance*, London: Lynne Rienner.

Gray, J. (1998), *False Dawn: The Delusions of Global Capitalism* (2nd edn), London: Granta.

Green, A. (1997), *Education, Globalization and the Nation State*, Basingstoke: Macmillan.

Hallerberg, M., and Basinger, S. (1998), Internationalization and changes in taxation policy in OECD countries: the importance of domestic veto players, *Comparative Political Studies*, 31, 3: 321–52.

Hay, C. (1998), Globalization, welfare retrenchment and the 'logic of no alternative': why second-best won't do, *Journal of Social Policy*, 24, 4: 525–32.

Hirst, P., and Thompson, G. (1996), *Globalization in Question: the International Economy and the Possibilities of Governance*, Cambridge: Polity Press.

Holton, R. J. (1998), *Globalization and the Nation-State*, Basingstoke: Macmillan.

Jefferys, S. (1996), France 1995: the backward march of labour halted, *Capital and Class*, 59: 7–21.

Jordan, B. (1998), *The New Politics of Welfare*, London: Sage.

Koivusalo, M., and Ollila, E. (1997), *Making a Healthy World: Agencies, Actors and Policies in International Health*, London: Zed Books.

Lee, E. (1997), Globalization and labour standards: a review of issues, *International Labour Review*, 136, 2: 173–89.

Leibfried, S., and Pierson, P. (1995), Semisovereign welfare states: social policy in a multitiered Europe. In S. Leibfried and P. Pierson (eds), *European Social Policy: Between Fragmentation and Integration*, Washington DC: Brookings Institution.

Leibfried, S., and Pierson, P. (1996), Social Policy. In H. Wallace and W. Wallace (eds), *Policy-Making in the European Union*, Oxford: Oxford University Press.

Meehan, E. (1992), *Citizenship and the European Community*, London: Sage.

Meeker-Lowry, S. (1996), Community money: the potential of local currency. In J. Mander and E. Goldsmith (eds), *The Case Against the Global Economy and For a Turn Toward the Local*, San Francisco: Sierra Club Books.

Meiksins-Wood, E. (1997), Modernity, postmodernity or capitalism?, *Review of International Political Economy*, 4, 3: 539–60.

Mishra, R. (1996), The welfare of nations. In R. Boyer and D. Drache (eds), *States Against Markets: the Limits of Globalization*, London: Routledge.

Mishra, R. (1999a), *Globalization and the Welfare State*, Cheltenham: Edward Elgar.

Mishra, R. (1999b), Beyond the nation states: social policy in an age of globalization. In C. Jones Finer (ed.), *Transnational Social Policy*, Oxford: Blackwell.

Mittelman, J. H. (1996), How does globalization really work? In J. H. Mittelman (ed.), *Globalization: Critical Reflections*, London: Lynne Rienner.

Moran, M., and Wood, B. (1996), The globalization of health care policy? In Philip Gummett (ed.), *Globalization and Public Policy*, Cheltenham: Edward Elgar.

Nader, R., and Wallach, L. (1996), GATT, NAFTA and the subversion of the democratic process. In J. Mander and E. Goldsmith (eds), *The Case Against the Global Economy and for a Turn Toward the Local*, San Francisco: Sierra Club Books.

Norberg-Hodge, H. (1996), Shifting direction: from global dependence to local interdependence. In J. Mander and E. Goldsmith (eds), *The Case Against the Global Economy and for a Turn Toward the Local*, San Francisco: Sierra Club Books.

Paccione, M. (1997), Local exchange trading systems as a response to the globalization of capitalism, *Urban Studies*, 34, 8: 1179–99.

Patel, P., and Pavitt, K. (1991), Large firms in the production of the world's technology: an important case of non-globalization, *Journal of International Business Studies*, First Quarter: 1–21.

Perraton, J., Goldblatt, D., Held, D., and McGrew, A. (1997), The globalization of economic activity, *New Political Economy*, 2, 2.

Petrella, R. (1996), Globalization and internationalization: the dynamics of the emerging world order. In R. Boyer and D. Drache (eds), *States against Markets: the Limits of Globalization*, London: Routledge.

Pierson, C. (1998), *Beyond the Welfare State: the New Political Economy of Welfare*, 2nd edn, Cambridge: Polity Press.

Pierson, P., and Leibfried, S. (1995), Multitiered institutions and the making of social policy. In S. Leibfried and P. Pierson (eds), *European Social Policy: Between Fragmentation and Integration*, Washington DC: Brookings Institution.

Pitelis, C. (1991), Beyond the nation state? The transnational firm and the nation state, *Capital and Class*, 43: 131–52.

Pooley, S. (1991), The state rules, OK? The continuing political economy of nation states, *Capital and Class*, 43: 65–82.

Rhodes, M. (1996), Globalization and West European welfare states: a critical review of recent debates, *Journal of European Social Policy*, 6, 4: 305–27.

Robinson, W. (1996), Globalization: nine theses on our epoch, *Race and Class*, 38, 2: 13–31.

Rowbotham, S., and Mitter, S. (eds) (1994), *Dignity and Daily Bread: New Forms of Economic Organizing Among Poor Women in the Third World and the First*, London: Routledge.

Ruigrok, W., and Van Tulder, T. (1995), *The Logic of International Restructuring*, London: Lawrence and Wishart.

Sanger, M. (1998), *MAI: Multilateral Investment and Social Rights*. Paper presented to the GASPP seminar on International Trade and Investment Agreements and Social Policy, Sheffield, December.

Shaw, L. (1996), *Social Clauses*, London: Catholic Institute for International Relations.

Stewart, M. (1984), *The Age of Interdependence: Economic Policy in a Shrinking World*, Cambridge MA: MIT Press.

Strange, S. (1996), *The Retreat of the State: The Diffusion of Power in the World Economy*, Cambridge: Cambridge University Press.

Streeck, W. (1995), From market making to state building? Reflections on the political economy of European social policy. In S. Leibfried and P. Pierson (eds), *European Social Policy: Between Fragmentation and Integration*, Washington DC: Brookings Institution.

Streeck, W. (1996), Neo-voluntarism: a new social policy regime? In G. Marks, F. W. Scharpf, P. C. Schmitter and W. Streeck (eds) (1996), *Governance in the European Union*, London: Sage.

Stryker, R. (1998), Globalization and the welfare state, *International Journal of Sociology and Social Policy*, 18, 2/3/4: 1–49.

Taylor-Gooby, P. (1997), In defence of second-best theory: state, class and capital in social policy, *Journal of Social Policy*, 26, 2: 171–92.

Teeple, G. (1995), *Globalization and the Decline of Social Reform*, Toronto: Garamond Press.

Townsend, P., and Donkor, K. (1996), *Global Restructuring and Social Policy: the Need to Establish an International Welfare State*, Bristol: Policy Press.

Vander Stichele, M., and Pennartz, P. (1996), *Making it our Business – European NGO Campaigns on Transnational Organizations*, London: Catholic Institute for International Relations.

Walton, J. (1987), Urban protest and the global political economy: the IMF riots. In *The Capitalist City*, Oxford: Blackwell.

Wilding, P. (1997), Globalization, regionalism and social policy, *Social Policy and Administration*, 31, 4: 410–28.

Chapter 1.4

Analysing transnational policy formation: the case of pensions privatization

Mitchell A. Orenstein

Introduction

[...]

This [study] analyzes the role of transnational policy actors in spreading pension privatization ideas and practices worldwide. Transnational policy actors are defined broadly as organizations (multiltateral state, or non-state) or individuals that seek to develop and advocate well-elaborated policy proposals in multiple national contexts. Through a detailed study of the privatization of state social security systems, this study seeks to answer several fundamental questions: Are national policy makers influenced by transnational policy actors who sell policy ideas from country to country? How much influence do transnational actors have on policies such as pension reform that have long been dominated by powerful domestic interest groups? If transnational actors are important, how are they important? What are the sources of their influence and when do they exert it?

This [study] addresses these questions by exploring the spread of pension privatization, which I also refer to as the new pension reforms, a set of policy reforms that have radically altered the post-war domestic social contract in more than thirty countries around the world. Pension privatization involves the partial or full replacement of social security type pension systems by ones based on private, individual pension savings acccounts. Transnational policy actors, including the World Bank, the U.S. Agency for International Development (USAID), and other multilateral and bilateral aid agencies, transnational policy entrepreneurs, and expert networks, have been deeply involved in the development, diffusion, and implementation of these reforms. While pension privatization has affected mostly middle-income developing countries, these reforms also have been implemented in Sweden and the United Kingdom and proposed in the United States as well as in other developed countries.

[...]

Transnationalization of domestic policy

In conducting further research for this project, I dug deeply into the growing literature on transnational public policy, a literature with roots in international relations theory and organizational sociology (DiMaggio and Powell 1983; Strang and Meyer 1993; Meyer et al. 1997; Strang and Soule 1998; Tolbert and Zucker 1983). In this literature, I found company with a group of scholars who argue that transnational and non-state actors are playing an increasing role in domestic policy development in countries around the world (Reinecke 1998). Pioneering works focused on transnational activist networks (Keck and Sikkink 1998), epistemic communities (Haas 1992), and a variety of other international actors that play a greater role than many scholars had previously thought in the making of domestic policy (Orenstein and Schmitz 2006).

National and transnational perspectives on policy are distinguished largely by their position on the autonomy of transnational actors. Transnationalist scholars believe that transnational actors and institutions play a fundamental and relatively autonomous role in policy making in multiple states (Reinecke 1998; Hewson and Sinclair 1999; Kaul et al. 1999; Stone 2003; Barnett and Finnemore 2004), while those working in a national politics or realist tradition see transnational actors as dependent on states that remain the final arbiters of policy decisions. Because the transnational actors that I observed seemed to have a great deal of control over their own agendas, I felt that it was important to integrate the transnational and national perspectives in order to explain the rise of pension privatization.

Ideas and influence

If transnational actors are relatively independent, what is the source of their influence? One source is their normative and ideological influence. Transnational actors have become vessels for ideational influence on politics worldwide through the creation and diffusion of new policy ideas, norms, metrics, values, and technical expertise. Whereas many previous studies of transnational actors such as international organizations and multi-national companies have emphasized their ability to coerce countries into adopting certain policies, I emphasize their persuasive as well as coercive powers. It is often difficult to separate these two forms of influence, however. Following Jacoby (2004) and Epstein (2008), I question the usefulness of the 'norms' versus 'incentives' debate and instead focus on discerning specific mechanisms of influence that may combine both norms and incentives. Norms are defined here as principled ideas about how policies should be designed. Norms and ideas are said to be 'new' to the extent they have not been previously adopted in a particular domestic context.

Studies that emphasize incentives and coercion, rather than norms and ideas, tend to start from a hard rational or materialist perspective on politics that assumes that the interests of policy actors are fixed. Therefore actors must be coerced to change their positions. Ideational approaches to politics tend to start from the assumption that rational actors face considerable uncertainty about their interests or how to pursue them; their rationality is bounded by the limits of information and cognition (March and Simon 1993; Druckman 2004). Introducing new normative ideas or information can cause actors to reshape their policy preferences. As a result, interests are less stable than hard rationalists would predict (Druckman 2004). […] I found many actors who initially opposed such reforms but later ended up supporting them because they gained new information or were persuaded of the normative case for these reforms by reform advocates. Some were also offered selective incentives to encourage compliance. As Juliet Johnson (2008) points out, some actors may be more influenced by norms, while others may only be influenced by material incentives. The most powerful transnational actors use a range of both ideational and material resources as circumstances permit. They apply all the tools they have in an effort to pursue their policy agendas to a successful conclusion.

In presenting an argument that combines both ideas and incentives this work follows Blyth (2002), who argues that norms and ideas partly constitute actors' interests and policy preferences. Blyth suggests that ideas can help to reduce uncertainty in times of crisis by providing problem definitions that enable actors to understand the situation that they are in. Second, ideas can make collective action and coalition building possible by allowing agents to redefine their interests under conditions of uncertainty and to link up with other actors behind new programs. Third, ideas can be weapons in the struggle over existing institutions. They help to delegitimize current institutions and the norms and ideas of opponents as well as justify policy preferences of reform advocates. Fourth ideas can act as blueprints for new institutions, suggesting policies and methods of achieving stated goals. Finally, ideas can make institutional stability possible by providing justifications for institutions' existence and the policies that they transmit (Blyth 2002, 34-41).

Transnational actors, including international organizations, transnational non-governmental organizations (NGOs), expert networks, and individual policy entrepreneurs, have become leading sources of policy norms and ideas in countries worldwide in areas that often exceed their original mandate. Their ability to exercise normative influence depends on their organizational and institutional legitimacy. Barnett and Finnemore (2004) argue that transnational actors often have a unique authority to pursue their goals. International organizations often possess 'delegated authority' explicitly granted by countries to pursue certain goals legitimately. Transnational actors may also have extraordinary 'moral authority' by virtue of their mission to pursue legitimate and seemingly disinterested moral objectives, such as poverty alleviation or environmental protection. Finally, transnational actors often enjoy 'expert authority' and are recognized as storehouses of global expertise in certain areas. Each of these sources of authority enables transnational actors to persuade other actors and organizations to accept their desired policy norms and ideas and join them in global campaigns.

Reshaping preferences

In exerting their independent influence on policy, transnational actors use a variety of means to reshape the preferences of transnational and national policy makers. In the pension reform arena, transnational actors have successfully advocated new pension reforms that radically alter existing social contracts and affect the core material interests of numerous groups in society. Transnational actors have often been the first in a country to advocate pension privatization. By forging alliances with like-minded domestic partners (Jacoby 2008) and working with them to change the preferences of key veto players and other social groups, transnational actors have been highly successful in spreading pension privatization. Transnational actor interventions cannot explain all adoptions or non-adoptions of pension privatization. However, their role is crucial to explaining a very high proportion of existing cases. Transnational actors have been particularly influential in middle-income developing countries where domestic policy-making resources are relatively weak and the willingness to undertake risky reforms is relatively high. In such contexts, decision makers have been highly influenced by transnational actors, their normative policy ideas and campaigns, their legitimacy, and their resources.

[...]

Conceptual and methodological issues

Any study of the impact of transnational actors on policy faces serious conceptual and methodological challenges. [...] One of the most fundamental problems in analyzing the role of transnational actors is that scholars often differ in their definitions of transnational actors. Many scholars tend to equate transnational influence with that of a single organization or type of transnational actor, such as international financial institutions, transnational activist networks, or policy entrepreneurs, while ignoring other transnational actors that may operate in the same policy domain or regime. Narrow definitions of transnational actors may obscure their influence. Similarly, scholars have a tendency to miscode organizations and individuals with deep transnational ties and activities as purely domestic. This suggests that identifying and distinguishing transnational and national actors can be a difficult analytical task. A second analytical difficulty is that since transnational actors necessarily act in partnership with domestic policy makers, it can be difficult to untangle the influence of transnational actors from that of the domestic actors they advise. This study provides evidence that transnational actors have not only been deeply involved in partnerships with domestic proponents of the new pension reforms, but they have been instrumental in putting these reforms on the policy agenda in country after country and providing the technical support to enable their domestic allies to push reform through. Finally, transnational actors tend to work together in global policy campaigns to advance policy reforms in multiple countries, often creating donor councils or meetings to divide responsibilities. This makes it difficult to analyze the impact of individual transnational actors.

Perhaps the best way to address these conceptual complications is to study the behavior of transnational actors in global policy campaigns through a case study method that allows close observation of the full range of transnational actors involved, their interventions in particular countries, and internal decision making. Such a method avoids making false or stylized assumptions about who transnational actors are and what they do. It allows for a more nuanced analysis of transnational actor behavior and its effects in particular countries and organizations. However, case study analysis also has its faults, creating the potential for observer bias and limited generalizability of findings. To remedy these problems, this study supplements case studies of organizations and country experiences with an analysis of the full range of transnational actor interventions in the pension reform arena. This is pursued through a comprehensive study of World Bank documents as well as through representative case studies of the full range of reform and non-reform cases. While most studies of the new pension reforms (Madrid 2003; Weyland 2005) and indeed of other transnational policy campaigns (Jacoby 2004; Kelley 2004) take either a regional approach or select a small number of representative cases for analysis, this study provides a comprehensive analysis of transnational actor involvement in the rise and spread of pension privatization worldwide. It studies their involvement over a broad scope of time, from agenda setting to implementation, and of space, from Central and Eastern Europe to Latin America to Asia to Africa. Taking such a comprehensive approach provides new perspective on the importance of transnational actors in setting domestic policy.

Generalizability

How easy is it to generalize conclusions about pension privatization to other areas of transnational public policy? Every policy area is somewhat unique. Developments may vary according to the nature of policy issues, the types of organizations involved in them, their motivations, and the intensity of domestic politics (Jacoby 2004). Nelson (2004) has argued that the pension policy area is unusual in being dominated by a clear set of ideas promoted by a powerful international organization and its partners. Other policy areas may display greater fragmentation in transnational policy advice, less focused transnational campaigns, and more resistant domestic politics. No doubt, the campaign for pension privatization has been particularly well organized and successful.

Yet in some ways, the campaign for pension privatization is typical of transnational policy making in the world today. Pension privatization typifies the spread of a vision of economic 'best practice' by transnational actors. These reforms provide a technocratic fix to the problem of population aging and are part of a broader set of neoliberal economic policies that have spread worldwide (Biersteker 1990; Graham 1998; Campbell and Pedersen 2001; Fourcade-Gourinchas and Babb 2002). In nearly every public policy sphere, a variety of types of organizations – state, non-state, and intergovernmental – are active in global policy campaigns advocating economic reform solutions. They interact with domestic partners in broadly similar ways and seek to have similar impacts on national policy in multiple jurisdictions. While specific features of the pension privatization process are no doubt distinctive, the general model of the transnational policy process presented here should be relevant to other areas.

Pension privatization provides an appropriate and extremely useful venue in which to test the influence of transnational actors on national policy. Previous studies have attempted to evaluate transnational actor influence in areas where one would expect to find it. Environmental policies, for instance, often have externalities that invite transnational actor interventions (Young 1999). Human rights policies similarly carry strong rationales for transnational intervention, such as the potential for civil conflict that may spill over into international conflict (Risse et al, 1999). By contrast, pension policies of states rarely create problems that require outside actor interventions. Transnational actors do not need to get involved in national pension reforms because of their interests. They do so rather because of their normative beliefs and organizational priorities.

Pension privatization does not provide an open and shut case for demonstrating the impact of transnational policy actors. Quite the opposite, pension policy provides a particularly challenging venue for testing the influence of transnational actors, where most previous literature has emphasized domestic causes. To demonstrate that transnational actors have had a significant influence on the spread of the new pension reforms is to show that transnational actors have a far greater influence than is commonly understood on many areas of 'domestic' politics. If transnational actors are important in shaping national pension policies, the domestic models of the policy process that are commonly employed to explain policy in a wide range of areas require substantial revisions. [T]his study thus hold[s] important implications for public policy research more generally.

[…]

Evaluating the Impact of transnational actors

Transnational actors have been directly involved in the enactment of pension privatization in countries around the world, but have they been important or only tangentially involved? How does one evaluate their impact and limits?

[…]

[A]ssessing the importance of transnational actors in the diffusion of pension privatization requires taking a global perspective and considering the full range of cases, including (1) any cases where transnational policy actors were involved and pension privatization was implemented, (2) any cases where transnational policy actors were involved but pension privatization was not implemented, and (3) any cases where transnational policy actors were not involved but pension privatization was implemented.

[…]

Problems of conceptualization and measurement

Despite considerable disagreement about the role and influence of transnational policy actors in the new pension reforms, data and methods for studying transnational policy actor involvement have been surprisingly weak and biased against findings of transnational actor influence. The approaches adopted by many studies tend to underestimate the impact of transnational actors in three ways. First, scholars have differed in their identification of transnational actors. Some actors, such as Chilean economists and reform advocates, have been defined as domestic or regional actors in some studies and as transnational reform advocates in others. Second, scholars have often made simplistic assumptions about what transnational actors want, rather than studying the complex decision-making processes of transnational actors and their differentiated advice in different countries. Third, most studies focus on the World Bank and ignore the ways that transnational actors cooperate in campaign coalitions, sometimes magnifying their influence beyond that exerted by any one organization. [...]

Who transnational actors are

One of the most surprising issues of the current literature on the political economy of pension reform has been the difficulty of coding policy actors as 'transnational' or 'domestic.' Some studies that have found a low influence for transnational actors have simply coded them as local when they may be more appropriately seen as transnational. For instance, Tavits's (2003) work on policy learning in Latvia and Estonia argues that Latvia reproduced international models in its pension reforms under the influence of the World Bank, while Estonia designed its program independently. Estonia reportedly rejected resources from the World Bank 'because of the reluctance to create any kind of dependency on international organizations' (2003, 655). Both countries adopted similar new pension reforms around the same point in time. Lindemann (2004, 12), a prominent international adviser on pension reform, likewise reports that Estonia's pension reforms were 'home grown.'

Other sources contradict the view that Estonia designed its reforms independently of transnational influence. The Republic of Estonia's (2000) Memorandum of Economic Policies to the International Monetary Fund (IMF) shows that Estonia promised the IMF to implement pension privatization quickly, while receiving technical advice from the World Bank. World Bank evaluations also show deep involvement of World Bank advisers in Estonia (World Bank 2005, 30). Estonian researchers Kulu and Reiljan (2004, 32) report that 'an international seminar was organized in Estonia in 1999 including World Bank staff and other pension experts, where specific design issues of the Estonian pension system were discussed.' Toots (2002) points out that Estonia not only benefited from international financial institutions' support for its pension privatization process, but also that the 'independent' policymakers whom Tavits (2003) suggests were carefully insulated from World Bank influence in fact had close ties to the World Bank. Of the five Estonian members of the Commission on Social Security Reform that designed the Estonian reforms, one (A. Hansson) had worked as an expert of the World Bank, and a second (M. Jesse) had been a local counselor to the World Bank and later coordinator of the World Bank/Estonian Health Policy Project (Toots 2002, 2-3).

Weyland's (2005) study on pension reforms in Latin America raises similar definitional quandaries. While Weyland argues that international financial institution (IFI) influence has been limited, he places a great deal of explanatory weight on the role of Chilean policy advisers in Latin American reforms. Yet Chilean advisers may also be regarded as transnational policy entrepreneurs. After pension privatization in Chile in the early 1980s, Chilean Secretary of Labor and Social Policy Jose Piñera began a long career advising countries that were considering replacing their social security systems with private, individual pension savings accounts. According to Piñera, he has worked in twenty-three countries that adopted pension privatization (interview, January 2006) in Latin America and Europe. Piñera has also worked closely with the World Bank and USAID in the provision of pension policy advice. While not an IFI, Piñera can undoubtedly be seen as a transnational policy entrepreneur with a global policy agenda. Thus, constraining the definition of transnational actors to IFIs alone excludes consideration of transnational actors that have been important in spreading reform in Latin America, such as Chilean policy entrepreneurs.

Such disparities indicate the difficulties comparative politics scholars face in coding 'domestic' versus 'transnational' actors. In part, differences stem from the mental model of the reform process that researchers apply. To a researcher attuned to the study of domestic politics, it may appear that Estonian reformers are domestic actors, while a student of transnational politics and policy may be sensitized to the ways that Estonian reformers are connected to transnational networks. Such networks can be difficult for scholars to recognize, because they depend on consulting and other relationships that may not be immediately visible. For instance, IFIs may co-opt local actors as one mode of influence, offering national officials a high-paying career route to policy advisory capacities in other countries, a lucrative stint in Washington, or speaking engagements at instructional conferences (Hunter and Brown 2000, 119). IFI incentives, which are often studied at the country level, may operate more effectively at the individual level. IFI officials may also appoint their own employees to high positions in reforming country policy teams. This has occurred in Poland, Hungary, and Croatia, where top-ranking IFI bureaucrats took leading positions in national teams dedicated to pension privatization [...]. In some cases, these officials were citizens of the reforming country; in other cases not. Thus, for a variety of reasons, it becomes difficult to ascertain the localism or transnationalism of policy reform teams. Is a reform team with all Estonian members 'local' if two of the members have run World Bank projects in the past? Or are they better understood as local members of a transnational policy network?

What transnational actors want

A second key problem in analyzing transnational influence is the difficulty in defining what transnational actors want. Studies of the influence of transnational actors often begin from stylized assumptions about what transnational actors are trying to achieve. Such assumptions are usually made in the spirit of theoretical and empirical parsimony, but they are sometimes inaccurate. Ascertaining the goals of transnational actors often requires careful attention to the complex internal decision making of actors with diverse centers of power and multiple stakeholders. By ignoring the internal politics of transnational actors, studies often make overly broad assumptions that cannot be backed up by systematic evidence.

For instance, in quantitative studies, it has become standard in the political economy of pension reform literature to use total World Bank lending to a country as a proxy measure for transnational influence (Madrid 2003; Brooks 2005). Doing so requires making a number of assumptions. First, it assumes that the World Bank wants the same outcome and therefore gives the same advice in each country. However, Holzmann and Hinz (2005) and World Bank (2006) show that this is not the case. Transnational actors do not treat all countries equally. Some countries are more strategic than others; transnational actors may make internal decisions to focus on implementing reform in one country or region over another.

Further, transnational actors may have a most preferred reform outcome and a second-choice outcome (Müller 1999, 28). The only way to understand the priorities of transnational actors is to learn more about their internal policy decisions. Madrid (2003) begins to unpack this complexity by using two measures of World Bank influence: the existence of a World Bank pension mission and total loans as a share of GDP. He finds, like Brooks (2005), no effect for total loans, but a strong and significant relationship between the World Bank sending a pension reform mission and enactment of pension privatization.

However, observing the dispatch of a World Bank mission does not imply knowing what advice it gives. Holzmann and Hinz (2005) find that the Bank has dispensed a wide variety of advice on pension issues, depending on country circumstances. Studies that assume that the World Bank offers standard advice and that use a simple proxy measure for World Bank influence or involvement without looking into the content of the advice offered may underestimate the extent of its influence. Advice may vary based on organizational characteristics. In some organizations, individual consultants may determine the nature of advice, while other organizations are more centralized and consistent. Such consistency cannot be assumed.

Finally, total World Bank lending to a country may not be an accurate predictor of the amount of pressure the Bank is able to bring to bear on pension reform issues. Pension lending is typically a small part of total lending to a country (Holzmann and Hinz 2005; World Bank 2006), and countries with high total lending may not be under pressure to adopt pension privatization. For instance, the World Bank may judge a poor, highly indebted country to have insufficient administrative capacity to implement pension privatization. A better measure of influence may be total World Bank pension lending to a country. However, such data is difficult to obtain. A recent World Bank internal evaluation found that most pension lending took place in the context of broader social sector or structural adjustment loans (World Bank 2006). Determining the amounts spent on pensions proved difficult even for World Bank personnel with full access to this data, and the data have not been made fully available to other analysts. Data availability can be a problem, despite the increasing transparency of transnational organizations.

In summary, standard methods for evaluating the impact of transnational actors tend to make strong assumptions about what transnational actors want that are not always backed up by empirical evidence. Yet the study of what transnational actors want and how they behave is complex and requires careful examination of their internal decision making and behavior.

Campaign coalitions

A third issue for the literature on pension privatization is the difficulty of studying the coalitions of transnational policy actors that appear to have influenced these reforms. Most studies of global governance focus on a single actor, such as the IMF (Stone 2002), or one type of actor, such as transnational advocacy networks (Keck and Sikkink 1998), international organizations (Barnett and Finnemore 2004), or transgovernmental networks (Slaughter 2004). Such approaches offer analytic clarity, particularly for international relations theory. However, if policies are being spread by voluntary, temporary, but intensively involved 'campaign coalitions' (Tarrow 2005) of actors that rally around particular issues, creating informal coalitions to pressure states, then the influence of these informally organized networks must be taken into account.

Tarrow (2005, 179) argues that transnational campaign coalitions are the most efficacious form of transnational activist cooperation. Campaign coalitions are issue-focused, not venue-focused, so they have the opportunity to switch venues when necessary and to work at multiple levels of the policy process. They are flexible, not highly institutionalized, and thus depend on voluntary compliance by their members, but their goals and activities are long-term and highly involved. Tarrow contrasts campaign coalitions to event-driven campaigns, which are more short-term, and instrumental coalitions and federations, which involve lower levels of engagement.

Similarly, transnational actors within campaign coalitions may coordinate by dividing responsibility for certain countries and elements of reform. Mechanisms of coordination are often informal, with no public access and no paper trail. While the World Bank has played a central role in spreading pension privatization, it is important to remember that USAID and other organizations such as the Asian Development Bank, Inter-American Development Bank, Organization for Economic Cooperation and Development, Cato Institute, and many other organizations and individual policy entrepreneurs have also played an important role. Therefore, measuring

World Bank influence alone may underestimate overall transnational policy actor influence on reform processes.

This section has laid out three issues scholars have faced in analyzing the influence of transnational actors on pension privatization. It has argued for a better understanding of who transnational actors are, what they want, and how they cooperate with a range of oranizations to pursue their objectives in multiple national policy arenas [...]

[...]

Analysing transnational public policy

Sources of authority

[A] leading source of impact of transnational policy actors lies in their ability to set policy agendas through knowledge creation and expert and moral authority (Barnett and Finnemore 2004). While scholars have attempted to distinguish the impact of 'norms-teaching' versus 'resource-leveraging' activities (Chwieroth 2003; Brooks 2005), modes and mechanisms of transnational policy actor influence often combine ideational and material forms of influence (Epstein 2008; Jacoby 2008). For instance, the training courses and seminars that provide many world leaders with their first understanding of pension privatization constitute one mechanism for the transfer of knowledge and information. Such seminars are primarily a mechanism of knowledge transfer. However, they are also very costly to run. Dissemination of technical know-how globally cannot be done without substantial resources. Costly too are the enormous publication series of the World Bank, whose publications budget exceeds the total budget of many smaller transnational policy actors. It is so large that the Bank has become the largest single source of development-related research in the world (Stone and Wright 2007, 9). Publication activities on this scale require ideas; they also require resources. In many cases, resource-leveraging and norms-teaching methods of influence are analytically inseparable.

Transnational actors not only teach norms, they also help to create them. In the pension reform area, the World Bank publication *Averting the Old Age Crisis* catalyzed thinking within expert communities on the importance of private, funded pension systems. It created new problem definitions (old-age crisis) and new metrics and indicators (implicit pension debt) and provided a comprehensive set of policy solutions to address these problems. It was the World Bank's role in creating new, authoritative knowledge about pension reform that was perhaps most crucial in the spread of pension privatization. This suggests that much greater attention needs to be paid in empirical studies to the ways that international organizations generate authority around the development of new knowledge and how they make decisions about which ideas to promote. [...] [T]hese choices may depend on organizational circumstances and the outcomes of internal debates rather than on systematic structural factors alone.

Transnational actors and the role of ideas

Many traditional studies of political economy give short shrift to the explanatory role of ideas, treating them, as Marx did, as 'epiphenomena' dictated by the interests of powerful groups. Materialist explanations are particularly prominent in rational choice theory in political science and economics. This study gives norms and ideas a more prominent role in causal explanation. It shows that norms and policy proposals pushed by leading transnational actors have had an enormous influence on economic policy in countries around the world. New policy ideas and norms have caused domestic political actors to reshape their policy preferences, imagine new political coalitions, and create new institutions. New ideas have helped to discredit competing policy proposals and win support for new actors in the pension reform policy area (Blyth 2002). The rise of pension privatization cannot be reduced to material interests alone. As case studies have shown, a wide variety of actors have supported the new pension reforms, including those whose material interests would seem to make them likely opponents. Political economy needs to come to terms with the role of ideas and proposal actors in shaping policy discourse, influencing perceptions of interest, and determining policy (Blyth et al. forthcoming). Rational and ideational explanations can and should be combined to make sense of reform outcomes.

Veto and proposal actors

Transnational actors are influential bearers of policy ideas worldwide. This study has suggested viewing transnational policy actors as 'proposal actors' in domestic policy contexts. A number of policy scholars have analyzed domestic policy processes as arenas for contestation between 'veto players' (Immergut 1990; 1992; Tsebelis 2002; Immergut and Anderson 2007). Veto players analysis provides a parsimonious and comparable way to study and compare complex domestic policy processes. However, it tends to focus attention exclusively on veto players while excluding consideration of principled advocates and other non-veto players in policy choice.

[...]

What is missing from the veto players analysis is attention to the ways that 'proposal actors' operate and shape the preferences of domestic veto players. Proposal actors are defined here as domestic or transnational actors who develop well-elaborated policy proposals and encourage veto players to adopt them as their own. Proposal actors include domestic think tanks, individual policy entrepreneurs, NGOs, specialized government agencies, and transnational actors. Transnational proposal actors develop well-elaborated policy proposals and advocate them in a transnational political space.

Proposal actors have power because veto players often do not have well formed preferences in certain areas of policy or because these preferences can be reordered when proposal actors present new information or proposals that promise to achieve or maximize material interests in ways not previously considered. Blyth (2002, 9) argues that preferences can be highly malleable under conditions of 'Knightian uncertainty,' 'situations regarded by contemporary agents as unique events where the agents are unsure as to what their interests actually are, let alone how to realize them,' for instance, in periods of crisis. Under such conditions, proposal actors can be remarkably influential by presenting ideas that help to organize new political coalitions and underpin the development of new institutions. Proposal actors do not supplant the material interests of veto players, but rather exert informational, ideational, or programmatic influence that causes preferences to shift. This perspective is consistent with that of McCarty (2000), who argues that veto players theory suffers from a lack of attention to proposal rights. It is also consistent with constructivist scholarship, which has long emphasized the role of ideas and perceptions in the constitution of material interests (Checkel 2001).

The veto players and proposal actors framework [...] is useful because it enables comparisons between countries, sheds light on the nature of coalitions across the transnational/domestic divide, and emphasizes their joint operations and resources. It provides a clear framework for combining ideational and material analysis and captures the most significant dynamics between transnational policy entrepreneurs and their domestic partners.

Cooperation and contestation in transnational agenda setting

Because transnational policy actors have become highly influential in setting policy agendas worldwide, they have also become critical sites for contestation between competing advocacy networks and epistemic communities. Control over transnational actors provides an important potential resource for policy advocates and entrepreneurs. Gaining key positions in a transnational actor or organization can provide control of transnational actor agendas, positions, resources, and legitimacy. It is not surprising, then, that multiple different expert communities fight to gain ascendancy within transnational actors, resulting in conflict over policy agendas within and between transnational actors.

In the case of pension privatization, a particular epistemic community was able to take positions of power within the World Bank and other influential organizations in order to organize a global campaign. [...] Nelson (2004) draws attention to the fact that the relatively united transnational coalition for pension privatization set it apart from other social sector spheres such as health policy, where transnational actor advice has been more variable. Prior to 1994, World Bank pension advice also encompassed a range of competing perspectives. This may be the norm in many large transnational policy actors. The creation of unified policy agendas that monopolize the orientation of action within and between organizations may be relatively unusual.

Why did pension privatization advocates take power within the World Bank while other advocacy groups did not achieve such dominance? One might hypothesize that it had something to do with the structure of the policy area, the ideas, or the interests involved. Nelson (2004), for instance, suggests that pension reforms may be less contentious than health sector reforms, where many interest groups are involved in day-to-day administration. However, this study suggests an alternative explanation. It raises the possibility that the rise in power of this particular epistemic community could have depended on more internal organizational factors, such as leadership. The rise of pension privatization may have owed less to structural factors affecting pension systems and more to the idiosyncratic occurrence of a particularly successful World Bank research and advocacy project. Had Lawrence Summers not commissioned a major report on pensions, had Nancy Birdsall not taken charge of it, and had Estelle James not led the pension reform team, it is likely that the spread of pension privatization would have proceeded far more slowly.

Policy outcomes worldwide may depend on the outcomes of internal struggles within transnational policy actors. If this is true, scholars should pay greater attention to conflicts and agenda setting within transnational policy actors and the ways that these actors make decisions, allocate resources, and distribute power. The domestic politics of transnational policy actors is an important yet understudied area (Orenstein and Schmitz 2006).

A transnational policy model

How can one integrate a new understanding of the role of transnational policy actors into standard domestically based models of the policy process? Such a synthesis requires adopting a multi-level model of the policy process. [...] This model pays greater attention to policy actors whose scope is global, transnational, or regional. It suggests that the involvement of transnational policy actors extends over three distinct periods or phases of reform: policy development, policy transfer, and policy implementation. It shows that transnational policy actors rely on multiple modes and mechanisms of influence, because they lack the veto power that would give them more concentrated authority.

This transnational policy perspective differs in important ways from the structural political economy model employed in much of the pension reform literature. Instead of focusing on a single decision point, in which domestic reformers are faced with economic crisis and a set of economic and political conditions, the transnational policy model presented here encompasses a longer period of time, in stages, with multiple modes of influence. Domestic actors often do not act alone. Instead, they are connected in transnational or transgovernmental networks or communities of policy makers (Slaughter 2004) that have the capacity to develop well-elaborated policy proposals, tailor them to local circumstances, promote them vigorously, and provide help with policy implementation. Transnational actors do not replace domestic ones in most cases, but are continuously involved in policy decisions in multiple states

[…] While the international and national political spheres often have been regarded as distinct, with different rules and procedures, the boundaries between domestic and international actors and influences increasingly are blurred. New advances in transnational politics and policy scholarship will tend to erode the coding of actors as either international or domestic. For instance, Chwieroth (2003) regards domestic policy actors trained at certain U.S. universities as 'neoliberals' and suggests that they have an independent effect on policy. Such actors may be understood as part of transnational epistemic communities, having more in common with their counterparts in international organizations than with many citizens of their own countries. Another useful way of looking at this may be through the lens of career tracks. Some individuals clearly see international organizations and work in foreign countries as part of their career path; this may be becoming more common in an era of globalization. It may be more sensible to divide policy actors into 'cosmopolitans' and 'locals' (Haas 2006) in ways that cut across the domestic–international divide.

In sum, the transnational policy model presented here suggests a mode of studying policy development that focuses on new actors, new data sources, and new ways of coding variables that leads to a richer and more accurate understanding of the transnationalization of domestic policy.

References

Barnett, M. and Finnemore, M. (2004) *Rules for the World: International Organizations in Global Politics*, Ithaca, NY: Cornell University Press.

Biersteker, T. (1990) 'Reducing the role of the state in the economy: a conceptual exploration of IMF and World Bank prescriptions', *International Studies Quarterly*, 34: 477–92.

Blyth, M. (2002) *Great Transformations: Economic Ideas and Institutional Change in the Twentieth Century*, Cambridge: Cambridge University Press.

Blyth, M., Rawi, A. and Parsons, C. (eds) *Constructivist Political Economy*.

Brooks, S.M. (2005) 'Interdependent and domestic foundations of policy change: the diffusion of pension privatization around the world', *International Studies Quarterly*, 49: 273–94.

Campbell, J.L. and Pedersen, O.K. (eds) (2001) *The Rise of Neoliberalism and Institutional Analysis*, Princeton: Princeton University Press.

Checkel, J.T. (2001) 'Why comply? Social learning and European identity change', *International Organization*, vol 59, no 4: 801–26.

Chwieroth, J. (2003) 'Neoliberal norms and capital account liberalization in emerging markets: the role of domestic-level knowledge-based experts', paper presented at the annual meeting of the American Political Science Association, Philadelphia.

DiMaggio, P.J. and Powell, W.M. (1983) 'The iron cage revisited: institutional isomorphism and collective rationality in organizational fields', *American Sociological review*, vol 48, no 2: 147–60.

Druckman, J.N. (2004) 'Political preference formation: competition, deliberation, and the (ir)relevance of framing effects', *American Political Science Review* 98, no 4: 671–86.

Epstein, R. (2008) 'Transnational actors and bank privatization', in M.A. Orenstein, S. Bloom and N. Lindstrom (eds) *Transnational Actors in Central and East European Transitions*, Pittsbugh: University of Pittsburgh Press.

Fourcade-Gourinchas, M. and Babb, S.L. (2002) 'The rebirth of the liberal creed: paths to neoliberalism in four countries', *American Journal of Sociology* 108, no 3: 533–79.

Graham, C. (1998) *Private Markets for Public Goods: Raising the Stakes in Economic Reform*, Washington DC: Brookings Institution.

Haas, M.R. (2006) 'Acquiring and applying knowledge in transnational teams: the roles of cosmopolitans and locals', *Organization Science* 17, no 3: 367–84.

Haas, P.M. (1992) 'Introduction: epistemic communities and international policy coordination', *International Organization* 46, no 1: 1–35.

Hewson, M. and Sinclair, T.J. (1999) 'The emergence of global governance therory', in M. Hewson and T.J. Sinclair (eds) *Approaches to Global Governance Theory*, Albany: State University of New York Press: 3–22.

Holzmann, R. and Hinz, R. (2005) *Old Age Income Support in the 21st Century: An International Perspective on Pension Systems and Reform*, Washington DC: World Bank.

Hunter, W. and Brown, D.S. (2000) 'World Bank directives, domestic interests and the politics of human capital development in Latin America', *Comparative Political Studies* 33, no 1: 113–43.

Immergut, E.M. (1990) 'Veto points, and policy results: a comparative analysis of health care', *Journal of Public Policy* 10, no 4: 391–416.

Immergut, E.M. (1992) 'The rules of the game: the logic of health policy-making in France, Swizterland and Sweden', in S. Steinmo, K. Thenlen and F. Longstreth (eds) *Structuring Politics: Historical Institutionalism in Comparative Perspective*, Cambridge: Cambridge University Press.

Immergut, E.M. and Anderson, K.M. (2007) 'Editors introduction: The dynamics of pension politics', in E.M. Immergut, K.M. Anderson and I. Schulze (eds) *The Handbook of West European Pension Politics*, Oxford: Oxford University Press.

Jacoby, W. (2004) *The Enlargement of the European Union and NATO: Ordering From the Menu in Central Europe*, Cambridge: Cambridge University Press.

Jacoby, W. (2008) 'Minority traditions and post-Communist politics: how do IGOs matter?', in M.A. Orenstein, S. Bloom and N. Lindstrom (eds) *Transnational Actors in Central and East European Transitions*, Pittsburgh: University of Pittsburgh Press.

Johnson, J. (2008) 'Two-track diffusion and central bank embededness: the politics of Euro adoption in Hungary and the Czech Republic', in M.A. Orenstein, S. Bloom and N. Lindstrom (eds) *Transnational Actors in Central and East European Transitions*, Pittsburgh: University of Pittsburgh Press.

Kaul, I., Grunberg, I. and Stern, M.A. (eds) (1999) *Global Public Goods: International Cooperation in the 21st Century*, Oxford: Oxford University Press.

Keck, M. and Sikkink, K. (1998) *Activists Beyond Borders: Advocacy Networks in International Politics*, Ithaca, NY: Cornell University Press.

Kelley, J.G. (2004) *Ethnic Politics in Europe: The Power of Norms and Incentives*, Princeton, NJ: Princton University Press.

Kulu, L. and Reiljan, J. (2004) *Old-age Pension Reform in Estonia on the Basis of the World Bank's Multi-Pillar Approach*, Tartu: University of Tartu, Faculty of Economics and Business Administration.

Lindemann, D.C (2004) 'Review of recent pension reforms in the Baltic region', in *Pension Reform in the Baltic Countries*, OECD Private Pension Series 5, Paris: OECD 7–24.

Madrid, R.L. (2003) *Retiring the State: The Politics of Pension Privatization in Latin America and Beyond*: Stanford: Stanford University Press.

March, J. and Simon, H. (1993) 'From organizations: Cognitive limits on rationality', reprinted in F. Dobbin (ed) *The New Economic Sociology: A Reader*, Princeton: Princeton University Press.

McCarty, N. (2000) 'Proposal rights, veto rights, and political bargaining', *American Journal of Political Science* 44, no 3: 506–22.

Meyer, J.W., Boli, J., Thomas, G.M. and Ramirez, F.O. (1997) 'World society and the nation-state', *American Journal of Sociology* 103, no 1: 144–81.

Müller, K. (1999) *The Political Economy of Pension Reform in Central-Eastern Europe*, Aldershot: Edward Elgar.

Nelson, J.M. (2004) 'External models, international influence, and the politics of social sector reforms', in K. Weyland (ed) *Learning from Foreign Models in Latin American Policy Reform*, Washington DC and Baltimore: Woodrow Wilson and Johns Hopkins University Press.

Orenstein, M.A. and Schmitz, H.P. (2006) 'The new transnationalism and comparative politics', *Comparative Politics* 38, no 4: 479–500.

Reinecke, W.H. (1998) *Global Public Policy: Governing Without Government?*, Washington DC: Brookins Institution Press.

Republic of Estonia (2000) Memorandum of Economic Policies, Washington DC: International Monetary Fund (February 14).

Risse, T., Ropp, S.C. and Sikkink, K. (eds) (1999) *The Power of Human Rights: International Norms and Domestic Change*, Cambridge: Cambridge University Press.

Slaughter, A.M (2004) *A New World Order*, Princeton: Princeton University Press.

Stone, D. (2003) 'Transnational transfer agents and global networks in the 'internationalisation' of policy', Paper presented at the Workshop on Internationalisation and Policy Transfer, Murphy Institute, Tulane University, New Orleans, 11-12 April.

Stone, R. (2002) *Lending Credibility: The International Monetary Fund and the Post-Communist Transition*, Princeton: Princeton University Press.

Stone, D. and Wright, C. (2007) 'The currency of change: World Bank lending in the Wolfensohn era', in D. Stone and C. Wright (eds) *The World Bank and Governance: A Decade of Reform and Reaction*, Routledge Series in Globalisation, Abingdon, UK and Routledge, New York.

Strang, D. and Meyer, J.W. (1993) 'International conditions for diffusion', *Theory and Society* 22, no 4: 487–511, August.

Strang, D. and Soule, S.A. (1998) 'Diffusion in organizations and social movements: from hybrid corn to poison pills', *Annual Review of Sociology* 24: 265–90.

Tarrow, S. (2005) *The New Transnational Activism*, Cambridge: Cambridge University Press.

Tavits, M. (2003) 'Policy learning and uncertainty: the case of pension reform in Estonia and Latvia', *Policy Studies Journal* 31, no 4: 643–60.

Tolbert, P.S. and Zucker, L.G. (1983) 'Institutional sources of change in the federal structure of organizations: the diffusion of civil service reform, 1880–1935', *Administrative Science Quarterly* 28: 22–39.

Toots, A. (2002) 'International and national actors in Estonial pension reform', Paper presented at the NISPA CEE Annual Conference, Krakow, Poland.

Tsebelis, G. (2002) *Veto Players: How Political Institutions Work*, New York and Princeton: Russell Sage Foundation and Princeton University Press.

Weyland, K. (2005) 'Theories of policy diffusion: lessons from Latin American policy reform', *World Politics* 57: 262–95.

World Bank (1994) *Averting the Old Age Crisis: Policies to Protect the Old and Promote Growth*, Oxford: Oxford University Press.

World Bank (2005) *Economies in Transition: An OECD Evaluation of World Bank Assistance*, Washington DC: World Bank.

World Bank (2006) *Pension Reform and the Development of Pension Systems: An Evaluation of World Bank Assistance*, Independent Evaluation Group Report, Washington DC: World Bank.

Young, O.R. (1999) *Governance in World Affairs*, Ithaca, NY: Cornell University Press.

Section 2

Global poverty and inequality

This section focuses on poverty and inequality in order to illustrate the conceptual and methodological issues raised by global social policy analysis, but it should be noted from the outset that similar issues apply to all of the other policy areas usually included within social policy analysis. As Section 1 discussed, the move from a national, or even international, focus to a global one inevitably involves a range of questions about how we should conceptualise, measure and respond to social problems globally. A focus on poverty and inequality is a useful way of examining these conceptual and methodological issues.

A large body of research now exists about the extent of poverty and inequality in national contexts, and definitions and measures of the central concepts are well established (although still subject to contestation and debate). However, analysis has usually focused on problems of definition and measurement of poverty levels and inequality among populations *within* the boundaries of particular states. Sometimes such analysis is widened to include comparative studies of different countries, and encouragingly this increasingly includes analysis of 'developing' countries as well as 'developed' ones. Nevertheless, such studies often continue to suffer from 'methodological nationalism' – an inability to think outside of the constraints of the 'nation state'. Once we broaden our focus from this relatively parochial view to the globe as a whole, we need to confront some difficult questions. How can we best measure poverty, inequality and other social problems at the global level? Can concepts and tools developed at the national level simply be transferred to the global level? What is the source of the dominant ideas about how poverty and inequality should be defined and measured globally and in developing countries, and how do these definitions affect the policies that are adopted by governments and international organisations?

The first reading in this section, by Peter Townsend, identifies the need for a robust *international* standard for poverty measurement in order to quantify and address growing social polarisation worldwide. As Townsend argues, without such a scientific approach, causes cannot be identified and appropriate policy responses cannot be put in place. The policies of the international financial institutions of the World Bank and the International Monetary Fund (IMF) are identified as a key cause of growing social polarisation. The approach of the World Bank, in particular, to the measurement and targeting of poverty has had a disproportionate influence globally, argues Townsend, and its emphasis on targeting the poorest has served to increase inequality.

The importance of the World Bank in influencing policy towards poverty and inequality is also testified to by the readings that follow by David Gordon, Robert Hunter Wade, and Jane Falkingham and Angela Baschieri, all of which offer critiques of its approach. Gordon provides a detailed analysis of how different international organisations, including the World Bank, define and measure poverty. He argues that none of these correspond to any internationally agreed definition of poverty. However, one such definition was agreed at the UN World Summit on Social Development in 1995, and Gordon outlines one example of how this definition could be operationalised so that it is comparable across countries. As at the national level, both Townsend and Gordon favour a relative definition of poverty at the international level that would take account of the level of income that is necessary to maintain people within the context of the particular social circumstances of their country, and more universalistic policy responses rather than the narrow targeting approach of the World Bank.

Most of the international poverty definitions and measures discussed by Gordon were designed to facilitate the comparison of poverty rates between countries. Despite its problems, the World Bank approach does at least appear to allow for estimates to be made of the absolute number of people living in extreme poverty worldwide. However, the reading from Wade provides a further critique of the Bank's approach, highlighting a number of weaknesses in its methodology. Since Bank statistics are often used to justify the neo-liberal argument that liberalisation inevitably brings growth and therefore poverty reduction, these methodological weaknesses render such claims questionable. The problems with the World Bank's approach to measuring world poverty underline the necessity for independent social research on such questions.

This point is reinforced by the reading from Falkingham and Baschieri, which demonstrates some of the gender implications of the Bank's approach. Indeed, it is in the analysis of poverty that the need to gender global social policy is particularly evident. Whilst in 2001 the World Bank called for the 'mainstreaming' of gender equality issues in the Poverty Reduction Strategy Papers (PRSPs) that it now requires countries receiving conditional loans to prepare, the poverty assessments that inform PRSPs may ignore or underestimate gendered differences in poverty. These poverty assessments are often based on analysis of living standard measurement surveys and utilise a unitary model of the household which assumes the equal pooling of household resources. These issues have been a subject of debate in poverty analysis for some time, and Falkingham and Baschieri illustrate the need for future global poverty analysis and policy also to pay more attention to understanding how resources are allocated within households.

Focusing upon income inequality, the reading from Branko Milanovic clarifies the conceptual differences between international and global measurements, before exploring the extent of these inequalities in some detail. Whilst *international inequality* measures inequalities between nations (or, specifically, the mean incomes of nations), *global inequality* measures inequality between all individuals regardless of where they live in the world, i.e. as though the entire world were one country. Milanovic explains three concepts of inequality: 'unweighted international inequality', which measures inequality in the mean incomes of different nations using per capita Gross Domestic Income (GDI); a measure of international inequality which also uses per capita GDI, but which weights this by population; and global inequality, which measures inequality between all individuals in the world using household survey data. He argues that global inequality matters, since as globalisation processes increase people's awareness of each other and highlight income disparities, poverty and inequality elsewhere will increasingly impact on us wherever we are in the world. As Wade has put it (in a section of his reading not reproduced here): 'We would not be interested in measuring income inequality within the United States by calculating the average income for each state and weighting it by their populations if we had data for all households.' In response to the extreme global inequality which his analysis reveals, Milanovic argues for global transfers that conform to three conditions: transfers should flow from a rich country to a poor country; transfers should be 'globally progressive', i.e., go from a richer person to a poorer person; and transfers should preserve 'national progressivities', i.e., should not worsen national income distributions. Section 5 of the Reader discusses the issue of global transfers in more detail.

Whilst Milanovic focuses on global inequality in income, James B. Davies et al provide an analysis of global inequality in wealth. Wealth here is defined as 'net worth', i.e. the value of physical and financial assets less liabilities, or 'capital'. As Davies et al point out, whilst capital is only one component of personal resources, it has a disproportionate impact on household well-being and economic success, as well as on broader economic development. However, the composition of wealth varies between countries, with financial assets and shareholdings being more important in rich countries with highly developed financial markets and/or reliance on private pensions, and real assets such as land and farm assets being more important in developing countries. Davies et al draw on data from Household Balance Sheets (HBS) supplemented by household wealth surveys, national accounts, tax data, and other data reported by financial, government and statistical agencies. Whilst we omit much of the detailed methodology from this reading, the results indicate extreme inequalities of wealth within countries, between countries and for the world taken as a whole. Global inequality in wealth is even greater than global inequality in income.

The readings in this section thus attest to the difficulty and complexity of measuring poverty and inequality globally, and the necessity for conceptual clarity about what is being measured and how. Together these readings, and others like them, provide the foundation for the further development of methodologies to determine the scope of global poverty, inequality and associated problems, and thus provide the basis for the development of appropriate global policy responses.

Chapter 2.1

Poverty, social exclusion and social polarisation: the need to construct an international welfare state

Peter Townsend

During the last half-century, the conventional wisdom has been that poverty can be diminished automatically through economic growth. This has got to change. During the next half-century, the world's most fundamental problem – as agreed by the biggest international agencies and a growing number of governments – is that wealth and poverty are becoming increasingly polarised, and that a different priority has to be followed.

Any resolution of this problem depends on connecting three concepts – *poverty*, *social exclusion*, and *social polarisation* – and bringing them into sharper and more distinguishable focus. Together they provide the basis for the scientific breakthrough to explain the problem, and develop the exact policies required to deal with it, as well as steer the international community away from impending disaster.

[...]

Building on international agreement

There is scope [...] for an analytical ground-clearing operation. However, if we are to adopt practical policies to reduce the two problems of poverty and social exclusion, we need to be clear about how to distinguish them, as well as how they are to be applied cross-nationally, rather than erratically and variously in different cultures. I say 'erratically' because the links between country- or region-specific definition and international definition have neither been investigated thoroughly nor justified – even when we can acknowledge that the research in question is helpful in understanding some internal conditions. 'Erratically' also, because the absence of scientific precision makes for political ambiguity – the great escape for holders of wealth. 'Erratically' too in relation to the international agencies. Here the World Bank's adoption of the crude criterion of $1 per day at 1985 prices for the poorest countries, $2 per day for Latin America, and $4 per day for the transitional economies, without regard to the changing conditions of needs and markets, affronts science as it affronts reasoned development of priorities in international policies. In 1997, UNDP topped this absurdity by suggesting that the US criterion of $14.4 per day might be applied to the Organisation for Economic Co-operation and Development (OECD) countries (UNDP, 1997).

If measurement is arbitrary and irrational, it is impossible either to concoct the right policies for the alleviation or eradication of poverty, or monitor their effects closely. The World Bank persists broadly with the anti-poverty approach of the 1960s, despite continuing evidence of that approach's failure. Thus, following reports in the early 1990s (for example, World Bank, 1990, 1993), there was little sign in the Bank's reports of the mid- and late 1990s of a change in the threefold strategy that continued to be stated time and again:

- broad-based economic growth;
- development of human capital;
- social safety nets for vulnerable groups (World Bank, 1996, 1997a, 1997b, 1997c; Psacharapoulas et al, 1997).

Each of these three requires detailed exposition, documentation and discussion.

The job of social policy analysis is to keep alive alternative strategies and policies that seem to fit the account of global problems and needs. For purposes of illustration, one alternative strategy might consist of:

- equitable tax and income policies;
- an employment creation programme;
- regeneration or creation of collective, or 'universal', social security and public social services;
- accountability and a measure of social control of transnational corporations and international agencies.

There are no signs yet of a debate taking place about the merits of even two alternative strategies, or sets of policies, to establish beyond reasonable doubt which alternative is the most successful – or indeed popular in democratic terms – in reducing poverty and contributing to social development.

[...]

A global trend

[...] Reporting in mid-1999, UNDP found that income inequality had increased 'in most OECD countries in the 1980s and early 1990s. Of 19 countries only one showed a slight improvement' (1999, p 37). Data on income inequality in Eastern Europe and the CIS 'indicate that these changes were the fastest ever recorded. In less than a decade income inequality, as measured by the Gini coefficient, increased from an average of 0.25-0.28 to 0.35-0.38, surpassing OECD levels' (1999, p 39). In China 'disparities are widening between the export-oriented regions of the coast and the interior: the human poverty index is just under 20 per cent in coastal provinces, but more than 50 per cent in inland Guizhou' (1999, p 3). Other East and South East Asian countries that had achieved high growth while improving income distribution and reducing poverty in earlier decades, like Indonesia and Thailand, were similarly experiencing more inequality (UNDP, 1999, p 36).

The gap *between* countries, as well as within them, has also widened. The latest studies show how the trend has accelerated: the average income of the world population's [richest] 20% was 30 times as large as the average income of the poorest 20% in 1960, but 74 times as large by 1997 (UNDP, 1999, p 36).

Of course, widening inequality has to be addressed at both ends of the spectrum. Executives' pay, and the disposable income and wealth of the richest people in the world, has been growing at an astonishing rate. For example, the UNDP points out that 'the assets of the 200 richest people are more than the combined income of 41% of the world's people' (1999, p 38). The top three have more than the combined GNP of the 43 least developed countries.

A new report for the World Institute for Development Economic Research of the United Nations University confirms the trend. An econometric analysis of 77 countries (accounting for 82% of world population), found rising inequality in 45, slowing inequality in 4, no definite trend in 12, and falling inequality in only 12 (Cornia, 1999a, pp vi and 7). 'For most countries, the last two decades have brought about slow growth and rising inequality.... Growing polarisation among countries has been accompanied by a surge in inequality between countries.... Income concentration has risen in many nations of Latin America, Eastern Europe and the former Soviet Union, China, a few African and Southeast Asian economies and, since the early 1980s, almost two-thirds of the OECD countries' (Cornia, 1999a, p 2).

> Since the early 1990s, the international community has made the eradication of poverty its foremost development objective. Yet, the decline of poverty in the years ahead depends also on trends in income inequality, a fact which still attracts little concern by the policymakers. Much of the recent rise in income inequality must thus be viewed with alarm, as it may well prove to be incompatible with poverty reduction objectives. (Cornia, 1999a, p vi)

Explaining polarisation

Defective structural adjustment policies

What are the reasons for this structural change? There is an international analysis that has to be tied in with nationally circumscribed investigation. What has to be accepted is the increasing impact of international developments on national subgroups and local populations. I mean that exposition of familiar problems to do with gender, ageing, disabilities, and families with children, for example, now displays overriding international determinants. I mean also that local problems, such as conflict on inner city housing estates, drugs, closure of local factories, and unsatisfactory privatisation of local services, are generated or enlarged by global market and other international factors.

Among the major policies of the international agencies, national governments and transnational corporations, for which a powerful consensus had been built up during the 1980s and 1990s, are the stabilisation, liberalisation, privatisation and welfare targeting and safety net programmes adopted as a result of the worldwide influence of monetarist theory. For example, the so-called *stabilisation and structural adjustment programmes*, that were advocated and supported by the international agencies, have entailed the reduction of subsidies on food, fuel and other goods, retrenchments in public employment, cuts in public sector wages and other deflationary measures. This not only generates recession, but also distributional outcomes which, as Cornia has argued (1999b, pp 11-12) are adverse in the poorer countries compared with industrialised countries, where wage systems are strongly institutionalised and self protecting, and where long-established social security provides a better cushion for downturns in the economy. Policies to cut public expenditure, and target welfare on the poorest (for example through means testing and the introduction of healthcare charges), have increased inequality and perpetuated poverty, especially in countries where, because of globalised trade and growing influence of transnational corporations, there has been a particularly rapid concentration of wealth.

In recognising what policies have brought about greater inequality within and between countries we have to understand the similarity of the programmes influencing developments throughout the world, at the same time as we recognise that they are calculated to vary in extent and force in different regions. The terminology is not always consistent. Governments as well as international agencies are often eager to adopt new names for conformist (rather than 'convergent') policies, especially when evidence that they are not working begins to accumulate.

In a remarkable shift from its long-standing policies, the World Bank has admitted that poverty has tended to increase during recessions in sub-Saharan Africa, Eastern Europe, and Latin America and not to decrease to the same extent during economic recoveries. Examples were given in a report showing that 'crises and recessions may result in irreversible damage to the poor: malnutrition or death from starvation (in extreme cases) and lower schooling levels' (World Bank, 1999, p 109). Higher food prices in the stabilisation programme in Côte d'Ivoire and elsewhere are cited. 'Sudden fluctuations in income or food availability can be fatal to already malnourished children'. Consequences include lower IQ, retarded physical growth, mental disabilities, lower resistance to infections, and associated problems like dropout from schools (World Bank, 1999, p 103; see also Huther et al, 1997).

Greater sensitivity to the encroachments of poverty also helps to explain the reactions of the international agencies to the financial crisis in East and South East Asia. The magic wand of liberalisation and structural adjustment programmes could no longer be waved, as it had been in Latin America and Africa and then in Eastern Europe and the Commonwealth of Independent States (and in similar strategic form in the industrial countries). The World Bank expected poverty rates, especially in Indonesia, to rise very sharply. Revealingly, the Bank no longer emphasises privatisation and extreme targeting. At one point it even suggests that the possible remedies in a difficult situation 'include waiving charges for the poor and extending health care to workers dismissed from their jobs' (World Bank, 1999, p 109).

[...]

The shortcomings of targeting and safety nets

In developing their structural adjustment programmes, first in Latin America and Africa, and then in the 'transition' countries of Eastern Europe and the former Soviet Union, the IMF and the World Bank tried to balance the unequal social consequences of liberalisation, privatisation and cuts in public expenditure with proposals to target help on the most vulnerable groups in the population. For some years, and still to a large extent today, this has been presented within the principle of means testing. Even if coverage was poor, large sums of money would be saved if the 'almost poor' were no longer subsidised by public funds.

Therefore, a report for the IMF (Chu and Gupta, 1998) seeks to pin responsibility on the transition countries for a failure to transform universal services into targeted and partly privatised services. Unfortunately, this report also reveals serious amnesia about the institutional history of the introduction of legislation establishing public services and social security in particular (see, for example, pp 90-2, 111-12). Ways in which former universal provisions might be modified to allow market competition to grow but not create penury among millions were not seriously considered.

IMF loan conditions demanding lower government expenditures in the poorest countries have led to sharp reductions in general social spending at a time when the poorest fifth of the population in those countries have been receiving only about half their share of education and health expenditures – thus making access worse. This is evidence drawn from the IMF's own studies (IMF, 1997), which shows that 'the poorest three-fifths of these nations are being excluded from whatever social "safety net" exists for education, health, housing and social security and welfare' (Kolko, 1999, p 56).

However, loan conditionalities affect economic security in other ways. There are cuts in the number of government employees and in their salaries, and there are private sector cuts and lay-offs, both of which are designed to raise cost-effectiveness in the world's export markets. Price subsidies for commodities such as bread and cooking oil are cut. Higher value added taxes that are advocated are regressive on income distribution.

In December 1987, the IMF introduced a new stage of its existing structural adjustment programme – the 'Enhanced Structural Adjustment Facility' (ESAF). Of the 79 countries eligible for these ESAF loans – on condition they complied with the IMF in setting 'specific, quantifiable plans for financial policies' – 36 had done so. Since World Bank aid also depends on fulfilling IMF criteria there is intense pressure on governments to accede. Critics have now concluded that countries which stayed out of the ESAF programme 'began and remained better off by not accepting its advice'. Those accepting the programme 'have experienced profound economic crises: low or even declining economic growth, much larger foreign debts, and the stagnation that perpetuates systemic poverty'. The IMF's own studies provided 'a devastating assessment of the social and economic consequences of its guidance of dozens of poor nations' (Kolko, 1999, p 53).

The problem applies sharply to rich and not only poor countries. The biggest struggle of the coming years is going to be between restriction of social security, or 'welfare', largely to means-tested benefits. Those who have assembled evidence for different European countries over many years (for example, van Oorschot, 1999) point out that such policies are poor in coverage, administratively expensive and complex, provoke social divisions, are difficult to square with incentives into work, and tend to discourage forms of saving. What is notable is the recent tempering of World Bank and other agency reactions. It is now conceded that targeting can include 'categorical' policies affecting vulnerable or disadvantaged groups in the population. [...]

Conclusion: the invention of the international welfare state

Where does this analysis lead? [...] An alternative international strategy and set of policies concerned with arresting the growth of inequality and radically reducing poverty has been outlined. [...]

What elements might the overall international strategy include? First, unless a scientific consensus is achieved in operationally defining, and measuring, international forms of poverty and social exclusion, the fact that the defeat of poverty worldwide has been put at the top of the international agencies' agenda will turn out to be empty rhetoric. [...]

Second, unless, the *policy-related causes* of poverty and social exclusion are properly traced and publicised in relation to structural trends in all societies, we will find it difficult to discriminate effectively between what are the successful, unsuccessful and even counterproductive measures working towards, or against, the agreed objectives.

Third, since poverty and social exclusion can neither be traced nor explained except in the context of the structural changes embodied in social polarisation, it is this phenomenon that has to be explained.

The effect of policies that have been tried has to be clarified. The *stabilisation and structural adjustment programmes* of the 1980s and 1990s are alleged to have contributed to growing inequality. Policies contributing to the *institutionalisation of unequal power* are argued to deepen that process. Far more attention has to be given to the entire hierarchical *system*, and especially rich institutions and rich individuals at the top. The international agencies, regional associations and national governments must begin to analyse the extraordinary growth of transnational corporations, and ask what reasonable limits can be placed upon their powers. [...]

Policies representing the principles, or ideologies, of *targeting and safety nets* also deserve better assessment. There are grave doubts that they provide the right strategy to compensate for the inequalities and impoverishment induced by liberalisation and the enhanced power of markets. The international agencies are beginning to recognise that, as policy, means testing is neither easy to introduce nor successful. The advantages of modernised social insurance, for developing as well as industrialised countries, are beginning to earn renewed international interest. This is a sign of hope.

There are of course new policies that have to be found as well as existing policies that deserve to be abandoned or corrected if the damaging structural trend of social polarisation is first to be halted, and then turned round. There seem to be two stages. At the first stage the whole critique has to be pulled together and made more forceful. This includes the reformulation of the measurement of poverty, social exclusion and unemployment. It includes insistence on the monitoring and determined fulfilment of international agreements. And it includes the mobilisation of new coalitions or alliances across countries – of parties, unions, campaigning groups and voluntary agencies – to question the conventional wisdom and promote alternative strategies. At the second stage measures for international taxation, regulation of transnational corporations and international agencies, reform of representation at the UN, and new guarantees of human rights, including minimal standards of income, have to be introduced and legally enforced.

Recognition of social insurance as one of the best means of building an 'inclusive' society and preventing the slide into poverty, as well as contributing to social and economic stability, would represent one major step forward.

New legal and political institutions for social good in a global economy have to be built. A start would come with new international company and taxation law, combined with the modernisation and strengthening of social insurance and more imaginative planning and investment in basic services, such as health and education, so that they reflect international and not just national or regional standards.

This amounts to calling for an *international* welfare state (Townsend with Donkor, 1996). One hundred years ago, different governments, including those of Britain and Germany as well as of smaller countries like New Zealand and Norway, responded to the manifest problems of poverty in those days. There were innovations which led to the establishment of national welfare states and a more civilised form of economic development.

Early in the 21st century the prospect of even greater social self-destruction, experienced as an accompanying feature of social polarisation, looms before us – unless urgent countervailing measures are taken. Collaborative scientific and political action to establish a more democratic and internationalised legal framework to protect human living standards has become the first priority.

[...]

References

Chu, Ke-Y. and Gupta, S. (eds) (1998) *Social safety nets: Issues and recent experiences*, Washington, DC: IMF.

Cornia, G.A. (1999a) *Liberalisation, globalisation and income distribution*, Working Paper no 157, Helsinki: UNU World Institute for Development Economic Research.

Cornia, G.A. (1999b) *Social funds in stabilisation and adjustment programmes*, Research for Action 48, Helsinki: UNU World Institute for Development Economic Research.

Huther, J., Roberts, S. and Shah, A. (1997) *Public expenditure reform under adjustment lending: Lessons from the World Bank Experience*, World Bank Discussion Paper no 382, Washington, DC: World Bank.

Kolko, G. (1999) 'Ravaging the poor: the International Monetary Fund indicted by its own data', *International Journal of Health Services*, vol 29, no 1, pp 51-7.

Psacharapoulos, G., Morley, S., Fiszbein, A., Lee, H. and Wood, B. (1997) *Poverty and income distribution in Latin America: The story of the 1980s*, World Bank Technical Paper no 351, Washington, DC: World Bank.

Townsend, P. with Donkor, K. (1996) *Global restructuring and social policy: An alternative strategy: Establishing an international welfare state*, International Seminar on Economic Restructuring and Social Policy, sponsored by UNRISD and UNDP, United Nations, New York, 1995, Bristol: The Policy Press.

UNDP (1997) *Human development report 1997*, New York and Oxford: Oxford University Press.

UNDP (1999) *Human development report 1999*, New York and Oxford: Oxford University Press.

van Oorschot, W. (1999) *Targeting welfare: On the functions and dysfunctions of means-testing in social policy*, Research in Europe Budapest conference on developing poverty measures.

World Bank (1990) *World development report 1990: Poverty*, Washington, DC: World Bank.

World Bank (1993) *Implementing the World Bank's strategy to reduce poverty: Progress and challenges*, Washington, DC: World Bank.

World Bank (1996) *Poverty reduction and the World Bank: Progress and challenges in the 1990s*, Washington, DC: World Bank.

World Bank (1997a) *Safety net programs and poverty reduction: Lessons from cross-country experience*, Washington, DC: World Bank.

World Bank (1997b) *Poverty reduction and the World Bank: Progress in fiscal 1996 and 1997*, Washington, DC: World Bank.

World Bank (1997c) *World development report 1997: The state in a changing world*, Washington, DC and New York, NY: Oxford University Press.

World Bank (1999) *Global economic prospects and the developing countries 1998/99: Beyond financial crisis*, Washington, DC and New York, NY: Oxford University Press.

The international measurement of poverty and anti-poverty policies

David Gordon

Introduction

This chapter will describe briefly how international social policy and academic research on poverty has been changing in the past decade and, in particular, how a widening chasm is developing between the anti-poverty policies being advocated by UN agencies and those of the EU. These latter evolving anti-poverty policies have a number of profound implications for the measurement of poverty by international organisations and national statistical offices (NSOs). Without good comparable measures of poverty, it will be impossible to determine if anti-poverty policies are working effectively and efficiently.

International anti-poverty policies

It has long been a dream of humanity to remove poverty from the face of the earth. There have been many fine words and failed attempts to achieve this in the past. However, there is now a strong desire among most of the world's governments to end poverty during the 21st century and a growing international momentum to take concrete action to eradicate poverty on a global scale. If this result is achieved (even partially) then it will have a number of dramatic effects including a significant improvement in the health of the people of the world (WHO, 1995, 1998).

Although there is now widespread agreement on the need to end poverty, there remains considerable international disagreement on the best way this can be achieved. In particular, there is a growing divide between the policies being pursued by the US and the Bretton Woods institutions (such as the World Bank and International Monetary Fund [IMF]) and the EU.

For 40 years, the World Bank, the IMF and other UN agencies have been pursuing what is, basically, the same set of anti-poverty policies (Townsend and Gordon, 2000). These have three elements:

- broad–based economic growth;
- development of human capital, primarily through education;
- minimum social safety nets for the poor.

These policies have been unsuccessful. The number of poor people in the world has continued to increase and, in particular, these same policies have resulted in terrible consequences in many parts of Sub–Saharan Africa, South America and in the countries of the former Soviet Union. [...]

European Union anti-poverty policies

Emerging EU policies on a 'social' Europe are very different to those outlined above. They are based on ideas of social inclusion and social quality. Inter-governmental agreements at Lisbon, Nice and Amsterdam have rejected a 'race to the bottom' for labour conditions and established anti-poverty policy based on:

- active labour market intervention to help create jobs and improve working conditions;
- progressive taxation and redistribution through a comprehensive welfare state.

The 1990s witnessed increasing concern about the high levels of unemployment and poverty in Europe. Widespread unemployment was problematic because European welfare states were founded on the assumption of full employment. They still require high levels of employment to function adequately and also to maintain economic growth in Europe. The EU responded to this challenge by shifting its focus from being virtually exclusively concerned with economic policies (for example, promoting the free movement of commodities, labour, services and capital) towards a more integrated approach of both social and economic policy, particularly in the sphere of employment policy.
[...]
  EU member states' policies do not just cover improved education and training for the workforce (social capital interventions) but also such strategies as minimum wages, minimum income guarantees to 'make work pay' and government-backed job creation schemes. European research into social inclusion measures (Gordon and Townsend, 2000) has shown that effective and efficient international anti-poverty policies would ideally include:

- an employment creation programme, designed deliberately to introduce labour-intensive projects to counterbalance patterns of job–cutting

in many countries that are often indiscriminate in their social effects.
Working conditions of the low paid would also be internationally
regulated;

- regeneration or creation of collective, or 'universal' social insurance
  and public social services – the 'basic needs services' – by introducing
  internationally sanctioned minimum wages and levels of benefit;
- the introduction of greater accountability and social and democratic
  control over transnational corporations and international agencies.
  Growing concern in the 1990s about the 'democratic deficit' invited
  collaborative international action on a regional – if not wider – basis.

Europe has over 100 years of social policy experience, and this has resulted
in a widespread consensus that comprehensive welfare states are the most
cost-effective and efficient mechanisms for combating poverty. In the EU,
almost everyone pays into the welfare state and everyone gets something
back. In 1996, nearly three quarters of EU households, on average, received
direct cash payments from the welfare state each month (or week) through
state pensions, child support and other benefits (Gordon and Townsend,
2000; Marlier and Cohen-Solal, 2000). On average, EU member states
spend 28% of their GDP on social protection benefits (Clotuche, 2001).
Their comprehensive welfare states not only provide effective and efficient
mechanisms for alleviating poverty, they also protect and improve the welfare
of all Europeans. They all redistribute income from 'rich' to 'poor' and from
men to women. However, they also equalise income distribution across
an individual's lifespan by taxing and reducing income levels in middle
age balanced with then paying social benefits to increase income during
childhood and old age.

There is considerable debate within Europe on which is the best kind
of comprehensive welfare state. Esping-Andersen, for example, uses the
principle of the 'commodification' of welfare to identify those countries
that characterise a liberal welfare state, a conservative-corporatist welfare
state and a social democratic welfare state and argues that social democratic
welfare states are the most desirable (Esping-Andersen, 1990, 1996; Goodin
et al, 1999). Many European countries (Ireland, for example) do not fit
easily into this classification scheme. Nevertheless, it is self evident that
– all things being equal – the more comprehensive the redistribution via
the welfare state, the lower the rates of poverty will be and international
comparative analyses of income poverty lines have clearly demonstrated this
fact. Figure 2.2.1 shows a recent OECD analysis of income poverty (50%
median income) in industrialised countries in the mid-1990s.

Countries like Sweden, France, Belgium, the UK and Ireland all have
much higher rates of low income/poverty than the US – before allowing
for taxes and transfers. However, the more comprehensive welfare states in

Figure 2.2.1: OECD analysis of income poverty rates in the 1990s, pre- and post-transfers

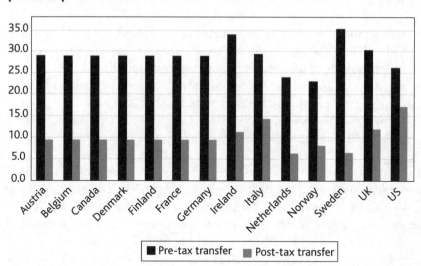

these European countries result in much lower poverty rates than the US after redistribution of national income by taxes and transfers (Förster and Pellizzari, 2000). Similar results have also been reported using other low-income thresholds (Förster, 1994) and by UNICEF researchers with respect to child poverty rates in rich countries (UNICEF, 2000).

There is unanimity within the EU that comprehensive social security provision is a fundamental human right. Article 12 of the revised European Social Charter (Council of Europe, 1996) guarantees the right to social security for 'all workers and their dependants'. No country can join the EU without having signed and ratified the European Code of Social Security which sets standards for health and welfare benefits and pensions 'at a higher level than the minimum standards embodied in International Labour Convention No. 102 concerning Minimum Standards of Social Security'. This International Labour Organisation convention (ILO, 1952) provides for minimum standards in nine distinct branches of social security (medical care, sickness, unemployment, old age, employment injury, family, maternity, invalidity, and survivors' benefits) and has been ratified by 40 countries.

Many European social scientists (and policy makers) believe that the World Bank and IMF would have had much greater success at reducing poverty if they had required that countries seeking aid complied with the ILO's convention on Minimum Standards of Social Security rather than pursuing the neo-liberal 'Washington consensus' policies described above. EU countries have flatly rejected the World Bank's ideas about minimum social safety nets for the poor being the best way to combat poverty.

At the Nice Summit (EC, 2001a) in December 2000, EU countries agreed to produce and implement a two-year (July 2001–June 2003) National Action Plan on Social Inclusion (NAPincl) designed to promote social inclusion and combat poverty and social exclusion (see EC, 2001b). These detailed plans are a key component of the member states' commitment to make a decisive impact on the eradication of poverty and social exclusion in Europe by 2010. The EU's aim is to be the most dynamic knowledge-based economy in the world, with full employment and increased levels of social cohesion by 2010. The accurate measurement of poverty and social exclusion is an integral component of this strategy and the recent Laeken European Council concluded that:

> ... the establishment of a set of common indicators constitute important elements in the policy defined at Lisbon for eradicating poverty and promoting social inclusion, taking in health and housing. The European Council stresses the need to reinforce the statistical machinery and calls on the Commission gradually to involve the candidate countries in this process. (EC, 2001c, s 28)

In Europe, during 2001, considerable scientific efforts were made to improve the measurement of poverty and social exclusion (Atkinson et al, 2002)[1] and the proposed new set of statistics and indicators will be a major improvement on previous EU analyses (Eurostat, 1990, 1998, 2000; Hagenaars et al, 1994; Atkinson, 2000; Mejer and Linden, 2000; Mejer and Siermann, 2000).

Implications for poverty measurement

There are a number of serious implications for internationally comparative measures of poverty. Over the past 30 years, there have been a number of international agreements which have clearly defined poverty. In 1975, the Council of Europe defined those in poverty as:

> ... individuals or families whose resources are so small as to exclude them from a minimum acceptable way of life in the Member State in which they live. (EEC, 1981)

The concept of 'resources' was further defined as 'goods, cash income, plus services from other private resources'.
In 1984, the EC extended the definition as:

> ... the poor shall be taken to mean persons, families and groups of persons whose resources (material, cultural and social) are so limited

as to exclude them from the minimum acceptable way of life in the Member State in which they live. (EEC, 1981)

These are *relative* definitions of poverty in that they all refer to poverty not as some 'absolute basket of goods' but in terms of the minimum acceptable standard of living applicable to a certain member state and within a person's own society.

There is now widespread agreement on the scientific definition of poverty as both low income and low standard of living (Gordon and Pantazis, 1997; Gordon et al, 2000). These ideas were enshrined in both the EU's definition of poverty and also in the two definitions of poverty adopted by 117 governments at the World Summit on Social Development in 1995.

These EU definitions are similar to the relative poverty definition devised by Peter Townsend (Townsend, 1979). However, they differ quite substantially from the definitions of poverty that were being used when the welfare state was first established in the UK and other EU countries. In the UK, Beveridge adopted the concept of 'subsistence' which was based on the minimum standards to maintain physical efficiency and was developed from the work of the pioneers of poverty research such as Rowntree. A minimum basket of goods was costed, for emergency use over a short period of time, with 6% extra added for inefficiencies in spending patterns, in order to draw up the welfare assistance rates (National Assistance rates). This was designed to be an emergency level of income and never meant to keep a person out of poverty for any length of time, however, these rates became enshrined into the Social Security legislation.

The current relative poverty definitions used in the EU deliver a much higher poverty line. They are also concerned with participation and membership within a society.

Absolute and overall poverty

There has been much debate about 'absolute' and 'relative' definitions of poverty and the difficulties involved in comparing poverty in industrialised countries with that in the developing world. However, these debates were resolved in 1995 at the UN World Summit on Social Development at which the governments of 117 countries – including all EU governments – agreed on two definitions of poverty – *absolute* and *overall* poverty. They adopted a declaration and programme of action which included commitments to eradicate absolute poverty by 2015 and also reduce overall poverty, by at least half, by the same year (UNDP, 1995).

Absolute poverty was defined by the UN as:

... a condition characterised by severe deprivation of basic human
needs, including food, safe drinking water, sanitation facilities, health,
shelter, education and information. It depends not only on income
but also on access to services.

Overall poverty was considered to take various forms, including:

... lack of income and productive resources to ensure sustainable
livelihoods; hunger and malnutrition; ill health; limited or lack of
access to education and other basic services; increased morbidity
and mortality from illness; homelessness and inadequate housing;
unsafe environments and social discrimination and exclusion. It
is also characterised by lack of participation in decision-making
and in civil, social and cultural life. It occurs in all countries: as
mass poverty in many developing countries, pockets of poverty
amid wealth in developed countries, loss of livelihoods as a result
of economic recession, sudden poverty as a result of disaster or
conflict, the poverty of low-wage workers, and the utter destitution
of people who fall outside family support systems, social institutions
and safety nets.

The Copenhagen agreements and the EU definitions of poverty are both
accepted by all EU countries.

Income is important but access to public goods – safe water supply, roads,
healthcare, education – is of equal or greater importance, particularly in
developing countries. These are the views of the governments of the world
and poverty measurement clearly needs to respond to them.

The need to measure precisely the extent of global poverty is becoming
increasingly urgent. At the United Nations Millennium Summit (UN,
2000), an unprecedented 191 countries committed themselves to halving
poverty by the year 2015 and to meeting related development targets as
described in the Millennium Declaration (see Johnston, 2001). Valid, reliable
and comparable measures of poverty are needed in order to monitor the
efficiency and effectiveness of anti-poverty policies.

The measurement of poverty by international agencies

There are currently three UN agencies which produce worldwide
measurements of poverty[2] – the International Fund for Agricultural
Development (IFAD) – which uses administrative statistics on health,
education, income and food security; the UN Development Programme
(UNDP) – which uses five indicators from administrative statistics on health,
education and water supply; and the World Bank – which uses microdata

from social surveys to calculate its $1 per day poverty line. This income poverty line is not applied universally and varies from region to region, for example, $2 per day in Latin America and $4 per day in former Soviet states. It is very unclear what standard of living people have who live below these income thresholds in different countries (Gordon and Spicker, 1999). These methods are described in more detail below.

International Fund for Agricultural Development

The IFAD is one of the world's foremost authorities on rural poverty and it has constructed four poverty indices which are designed to measure rural poverty and deprivation (Jazairy et al, 1995):

- The Food Security Index (FSI) attempts to measure the composite food security situation of a country. This index combines relevant food production and consumption variables, including those reflecting growth and variability. The index can take values of zero and above, with 1 being a cut-off point between countries which are relatively food secure and those which are not.
- The Integrated Poverty Index (IPI) is an economic index which is calculated by combining the headcount measure of poverty with the income-gap ratio, income distribution below the poverty line and the annual rate of growth of per capita GNP. According to the IFAD, the headcount index represents the percentage of the rural population below the poverty line. The income-gap ratio is a national measure, the difference between the highest GNP per capita from among the 114 developing countries and the individual country GNP per capita expressed as a percentage of the former. Life expectancy at birth is used as a surrogate measure of income distribution below the poverty line. The IPI follows Amartya Sen's composite poverty index (Sen, 1976) and can take values between zero and 1 with values closer to 1 indicating a relatively worse poverty status.
- The Basic Needs Index (BNI) is designed to measure the social development of rural areas and is composed of an education index and a health index. The education index covers adult literacy and primary school enrolment while the health index includes population per physician, infant mortality rate and access to services such as health, safe water and sanitation. The BNI can take values between zero and 1. The closer the value is to 1, the higher the basic needs status of the population of a country.
- The Relative Welfare Index (RWI) is the arithmetic average of the other three indices (FSI, IPI, BNI). With the FSI normalised to take values between zero and 1, the RWI takes values within the same range.

The IFAD also produces the Women's Status Index (WSI) which is designed to measure the situation of women in order to derive concrete policy recommendations to help improve the status of poor rural women in developing countries.

Having said this, the most recent IFAD (2001) report on rural poverty makes extensive use of the World Bank's $1 per day poverty measure, broken down by area type (for example, urban and rural).

United Nations Development Programme

The UNDP has produced a large number of different indices that are designed to measure poverty, inequality and other developmental issues. Since 1990, these have been published in its annual Human Development Reports. The 1997 *Human Development Report* was entirely devoted to poverty as part of the United Nations International Year for the Eradication of Poverty.

The UNDP's concept of poverty is incorporated within the broader concept of human development, which is defined as (UNDP, 1995):

> Human development is a process of enlarging people's choices. In principle, these choices can be infinite and can change overtime. But at all levels of development, the three essential ones are for people to lead a long and healthy life, to acquire knowledge and to have access to the resources needed for a decent standard of living. If these essential choices are not available, many other opportunities remain inaccessible.

> But human development does not end there. Additional choices, highly valued by many people, range from political, economic and social freedom to opportunities for being creative and productive and enjoying personal self-respect and guaranteed human rights.

> Human development thus has two sides. One is the formation of human capabilities – such as improved health, knowledge and skills. The other is the use people make of their acquired capabilities – for productive purposes, for leisure or for being active in cultural, social and political affairs. If the scales of human development do not finely balance the two sides, much human frustration can result.

> According to the concept of human development, income clearly is only one option that people would like to have, though certainly an important one. But it is not the sum-total of their lives. The purpose of development is to enlarge *all* human choices, not just income.

The most influential index produced by the UNDP is the Human Development Index (HDI) which was constructed to reflect the most important dimensions of human development. The HDI is a composite index based on three indicators: longevity – as measured by life expectancy at birth; educational attainment – as measured by a combination of adult literacy (two thirds weight) and combined primary, secondary and tertiary enrolment ratios (one third weight); and standard of living – as measured by real GDP per capita (PPP$). However, there have been a number of changes made to the way the HDI is constructed since it was first produced in 1990 (UNDP, 1990, 1996).

The 1997 *Human Development Report* defined poverty within the human development perspective and introduced the term Human Poverty. This drew heavily on Sen's capability concept and defined poverty as 'the denial of choices and opportunities for a tolerable life' (UNDP, 1997) . The *human poverty index* (HPI) attempted to operationalise this concept by focusing on those groups whose choices are heavily constrained in each of the three areas used in the HDI. While the HDI focuses on the average achievements of a country, the HPI focuses on the most deprived. The HPI is made up of five weighted components (UNDP, 1997):

- the percentage of people expected to die before 40 years of age;
- the percentage of adults who are illiterate;
- the percentage of people with access to health services;
- the percentage of people with access to safe water;
- the percentage of children under five years of age who are malnourished.

Aspects of human poverty that are excluded from the index due to lack of data or measurement difficulties are – lack of political freedom, inability to participate in decision making, lack of personal security, inability to participate in the life of the community and threats to sustainability and intergenerational equity. Human Poverty Indices (HPI-2) have also recently been calculated at small area level within the UK to compare local pockets of human poverty (Seymour, 2000).

World Bank

The World Bank has produced the most influential measurement of world poverty and devoted its annual reports in both 1990 and 2000 to poverty eradication issues. The World Bank produces a 'universal poverty line [which] is needed to permit cross-country comparison and aggregation' (World Bank, 1990, p 27). Poverty is defined as 'the inability to attain a minimal standard of living' (World Bank, 1990, p 26). Despite its acknowledgement of the difficulties in including, in any measure of poverty, the contribution to living standards of public goods and common-property resources, the World Bank settles for a standard which is 'consumption-based' and which comprises:

> ... two elements: the expenditure necessary to buy a minimum standard of nutrition and other basic necessities and a further amount that varies from country to country, reflecting the cost of participating in the everyday life of society. (World Bank, 1990, p 26)

The first of these elements is stated to be 'relatively straightforward' because it could be calculated by 'looking at the prices of the foods that make up the diets of the poor' (World Bank, 1990, pp 26-27). However, the second element is 'far more subjective; in some countries indoor plumbing is a luxury, but in others it is a "necessity"' (World Bank, 1990, p 27). For operational purposes, the second element was set aside and the first assessed as Purchasing Power Parity (PPP) – $370 per person per year at 1985 prices for all the poorest developing countries. Those with incomes per capita of less than $370 were deemed 'poor' while those with less than $275 per year were 'extremely poor'. This approximate $1 of consumption per person per day poverty line was chosen from a World Bank study of minimum income thresholds used in 8 of the 33 'poorest' countries to assess eligibility for welfare provision (Ravallion et al, 1991).[3]

The *World Development Report on poverty* in 2000 used a similar methodology to revise the poverty line estimate as $1.08 per person per day at 1993 Purchasing Power Parity (Chen and Ravallion, 2000). However, the poverty threshold is now set at the median value of the ten poorest countries with the lowest poverty lines; that is, world poverty rates are set at the level of the country with the fifth lowest welfare benefit eligibility threshold. No explanation has yet been provided for this change.

Equivalent consumption expenditures of $1.08 are calculated for each country using PPP conversions, which are primarily designed for comparing aggregates of national accounts[4] not the consumption of poor people. It is very unclear what the World Bank's poverty line means or even if the new $1.08 at 1993 PPP poverty line is higher or lower than the old $1 a day poverty line at 1985 PPP because the 1985 and 1993 PPP tables are not directly comparable (Reddy and Pogge, 2002).

No allowance was made by the World Bank in either 1990 or 2000 for the second 'participatory' element of its poverty definition. The logic of the Bank's own argument is not followed, the minimum value of the poverty line is underestimated and the number of poor in the World are therefore also underestimated.[5]

Poverty measurement in the European Union

Although poverty has been clearly defined in Europe as an unacceptably low standard of living caused by low income, the measurement of poverty within Europe has almost exclusively concentrated on measuring only low incomes. The major comparative studies by the European Community Statistical Office (EUROSTAT) have been based on either the European Community Household Panel (ECHP) survey or harmonised national household budget surveys. A range of arbitrary low income thresholds have been used as proxies for poverty, for example, half average expenditure, half average income, less than 60% of median income, less than 50% of median income, and so on.

[...]

Producing meaningful and internationally comparable poverty statistics

The major problem with all the poverty measures produced by IFAD, UNDP, the World Bank and EUROSTAT is that they are of little value for measuring poverty *within* a country or for helping developing or industrialised countries to assess the effectiveness of their own anti-poverty policies. Nor do they correspond to any internationally (or even nationally) agreed definitions of poverty.

The main problem with the World Bank's $1 a day poverty lines is that they are essentially meaningless. It is impossible to tell from the World Bank poverty line whether or not a household with an income below this threshold has sufficient money to live decently or not. It would be much more meaningful to produce low income statistics which show how many households do not have an adequate income to allow them to meet their basic needs (*absolute poverty*) and/or participate in the economic, social, cultural and political life of the country in which they live (*overall poverty*). Low income thresholds and statistics should measure adequacy not arbitrary thresholds and the most widely used method of achieving this goal is to use a 'budget standards' approach.

A budget standard is a specified basket of goods and services which, when priced, can represent a particular standard of living. Budgets can be devised to represent any living standard (Bradshaw, 1993) and, for example, national statistical offices could produce budget standards which corresponded with the *absolute* and *overall* poverty definitions agreed at the World Social Summit (discussed earlier in this chapter). This would produce income poverty thresholds which are both nationally and internationally meaningful.

Budget standards are probably the oldest scientific method of exploring low living standards. Pioneered by Rowntree (1901) in the UK, in his famous

studies of poverty in York, they have since been used in many countries to
measure income poverty, for example, in the USA, at both national and state
level (Orshansky, 1965; Watts, 1980; NYCC, 1982; Renwick, 1993; Citro and
Michael, 1995); Canada (Social Planning Council, 1981); the Netherlands
(Hagenaars and de Vos, 1988); New Zealand (Stephens, 1995); Hong Kong
(MacPherson, 1994); the UK (Piachaud, 1979; Bradshaw, 1993; Parker, 1998,
2000); and in Australia (Saunders, 1998).

Indeed, Mark Malloch Brown, the UN Development Program (UNDP)
administrator, recently argued that: 'We need a global Rowntree.... A
clearer benchmarking of poverty and of its contributing elements, such as
child education and healthcare, could provide the political space and focus
for action at the community, national and global levels' (Malloch Brown,
2001).

While budget standards-derived income poverty thresholds, using
internationally agreed definitions of poverty, would produce meaningful
and comparable income poverty statistics for individuals and households,
additional (direct) measures of deprivation (low standard of living) are also
needed for international poverty comparisons and anti-poverty policy
monitoring. This is because poverty is not only dependent on personal/
household income but also on the availability of public goods, for example,
clean water supplies, hospitals, schools, and so on. One example of how this
could be achieved is discussed below.

International measurement of standard of living (deprivation)

During the 1990s, advances in social survey methodology in developing
countries have made available a wealth of new data, some of which can be
used to measure low standard of living and deprivation. This section outlines
some recent work that has been carried out in the UK by the Townsend
Centre for International Poverty Research, on behalf of UNICEF, which
attempts to operationalise the absolute definition of poverty agreed at the
World Summit on Social Development to measure child poverty in the
developing world.

There are currently no consistent estimates of the extent or severity of
child poverty in developing countries. While many countries do have detailed
anti-poverty strategies and statistics on child poverty, these estimates tend to
use different methods and definitions of poverty which makes comparison
extremely difficult.

The World Bank's method of measuring poverty by low per capita
consumption expenditure is singularly unsuitable for measuring child
poverty and does not conform with the internationally agreed definitions
of poverty adopted at the World Social Summit. For example, the definition
of absolute poverty implies that a child is poor if she suffers from severe

educational deprivation. In accordance with a number of UN resolutions, this could be operationalised as her lack of receipt of primary education (Gordon et al, 2001). There might be a number of reasons why a child does not receive primary education and low family income is often a very important factor. However, a lack of government investment in schools and infrastructure can also prevent children from being educated as can prejudice and discriminatory attitudes that consider that certain children are not 'worth' educating. Whichever of these reasons is true, either singularly or in combination, the end result will be the same in that the child will suffer from severe educational deprivation.

Therefore, there is a need to look beyond the World Bank's narrow focus on per capita consumption expenditure and at both the effects of low family income *and* the effects of inadequate service provision for children (Vandemoortele, 2000), as it is a lack of investment in good quality education, health and other public services in many parts of the world that is as significant a cause of child poverty as low family incomes. Nobel Laureate, Amartya Sen, has argued that, in developing countries, poverty is best measured directly using indicators of standard of living rather than indirectly using income or consumption measures.

> In an obvious sense the direct method is superior to the income method ... it could be argued that only in the absence of direct information regarding the satisfaction of the specified needs can there be a case for bringing in the intermediary of income, so that the income method is at most a second best. (Sen, 1981, p 26)

Such direct measures of need or low standard of living are often referred to as *deprivation* measures. Deprivation can be conceptualised as a continuum which ranges from no deprivation, through mild, moderate and severe deprivation to extreme deprivation at the end of the scale. Figure 2.2.2 illustrates this concept.

Figure 2.2.2: Continuum of deprivation

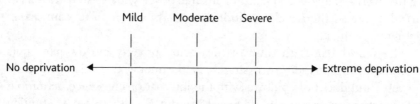

In order to measure absolute poverty among children using the World Social
Summit definition, it is necessary to define the threshold measures of severe
deprivation of basic human need for:

- food;
- safe drinking water;
- sanitation facilities;
- health;
- shelter;
- education;
- information;
- access to services.

Comparable information on severe deprivation of basic human need among
children is available from high quality microdata from the Demographic and
Health Surveys (DHS)[6] carried out in 68 countries during the 1990s. The
DHS are nationally representative household surveys with sample sizes of
about 5,000 households and an estimated cost of $200 per household (Loup
and Naudet, 2000). A major advantage of the DHS is their random cluster
sampling methodology. On average, 3,000 to 9,000 women of childbearing
age were interviewed in each country (average 5,400) and each survey
contains between 150-300 clusters, with an average of 200 clusters. Cluster
size is around 2-3 km or smaller in urban areas (Gerland, 1996).

Table 2.2.1 shows the operational definitions of deprivation for the eight
criteria in the World Summit definition of absolute poverty that have been
used for the UNICEF study of child poverty using DHS microdata.

Children who suffer from *severe deprivation of basic human need* – as shown
in the fourth column of Table 2.2.1 – are living in absolute poverty as
defined at the World Social Summit, that is, 'Absolute poverty is a condition
characterised by severe deprivation of basic human needs, including food,
safe drinking water, sanitation facilities, health, shelter, education and
information. It depends not only on income but also on access to social
services' (UNDP, 1997).

Cost of ending poverty

The EUROSTAT analysis of poverty indicates that almost sixty million
people in the EU are 'poor' (have an income of less than half the average).
Poverty analyses by the World Bank (2001) have demonstrated that over
one billion people in developing countries have to live on the equivalent of
less than $1 per day. These are huge numbers of people so a major question
remains – is the world's desire to end poverty in the 21st century realistic
and affordable?

Table 2.2.1: Operational definitions of deprivation for children

Deprivation	Mild	Moderate	Severe	Extreme
Food	Bland diet of poor nutritional value	Going hungry on occasion	Malnutrition	Starvation
Safe drinking water	Not having enough water on occasion due to lack of sufficient money	No access to water in dwelling but communal piped water available within 200 metres of dwelling or less than 15 minutes' walk away	Long walk to water source (more than 200 meters or longer than 15 minutes). Unsafe drinking water (for example, open water)	No access to water
Sanitation facilities	Having to share facilities with another household	Sanitation facilities outside dwelling	No sanitation facilities in or near dwelling	No access to sanitation facilities
Health	Occasional lack of access to medical care due to insufficient money	Inadequate medical care	No immunisation against diseases. Only limited non-professional medical care available when sick	No medical care
Shelter	Dwelling in poor repair. More than one person per room	Few facilities in dwelling, lack of heating, structural problems. More than three persons per room	No facilities in house, non-permanent structure, no privacy, no flooring, just one or two rooms. More than five persons per room	Roofless – no shelter
Education	Inadequate teaching due to lack of resources	Unable to attend secondary but can attend primary education	Child is seven years of age or older and has received no primary or secondary education	Prevented from learning due to persecution and prejudice
Information	Cannot afford newspapers or books	No television but can afford a radio	No access to radio, television or books or newspapers	Prevented from gaining access to information by government, and so on
Basic social services	Health and education facilities available but occasionally of low standard	Inadequate health and education facilities nearby (for example, less than one hour travel)	Limited health and education facilities more than one hour travel away	No access to health or education facilities

The costs of ending poverty are much less than the large numbers of poor people would indicate. Table 2.2.2 below shows how much of the income of the non-poor population would have to be transferred (given) to the poor people in each EU country to eliminate poverty using a 50% and 60% of the median income poverty line in each country (Fouarge, 2001).

In the UK, 1.5% of the income of non-poor households would have to be transferred to poor households in order to raise every person's income above the 50% median income poverty threshold. Similarly, in the UK, 3.0% of income would need to be transferred to poor people to raise their incomes above the 60% median income poverty threshold. The corresponding figures for ending income poverty in Finland are 1% and 1.8% respectively, and, for the EU as a whole, 1.7% and 3%. The cost of ending income poverty in the EU is therefore not unfeasibly large.

UNICEF has carried out a similar analysis on the costs of eradicating *child* poverty in 'rich' countries. Table 2.2.3 shows how much national income (percentage of GNP) would be needed to close the child poverty gap in 17 OECD countries.

The table shows that relatively little national income needs to be transferred to poor families to eliminate child income poverty – using UNICEF's definition of income poverty (less than 50% of the national median income). In Finland, less than 1% of GNP would need to be spent on helping poor families with children and, even in the UK, which has very

Table 2.2.2: Cost of ending poverty in the EU: % of income needed to be transferred from the non-poor to the poor in each country

Country	Cost of ending poverty (50% of median income poverty line)	Cost of ending poverty (60% of median income poverty line)
Luxembourg	0.8	1.5
Denmark	0.8	1.7
Austria	1.0	1.8
Finland	1.0	1.8
France	1.1	2.2
Ireland	1.1	2.2
Belgium	1.5	2.8
Netherlands	2.0	3.0
UK	1.5	3.0
Spain	1.8	3.1
Germany	2.2	3.3
Italy	2.2	3.6
Portugal	2.3	3.8
Greece	2.3	3.9
EU	1.7	3.0

high rates of child poverty, less than 0.5% of GNP is needed.

The reason why so much poverty can be ended at comparatively little cost is that welfare states are reasonably good at preventing people from falling into very deep poverty. Most poor households have incomes which are relatively close to the income poverty thresholds that are used in these kinds of analyses. Therefore, relatively small transfers of income will raise a large number of people above these income poverty thresholds.

Lack of good income information has meant that detailed costs of ending poverty analyses, that are available for rich countries, are not available for developing countries. However, the UNDP has estimated (UNDP, 1997) the annual cost over ten years of providing every person in the world with basic social services (Table 2.2.4).

The UNDP estimated that the additional cost of achieving basic social services for all in developing countries at about $40 billion a year over ten years

Table 2.2.3: Percentage of GNP required to end child poverty in 17 OECD countries

Country	% of GNP
Sweden	0.07
Finland	0.08
Belgium	0.09
Luxembourg	0.09
Norway	0.12
Denmark	0.12
France	0.14
Hungary	0.24
Germany	0.26
Spain	0.31
Netherlands	0.31
Australia	0.39
Canada	0.46
UK	0.48
Italy	0.50
Poland	0.56
USA	0.66

Source: UNICEF (2000)

(1995–2005). This is less than 0.2% of world income and represents about 1% of developing country income. The cost of providing basic health and nutrition for every person in the world was estimated at just $13 billion per year for ten years. This seems a very large figure but, to put it in perspective, in 2000 the US population spent $11.6 billion on dog and cat food (Euromonitor International, 2001). Europe and the US together spend a lot more on pet food than is needed to provide basic health and nutrition for all the world's people.

Table 2.2.4: The cost of achieving universal access to basic social services

Need	Annual cost (US$ billions)
Basic education for all	6
Basic health and nutrition	13
Reproductive health and family planning	12
Low-cost water supply and sanitation	9
Total	40

Ending poverty is largely a matter of lack of political will. It is not a problem
of lack of money or scientific knowledge on how to eradicate poverty.

Conclusions

Poverty is the world's most ruthless killer and the greatest cause of suffering
on earth. The 1995 World Health Organisation (WHO) report argued
that:

> Poverty is the main reason why babies are not vaccinated, clean
> water and sanitation are not provided, and curative drugs and other
> treatments are unavailable and why mothers die in childbirth.
> Poverty is the main cause of reduced life expectancy, of handicap
> and disability, and of starvation. Poverty is a major contributor to
> mental illness, stress, suicide, family disintegration and substance
> abuse. (WHO, 1995)

Yet the costs of meeting the basic needs of every person in the world
are relatively small compared with the vast wealth available. The practical
policies and institutional mechanisms needed to end world poverty are well
known and widely understood. No scientific breakthroughs are required
to provide everybody with a safe water supply, a nutritious diet, adequate
housing and basic healthcare. No new knowledge is needed to provide all
children with an education. A wide range of comprehensive welfare state
models in European countries have been proven to be effective mechanisms
for delivering social security and welfare. International agreements are
already in place which provide guidance on what the minimum levels of
social security benefits should be and the governments of the world have
repeatedly made commitments to reduce and eventually end poverty in
the 21st century.

The neo-liberal 'Washington Consensus' policies pursued by the World
Bank and IMF have failed to even reduce poverty (let alone end poverty)
nor are the methods that they (and other international organisations) use
to measure poverty adequate. In particular, the World Bank's consumption-
based poverty measures ($1.08 per day) are not reliable, valid or particularly
meaningful and cannot be used to measure the effectiveness of anti-poverty
policies.

New advances in social science *are* needed to produce scientific
measurements of poverty which are both internationally comparable and
also of use to policy makers within countries – one possible approach has
been discussed in this chapter. New research is also needed to identify the
best methods of building comprehensive welfare states in countries where
currently only residual welfare states exist.

Notes

[1] See vandenbroucke.fgov.be/Europe%20summary.htm for a summary of the new EU poverty and social exclusion indicators and www.vandenbroucke.fgov.be/T-011017.htm for discussion.

[2] In the past, the Food and Agricultural Organisation (FAO) has also produced estimates of absolute poverty using per capita food expenditure (Engle coefficients): 59% and over indicated absolute poverty, 50-59% hand to mouth existence, 40-50% a better off life, 30-40% affluence and 30% and below, the richest (Ruizen and Yuan, 1992).

[3] '[A] representative, absolute poverty line for low income countries is $31, which (to the nearest dollar) is shared by six of the countries in our sample, namely Indonesia, Bangladesh, Nepal, Kenya, Tanzania, and Morocco, and two other countries are close to this figure (Philippines and Pakistan)' (Ravallion et al, 1991).

[4] See the OECD FAQ's about PPP at www.oecd.org/oecd/pages/home/displaygeneral/0,3380,EN-faq-513-15-no-no-322-513,FF.html.

[5] For a more comprehensive review of the problems with the World Bank's 2000/01 *World Development Report on attacking poverty* see the review by the International Social Science Council's Comparative Research Programme on Poverty (CROP, 2002).

[6] For more information see the Measure *DHS+* website at www.measuredhs.com.

References

Atkinson, T. (2000) 'A European social agenda: poverty benchmarking and social transfers', Unpublished paper (www.nuff.ox.ac.uk/users/atkinson/CAE2000final.pdf).

Atkinson, T., Cantillon, B., Marlier, E. and Nolan, B. (2002) *Social indicators – the EU and social inclusion*, Oxford: Oxford University Press.

Bradshaw, J. (ed) (1993) *Budget standards for the United Kingdom*, Aldershot: Avebury.

Chen, S. and Ravallion, M. (2000) *How did the world's poorest fare in the 1990s?*, World Bank Occasional Paper, New York (www.worldbank.org/research/povmonitor/pdfs/methodology.pdf).

Citro, C.F. and Michael, R.T. (eds) (1995) *Measuring poverty. A new approach*, Washington, DC: National Academy Press.

Clotuche, G. (2001) 'The social protection in the CEEC in the context of the enlargement', *Belgian Review of Social Security*, vol 43, pp 21-8 (socialsecurity.fgov. be/bib/index.htm).

Council of Europe (1996) European Social Charter (revised), conventions.coe. int/Treaty/EN/Treaties/HTML/163.htm

CROP (Comparative Research Programme on Poverty) (2002) 'A critical review of the World Bank report: *World Development Report 2000/2007. Attacking poverty*', (www.crop.org/publications/files/report/Comments_to_WDR2001_2002_ ny.pdf).

EC (2001a) 'Social exclusion: Commission takes first step towards EU poverty strategy', (www.europa.eu.int/comm/employment_social/news/2001/oct/ i01_1395_en.html).

EC (2001b) 'NAPs/incl: National Action Plans on social inclusion', (www.europa. eu.int/comm/employment_social/news/2001/jun/napsincl2001_en.html).

EC (2001c) 'European Council Laeken: Conclusions of the presidency', (www. europarl.eu.int/summits/pdf/lae_en.pdf).

Esping-Andersen, G. (ed) (1990) *The three worlds of welfare capitalism*, London, Princeton, NJ: Polity Press and Princeton University Press.

Esping-Andersen, G. (ed) (1996) *Welfare states in transition: National adaptations of global economics*, London: Sage Publications.

Euromonitor International (2001) *Pet foods and accessories in the USA 2001*, London (www.majormarketprofiles.com).

Eurostat (1990) *Poverty in figures: Europe in the early 1980s*, Luxembourg: Eurostat.

Eurostat (1998) *Recommendations of the Task Force on Statistics on Social Exclusion and Poverty*, Luxembourg: Eurostat.

Eurostat (2000) *Income, poverty and social exclusion*, Luxembourg: Office for Official Publications of the European Communities.

Förster, M.F. (1994) *Measurement of low incomes and poverty in a perspective of international comparisons*, Labour Market and Social Policy Occasional Papers no 14, Paris: OECD (www1.oecd.org/els/health/docs.htm).

Förster, M.F. and Pellizzari, M. (2000) *Trends and driving factors in income distribution and poverty in the OECD area*, Labour Market and Social Policy Occasional Papers no 14, Paris: OECD (www1.oecd.org/els/health/docs.htm).

Fouarge, D. (2001) *Subsidiarity and poverty in the European Union. Fiscal competition or co-ordination?*, Tilburg: Tilburg University (www.sbu.ac.uk/euroinst/EXSPRO/ wp3.pdf).

Gerland, P. (1996) 'Socio-economic data and GIS: datasets, databases, indicators and data integration issues', Paper presented to UNEP/CGIAR (Consultative Group on International Agricultural Research), Arendal III Workshop on *Use of GIS in agricultural research management*, Norway, 17-21 June (www.un.org/Depts/unsd/ softproj/papers/pg_cgiar.htm).

Goodin, R.E., Headey, B., Muffels, R.J.A. and Dirven, H.J. (1999) *The real worlds of welfare capitalism*, Cambridge: Cambridge University Press.

Gordon, D. and Pantazis, C. (eds) (1997) *Breadline Britain in the 1990s*, Aldershot, Brookfield, Hong Kong, Singapore and Sydney: Ashgate.

Gordon, D. and Spicker, P. (eds) (1999) *The international glossary on poverty*, London: Zed Books.

Gordon, D. and Townsend, P. (eds) (2000) *Breadline Europe: The measurement of poverty*, Bristol: The Policy Press.

Gordon, D., Adelman, A., Ashworth, K., Bradshaw, J., Levitas, R., Middleton, S., Pantazis, C., Patsios, D., Payne, S., Townsend, P. and Williams, J. (2000) *Poverty and social exclusion in Britain*, York: Joseph Rowntree Foundation (www.bris. ac.uk/poverty/pse).

Gordon, D., Pantazis, C. and Townsend, P. (2001) 'Child rights and child poverty in developing countries', Unpublished report for UNICEF, Bristol: Townsend Centre for International Poverty Research.

Hagenaars, A.J.M. and de Vos, K. (1988) 'The definition and measurement of poverty', *Journal of Human Resources*, vol 23, no 2, pp 211-21.

Hagenaars, A.J.M., de Vos, K. and Zaidi, A. (1994) *Poverty statistics in the late 1980s*, Luxembourg: Eurostat.

ILO (International Labour Organisation) (1952) *Social Security (Minimum Standards) Convention, 1952 (No 102)*, Geneva: ILO (ilolex.ilo.ch:1567/scripts/convde. pl?C102).

IFAD (International Fund for Agricultural Development) (2001) *Rural poverty report 2001: The challenge of ending rural poverty*, Oxford: Oxford University Press.

Jazairy, I., Alamgir, M. and Panuccio, T. (1995) *The state of world rural poverty*, London: IFAD.

Johnston, R. (2001) *Road map towards the implementation of the United Nations Millennium Declaration: Report of the Secretary-General*, UN General Assembly 56th Session, 6 September, follow-up to the outcome of the Millennium Summit, UN, New York (www.ibge.gov.br/poverty/pdf/millennium_road_map.pdf; see also www.un.org/millennium).

Loup, J. and Naudet, D. (2000) *The state of human development data and statistical capacity building in developing countries*, Human Development Report Office, Occasional Papers no 60 (www.undp.org/hdro/occ.htm#2).

MacPherson, S. (1994) *A measure of dignity. Report on the adequacy of public assistance rates in Hong Kong*, Hong Kong: Department of Public and Social Administration, City Polytechnic of Hong Kong.

Malloch Brown, M. (2001) 'Child poverty and meeting the 2015 targets', statement, London, 26 February (www.undp.org/dpa/statements/administ/2001/february/ 26feb01.html).

Marlier, E. and Cohen-Solal, M. (2000) 'Social benefits and their redistributive effect in the EU', *Statistics in Focus*, Population and Social Conditions, Theme 3–9/2000, Luxembourg: Eurostat.

Mejer, L. and Linden, G. (2000) 'Persistent income poverty and social exclusion in
the European Union', *Statistics in Focus*, Population and Social Conditions, Theme
3–13/2000, Luxembourg: Eurostat.

Mejer, L. and Siermann, C. (2000) 'Income poverty in the European Union: children,
gender and poverty gaps', *Statistics in Focus*, Population and Social Conditions,
Theme 3–12/2000, Luxembourg: Eurostat.

NYCC (Community Council for Greater New York) (1982) *A Family Budget
Standard*, New York, NY: NYCC.

Orshansky, M. (1965) 'Counting the poor: another look at the poverty profile',
Social Security Bulletin, June, pp 3-29.

Parker, H. (ed) (1998) *Low cost but acceptable: A minimum income standard for the UK:
Families with young children: How much is enough?*, Bristol: The Policy Press.

Parker, H. (2000) *Low cost but acceptable: Incomes for older people. A minimum income
standard for households aged 65-74 years in the UK*, Bristol: The Policy Press (www.
bris.ac.uk/Publications/TPP/pages/rp032.html).

Piachaud, D. (1979) *The cost of a child: A modern minimum*, London: Child Poverty
Action Group.

Ravallion, M., Datt, G. and Van de Walle, D. (1991) 'Quantifying absolute poverty
in the developing world', *Review of Income and Wealth*, vol 37, pp 345-61.

Reddy, S.G. and Pogge, T.W. (2002) 'How not to count the poor', Unpublished paper,
Columbia University (www.google.com/search?q=cache:S3mzMaVx31UC:
www.ids.ac.uk/ids/pvty/Count.pdf+how+not+to+count+the+poor&hl=en).

Renwick, T.J. (1993) 'Budget-based poverty measurement: 1992 Basic Needs
Budgets', *Proceedings of the American Statistical Association*, Social Statistics Section,
pp 573-82.

Rowntree, B.S. (1901) *Poverty. A study of town life*, London: Macmillan (republished
in 2000 by The Policy Press, Bristol: www.bris.ac.uk/Publications/TPP/pages/
at036.htm).

Saunders, P. (1998) *Using budget standards to assess the well-being of families*, Social
Policy Research Centre Discussion paper 93, Sydney, University of New South
Wales (www.sprc.unsw.edu.au/dp/dp093.pdf).

Sen, A.K. (1976) 'Poverty: an ordinal approach to measurement', *Econometrica*, vol
44, no 2, pp 219-31.

Sen, A.K. (1981) *Poverty and famines. An essay on entitlement and deprivation*, Oxford:
Clarendon Press.

Seymour, J. (ed) (2000) *Poverty in plenty: A human development report for the UK*,
London: Earthscan.

Social Planning Council (1981) *The budgets guide methodology study*, Toronto: Social
Planning Council of Metropolitan Toronto.

Stephens, R. (1995) 'Measuring poverty in New Zealand, 1984-1993', in P. Saunders
and S. Shaver (eds) *Social policy and the challenges of social change*, Volume 1, Reports
and Proceedings no 122, Sydney: Social Policy Research Centre, University of
New South Wales, pp 229-42.

Townsend, P. (1979) *Poverty in the United Kingdom*, Harmondsworth: Penguin.

Townsend, P. and Gordon, D. (2000) 'Introduction: The measurement of poverty in Europe', in D. Gordon and P. Townsend (eds) *Breadline Europe: The measurement of poverty*, Bristol: The Policy Press, pp 1-22.

UN (2000) 'Millennium Assembly' (www.un.org/millennium).

UNDP (United Nations Development Programme) (1990) *Human Development Report 1990: Concepts and measurement of human development*, New York, NY: Oxford University Press (hdr.undp.org/reports/global/1990/en/).

UNDP (1995) *The Copenhagen Declaration and Programme of Action: World Summit for Social Development 6-12 March 1995*, UN Department of Publications, sales no E.96.IV.8, New York (www.visionoffice.com/socdev/wssd.htm).

UNDP (1996) *Human Development Report 1996: Sustainability and human development*, New York, NY: Oxford University Press (hdr.undp.org/reports/global/1997/en/).

UNDP (1997) *Human Development Report 1997: Human development to eradicate poverty*, New York, NY: Oxford University Press (hdr.undp.org/reports/global/1999/en/).

UNICEF Innocenti Research Centre (2000) *Innocenti Report Card No. 1. A league table of child poverty in rich nations*, UN Children's Fund, Florence (www.unicef-icdc.org/cgi-bin/unicef/Lunga.sql?ProductID=226).

Vandemoortele, J. (2000) *Absorbing social shocks, protecting children and reducing poverty: The role of basic social services*, UNICEF Working Papers, New York.

Watts, H. W. (1980) *New American Budget Standards: Report of the Expert Committee on Family Budget Revisions*, Special Report Series, Institute for Research on Poverty, University of Wisconsin, Madison.

WHO (World Health Organisation) (1995) *The World Health Report 1995: Bridging the gaps*, Geneva: WHO.

WHO (1998) *The World Health Report 1998: Life in the 21st century a vision for all*, Geneva: WHO.

World Bank (1990) *World Development Report 1990: Poverty*, Washington, DC: World Bank.

World Bank (2001) *World Development Report 2000/2001: Attacking poverty*, New York, NY/Oxford: Oxford University Press.

Chapter 2.3

Globalization, poverty and income distribution: does the liberal argument hold?

Robert Hunter Wade

[...]

Poverty

As the economist Richard Cooper says, the record on poverty alleviation in the late twentieth century is 'unambiguously positive'.[1] Things may have got worse in Africa, he admits, but the improvements in China and India mean that 'the fraction of the world's population living in poverty has gone way down'.

These and other such statements are based on World Bank figures, for the Bank is effectively the sole producer of the world poverty headcount. It declares in the opening sentence of the World Development Indicators 2001, 'Of the world's 6 billion people 1.2 billion live on less than $1 a day'.[2] This number, says the Bank, was the same in 1998 as in 1987. Since world population increased, the proportion of the world's population in absolute poverty fell sharply in only 11 years from around 28 percent to 24 percent, an extraordinary historical reversal of trend.

Other Bank sources give different numbers, however. *The World Development Report 2000/2001:Attacking Poverty* says that the number of people living on less than $1 a day *increased* by 20 million from 1.18 billion in 1987 to 1.20 billion in 1998. Less than two years later *Globalization, Growth, and Poverty: Building an Inclusive World Economy* claimed that the number of people living in poverty *decreased* by 200 million in the 18 years from 1980 to 1998.[3]

My strong conclusion is that we cannot have much confidence in the Bank's numbers.[4] My weaker conclusions are that the absolute numbers in extreme poverty are probably higher than the Bank's, that the trend is probably upwards, and that, nevertheless, the proportion of the world's population living in extreme poverty has indeed probably fallen over the past twenty years, as the liberal argument claims.

The Bank's world poverty headcount emerges from a process in which it first calculates an international 'extreme poverty' line (defined in terms of income or consumption) from the official national poverty lines in a sample of countries. It applies purchasing power parity exchange rates (PPP exchange rates, expressed as so many units of national currency per US dollar), rather than current market exchange rates, to the national poverty lines in order to arrive at the international poverty line defined in US dollars. When the Bank began this world poverty headcount exercise in 1990[5] it took a sample of 33 low- and middle-income countries (using a selection criterion that it has not explained), and found that a cluster of eight countries had poverty lines at around $31 per month or $1 per day, using the Penn World Tables to get the PPP exchange rates between national currencies and US dollars for 1985. This 'typical' line is the origin of the famous '$1/day' extreme poverty line. National poverty lines so calculated were then adjusted by the national consumer price index for years after 1985. (The Penn World Tables are based on a large-scale international price comparison made in 1985. It took a large number of goods and services and compared the prices for a given unit in the US against the prices in other countries. So the price comparison showed the US$ price of a kilo of wheat over the price of a kilo of wheat in India expressed in rupees, the US$ price of a massage in the United States over the rupee price of a massage in India, and so on. This gave a purchasing power parity exchange rate for each good or service with respect to the US and India. These individual PPP exchange rates were then aggregated into a single PPP exchange rate between the US$ and the Indian rupee, taking some account of regional price variation within countries. The same exercise was done for all countries in the survey using the same basket of goods and services.)

In the late 1990s, the Bank changed the poverty headcount methodology. It took the same 33 countries and the same basket of goods and services that had been included in the earlier poverty line, and revalued them using a new international price survey of 1993. With the 1993 prices the earlier cluster of national poverty lines around $31 per month disappeared. So the Bank arbitrarily took the 10 lowest of the 33 national poverty lines and selected the median, roughly the fifth lowest. This gave a 'rebased' international poverty line of $PPP 1.08 per day. The Bank then used the new set of 1993 prices to convert this new international poverty line back into national poverty lines expressed in national currencies. Then it recalculated the number of people in each country, and the world, living on incomes below this new level. In short, the Bank's change of methodology in the late 1990s (the new results were published in *World Development Report 2000/01*) amounted to: (1) a change in the way the international poverty line was calculated from a set of official poverty lines for a sample of low- and middle-income countries, (2) a change in the international poverty line from $PPP 1 per day to $PPP 1.08 per day, and (3) a change in the procedure for aggregating the relative price changes between 1985 and 1993 for each of the goods and services in the standard bundle for each country (a change that the Bank has never reported publicly, let alone explained).[6]

Some of the reasons for agnosticism about the number of people in extreme poverty come from the change in methodology, others from problems that the change did not address.

First, the Bank's comparison between 1980 and 1998 – 1.4 billion in extreme poverty in 1980, 1.2 billion in 1998 – is not legitimate, because the two figures are calculated using different methodologies. The Bank has recalculated the poverty numbers with the new methodology only back to 1987. We do not know what the 1980 figure would be if calculated by the same methodology as the later figures.

Second, we do know that the Bank's new methodology using the relative prices from the 1993 survey caused a huge change in the poverty count even for the same country in the same year using the same survey data. Table 2.3.1 shows the impact of the revision in terms of the poverty rate in different regions, for 1993. Angus Deaton concludes from these figures, 'Changes of this size risk swamping real changes, and it seems impossible to make statements about changes in world poverty when the ground underneath one's feet is changing in this way'.[7]

Table 2.3.1: 1993 poverty rate, using old and new World Bank methodology

	Old poverty rate (%)	New poverty rate (%)
Sub-Saharan Africa	39.1	49.7
Latin America	23.5	15.3
Middle East/North Africa	4.1	1.9

Note: The poverty rate is the proportion of the population living on less than $1 a day. The old rate is based on the 1985 PPP benchmark survey, the new rate is based on the one of 1993.
Source: Deaton, "Counting the world's poor".

Third, the new methodology did not address a basic problem with the Bank's global (old or new) poverty line to do with *which* goods and services are included in the bundle against which relative purchasing power is being measured. The problem is that the Bank's line relates to a 'general consumption' bundle, not to a basket of goods and services that makes sense for measuring poverty, such as food, clothing and shelter (though '$1 per day' does have intuitive appeal to a western audience being asked to support aid). We have no way of knowing what proportion of food–clothing–shelter needs the Bank's poverty line captures. If the Bank used a basic needs poverty line rather than its present artificial one the number of absolute poor would probably rise, because the national poverty lines equivalent to a global basic needs poverty line expressed in US dollars would probably rise by a lot (maybe 25-50%). They would rise a lot because the present PPP price indices include many services that are very cheap in developing countries (e.g. massages) but irrelevant to the poor – to the consumption bundle needed to avoid poverty – and therefore give a misleadingly high measure of the purchasing power of the incomes of the poor. Food and shelter are relatively expensive, and if they alone were included in the PPP exchange rate used to express the incomes of the poor in US dollars, national poverty lines would go up.[8] Indeed, the rates of 'extreme poverty' for Latin American countries using poverty lines based on calorific and demographic characteristics are roughly twice as high as those based on the World Bank's $1/day line.[9]

Fourth, the poverty headcount is very sensitive to the precise level of the global poverty line because income distribution in the vicinity of developing country poverty lines is typically fairly flat. Even a small increase in the line brings a large increase in the number of people below it. Hence we can expect that a shift to a poverty line based on basic needs, excluding services that are very cheap but irrelevant to the poor, would raise the number of people in extreme poverty by a significant amount.

Fifth, the Bank's poverty headcount comes from household surveys. Household surveys have a number of limitations that add up to a large margin of error in national poverty numbers and so also in the world totals. Some are well known, such as the exclusion of most of the benefits that people receive from publicly provided goods and services. Others are less well known, such as the sensitivity of the poverty headcount to the recall period used in the survey. The shorter the recall period the more expenditure is reported. India provides a striking example. A recent study suggests that a switch from the standard 30 day reporting period to a 7 day reporting period itself lifts 175 million people from poverty using the Indian official poverty line, a nearly 50 percent fall. Using the $1/day international line, which is higher, the fall would be even greater.[10]

Sixth, when new household surveys for a country are not available the Bank assumes that income distribution is the same as it was under the last available household survey and then increases the consumption of the poor in the old survey by the growth in *average* consumption in the national accounts data, no matter that national income distribution may have changed a lot. This procedure can make poverty fall as an artifact of the methodology.

Seventh, the PPP-adjusted income figures for China and India – the two most important countries for the overall trend – contain an even bigger component of guess work than for most other significant countries. I noted earlier that the main sources of purchasing power parity income figures (the Penn World Tables and the International Comparison Project) are based on two large-scale international price benchmarking exercises for calculating purchasing power parity exchange rates, one in 1985, the second in 1993, carried out in 60 countries in 1985, 110 countries in 1993.[11] The government of China declined to participate in both. The purchasing power parity exchange rate for China is based on guestimates from small, ad hoc price surveys in a few cities, adjusted by rules of thumb to take account of the huge price differences between urban and rural areas and between eastern and western regions. The government of India declined to participate in the 1993 exercise. The price comparisons for India are extrapolations from 1985 qualified by small, ad hoc price surveys in later years. The lack of reliable price comparisons for China and India must compromise any statement about trends in world poverty.[12]

Finally, we need to bear in mind that the number of absolute poor is a politically sensitive number, because critics use it to attack the Bank. The majority report of the Meltzer Commission, for the US Congress, said the Bank was failing at its central task of poverty reduction – as shown by the fact that the number of people in absolute poverty remained constant at 1.2 bn between 1987 and 1998.[13] (A spurious argument if ever there was one.) People who calculate politically sensitive numbers – in the Bank or anywhere else – may be inclined to make choices that flatter the result even if they remain within the bounds of the professionally defensible, even if they remain far from behavior that could be construed as 'cooking the books'.

In short, we should be cautious about accepting the World Bank's poverty headcount as approximately correct; we should acknowledge the large margin of error. We do not know for sure whether the late 1990s' revisions to the methodology and to the PPP numbers have the effect of raising or lowering the poverty headcount, and whether they alter the direction of the trend over the 1980s and 1990s. But it is likely that (a) the Bank's numbers underestimate the true numbers, and (b) the new methodology applied in the late 1990s underestimates the true numbers by more than the old methodology and by more in later years than in earlier years. The new methodology makes the trend look better than it really is because the new international poverty line of $PPP 1.08 translates into *lower* national poverty lines in most countries (to be exact, in 77 percent of the 94 countries for which data are available, containing 82 percent of their population). The new international line lowers the old national line for China by 14 percent, for India, by 9 percent, for the whole sample by an average of 13 percent.[14] It is likely that future 'updating' of the international poverty line will continue to depress the true trend, because worldwide average consumption patterns (on which the international poverty line is based) are shifting toward services whose relative prices are much lower in poor than in rich countries, giving the false impression that the increase in the cost of the basic consumption goods required by the poor is lower than it is.

Some people argue that the whole exercise of constructing a global poverty line and then counting the number of poor below is futile; not only are our current numbers not meaningful, they *could not* be meaningful. They propose to use national poverty lines to count the number of poor in each of the world's 200+ countries, and then make an interpretation based on 200 data points for one year, or 400 data points for two years. The problem is obvious. My response is that if we are to assess globalization as a world-scale phenomenon and not simply as the aggregate of national phenomena we need world aggregate data to measure the overall trends. Our task is to find measures that survive scrutiny. For this we need measures and price indices specifically related to poor people, in contrast to what is presently available.

Having said all this, I think it is quite plausible that the proportion of the world's population living in extreme poverty (facing periods of food consumption too low to maintain health and wellbeing) has indeed fallen over the past twenty years or so, thanks largely to fast economic growth in China and India. The broad trends in national data for these two countries, including life expectancy and other non-income measures, give grounds for confidence in this conclusion, even allowing for large margins of error. Moreover the magnitude of world population increase over the past twenty years is so big that the Bank's poverty numbers would have to be *huge* underestimates for the proportion in extreme poverty not to have fallen. But any more precise statement about the absolute number of the world's people living in extreme poverty and the change in the number over time currently rests on statistical quicksand.

The statistical problems behind the poverty numbers also mean that we cannot give a confident answer to one of the most central of all questions about economic development – the effect of economic growth on the number of people living in extreme poverty. The liberal argument says that economic growth lifts people out of poverty. Indeed, some analysts claim that the income of the poor rise 'one-to-one' with average income.[15] Other analysts say, on the contrary, that the lack of a fall in the number of people in extreme poverty despite historically high rates of economic growth – both in the world as a whole and in specific countries (notably India) – suggests that economic growth may do little to reduce poverty. The truth is that our currently available data preclude a confident conclusion.[16] The reason is not only the uncertainty in the poverty numbers, but also the fact that the poverty numbers and the economic growth numbers come from different and quite inconsistent sources. The poverty numbers come from household surveys, while the economic growth measures come from the national income accounts, and in many countries there are large and growing discrepancies between income and consumption estimates from the two sources. In Asia the consumption estimates from household surveys tend to be well *below* the consumption estimates from the national accounts. The ratio of household survey-based consumption to national accounts-based consumption in India (the biggest single contributor to the world poverty count) fell from around unity in the 1950s to little more than 50 percent in recent years. A similar drift is found in China, the second biggest contributor to the world poverty count; and also in Pakistan, Bangladesh, and Indonesia. In some sub-Saharan African countries, on the other hand, the estimate of consumption from household surveys is two to three times *above* the estimate from the national accounts. As Angus Deaton concludes, we have no consistent empirical basis for conclusions about the extent to which economic growth reduces poverty.

[...]

Notes

[1] Richard Cooper, quoted in Jim Hoagland, 'Is the global economy widening the income gap?', *International Herald Tribune*, 27 Apr 1999, p.8.

[2] *World Development Indicators 2001*, The World Bank, p.3. The $1 a day is measured in purchasing power parity.

[3] *Globalization, Growth, and Poverty: Building an Inclusive World Economy*, World Bank and Oxford University Press, 2002. See Angus Deaton, 'Is world poverty falling?', *Finance and Development*, forthcoming as of May 2002.

[4] I am indebted to Sanjay Reddy for discussions of the points made here. His paper with Thomas Pogge, ' How not to count the poor', typescript, June 2002, at www. socialanalysis.org , discusses them in much greater detail. Also, Massoud Karshenas, 'Measurement and nature of absolute poverty in least developed countries', typescript, Economics Department, SOAS, University of London, January 2002.

[5] *World Development Report 1990*, World Bank, 1990.

[6] From the Geary-Khamis method to the EKS method.

[7] Angus Deaton, 'Counting the world's poor: problems and possible solutions', *The World Bank Research Observer*, 16 (2), 2001, 125-47, p.128.

[8] It is remarkable that the International Comparison Project (ICP), which has orchestrated systematic collection of international price data since its founding in 1967, held its first ever panel meeting to discuss designing a purchasing power parity factor specifically relevant to the consumption bundle of the poor as recently as March 2002, yet has been chaired by the World Bank for the past decade. The ICP's central concern has been to design ways of comparing GDPs.

[9] For example, Brazil's extreme poverty rate according to the CEPAL line was 14%, according to the World Bank for roughly the same recent year, 5%; Bolivia, 23%, 11%; Chile, 8%, 4%; Colombia, 24%, 11%, Mexico, 21%, 18%. *Panorama Social de America Latina 2000-01*, CEPAL, September 2001, p.51.

[10] Reported in Deaton, 'Counting the world's poor'.

[11] An ICP benchmark survey was also done in 1996, but the quality of the data was poor because many more countries participated than expected and resources were insufficient for central coordination and data quality control.

[12] See Reddy and Pogge, above.

[13] United States Congressional Advisory Commission on International Financial Institutions (Meltzer Commission), *Report to the U.S. Congress on the International Financial Institutions*, 2000. Available at www.house/gov/jec/imf/ifiac. Meltzer later described the fall in the proportion of the world's population in poverty from 28% in 1987 to 24% in 1998 as a 'modest' decline, the better to hammer the Bank (Allan Meltzer, 'The World Bank one year after the Commission's report to Congress', hearings before the Joint Economic Committee, U.S. Congress, March 8, 2001).

[14] Reddy and Pogge, 'How not to count the poor'.

[15] '[O]n average there is a one-to-one relationship between the growth rate of income of the poor and the growth rate of average income in society', *Globalization, Growth, and Poverty*, World Bank and Oxford University Press, 2002, p.48.

[16] Deaton, 'Counting'.

Chapter 2.4

Gender and poverty: how misleading is the unitary model of household resources?

Jane Falkingham and Angela Baschieri

Introduction

Since December 1999, all countries wishing to access concessional lending from the International Monetary Fund (IMF) and World Bank are required to prepare a Poverty Reduction Strategy Paper (PRSP) outlining the country's policy framework for addressing the challenges of poverty reduction. The diagnosis and causal analysis of poverty within PRSPs are, in turn, often based on 'poverty assessments' carried out either by, or in conjunction with, the World Bank. Many of these poverty assessments are based on analysis of living standard measurement surveys (LSMS) and invariably use a monetary measure of welfare and adopt a unitary model of the household in their analyses. This unitary model envisages the household as a single unit, implying the existence of a single household welfare function reflecting the preferences of *all* its members, and assumes that all members of the household pool their resources. As a result all members of the household are assumed to enjoy the same level of welfare. This has implications for the subsequent profile of poverty and the policies to combat poverty that are put in place. One important consequence is that gender differentials in welfare are often hidden with the result that policies to combat poverty may be poorly targeted on women and children.
[...]

The unitary model of the household, intra-household allocation of resources and gender

Standard economic analyses of poverty such as those frequently carried out *inter alia* by the World Bank invariably use a unitary model of the household.[1] This model envisages the household as a single unit, implying the existence of a single household welfare function reflecting the preferences of *all* its members. However, as Chiappori et al. (1993: 4) suggests, this is an assumption that is 'by no means an innocuous assumption' as individual household members are likely to have different preferences. Another fundamental assumption of the unitary model of the household is the pooling of all household resources, with the result that all members are assumed to enjoy the same level of welfare. However, sociological and anthropological studies show that this is rarely the case (Bruce and Dweyer, 1988; Chant, 2007; Evans, 1989; Moore, 1992). In particular, men are found to retain part of their income and 'spend some of their income on goods for their personal consumption' (Haddad et al., 1994: 31). By contrast, women are believed to be more likely to purchase goods for children and for general household consumption. A study in Kerala in India suggested that a child's nutritional level is positively correlated with the size of mother's income, whereas there were no significant effects with the increase of parental income (Kumar, 1977).

Finally, the unitary model often relies on an assumption that the household head is an altruist, taking the well-being of others into account. 'This assumption is difficult to maintain when the individual who is assumed to be altruistic is also the perpetuator of physical violence' (Haddad et al., 1994: 41). As Haddad et al. (1994: 41) notes, 'sociological and cross-cultural ethnographic studies show that wife-beating occurs in virtually all societies'.

Chiappori et al. (1993) argue that a better representation of real life may be provided by the collective model of the household. They suggest that there are two types of collective models, the cooperative and non-cooperative. In the non-cooperative models 'individuals within the household not only have differing preferences, but act as autonomous sub economies. Each individual controls their own income, and purchases commodities subject to an individual (non pooled) income constraint' (Haddad et al., 1994: 17). In the cooperative model, individuals have a choice of remaining single or of forming a household. The household decisions are an outcome of some bargaining process. This model does not assume the pooling of *all* resources, but rather that men and women choose to pool some resources and retain sole control over others. Thus the key issues within the cooperative collective model are the extent to which resources are pooled and the relative strength of men and women in the bargaining process.

Studies that have looked at the intra-household allocation of resources have largely concentrated on the relationship between the share of the wife's income and the share of expenditure, treating the household as units of both production and consumption. Ulph (1988: 45) noted 'a very clear relationship between the share of expenditure on commodities and the share of household income accruing to the wife', whereas Von Braun (1988) found a positive relationship between the proportion of cereals produced under women's control and household consumption of calories in Gambian households. Garcia (1990) found that the higher the women's share in the overall household income, the higher is the amount of calories and protein consumption. Thomas (1990) illustrated that unearned income in the hands of the mother has larger positive effects on child health than income managed by the father. Hoddinott and Haddad (1995), using Ulph's (1988) non-cooperative bargaining model of household expenditure and nationally representative data from the Ivory Coast, examined the extent to which a bargaining model of household behaviour could be used to explain patterns of expenditure. They showed that increasing wives' share of cash income increases the budget share of food, and reduces the budget share of alcohol and cigarettes. Their findings support the view that the 'household [is] better modelled by collective entities in which bargaining occurs among members' (Hoddinott and Haddad, 1995: 94).

Haddad and Kanbur (1990) argue that if resources are unequally allocated within the household, poverty measures will be sensitive to intra-household inequality. This suggests that if the assumption of equal sharing of household resources is found *not* to be valid, estimates of poverty amongst women and men might change dramatically according to the extent of intrahousehold inequalities. As a consequence, a gendered analysis of poverty that uses the unitary household assumption might provide an entirely erroneous picture of the relative levels of poverty among men, women and children.

[...]

Conclusions

[...]

In late 2001, the World Bank called for the 'mainstreaming' of gender equality issues in PRSPs (World Bank, 2002). If we are serious about 'gendering development' then it is important that the evidence base used for policy making is gender sensitive. The opening paragraph of Chapter 10 in the *PRSP Sourcebook*, a guide produced to 'assist countries in the development and strengthening of poverty reduction strategies' (Klugman, 2002: vii), states:

> Poverty is experienced differently by men and women. A full understanding of the gender dimensions of poverty can significantly change the definition of priority policy and program interventions supported by the PRS. Evidence is growing that gender-sensitive development strategies contribute significantly to economic growth as well as to equity objectives by ensuring that all groups of the poor share in program benefits. Yet differences between men's and women's needs are often not fully recognized in poverty analysis

and participatory planning, and are frequently not taken into consideration in the selection and design of poverty reduction strategies. It is essential, then, to integrate gender analysis into poverty diagnosis. (Bamberger et al., 2002: 335)

We would argue that the standard approach to measuring poverty employed in most World Bank poverty assessments fails on this count. Quisumbing and McClafferty (2006) powerfully argue that understanding how resources are allocated within households can profoundly affect policies associated with the design and implementation of development projects. We agree. For future poverty analysis to be more meaningful and reflexive of the reality of women's lives it is essential that the 'black box of the household' is unpacked and that greater attention is paid to intra-household resource allocation patterns, however difficult that may be.

Note

[1] It has also been called the 'common preferences' model or the 'altruism' model.

References

Bamberger, M., Blackden, M., Fort, L. and Manoukian, V. (2002) 'Gender', J. Klugman (ed.) *A Sourcebook for Poverty Reduction Strategies* (pp. 333–75). Washington, DC: World Bank.

Bruce, J. and Dweyer, D. (1988) *A Home Divided: Women and Income in the Third World*. Stanford, CA: Stanford University Press.

Chant, S. (2007) *Gender, Generation and Poverty: Exploring the 'Feminisation of Poverty' in Africa, Asia and Latin America*. Cheltenham: Edward Elgar.

Chiappori, P.A., Haddad, L., Hoddinott, J. and Kanbur, R. (1993) 'Unitary versus Collective Models of the Household: Time to Shift the Burden of Proof?', Policy Research Working Paper 1217. Washington, DC: World Bank.

Evans, A. (1989) 'Gender Issues in Rural Household Economics', IDS Discussion Paper 254. Brighton: Institute of Development Studies.

Garcia, M. (1990) 'Resource Allocation and Household Welfare: A Study of Personnel Sources of Income on food Consumption, Nutrition and Health in the Philippines', PhD thesis, Institution of Social Studies, The Hague.

Haddad, L., Hoddinott, J. and Alderman, H. (1994) 'Intrahousehold Resource Allocation: an Overview', Policy Research Working Paper 1255. Washington, DC: World Bank.

Haddad, L. and Kanbur, R. (1990) 'How Serious is the Neglect of Intrahousehold Inequality', mimeo. Washington, DC: International Food Policy Research Institute.

Hoddinott, J. and Haddad, L. (1995) 'Does Female Income Share Influence Household Expenditure?: Evidence from Ivory Coast', *Oxford Bulletin of Economics and Statistics* 57(1): 77–96.

Klugman, J. (2002) *A Sourcebook for Poverty Reduction Strategies*. Washington, DC: WorldBank.

Kumar, S. (1977) 'Composition of Economic Constraints in Child Nutritional: Impact from Maternal incomes and Employment in Low Income Households', PhD thesis, Cornell University.

Moore, H. (1992) 'Households and Gender Relations: The Modelling of the Economy', in S. Ortiz and S. Lees (eds) *Understanding Economic Process* (pp. 131–51). New York: University Press of America.

Quisumbing, A. and McClafferty, B. (2006) *Using Gender Research in Development*. Washington, DC: International Food Policy Research Institute.

Thomas, D. (1990) 'Intrahousehold Resource Allocation: An Inferential Approach', *Journal of Human Resources* 25(4): 635–64.

Ulph, D. (1988) 'A General Noncooperative Nash Model of Household Consumption Behaviour', mimeo. Bristol: University of Bristol.

Von Braun, J. (1988) 'Effects of Technological Change in Agriculture on Food Consumption and Nutrition: Rice in a West African Setting', *World Development* 16(9): 1083–98.

World Bank (2002) *Integrating Gender into the World Bank's Work: A Strategy for Action*. Washington, DC: World Bank.

Chapter 2.5

Globalization and inequality

Branko Milanovic

Definitions and concepts

In our efforts to understand the state of inequality today, we need first to define the key concepts and terms. Most crucially, we need to distinguish between international and global inequality in order to avoid terminological confusion. I explore these two concepts throughout the essay. Here it suffices to say that international inequality denotes the inequality between nations, more exactly between mean incomes of nations. Global inequality (also known as 'world inequality'), on the other hand, is an inequality between individuals in the world regardless of their nation, regardless of where they live. In other words when measuring global inequality, we see the entire world as if it were one country.

In this essay I will utilize three concepts of inequality in order to explore the patterns of *international* and *global* inequality and map out changes in inequality over time. I will call these three different ways of assessing inequality Concept 1, Concept 2 and Concept 3.

Concept 1 inequality

Concept 1 measures *unweighted international inequality*. As previously explained, international inequality measures the inequality between mean incomes of different nations. This sort of inequality is captured in statements like 'the mean income in the United States is higher than the mean income in Pakistan'. In measuring this inequality, we generally rely on national accounts, that is Gross Domestic Income (GDI) of the countries. We compare the GDIs of countries to each other to grasp Concept 1 inequality. Because populations of countries are left out, Concept 1 is unweighted international inequality. Notice also that inequality *within* countries is ignored.

Concept 2 inequality

Concept 2 inequality is similar to Concept 1. Like Concept 1, Concept 2 measures international inequality by relying on the representative income of a country: GDI per capita. Differently from Concept 1, however, Concept

2 takes into consideration the population of countries. In these calculations China's weight is approximately 20 per cent of the world rather than, as in Concept 1, having the same weight as any other country. Consequently, when calculating the inequality of Concept 2, the role of China and India would be very important. To make the difference clear, note that Concept 1 inequality is akin to the UN General Assembly: there is one ambassador for each country and each country is represented by its GDI per capita. In contrast with Concept 1, here we have 6 billion ambassadors (the world's population) and all the ambassadors from, say, China display the mean income of China, all ambassadors from India display the mean income of India and so forth. Hence with Concept 2, each country would be represented in accordance with its population but it would be still represented by ambassadors having *representative* incomes of their nations – not actual incomes of people who live there. Thus Concept 2 also ignores differences in incomes within countries.

Concept 3 inequality

The final type of measurement we will rely on to explore inequality in this chapter is Concept 3 inequality. Concept 3 denotes *world inequality* or *global inequality*. Differently from international inequality, this concept captures inequality between individuals. To use the previous metaphor, we dispense with ambassadors: every individual enters into the calculations with his/her actual income. The only source of data from which we learn about people's incomes is household surveys. Ideally, we should have a world household survey to find out what is world income distribution. But short of that we have to use individual country's household surveys, collate them and derive a world distribution of income across individuals. This further differentiates Concept 3 from the other two Concepts: it relies on an entirely different source of data, income distribution data obtained from household surveys. Thus the data requirements are much more formidable than they are for Concepts 1 and 2 where we need respectively only one variable (GDI per capita) or two (GDI per capita and population). This huge jump in the data requirement makes the move from Concept 2 to Concept 3 even more problematic because of the difference between disposable income from household surveys (our welfare aggregate in Concept 3 calculations) and national accounts data from which we get our GDIs per capita. The largest part of the difference is definitional: household disposable income is after-tax income and it excludes publicly provided health, education and other government services and goods. The latter are, of course, included in Gross Domestic Income. Another part of the discrepancy comes from the undersurvey of rich people and their income sources (mostly property income) in household surveys. These sources are better captured by national accounts simply because rich people are loath to fully reveal their actual income to survey enumerators. These points will be discussed further. Table 2.5.1 summarizes the three Concepts and their sources of data.

Table 2.5.1: Three concepts of inequality summarized

	Concept 1: Unweighted international inequality	Concept 2: Weighted international inequality	Concept 3: Global or world inequality
Main source of data	National accounts	National accounts	Household surveys
Unit of observation	Country	Country (weighted by its population)	Individual
Welfare concept	GDI per capita	GDI per capita	Mean per capita disposable income or expenditures
National currency conversion	Market exchange rate or PPP exchange rate		
Within-country distribution (inequality)	Ignored	Ignored	Included

Source: Milanovich (2005)

Patterns of inequality

Let us now see how Concepts 1, 2 and 3 have moved over time in order to explain the changing patterns of inequality. I will start with a historical perspective before discussing the contemporary patterns of inequality. This historical perspective applies primarily to Concepts 1 and 2. We do not know much about how Concept 3 has moved over time simply because we lack the relevant data on household surveys. Since incomes or expenditures from household surveys are not available for a historical period, we shall focus on a briefer period, 1988–98.

Historical perspective

Figure 2.5.1 displays the historical movement of Concept 1 inequality. This Figure, based on Maddison (2004) GDI per capita data which are the only source of long-run historical income statistics, shows that between 1820 and 1870 international inequality was on the rise. The increase is present whether measured by the Gini coefficient or Theil Index.[1] Inequality also ascended during 1870–1913, although it declined or stabilized during the inter-war period of 'deglobalization', 1913–38. Following this period, we witness a sharp increase in Concept 1 inequality between 1938 and 1952. This is related to the Second World War and the fact that some of the rich countries (United States, Australia, New Zealand, Argentina) did very well while most of the rest of the world lost out. From roughly 1952 to 1978, Concept 1 inequality remains at the same level as measured by the Gini and declines rather substantially as measured by the Theil Index. For the less developed countries, this was the period associated with decolonization and application of import substitution policies including a strong role of the state. For the rich world that was the period of unmatched growth that became known as the 'Golden Age'. But despite the rich world's fast growth, there was clearly, on average, a catch up of poor and middle-income countries or income convergence; it proved short-lived. Starting from around 1978, the beginning of the 'neoliberal regime', there is a sharp turnaround and Concept 1 inequality rises whether measured by the Gini or Theil.

Figure 2.5.1 demonstrates that Concept 1 inequality has generally been on an upward trend from 1820 up to today. This finding tells us that differences between mean incomes of countries are much greater today than they were some 200 years ago. It is also true that our sample size has gone up because originally in Maddison's data we had approximately only 35 or 40 countries, but over time the number of countries has increased to 50, 60 or 80. Today we have more than 150 nations in the sample. Thus a *part* of the increase

Figure 2.5.1: Concept 1 inequality, 1820–2000

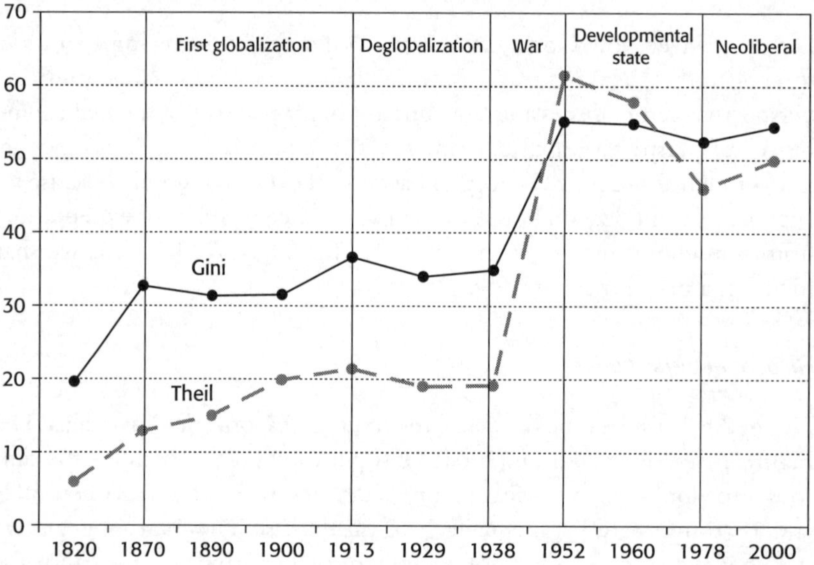

Source: Calculated from Maddison (2004)

in Concept 1 inequality can be explained by the increase in the sample size (that is, in the number of independent states in the world). But, it is important to emphasize that only a part of the change can be attributed to this factor. If we were to take only the countries for which we have data over the entire period 1820–2000, we would still find that international inequality of this sort has been on the rise.

When we use Concept 2 inequality, we observe a different picture. Here, I use the same data as I did for Concept 1 inequality above, viz. the same GDI per capita data from Maddison (2004) and the same countries, but this time around the data are weighted by population. I will discuss later some pitfalls of the data on China but let us assume here that these data are reliable. Figure 2.5.2 demonstrates the historical journey of Concept 2 inequality. As this figure shows, during the period from 1850, which is the first year in the figure, to about 1950, which represents a peak, there is a clear upward trend. From the mid-1950s to today, Concept 2 inequality remains broadly stable (or just slightly decreasing). This finding is confirmed by Bourguignon and Morrisson (2002).

Contemporary patterns of inequality

Now let us move from this very brief historical sketch to a focus on what inequality is today, analysing the period 1950–2000. To paraphrase a well-known dictator, Figure 2.5.3 illustrates the 'mother of all inequality disputes'.

Figure 2.5.2: Concept 2 inequality (Gini coefficient), 1820–2000

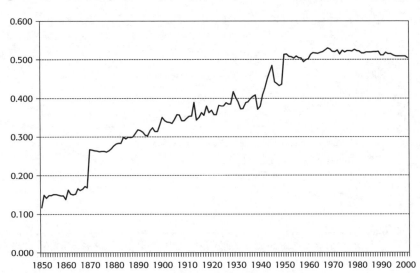

Source: Calculated from Maddison (2004)

The essence of the dispute is about what happened to inequality roughly between 1950 and 2000.

Figure 2.5.3 examines inequality during this period using the three Concepts of inequality. As we see from the figure, unweighted international inequality – the Concept 1 inequality – has gone up. Of particular importance to note is that it has been going up over the last 20 years. Moreover, we see that the 'watershed years' 1978–80 – the term coined by Paul Bairoch (1997) – characterized by rising oil prices and real interest rates, the onset of the debt crisis and the beginning of the Thatcher and Reagan rule in Great Britain and the United States, were at the origin of this unmistakable upward trend which has persisted ever since.

Concept 2 inequality charts a very different course. As Figure 2.5.3 shows, Concept 2 inequality has declined over precisely the same time during which Concept 1 inequality rose. Moreover Concept 2 inequality begins its downward trend exactly around 1978–80. The decline is driven by the fact that China has grown very fast ever since 1978 when the responsibility system was introduced in the countryside and communes were dismantled by the Deng Xiaoping regime. China was a very poor country with a huge population, and as people in China have become richer, overall inequality in the world has tended to go down. The role of China is crucial, as it becomes clear when we calculate Concept 2 inequality without China: we see that inequality of this sort has been stable or even rising (see the dotted line in

Figure 2.5.3: The three concepts of inequality, 1950–2000

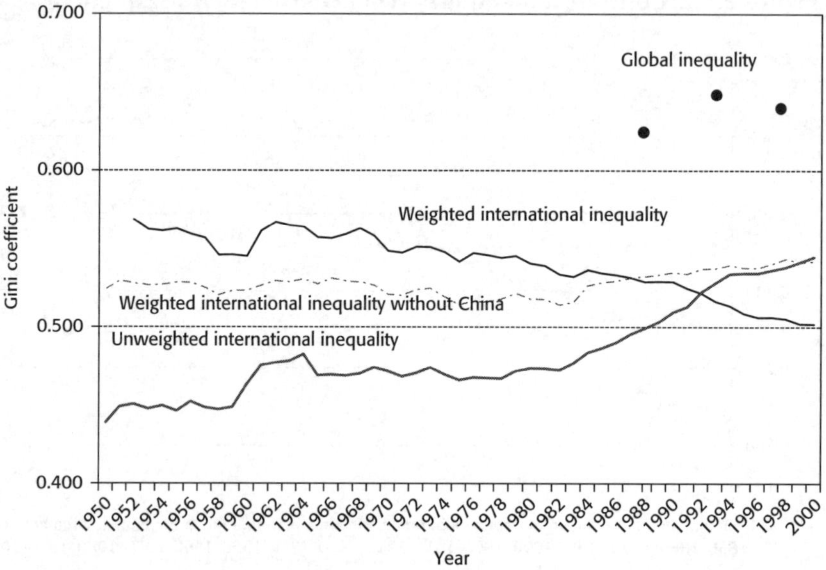

Source: Calculated using World Bank *WDI* data

Figure 2.5.3). In sum, *inequalities between countries have been rising since around 1978, although population-weighted inequality between countries has been decreasing since 1978 thanks to growth in China and more recently in India.*

Let us now look at global inequality, Concept 3. Based on my own calculations, Figure 2.5.3 displays three dots – years 1988, 1993 and 1998 – that capture global inequality. These three dots are based on household survey data. There are some important points to highlight here. To begin with, we cannot really extract similar data for the past because we do not have household surveys for many important parts of the world (China, the Soviet Union, most of Africa) for any years before the early 1980s. As we see in Figure 2.5.3, these three years do not follow a pattern: there is first a strong increase in inequality followed by a more modest decline. The gap between global inequality (the three dots) and weighted international inequality is explained by inequality within nations. We can write it out as,

(1) Global inequality = Concept 2 inequality (or between-country inequality) + within-country inequality

Overall, the three dots inform us that *inequality among people in the world today is extremely high, though its direction of change is unclear.* The Gini Index of inequality between people in the world lies between 62 and 66. A Gini of 62, which is a very high number, is a higher level of inequality than what is found in any individual country: for instance, Brazil's inequality is in the upper 50s level; South Africa is in the low 60s. This level of inequality is perhaps unparalleled in world history. If such extreme inequality existed in smaller communities or in a nation-state, governing authorities would find it too destabilizing to leave it alone, or revolutions or riots might break out. The fact that such extreme levels of inequality exist on the global level perhaps causes us to react against it relatively less severely.

A number of different forces impact upon global inequality, causing a very complicated pattern to emerge. First, fast economic growth in China and India – populous nations that were very poor and are still relatively poor – pushes world inequality down. Second, the relative decline of many poor and middle-income countries has the opposite effect: it contributes to global inequality. Third, higher inequality within large nations, such as the United States, China, India, and Russia, adds to global inequality, pushing the dots in Figure 2.5.3 further upwards from the line that captures Concept 2 inequality. Thus as one force reduces global inequality, the other one or two increase it.

Regionally, the last 20 to 25 years have been characterized by the following basic trends: China and India pulled ahead, Latin America and Eastern Europe – the middle-income countries – declined, and Africa's position became even worse. The rich world (Western Europe, North America and Oceania)

grew relatively fast. As for within–nation inequalities, they increased almost everywhere. *We are witnessing the Africanization of poverty*, since most of the African nations are now extremely poor and many of them are actually poorer than they were in 1960. The correlation between being poor and being African is probably stronger than ever in recorded history. Another interesting fact is that, for the first time since the early nineteenth century, all Latin American nations are poorer in per capita terms than the poorest West European country (Portugal).

The complicated way in which different forces impact upon global inequality should encourage us to avoid broad generalizations. The difficulty of saying what happens to global inequality stems, in part, from the fact that it is hard to calculate because it requires access to detailed household survey data from most countries in the world. While there is no dispute that global inequality is extremely high today, there remains a debate on the direction of change in global inequality as well as on the significance and meaning of this putative change. We would also like to draw some sort of causal link between globalization and global inequality. This is exceedingly difficult because globalization affects differently the growth rates of GDIs per capita of poor and rich nations, within-national inequalities in poor and rich countries, and may influence differently the populous and small nations. Sometimes these effects may work in the same direction, for example if greater openness helps accelerate growth of poor countries and reduces within-nation inequalities, and sometimes they may offset each other, for example if openness helps poor countries but widens their internal income distributions.

The three concepts explored further

[...]

How solid is the Concept 2 inequality decline?

In my analysis Concept 2 inequality derives its significance because it is the lower bound to Concept 3 inequality. Concept 3 inequality is critical if we want to know what is happening to the income of individuals in the world, but, as I said before, oftentimes we lack the necessary data to calculate it. Given such difficulties with data, some authors have used a shortcut to Concept 3 inequality by calculating Concept 2, the population-weighted international inequality. They have done so because (a) Concept 2 inequality accounts for a large part of global inequality, and (b) it can be calculated relatively easily with the knowledge of only two data points for each country (GDI per capita and population). Notice that at the extreme, Concept 2 inequality becomes global inequality: to see this, break the countries into finer and finer partitions continuing all the way to a situation where each individual is a country. Then, clearly, Concepts 2 and 3 coincide.

We can move somewhat in that direction (raising as it were the lower bound to global inequality) by breaking large countries into their provinces and rural/urban areas. If after doing this, we find that this new more detailed Concept 2 inequality has been more or less stable over the last two decades, then Concept 3 inequality cannot have gone down. The reason is as follows: we know that the within-component (see equation 1) of global inequality has gone up during the last two decades driven by the almost unanimous increase in within-national inequalities.

So let us see how the previously calculated Concept 2 decline is affected by data modifications and improvements. We can recalculate Concept 2 inequality by doing three things. First, we can use alternative GDI per capita data for China. The data on the Chinese GDP remains subject to intense debate amongst specialists. While most economists agree that the current levels of Chinese GDI are accurate, they disagree about the historical statistics, and in particular about the officially claimed growth rates. The problem with them is that if they are extrapolated all the way back into the past, the 1952 level of China's GDI per capita becomes unreasonably, and even impossibly, low: less than $PPP 300 at 1990 prices. It is very difficult to believe that China, which indeed was poor, was below the subsistence level (on average). Thus Maddison's 2004 data, based on his detailed study of long-run Chinese growth (Maddison 1998), display lower growth rates than the official Chinese sources.[2] If China was less poor in the 1950s, 1960s, and so on then its catch up with the rich world was less, and the decrease in Concept 2 inequality was less too. If we recalculate Concept 2 using all the same World Bank data as before, except for China for which we use Maddison's GDI numbers, the decline of Concept 2 inequality which was 3.3 Gini points previously becomes only 1.9 Gini points (see Table 2.5.2 and Figure 2.5.4). This shows the extreme sensitivity of Concept 2 and global inequality calculations to the assumptions about Chinese growth.

Second, we can assess the firmness of the data on Concept 2 inequality by breaking five most populous countries (China, India, United States, Indonesia, and Brazil) into their provinces/states. In addition, we know that for both China and India there are serious and apparently growing rural–urban disparities. By taking an aggregate number for China, we fail to show the inequality which exists between rural and urban areas or between poor and rich provinces. So we can further break each Chinese province into rural and urban parts, using of course for each province mean rural and mean urban income. What we do thereby is to vastly improve the precision of our estimates: rather than using one GDI per capita number for China, we now use either 28 numbers (means for each province) or even 56 numbers (28 provinces times two – for rural and for urban). The same is done for the other four countries: for example, instead of one value for the United States, we have fifty.

Table 2.5.2: Change in Concept 2 inequality between 1985 and 2000 using different data sources and finer partitions (in Gini points)

	World Bank data	World Bank data except Maddison for China	Maddison data
Whole countries	−3.3	−1.9	−1.1
Populous countries* divided in states or provinces (the rest unchanged)	−3.8	−2.3	−1.5
Adding rural–urban divide for China	−3.3	n/a	−1.0

Note: * 'Populous countries' are China, India, United States, Indonesia and Brazil.
Source: Calculated from Maddison (2004) and World Bank *WDI*

Third, we can broaden our coverage of countries. World Bank data have a more restricted country coverage because a number of war-torn or 'excluded' countries like the Congo, Sudan, Cuba, North Korea, Afghanistan and Somalia are not part of the database. This omission, however, is not random: these are mostly poor countries and their inclusion raises Concept 2 inequality and may also slow down its downward slide (since these countries have tended to fall further behind the rich world, thus adding to inequality). Maddison data do include all these countries: for example, in 2000, Maddison data include 160 countries while the World Bank data include only 138 countries.

Figure 2.5.4 demonstrates the sensitivity of Concept 2 inequality to different data sources as well as the remarkable importance of China in these calculations. If we use Maddison's data, we find – between 1985 and 2000 – only a minimal decrease in Concept 2 inequality of 1.1 Gini points (see Table 2.5.2). This is less than a third of the decrease as calculated using World Bank numbers. Finally, if we break the five most populous countries into their provinces/states and use the rural–urban divide for China, Maddison's data yield a decrease of only 1 Gini point. This finding suggests that Concept 2 numbers are not as firm as we originally might have thought. Another important implication is that the likelihood that Concept 3 inequality decreased over the 1985–2000 period is also significantly less; if Concept 2 inequality – which is the main driving force behind a possible decrease in global inequality – went down by only 1 rather than by 3.3 Gini points, it is quite possible, even likely, that the increase in within-national inequalities offset this decline, and that global inequality remained about the same.

Figure 2.5.4: Concept 2 inequality recalculated using three different GDI databases

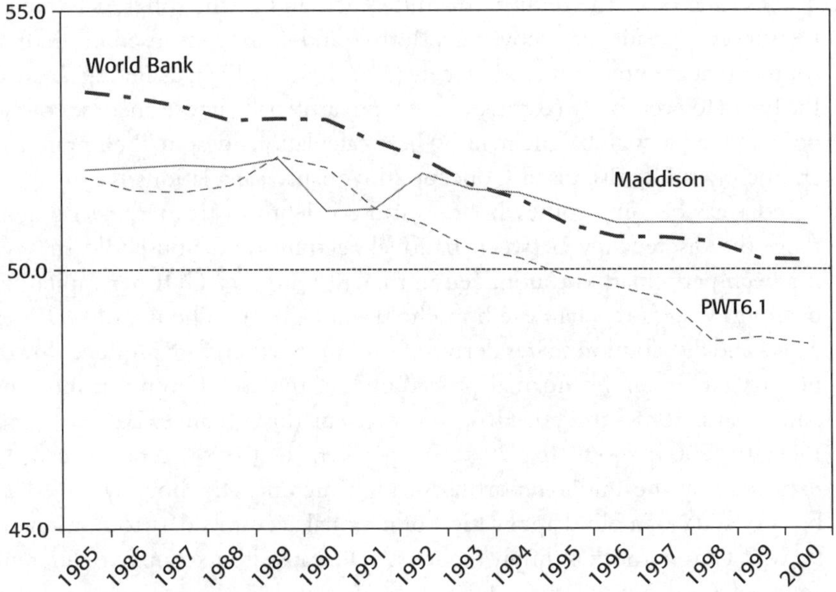

Source: Calculated from Maddison (2004), World Bank *WDI* and Penn World Table 6.1

This last point is illustrated in Table 2.5.3. It displays the within-component of global inequality. It increased between 1988 and 1998 by 0.8 Gini points, about as much as Concept 2 inequality, according to Maddison's data, has gone down.

There also remains a technical issue, to which I alluded above. There is a discrepancy between the movements in national accounts and movements in household survey data, making comparisons of results using the two sources difficult. In some calculations of global inequality which are not based directly on household surveys, the authors (e.g., Bhalla 2002 and Sala-i-Martin 2002) mix GDI per capita data from national accounts and some fragmentary (quintile) distributions from household surveys. Thus they apply to a distribution not of its own mean but a mean derived from another source (national accounts). As explained before, GDI is by definition greater than household disposable income. In addition, the difference is magnified because of

Table 2.5.3: The within-component of global inequality (in Gini points)

Year	Gini index
1988	13.7
1993	14.5
1998	14.5

Source: Milanovic (2005)

inadequate coverage of property incomes by household surveys. Call this total difference between GDI per capita and mean household per capita income d, consisting of d_1, the definitional difference, and d_2, the difference due to the survey of inadequate coverage. Both d_1 and d_2 are composed of income sources that are predominantly received by the rich. Then assigning d across the board to everybody (as these authors do) artificially boosts incomes of the poor and reduces global inequality. These calculations, despite their pretence, are merely thinly disguised Concept 2 inequality calculations.[3]

India has become somewhat of a cause célèbre in this respect because there the discrepancy between national accounts and household surveys has been particularly pronounced in the last ten years. GDI per capita has been growing faster than the household survey mean. The use of GDI per capita and distribution shares derived from surveys therefore produces lower poverty rates than the 'normal' procedure (i.e., the use of both distributions and means from surveys). However, even in this instance, Banerjee and Picketty (2005) show that 20 to 40 per cent of the discrepancy can be explained by the under-reporting of high incomes. In short, we need to be very wary of a blind application of national accounts data to household surveys. The approach is simply inconsistent because it mixes up two different aggregates and ignores their differences.

Inequality between world citizens today

Having explored the relationship between different concepts of inequality, we can revisit the 'true world inequality' – the Concept 3 inequality and where it stands today. As emphasized before, we find extreme inequalities today. Earlier in the chapter I indicated that the world inequality today varies between 62 and 66 Gini points and emphasized how such levels of inequality surpass the disparities seen in some very unequal countries, such as Brazil and South Africa. Table 2.5.4 shows the evolution of global inequality in three different years (recall our three dots in Figure 2.5.3 above). Global

Table 2.5.4: Global inequality, distribution of persons by $PPP and dollar incomes per capita

	Gini index	
	International dollars ($PPP)	US dollars
1988	61.9 (1.8)	77.3 (1.3)
1993	65.2 (1.8)	80.1 (1.2)
1998	64.2 (1.9)	79.5 (1.4)

Note Gini standard errors are given between brackets
Source: Milanovic (2005)

inequality calculated using current exchange rates (displayed in column 3) is even greater: its Gini is probably the highest ever recorded, around 80.

The ratios displayed in Table 2.5.5 below show the extreme levels of contemporary inequalities. These ratios help us understand the significance of a Gini of 62–66. If we look at incomes expressed in international dollars received by the various fractiles of the distribution, we find that the top 5 per cent of highest earners in the world receive one-third of the world income, whereas the bottom 5 per cent receive only 0.2 per cent. Consequently, the ratio of the top 5 per cent to the bottom 5 per cent is 165 to 1. Differently, the top 10 per cent of people in the world get around one-half of world income, leaving the remaining 90 per cent of the world's population the other half of the global income. If we do the same calculations in US dollars, the ratio of the top 5 per cent to the bottom per cent becomes 300 to 1.

Table 2.5.5: Share of total global income received by various fractiles of global distribution

	Top	Bottom	Ratio top to bottom
In $PPP			
5%	33%	0.2%	165–1
10%	50%	0.7%	70–1
In current US dollars			
5%	45%	0.15%	300–1
10%	67.5%	0.45%	150–1

Source: Milanovic (2005)

Key determinants of global inequality summarized

In discussing the three concepts of inequality, this chapter has already touched upon the contradictory movements which influence global inequality today. Here, I expand upon these discussions before offering policy recommendations. In order to understand inequality today, we need to focus on the interaction between: (a) the rich countries of the West; (b) urban incomes in China and India; and (c) rural incomes in these two countries. It is necessary for us to separate China and India into urban and rural categories because the urban–rural income gap in both countries, and indeed in most Asian nations such as Indonesia and Thailand, is large and has been growing rapidly. Thus if mean incomes in urban China and India increase fast enough, they will move closer to mean incomes of the rich countries in the West. That would be good news for world equality. However, if urban incomes in China and India increase very fast but people in rural China and India fall behind, then we have an offsetting effect, namely, rising differences between these two parts (urban and rural) that add to global inequality. This is particularly so because we are talking about massive numbers of people: 800 million rural dwellers versus almost 500 million urban in China, and 750 million rural versus 300 million urban in India. The crucial thing for global inequality is, then, how these three 'components', (a) to (c), evolve.

Position of people from different countries in the global income distribution

We need also to compare the distributions of different countries. This is, as we shall argue below, especially pertinent when making policy recommendations. We do this in Figure 2.5.5 which plots the position of each 5 per cent (ventile) of different countries' distributions in the global income distribution. Consider the line for France. We calculate the mean income (in international dollars) of each French ventile from the lowest (first) to the highest – arrayed on the horizontal axis – and then find their positions in global income distribution. The bottom ventile of the population in France represents people with the lowest incomes in France. In terms of world distribution of income, they are placed around the 72nd percentile of the world. This statistic tells us that the poorest Frenchmen are actually richer than 72 per cent of people in the world. The top 5 per cent of people in France (and also in the rest of Western Europe and the United States; not shown here) are in the top percentile of the world. Let us now look at the distribution (by ventiles) in rural India (bottom line in Figure 2.5.5). Even the richest 5 per cent of people in rural India are poorer than the poorest 5 per cent of people in France. These findings have the following policy significance. If there is aid from a richer to a poorer country, when income distributions do not overlap at all it is very difficult *not* to transfer from a richer person to a poorer person. In other words, the chance of a regressive transfer is very small. If one argues in favour of some transfer of income from the rich to the poor then these are relatively easy situations since the danger of a mistransfer (regressive transfer) is almost nil. One could tax a Frenchman around the median of income distribution and distribute aid to rural India randomly: there would be no danger of a regressive transfer.

In making transfers from rich to poor countries, we can use results from the Figures, for example Figure 2.5.5, as our guidance (obviously, the position of each country can be charted): for instance, the distribution of Kazakhstan can be used as a proxy for transition countries. In Figure 2.5.5, the Brazilian distribution presents a very interesting case. Brazil's distribution essentially mimics the world (world distribution would have been a straight line). Brazil approximates the world because the poorest people in Brazil are poorer than almost everybody else and the rich people in Brazil are as rich as rich Western Europeans and Americans. This is a crucial piece of information because, if we envisage a transfer from France to Brazil, we run the risk of making a regressive transfer unless appropriate targeting is made. In other words, there are countries for which the likelihood of conducting a regressive transfer is not negligible: for instance, it could well be that somebody who is in the bottom decile or quintile in France subsidises the income of someone who is richer than himself in Brazil. The perception that aid is misguided in the sense that the middle class in rich countries transfers a portion of its income to the rich people in poor countries is responsible for a great deal of resentment against aid. While only at times accurate, this perception contributes to the aid fatigue. The key lesson to take from Figure 2.5.5 is that income distribution of the recipient country must be taken into account when decisions on aid are made: given an equally poor country and lack of knowledge regarding targeting of transfers a country with more equal distribution should be preferred.

[...]

Figure 2.5.5: The position of different countries' ventiles in global income distribution

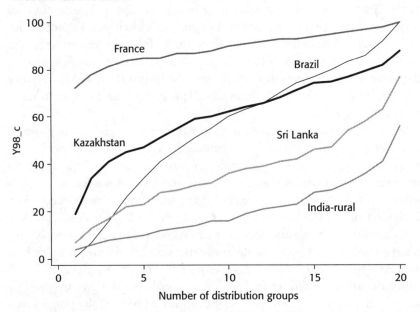

Source: Calculated from World Income Distribution (WID) data, at http://econ.worldbank.org/ projects/inequality

Does global inequality matter?

[...]

If [...] globalization increases awareness of what other people are receiving, then to a person living in a poor country, the income with which he or she would normally be satisfied may no longer seem enough. The very process of globalization might influence our perception and our satisfaction with a given level of income. This is a crucial point: as the process of globalization enfolds how much will it influence our perception of our own position in it? If it does, maintaining large inter-country income differences becomes more and more difficult. But in the face of greater mutual interaction between people and declining travel costs, the rich world will have to become a fortress in order to keep the poor people out; but this is almost impossible. So, what else can be done?

What can we do about global inequality?

There exists a litany of literature on the remedies for global inequality, but I would like to make one more radical proposal. Some of the usual recommendations to alleviate global inequality include changing the rules of the international trading system to benefit the poor. The removal of agricultural subsidies in rich countries is one such change. Like some other authors [...], I also believe that changing the WTO rules and ensuring the decision-making at the global level is more democratic, not least transforming the current voting rights in the IMF and the World Bank, would be very important. We can also think about special programs for Africa (for instance on combating AIDS).

My own, perhaps more radical, proposal to reduce global inequality is to establish 'global transfers', a concept akin to a 'global safety net'. If we really think of the world as a whole, we have to start thinking about an arrangement that would constitute a very modest *global* safety net. But if we do so, we also need some rules for the functioning of this safety net. I envision the first rule of this global safety net to be the 'Progressivity 1 Condition': transfers should flow from a rich country to a poor country. This is not a controversial point, as obviously transfers already flow from rich to poor nations. Second, we should also require that transfers at the global level satisfy the same conditions that within-national transfers are supposed to satisfy at the national level, that is that they should be 'globally progressive'. In other words, we need to ensure the transfers go from a richer person (taxpayer) to a poorer person (beneficiary). It is not desirable, for instance, for a middle-class Frenchman to make a transfer to somebody who is very rich in South Africa or Brazil. This is where national income distributions and the data displayed in Figure 2.5.5 become relevant.

The third condition that should govern global transfers is to preserve 'national progressivities'. Progressive transfers at the global level should not worsen national distributions. Taxation should not only be 'globally progressive' but also be sensitive to 'national progressivities'. To illustrate this point examine Figure 2.5.6 below.

In this figure we have T (tax payer) and B (aid beneficiary) across the two distributions, with the rich country (obviously) on the right and the poor country on the left. Now a transfer from T_1 to B_1 does satisfy the axiom of 'global progressivity' because the person in the rich country is better off than the beneficiary B. Yet such a transfer would also make national distributions in *both* countries worse simply because the tax would be borne by somebody who is relatively poor in the United Kingdom or France and benefits would be received by a person who is relatively well off in an African nation. Globally progressive transfer is compatible with making both national distributions (of the participant countries) more unequal. This is not desirable. We would like to ensure that we tax rich people in rich countries in favour of poor people in poor countries because only then can we hope to improve the distributions within–nations. This would probably also help reduce the opprobrium in which aid is currently held in some quarters. All in all, paying attention to 'national progressivities' requires that tax payers from the rich world that finance global transfers should indeed be rich even within their own countries, and that the beneficiaries should be poor even within their own (poor) countries – a transfer should flow from T_2 to B_2.

Figure 2.5.6: Globally progressive transfers

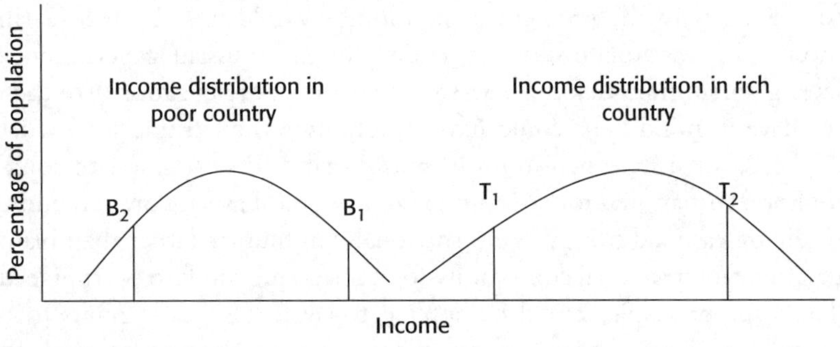

T = tax payer   B = aid beneficiary.

These three principles of global transfers – 'progressivity 1', 'global progressivity', and 'national progressivities' – need to be coupled with a supranational taxation authority which would collect taxes and distribute aid. The first component of this proposal (taxation) is easy to understand, as we have already had a number of writers argue for a Tobin tax – a global tax assessed on some particularly income elastic commodities or activities. The tax would be paid by the globally (and nationally) rich. The second part of the 'equation' concerns the allocation of thus collected money, that is disbursement of aid. We have already explained the key principles which should govern it, but if we are thinking about 'global tax' we must also accept 'global aid', that is aid that flows directly to the poor individuals in poor countries without their government's intermediation. If some sovereignty is conceded by the rich countries to the new global safety net agency (due to the vesting of taxing rights in the agency), then some sovereignty must be conceded by the poor countries as well. Rather than their governments being recipients of aid, aid would go directly to citizens. The global safety net should introduce a relationship between the global authority and individuals in poor countries or poor people wherever they are.

In other words, we would like to eliminate the filter of state-to-state relationship because we know that this filter has not been very successful. This change in approach to handling global inequality is necessitated by the lessons of the past. I have already outlined the need to adopt a global approach to global problems. In addition, we know that development approaches done in the fifties and the sixties have not been successful. We also know that structural adjustment has failed to deliver. We thus need direct transfer of purchasing power; we need to give money to people who are unemployed or people who are very poor, handicapped, sick and generally disenfranchised. Such transfers of money already take place in rich countries. We simply need to apply this on a global level. This idea dawned on me more than a decade ago when I observed the situation in Russia and the plight of Russian pensioners. Both the ethical and pragmatic approach to dealing with the problem of pensioners would have been to earmark money for pensions instead of lending to the Russian government and letting corruption suck it away. An international organization, like the one we have in mind here, could have simply used the existing infrastructure of the Russian state, pension rolls, and distributed cash grants to some 20 million Russian pensioners. And citizens would have fondly remembered receiving cash aid from the international community rather than blaming that same international community for transferring funds to corrupt leaders. The same principles could be applied today to give cash grants to (say) mothers of all kids under a certain age in a state in Nigeria or to all landless peasants in a district in India.

The approach I advocate here is based on four simple principles:

1 *symmetry*: global agency limits sovereignty of both rich and poor nation-states;

2 *grants*: transfers are pure grants but they are not charity;

3 *cash*: money is disbursed to individuals in cash; and

4 *categorical targeting*: instead of trying to implement fine-grained targeting, cash grants should be disbursed to vulnerable categories of people.

Notes

[1] Both Gini and Theil are commonly used measures of inequality. The Gini coefficient ranges from 0 (all recipients have the same income) to 1 (or 100 as expressed in percentages) when only one recipient takes the entire income. The Theil Index of entropy begins at 0 (perfect equality) but does not have an upper bound. Obviously, the greater the value of each index the greater the inequality. However, Gini is more sensitive to what is happening around the mode of the distribution and Theil is more sensitive to the extremes.

[2] The latter are basically also reproduced by the World Bank.

[3] For a critique, see Milanovic (2002).

References

Bairoch, Paul 1997. *Victoires et déboires: Histoire économique et sociale du monde du XVIe siècle à nos jours*, vol. 2. Paris: Folio Histoire Gallimard.

Banerjee, Abhijit and Piketty, Thomas 2005. 'Top Indian Incomes, 1956–2000.' *World Bank Economic Review*, 19 (1): 1–20.

Bhalla, Surjit 2002. *Imagine There's No Country*. Washington, DC: Institute for International Economics.

Bourguignon, François and Morrisson, Christian 2002. 'The Size Distribution of Income Among World Citizens, 1820–1990.' *American Economic Review*, September: 727–44.

Maddison, Angus 1998. *Chinese Economic Performance in the Long Run*. Paris: OECD, Development Centre.

Maddison, Angus 2004. 'World population, GDP and GDP per capita, 1–2000 AD.' At www.ggdc.net/maddison/.

Milanovic, Branko 2002. 'The Ricardian Vice: Why Sala-i-Martin's Calculations of World Income Inequality are Wrong.' At SSRN: http://ssrn.com/abstract 403020.

Milanovic, Branko 2005. *Global Inequality*. Princeton: Princeton University Press.

Sala-i-Martin, Xavier 2002. 'The Disturbing "Rise" of Global Income Inequality.' NBER Working Paper, no. 8904, April. At www.nber.org/papers/w8904.

Chapter 2.6

The world distribution of household wealth

James B. Davies, Susanna Sandstrom,
Anthony Shorrocks and Edward N. Wolff

Introduction

Much attention has recently been focused on estimates of the world distribution of income (Bourguignon and Morrison, 2002; Milanovic, 2002 and 2005). The research shows that the global distribution of income is very unequal and the inequality has not been falling over time. In some regions poverty and income inequality have become much worse. Interest naturally turns to the question of global inequality in other dimensions of economic status, resources or wellbeing. One of the most important of these measures is household wealth.

In everyday conversation the term 'wealth' often signifies little more than 'money income'. On other occasions economists interpret the term broadly and define wealth to be the value of all household resources, both human and non-human, over which people have command. Here, the term is used in its long-established sense of net worth: the value of physical and financial assets less liabilities.[1] Wealth in this sense represents the ownership of capital. While only one part of personal resources, capital is widely believed to have a disproportionate impact on household wellbeing and economic success, and more broadly on economic development and growth.

Wealth has been studied carefully at the national level since the late nineteenth or early twentieth centuries in a small number of countries, for example Sweden, the UK and the US. In some other countries, for example Canada, it has been studied systematically since the 1950s. And in recent years the number of countries with wealth data has been increasing fairly quickly. The largest and most prosperous OECD countries all have wealth data based on household surveys, tax data or national balance sheets. Repeated wealth surveys are today also available for the two largest developing countries – China and India, and a survey that inquired about wealth is available for Indonesia. Forbes magazine enumerates the world's US$ billionaires and their holdings. More detailed lists are provided regionally by other publications, and Merrill-Lynch estimate the number and holdings of US$ millionaires around the world. National wealth has been estimated for a large number of countries by the World Bank.[2] In short, there is now an impressive amount of information on wealth holdings. We believe the time has therefore come to estimate the world distribution of household wealth.[3]

In this paper we show, first, that there are very large intra-country differences in the level of household wealth. The US is the richest country, with mean wealth estimated at $144,000 per person in the year 2000.[4] At the opposite extreme among countries with wealth data, we have India with per capita wealth of about $6,500 in purchasing power parity (PPP) terms. Other countries show a wide range of values. Even among high income OECD countries there is a range from figures of $56,000 for New Zealand and $66,000 for Denmark to $129,000 for the UK (again in PPP terms).

We also look at international differences in the *composition* of wealth. There are some regularities but also country-specific differences – such as the strong preference for liquid savings in a few countries, such as Japan. Real assets, particularly land and farm assets, are more important in less developed countries. This reflects not only the greater importance of agriculture, but a lack of financial development that is being corrected in some of the most rapidly growing LDCs. Among rich countries, financial assets and share-holding tend to bulk largest in those with more reliance on private pensions and/or the most highly developed financial markets, such as the UK and US.

The concentration of wealth within countries is high. Typical Gini coefficients in wealth data lie in the range of about 0.65–0.75, while some range above 0.8. In contrast, the mid-range for income Ginis is from about 0.35–0.45. The mid value for the share of the top 10 per cent of wealth-holders in our data is 50 per cent, again higher than is usual for income.

While inter-country differences are interesting, our goal is to estimate the world distribution of wealth. In order to do so we need estimates of the levels and distribution of wealth in countries where data on wealth are not available. Fortunately for our exercise, the countries for which we have data included 56 per cent of the world's population in the year 2000 and, we estimate, more than 80 per cent of its household wealth. Careful study of the determinants of wealth levels and distribution in the countries that *have* wealth data allows imputations to be made for the 'missing countries'.

[...]

World distribution

[...]

The interpretation of data on personal wealth distribution hinges a great deal on the underlying population deemed to be relevant. Are we concerned principally with the distribution of wealth across all individuals, across adult persons, or across households or families?[5] When examining the analogous issue of global income distribution, we support the common practice of assuming (as a first approximation) that the benefits of household expenditure are shared equally among household members, and that each person is weighted equally in determining the overall distribution. However, the situation with wealth is rather different. Personal assets and debts are typically owned by named individuals, and may well be retained by those individuals if they leave the family. Furthermore, while some household assets, especially housing, provide a stream of communal benefits, it is highly unlikely that control of assets is shared equally by household members or that household members will share equally in the proceeds if the asset is sold. Membership of households can be quite fluid (for example, with respect to children living away from home) and the pattern of household structure varies markedly across countries. For these and other reasons, the total number of households is not readily available for many countries. Thus, despite the fact that most of the datasets listed in Table 2.6.1 are constructed on a family or household basis, we believe that the distribution of global wealth is best interpreted in terms of the distribution across adults, on the grounds that those under 20 years of age have little formal or actual wealth ownership, and may therefore be neglected in global terms.[6]

Tables 2.6.2 and 2.6.3 summarise our estimates of the distribution of wealth across the global population of 3.7 billion adults with wealth measured at official exchange rates for the year 2000. The results indicate that only $2161 was needed in order to belong to the top half of the world wealth distribution, but to be a member of the top 10 per cent required at least $61,000 and membership of the top 1 per cent required more than $500,000 per adult. This latter figure is surprisingly high, given that the top 1 per cent group contains 37 million adults and is therefore far from an exclusive club. The entrance fee has presumably grown higher still in the period since the year 2000.

The figures for wealth shares show that the top 10 per cent of adults own 85 per cent of global household wealth, so that the average member of this group has 8.5 times the global average holding. The corresponding figures for the top 5 per cent, top 2 per cent and top 1 per cent are 71 per cent (14.2 times the average), 51 per cent (25 times the average) and 40 per cent (40 times the average), respectively. This compares with the bottom half of the distribution which collectively owns barely 1 per cent of global wealth. Thus the top 1 per cent own almost 40 times as much as the bottom 50 per cent. The contrast with the bottom decile of wealth holders is even starker. The average member of the top decile has nearly 3000 times the mean wealth of the bottom decile, and the average member of the top percentile is more than 13,000 times richer.

Table 2.6.1: Wealth shares for countries with wealth distribution data, official exchange rate basis

Country	Year	Unit	share of lowest											share of top					
			10%	20%	25%	30%	40%	50%	60%	70%	75%	80%	90%	10%	5%	2%	1%	0.5%	0.1%
Australia	2002	household	0.0	0.0		1.0	4.0	9.0	16.0	25.0		38.0	56.0	45.0	32.0				
Canada	1999	family unit											47.0	53.0					
China	2002	person	0.7	2.8		5.8	9.6	14.4	20.6	29.0		40.7	58.6	41.4					
Denmark	1975	household											35.0	65.0	48.0		25.0		
Finland	1998	household	-0.9	-0.9		-0.3	2.2	7.4	15.0	25.0		38.6	57.7	42.3					
France	1994	person?											39.0	61.0			21.3		6.3
Germany	1998	household	-0.3	-0.2		0.3	1.5	3.9	9.0	18.9		34.0	55.7	44.4					
India	2002	household	0.2	1.0		2.5	4.8	8.1	12.9	19.8		30.1	47.1	52.9	38.3		15.7		
Indonesia	1997	household	0.0	0.4		1.3	2.8	5.1	8.5	13.5		21.1	34.6	65.4	56.0		28.7		
Ireland	1987	household	0.0	0.2		2.5	6.6	12.2	18.9	28.5		40.4	57.7	42.3	28.7		10.4		
Italy	2000	household					7.0					36.2	51.5	48.5	36.4		17.2		
Japan	1999	household	0.5	2.1		4.8	8.7	13.9	20.7	29.8		42.3	60.7	39.3					
Korea, South	1988	household	0.5	1.8		4.0	7.4	12.3	18.9	27.9		39.9	56.9	43.1	31.0		14.0		
New Zealand	2001	tax unit											48.3	51.7					
Norway	2000	household	0.1	0.7		2.6	5.8	10.4	16.4	24.2		34.6	49.6	50.5					
Spain	2002	household			2.1			13.2			34.7		58.1	41.9					
Sweden	2002	household	-5.7	-6.8		-6.9	-6.6	-4.8	-0.6	7.1		19.9	41.4	58.6					
Switzerland	1997	family											28.7	71.3	58.0		34.8	27.6	16.0
UK	2000	adult						5.0			25.0		44.0	56.0	44.0	31.0	23.0		
USA	2001	family						2.8					30.2	69.8	57.7		32.0		

Table 2.6.2: Global wealth distribution in 2000, official exchange rate basis

	Decile 1	Decile 2	Decile 3	Decile 4	Decile 5	Decile 6	Decile 7	Decile 8	Decile 9	Top 10	Top 5	Top 1	Adult population (000s)	Population share	Wealth per adult	Wealth share
World wealth shares	0.003	0.09	0.2	0.3	0.5	0.8	1.4	2.8	8.8	85.1	70.6	39.9				
Minimum wealth	0	192	464	890	1405	2161	3517	6318	14169	61041	150145	514512				
Population proportions by region																
North America	0.2	0.5	0.9	1.2	1.8	2.8	4.5	8.0	14.1	27.1	28.6	39.1	225719	6.1	190653	34.3
Latin America and Caribbean	5.5	6.7	6.9	5.7	6.2	7.9	10.2	13.2	14.7	5.0	3.1	2.1	302915	8.2	18163	4.4
Europe	8.6	8.3	9.2	7.9	8.8	10.4	12.8	16.8	30.1	36.1	35.7	26.2	550579	14.9	67232	29.5
Asia: China	6.8	14.6	16.9	36.9	40.8	38.0	35.5	29.1	8.9	0.2	0.0	0.0	842063	22.8	3885	2.6
Asia: India	27.3	27.5	27.3	19.4	16.5	14.8	11.4	7.4	2.5	0.2	0.0	0.0	570595	15.4	1989	0.9
Asia: high income	0.0	0.0	0.1	0.2	0.4	0.7	1.6	3.8	12.0	26.3	29.5	31.0	166532	4.5	172414	22.9
Asia: other	24.1	24.7	24.4	19.3	17.4	17.7	16.6	14.8	12.2	2.5	1.2	0.6	642421	17.4	5952	3.1
Africa	27.3	17.5	14.1	9.2	7.8	7.4	7.0	6.4	4.4	0.7	0.3	0.2	376292	10.2	3558	1.2
Oceania	0.2	0.2	0.3	0.3	0.3	0.2	0.4	0.4	1.2	2.0	1.5	0.8	20405	0.6	72874	1.2
World	100	100	100	100	100	100	100	100	100	100	100	100	3697518	100	33893	100

Table 2.6.3: Global wealth distribution in 2000, selected country details, official exchange rate basis

	Decile 1	Decile 2	Decile 3	Decile 4	Decile 5	Decile 6	Decile 7	Decile 8	Decile 9	Top 10	Top 5	Top 1	Adult population	Population	Wealth per	Wealth	Gini
USA	0.2	0.5	0.9	1.2	1.7	2.6	4.2	7.1	11.6	24.9	26.7	37.4	202865	5.5	201319	32.6	0.801
Japan	1.4	0.8	0.9	0.4	0.9	0.1	0.4	1.3	5.0	20.5	25.1	26.8	100933	2.7	227600	18.3	0.547
Germany		0.8	0.9	0.4	0.9	0.5	0.4	1.0	3.6	7.6	9.8	3.7	64810	1.8	109735	5.7	0.671
Italy			0.1	0.1		0.1	0.3	1.1	4.4	6.6	5.0	3.9	46416	1.3	122250	4.5	0.609
UK			0.1	0.1	0.2	0.4	0.9	1.7	2.5	5.9	7.8	6.3	43871	1.2	169617	5.9	0.697
France			0.1	0.1	0.2	0.4	0.8	1.8	4.3	4.2	4.1	5.2	44358	1.2	114650	4.1	0.730
Spain					0.1	0.3	0.5	0.7	3.0	3.9	2.5	1.3	32165	0.9	86958	2.2	0.565
Canada						0.1	0.3	0.9	2.5	2.2	1.9	1.7	22764	0.6	95606	1.7	0.663
Australia		0.1	0.2	0.2	0.2	0.1	0.2	0.2	0.8	1.8	1.3	0.7	13690	0.4	94712	1.0	0.622
China, Taiwan						0.1	0.3	0.5	1.5	1.8	1.5	1.2	15476	0.4	105613	1.3	0.654
Korea, South			0.1	0.1	0.3	0.4	0.7	1.6	4.2	1.7	0.6	0.5	33242	0.9	41777	1.1	0.579
Netherlands						0.1	0.1	0.3	1.0	1.7	1.7	1.5	12046	0.3	144406	1.4	0.649
Brazil	1.9	2.7	2.3	2.0	2.2	2.9	3.6	4.4	4.5	1.5	0.9	0.6	104213	2.8	15958	1.3	0.783
Mexico	0.4	0.8	1.2	0.8	1.0	1.3	1.9	2.8	3.6	1.2	0.8	0.5	56132	1.5	23305	1.0	0.748
Argentina	0.1	0.2	0.3	0.4	0.3	0.5	0.6	1.0	1.9	1.0	0.7	0.5	23307	0.6	40225	0.7	0.740
Switzerland							0.1	0.3	0.5	0.6	0.7	1.3	5497	0.1	222641	1.0	0.803
Turkey	0.2	0.6	1.0	0.7	0.8	1.1	1.5	2.2	2.2	0.6	0.3	0.1	40391	1.1	16218	0.5	0.717
China	6.8	14.6	16.9	36.9	40.8	38.0	35.5	29.1	8.9	0.2			842063	22.8	3885	2.6	0.550
India	27.3	27.5	27.3	19.4	16.5	14.8	11.4	7.4	2.5	0.2			570595	15.4	1989	0.9	0.669
Russia	3.8	3.5	3.5	3.1	3.2	3.7	3.9	2.8	1.5	0.1	0.1		107493	2.9	4140	0.4	0.698
Thailand	0.7	1.4	1.1	1.0	1.1	1.3	1.5	1.6	1.0	0.1			40160	1.1	6717	0.2	0.709
Indonesia	7.7	5.9	5.6	4.0	3.2	2.8	2.7	0.6	0.9	0.1	0.1		124446	3.4	2421	0.2	0.763
Nigeria	5.9	3.0	2.1	1.1	0.6	0.5	0.4	0.2	0.1				51431	1.4	862	0.0	0.735
Pakistan	2.5	3.0	3.1	2.6	2.3	2.2	1.0	1.0	0.6				67968	1.8	2633	0.1	0.697
Bangladesh	2.4	2.9	3.0	2.4	2.2	2.1	1.6	1.0	0.4				66483	1.8	2424	0.1	0.658
Viet Nam	2.3	2.0	2.0	1.6	1.3	1.1	0.8	0.5	0.2				44025	1.2	1986	0.1	0.680
World	100	100	100	100	100	100	100	100	100	100	100	100	3697518	100	33893	100	0.892

Note: Blank cells indicate values less than 0.05 per cent.

Table 2.6.3 supplements these results with details of the Gini coefficient for individual countries and for the world as a whole. As mentioned earlier, wealth distribution is unambiguously more unequal than income distribution in all countries which allow comparison. Our wealth Gini estimates for individual countries range from a low of 0.547 for Japan to the high values reported for the USA (0.801) and Switzerland (0.803), and the highest values of all in Zimbabwe (0.845) and Namibia (0.846). The global wealth Gini is higher still at 0.892. This roughly corresponds to the Gini value that would be recorded in a 10-person population if one person had $1000 and the remaining 9 people each had $1.

By way of comparison Milanovic (2005, p. 108) estimates the Gini for the world distribution of income in 1998 at 0.795 using official exchange rates. It is interesting to note that, while wealth inequality exceeds income inequality in global terms, the gap between the Gini coefficients for world wealth and income inequality – about 10 percentage points – is less than the gap at the country level, which averages about 30 percentage points. This is unavoidable given that an income Gini of 0.795 and a Gini upper bound of 1, limits the possibilities for higher Gini values.[...]

We now turn to the composition of each of the wealth quantiles. Table 2.6.2 provides a regional breakdown where, due to their population size, China and India are reported separately. It is also convenient to distinguish the high income subset of countries in the Asia-Pacific region (a list which includes Japan, Taiwan, South Korea, Australia, New Zealand and several middle eastern states) from the remaining (mainly low income) nations.

'Thirds' feature prominently in describing the overall pattern of results. India dominates the bottom third of the global wealth distribution, contributing a little under a third (27 per cent to be precise) of this group. The middle third of the distribution is the domain of China which supplies more than a third of those in deciles 4–8. At the top end, North America, Europe and high-income Asia monopolise the top decile, each regional group accounting for around one third of the richest wealth holders, although the composition changes a little in the upper tail, with the North American share rising while European membership declines. Another notable feature is the relatively constant membership share of Asian countries other than China and India. However, as the figures indicate, this group is highly polarised, with the high-income subgroup populating the top end of the global wealth distribution and the lower income countries (especially, Indonesia, Bangladesh, Pakistan and Vietnam) occupying the lower tail. The population of Latin America is also fairly even spread across the global distribution but Africa, as expected, is heavily concentrated at the bottom end.

Table 2.6.3 provides more details for a selection of countries. The list of countries include all those which account for more than 1 per cent of global wealth or more than 1 per cent of those in the top decile, plus those countries with adult populations exceeding 45 million. They have been arranged in order of the number of persons in the top global wealth decile.

The number of members of the top decile depends on three factors: the size of the population, average wealth, and wealth inequality within the country. As expected, the US is in first place, with 25 per cent of the global top decile and 37 per cent of the global top percentile. All three factors reinforce each other in this instance: a large population combining with very high wealth per capita and relatively unequal distribution. Japan features strongly in second place – more strongly than expected, perhaps – with 21 per cent of the global top decile and 27 per cent of the global top percentile. The high wealth per adult and relatively equal distribution accounts for the fact that the number of Japanese in the bottom half of the global wealth distribution is insignificant according to our figures. Italy, too, has a stronger showing than expected, for much the same reasons as Japan.

Further down the list, China and India both owe their position to the size of their population. Neither country has enough people in the global top 5 per cent in 2000 to be recorded. While the two countries are expected to be under-represented in the upper tail because of their relatively low mean wealth, their absence here from the top 5 per cent seems anomalous. It may well reflect unreliable wealth data drawn from surveys that do not over-sample the upper tail, data which could be improved by making corrections for differential response and under-reporting. The representation of both China and India has been rising in the annual Forbes list of billionaires, so these countries should not only be represented in an accurate estimate of the membership of the top 5 per cent or top 1 per cent, but also likely supply an increasing number of people in these categories.

For the world's super rich it is natural to compare the wealth of people in different countries using official exchange rates. In today's world capital is highly mobile internationally, and rich people from most countries travel a great deal and may do a considerable amount of their spending abroad. The wealth of one millionaire goes just as far as that of another in Monte Carlo or when shopping at Harrods, irrespective of which country he resides in. Lower down the scale, however, the benefits (and valuations) of asset holdings may depend heavily on the local prices of goods and services. In this case it may be more appropriate to evaluate wealth in terms of what it would buy if liquidated and spent on consumption locally. To address this point, Tables 2.6.4 and 2.6.5 provide a second set of wealth distribution estimates based on PPP comparisons rather than official exchange rates.

Applying the PPP adjustment increases average wealth levels in most countries, and hence the global average, which rises from $33893 per adult to $43628 per adult. The admission fee for membership of the top wealth groups also increases. The price for entry to the top 10 per cent rises from $61041 to $88035, but entry to the top 1 per cent increases more modestly,

Table 2.6.4: Global wealth distribution in 2000, PPP values

	Decile 1	Decile 2	Decile 3	Decile 4	Decile 5	Decile 6	Decile 7	Decile 8	Decile 9	Top 10	Top 5	Top 1	Adult population (000s)	Population share	Wealth per adult	Wealth share
World wealth shares	0.1	0.3	0.6	1.1	1.6	2.4	3.7	6.2	12.9	71.1	57.0	31.6				
Minimum wealth	2	826	1978	3693	5724	8399	12749	20299	35954	88035	170467	523264				
Population proportions by region																
North America	1.4	2.6	3.5	3.3	3.5	4.0	5.2	6.2	9.6	21.6	25.7	39.3	225719	6.1	193147	27.0
Latin America and Caribbean	10.3	9.1	8.1	6.8	6.7	7.5	8.2	9.0	9.3	6.9	6.4	6.1	302915	8.2	34956	6.6
Europe	9.1	9.2	10.1	9.1	9.3	12.0	14.1	18.1	22.7	35.0	35.8	31.2	550579	14.9	81890	27.9
Asia: China	6.8	14.3	14.8	33.5	37.5	34.2	32.4	29.4	20.7	4.1	1.4	0.0	842063	22.8	16749	8.7
Asia: India	21.0	21.9	25.2	18.1	16.3	15.8	14.2	11.6	8.0	2.3	1.2	0.0	570595	15.4	11655	4.1
Asia: high income	0.0	0.3	0.9	1.2	1.5	2.0	2.4	5.0	12.1	19.6	21.0	17.1	166532	4.5	138750	14.3
Asia: other	22.2	24.1	23.1	18.7	17.5	17.7	17.2	15.0	11.9	6.4	4.9	3.7	642421	17.4	18266	7.3
Africa	28.7	17.9	14.0	9.1	7.3	6.6	6.1	5.3	4.6	2.2	1.7	1.2	376292	10.2	11730	2.7
Oceania	0.4	0.5	0.4	0.2	0.3	0.2	0.2	0.3	1.0	1.9	2.0	1.4	20405	0.6	99634	1.3
World	100	100	100	100	100	100	100	100	100	100	100	100	3697519	100	43628	100

Table 2.6.5: Global wealth distribution in 2000, PPP values: selected country details

	Decile 1	Decile 2	Decile 3	Decile 4	Decile 5	Decile 6	Decile 7	Decile 8	Decile 9	Top 10	Top 5	Top 1	Adult population (000s)	Population share	Wealth per adult	Wealth share	Gini
USA	1.4	2.6	3.4	3.1	3.3	3.6	4.6	5.3	8.1	19.6	23.5	36.8	202865	5.5	201319	25.3	0.801
Japan		0.1	0.3	0.6	0.6	0.8	0.9	2.5	7.3	14.2	15.9	11.7	100933	2.7	157146	9.8	0.547
Germany	3.0	1.2	0.8	0.4	0.1	0.7	1.1	1.5	1.9	7.0	8.9	3.9	64810	1.8	114185	4.6	0.671
UK	0.1	0.3	0.5	0.6	0.7	0.9	0.7	1.2	0.8	5.9	6.0	6.3	43871	1.2	172461	4.7	0.697
Italy			0.1	0.2	0.3	0.5	0.9	1.7	3.1	5.8	5.5	5.3	46416	1.3	148843	4.3	0.609
China	6.8	14.3	14.8	33.5	37.5	34.2	32.4	29.4	20.7	4.1	1.4		842063	22.8	16749	8.7	0.550
Spain		0.1	0.3	0.3	0.4	0.5	0.3	0.7	2.5	3.7	3.2	2.3	32165	0.9	116782	2.3	0.565
France	0.1	0.3	0.5	0.6	0.7	0.9	1.2	1.7	2.6	3.5	3.9	5.6	44358	1.2	125254	3.4	0.730
Brazil	3.9	3.1	2.8	2.3	2.4	2.6	2.7	2.9	3.0	2.4	2.3	2.3	104213	2.8	35188	2.3	0.783
India	21.0	21.9	25.2	18.1	16.3	15.8	14.2	11.6	8.0	2.3	1.2		570595	15.4	11655	4.1	0.669
Canada		0.1	0.1	0.2	0.2	0.4	0.6	0.9	1.6	2.0	2.2	2.5	22764	0.6	120326	1.7	0.663
Korea, South		0.2	0.4	0.4	0.5	0.7	0.9	1.5	2.7	1.8	1.1	0.9	33242	0.9	64521	1.3	0.579
China, Taiwan			0.1	0.1	0.2	0.3	0.3	0.5	1.0	1.7	1.8	1.9	15476	0.4	143405	1.4	0.654
Australia	0.2	0.3	0.2		0.2	0.1	0.1	0.2	0.8	1.7	1.7	1.2	13690	0.4	126635	1.1	0.622
Russia	2.9	3.0	2.9	2.7	2.6	3.1	3.5	3.8	3.0	1.5	1.0	0.9	107493	2.9	24011	1.6	0.698
Netherlands			0.1	0.1	0.1	0.2	0.2	0.4	0.8	1.4	1.6	1.7	12046	0.3	158484	1.2	0.649
Mexico	1.4	1.7	1.4	1.2	1.2	1.4	1.7	1.9	2.0	1.4	1.3	1.2	56132	1.5	38324	1.3	0.748
Turkey	0.5	1.1	0.9	0.8	0.9	1.1	1.3	1.5	1.6	1.1	0.9	0.8	40391	1.1	40202	1.0	0.717
Argentina	0.4	0.5	0.4	0.4	0.4	0.5	0.6	0.8	1.1	1.0	1.0	0.9	23307	0.6	60917	0.9	0.740
Indonesia	6.7	4.9	5.1	3.7	3.4	3.0	2.9	2.2	0.7	0.9	0.7	0.7	124446	3.4	13401	1.0	0.763
Thailand	1.0	1.4	1.2	1.1	1.0	1.1	1.2	1.2	1.1	0.5	0.4	0.2	40160	1.1	22678	0.6	0.709
Switzerland				0.1	0.1	0.1	0.2	0.2	0.3	0.4	0.6	1.0	5497	0.1	187998	0.6	0.803
Pakistan	2.0	2.8	2.8	2.3	2.3	2.1	1.7	0.9	0.9	0.4	0.3	0.2	67968	1.8	13214	0.6	0.697
Bangladesh	1.9	2.7	2.6	2.2	2.1	2.1	1.9	1.4	0.9	0.3	0.2	0.2	66483	1.8	12389	0.5	0.658
Viet Nam	2.0	1.9	1.9	1.5	1.2	1.2	1.0	0.7	0.5	0.1	0.1		44025	1.2	10066	0.3	0.680
Nigeria	7.6	2.9	1.6	0.6	0.4	0.3	0.2	0.1	0.1				51431	1.4	2194	0.1	0.735
WORLD	100	100	100	100	100	100	100	100	100	100	100	100	3697519	100	43628	100	0.802

Note: Blank cells indicate values less than 0.05 per cent.

158

from \$514512 to \$523264, reflecting the small impact of PPP adjustments within the richest nations.

Because the PPP adjustment factor tends to be greater for poorer countries, switching to PPP valuations compresses the variation in average wealth levels across countries and hence provides a more conservative assessment of the degree of world wealth inequality. As a consequence, the estimated share of wealth owned by the richest individuals falls: from 85.1 per cent to 71.1 per cent for the top 10 per cent of wealth holders, for example, and from 39.9 per cent to 31.6 per cent for the top 1 per cent. The overall global Gini value also declines, from 0.892 to 0.802 (although the Gini values for individual countries are unaffected).[7]

The overall picture suggested by Tables 2.6.4 and 2.6.5 is much the same as before. India moves a little more into the middle deciles of the global wealth distribution, and both India and China are now deemed to have representatives in the global top 5 per cent, although not the top 1 per cent. Membership of the top 10 per cent is a little more spread regionally, principally due to a decline in the share of Japan, whose membership of the top 10 per cent falls from 20.5 per cent to 14.2 per cent as a result of the decline in wealth per adult from \$227600 to \$157146 when measured in PPP terms.

As regards the rankings of individual countries, Brazil, India, Russia, Turkey and Argentina are now all promoted into the exclusive class of countries with more than 1 per cent of the members of the global top wealth decile. The most dramatic rise, however, is that of China which leapfrogs into fifth position with 4.1 per cent of the members. Even without an increase in wealth inequality, a relatively modest rise in average wealth in China will move it up to third position in the global top decile, and overtaking Japan is not a remote prospect.

In summary, it is clear that household wealth is much more concentrated, both in size distribution and geography, when official exchange rates rather than PPP valuations are employed. Thus a somewhat different perspective emerges depending on whether one is interested in the power that wealth conveys in terms of local consumption options or the power to act and have influence on the world financial stage.

[...]

Conclusion

This paper has provided a first estimate of the world distribution of household wealth. We have seen that the distribution is highly concentrated – in fact much more concentrated than the world distribution of income, or the distribution of wealth within all but a few of the world's countries. While a typical share of the top 10 per cent of wealth-holders within a country would be about 50 per cent, and the median Gini around 0.7, we have estimated that for the world as a whole the share of the top 10 per cent was 85 per cent in the year 2000 and the Gini equalled 0.892 using official exchange rates, Milanovic (2005) estimates that the world income Gini was 0.795 in 1998. While wealth (and income) concentration is somewhat less when the estimates are done on a PPP basis, we have argued that the large share of wealth that is owned by people who can readily travel and invest globally means that converting at official exchange rates is preferable for many purposes when one is studying the distribution of wealth, rather than income distribution or poverty.

Much of the data that is used here comes from household surveys. For the wealthiest country, the US, which supplies 25 per cent of the world's top 10 per cent of wealth-holders on an official exchange rate basis (20 per cent using PPP), this is not a big problem. Sophisticated techniques have been used by the Federal Reserve Board to make its triennial Survey of Consumer Finance a reliable instrument. Less striking, but still effective steps have been taken in some of the other wealthiest countries. While the super rich are not represented in these data, in terms of measuring the overall degree of inequality we have seen that that is not a major deficiency. On the other hand, surveys in the major developing countries appear to have a particular problem in capturing the upper tail. This means that while we have reasonable confidence in our estimates, there is a non-negligible error bound that must be placed on them.

In evaluating the results obtained here it is important to keep in mind that the quality of the estimates depends only in part on the accuracy of the *distributional* information that has been assembled. It also depends on the accuracy of our estimates of mean household wealth in the countries studied. Here we are on safer ground. For 33 countries, including all of the world's major OECD economies, we have data on the household sector's financial balance sheet. And for 18 of those countries we also have reasonable estimates of non-financial assets. These estimates are often formed in conjunction with Flow of Funds numbers or the National Accounts. There is a solid basis of good numbers from financial institutions and government statistical agencies in these exercises.

Our study of wealth levels and composition across countries is not only important in providing a key ingredient in estimating the world distribution of wealth. It is also of independent interest. First, it gives us a picture of how wealth composition varies, not only with the stage of development, but across countries at similar income levels due to institutional and traditional differences, varying importance of public pensions, and other factors. Our empirical work has shown how the importance of both financial assets and borrowing rises sharply with per capita income and the development of financial markets. Conversely, we have seen how balance sheets in poor countries are still dominated by land and other tangible assets. Secondly, we get a snapshot of what Milanovic (2002, 2005) and others refer to as 'international inequality', that is inequality *between* countries. On an official exchange rate basis per capita household wealth ranged from about $1,100 for India to $144,000 for the United States in the year 2000. We have also found that differences are large even for countries at a similar stage of development. Thus, differences between countries make an important contribution to inequality in the world distribution of household wealth. Even if the current level of wealth inequality within countries proved to be enduring, one may hope for a significant reduction in world wealth inequality as convergence takes place in wealth between nations.

Two caveats to conclusions about wealth inequality between countries ('international inequality') are that the concentration is smaller when we measure on a PPP basis, and also less on a per adult basis. Thus, for example, while the coefficient of variation for international inequality is 2.141 on a per capita and official exchange rate basis, it is only 1.298 on a per adult and PPP basis.

There is huge room for improvement in the study of household wealth from a global perspective. Household balance sheets and wealth surveys need to be generated in more countries. These are completely lacking in Latin America, and almost completely absent in Africa and most of Asia as well. Financial development is a key aspect of economic growth and human development. Without the relevant data it is impossible to see what progress is being made. Improvements in data quality, particularly in survey data, must also occur. The task is far from hopeless, however, and great strides have been taken in quite a few countries. The mere fact that regular wealth surveys are conducted in the world's two largest and most dynamic developing countries, China and India, is very encouraging. As surveys are conducted in more developing and transition countries, and as techniques for achieving greater accuracy, especially in the upper tail, are applied in more countries, we will get a much better picture of the composition and distribution of household wealth around the globe.

Notes

[1] In some work attempts have been made to include 'social security wealth', that is the present value of expected net benefits from public pension plans in household wealth. We exclude social security wealth here, in part because estimates are available for only a few countries.

[2] See World Bank (2005). National wealth differs from household wealth in including the wealth of all other sectors, of which corporations, government and the rest-of-the-world are important examples.

[3] One sign of the growing maturity of household wealth data is the launching of the Luxembourg Wealth Study (LWS) parallel to the long-running Luxembourg Income Study (LIS). See http://www.lisproject.org/lws.htm. In its first phase the LWS aims to provide comparable wealth data for nine OECD countries, with the cooperation of national statistical agencies or central banks. The LWS initiative differs from ours in that its aim is not to estimate the world distribution of wealth, but to assemble fully comparable wealth data across an important subset of the world's countries.

[4] All our wealth estimates are for the year 2000. Wealth data typically become available with a significant lag, and wealth surveys are conducted at intervals of three or more years. The year 2000 provides us with a reasonably recent date and good data availability.

[5] Note that each of these bases was used by at least one country listed in Table 2.6.1.

[6] The original country level data are generally based on households. We implicitly assume that the shape of the distribution of wealth among adults is the same as that among households, an assumption which would be true if all households contained two adults, if children had zero wealth, and if wealth was equally divided between the adult members.

[7] Milanovic (2005, p. 108) reports a world income Gini of 0.642 using PPP. Thus the gap between the world wealth and income Ginis appears to be larger, in absolute terms, on a PPP basis than using official exchange rates, where the gap reported earlier was $0.892 - 0.795 = 0.097$.

References

Bourguignon, François and Morrisson, Christian (2002). 'The Size Distribution of Income Among World Citizens, 1820–1990.' *American Economic Review*, September: 727–44.

Milanovic, Branko (2002). 'True World Income Distribution, 1988 and 1993: First Calculation Based on Household Surveys Alone', *Economic Journal* 112: 51-92.

Milanovic, Branko (2005). *Global Inequality*. Princeton: Princeton University Press.

World Bank (2005). *Where is the Wealth of Nations? Measuring Capital for the XXI Century*. Washington, DC.

Section 3

Global policy actors, institutions and processes

A fundamental contradiction lies at the heart of the world political economy, in that whilst processes of economic globalisation increasingly tie the interests of people living in different countries together, the world polity remains divided between nation states that have varying levels of power. This section addresses themes and debates regarding institutional and governance issues at the global level as they affect social policy, particularly those that are concerned with the problems of collective action beyond nation states and governments to address global social policy issues. The world's existing international institutions are primarily *multilateral* organisations, that is to say, they are run by or on behalf of their member country governments. These governments have varying degrees of economic and military resources to draw upon, and whilst international organisations may have a degree of 'relative autonomy' from the governments that created them, their governance structures usually reflect these disparities of power. International institutions are further fragmented between a range of different organisations and agencies that have responsibility for aspects of global governance that are relevant to social policy. The place of nation states at the heart of the international system, together with this organisational fragmentation, sometimes leaves what might be called a 'governance gap', as the problems facing humanity become more global whilst the existing international institutions have limited capacity to respond effectively to these problems. However, as processes of globalisation have gained pace, new actors have increasingly gained access to governance mechanisms at the global level. These include transnational businesses, which have become increasingly influential in a range of governance areas, but also emerging global civil society groups, associations and movements which organise and mobilise citizens across the borders of their countries of residence.

The first reading in this section, by Robert O'Brien, highlights the fact that most of our current international organisations were born out of the conflict of the Second World War, in an attempt to avoid further global conflict and provide a stable institutional basis for global economic exchange. This historical relationship between political/economic shocks (such as depression and war) and innovation in international organisation, O'Brien argues, suggests a greater possibility of reforming existing international organisations in socially progressive ways than of replacing them with a radically new set of institutions (although following the global financial crisis that began in 2007, we might argue that there is now both the opportunity and the necessity for a fundamental re-examination of the global system of economic governance).

O'Brien further points out that whilst some international organisations have rule-creating and rule-supervisory functions, and therefore a degree of coercive power, others must rely on moral suasion and argument. Most of the organisations that champion progressive social policy (such as the International Labour Organization) tend to be of the latter kind, whilst those that govern the world economy (and therefore also have a profound impact on social policy) tend to be of the first kind. The rule-creating and supervisory economic institutions of the International Monetary Fund (IMF), World Bank and World Trade Organization (WTO) all subscribe to a technocratic modus operandi allied to strongly neo-liberal economic prescriptions, something O'Brien terms 'neoclassical functionalism'. The closed and sometimes 'pathological' practices that this produces could be challenged by opening up international organisations to outside influences, such as those of civil society groups, or by better integrating policies across international institutions. However, any strategy for change will need to take account of the importance of states in the international system and of the balance of social forces.

The reading by Kevin Farnsworth addresses this issue of social forces by examining the respective positions of business and labour organisations at the international level. Farnsworth argues that the balance of power between capital and labour globally has shifted towards capital in recent years as a result of a number of factors, including the development of a neo-liberal hegemony among key international organisations since the 1980s; the relative success of businesses in organising beyond the nation state; the lack of legal rights to institutional participation at the international level and the related importance of informal networks to accessing decision makers; and the relative dependence of labour upon business investment. Having surveyed the social policy preferences of international business and labour organisations as advanced within the context of one international organisation, the OECD, Farnsworth concludes that international governmental organisations have internalised a bias towards the needs and preferences of business over labour.

While the relative influence of organised labour has declined since the 1980s, a heterogeneous variety of actors and social movements have come to the foreground and are increasingly organised at the global level. These include civil society organisations and Transnational Corporations (TNCs), and the role of TNCs in global social governance and policy is a key concern of the next three readings in this section.

One of the significant shifts in the role of businesses in recent years has involved the development of 'global public–private partnerships' (GPPPs), particularly in the health field. These involve large corporations or industry associations collaborating with an intergovernmental organisation and a range of other potential partners, such as national governments or health ministries. Buse and Walt outline how this has entailed a relative shift from 'vertical' governance mechanisms involving formal, hierarchical, representation of states within the UN system, to 'horizontal' governance mechanisms involving more ad hoc participation of non-state actors in more complex networks of relationships. They argue that GPPPs have the potential to further fragment international cooperation in health and to undermine some of the key functions and attributes of the World Health Organization (WHO). The shift to 'horizontal' forms of involving private interests in global health governance may undermine a number of features of 'good governance', including the 'representative legitimacy' and accountability mechanisms present in established forms of state representation in the United Nations (UN) system.

Whilst Buse and Walt examine the relationship between corporations and the UN system, Pearson and Seyfang examine the broader field of voluntary corporate codes of conduct relating to labour conditions. Such codes are 'voluntary self-regulatory tools that are applicable to specific firms, or groups of firms, and thus to certain groups of workers at certain times'. Pearson and Seyfang argue that these voluntary codes have attained a greater significance in the current period, as a result of the relative decline in support for strong statutory codes of social regulation from governments and international organisations and the accompanying labour market deregulation. Their analysis indicates that firms tend to adopt voluntary codes for reasons of reputation management and to deflect proposals for stronger codes or forms of regulation, and suggests that where codes are adopted they may lead to temporary 'enclave' social policy that benefits only particular groups of workers at particular times. Nevertheless, positive features exist where the process expands the scope for previously excluded groups to have a say in labour negotiations, such as marginalised or women workers and non-governmental organisations (NGOs).

The reading by Jeff Collin, Kelley Lee and Karen Bissell addresses a number of overlapping themes relevant to the section as a whole: the emergence of innovative forms of global governance; the need for coordination and policy coherence between international organisations; the increasing participation of civil society actors alongside states and multilateral organisations; the need to effectively regulate TNCs; and the need to address the concerns of developing countries alongside those of developed countries. The case of the Transnational Tobacco Companies (TTCs) highlights a number of issues related to the activities of TNCs, such as the political influence they have sometimes exerted over national governments, and the role of international organisations like the WTO in facilitating their expansion in developing countries. The WHO's Framework Convention on Tobacco Control (FCTC), which came into force in 2005, has resulted from a process in which the WHO has for the first time utilised its authority to develop an international treaty, and has involved a number of significant features. These include the recognition by member states of tobacco control as a global, rather than simply national, issue, the development of world-regional groupings of states within the negotiating process to coordinate and give effective weight to the voices of developing countries, and an unusual degree of formal participation in a multilateral negotiating process by civil society actors.

The section concludes with four milestone documents from international organisations that provide, each in their own way, key embodiments of global social policy. The statements of intent articulated in these declarations have proved in practice to be highpoints of global social policy articulation by the existing multilateral organisations, with their principles breached as often as they have been adhered to and their objectives often only partially met. Yet they are evidence of a powerful discourse of human rights that, beginning in the aftermath of the destruction wrought by the Second World War, has continued to provide a basis for global social progress. The documents reproduced here serve as key reference points on the way to a more socially just world.

Chapter 3.1

Organizational politics, multilateral economic organizations and social policy

Robert O'Brien

Many analysts writing on the subject of globalization and social policy have noted the significant role of multilateral economic organizations (MEOs) such as the International Monetary Fund (IMF), World Bank and World Trade Organization (WTO). These institutions are often identified as the carrier and enforcer of policies that lead to the undermining of social policies. Mishra (1999: 122–4), for example, argues that the IMF and World Bank see social policy as an economic burden. He suggests that they use the influence generated by being the grantor of loans and dispenser of economic expertise to undermine social policy in industrialized and developing states. Deacon et al.'s (1997: 198–202) study of the contest between social policy models in Eastern Europe paints a picture of the IMF and the World Bank advocating very liberal approaches against the more corporatist strategies of the International Labour Organisation (ILO) and Council of Europe. Some social activists go much further than this, calling for the outright abolition of the Fund, Bank and WTO in a form of social policy self-defense (Danaher, 1994).

While such concerns are often well founded, the relationship between MEOs and social policy would benefit from increased attention of international relations scholars. In this article the term social policy is being used to refer to the 'activities of governments and other actors which modify the free play of market forces to shape social redistribution, social regulation and social rights' (Deacon, 2001: 5). As a short form, the article will refer to 'redistributive' social policy. The social policy issue is one of many that emerge from a general examination of the functioning and role of international organizations. The international relations literature provides insights into several aspects of international organizations that may be of concern to social policy analysts. The key elements this article considers are: the significance of international organizations, the pitfalls of organizational politics, the challenge of harnessing state interests, and the role of social forces.

This article contributes to the debate over social policy and multilateral economic institutions by suggesting that advocates seeking to strengthen or defend socially redistributive social policy in the face of such institutions encounter a threefold challenge. The present antagonism between forms of social policy that 'intervene in the operations of the free market in the interests of social protection and social welfare' (Deacon et al., 1997: 1) and MEOs emerges from a series of conflicts in the realm of organizational politics, state interest and clashing social forces. A more supportive environment for redistributive social policy will require action in each of these areas. While organizational design and politics can account for many of the difficulties in the relationship between MEOs and social policy, solutions require a shift in the approach of key states and in the balance of social forces in civil society.

The article is divided into four sections. The first section reviews the rise of international organizations and the increasing importance of MEOs. The second section examines the particular organizational politics that have led to the emergence of what can be termed 'neoclassical functionalism'. The issue of pathological behavior evident from neoclassical functionalism is examined. This problem can be ameliorated by trying to open up the organizations to participation from a wider range of actors or developing mechanisms that integrate social and economic policy across organizations. However, reform of MEOs depends crucially upon developments in two arenas – interstate and civil society. Section three examines how state actors are central to the functioning of MEOs and highlights some alignments that might produce policy change. It suggests a need for a more assertive role for Europe, Japan and developing countries within MEOs. The fourth section discusses the escalating contest between social forces played out through the operation of MEOs. Pressure for changes in organizational and state policy are most likely to emerge from a contest over ideas in the intellectual realm and direct action by civic associations.

Before proceeding on to the argument, a brief explanation about the term 'multilateral economic organization' may be helpful. Entities such as the IMF and WTO are sometimes referred to as 'organizations' and sometimes as 'institutions'. This can generate confusion because institutions need not be formal organizations and the term 'international organization' can refer to a method of ordering international affairs rather than a formal institution. Such entities are also usually described as 'international', although that term also applies to regional groupings such as the European Union. I am using the term multilateral to signify bodies that aspire to near universal or global membership (as opposed to regional or sectoral). Economic refers to those actors that are primarily concerned with the rules that govern the exchange of money, services and commodities. Finally, I use the term organization to signify formal institutions that have buildings and permanent secretariats.

The significance of international organizations

In laying the groundwork for an analysis of MEOs and social policy, it is helpful to situate the subject in the context of international organizations in general. The 20th century witnessed a long struggle to channel conflict between states through the more peaceful path of international organizations. However, the creation of effective international organizations is a difficult task that is very dependent upon broader structural factors, such as the establishing of a new international order following a systemic conflict. This suggests that there is a much greater possibility of reforming existing organizations in a more social policy friendly direction than there is of replacing existing organizations with a new set of institutions following different principles.

The opposition to MEOs sometimes obscures the fact that these organizations were created with great difficulty and that their fate is closely tied to general developments in the international system.

The proliferation of international organizations is one of the most striking developments in the international relations of the 20th century. They have increased both in number and in importance. Their growth has been both a product of industrial change and facilitated the growth of an international and a global economy (Murphy, 1994). Regional organizations have joined the UN multilateral organizations to provide a web of coverage across issues and between states. Non-state actors have rushed to keep up with the proliferation of interstate organizations as 'transborder' activities become important to all sectors of societies. Boli and Thomas (1999) have gone as far as to suggest that the spread of international NGOs is contributing to the emergence of a world polity.

Although international organizations have many different characteristics, a useful distinction is between those that have some degree of coercive power and those that rely upon dispensing advice. Almost 30 years ago Cox and Jacobson (1974: 426–7) highlighted the difference between those international organizations that have rule-creating and rule-supervisory powers and those organizations which must rely upon moral suasion and argument. Some examples of organizations relying upon argument are the ILO, the United Nations Conference on Trade and Development (UNCTAD) and the UN General Assembly. The IMF, World Bank, the WTO and the UN Security Council are examples of organizations that create, supervise and enforce rules. Those institutions that champion social policy tend to be in the advisory category while some of the strongest rule-creating and rule-supervisory institutions advocate economic liberalism with little concern for social policy.

The distinction between coercive and advisory international organizations is nicely illustrated in the debate over trade and core labor standards. During the 1990s, international labor federations adopted a strategy of trying to link core labor standards to the enforcement power of the World Trade Organization. Their goal was to move beyond the advisory powers of the ILO to the more powerful coercive mechanisms of the WTO (O'Brien et al., 2000: 67–108).

There is a close relationship between political/economic shocks in the international system and transformation in international organizations. International organizations were first used to bolster peace and security, as well as facilitate economic exchange, on a large scale in the wake of the First World War. The League of Nations was created by those who believed that international organizations were essential to fostering peaceful coexistence and economic well-being. A second wave of using international organizations as a cornerstone for world order followed the Second World War. Systemic change or crisis is required before the political will can be generated to create new, elaborate international organizations.

Looking specifically at the IMF, World Bank and WTO we can see that broader developments in the international system were crucial to their creation and evolution. The IMF and Bank were created in negotiations dominated by the USA and UK in the final days of the Second World War (Helleiner, 1994: 25–50). Allied planners were convinced that the economic and political turmoil of the 1930s could only be avoided by creating a series of institutions that would govern the international economy. A sister trade organization, the International Trade Organization, died on the drawing board because it was not liberal enough for the tastes of US business and the US Congress. Although many states participated in the General Agreement on Tariffs and Trade (GATT), the creation of the WTO would await the end of another global military confrontation – the Cold War.

Whereas the creation of these institutions required the demise of military confrontation, their evolution was conditioned by transformation in the global economy. The explosion of the debt crisis in the early 1980s provided the opportunity for the Fund and Bank to change their role. The IMF evolved from providing short-term stabilization funding to designing medium and long-term structural adjustment packages (James, 1996). Structural adjustment programs have had the effect of greatly reducing the autonomy of recipient states (Denters, 1996). The World Bank has also gone through an extensive transition in the past 20 years. It has moved away from financing particular development projects to supporting policies that facilitate structural adjustment (Gilbert et al., 1996). In the case of the founding of the WTO, a new institution was created to replace the GATT. The key features of the WTO are an expansion in its mandate to new areas of economic activity and a strengthened legal structure (Croome, 1995). The strengthening of its dispute settlement mechanism endows the WTO with greater coercive powers over incompatible state policies.

Since voices have been raised from the right and the left suggesting that some or all of the MEOs should be abolished (Bond, 2001; Shultz et al., 1999) it is worth pointing out that they play important roles in the global economy. The IMF is designed to bolster international monetary stability by helping countries weather temporary balance of payments problems. A country faced with the prospect of no longer being able to buy imports due to a lack of foreign currency can turn to the Fund for assistance. The World Bank is charged with assisting non-industrialized countries rebuild and develop their economies through the provision of long-term financing. The WTO is designed to facilitate the free exchange of goods and services and to mediate between states when disputes arise. One can certainly argue about how well the organizations fulfill these roles, about the costs they impose upon other actors and whether they have strayed from their mandates. However, abolishing the organizations means that either new organizations are required to fulfill the same tasks or the services will not be provided by public authorities. Neither of these options is appealing or practical. As outlined above, the creation of new organizations is heavily dependent upon favorable systemic factors such as the end of a large-scale war or an economic crisis that threatens the entire system. The prospect of a global economy functioning in the absence of such stabilizing institutions is poor.

International organizations are both a tool for implementing policy of powerful actors and an arena for contesting the content of that policy (Cox and Sinclair, 1996: 364, 526). International organizations institutionalize particular power configurations from their time of origin. They continue to reflect the power of particular actors as they mature. However, international organizations are also arenas for a contest between social forces, ideas and states. The ILO's evolution is an example of these patterns. At the time of its creation in 1919, western governments felt threatened by the Bolshevik revolution and the rising tide of communism in the working class. Their response was to institutionalize labor's concerns in the ILO. They went as far as to create a tripartite decision-making structure involving state, employer and organized labor representatives. It is unlikely that organized labor would have the power to secure such representation if the institution was being created today rather than 100 years ago. In this sense, the ILO's structures froze a balance of power between organized labor, employers and the state that resonates with the early years of communist insurgency rather than today's political environment. Yet, the ILO is capable of changing to address other issues and social forces that are more prominent today. In recent years the ILO has taken on issues of homeworking and the informal sector (Prugl, 1999). It is moving beyond the traditional constituency of the institution to address new issues and problems. Although its structure is dated, the institution has successfully been used as an arena to bring forward a different agenda and struggle (Vosko, 2002).

Organizational politics and neoclassical functionalism

With rare exceptions (Ashworth and Long, 1999), the functional approach to international organizations and international relations has not received much recent attention. This is unfortunate because one of the ways of understanding why redistributive or universal forms of social policy are disadvantaged by today's international architecture is to see existing arrangements as a fusion of functionalism and neoclassical economic theory. This produces a practical type of organizational politics and organizational ideology (Williams, 1994: 42–3) that favors liberal market-based responses to social policy and services. This section outlines the complicated connections binding functionalism and neoclassical economics.

The functionalist approach to international relations proposed that a series of international organizations be created to address the technical problems of maximizing welfare across state borders (Mitrany, 1964). Neo-functionalists stressed the role of interest groups, the process of spillover into new areas of activity and the possibility that integration was more likely on a regional than world level (Haas, 1964). The strategy of functionalists and neo-functionalists has been to gradually build up a series of international organizations working on uncontroversial technical issues that would progressively expand to cover more and more aspects of people's daily lives. This ongoing expansion of technical institutions would overshadow narrow state interests as people increasingly identified with international organizations and the services they provided. This strategy of incrementally institutionalizing interstate relations to avoid overt conflict between countries has been the primary method of building formal regional integration in Western Europe (Tranholm-Mikkelsen, 1991).

One of the difficulties of a functional approach is that breaking organizational responsibility into particular functional areas ignores the need to integrate different policy domains in an overall strategy. It fosters a technocratic approach to decision making which can lead to social closure and poor, even pathological policy outcomes.

In a discussion of public participation in policy making DeSario and Langton (1987: 5) defined technocracy as 'the application of technical knowledge, expertise, techniques and methods to problem solving'. Taken to an extreme, technocracy can characterize a system of governance when *major* decisions are taken and implemented by officials employed because of their expertise in a particular subject. It is rule by the technically competent. Experts rule 'by virtue of their specialized knowledge and position in dominant political and economic institutions' (Fischer, 1990: 17).

While technocratic forms of governance and the institutionalizing of relations [have] facilitated cooperation between states and offset inequalities of power to some degree, rampant technocracy enforces social closure and increases the incidence of pathological behavior by international institutions. Rising levels of global technocracy increase incidents of what Weberian sociologists call 'social closure'. Social closure 'refers to the process of subordination whereby one group monopolizes advantages by closing off opportunities to another group of outsiders beneath it which it defines as inferior and ineligible' (Murphy, 1988: 8). Technocrats exclude non-technocrats and technocrats in other policy areas from policy formulation and implementation. In the context of international organizations exclusion can take place by: hoarding information; refusing to engage in discussion with those lacking the appropriate credentials; denying access to agenda-setting sessions; and insulating decision-making arenas from public pressure.

The functionalist Mitrany did not anticipate that his approach would lead to such closure. On the contrary, he saw functionalism as opening up the political process because it replaced the dysfunctional politics of state interests with a more open system of states, international organizations and concerned public interests. There were two errors in this approach. The first was to assume that the technocrats at the functional institutions would seriously engage with all the groups concerned with a particular issue area. Rather than a healthy dialogue, technocrats can dismiss the views of others as uninformed. The second was an assumption that concerned groups would have equal access to the process. Civil society contains groups with vastly different possibilities of engaging with technocrats. Some are excluded because of lack of resources, unrecognized sources of knowledge, language or locational barriers. Although functionalism and technocratic governance has contributed to international public policy, [they have] also restricted participation by depoliticizing issues and moving them beyond the reach of citizens.

An additional effect of technocracy and social closure is that technocrats can increase the pathology of international organizations. Barnett and Finnemore (1999) have highlighted how bureaucratic culture can cause pathological behavior by pursuing activities that undermine their mandate and mission. They focus upon five elements: (1) pursuing rules past the boundaries of rationality; (2) universalizing prescriptions to inappropriate cases; (3) normalizing deviance; (4) insulation of bureaucrats; and (5) institutions divided by cultural disputes. Although they do not argue it in these terms, one can see that the first four dysfunctional behaviors can be traced to a lack of accountability of the bureaucratic culture to outside interests. Technocratic policy prescriptions in a particular issue area can loose [sic] touch with the public interest when they are isolated from other views. The result is that 'those who might offer practical wisdom are excluded by deficiencies of technical expertise, whereas those schooled in technical knowledge are the most improbable sources of practical wisdom' (Beiner, 1988: xi). This policy insulation is counterproductive because the exclusion of interests effected by the activity of international organizations risks undermining their legitimacy. International organizations lacking legitimacy have increased difficulty implementing their policies because of resistance from their members or the public in key states.

[...]

While functionalist and technocratic approaches to international organizations create issues that need to be addressed, an additional problem for most social policy advocates is that the rule-enforcing and supervisory international organizations became married to neoclassical economic principles in the early 1980s. This was part of a general 'triumph of neoclassical economics' (Biersteker, 1992) that took place in a wide range of developed and developing countries, as well as at the MEOs. Structural adjustment programs concentrated on reducing the size of the state, reorienting the economy to export-led growth and increasing the role of the private sector (and NGOs) in providing social services. Social policy suffered because it was seen as expendable in the rush to make economies more competitive. In the case of the WTO, a dispute settlement mechanism was created to ensure that domestic policies would be trade friendly. Fears were raised about the effects on social policy because the WTO acts as a protector of corporate rights in disputes with governments. In the health area the concern was that the WTO would force a higher standard of proof on states restricting private enterprise in the cause of public health and that the protection offered to drug companies for their intellectual property rights would place essential drugs beyond the reach of poor countries and citizens (Koivusalo and Ollila, 1997: 85–6, 174–5).

[...] Kapstein and Milanovic (2001: 197) suggested that the liberal economic policy advanced in the Washington Consensus through MEOs was not intentionally hostile to social policy. Social policy was simply not one of the areas seen as being crucial to economic reform. The view from activists in developing countries leaves some doubt about the intentionality question (Danaher, 1994, 2001), but one can say that the marriage of functionalism and neoclassical economics led to an undermining of social policy, whether intentional or not. Neoclassical economics advances market-based solutions to development issues and the insulation of MEOs from other actors and organizations in the international system permitted the neglect of social policy when designing programs or creating rules. The fact that neoclassical economics became embedded in the rule-supervisory organizations while alternative approaches retreated to advisory organizations further marginalized social policy.

Possible institutional remedies

There are two methods by which MEO neoclassical functionalism can be mitigated. Both methods entail the tempering of neoclassical liberal principles and technocratic practices by exposing the organizations to other influences. Each initiative, however, also brings its own set of problems. The first method is to open up the organizations to greater participation from outside groups. The second is to create or expand mechanisms that would encourage policy integration across international organizations.

One option is for international organizations to involve non-state or civil society actors in policy design, implementation and decision making. This can include consultations with advocacy groups, research institutes and other civic associations. Non-state actors can advance social concerns that may not be championed within the institutions. They can also bring new sources of information and knowledge to the attention of technocrats designing programs or drafting policy changes. Many civil society groups have been campaigning at the IMF, World Bank and WTO for such inclusion (O'Brien et al., 2000). The response from these and other international organizations in terms of institutional access varies greatly (ICTSD, 1999; Stiles, 1998). This process creates a number of problems.

One problem is a trend in which the more powerful an institution is the less likely it is to welcome civil society participation. The less 'social' a mandate an institution has, the less it is inclined to provide for civil society participation. The closer an institution gets to central economic functions – exchange of goods, services and money – the less likely it is to let non-technocrats have input into policy development or implementation. One can visualize a participation pyramid structure with the IMF and WTO sitting at the top and a series of other international organizations filling up the base. The powerful institutions guide general economic policy with little public input while the institutions responsible for social matters are more open to public participation, but must labor in the shadow of their technocratic superiors.

A second problem arises from fears about the nature of the groups participating and their potential to undermine the representative functions of national governments. Some have argued that civil society actors themselves must be subjected to standards of accountability and good governance in their dealings with international organizations (Woods, 1999: 45). For example, some NGOs are more accountable to their donors than the people they claim to aid. Another worry is that civil society groups from northern states may be overrepresented in their dealings with institutions because of resource, locational, expertise and ideological advantages (O'Brien et al., 2000: 224–5). In the case of the WTO, many developing states support technocratic governance and oppose the integration of other policy issues because they fear protectionism from developed states.

A third issue is that some institutions were not designed to be anything other than technocratic bodies. Opening them up to public input may violate their mandates or frustrate the policies they are designed to promote. Specialization has its advantages and asking an institution to deal with a wide series of policy issues may overwhelm the institution and make it ineffective. Rather than opening all institutions up to all issues, it might be possible to think about selective ways in which policies can be integrated across institutions.

This leads to a second strategy, which is to develop mechanisms for integrating policies across institutions. This solution implies that the problem is not the institutions themselves, but that their policy agendas are not tempered by other institutional agendas. In national politics rival policy agendas are resolved and integrated through cabinet meetings of the executive. No such integration takes place at the international level. The nature of international integrative mechanisms could range from increased institutional contact to an overreaching coordinating body.

The institutions discussed in this study have increased their interactions and exchange with each other and outside institutions. An interesting example is the joint role that the Fund and the Bank are playing in assisting countries in developing Poverty Reduction Strategy Papers (PRSPs). These papers are designed to ensure that 'social and sectoral programs aimed at poverty reduction will be taken fully into account in the design of economic policies for promoting faster sustainable growth' (IMF, 1999). The papers must be approved by both the Bank's and the Fund's Boards; indicating that some technocratic interchange is taking place.

However, it is unclear whether increased contact results in any policy changes or the diluting of technocratic governance. In many cases coordination is conceptualized as coordination between the three key MEOs. For example, in an IMF speech to UNCTAD, the Fund's former managing director discussed multilateral cooperation against poverty almost solely in terms of IMF/World Bank/WTO cooperation (Camdessus, 2000). Similarly, academic discussion of building better institutional relationships often focuses on the IMF/Bank/WTO relationship (Sampson, 1999; Vines, 1999). While the Bank might be able to highlight some social policy issues for the Fund, it is less clear that the three dominant economic institutions internalize the knowledge of other organizations.

Following the reassessment of organizational roles in the wake of the [1997] Asian financial crisis the IMF, World Bank and WTO officials may be more aware of policies at other institutions, but this does not mean that they adjust their own policies in light of other institutions' goals. The structural imbalance remains even if officials meet on a regular basis. The relations between the liberalization trinity and other institutions are probably reflected in the relationship between the WTO and the ILO. In response to the debate about labor standards, the 1996 WTO Ministerial Declaration declared the devotion of trade ministers to core labor standards and existing WTO–ILO cooperation. At the time very few people had any idea what that cooperation entailed. This section of the declaration had more to do with keeping labor issues out of the WTO and keeping the ILO at a safe distance.

An advance upon increased contact would be some form of integrative body that brought policy making from the different organizations together in a single arena. The Commission on Global Governance revived the idea of an Economic Security Council (ESC). The ESC would be modeled on the UN Security Council and would be tasked with 'assessing the overall state of the world economy and the interaction between major policy areas' (CGG, 1999: 156). Although there are many controversial details about such a proposal, the significant element is that it proposes a body that would coordinate policies between international organizations. The process of coordination would force a dilution of technocratic governance as varying agendas, proposals and strategies emerged for debate within the coordination process. This would force a re-politicization of the decision-making process as choices between contending values and priorities would be a matter for debate rather than simply implemented according to a technocratic consensus.

The importance of state interests

[...]

Efforts to address the problems of organizational politics outlined above must acknowledge that MEOs are interstate organizations and that they respond to the demands and interests of some states more than others. The Group of 7 industrialized states and the USA, in particular, have disproportional voice in the operation of MEOs. In some cases this influence can be seen in the formal organizational structures of the institutions. For example, the IMF and the Bank both operate with a system of voting that is roughly proportional to states' financial contributions. The USA and the G-7 are the largest contributors and exercise the most influence. This formal influence is bolstered by the power that key states are able to exercise outside of the organizations. The USA was able to press the IMF into supporting its 1994 bailout of Mexico without consulting the Europeans and it was able to derail the Japanese plan for an Asian Monetary Fund. At the WTO decisions are taken by consensus, but the USA is able to use its market power to prod reluctant states in its direction. US trade negotiators bolster their arguments within the WTO by threatening states with bilateral sanctions through US trade law.

Within the industrialized world, the USA is known for having one of the most liberal and market-based forms of social policy (Esping-Andersen, 1990). It also contains many of the largest financial interests, which exercise immense influence on US foreign economic policy. Although the fate of MEOs provokes debate within the USA, it would be unrealistic to expect the country with such a limited welfare state to make social policy a concern at the IMF or WTO. If some of the reforms suggested above are to take place, states other than the USA must actively challenge the leading power's policy privileges. [...]

MEOs do impose constraints on national policy, especially upon weaker states. However, all states have some degree of manoeuvrability if their domestic policy priorities differ from those of the MEOs. Furthermore, MEOs evolve and concerted action to influence state policy can bring results. It is possible to envisage a coalition of states creating more space for social policy under the MEO umbrella.

The contest of social forces

Outside MEOs and states, the struggle for change is played out as a contest between social forces. On one side are actors seeking to construct a global economy that grants legal protection to investors and corporations while restricting the rights of governments and citizens (Gill, 2000; Sklair, 1997). For example, one can trace the connections between the interests of Wall Street financial firms, the US Treasury and the provisions of South Korea's IMF package (Blustein, 2001: 145). One can also see the connection between the companies such as CBS, General Motors, Pfizer, and the WTO's defense of intellectual property rights (Sell, 1999). On the other side is an even more diverse range of actors seeking to restrain corporate freedom and build social protection (O'Brien et al., 2000). These social forces engage in combat on two plains – that of ideas and action.

In the terrain of ideas, Stone (2001) has pointed out the significance of think tanks in moving the social policy agenda while Weiss and Carayannis (2001) have suggested that the UN system itself is a source of ideas about how the world should be ordered. Perhaps the most significant development to counter the neoclassical economic neglect of social policy is the idea that redistributive social policy and social cohesion foster economic growth (Dayton-Johnson, 2001). This is an attempt to insert social policy concerns into the dominant discourse of economic growth and economic liberalization.

[...]

As important as the intellectual debate is to social change, the best ideas need powerful allies if they are to have an impact upon public policy. Even before the media-attracting spectacle of the WTO protests in Seattle some analysts were drawing attention to the fact that a wide spectrum of civic associations were challenging the governing principles of the IMF, Bank and WTO (O'Brien et al., 2000). In the face of what seemed to be state impotence, social movements were acting as the unofficial opposition to MEO socially destructive policies. Civic associations already engaged in lobbying the institutions were joined by others that took a more oppositional stance. Combining traditional social movement protest strategies with internet activism, the role of MEOs has been thrust onto the political agenda in many states.

Protest and lobbying on global social issues has become institutionalized with the creation of the World Social Forum (WSF) (http://www. forumsocialmundial.org.br). Timed to coincide with the World Economic Forum, the WSF brings together social activists to network and plan strategy in the long struggle of building and protecting social rights. The WSF builds a global public space that allows the forces for social change to organize and learn from each other's struggles. While the WSF has its own contradictions and problems, it is the latest sign that the self-defense of society in the face of destructive liberal policies that Polanyi (1957) theorized on a national scale is also taking place on a global stage.

[...]

The combination of valorizing broad-based social policy in the intellectual debate and direct action against MEOs and governments provides some incentive for state action and incremental MEO reform.

Conclusion

A globalizing economy offers rewards and risks for governments and citizens. Pauly (1997) has argued that institutions such as the IMF potentially provide mechanisms to regulate the global economy so that stability is nurtured and citizens can hold governments accountable. They bridge the desire to reap the benefits of foreign capital and markets with the need to exercise political control over unstable economic structures. The influence of MEOs is significant in some circumstances (especially in their relationships with weaker states), but their authority is limited by the nearly universal desire to retain as much national policy autonomy as possible.

The IMF, the World Bank and the WTO are likely to continue functioning as significant regulatory organizations in the global economy. Despite widespread opposition to some of their policies, their future is secure unless the major powers decide they are no longer of use or there is a systemic economic crisis. For social policy advocates, the challenge is to engage the organizations so that their activity is social policy neutral if not redistributive social policy friendly. MEOs need to [be] sensitized to the reality that the liberal market-based approach to social policy is only one of several efficient policy responses. This requires work on a number of levels to mitigate the effect of MEOs on national social policies and to improve social rights on a global scale.

[...]

References

Ashworth, L. M. and Long, D. (eds) (1999) *New Perspectives on International Functionalism.* Basingstoke: Macmillan.

Barnett, M. N. and Finnemore, M. (1999) 'The Politics, Power and Pathologies of International Organizations', *International Organization* 53(4): 699–732.

Beiner, R. (1988) 'Introduction', in R. B. Day, R. Beiner and J. Masciulli (eds) *Democratic Theory and Technological Society* (pp. ix–xii). London: M. E. Sharpe.

Biersteker, T. J. (1992) 'The Triumph of Neoclassical Economics in the Developing World', in J. N. Rosenau and E. Czempiel (eds) *Governance Without Government: Order and Change in World Politics* (pp. 102–31). Cambridge, UK: Cambridge University Press.

Blustein, P. (2001) *The Chastening: Inside the Crisis that Rocked the Global Financial System and Humbled the IMF.* New York: Public Affairs.

Boli, J. and Thomas, G.M. (eds) (1999) *Constructing World Culture: International Nongovernmental Organizations since 1875,* Stanford, CA: Stanford University Press.

Bond, P. (2001) 'Defunding the Fund, Running on the Bank', in K. Danaher (ed.) *Democratizing the Global Economy: The Battle Against the World Bank and the IMF* (pp. 163–76). Philadelphia, PA: Common Courage Press.

Camdessus, M. (2000) 'Development and Poverty Reduction: A Multilateral Approach', address by Managing Director of the International Monetary Fund to the Tenth United Nations Conference on Trade and Development Bangkok, Thailand, 13 February.

CGG (Commission on Global Governance) (1999) *Our Global Neighbourhood: The Report of the Commission on Global Governance.* Oxford: Oxford University Press.

Cox, R. W. and Jacobson, H. K. (eds) (1974) *The Anatomy of Influence: Decision Making in International Organization.* New Haven, CT: Yale University Press.

Cox, R. W. with Sinclair, T. J. (1996) *Approaches to World Order.* Cambridge, UK: Cambridge University Press.

Croome, J. (1995) *Reshaping the World Trading System.* Geneva: World Trade Organization.

Danaher, K. (ed.) (1994) *50 Years is Enough: The Case Against the World Bank and the International Monetary Fund.* Boston, MA: South End Press.

Danaher, K. (ed.) (2001) *Democratizing the Global Economy: The Battle Against the World Bank and the IMF.* Philadelphia, PA: Common Courage Press.

Dayton-Johnson, J. (2001) *Social Cohesion & Economic Prosperity*. Toronto: James Lorimer.

Deacon, B. (2001) 'Editorial', *Global Social Policy* 1(1): 5–6.

Deacon, B. with Hulse, M. and Stubbs, P. (1997) *Global Social Policy: International Organizations and the Future of Welfare*. London: Sage.

Denters, E. (1996) *Law and Policy of IMF Conditionality*. Dordrecht: Kluwer.

DeSario, J. and Langton, S. (1987) 'Citizen Participation and Technocracy', in J. DeSario and S. Langton (eds) *Citizen Participation in Public Decision Making* (pp. 3–18). New York: Greenwood Press.

Esping-Andersen, G. (1990) *The Three Worlds of Welfare Capitalism*. Cambridge, UK: Polity Press.

Fischer, F. (1990) *Technocracy and the Politics of Expertise*. Newbury Park, CA: Sage.

Gilbert, C. L., Hopkins, R., Powell, A. and Roy, A. (1996) 'The World Bank: Its Functions and Its Future', *Working Paper No. 15* (July), Global Economic Institutions.

Gill, S. (2000) 'The Constitution of Global Capitalism', paper presented to the International Studies Association Conferences, Los Angeles, 14 March.

Haas, E. B. (1964) *Beyond the Nation-State: Functionalism and International Organization*. Stanford, CA: Stanford University Press.

Helleiner, E. (1994) *States and the Reemergence of Global Finance: From Bretton Woods to the 1990s*. Ithaca, NY: Cornell University Press.

ICTSD (1999) *Accreditation Schemes and Other Arrangements for Public Participation in International Fora*. Geneva: International Centre for Trade and Sustainable Development.

IMF (1999) 'Communiqué of the Interim Committee of the Board of Governors of the International Monetary Fund', 26 September.

James, H. (1996) *International Monetary Cooperation since Bretton Woods*, New York: IMF/Oxford University Press.

Kapstein, E. B. and Milanovic, B. (2001) 'Responding to Globalization: Social Policy in Emerging Markets', *Global Social Policy* 1(2): 191–212.

Koivusalo, M. and Ollila, E. (1997) *Making a Healthy World: Agencies, Actors and Policies in International Health*. London: Zed Books.

Mishra, R. (1999) *Globalization and the Welfare State*. Cheltenham: Edward Elgar.

Mitrany, D. (1964) *A Working Peace System*. Chicago, IL: Quadrangle Books.

Murphy, C. N. (1994) *International Organization and Industrial Change: Global Governance since 1850*. Cambridge, UK: Polity Press.

Murphy, R. (1988) *Social Closure: The Theory of Monopolization and Exclusion*. Oxford: Clarendon Press.

O'Brien, R., Goetz, A.M., Scholte, J.A. and Williams, M. (2000) *Contesting Global Governance: Multilateral Economic Institutions and Global Social Movements*, Cambridge, UK: Cambridge University Press.

Pauly, L. W. (1997) *Who Elected the Bankers? Surveillance and Control in the World Economy*. Ithaca, NY: Cornell University Press.

Polanyi, K. (1957) *The Great Transformation.* Boston, MA: Beacon Hill.

Prugl, Elisabeth (1999) *The Global Construction of Gender: Home-Based Work in the Political Economy of the 20th Century.* New York: Columbia University Press.

Sampson, G. (1999). 'Greater Coherence in Economic Policy Making: A WTO Perspective', in A. O. Krueger (ed.) *The WTO as an International Organization* (pp. 257–70). Chicago, IL: University of Chicago Press.

Sell, S. (1999) 'Multinational Corporations as Agents of Change: The Globalization of Intellectual Property Rights', in C. A. Cutler, V. Haufler and T. Porter (eds) *Private Authority and International Affairs* (pp. 169–97). Albany, NY: State University of New York Press.

Shultz, G. P., Simon, W. E. and Wriston, W. B. (1999) 'Who Needs the IMF?', in L. J. McQuillan and P. C. Montgomery (eds) *The International Monetary Fund: Financial Medic to the World?* (pp. 197–200). Stanford, CA: Hoover Institution Press.

Sklair, L. (1997) 'Transnational Social Movements for Capitalism', *Review of International Political Economy* 4(4): 514–38.

Stiles, K. W. (1998) 'Civil Society Empowerment and Multilateral Donors: International Institutions and New International Norms', *Global Governance* 4(2): 199–216.

Stone, D. (2001) 'Think Tanks, Global Lesson-Drawing and Networking Social Policy', *Global Social Policy* 1(3): 338–60.

Tranholm-Mikkelsen, J. (1991) 'Neo-Functionalism: Obstinate or Obsolete? A Reappraisal in the Light of the New Dynamism of the EC', *Millennium* 20(1): 1–22.

Vines, D. (1999) 'The WTO in Relation to the Fund and the Bank: Competencies, Agendas, and Linkages', in A. O. Krueger (ed.) *The WTO as an International Organization* (pp. 59–82). Chicago, IL: University of Chicago Press.

Vosko, L. (2002) 'Labour and Hegemony in a Different Register? The Shifting Role of the ILO and the Struggle for Global Social Justice', *Global Social Policy* 2(1): 19–46.

Weiss, T. G. and Carayannis, T. (2001) 'Wither United Nations Economic and Social Idea? A Research Agenda', *Global Social Policy* 1(1): 25–47.

Williams, M. (1994) *International Economic Organizations and the Third World.* New York: Harvester Wheatsheaf.

Woods, N. (1999) 'Good Governance in International Organizations', *Global Governance* 5(1): 39–61.

Chapter 3.2

International class conflict and social policy

Kevin Farnsworth

Introduction

Capital and labour are today better organised and have stronger voices at the international level than ever before. The increased role and responsibility of global and regional decision-making bodies has meant that lobbying solely at the national level risks unfavourable policy outcomes being introduced internationally. As a result, there has been an explosion in the number of international business, trade union, NGO and private consultancy organisations, and this has provided greater opportunities for the development of international coalitions and unity amongst various organisations (Balanya et al., 2000: 3; Coen, 1998: 78; Sklair, 2001; O'Brien et al., 2000). Certain capital and labour organisations have also become more institutionally embedded within IGO decision-making structures. This brief paper presents an analysis of power in the global economy before investigating the social policy preferences of key international capital and labour organisations, taking a lead from Therborn's (1984) important but underutilised work on class mobilisation and welfare states. It then briefly examines the social policies of key international governmental organisations, arguing that the apparent move towards a more socially responsible globalisation in recent years in fact represents a move closer to the position of international capital.

The relative power of capital and labour within the international sphere

Although capital and labour are both capable of wielding power within national and international policy arenas, their actual influence depends a great deal on the prevailing political and economic conditions. Because it has transformed these conditions, globalisation has had a major impact on power relations between the classes and key governing interests, although it is capital rather than labour that has benefited most from this for several reasons. First, capital is able to exercise structural power where labour cannot. Although at the international level structural power is less salient than at the national level, largely because in this instance the threat of exit disappears, structural power is nonetheless reinforced and exercised *through* international governmental organisations. One of the key ways this occurs is through the promotion of a global neoliberal hegemony, which is pushing international governmental organisations (IGOs) and nation states towards unregulated and flexible labour markets and de-regulated and open industrial and financial markets, all in the name of greater competitiveness (Cerny, 1997: 259; Martin and Schumann, 1997: 7; Gill and Law, 1989; Crouch and Streeck, 1997; see also Cox, 1977 for a discussion of the adoption and promotion of capitalist hegemony by the ILO). This neoliberal hegemony has, according to many, become firmly embedded within all the major IGOs, including the European Union (Gill and Law, 1988: Ch. 16; Held, 1991: 220–222; Strange, 1988: 112–114, 1996; Van Apeldoorn, 2000; Balanya et al., 2000; Mishra, 1999).

Second, although the opportunities to engage in policy processes at the international level have increased for both interests, capital has been far more successful in organising and exploiting new openings beyond nation states. International capital has, for instance, been able to present a relatively united front across borders and form linkages with important non-economic elites within IGOs (Sklair, 2001). This has been made easier because capital's needs, in contrast to labour's, are relatively straightforward to define, defend and unite behind according to Miliband (1969: 139–148) and Coates (1984: 59). The interests of international labour, however, are often mired in conservatism and competing national interests. Labour's multitudinal needs and wants, together with its structural dependence on capital, makes it difficult for international labour to find common ground on which to unite, especially beyond North and South divisions (Traxler, 1993: 675). Labour also lacks the financial advantages of capital, which are even more important in facilitating unity at the international level than the national level (Gallin, 2002). All of this is a problem for labour, since its power lies in its human capital and organisational capacity, especially its success in generating numerical support (Korpi, 1983).

Third, the absence of institutionalised voting rights at the international level, or in the European case the weakness of democratic institutions, rules out legal rights to institutional participation in most cases (although some institutions do have a statutory duty to consult with major interests) and effectively means that access to decision makers is highly dependent on informal networks, the ability of different groups to amass political favours and the willingness of institutions to consult with external bodies. All this has an impact on relative power, and, in most cases, the net effect is to privilege capital above labour (O'Brien et al., 2000; Van Apeldoorn, 2000). Moreover, IGOs have gone out of their way to incorporate business interests within various committees and decision-making bodies, where labour has not been afforded the same advantages (Stiglitz, 1998, 2002; Korten, 1997; Tesner, 2000). This has been motivated by a desire to learn from business how states might develop attractive investment environments, and to obtain the backing of powerful business interests for international projects that might then be easier to 'sell' to governments. This relationship is further enhanced through transnational elite gatherings, including the World Economic Forum which brings together senior business people from the largest global corporations as well as senior politicians and the heads of the major IGOs.

Fourth, neo-Marxists (Offe and Wiesenthal, 1980) and elite pluralists, such as Lindblom (1977), have pointed out that labour occupies a greater dependency on capital than the other way around, and the political repercussions from this extend to the international level (Traxler, 1993). International labour must effectively steer a course between, on the one hand, countering capital and defending workers, and on the other, ensuring that capital continues to thrive, since the interests of its own members are synonymous with the continued profitability and accumulation of firms (Vosko, 2002). Whilst increased international capital investment is necessary to anti-poverty strategies, labour constantly has to struggle against the inevitable outcome of this in the form of low wages, poor working conditions and even environmental destruction, but whenever labour recommends tighter controls and regulations on capital, it is accused of standing in the way of economic and social development (Offe and Wiesenthal, 1980). Moreover, as international labour has broadened its scope to cover a whole range of individuals that traditionally were not well represented, including women, non-waged labour and workers in developing countries (Vosko, 2002: 29), this has made global solidarity harder still. Capital, in contrast, can defend its interests on the grounds that profitability and growth are essential to future economic and social development (Block, 1990; Lindblom, 1977), and can be safe in the knowledge that the international hegemony favours its position.

International class preferences and social policy

This next section investigates class preferences at the international level, represented primarily by the business and industry advisory committee (BIAC) and the trade union advisory committee (TUAC) to the OECD. Focusing on these two organisations is especially valuable, since their remit is to consult with and represent their key constituencies (consisting of national and international business and trade union interests) and because both are consulted regularly by the OECD in the formulation of its labour and social policies. Most pertinently, both were invited, as representatives of capital and labour, to submit contributions to two important OECD ministerial level meetings on social policy in 1981 and 1998. Together, these inputs provide an opportunity to examine the class positions of capital and labour on social policy. However, because it limits its focus in this way, this approach does neglect many forms of agitation, class struggle and fields of negotiation.

The social policy preferences of international capital

The bottom line for international capital is that state social provision is justified only if it contributes directly to economic growth or at least does not undermine it, and is affordable only if it exists in an environment populated by profitable and successful firms. International capital has therefore urged governments to address impediments to job creation, which are argued to include generous social provision, inefficient welfare services, and high levels of state spending. The basic position is captured well in the following statement submitted to the OECD by the BIAC in 1981:

> social policy must be shaped in such a way that it is compatible with the long-term possibilities of the economy. High social benefits can only be financed by a corresponding high level of economic performance ... [I]ncreased expenditure for additional social benefits is only possible within the limits of real economic growth. (BIAC, 1981: 84)

International capital has accordingly lobbied hard against those forms of provision that are perceived to undermine economic growth and has embarked on a strategy to steer social policy towards more productive provision. Outside of education and training its priority has been to place pressure on governments to reduce expenditure and taxation (especially on corporations) and to utilise social provision to reduce disincentives to work, halt the propensity towards early retirement and increase the productivity of firms.

On the question of service delivery, capital has pushed for greater private sector integration into service delivery; indeed, BIAC, amongst other representatives of business, has engaged in concerted efforts to liberalise the international trade in services, since this represents tremendous opportunities for future private sector expansion (BIAC, 1996). The general perception of capital is that state services tend to be inefficient and costly (BIAC, 1981: 86). Therefore, although the state's role in the regulation and funding of education and training services is defended by business, capital advocates a far greater role for the private sector in education, especially in tertiary education. For international business, states must do more to address the direct skills needs of employers and increase the flexibility and adaptability of labour (BIAC, 2002), whilst removing the financial burden faced by firms who have to make up for poor schooling (BIAC, 1998a).

As for social protection, capital has pushed for benefit reforms that increase, for it, employability, affordability and personal responsibility. For capital, high social security costs and accompanying administrative burdens undermine profitability and discourage firms from employing new workers (BIAC, 1998b), although temporary benefits are defended as key to smoothing out employment markets as is made clear in the following statement from BIAC:

> there will always be people who experience difficulties in adjusting to change despite their personal willingness to adapt. These individuals . . . deserve targeted programmes to facilitate re-integration to the labour market. While the precise measures may vary . . . such programmes might include temporary income support combined with re-training and re-location assistance. (BIAC, 1997: 5)

Noteworthy here is the fact that capital has not, on the whole, tried to push for the abolition of social security and pensions, but has instead argued for the imposition of conditional qualifying requirements to social protection that provides 'what is necessary' rather than 'what is desirable' for the poor (BIAC, 1981) and in a time-limited and work-focused way. It has also argued for the creation of sufficiently wide gaps between benefits and the lowest pay rates (BIAC, 1981: 87) in order to maintain work incentives. Such basic principles are important, according to BIAC, if social protection systems are to remain viable (BIAC, 1998b).

On the question of funding, capital has pushed for welfare systems that are financed primarily through taxation on workers, with redistribution occurring across lifetimes rather than between rich and poor. In the case of pensions, capital has advocated greater private provision and argued for more flexibility in the age of retirement (BIAC, 1998b), but has defended basic compulsory state pensions as an important source of income for the poorest pensioners, supplemented by second tier occupational and private pensions and third tier individual tax-exempt savings (ibid.). Whether in pensions or other forms of social protection, the key for business is that employers should be able to shed surplus labour with relative ease, but retain workers as economic conditions dictate.

All this suggests a relatively clear and coherent message on social policy, including over time. There is little discernible movement in the basic questions towards welfare provision over time, although the position of capital has grown in confidence. Indeed, by the end of the 1990s, capital appears to feel that it had won the major arguments concerning welfare reform, suggesting to government ministers in 1998 that:

> When commentators look back on the history of the twentieth century, the major trend that will stand out will be that of the engagement of the state in the economy in the first half of [the] century and its withdrawal towards the end of the second half – a development that has happened in an evolutionary manner where the private sector has been allowed to explore and experiment, and in a revolutionary manner where it was suppressed. (BIAC, 1998a: 13)

This hardly suggests wholehearted support for state welfare systems on the part of capital, yet neither does the above summary of its position suggest the type of rampant anti-welfare stance that business is often credited with. It is probably more accurate to describe capital's approach to social policy as pragmatic, informed more by self-preservation, practical politics and the simple reality that state provision is essential to future profitability, than by a tight ideological framework. Overall, capital favours those forms of social provision that reduce the relative costs of labour whilst increasing its availability, flexibility and skills set. It has opposed most forcefully those forms of social provision that reduce the availability of labour or force up labour costs. In this respect, capital has acted to exploit its structural advantage through agency by pushing most strongly the message that social policy should be steered towards the needs of business, since only a competitive economy is able to sustain social provision.

The social policy preferences of international labour

The key strategy of international labour as far as social policy is concerned has been to try to safeguard social provision from the international drive towards capital-centred priorities. For TUAC, it is as important to integrate social objectives within economic policies as it is for social policy to take account of economic policy objectives (TUAC, 1981) and, although labour accepts that economic growth is important to the future sustainability of social policy, the prioritising of economic over social goals leads to greater problems, such as deprivation and social disharmony, which undermine competitiveness.

> Uncontrolled economic growth, considered by some as the panacea to solve all our problems and reach all goals, has been accompanied by pollution, new health and safety risks, ever-increasing monotony of work, and an increasingly complex and elusive decision-making process in the industries and in society ... Growth has never solved social problems alone. Even selective growth does not eliminate

tensions between social and economic aims. (TUAC, 1981: 90–91)

Moreover, labour views many of the problems associated with social provision as stemming from failures in economic policy to accommodate social objectives, such as full employment, which has consistently been held up as the central priority for labour.

The ascendance of economic priorities since the 1970s has, according to labour, led to growing levels of inequality, insecurity and fear of unemployment, and risks undermining the foundations of market societies (TUAC, 1998).

On the question of provision, labour has, in the past, defended vehemently state services as crucial to the advancement of equity within market economies and accordingly fought hard against the privatisation agenda. It is therefore interesting and important to note that the position of TUAC appears to have shifted slightly between the early 1980s and the late 1990s so that it now accepts that there might be some scope for the expansion of private markets (TUAC, 1998):

> Trade unions are aware that social responsibility of the state does not necessarily mean state provision. Trade unions also agree with proposals in favour of an enabling state. But they strongly oppose approaches to social policy which are guided by ideological or self serving thinking that 'private is better'.

However, on the question of gearing social provision towards the needs of business, labour is more firmly opposed:

> Despite the need to change the role of the state in the field of social policy, markets alone cannot and should not play the major agenda setting role in the provision of social services . . . Market outcomes are strongly influenced by existing inequalities of economic and political power. (TUAC, 1998)

Labour is especially adamant of this in the case of educational services, where it is feared that short-termism might steer services away from the longer-term interests of both employees and employers.

As for the question of the sustainability of welfare, including social security policy and pensions, such questions only arise, according to labour, because of the failure of economic policy and of national governance. The real problem, for labour, is that persistently high levels of unemployment, which governments have come to tolerate, undermine the affordability and operation of welfare services (TUAC, 1981). Hence, for labour, tackling unemployment remains a top priority, alongside related issues, such as eradicating poverty and social exclusion. Labour takes a similar line in response to international concerns about the sustainability of pensions. For it, full employment will increase the affordability of pensions by increasing contributions into state schemes and help to tackle the problem of early retirement. On this note, labour has again adjusted its position slightly, shifting from a defence of fixed retirement ages to advocating more flexible retirement, although, in contrast to capital, labour argues that employees should neither be forced to retire nor to continue working when they reach notional pensionable ages (TUAC, 1998).

To summarise, the position of labour on social policy is again a relatively coherent one, although it often also appears as a defensive one. Further, labour appears to be more willing to accommodate the views of capital than has been the case the other way around; in many ways this is an inevitable outcome of the relative power and confidence of capital since the 1980s. Its message on the centrality of full employment and its defence of social policy as essential to future competitiveness do remain constants in labour's social policy strategy, however.

Class preferences and international social policy development

The question that remains is how has international social policy responded to these demands of capital and labour? Two contrasting answers to this question stand out in the social policy literature. The first, which I have already outlined above, suggests that labour interests have been sidelined within the international social policy discourse by a dominant neoliberal corporate agenda. A second, more recent approach, suggests that some IGOs have responded to criticisms from the labour movement and beyond, by adopting what Deacon (1999, 2000, 2002) has referred to as a more *socially responsible* globalisation. Evidence for this is gleaned from a number of sources. The World Bank, Deacon argues, is argued to have shifted its position so that it now focuses more on poverty alleviation, empowerment, increased economic security and environmental protection (Deacon, 2000; see also Wade, 2002). Deacon (2000) also identifies the OECD's 1999 report entitled *A Caring World* as being a watershed moment, where the organisation accepted the need for social provision within a globalising world.

Whilst Deacon's identification of this shifting social policy discourse at the international level is not in question, what is less clear is that this is as significant for social policy as Deacon suggests, or that it represents a progressive response to the demands of labour. If we focus on recent developments in those IGOs that are considered to be the most sympathetic to social policy, the OECD and the EU, and compare these with the class positions of capital and labour, international social policy discourse appears, if anything, to have actually shifted closer to the business agenda. The OECD's Jobs Study, for instance, recommended that governments: tackle inflation, increase wage and employee flexibility, eliminate 'impediments to the creation and expansion of enterprises', relax regulations on employment, increase employee skills and reform social protection systems to ensure they do not impinge on labour markets (OECD, 1994). *A Caring World*, meanwhile, argued that social protection 'can ensure that those who lose their jobs are insured against loss of all their income during the period while they search for a new job' and can 'assist displaced workers to readjust to the new labour market opportunities'. It went on to argue that 'well administered' social provision can 'reduce resistance to change and new working practices' and enhance 'the attractiveness of the country concerned as a business location' (OECD, 1999: 137). Although it concluded that 'one effect of globalisation could be to increase the demand for social protection', it went on to suggest that governments, under financial pressures, should make 'more effective use of the networks and skills of non-government organisations' including 'outsourcing some activities ... to the private and not-for-profit sector' in order to 'benefit from cost-efficiencies and competitive tendering' (ibid. 126). Finally, it argued that, because globalisation increases capital mobility, it is likely to lead to an increased burden of taxation being borne by workers, and because this will distort the labour market, this may mean that 'regardless of the need for it social protection may become more difficult to finance' (ibid: 137).

Within the European Union there has been growing emphasis on competitiveness and a more capital-centred social policy since the 1990s. The 1997 Amsterdam summit, for example, urged that 'more attention be given to improving European competitiveness as a prerequisite for growth and employment' through the development of a 'skilled and adaptable workforce responsive to economic change'. It went on to recommend 'a reduction in the overall tax burden' and 'training and lifelong learning in order to increase employability' (Balanya et al., 2000: 64–65). More recently, and more importantly, the Lisbon Agenda has, since 2000, pushed member states towards making improvements to education and training provision, cutting regulations and red tape on corporations, increasing work incentives, cutting non-wage labour costs and completing the internal market in services, with the aim of making Europe 'the most competitive and dynamic knowledge-based economy in the world' by 2010 (EC, 2003, 2004).

Such shifts in emphasis are part of a wider move towards more business-centred social policy. The social policy discourse of the OECD and EU clearly places capital rather than labour at its centre. Similar processes have also taken place within the other major IGOs (see Farnsworth, 2004 for a review). It is not clear, therefore, that the move towards a more socially responsible globalisation represents much more than a shift towards a capital-centred international social policy.

Conclusion

The above analysis suggests that labour faces an international bias towards capital, promoted by the institutional privileging of business interests within IGOs and a powerful state sponsored neoliberal agenda. On the other hand, organised capital demonstrates a less antagonistic position towards social provision, informed primarily by its own need for targeted state intervention in a range of social and economic policy areas in order to remain profitable. Capital's approach to social policy remains conservative and pragmatic however, and is in direct opposition to labour's traditional class perspective. But, whilst capital's position has remained constant, there are signs that labour has become more accommodating of business preferences over time. Similarly, there has been some movement in international discourse, away from a crude neoliberalism and towards a positive view of social policy. Whilst this is to be welcomed, this shift also has to be recognised as still further evidence of the ascendance of capital; social policy continues to be driven primarily by the needs of business rather than the needs of labour and this is only marginally preferable to crude neoliberalism. It is also as likely to take us further away from a progressive international social policy than closer towards it. Rather, what is needed at the international level is the strengthening of labour's voice in tripartite negotiations. Policy outcomes that were more of a genuine compromise between capital and labour would certainly look quite different to the current international business–centred social policy.

References

Balanya, B., Doherty, A., Hoedeman, O., Ma'anit, A. and Wesselius, E. (2000), *EuropeInc.: Regional and Global Restructuring and the Rise of Corporate Power*, London: Pluto Press.

BIAC (1981), 'A view from the entrepreneurs', presented to the Conference on Social Policies in the 1980s', OECD, Paris, October. Published as OECD, *The Welfare State in Crisis*, Paris: OECD.

BIAC (1996), *Productivity to the Rescue of Social Protection*, Paris: BIAC.

BIAC (1997), 'Addressing the social impact of globalisation: promoting the benefits of change', submission to the OECD Liaison Committee with International Non-Governmental Organisations, BIAC, Paris.

BIAC (1998a), 'Views on lifelong learning' (based on comments made by members of the BIAC Expert Group on Education at the OECD Seminar on Lifelong Learning), 18 November 1998, BIAC, Paris.

BIAC (1998b), 'Statement to the meeting of the Employment, Labour and Social Affairs Committee at Ministerial Level on Social Policy', 23–24 June, BIAC, Paris.

BIAC (2002), *Employment and Learning Challenges for the 21ˢᵗ Century*, Paris: BIAC.

Block, F. (1990), 'Political choice and the multiple "logics" of capital', in S. Zukin and P. DiMaggio (Eds.), *Structures of Capital: The Social Organisations of the Economy*, Cambridge University Press: Cambridge.

Cerny, P. (1997), 'Paradoxes of the competition state: the dynamics of political globalization', *Government and Opposition*, 32, 251–274.

Coates, D.(1984), *The Context of British Politics*, London: Hutchinson.

Coen, D.(1998), 'The evolution of the large firm as a political actor in the European Union', *Journal of European Public Policy*, 18, 75–100.

Cox, R.W. (1977), 'Labor and Hegemony' *International Organization* 31(3), 385–424.

Crouch, C. and Streeck, W. (1997), *Political Economy of Modern Capitalism: Mapping Convergence and Diversity*, London: Sage.

Deacon, B. (1999), 'Towards a Socially Responsible Globalisation: International Actors and Discourses', GASPP Occasional Papers. No. 1, STAKES, Helsinki.

Deacon, B. (2000), 'Socially responsible globalization: the challenge for social security', Paper presented to the International Social Security Association (ISSA).

Deacon, B. (2002), 'Prospects for equitable social provision in a globalising world', Paper presented to the 5th Annual Conference of the Centre for the Study of Globalisation and Regionalisation, 15–17 March, University of Warwick.

EC (2003), 'Jobs, jobs, jobs: creating more employment in Europe', Report of the Employment Taskforce, European Commission, Brussels.

EC (2004), *Facing the Challenge: The Lisbon Strategy for Growth and Employment*, Brussels: European Commission.

Farnsworth, K.(2004), *Corporate Power and Social Policy in Global Economy: British Welfare under the Influence*, Bristol: The Policy Press.

Gallin, D. (2002), 'Labour as a global social force: past divisions and new tasks', in J. Harrod and R. O'Brien (Eds.), *Global Unions?: Theory and Strategies of Organised Labour in the Global Political Economy*, London: Routledge.

Gill, S.R. and Law, D. (1989), 'Global hegemony and the structural power of capital', *International Studies Quarterly*, 33, 475–499.

Gill, S. and Law, D. (1988), *The Global Political Economy: Perspectives, problems, and Policies*, London: Harvester Wheatsheaf.

Held, D. (1991), *Democracy, the Nation-State and the Global System*, Cambridge: Polity Press.

Korpi, W.(1983), *The Democratic Class Struggle*, London: Routledge.

Korten, D. (1997), 'The United Nations and the Corporate Agenda' *Global Policy* www.globalpolicy.org/ reform/korten.htm – accessed April 2003.

Lindblom, C. E.(1977), *Politics and Markets*, New York: Basic Books.

Martin, H.P. and Schumann, H.(1997), *The Global Trap: Globalization and the Assault on Democracy and Prosperity*, London: Zed.

Miliband, R. (1969), *The State in Capitalist Society*, London: Quartet Books.

Mishra, R. (1999), *Globalization and the Welfare State*, Cheltenham: Edward Elgar.

O'Brien, R., Goetz, A.M., Scholte, J.A. and Williams, M. (2000), *Contesting Global Governance: Multilateral Economic Institutions and Global Social Movements*, Cambridge: Cambridge University Press.

OECD (1994), *Jobs Study: Facts, Analysis, Strategies*, Paris: OECD.

OECD (1999), *A Caring World: A New Social Policy Agenda*, Paris: OECD.

Offe, C. and Wiesenthal, H. (1980) 'Two logics of collective action: theoretical notes on social class and organisational form', in M. Zeitlin (Ed) *Political Power and Social Theory*, Greenwich CN: JAI Press.

Sklair, L. (2001), *The Transnational Capitalist Class*, Oxford: Blackwell Publishers.

Stiglitz, J. (1998), 'More instruments and broader goals: moving towards the post-Washington consensus', Wider Annual Lecture, UN World Institute for Development Economics Research, New York.

Stiglitz, J. (2002), *Globalization and Its Discontents*, London: Norton House.

Strange, S.(1988), *States and Markets*, 2nd edition, London: Pinter.

Tesner, S. (2000), *The United Nations and Business: A Partnership Recovered*, London: Macmillan.

Therborn, G. (1984), 'Classes and state: welfare state developments, 1881–1981', *Studies in Political Economy*, 13, 7–42.

Traxler, F. (1993), 'Business associations and labor unions in comparison: theoretical perspectives and empirical findings on social class, collective action and associational organizability', *British Journal of Sociology*, 44, 2, 673–691.

TUAC (1981), 'A view from the trade unions', presented to the OECD's Conference on Social Policies in the 1980s, OECD, Paris, October. Published as OECD, *The Welfare State in Crisis*, Paris: OECD.

TUAC (1998), 'Statement to the OECD Ministerial Meeting on Social Policy', 23–24 June, Paris.

Van Apeldoorn, B. (2000), 'Transnational class agency and European governance: the case of the European round table of industrialists', *New Political Economy*, 5, 2.

Vosko, L. (2002), '"Decent Work": the shifting role of the ILO and the struggle for global justice' *Global Social Policy*, 2(1), 19–46.

Wade, R.H.(2002), 'US hegemony and the World Bank: the fight over people and ideas', *Review of International Political Economy*, 9, 2.

Chapter 3.3

The World Health Organization and global public-private health partnerships: in search of 'good' global health governance

Kent Buse and Gill Walt

The past decade has witnessed dramatic changes in international cooperation through the United Nations and its organizations. Two interrelated trends stand out. First, as a function of globalization – defined as the accelerated diffusion of capital, traded goods, people, ideas, etc. across increasingly porous national boundaries – it is progressively more evident that a variety of challenges cannot be met efficiently at the national level, but require additional collective international, if not global, approaches (Kaul et al., 1999). Moreover, the ascendancy of organized capital over the power of the nation–state adds impetus to the need for intergovernmental cooperation. It has been argued that 'short of a backlash against globalization, states will have little choice but to pool their sovereignty to exercise public power in a global environment now mostly shaped by private actors' (Reinicke & Witte, 1999). Consequently, globalization has highlighted the need for strengthened international cooperation and has resulted in significant discussion of reform within existing multilateral institutions, as well as the establishment of new ones with distinctive characteristics – for example, a World Trade Organization lying outside of the UN system that can exercise unprecedented and binding authority over its member states.

A second significant trend in international cooperation within the United Nations involves a shift from vertical representation to horizontal participation (Walt, 2000). Vertical representation describes a hierarchical, bureaucratic relationship between the state and its representation in the international organizations that make up the UN. Representation through this process provides, at least in theory, both a form of democracy and accountability (i.e., citizens represented through member states, and member states represented in decision-making bodies, with decision-making bodies responsible to member states). Horizontal participation is more typical of the network society, in which states and non-state organizations, including the UN and private for-profit organizations, form less hierarchical and less bureaucratic interorganizational relationships. Global public-private partnerships (GPPPs) provide a form of interorganizational networking.

While there is, as yet, relatively little experience in determining how well these horizontal public-private partnerships work, it is clear that, in addition to their many potential benefits, they also pose a variety of potential challenges and threats in relation to international cooperation in health. The purpose of the United Nations, at the point of its establishment, was to further peaceful and cooperative relations among states. As one of its specialized agencies, the World Health Organization's role was to coordinate activities in health against a very broad constitutional mandate that saw health as a fundamental right and WHO's main objective as 'the attainment by all peoples of the highest possible level of health' (WHO, 1946). An international civil service was established to provide support to countries and actions to advance this mandate. While the UN and WHO have always been constrained in their ability to achieve these lofty goals, and although we acknowledge significant weaknesses in many UN organizations, we nevertheless argue that the UN plays critical functions with respect to global health, among other things. Our concern is that horizontal participation, as evidenced in the growth of public-private partnerships at the global level, will further fragment international cooperation in health and undermine UN aims for cooperation and equity among states.

Our chapter begins with a short discussion of the meaning of partnership. We then describe the context in which public-private partnerships have emerged, drawing particular attention to the shift from 'international' to 'global' governance in the health as well as other sectors. Thereafter, we enumerate the interests that private and public actors pursue in relation to partnership, as these carry important consequences for the impact of GPPPs for international cooperation in health. We review the critical functions performed by the UN in relation to health and argue that these are made possible by a number of facilitating attributes which characterize UN organizations such as WHO. The manner in which partnerships with the for-profit sector may impinge, both positively and negatively, upon these facilitating attributes is explored. The chapter concludes that more care needs to be exercised in relation to preserving these important functions and attributes as partnerships proliferate. Although our primary interest is with health partnerships and, consequently, WHO, we make an attempt to situate our discussion in a broader context and include examples that involve other UN organizations.

Defining partnerships

Elsewhere we have described how the conceptual understanding of partnership has evolved over the past few decades (Buse & Walt, 2000a). In

relation to development cooperation, the term was most frequently employed
to describe aspirational relationships between official donor agencies and
recipient ministerial bodies in developing countries. Today, a profusion of
interpretations surround the term. We submit that the notion of partnership
has become a cognitive device that groups similar things and thereby permits
recognition and communication. However, when subjected to scrutiny,
it becomes apparent that the notion of partnership is imbued with very
different characteristics in different contexts. Although partnering (and the
term *partnership*) clearly implies a tendency toward collaboration, it is also
used to describe a wide range of relationships and activities. Consequently,
there is the risk that the term often obscures more than it reveals. To assess
the impact of partnerships on international cooperation for health and to
judge under which circumstances partnerships are likely to be suitable and
effective or what rules of engagement should guide partners' activities, we
need greater specificity with respect to our object of analysis.

For this discussion, we employ a narrow and specific definition of a
global public-private partnership for health. Health GPPPs are collaborative
relationships that transcend national boundaries and bring together at least
three parties – among them a corporation and/or industry association and
an intergovernmental organization – so as to achieve a shared health-creating
goal on the basis of a mutually agreed and explicitly defined division of labor
(adapted from Buse & Walt, 2000a). While other parties, such as civil society
organizations and private foundations, are often also critical partners in
GPPPs, here our unit of analysis comprises for-profit and intergovernmental
organizations.

Context

Globalization provides the defining contextual shift marking the widespread
emergence of global public-private partnership. As noted above, international
cooperation is affected in two major ways by increased global integration.
First, globalization circumscribes some functional sovereignty of the
nation-state and thereby reinforces recognition of the need for multilateral
cooperation for solutions to common problems (Kaul et al., 1999).
Second, globalization, particularly through advances in communication
technologies, facilitates horizontal and network-oriented approaches to
governance (Reinicke, 1998). Consequently, multilateral cooperation has
increasingly and purposefully looked toward the potential for public-private
collaboration. For example, in his 1999 address to the annual meeting of
the World Economic Forum, UN Secretary-General Kofi Annan reflected
that 'the United Nations once dealt only with governments. By now we
know that peace and prosperity cannot be achieved without partnerships
involving governments, international organizations, the business community,

and civil society' (Annan, 1999). Reflecting Annan's observations on the UN and relating these to the concept of governance, Mark Malloch Brown, administrator of the United Nations Development Program (UNDP), wrote in the foreword to the 1999 Human Development Report:

> We are seeing the emergence of a new, much less formal structure of global governance, where governments and partners in civil society, the private sector, and others are forming functional coalitions across geographic borders and traditional political lines to move public policy in ways that meet the aspirations of a global citizenry. . . . These coalitions use the convening power and the consensus-building, standard-setting, and implementing roles of the United Nations, the Bretton Woods institutions, and international organizations, but their key strength is that they are bigger than any of us and give new expression to the UN Charter 'We, the peoples.' (UNDP, 1999)

In so far as global governance involves the formal and informal 'institutions and organizations through which the rules and norms governing world order are (or are not) made and sustained' (Held et al., 1999), Malloch Brown is correct in viewing partnership not solely as a reflection of globalization, but as a response to its processes as well. This is particularly the case where new principles, norms, and standards are elaborated within the framework of partnerships.

The emergence of GPPPs can be traced to a number of additional dynamics that marked the 1990s. [...]

[One] contextual shift that fuelled the rise of GPPPs involved the growing *disillusion with the UN* and its organizations. Concerns about the effectiveness of the UN, including increasing evidence of overlapping mandates and interagency competition, led directly towards establishing partnerships to deal with specific and limited issues. Partnerships that are housed outside of the UN bureaucracy are viewed as a way of getting things done, and where industry is involved, getting things done efficiently. In relation to the Medicines for Malaria Venture (a public–private drug research partnership), for example, it was agreed that 'the organization should run as a not-for-profit-business and be based on operational paradigms of industry, not the public sector' (Ridley et al., 1999). It has been suggested that the UN may see the benefits of industry partnership as 'relegitimizing' the UN and thereby enabling it to regain a more central position in global policymaking. For example, the Corporate Europe Observatory argues that 'working with the International Chamber of Commerce diversifies the UN's image, which in some countries, including the United States, is not ideal' (CEO, 1998).

Negative perceptions of UN effectiveness, among other things, have provided *financial impetus for partnerships* in that donors have imposed a policy of zero real growth in UN budgets and shifted toward supplementary (i.e., voluntary and earmarked) funding. These funding trends have made GPPPs attractive (and perhaps necessary) to the UN. Resources provided by the private sector 'are more than welcome; they are necessary' (Beigbeder, 1996). Beyond the commercial sector, important new sources of funding for UN partnerships are those from the new philanthropists (i.e., Bill Gates, George Soros, and Ted Turner).

[...]

Changes in business–UN relations, as expressed by the formation of GPPPs, may also reflect the impact of globalization on the *structure of the global economy* (and within various industries) and on ways of doing business. In particular, three possibly interrelated elements stand out. First, as noted above, transnational corporations have become the lynchpins of the world economy; the globalization of production has entrenched the power of organized corporate capital vis-à-vis state power (Held et al., 1999). This has undoubtedly emboldened corporations to demand a voice in intergovernmental decision-making, for example in the WTO and WHO. Second, increasing concentration empowers individual megacompanies in relation to both state and intergovernmental organizations, but also increases the possibilities for industry-wide association and organization (Mytelka & Delapierre, 1999). Consequently, we have seen a rise in self-organization and private-sector-influenced regulation at the global level (Cutler et al., 1999). Third, there have been changes in the form of business organization. It has been argued that globalization is fuelling corporate alliances (and may, indeed be replacing mergers). It is speculated, for example, that whereas 'the average large company, which had no alliances a decade ago, now has in excess of 30' (*Business Week*, 1999). These are love affairs, rather than marriages: competitors in one market can collaborate in others, and it is natural that the commercial world extends this form of organization to its relations with governmental entities.

Finally, the trend towards global public-private partnerships may be related to the change in public attitudes and the growing response of the private sector to concerns and vocal demands for *corporate responsibility and accountability*. Corporations themselves have realized their need to take into account broader responsibilities to society (Control Risks Group, 1997). This recognition has been stimulated by the strength of consumer, environmentalist, and other civil society group actions in industrialized countries, which have challenged international companies' policies in a number of spheres and won considerable concessions (Wapner, 1995). GPPPs offer the possibility to improve corporate image. One company executive explained that public pressure was of highest consideration in terms of why his company sought partnerships with the public health sector (Auty, 1999). [...]

Partner interests in global public-private partnerships differ

The specific interests that each party to a particular partnership pursues, the extent to which the party seeks to realize those interests through the partnership, as well as its relative influence within the partnership arrangement will have some bearing on the effectiveness and outcomes of the partnership activity, but may equally play some transformative role within each partner organization. Here we enumerate some of the interests pursued by the private for-profit sector and United Nations (and WHO) through partnership generally before analyzing how the pursuit of these interests may alter characteristics of the UN. In the ensuing discussion, we have made generalizations about both the UN and the private sector. In practice, neither sector is comprised of homogeneous entities (nor indeed are GPPPs). There is a great diversity in size, competence, and efficiency among UN and for-profit organizations. Some divisions of UN bodies have been charged with malpractice, while firms are differentiated, among other things, by their willingness to comply with the rule of law and their interest in philanthropy and partnership. Moreover, private firms are also not solely driven by short-term economic imperatives to maximize profits. They may singly or collectively construct a variety of organizational arrangements that structure their own and others' behavior with a view to longer-term interests, and GPPPs provide one vehicle for so doing.

Private interests in global public-private partnerships

Incorporating industry interests in global governance

> We want neither to be the secret girlfriend of the WTO nor should the ICC have to enter the World Trade Organization through the servant's entrance. Helmut Maucher (1997), ICC President

As the processes of globalization intensified during the 1990s, industry came to recognize the potential benefits of alliances with the United Nations. For example, according to Maria Cattaui, secretary general of International Chamber of Commerce (ICC), 'Business believes that the rules of the game for the market economy, previously laid down almost exclusively by national governments, must be applied globally if they are to be effective. For that global framework of rules, business looks to the United Nations and its agencies' (Cattaui, 1998a). Maucher (1998) supports this position, arguing that 'in this process of modernization and globalization of rules, ICC is making a positive contribution, both as an advisor and through its own standard setting. . . . Broader efforts should now follow in order to foster rules-based freedom for business, with the WTO assuming a key role.' While the ICC conceded the need for additional authority for intergovernmental organizations, this was 'with the proviso that they must pay closer attention to the contribution of business.' The ICC was, however, concerned that the 'power of world business' has been 'poorly . . . organized on the international level to make its voice heard' (quoted in CEO, 1998). Consequently, the ICC established, in its words, a 'systematic dialogue with the United Nations' in an effort to redress this perceived threat to its interests (Cattaui, 1998b).

Industry has embarked upon a multipronged strategy to influence UN decision making. For example, in June 1997 the executive director of the World Business Council on Sustainable Development (WBCSD) cohosted a high-level public-private sector meeting with the president of the UN General Assembly to 'examine steps toward establishing terms of reference for business sector participation in the policy setting process of the UN and partnering in the uses of UN development assistance funds' (Korten, 1997). The meeting concluded that 'a framework' for corporate involvement in UN decision making be worked out under the auspices of the UN Commission on Sustainable Development (Korten, 1997). The ICC also conceived the Geneva Business Partnership. Established in September 1998, the Partnership enabled 450 business leaders to meet with representatives of international organizations so as to determine 'how to establish global rules for an ordered liberalism' (CEO, 1998). One outcome of the industry effort is a joint UN-ICC statement on common interests which includes a call to 'intensify the search for partnerships' (United Nations, 1998). Interaction among the commercial and public sectors, while neither new nor ipso facto 'partnership,' reflects the increased intensity, extent, and purpose of growing private-sector interests in public-sector decision making.

GPPPs and emerging market penetration

> Corporate success will be increasingly dependent on harnessing
> these new markets and production opportunities. (UNDP, 1998)

Globalization is perhaps most advanced in the economic sphere. Nonetheless, according to the World Bank, more people live in poverty than ever before. The United Nations portrays poverty as a 'downside of globalization' but also suggests that poverty is both a threat and an opportunity to industry interests. It is a threat in the sense that mass poverty could lead to destabilization, thereby jeopardizing the smooth functioning of the market, and an opportunity in terms of the poor being a potential market-in-waiting. Companies such as Dupont, Unilever and Johnson and Johnson are experimenting with rural poor markets as they see most growth potential at the bottom of the pyramid (Slavin, 2001). Market creation is the explicit goal of a number of UN–industry partnerships. For example, through the Global Sustainable Development Facility (GSDF), leading corporations and UNDP aimed to include two billion new people in the global market economy by the year 2020 (UNDP, 1998). The GSDF was to be established as a separate legal entity outside the UN system that would be 'primarily governed by participating corporations and will benefit from the advice and support of the UNDP through a special relationship' (UNDP, 1998). The GSDF was addressed, among other things, to 'developing products and services adapted to the emerging markets of the poor' (UNDP, 1998). Despite early interest and participation of numerous corporations, UNDP aborted the initiative due to the controversy that it provoked (New, 2000).

Thus public-private partnerships are sometimes proposed as priming-the-pump of economic globalization in those areas where the market is not well enmeshed in the global economy, but also as an opportunity for individual firms to penetrate specific markets. As the president of the medical systems unit of Becton Dickinson & Co. has remarked, 'Of course we want to help eradicate neonatal tetanus, but we also want to stimulate the use of non-reusable injection devices, and to build relationships with ministries of health that might buy other products from us as their economies develop' (Deutsch, 1999).

GPPPs and corporate citizenship

Kofi Annan has warned that because 'globalization is under intense pressure ... and business is in the line of fire ... business must be seen to be committed to global corporate citizenship' (Annan, 1999). Emerging public-private relationships often move beyond the simple philanthropy (gift giving) of the past and can be differentiated by a range of motivations including corporate responsibility (obligation-oriented), corporate citizenship (rights and responsibilities) and, as noted above, strategic gain (Waddell, 1999). Collaboration is in part due to the fact that the commercial sector has been increasingly challenged to show greater social responsibility, to invest in the well being of populations, to adhere to global labor and environmental standards, and to invest in research and development that benefits the poorest. Debate surrounding the WTO Agreement on Trade-Related Aspects of Intellectual Property Rights (TRIPS) is illustrative of the manner in which GPPPs provide industry an opportunity to demonstrate its corporate citizenship. Concerns have been raised that implementation of the TRIPS Agreement will increase the costs and, thereby, limit access to essential drugs in developing countries (pursuant to strengthened patent protection on process and product and controls on the manufacturing and export/import of generic drugs) (Velasquez & Boulet, 1999). Industry acknowledges that access to medicines in poorer countries is an issue but suggests that the 'long-term donation programs instituted by pharmaceutical companies for such debilitating diseases as trachoma, filariasis and river blindness' (i.e., high profile GPPPs) provide a means to redress the access problem (Bale, 1999). [...]

United Nations interests in global public-private partnerships

The interests that the United Nations and its organizations pursue through participation in GPPPs have already been alluded to. First, there is the financial imperative. Budgets throughout the system have been frozen and/or reduced. Partnership with the private sector enables the UN system to leverage its own resources and advice and to access new resources that enable it to fulfill its mandate. This carries weighty implications for the power and influence that the UN organizations bring to various partnership arrangements. Second, the UN has increasingly accepted the prevailing orthodoxy that suggests that partnership is the way to overcome market and government failure. It therefore has an interest in experimenting with partnership strategies and mechanisms that might overcome these failures to produce global public goods. Finally, in recognition of the rise of corporate power and influence, partnership allows the UN to maintain a voice in arrangements of global governance.

WHO's enthusiasm for partnership mirrors that of the UN. Nonetheless, WHO's approach is distinct because of its explicit focus on health – the specific health goals pursued by the organization as well as the underlying ethical values that support its mission (Buse, 2001). WHO tends to enter into partnerships which have well-defined and specific health outcomes such as those that are disease or risk-factor oriented. Through partnership with the commercial sector, WHO seeks (in addition to the broad motivations described above) to achieve a range of objectives that include:

- To encourage industry to adopt and abide by the universal health principles established in Health For All
- To facilitate universal delivery and access to existing essential drugs and health services
- To accelerate research and development of vaccines, diagnostics, and drugs for neglected diseases
- To prevent premature mortality, morbidity, and disability
- To encourage industry to develop 'healthier' products in ways that are less harmful to workers and the environment
- To integrate health in all sectors for sustainable development

- To absorb and acquire knowledge and expertise from the private sector
- To enhance the organization's image among constituencies hostile to the UN.

Functions and attributes of the United Nations – What implications partnership?

The preceding discussion suggests that public and private actors pursue a variety of interests through partnership, and that these may affect the particular objectives of any individual partnership. In that the partnering process may be transformative, it is arguable that the pursuit of the aforementioned interests may influence the work of either sector. Such influence may be positive or negative. Partnering, for example, may imbue the UN with entrepreneurial talent and business culture which some might argue may thereby improve its efficiency. Similarly, the business community may adopt norms and values espoused by the UN in relation to workers' rights or occupational health, for example. Alternatively, less beneficial outcomes from partnering might obtain. The values and norms of the UN might be captured or diluted, and its decision-making structures subject to commercial considerations. Business may become mired in public-sector bureaucratic procedures.

Although it is still unclear exactly how public-private partnerships between the United Nations and the for-profit sector will influence the work of the UN, this section explores some of the potential changes in relation to public health. The section is organized around a framework that proposes that multilateral organizations such as WHO play four critical functions with respect to global health, enabled, to varying degrees, by a variety of facilitating attributes. The manner in which partnership impinges upon these attributes constitutes the substance of this section (summarized in Table 3.3.1). In presenting this idealized model of the functions of WHO, we are not suggesting that the organization has fulfilled them consistently in an effective and efficient manner. We fully acknowledge that the UN in general and WHO in particular have a variety of shortcomings that have inhibited them from fulfilling these functions (Godlee, 1994; Walt, 1996). However, we believe that every effort should be made to enable the UN to fulfill its potential and feel that attempts at reform of the organization of the past decade have been similarly motivated by such concern. We are also concerned that without due attention, global public-private partnerships may further compound the organization's difficulties.

Table 3.3.1: Functions and attributes of the World Health Organization and how these might change through partnerships with the private sector

Critical and unique functions	Enabling attributes	Positive influence of partnership	Negative influence of partnership
WHO acts as the world's health conscience (e.g., human rights and equity), providing a moral framework and agenda for health.	Moral authority deriving from near universal membership. Constitution specifies concern for health of all peoples and special attention to needs of poor.	Partnerships may provide resources that enable WHO to promote its moral framework more forcefully. Partnerships may encourage for-profit entities to support WHO mission and values.	Function and attributes potentially undermined through value diffusion by more powerful private-sector interests.
Establishing global norms and standards.	Legitimacy deriving from universality (particularly representation of poor countries and population groups), specialization, expert technical networks, and associated attributes of impartiality and neutrality.	Private sector may be more willing to abide by standards and norms elaborated through multilateral means if it has a voice in articulating them through its participation in partnerships.	Function potentially eroded if normative activities are shifted to GPPP expert committees where particularistic private interests may prevail.
Promotion and protection of the global commons (including creation of transnational public goods such as R&D capacity, information dissemination, and control of transnational externalities such as environmental risks, spread of pathogens, trade in illegal substances).	Mobilizing collective state action and resources through convening power and consensus building.	Enhanced for particular goods through access to additional resources from non-state actors. Potential to bring new resources into the control process. Potential to involve those private actors whose activities have the greatest impact on transnational externalities.	Depends on how private partner's interests are impacted by the creation of any good or control of any bad. Where conflicts of interest arise, private partners may seek to subordinate social and health standards to profit objectives thereby thwarting WHO objectives. May also entail shift to industry self-regulation.
Supportive cooperation at country level (particularly for unfashionable activities such as training and health systems support).	Reliant on members dues and bilateral (and other) donations to fulfill its mandate.	Potential to raise additional resources and engage additional partners to support health sector development in countries in greatest need.	EBF funding for country level activities may be reduced as 'profitable' activities hived off to GPPPs while difficult activities left with WHO. May lead to intercountry inequity as GPPPs focus on countries.

GPPPs and normative frameworks

The United Nations' so-called Charter Model aims to organize world affairs according to the principle, among others, that nation-states are bound to a series of 'universal' norms and values (Cassese, 1986). The UN plays a prominent role in providing a platform for the discussion, negotiation, and promotion of these norms and values.

This role, however, is not without tension. Norms and values are culturally based and regularly contested. For example, in societies characterized by goals of universality and equity, based on principles of risk pooling and resource redistribution, citizens have different expectations of the state than do those in societies driven by individualism and markets, with collective response often limited to instances of market failure. Perhaps because of these underlying differences in norms and values, differences also exist in the perception of the legitimacy of close connections between the corporate world and the public sector. In European societies organized along principles of solidarity, for example, there has been greater separation and less interaction between public and private sectors than in the United States. Thus the scope and extent of corporate philanthropy has differed. In Europe corporate philanthropy has a long tradition, but it has been low profile and relatively limited. In the United States corporate philanthropy has had a strong institutional presence and made significant investments in community and international development efforts.

Public and private sectors, similar to societies, social groups, and individuals, bring a number of different values to partnerships. At the one end of the continuum are the values of the UN: 'Our main stock in trade . . . is to promote values: the universal values of equality, tolerance, freedom, and justice that are found in the UN Charter' (Annan, 1999). Also at this end of the continuum is WHO, with its concern for the health of the marginalized and dispossessed, and its claim to be the world's health conscience. WHO's values flow from its constitutional mandate, while its claims to promoting universally held values derive from its wide membership (the majority of nation-states).

At the other end of the continuum are the 'bottom line' values and interests to maximize profits so as to increase shareholder value that are reflected in company policies, although such values are increasingly framed within explicit goals of social responsibility. For example, the Royal Dutch Shell Group sees their role 'not just as commercial operators, but as investors in communities, in people, in societies around the world.' Irrespective of one's interpretation of such rhetoric, two caveats are in order. First, as stated above, the corporate sector is diverse, and among the socially responsible business entities are those whose activities have been highly criticized for pursuing profits by aggressive marketing or poor labor practices. Second, despite encouraging signs of enhanced corporate social responsibility, the primary responsibility of any commercial enterprise remains a fiduciary one to its owners.

There has been, therefore, great debate over whether or not – despite shared partnership goals – private and public interests are mutually compatible. Several mechanisms have been identified through which profit maximization may undermine the goal of better health (Hancock, 1998). Within partnerships, the question arises as to whether or not private sector values will ultimately dominate as the UN and industry move closer towards jointly defining their goals through GPPPs – and as the values of the weaker partner are captured by the more powerful. It is possible that WHO's emphasis on and advocacy for the marginalized and the poor will be displaced as resource-rich partnerships dictate organizational priorities and strategies. It has been suggested, for example, that WHO's involvement in the Global Alliance for Vaccines and Immunizations (GAVI) has derailed the organization's commitment to equity in relation to the goal of universal vaccination with traditional vaccines as it joins with its partners in bringing 'new' vaccines to the relatively less hard to reach (Hardon, 2001). Similarly, it was argued that recent WHO-convened deliberations on breast-feeding were subject to censorship due, it is asserted, to considerations of the sensibilities of WHO's new commercial constituencies (Ferryman, 2000).

Alternatively, is it possible to ensure that core public and private identities and values are preserved as partnerships limit themselves to specific win-win situations? This will depend first on the selection of private partners. Hancock urges 'sober second thoughts' regarding the suitability of the pharmaceutical industry as a partner for WHO, at least in terms of health promotion, because of 'perceived or actual conflict of interests' (1998). Second, it will depend on the rules of engagement. In practice, given the financial imperatives that sometimes motivate UN organizations to enter into partnerships with the private sector (i.e., the stagnation of funding referred to above), they may find it difficult to refuse corporate offers that do not comply with internal guidelines.

Optimistically, many believe that increased interaction through partnership will be transformative in a more positive manner. In particular, that partnership will promote more socially responsible business entities and practices, which actively promote and uphold the values and norms enshrined within the UN Charter and subsequent conventions. And that some of the strategic, outcome-oriented methods of the private sector might be absorbed into the UN.

Establishing global norms and standards

The United Nations plays an important role in the area of developing normative standards governing activities in all spheres of social life – from shipping lanes to postal services. In the health sector, WHO has a mandate to develop standards (and international treaty law) in five areas: quarantine requirements; nomenclatures in respect to diseases, etc.; standards for diagnostics procedures; standards for safety, purity, and potencies of medications; and advertising, marketing, and labeling of health related goods. A series of attributes enable WHO to assume this role in global norm and standard setting, including relative legitimacy, technical competence and authority, impartiality, and neutrality. These attributes, which are in some ways interlinked, derive from and rest upon the governing arrangements of WHO. Partnerships with the commercial sector may entail reform of these arrangements and therefore raise questions of how to preserve these crucial attributes upon which global norms and standards are developed, particularly those which sustain or promote the ethical values described above. In relation to independent norm and standard setting within WHO, critics charge that partnership may subject WHO to commercial influences. It is argued, for example, that its impartiality was jeopardized during the elaboration of the Guidelines for the Management of Hypertension as a result of the influence of a firm that stood to benefit from them (Woodman, 1999).

Legitimacy concerns the extent to which authority is considered valid by those affected by it. Legitimacy confers upon its holder a recognized right to establish norms and standards. It is fair to argue that most UN organizations derive some of their legitimacy from near universal membership in their governing bodies. For example, the World Health Assembly is currently attended by 191 member states, all of which have equal voting rights irrespective of size of financial contribution. In contrast, representation in global public-private partnerships is both narrower and more eclectic. No health GPPP can claim near universal membership of nation states (which would make it unwieldy in any event), but, more importantly, few partnerships include low-income country representation, not all of them include WHO on their governing boards and technical committees, and in some cases it would appear that the private sector representation is ad hoc and based on personal contacts.

In recognition of the limitations of representative legitimacy, the legitimacy of many GPPPs will depend largely on the expert committees that are established to advise them. Whereas the specialized agencies of the UN, such as WHO, rely on extensive networks of technical experts and have established means for selecting and operating expert groups, there are concerns that GPPP expert groups may be chosen from exclusive epistemic communities, may (due to funding) suffer from a lack of independence, and may have circumscribed powers (Buse & Walt, 2000b). Although many analysts have drawn attention to the extent to which international agenda setting and formulation of policy is controlled by transnational policy elites (Haas, 1992), the implications of the increasing prominence of the private sector in policy networks on global standard setting has yet to receive much attention (Cutler et al., 1999). Sell's (1999) detailed account of the role of twelve CEOs of US firms in drafting the WTO TRIPS Agreement provides an exception.

Partnerships also raise difficult questions in relation to competence and appropriateness. WHO has a constitutional mandate to coordinate international efforts in relation to health. This has always been a difficult task, one which will be made more difficult as the sector is further fragmented through the advent of numerous and sometimes competing partnerships and initiatives. By 2001, there were, for example, several partnerships focusing on malaria, on vaccinations, and on anti-retroviral drugs for HIV/AIDS. The strong emphasis on infectious diseases attracted attention and financial resources, putting other health issues into shadow and undermining any role WHO might have played in forging a coherent global agenda. Moreover, as global responsibility for specific health issues is transferred from WHO programs to GPPPs, there is some danger that WHO will fail to continue to establish expert groups on these issues so as not to duplicate the technical committees established under the aegis of the partnerships (whose membership is usually vetted by the corporate sponsors). This raises the specter of the erosion of WHO's normative function. Where the private sector assumes a greater voice through partnership in WHO technical discussions, will global standards and norms not begin to more closely reflect private interests, thereby jeopardizing their credibility? For example, if a malaria vaccine is developed under the sponsorship of the Medicines for Malaria Venture partnership, there may be a risk that process and product standards concerning any vaccines developed will be unnecessarily high, thus discriminating against low- and middle-income countries.

The global health commons

As noted in the introduction, the determinants of health as well as the means to address them are increasingly subject to transnational forces. It can, therefore, be argued that the imperative for nation-state collaboration to address problems of the global health commons is more compelling than ever. The promotion of global public goods (i.e., those which are nonexcludable, nonrival, and exhibit significant positive externalities), such as research and development on health, the generation and dissemination of knowledge, norms and regulatory standards, and the control of negative international externalities such as transborder spillover of environmental risks, drug resistance, etc., are therefore gaining increased attention. A central role for the United Nations has been proposed in relation to the protection and promotion of the global commons (Kaul et al., 1999). This role derives from its ability to convene a broad array of actors, develop consensus, and mobilize resources.

A number of GPPPs have been established to address problems of the global health commons (such as the Stop TB Initiative). Consequently, it can be argued that the addition of private resources through GPPPs further enables collective international action on critical public health issues. Private resources may be provided to partnerships directly which aim to promote global public goods, or partnerships may encourage private behavior that minimizes negative transnational externalities or promotes positive transborder spillovers. The challenge remains, however, to establish systems for priority setting that are fair and just with respect to which public goods to produce and which externalities to control. At present this is decided in a somewhat ad hoc and opportunistic manner.

Supportive cooperation at the country level

In a world marked by increasing inequalities, the United Nations also plays a role of protecting the health of vulnerable populations and providing development support (e.g., capacity development) in low-income countries. While WHO shares this role with a host of other agencies, its aid need not be conditional upon political and economic objectives (as is often the case with bilateral aid) and can therefore be allocated according to objective measures of need – although this is patently not always the case (Michaud & Murray, 1994). The WHO is able to play this role as a function of the dues it receives from its members and it can allocate these resources according to nonpartisan criteria as a function of its relatively 'apolitical' nature. Public-private partnerships can enable the UN to further its work in poor countries and populations as demonstrated by the success of the African Program for Onchocerciasis Control to deliver drugs to the poorest Africans in the most remote settings.

On the negative side, those countries that do not benefit from partnerships might feel abandoned by the global community. And partnerships may increase inequities within societies: for example, the World Alliance for Community Health, which includes Rio Tinto, Placer Dome and other multinational corporations, aided by WHO, is helping companies develop a 'business plan' for health, 'to improve health of firms as well as ordinary people.' While potentially bringing better quality primary health services to workers and their families, such efforts may undermine universal health systems (*The Economist*, 1999). Worse yet, if activities that are in vogue are hived off to special partnerships, there is the potential that bilateral funds that might have been allocated to the UN may be redirected to GPPPs, thereby further imperiling the financial situation of the organizations, as well as undermining (or devaluing) government efforts, and possibly increasing inequity among countries.

There is also the danger that GPPPs focus on relatively narrow problems and solutions (drugs for malaria and TB, vaccines for HIV/AIDS) and pay insufficient attention to the strengthening of health service delivery systems, which are crucial if new proposals are to work. For example, Hardon (2001) has raised the concern that the Global Alliance on Vaccines and Immunization (GAVI) is focusing largely on the introduction of new vaccines to countries, while little attention and few funds have been allocated to making fragile health systems more effective. In such a situation, helping sustain health systems through training and support might be left to organizations such as WHO.

In summary, Table 3.3.1 suggests that there are potential pros and cons of partnerships in relation to WHO. While partnerships may reinforce some of WHO's functions, the potential threats enumerated above in relation to the organization's mandate, the manner in which global norms and standards are established, and which global public goods and countries receive WHO support, suggest that some caution should be exercised in the partnering process. WHO performs very specific functions based on particular values, institutional characteristics, and decision-making processes. Uncritical support for poorly designed partnership initiatives may undermine WHO's functions and further fragment intergovernmental health cooperation. The extent to which a partnership may impinge upon the work of WHO will depend not only on the nature of the problems and resources available to address it, but also, to a great extent, on the institutional arrangements by which it is governed. These include the selection of partners, the composition of the governing bodies, balance of power among private and public parties, the mechanisms by which decisions are made, and the systems established to ensure accountability and transparency.

Partnerships and governance

Governance can be defined as 'the process whereby an organization or society steers itself' (Rosenau, 1995). Broadly speaking, governance comprises the systems of rules, norms, processes, and institutions through which power and decision making are exercised. Good governance is thought to be based upon: (1) representative legitimacy; (2) accountability; (3) competency and appropriateness; and (4) respect for due process (World Bank, 1994).

A number of challenges to good governance confront the UN as it enters into partnerships with the private, for-profit sector. For example, in relation to representative legitimacy, it would appear that GPPPs provide the commercial sector and purposely selected (predominantly northern) scientists with improved access to decision making within the UN, which is not matched for recipient countries, not-for-profit agencies, southern scientists, and other marginalized groups. This carries significant risks and will have to be handled with caution 'Opening up participation to a broader group of non-state actors and NGOs ... there is a risk that institutions will simply increase access to representatives of US-based and European-based groups and further skew institutional participation and accountability away from the broader, more universal set of members' (Woods, 1999, p. 57).

Accountability, which is broadly concerned with being held responsible for one's actions, poses similar challenges. Public and private sectors have well-established mechanisms of accountability. In the private sector, management is accountable to the company's shareholders. In the public sector, administrative structures report to political structures, which are accountable to the ruled through the contestability of political power. We argued above that accountability within the UN rested upon representation of member states in its governing bodies. However, accountability within public-private partnerships may be less straightforward, partly because of the distance between the global partners and the beneficiaries and the length of time for any impact to be felt. Moreover, actually holding a partner accountable presents difficult challenges, as they are autonomous entities. Presently, systems of sanctions do not appear to have developed to apply to negligent partners. In a number of GPPPs, accountability appears to be predominantly oriented towards the commercial sponsors – e.g., the Mectizan Donation Program (Frost & Reich, 1998) – whereas in others, the management group reports to a governing body whose members report back to their respective organizations – e.g., the International Trachoma Initiative (J. Cook, personal communication, May 20, 1999).

In relation to competence and appropriateness, we have described how partnerships may shift the locus of technical groups outside of the remit of the UN organizations and how, through this process, global norms and standards may tend to more closely reflect private interests. We may also witness a brain-drain from WHO to 'competing' partnership institutions, which could affect the organization's capacity and technical authority. Due process, or the extent to which institutional regulations are observed, has yet to receive much attention in relation to the governance of GPPPs. Although WHO has developed provisional guidelines and a process for vetting partner companies, introduced conflict of interest forms, and established other internal procedures, these have provoked controversy – even among members of its executive board (WHO, 2001). While transparency of decision making to the public will be essential, conflicts of interest may well arise, with information controlled or censored. At present, although many high profile partnerships host a website and produce annual reports, these contain surprisingly little information on the arrangements through which the partnerships are governed.

Conclusions

Globalization necessitates novel arrangements for health governance in which international organizations and nation-states, as well as global and local private, for-profit, and civil society organizations work together. GPPPs provide one such mechanism – and an apparently popular one. While GPPPs have great positive potential they also raise a number of challenges in relation to the United Nations system, especially regarding the potential for further fragmentation of international health cooperation. UN organizations are well aware of some of these potential problems. Although positive towards GPPPs, UNICEF's present executive director has warned, 'it is dangerous to assume that the goals of the private sector are somehow synonymous with those of the United Nations, because they most emphatically are not' (Bellamy, 1999). WHO's provisional guidelines on involvement with the commercial sector reflect this and other concerns, particularly those dealing with real and perceived conflicts of interest (WHO, 1999). As these guidelines fall short on a number of counts (Buse, 2001), there are grounds for a wider debate on a regulatory framework that can differentiate between acceptable and unacceptable GPPPs by ensuring that the former meet specific minimum conditions. Accrediting GPPPs may allay concerns of critics while benefiting private sponsors of partnerships as well.

Falk (1999) reminds us that 'there is little, or no, normative agency associated with this emergent world order: it is virtually designer-free, a partial dystopia that is being formed spontaneously, and in the process endangering some of the achievements of early phases of statist world order.' Greater thought needs to be given to how the present patchwork of alliances and partnerships in health move towards a system of 'good global governance' without losing their energy and creativity. How far is it realistic to work towards *a global health governance network* that would build on existing organizations, common values, and agreed regimes (Kickbusch & Buse, 2000)? Although we are in a period of exploration and experimentation, it is not too late to ensure that, within the patchwork, the critical functions and attributes of the World Health Organization elaborated in this chapter remain intact. More research and debate on how to safeguard these functions, establish criteria for acceptable partnerships, and design a legitimate oversight body will undoubtedly prove more challenging than bringing public and private actors together to act on neglected health concerns, but it will ultimately prove equally rewarding.

References

Annan, K. (1999, June 8). United Nations Secretary-General address to the United States Chamber of Commerce [Press release]. Washington, DC.

Auty, R. (1999, June 8). Remarks made at parallel session number 7.1 at the Third Global Forum for Health Research, Geneva.

Bale, H. (1999, April 24). The globalization of the fight against disease [Advertisement sponsored by Pfizer written by the director general of the International Federation of Pharmaceutical Manufactures Associations]. *The Economist*, p. 26.

Beigbeder, Y. (1996, June 24–26). Another role for an NGO: Financing a WHO program – Rotary International and the eradication of poliomyelitis. Paper presented to 1996 ACUNS Ninth Annual Meeting, Turin, Italy, p. 8.

Bellamy, C. (1999). Public, private and civil society. Statement of UNICEF Executive Director to Harvard International Development Conference on 'Sharing responsibilities: public, private and civil society.' Cambridge, Mass, 16 April 1999. Available from: *http://www.unicef.org/exspeeches /99esps.htm*

Buse, K. & Walt, G. (2000a). Global public-private partnerships: Part 1 – A new development in health? *Bulletin of the World Health Organization*, 78(4), 549–561.

Buse, K. & Walt, G. (2000b). Global public-private partnerships: Part II – What are the issues for global governance? *Bulletin of the World Health Organization*, 78(5), 699–709.

Buse, K. (2001). Partnering for better health? Ensuring health gains through improved governance: A strategy for WHO. *Bulletin of the World Health Organization*.

In praise of business alliances. (1999, October 25). *Business Week*, p. 106.

Cassese, A. (1986). *International law in a divided world*. Oxford: Clarendon Press.

Cattaui, M. S. (1998a, August 3). Business and the UN: Common ground. *ICC Business World*.

Cattaui, M. S. (1998b, February 6). Business partnership forged on global economy [Press release]. Paris: ICC.

CEO (1998). The Geneva business dialogue. Business, WTO and UN: Joining hands to deregulate the global economy? [Online]. Available from: *www.globalpolicy.org/soce-con/trncs/maucher.htm*

Control Risks Group (1997). No hiding place: Business and the politics of pressure. Unpublished paper.

Cutler, A. C., Haufler, V., & Porter, T. (1999). Private authority and international affairs. In A. C. Cutler, V. Haufler, & T. Porter (Eds.), *Private authority and international affairs* (pp. 3–28). New York: SUNY.

Deutsch, D. H. (1999, December 10). Unlikely allies with the United Nations; for big companies, a strategic partnership opens doors in developing countries. *The New York Times*, p. C1.

Falk, R. (1999). *Predatory globalization: A critique*. Cambridge, U.K.: Polity Press.

Ferryman, A. (2000). WHO accused of stifling debate about infant feeding. *British Medical Journal*, 320, 1362.

Frost, L. & Reich, M. (1998). *Mectizan Donation Program: Origins, experiences, and relationships with coordinating bodies for onchocerciasis control.* Boston: Department of Population and International Health, Harvard School of Public Health.

Godlee, F. (1994). The World Health Organization: WHO in crisis. *British Medical Journal,* 309, 1424–1428.

Haas, P. M. (1992). Epistemic communities and international policy coordinates. *International Organization,* 46, 1–35.

Hancock, T. (1998). Caveat partner: Reflections on partnership with the private sector. *Health Promotion International,* 13(3), 193.

Hardon, A. (2001). Immunization for all? A critical look at the first GAVI partners meeting. *HAI-Lights,* 6(1). Available from: *http://www.haiweb.org/highlights/ mar2001*

Held, D., McGuire, A., Goldbatt, D., & Perraton, J. (1999). *Global transformations: Politics, economics and culture.* Stanford: Stanford University Press.

Kaul, I., Grunberg, I., & Stern, M.A. (1999). *Global public goods: International cooperation in the twenty-first century.* Oxford: Oxford University Press.

Kickbusch, I. & Buse, K. (2000). Global influences and global responses: International health at the turn of the twenty-first century. In M. Merson, R. E. Black, & A. J. Mills (Eds.). *International Health.* Gaithersberg: Aspen.

Korten, D. (1997, July). The United Nations and the corporate agenda [Online]. Available from: *http://www.igc.org/globalpolicy/reform/korten.htm.*

Maucher, H. O. (1998, September 24). The Geneva business declaration. Geneva: ICC.

Maucher, H. O. (1997, December 6). Ruling by consent [Guest column]. *The Financial Times,* FT Exporter, p. 2.

Michaud, C. & Murray, C. J. L. (1994). External assistance to the health sector in developing countries: A detailed analysis, 1972–1990. *Bulletin of the World Health Organization,* 72(4), 639–651.

Mytelka, L.K. and Delapierre, M. (1999) Strategic partnerships, networked oligoplies and the state. In A.C. Cutler, V. Haufler and T. Parker (Eds.) *Private Authority and International Affairs* (pp. 129-149). New York: SUNY.

New, W. (2000, June 1). Special report: NGOs wary of UN corporate links. *UN Wire Business Weekly* [Online serial]. Available from: *http:// www.unfoundation.org/*

Reinicke, W. H. (1998). *Global public policy: Governing with government?* Washington, DC: Brookings Institution Press.

Reinicke, W. H. & Witte, J. M. (2001). Interdependence, globalization and sovereignty: The role of non-binding international legal accords. In D. H. Shelton (Ed.), *Commitment and compliance: The role of non-binding norms in the international legal system* (forthcoming). Oxford: Oxford University Press.

Repositioning the WHO (1998, May 9). *The Economist.*

Ridley, R., Gutteridge, W. E., & Currat, L. J. (1999, June 8–11). *New Medicines for Malaria Venture: A case study of the establishment of a public sector-private sector partnership.* Paper presented at the Third Global Forum for Health Research, Geneva.

Rosenau, J. N. (1995). Governance in the twenty-first century. *Global Governance*, 1(1), 13–43.

Sell, S. K. (1999). Multinational corporations as agents of change: The globalization of intellectual property rights. In A. C. Cutler, V. Haufler, & T. Porter (Eds.), *Private authority and international affairs* (pp. 169–197). New York: SUNY.

Slavin, T. (2001, April 5–11). The poor are consumers too. *Guardian Weekly*, p. 27.

United Nations (1998, February 9). Joint statement on common interests by UN secretary-general and International Chamber of Commerce [Press Release SG/2043]. New York: Author.

UNDP (1999). *Human development report*. Foreword. New York: Author.

UNDP (1998, July). *The global sustainable development facility*. Internal document. New York: Author.

Velasquez, G. & Boulet, P. (1999). Essential drugs in the new international economic environment. *Bulletin of the WHO*, 77 (3), 288–291.

Waddell, S. (1999). The evolving strategic benefits for business in collaboration with nonprofits in civil society: a strategic resources, capabilities and competencies perspective. Providence, R.I.: Organizational Futures. Unpublished.

Walt, G. (1996). International organizations in health: The problem of leadership. Paper presented at Pocantico Retreat, Feb 1–3 1996. Rockefeller Foundation, Social Science Research Council, Harvard School of Public Health.

Walt, G. (2000). Global cooperation in international public health. In M. Merson, R. E. Black, & A. J. Mills (Eds.), *International Health*. Gaithersberg: Aspen.

Wapner, P. (1995). Politics beyond the state: Environmental activism and world civic politics. *World Politics*, 47, 311–340.

WHO (1999, July). *WHO guidelines on interaction with commercial enterprises* [Preliminary version]. Geneva: Author.

WHO (1946). Constitution of the World Health Organization. Geneva: Author.

WHO (2001, January 22). Minutes of the twelfth meeting of the WHO's executive board. Document EB 107/SR/12.

Woodman, R. (1999). Open letter disputes WHO hypertension guidelines. *British Medical Journal*, 318, 893.

Woods, N. (1999). Good governance in international organizations. *Global Governance*, 5, 39–61.

World Bank (1994). Governance: The World Bank's experience. Washington, DC: Author.

Chapter 3.4

New hope or false dawn? Voluntary codes of conduct, labour regulation and social policy in a globalizing world

Ruth Pearson and Gill Seyfang

[...]

[A]s Deacon, with Hulse and Stubbs (1997) points out, social policy in a globalizing world [...] 'includes the ways in which supranational organisations shape national social policy'. From this perspective recent activities in the field of private codes of conduct – which refer to voluntary measures taken by private sector firms involved in global chains of production and distribution, to ensure basic standards, conditions and remuneration for their workforce – should be understood both as part of the unfolding redefinition of the arena of social policy and as the process of supranational moulding of local conditions.

Key to this new conceptualization of social policy are: first, which aspects of labour rights emerge as the central entitlements for workers in the global labour force; and second, which voices and interests are represented in the transnational institutions and discourses that are constructing the new social policy framework, that is to say, what is on the agenda and who is being invited to the negotiating table? This new type of development has been greeted with enthusiasm by a range of actors who might be perceived as representing distinct interests and objectives – including governments, trade unions, development agencies, non-governmental organizations (NGOs), consumer and environmental pressure groups, and women's organizations in both the north and the south. [...]

This article briefly maps the contours of the complex and fast-changing terrain of voluntary codes of conduct that concern labour regulation and practices. It considers the perils and promises of these codes, and their implications in the context of current concerns and debates about the restructuring of social policy in a globalizing world. The discussion is based on an analysis of recent initiatives to develop labour codes that have universal applicability, and also analyses a range of codes that apply specifically to the garments, toys and footwear sectors.

Which actors, why now? The spread of voluntary codes of labour regulation

The rise and fall of statutory codes

The current wave of voluntary codes of conduct has emerged from the rise and fall of statutory codes. These come from the previous international institutional architecture, which reflected the settlement following international conflict of colonial expansionism and the First World War. They also embodied the (then) new voice of organized labour as a key actor in international and intranational political and economic policy dialogue.

The International Labour Organisation (ILO) was established in 1919 to represent the tripartite interests of state, capital and labour in drawing up universal labour standards. The ILO's constitution sets out three prime purposes: first, to address the needs of those who suffer hardship and social injustice through their working conditions; second, that this humanitarian concern should also pre-empt widespread civil unrest; and third, to create a 'level playing-field' whereby all countries should adhere to the same standards and so reduce the competitive advantage of social policy free riders in the international economy (Lee, 1997). The subsequent 60 years saw a growing adoption of international labour standards and conventions from the ILO, with 176 conventions and 174 member states (ibid.). The core ILO Human Rights conventions, which now form the basis of many voluntary codes, are Freedom of Association and Protection of the Right to Organise Convention, 1948 (no. 87); Right to Organise and Collective Bargaining Convention, 1949 (no. 98); Forced Labour Convention, 1930 (no. 29); Abolition of Forced Labour Convention, 1957 (no. 105); Discrimination (Employment and Occupation) Convention, 1958 (no. 111); Equal Remuneration Convention, 1951 (no. 100); Minimum Age Convention, 1973 (no. 138) (ILO, 1999).

However, in the last 20 years, there has been a significant decline in the political acceptability of strong institutional standards. The 1980s witnessed a rise in neo-liberal social policy (domestically and internationally, through bodies such as the International Monetary Fund), accompanied by labour market deregulation, and in particular restrictions on collective bargaining (Picciotto, 1999). This reflects the accelerated trend towards flexibility of labour, which was partly the result of the increasing competition from East Asian economies in the New International Division of Labour in the 1970s and 1980s, economies which were characterized by fewer labour rights and costs than those prevailing in industrialized welfare states (Standing, 1999: 63). Since then the global expansion of international trade has been largely based on unregulated labour as production for export markets has constructed new 'cheap' labour forces such as young women workers, who have never been protected by the institutions of organized labour (Pearson, 1998).

The declining international influence of organized labour over this period is reflected in the fact that ratification of ILO conventions was far from universal. Relatively few countries have ratified the specific regulations contained in more recent conventions on the extension of labour protection to areas such as occupational health and safety, training and health services (Standing, 1999: 56). In the UK, for instance, many of the labour standards that had been ratified by previous governments were revoked by the Conservative government in power between 1989 and 1997, keen to remove obstacles to a freer labour market and undermine trade union organizations further (Hepple, 1997). This reflected a new political landscape, which incorporated the values of neo-liberal economics, encompassed in the so-called 'Washington Consensus' of the World Bank and the IMF. This was further strengthened by the collapse of state socialism in Eastern Europe and the Soviet Union, which meant that widespread labour unrest was increasingly unlikely to become a major political force in the global economy (Lee, 1997).

Despite widespread ratification of many of the labour standards conventions, adverse judgements from the ILO were increasingly unenforced and unenforceable, and so for some years the prevailing mood was one of ever-increasing liberalization and lower standards – a so-called 'race to the bottom' (Hepple, 1997: 355). The lack of enforcement mechanism is a serious shortcoming of these universal standards, in spite of the tripartite nature of their sponsorship, although it has been argued strongly that their existence defines a set of minimum or best practice benchmarks against which other codes, including voluntary codes of conduct discussed below, can be measured (Murray, 1998; Zeldenrust and Ascoly, 1998; IRC, 1999).

The rise and rise of voluntary codes of conduct

What precisely is a 'code of conduct'? Here the term is used to refer to a voluntary measure taken by a private sector firm to impact upon some aspect of their labour conditions and workforce. By definition, and in contrast to universal standards such as the ILO conventions which are binding on countries rather than on individual producers, codes of conduct are voluntary self-regulatory tools that are applicable to specific firms, or groups of firms, and thus to certain groups of workers at certain times, rather than applying to all citizens or workers in particular states. There are a range of different levels of labour codes, some of which are developed by, and for, individual companies, and others which function as 'ready-made' codes for wider implementation by multiple firms, applicable to a cross-sectoral group of companies operating in a given market such as the Ethical

Trade Initiative (ETI), or to the whole of a given sector, for example the International Football Federation (FIFA) code of labour practice, concerned with football production.

The development of voluntary codes of conduct therefore reflects both the political and economic forces behind the demise of statutory codes – namely the expansion and deregulation of the global labour force and the shifting political context that undermines the interest of organized labour (Balasubramanyan, 1999). In its stead the interests of workers in the global production line are being carried, at the turn of the new millennium, by a pluralistic group of alternative actors. These include labour organizations and trade unions, pressure and advocacy groups, and individual corporations themselves, often pursuing a rights-based approach to the struggle for improved working conditions (Arthurs, 1996; Ferguson, 1999).

These organizations have focused their campaigns with, and on, workers' behalf by attempting to influence and regulate corporate practices indirectly via consumer behaviour as well as directly via investor pressure and the more traditional activities concerning state legislation. Consumer campaigns in support of workers' rights in global production chains have become increasingly visible and vocal in developed countries. This has articulated a diverse set of 'single issue' but connected social movements including environmental sustainability, campaigns against sweatshop and forced labour and exploitation of child labour, women workers' rights and freedom of organization (Kearney, 1999). These campaigns have intelligently utilized media and internet modes of communication and linked these to increasing market niche segmentation of global brands in the fashion and sportswear industry, making leading retailers and producers sensitive to the threat of adverse publicity or consumer boycott against particular products. Retailers involved in global production sourcing chains such as Gap, Nike, Levis, H&M, Sainsbury, C&A, CWS, Monsoon, Littlewoods, Tesco, River Island, Shell, and Unilever have already initiated or completed negotiations for company-based voluntary codes of conduct that, in theory, cover all their subcontractors and suppliers (Ferguson, 1998; IRENE, 1998; *Financial Times,* 1999; Fridd and Sainsbury, 1999). Thus the global nature of consumption has itself become a terrain of activism as NGO campaigns concerning workers' interests are articulated in the market place, where product choice and market shares are increasingly influenced by consumer preferences and perceptions about ethical labour practices.

This expression of social values in the market place, and a concurrent growth of shareholder activism (War On Want, n.d.) is in some ways parallel to the 'green consumerism' boom of the late 1980s, when corporations began to market their products as being environmentally-friendly (Dobson, 1990; Booth and Seyfang, 1991). There are earlier examples of shareholder activism combined with consumer boycotts to target individual companies considered to be infringing certain widely accepted principles. These include, for example, the Swiss conglomerate Nestlé, for flouting conventions on the promotion of baby milk formulas in developing countries (TIE, 1985), or the campaign against Barclays for disinvestment in the apartheid years, and the more recent response to Shell's environmental and social destruction of the Niger delta area and the response of the Ogoni people (Yearley and Forrester, 2000). More recently the growth of the ethical investment movement, reflecting both institutional and individual investors' concerns with socially and environmentally positive performances of companies, has further heightened corporate sensitivity to at least the public perception of the impact of their investment (UKSIF, 1998; Kahn, Peters and Poneman, 1999). Particular pressure has also been brought by organizations specifically concerned with the conditions of workers in particular situations, mainly developing world factories and plantations (WWW, 1998; Barrientos, McClenaghan and Orton, 1999; CAWN and WWW, 1999).

There has also been a deepening of companies' approaches to meeting social and environmental standards. Rather than being satisfied with 'glossy' offerings, different stakeholders – be they shareholders, staff, customers, labour or interest group organizations – are demanding much more focused and accurate reporting of social and ethical performance (Zadek, Pruzan and Evans, 1997). A further source of pressure that has one driving force behind them is the pressure afforded by consumer campaigns in the developed countries, concerned with issues around production, frequently in developing countries. This has added to the sensitivity of large companies, particularly those which are high street chains or brand name producers, and may in part explain the willingness of a number of leading UK companies to join the ETI. This was promoted by the UK government's Department for International Development, and was established in 1998 as:

> a collaborative alliance of companies, trade unions and not-for profit organisations with the UK government. It is committed to promoting fundamental human rights in employment and decent working conditions through the global supply and production chains, and is working to develop good practice in monitoring, independent verification and processes of improvement to ensure the effective application of codes of conduct based on internationally agreed minimum labour standards. (ETI, 1998)

The ETI includes 17 high-profile UK-based companies, together with 18 NGOs, as well as 4 domestic and international trade union federations; and currently has pilot projects in China (clothing), Zimbabwe (horticulture) and South Africa (wine). Its base code is derivative of the ILO core labour standards. In spite of the enthusiasm with which it has been greeted by industry, NGOs, labour organizations and government, its impact has been limited by the complexities of working out mechanisms of implementation, monitoring, local adaptation and accountability in terms of worksites and workforces in the South (Burgess and Burns, 1999; ETI, 1999; Green, 1999).

The ETI, together with its USA equivalent, the aborted White House Apparel Industry Partnership (WHAIP), represents an interesting shift in the role of the state in terms of labour regulation and global flexibility. The most striking shift has been the retreat of the state away from being a standard-setter and regulator, and towards a more facilitating role of setting up frameworks for the voluntary self-regulation of corporations, with or without the involvement of civil society groups as well (Haworth, 2000). Accompanying this has been the promotion of voluntary standards and best practice, rather than compulsory minimum standards. On the international stage, the Organisation for Economic Co-operation and Development (OECD), a coalition of mainly northern states, has been revising its guidelines for multinational companies, but once again, these are voluntary guidelines (OECD, 1997). The ILO's 1977 Tripartite Declaration of Principles Concerning Multinational Enterprises and Social Policy aims to address the specific issues raised by international businesses and the power they hold in the global economy, to 'encourage the positive contribution which multinational enterprises can make to economic and social progress and to minimize and resolve the difficulties to which their various operations may give rise' (ILO, 1978: clause 2). This set of ethical guidelines addresses a range of issues, drawing upon the above Human Rights Conventions. Unlike the ILO statutory conventions, this is a voluntary set of principles, which may be adopted by firms, rather than conventions binding on states. It can be seen as a voluntary corollary to the compulsory rights of corporations to equal treatment in foreign countries (Murray, 1998).

Individual firms' codes

As indicated above, a growing number of companies are adopting their own codes of conduct, producing a bewildering array of standards, social accounts and claims to ethical performance (Zadek et al., 1997). Reviews of corporate codes are now emerging, which compare and analyse the standards adopted by individual firms (Ferguson, 1998; Green, 1998; ILO, 1998; Investor Responsibility Research Center, 1998). Clare Ferguson's (1998) study of the scope and content of 18 individual corporate codes of conduct examined the statements of values that the firms purport to recognize in their operations. The codes examined were applicable to a diverse range of business settings (for example, retail, manufacturing, extractive industries, etc.), and so varied greatly in their coverage and emphasis.

Ferguson's review identifies three main issues to be addressed when considering individual firms' codes and the benefits they could give to vulnerable workers. The problematic areas are equally relevant when evaluating the umbrella (multi-firm or sector-wide) codes discussed below. However, when dealing with multiple individual firms' codes, the shortcomings are more easily spotted, and more important to highlight. The first issue is that the content of voluntary codes, when considered together, varies enormously (over and above variations expected due to different applicability). Checklists of standard issues to be covered (with reference to the ILO conventions) revealed that while all the codes included health and safety measures, the right to trade unions organization and collective bargaining was poorly represented (Ferguson, 1998). The US-based Investor Responsibility Research Center's (IRRC) report on corporate codes analysed the responses of 121 firms about their social and labour standards, paying particular attention to labour standards in developing countries (IRRC, 1998). It came to the same conclusions over which issues were most readily addressed, and which were least likely to be included in codes. These are the issues considered most newsworthy to consumer and advocacy groups in developed countries: child labour is mentioned in almost all codes, but less media-friendly issues such as the rights of women or migrant workers do not receive the same attention. This is due to the codes being adopted as a response to NGO campaigns, and being aimed primarily at developed country consumers, rather than tackling the problems faced by a diverse set of vulnerable worker groups.

The second issue is the scope of a code, and the question of exactly how far along a global supply chain does it apply? Multinational enterprises frequently use subcontractors, licensees and homeworkers in their production chains, and so a comprehensive code should also explicitly apply to these groups of workers. A third problem is in the wording of codes: they frequently contain broad generalizations and statements of intent, with very few concrete, achievable standards, and very little direct reference to ILO standards (ILO, 1998) – even where the ILO codes are referred to as benchmarks, their inclusion in corporate codes is rarely as detailed, inclusive or precise as the original standards. With the enormous variations in content, Ferguson (1998) found that this results in little comparability across firms, for standards, independent monitoring and verification (none of the 18 codes studied included this), scope and representation (none incorporated civil society organization involvement).

Umbrella and multi-firm codes

There is clearly a need for more standardization of codes, partly to make compliance easier for suppliers of several firms, and also to encourage second-tier firms, who do not have the resources to develop their own codes, but want to adopt a 'ready made' code (ETI, 1999). Examples of this type of code, frequently drawn up by coalitions of NGOs, workers' organizations, corporate associations and occasionally government support, include the Social Accountability standard SA8000, the UK's Ethical Trading Initiative Base Code, Amnesty International's Human Rights Principles for Companies, and the Clean Clothes Campaign's Code of Labour Practices for the Apparel Industry Including Sportswear [...]. One problem is that while trade associations might endorse codes of conduct, there is no commitment of their members to adopt them individually. In this field of umbrella, regional or industry-wide codes there are a great many different initiatives competing for the hearts and minds of consumers and corporate managers alike (Steelworkers Humanity Fund, 1998; Yanz, Jeffcott, Ladd and Atlin, 1999) [...].

Who instigates voluntary codes of conduct?

The great majority of the umbrella initiatives examined here originate in the global north. [...]

The umbrella codes of northern and international origin are of three main varieties. These are first, model or benchmark codes drawn up by international and national NGOs, consumer campaign organizations, pressure groups and workers groups with the purpose of providing an example of 'best practice' of the most effective and consistent language to use, to other organizations and firms, and lobbying industry associations to endorse the codes and encourage their members to adopt them; it is worth noting that all the model codes are based primarily on the ILO core conventions. [...]

A second group is those where (northern) governments have instigated codes to be adopted by domestic commercial companies in their overseas operations and supply chains by bringing together workers and NGOs with industry groups. These include the ETI (described above) [...].

The third group of umbrella codes comprises those put forward by trade associations and coalitions of commercial enterprises themselves as a self-regulatory mechanism. These include the International Council of Toy Industries (ICTI) and the British Toy and Hobby Association (BTHA) (Murray, 1998), the BGMEA and the PAECLSBI (IRC, 1999). Some of these were direct responses to stronger codes put forward by workers' organizations and pressure groups in those industries, and the content of these codes reflects this origin [...] – however, it is notable that it is this category of codes which is most likely to be adopted by firms.

Who participates in the development of codes of conduct?

Unlike the statutory standards, few of the voluntary codes involve stakeholders from state government; the more recent development of the UK ETI [...] might indicate a change in this trend. Furthermore the proposed European code of conduct, approved by the European Parliament, recommends a standardized code – again in consultation with representatives of pressure groups, labour organizations and trade unions, which it is intending should provide a best practice guideline for any European firms involved in global production chains (Howitt, 1999). However, there is a conspicuous absence of involvement of southern state governments, who tend to view international regulation of labour conditions as a form of disguised protectionism (Lee, 1997), a factor which has been evident in the as yet uncompleted WTO negotiations initiated in Seattle (Haworth, 2000) and Mexico's opposition to the revised OECD guidelines on labour and environmental standards for multinational firms (Denny, 2000). This position is reminiscent of the accusation in the 1970s that northern trade unions were supporting a 'new internationalism' of higher labour standards in order to offset the 'unfair' competition from low-wage developing countries that was leading to significant relocation of manufacturing jobs (Jenkins, 1984).

Who do they cover?

The scope of a code of conduct, in other words, exactly how far along a global supply chain a code applies, is a critical issue. Multinational enterprises frequently use subcontractors, licensees and homeworkers in their production chains (particularly in the fragmented and highly decentralized clothing and textiles industries), but many codes exclude these groups of workers (Brill, 2000; Homenet, 2000). Furthermore, in many manufacturing industries, while (largely male) factory workers might be covered by a company code and are traditionally backed up by trade unions organizations, the (largely female) 'casualized', homeworking labour force is more likely to be excluded from the coverage of these codes of conduct (Barrientos et al. 1999; Green, 1999). [...] [T]he more complex the nature of the subcontracting chain the more difficult it is in practice to apply uniform codes of labour standards in different contractual circumstances.

What they cover

Although often referred to generically as voluntary codes of conduct, the actual coverage of different codes reveals a broad dispersion of content and coverage. [A] checklist of issues (ILO conventions and further concerns) [...] reveals that while a majority refer to the ILO core conventions, few are comprehensive in their inclusion of those standards, and the standards selected reveal much about the interest groups governing each initiative.

First, in common with other studies (Ferguson, 1999), and as discussed above, it is clear that the most commonly cited labour standard is that relating to the minimum age of workers [...]. The widespread inclusion of this standard above all others is likely due to the high profile given to the controversial subject of child labour in northern consumer markets, both by campaign groups and the media. [...]

Issues such as the payment of non-wage benefits, health and safety issues, reproductive rights, the provision of information on standards, and banning physical abuse, are more likely to have been included in codes with their origins in workers' organizations, than any of the other interest groups. This is a first indication of the issues that are considered more important by workers than by, for example, NGOs, firms or state representatives. The issues that were most likely to be included in codes instigated by NGOs were: independent verification, the foundation model of verification, payment of minimum and living wages (see Seyfang, 1999).

[...] The minimum age convention is included in *all* codes that feature industry representation, confirming the view that firms adopt codes of conduct as a defensive measure against adverse publicity – since child labour is given the most sensational media coverage. While all codes with workers' organization and 80 percent of those with NGO representation protect the right to freedom of association, the right to organize and collective bargaining, only just over half of codes with industry involvement have these clauses. Codes associated with workers' organizations prioritize pay and working conditions, particularly freedom of association and right to collective bargaining, no discrimination, equal remuneration, health and safety, no physical abuse, information on standards, legally-due non-wage benefits, reproductive rights, and health service provision.

[...] It is notable that none of the codes make specific reference to prohibition of certain practices known to be a problem for workers in many export-processing factories, for example, restriction of toilet breaks and provision of safe transport home for women workers (Light, 1999; NICWJ, 1999). These kinds of issues are primarily experienced by women workers, and an emerging picture from this analysis is that whereas traditional labour concerns such as union organization are becoming more commonplace in codes of conduct, the topics of particular relevance to women do not get mentioned. In addition, many women workers organize themselves outside the traditional union framework, finding more favourable representation, in for example, dedicated women's organizations based around the workplace (Bickham-Mendez, 1999; Hadjipateras, 1999).

The perils of voluntary codes of conduct

The purely voluntary nature of these self-regulation initiatives must raise a number of questions concerning the motivation, credibility, and accountability of corporations involved in promoting and implementing codes of conduct concerning labour standards.

[...]

Codes of conduct as contingent and enclave social policy

In spite of their global reach, transnational corporations only engage with specific segments of the working population in the different countries involved in their value chains. By choosing to exercise their concerns for social responsibility and social policy within the context of their engagement in transnational production and exchange, the global citizenship of such corporations appears to be more enclave than universal, since their concerns and responsibilities are delineated not by the global potential of the universe in which they operate but the specific localization of particular production processes. The history of transnational production over recent decades, however, indicates a high degree of 'footlooseness' among suppliers, with competition between locations for a place in the global production line; many well-known brand names have switched their production from one cheap wage country to another. For example, in both garments and electronic components in Asia there has been a marked trend for investment and sourcing to shift to 'new' sources of even cheaper labour which has meant in practice a relocation from the original Asian tigers to South East Asia (Malaysia, Thailand, Indonesia) and more recently to Vietnam, China, Laos and Cambodia (Horton, 1996; Lo, 1999; Pearson, 2000). In this light the new social commitment of transnational corporations might just reflect an opportunistic and temporary liaison with all commitments to improvement of the pay and conditions of a particular group of workers being jettisoned as soon as global production conditions indicated a relocation in the name of commercial viability and profits.

Moreover, even for the time period in which transnational corporations continue their production in particular locations the social policy implications of codes of conduct are further restricted by the casual and temporary nature of many employment contracts. For example in many countries specific workforces are recruited into the production of manufactures for export; in garments and electronics it has long been established the employers prefer young, single and childless women as their ideal 'cheap' labour force (Elson and Pearson, 1981). This process of construction of 'cheap labour' implies a routine rotation of workers, with those who no longer fit the category of ideal workers – for instance when they are older, get married, have responsibility for children – being retrenched in favour of a fresh cohort of 'nimble-fingered' workers (Pearson, 1998). Codes of conduct might well offer an improvement in working conditions (CAWN and WWW, 1999). But only those who are currently employed in the global production chain are covered by the stipulations of the codes; those who have outlived their usefulness to transnational exporters and are forced into less favourable work in the informal sector or producing for the domestic market are no longer able to benefit from the regulation and protection offered by company codes of conduct. [...]

Thus, far from representing a commitment to ensuring protection of workers in global production chains, it could be argued that voluntary codes of conduct represent a commitment to a particular group of workers in particular locations only as long as production continues in that location, and/or those particular workers are employed in the corporation's global sourcing chains. For this reason they can be considered as social policy enclaves, entry to which is dependent on workers' position in the global production chain rather than in terms of global social entitlements. These enclaves offer contingent social benefits to workers only as long as they are engaged in particular production situations (Pearson, 1999). While it could be argued that all welfare regimes, particularly in developing countries, have always reflected enclave characteristics, in that they have for the most part protected only the formal sector 'labour aristocracy', codes of conduct offer neither the possibility of universal coverage nor any continuity for those within their reach.

The limited scope and reach of voluntary codes of conduct might well suggest that these initiatives fall short of moves towards a multi-stakeholder commitment to global social policy and the defence of labour standards and working conditions in the context of 'refigurations' in both global production and institutional policy architecture. Furthermore, as many actors and researchers have emphasized, the struggle to enforce the implementation of such codes in local production contexts has proved bitter and hazardous, even when the global spokespersons of transnational corporations have vocalized their commitment to upholding core labour standards through voluntary codes of conduct to their investors and to pressure groups communicating with their global headquarters. Activists report that the compliance with such codes is more significant in their breach. Even the much heralded Nicaraguan Women's Alternative Code of Ethics, whose recognition by the national Ministry of Labour and adoption by firms operating in the Free Trade Zone has been celebrated as an example of an effective worker-instigated code, has been called into question. Recent reports indicate that subsequent ministers have acted to support companies in out-manoeuvring workers' organization activity, firing activists, and ensuring a clampdown on union activity (NSC, 2000).

Codes and accountability: the monitoring problem

A key question that arises out of the voluntary and partial nature of voluntary codes of conduct concerns issues of monitoring and accountability. This is complicated by several factors. First, the plethora of codes makes it difficult to codify the key elements of the provisions of codes; second, the complexities of global production chains means that it may be difficult to know which enterprises, including subcontractors, are actually covered by the provisions of the codes. And third, the wide range of actors and interests groups, and the absence of any enabling structure provided by the local state, means that there is often not an obvious structure or agency which would take on the role of monitoring the implementation of the codes' provisions, and report back to the different stakeholders involved (NEF and CIIR, 1997).

The promises of voluntary codes of conduct

In spite of the obvious problems with codes of conduct detailed above, the increasing attention given to these developments from companies, workers' organizations, NGOs and international organization testify to their growing global significance. It would be premature, if not foolish, to dismiss Codes of Conduct as pure window dressing or regulation avoidance activity on the part of transnational corporations and their allies. [...] [T]here have been a number of positive effects – both intended and unintended – which suggest a positive role of such initiatives in the unfolding process of policy adjustment to globalization.

Expanding participation in negotiation

First, the various forums in which codes have been developed and discussed has changed the traditional institutional structure concerning labour negotiations. Different actors have been brought into contact with each other, and in particular previously excluded groups – such as women workers in export zones – have achieved a voice in the negotiations and a role in monitoring and evaluation (CIPAF, 1999; Murphy and Bendell, 1999). This is important not just symbolically but also in terms of the contents of labour agreements. It is not an accident that [...] the codes which include the immediate demands of women workers concerning sexual harassment, reproductive rights or even appropriate access to toilet facilities are those which have been developed with the active participation of women's groups.

New coalitions and initiatives have also been developed which have taken a more holistic approach to the demands and requirements of workers. An example is the development of the 'Broad Based Bargaining' strategy being developed in Canada to improve standards for garment workers. This approach, which assumes a multi-employer subcontracting environment, has explored additional measures such as joint and several liability for retailers and manufacturers, mechanisms for anonymous or third party complaints and a central registry for homeworkers. The Maquila Solidarity Network has been working with Central American garments workers in current negotiations concerning codes of conduct and examining ways in which the broad based bargaining approach can be applied to women workers in export production (Yanz, 2000).

Monitoring and implementation

Although the issue of monitoring and accountability is an ongoing challenge, several organizations are working towards a greater understanding of the need to measure and report on the social impact of firms, and are developing comprehensive, consistent frameworks for this, for example the Global Reporting Initiative (CERES, 1999), the Social Accountability SA8000 standard (CEPAA, 1997) [...], and The Prince of Wales Business Leaders Forum similarly promotes more socially-responsible business practices, and is working on indexes and indicators to measure societal performance (Nelson, 1998).

There are a number of ongoing approaches to this issue. One possible way forward is the use of a 'social labelling' scheme, which informs consumers that certain standards have been met; again, credibility and trustworthiness of corporations is a primary issue here (Yanz et al., 1999). The independent monitoring and verification of codes of conduct must be given equal attention (CCC, 1998). The SA (Social Accountability) 8000 international standard, referred to above, is devised by the US organization, the Council for Economic Priorities. Based on the seven core ILO standards, it is designed to work across countries and industries, and for companies of all sizes. Compliance will earn companies certification, offering a form of credibility and accountability to both consumer and labour rights interest groups.

Information sharing and communication

New forms of inter-actor communication, networking and coalition have encouraged and facilitated widespread access to information about core labour standards and international conventions and institutional support for the notion of universal rights for workers. Trade unions are now able to negotiate with international corporations on the basis of effective information about international production and trading patterns; and workers' organizations are able to exchange information about corporate practice – positive and negative – in different parts of the world. The Clean Clothes Campaign, for example, maintains an active email list that shares information about conditions, actions and labour conditions in different parts of the world. Enhanced communication of this type as well as the application of transnational voluntary codes can potentially constrain the freedom of global manufacturers to move from one country to another to avoid regulation of workers' rights and conditions.

[...]

Adding workers' interests to poverty discourses and policy

Initiatives to promote codes of conduct, such as those supported by bilateral agencies such as the Department for International Development (DfID) and multilateral agencies such as the ILO, have contributed to a tangible change in the policy discussions concerning poverty alleviation and the economic impact of globalization. Previously these have been discrete discourses, the former concerned with development cooperation and economic and social policy initiatives, the latter based on political economy critiques about globalization. This separation can be seen to underlie the separation of 'social' and 'economic' negotiating regimes so that social and environmental issues are excluded from the negotiations about international trade (de)regulation at the OECD and WTO. The move to assert the ethical dimensions of labour (and environmental) standards as part of the providence of international companies provides a basis for more inclusive negotiations of global trade and investment. Moreover, it links disparate or individual corporations taking 'ethical' stands with more global developments in the field of social responsibility. [...]

Codes of Conduct and Social Policy in a Globalizing Economy

The notion that international corporations might have some role if not responsibility in social development and policy is relatively new, and reflects both the extended global reach of transnational corporations and their escalating influence not just through direct control of affiliates but increasingly through joint ventures, strategic alliances and outsourcing (UNRISD, 2000: 76). But, more and more often global producers find themselves increasingly unable to remain insulated from demands for social responsibility, in the face of calls from a range of stakeholders, that they act as 'global citizens' rather than pursue a narrow insistence on a single bottom line to reflect the interests of their shareholders (CBI, 1999).

[...]

Direct pressure on corporations to develop, respect and enforce codes of conduct in global supply chains can therefore be understood as both the advance of a global social policy agenda and the re-articulation of labour interests within current debates about global social policy standards. This not only includes the previously ignored major stakeholder of transnational corporations, but also strengthens the traditional voices of organized labour – including the trade unions and the ILO – and also adds the voice of a set of previously unrepresented stakeholders – namely the workforce outside the organized formal centre who were beyond the scope or remit of trade unions or international agencies. The 'flexibilization' and casualization of labour associated with the integration of developing and emerging economies within the global market indicates the ways in which such countries have attempted to attract capital at any price, often on the basis of competing over low-cost and unprotected labour, necessitating a rational disregard for the emergence of global labour, environmental and social standards (Deacon, 1999). The pursuit of regulation of labour standards through codes of conduct thus reflects a re-grouping of those committed to pursuing labour interests, within a new configuration of institutional and policy debates concerning the elements and mechanisms of social policy in the changing context of globalization.

Deacon with Hulse and Stubbs (1997) question whether the broad coalition of stakeholders involved in developing and implementing (voluntary) codes of conduct [...] – a coalition which includes the very corporations accused and indicted of some of the worst excesses of economic, environmental and social exploitation of workers, localities and natural resources – [can] be – voluntarily – part of a solution that will rectify such abuses and deliver a win–win strategy for both international capital and workers? The impact of the ethical turn in business, including the effects of voluntary codes of conduct, may result in a number of different scenarios, which Zadek (2000) terms *oasis*, *desert* and *mecca*. The first refers to improvement for select groups of workers in specific consumer-sensitive industries – the enclave social policy effect discussed above. The second describes a situation where civil pressure for codes does not result in significant improvements, but at the same time their implementation undermines government regulation. These two scenarios present voluntary codes of conduct as a false dawn. However, in Zadek's third model, consumer pressure and voluntary codes reinforce statutory regulation to deliver a sustained improvement in labour standards, both nationally and internationally. The challenge lies in creating practical measures to ensure that this *mecca* is achieved.

[...]

References

Arthurs, H. (1996) 'Labour Law Without the State', *University of Toronto Law Journal* 46: 1–45.

Balasubramanyan, V.N. (1999) 'Foreign Direct Investment in Developing Countries', in S. Picciotto and R. Mayne (eds) *Regulating International Business: Beyond Liberalisation* (pp. 29–46). London: Macmillan.

Barrientos, S., McClenaghan, S. and Orton, L. (1999) *Gender and Codes of Conduct: A Case Study from Horticulture in South Africa*. London: Christian Aid.

Bickham-Mendez, J. (1999) 'Creating Alternatives from a Gender Perspective: Transnational Organising for Maquila Workers' Rights in Central America', submitted for inclusion in N. Naples and M. Desai (eds) *Globalisation from Below: Women's Community Activism for Social Change*.

Booth, F. and Seyfang, G. (1991) 'Is Green Consumerism Costing the Earth?', unpublished dissertation. Norwich: School of Development Studies, University of East Anglia.

Brill, L. (2000) 'Homenet Presentation: The Position of Homeworkers', paper presented at the Workshop on Emerging Issues in Ethical Trade, Westminster Central Hall, 22 March 2000.

Burgess, P. and Burns, M. (1999) 'Pilot Interim Review', ETI Report, accessed 6 July 2000, copy on file: http://www.ethicaltrade.org/_html/publications/report_1999–11/ content.shtml.

CAWN (Central America Women's Network) and WWW (Women Working Worldwide) (1999) *Women Workers and Codes of Conduct: Central America Workshop Report*. London: CAWN and Manchester: WWW.

CBI (Confederation of British Industry) (1999) 'Global Social Responsibility: Is the Business of Business just Business?', briefing prepared by the International Competitiveness Directorate. London: CBI.

CCC (Clean Clothes Campaign) (1998) 'Keeping the Work Floor Clean: Monitoring Models in the Garment Industry', accessed 9 March 1999, copy on file: http://www.cleanclothes.org/1/cleaner.htm.

CEPAA (1997) *Social Accountability 8000*, International Standard. London: CEPAA.

CERES (1999) 'Global Reporting Initiative (GRI)', CERES, accessed 19 March 1999, copy on file: http://www.ceres.org/reporting/globalreporting.html.

CIPAF (1999) 'Appuntes acerca de los codigos de conducta en las empresas transnacionales', document for the 'Trabajo si pero con dignidad' campaign. Santo Domingo: CIPAF/OXFAM.

Deacon, B. (1999) 'The Tobin Tax and Global Social Policy', copy on file: http://www.stakes.fi/gaspp/docs/tobin.doc.

Deacon, B. with Hulse, M. and Stubbs, P. (1997) *Global Social Policy: International Organisations and the Future of Welfare*. London: Sage.

Denny, C. (2000) 'Mexico Threatens to Scupper Labour Pact', *Guardian*, 1 July.

Dobson, A. (1990) *Green Political Thought*. London: Harper Collins.

Elson, D. and Pearson, R. (1981) 'Nimble Fingers Make Cheap Workers: An Analysis of Women's Employment in Third World Export Manufacturing', *Feminist Review* 7(Spring): 87–107.

ETI (Ethical Trading Initiative) (1998) Ethical Trade Newsletter, No. 1, June 1998, accessed 6 July 2000, copy on file:http://www.ethicaltrade.org/_html/ publications/ newsl_01/content.shtml.

ETI (Ethical Trading Initiative) (1999) *'Learning From Doing' Review: A Report on Company Progress in Implementing Ethical Sourcing Policies and Practices*. London: ETI.

Ferguson, C. (1998) *A Review of UK Company Codes of Conduct*. London: Department for International Development, Social Development Division.

Ferguson, C. (1999) *Global Social Policy Principles: Human Rights and Social Justice*. London: Department for International Development, Social Development Division.

Financial Times (1999) 'Responsible Business: A Financial Times Guide'. London, June.

Fridd, P. and Sainsbury, J. (1999) 'The Role of Voluntary Codes of Conduct and Regulation – A Retailer's View' in S. Picciotto and R. Mayne (eds) *Regulating International Business: Beyond Liberalisation* (pp. 221–234). Basingstoke: Macmillan.

Green, D. (1998) *Fashion Victims: Together We Can Clean Up the Clothes Trade: The Asian Garment Industry and Globalisation*. London: CAFOD.

Green, D. (1999) *Views from the South: Conference Report on Ethical Trade*. London: NGO Labour Rights Network.

Hadjipateras, A. (1999) *New Ways of Organising in a Free Trade Zone: A Case Study of NGO Organising*. London: Central American Women's Network.

Haworth, N. (2000) 'International Labour and its Emerging Role in Global Governance: Regime Fusion, Social Protection, Regional Integration and Production Volatility', paper presented to the 'Engaging Global Governance' workshop, University of Manchester, July 2000.

Hepple, B. (1997) 'New Approaches to International Labour Regulation', *Industrial Law Journal* 26(4): 353–66.

Homenet (2000) Newsletter, No. 13, Spring.

Horton, S. (1996) *Women and Industrialisation in Asia*. London: Routledge.

Howitt, R. (1999) *Report on EU Standards for European Enterprises operating in Developing Countries: Towards a European Code of Conduct*. Brussels: Committee on Development and Cooperation, European Parliament.

International Labour Organisation (1978) *Tripartite Declaration of Principles Concerning Multinational Enterprises and Social Policy*, OB Vol. LXI, 1978, Series A, No. 1. Geneva: ILO.

International Labour Organisation (1998) *Overview of Global Developments and Office Activities Concerning Codes of Conduct, Social Labelling and other Private Sector Initiatives Addressing Labour Issues,* Working Party on the Social Dimensions of the Liberalisation of International Trade, GB.273/WP/SDL/1(rev1). Geneva: ILO. Accessed electronically 9 March 1999, copy on file: http://www.ilo.org/public/english/20gb/docs/gb273/sdl-1.htm.

International Labour Organisation (1999) *Fundamental ILO Conventions,* accessed 7 July 1999, copy on file: http://www.ilo.org/public/english/50normes/whatare/fundam/index.htm.

Investor Responsibility Research Center (1998) *The Sweatshop Quandary: Corporate Responsibility on the Global Frontier.* Washington, DC: IRRC.

IRC (Interhemispheric Resource Centre) (1999) 'Blood, Sweat and Shears: Corporate Codes of Conduct', Corporate Watch, accessed 12 April 1999, copy on file: http:// www.igc.org/trac/feature/sweatshops/codes.html.

IRENE (International Restructuring Education Network Europe) (1998) 'Let's Go Fair: report of IRENE International Workshop on the Sports Shoes Campaigns in Europe', *News from IRENE* 26 (April): 50–1.

Jenkins, R. (1984) 'Divisions Over the International Division of Labour', *Capital and Class* 22: 28–57.

Kahn, H., Peters, G. and Poneman, L. (1999) 'Reputation Assurance: The Value of a Good Name', in *re: Business* (February), copy on file: http://www.pwcglobal.com/ rebusiness.

Kearney, N. (1999) 'Corporate Codes of Conduct: The Privatised Application of Labour Standards', in S. Picciotto and R. Mayne (eds) *Regulating International Business: Beyond Liberalisation* (pp. 205–220). Basingstoke: Macmillan.

Lee, E. (1997) 'Globalisation and Labour Standards: A Review of Issues', *International Labour Review* 136(2): 173–89. Accessed electronically 12 April 1999, copy on file: http://www.ilo.org/public/english/180revue/articles/lee97-2.htm.

Light, J. (1999) 'Engendering Change: The Long, Slow Road to Organising Women Maquiladora Workers', La Linea (Gender, Labor and Environmental Justice on the US–Mexico Border) Feature, Corporate Watch, accessed 10 August 1999; copy on file: http://www.corpwatch.org/trac/feature/border/women/engendering.html.

Lo, D. (1999) 'The East Asian Phenomenon: The Consensus, the Dissent and the Significance of the Present Crisis', *Capital and Class* 67: 1–23.

Murphy, D.Y. and Bendell, J. (1999) *Partners in Time?: Business, NGOs and Sustainable Development. UNRISD Discussion Paper 109.* Geneva: UNRISD.

Murray, J. (1998) 'Corporate Codes of Conduct and Labour Standards', *International Labour Organisation Bureau for Workers Activities (ACTRAV) Working Paper,* accessed 20 July 1999, copy on file: http://www.ilo.org/public/english/230actra/ publ/codes.htm.

NEF (New Economics Foundation) and CIIR (Catholic Institute for International Relations) (1997) *Open Trading.* London: NEF.

Nelson, J. (1998) *Building Competitiveness and Communities*. London: Prince of Wales Business Leaders Forum.

NICWJ (National Interfaith Committee for Worker Justice) (1999) 'Cross Border Blues: A Call for Justice for Maquiladora Workers in Tehuacan', accessed 25 November 1999, copy on file: http://www.guessboycott.org/mexico/mexico1.html

NSC (Nicaragua Solidarity Campaign) (2000) Nicaragua Network Hotline, 19 June 2000, email newsletter: http://www.gn.apc.org/nsc.

OECD (Organisation for Economic Co-operation and Development) (1997) *The OECD Declaration and Decisions on International Investment and Multinational Enterprises: Basic Texts*, OCDE/GD(97)36. Paris: OECD.

Pearson, R. (1998) '"Nimble Fingers" Revisited: Reflections on Women and Third World Industrialisation in the Late Twentieth Century', in C. Jackson and R. Pearson (eds) *Feminist Visions of Development: Gender Analysis and Policy* (pp. 171–188). London: Routledge.

Pearson, R. (1999) 'Codes of Conduct as Contingent and Enclave Social Policy', paper presented at DfID Global Social Policy Workshop, London, May 13–14.

Pearson, R. (2000) 'Gender, Globalization and Transitional Economies', Keynote Paper, Gender and IndoChina Conference Proceedings, Women's Action and Research Initiative, Bangkok, February.

Picciotto, S. (1999) 'Introduction: What Rules for the World Economy?' in S. Picciotto and R. Mayne (eds) *Regulating International Business: Beyond Liberalisation* (pp. 1–26). Basingstoke: Macmillan.

Seyfang, G. (1999) 'Private Sector Self-regulation for Social Responsibility: Mapping Codes of Conduct', Social Policy Research Programme, Working Paper No. 1. Norwich: Overseas Development Group, University of East Anglia.

Standing, G (1999) *Global Labour Flexibility: Seeking Resdistributive Justice*. Basingstoke: Macmillan.

Steelworkers Humanity Fund (1998) 'Review of Codes of Conduct and Labels Relevant for a Proposed Canadian Task Force on Sweatshop and Child Labour, SWF', accessed 11 August 1999, copy on file: http://www.web.net/fairtrade/other/ learning-circle.html.

TIE (Transnationals Information Exchange) (1985) Meeting the Corporate Challenge: A Handbook on Corporate Campaigns, TIE Report 18/19. Amsterdam: TIE.

UKSIF (UK Social Investment Forum) (1998) 'The UKSIF Newsletter', No. 8, Summer 1998, accessed 7 July 2000, copy on file: http://www.uksif.org/newsletter/ 1998_issue8/content.shtml.

UNRISD (2000) *Visible Hands: Taking Responsibility for Social Development*. Geneva: UNRISD.

War On Want (n.d.) *Invest In Freedom: Activate Your Pension*, resource pack. London: War On Want.

WWW (Women Working Worldwide) (1998) *Women Workers and Codes of Conduct: Asian Workshop Report*. Manchester: WWW.

Yanz, L. (2000) 'Broad Based Bargaining', paper presented to Women Working Worldwide conference, Manchester University, 27–28 September.

Yanz, L., Jeffcott, B., Ladd, D. and Atlin, J. (Maquila Solidarity Network, Canada) (1999) *Policy Options to Improve Standards for Women Garment Workers in Canada and Internationally*. Ottowa: Status of Women Canada. Accessed 13 March 1999, copy on file: http://www.swc-cfc.gc.ca/publish/research/yanz-e.html.

Yearley, S. and Forrester, J. (2000) 'Shell, a Sure Target for Global Environmental Campaigning?', in R. Cohen and S. M. Rai (eds) *Global Social Movements*. London: Athlone.

Zadek, S. (2000) *Ethical Trade Futures*. London: New Economics Foundation.

Zadek, S., Pruzan, P. and Evans, R. (1997) *Building Corporate Accountability*. London: Earthscan.

Zeldenrust, I. and Ascoly, N. (1998) *Codes of Conduct for Transnational Corporations: An Overview*. Tilberg: International Restructuring Education Network Europe (IRENE).

Chapter 3.5

The Framework Convention on Tobacco Control: the politics of global health governance

Jeff Collin, Kelley Lee and Karen Bissell

It is estimated that some four million deaths per year can currently be attributed to tobacco, a figure representing around one in 10 adult deaths. By 2030 both the total and the proportion of tobacco-related deaths are expected to have risen dramatically, to some 10 million or one in 6 adult deaths. Such figures suggest that around 500 million people alive today will eventually be killed by tobacco. Nor will this burden be equitably shared. Smoking related deaths were once largely confined to men in high-income countries, but the marked shift in smoking patterns among high- to middle- and low-income countries will be evident in due course by rapidly rising trends in tobacco-related diseases. By 2030 70% of deaths from tobacco will occur in the developing world, up from around 50% currently (WHO, 1999; Jha & Chaloupka, 1999).

These sobering statistics reflect a continuing struggle by the public health community to effectively address an issue that has long been understood scientifically. Since the first wave of publications linking smoking with lung cancer around 1950 (Levin *et al*, 1950; Wynder & Graham, 1950; Doll & Hill, 1950), much has been learned about the diverse health impacts of tobacco consumption. Despite the clear messages emerging from medical research, however, the establishment of effective regulatory frameworks of tobacco control has been sporadic, and they remain far from adopted in most countries.

The additional challenge in recent decades has been the globalisation of the tobacco industry. Globalisation is a set of processes leading to the intensification of human interaction across three types of boundaries – spatial, temporal and cognitive. The changes wrought by processes of global change are evident in many spheres of social activity, including the economic, political, cultural and technological (Lee, 2001). In terms of tobacco control, the specific challenges of globalisation are:

- facilitated access to markets worldwide by the tobacco industry through trade liberalisation and specific provisions under multilateral trade agreements;
- enhanced marketing, advertising and sponsorship opportunities via global communication systems;
- greater economies of scale ranging from the purchase of local cigarette manufacturers, improved access to ever larger markets and the development and production of global brands; and
- the ability of transnational corporations (TNCs) to undermine the regulatory authority of national governments.

It is therefore unsurprising that transnational tobacco companies (TTCs) have enjoyed record sales and profits since the early 1990s, with the main source of growth being the developing world. While demand has gradually declined in many high-income countries thanks to changing public attitudes towards tobacco use and stronger regulation, changes in the developing world are more than compensating for contraction of traditional markets. Indeed, by expanding their presence in middle- and low-income countries, TTCs will continue to remain viable and lucrative businesses in all countries.

This paper analyses the particular challenges that tobacco control poses for health governance in an era of accelerating globalisation. Traditionally health systems have been structured at the national level, and health regulation has focused on the needs of populations within individual countries. However, the increasingly global nature of the tobacco industry, and the risks it poses to public health, require a transnational approach to regulation. This has been the rationale behind negotiations for a Framework Convention on Tobacco Control (FCTC) by the Tobacco Free Initiative of the World Health Organisation (TFI/WHO). In recognition of the need to go beyond national governments, and to create a governance mechanism that can effectively address the transnational nature of tobacco issues, WHO has sought to involve a broad range of interests in negotiations. The contributions of civil society groups in particular in the negotiation process have been unusual. The paper explores the nature and effectiveness of these contributions. It concludes with an assessment of whether the FCTC constitutes a significant shift towards a new form of global health governance, exploring the institutional tensions inherent in attempting to extend participation within a state–centric organisation.

Thwarting health governance: the tobacco industry and the limits of tobacco control

> Tobacco use is unlike other threats to global health. Infectious diseases do not employ multinational public relations firms. There are no front groups to promote the spread of cholera. Mosquitoes have no lobbyists. (WHO Committee of Experts, 2000)

The progress of the global epidemic of tobacco-related deaths and disease reflects the extent to which the tobacco industry has been able to thwart the development and implementation of effective tobacco control policies at national, regional and international levels. [...]

The most striking examples of tobacco company influence in the conduct of the national policy process are provided by those cases where industry intervention via lobbying has apparently shaped the outcome of proposed legislation, resulting in its abandonment or significant amendment. Internal industry documents released as a result of litigation in the USA are illustrative of the scale of such efforts, the resources afforded to them and their frequency of success. A review of activities by Philip Morris International Corporate Affairs in 1986 proclaims, among other achievements, their success in blocking, diluting and reversing measures to control advertising:

> A law prohibiting tobacco advertising was passed in Ecuador but, after a mobilization of journalists from throughout Latin America and numerous organizations, it was vetoed by the President. A similar bill was proposed in Peru, but was sent back for reconsideration ... In Venezuela, we were successful in stopping a detrimental, self-regulating advertising code, and are now negotiating a new one. Our work in Senegal resulted in a new advertising decree which reversed a total advertising ban. (Whist, 1986)

A review of Philip Morris' corporate affairs activities across Asia–Pacific similarly notes that 'the region has been successful at fighting off anti-tobacco proposals', exemplified by events in the Philippines where 'we have successfully delayed the passage of national legislation and more recently local legislation' (Dollisson, 1989). Such lobbying success is not, of course, confined to low- and middle-income countries. In what was reportedly the most expensive sustained issue-advocacy campaign in the USA, the tobacco companies spent $43 million in the first half of 1998 in defeating federal legislation sponsored by Senator John McCain (Saloojee & Dagli, 2000).

[...]

In keeping with the primarily national basis of tobacco control to date, the efforts of the industry to minimise its impact have historically focused on policy processes within nation-states. Tobacco companies have, however, been quick to identify both the potential regulatory challenges and the enormous business opportunities inherent in regional and international organisations. [...]

Within the EU the gradual transfer of policy competence to the regional level has been accompanied by increasing concern among the major tobacco companies to monitor and intervene in policy making. The diversity of key issues handled by EU institutions, including food regulation, advertising practices, excise tax harmonisation, abolition of duty free and environmental tobacco smoke have encouraged major lobbying efforts by the industry. Analysis of industry documents reveals the astute exploitation of the complex decision-making procedures of EU institutions, as well as the high levels of access to and support within them that tobacco companies have secured. [...]

The tobacco industry has also sought to minimise the impact of potential control measures within international organisations, particularly WHO, while simultaneously exploiting the opportunities presented by trade liberalisation under GATT and WTO. Analysis of tobacco industry documents has revealed the scale of collaborative activities undertaken by transnational tobacco companies to undermine WHO efforts to reduce tobacco consumption. A committee of experts assembled by WHO Director-General Gro Harlem Brundtland identified diverse strategies to defuse the potential impact of WHO initiatives. Tobacco companies sought to influence policy by building relationships with WHO staff, including gaining contacts through hiring or offering future employment to officials, and placing industry consultants in positions within WHO. The industry exerted pressure on relevant WHO budgets in an attempt to further constrain its tobacco control activities, and targeted other UN agencies to detract attention from the scale of the health impact of tobacco. WHO's competence and priorities were attacked in orchestrated campaigns of media and political pressure, the International Tobacco Growers Association was established as a front for lobbying, and large events were staged to distract media attention from the World Conference on Tobacco or Health (WHO Committee of Experts, 2000).

[...]

The expansion and entrenchment of a liberal trading regime under the auspices of GATT and WTO represent an opportunity that TTCs have been quick to exploit. The operational context of the industry was transformed by the rapid political and economic changes coincident with the end of the Cold War. In 1993 the then BAT chairman Sir Patrick Sheehy noted that 'the tobacco markets open to our products have actually tripled in size in recent years, under the twin impact of sweeping market liberalisations across the northern hemisphere and the crumbling monolithic communism east of the river Elbe' (Sheehy, 1993). [...] Trade liberalisation has led to increased consumption of tobacco, but while it has no substantive effect on higher income countries, it has a large and significant impact on smoking in low-income countries and a significant, if smaller, impact on middle-income countries (Taylor *et al*, 2000).

Part of this expansion can be attributed to the willingness and ability of the tobacco transnationals to pursue their interests within the institutional architecture of the international trading regime. The most famous example here is the case of Thailand, where access to a previously closed cigarette market was enforced by a GATT arbitration panel in 1990 following a referral by the US Trade Representative that was prompted by US tobacco companies (Chantornvong & McCargo, 2000; Vateesatokit *et al*, 2000). The Thai case was part of a broader wave of threatened retaliatory sanctions by the USA between 1986 and 1990 that also involved Taiwan, South Korea and Japan. It has been estimated that the subsequent opening of these markets had by 1991 increased per capita cigarette consumption by an average of 10% (Chaloupka & Laixuthai, 1996). [...]

Revitalising health governance: the Framework Convention on Tobacco Control

> The Framework Convention process will activate all those areas of governance that have a direct impact on public health. Science and economics will mesh with legislation and litigation. Health ministers will work with their counterparts in finance, trade, labour, agriculture and social affairs ministries to give public health the place it deserves. The challenge for us comes in seeking global and national solutions in tandem for a problem that cuts across national boundaries, cultures, societies and socioeconomic strata. (Brundtland, 2000)

In a world where many health risks and opportunities are becoming increasingly globalised, influencing health determinants, status and outcomes cannot be achieved through actions taken at the national level alone. The intensification of transborder flows of people, ideas, goods and services necessitates a reassessment of the rules and institutions that govern health policy and practice. This is especially so as the determinants of health are being affected by factors outside the traditional parameters of the health sector – trade and investment flows, collective violence and conflict, illicit and criminal activity, global environmental change, and global communication technologies. Importantly, there is a widespread belief that the current system of international health governance (IHG), focused on the national governments of states, has a number of limitations and gaps. In the light of these challenges, the concept of global health governance (GHG) has become a subject of interest and debate in the field of international health (Dodgson et al, 2001).

The distinction between IHG and GHG arises from the challenges of globalisation, as defined above, to health governance. First, the spatial dimension of global change means that health determinants and outcomes are less defined by, and in some cases, disengaged from, territorial space. Traditionally, national health systems are by definition structured along national boundaries and deal with cross-border flows (eg infectious disease control) through international cooperation. Globalisation creates transborder flows that, in many cases, are 'deterritorialised' (unrelated to physical or territorial space) and may thus circumvent territorially based rules and institutions. In the case of tobacco control, trade in tobacco products remains largely within the regulatory control of national governments. However, the trend towards targeting selected populations within and across countries through marketing, advertising and sponsorship conveyed through global communications (eg satellites), for example, has the potential to circumvent national regulatory authority.

A recognition of the limitations of health governance, primarily structured around states, for controlling the global dimensions of the tobacco epidemic is the impetus behind the FCTC. While the convention formally remains an inter-governmental treaty, the involvement of non-state actors in the negotiation process reflects the need to go beyond the state. Civil society organisations have been especially active in tobacco control, and will represent a key resource for implementing and monitoring the provisions of FCTC. [...]

The FCTC process has thus been employed as a catalyst to encourage broader participation in and engagement with tobacco control issues. An obvious target for this inclusive approach has been WHO member states themselves, clearly the core constituency if a convention is to be adopted and implemented. The 1999 World Health Assembly unanimously adopted resolution 52.18 (World Health Assembly, 1999) to instigate a two-step process leading to negotiation of the FCTC, with working groups to establish its technical foundation, to be followed by the establishment of an Intergovernmental Negotiating Body (INB). A record 50 states took the floor to commit political and economic support (WHO, 2000a). The scale of subsequent member state involvement in the process has been generally impressive, with 148 countries attending the first session of the INB in October 2000 (WHO, 2000b). The demands of such attendance and participation have meant an expanded role for multi-sectoral collaboration on tobacco issues at the national level. Formal and informal committees have been established and regular inter-ministerial consultations in countries as diverse as Zimbabwe, China, Brazil, Thailand and the USA (Woelk et al,

2000; Wipfli *et al*, 2001). A notable development has been the negotiation of co-ordinated positions among regional groupings prior to the INB meetings. The Johannesburg Declaration on the FCTC (African Region Meeting 2001) was adopted by 21 countries of the African Region in WHO in March 2001. This common front was widely perceived as having added weight to their contributions to the INB session, emphasising a commitment to progressive control measures in combination with calls for assistance in agricultural diversification (Bates, 2001).

An additional objective of the WHO team handling the FCTC process has been to improve co-ordination and co-operation across UN agencies. A key step here was the 1999 decision to establish an Ad Hoc Inter-Agency Task Force on Tobacco Control under the leadership of WHO. This replaced the UN focal point, previously located within the UN Conference on Trade and Development (UNCTAD), the creation of which had 'opened the door to tobacco industry influence throughout the UN' (WHO Committee of Experts, 2000). Fifteen UN organisations as well as the World Bank, the International Monetary Fund and the WTO are participating in the work of the Task Force (Wipfli *et al*, 2001). Its technical work in support of the negotiation process has included projects on environmental tobacco smoke, deforestation, employment and the rights of the child (Taylor & Bettcher, 2001; WHO & UNICEF, 2001). Success in engaging the World Bank in tobacco control issues has been of particular importance in adding credibility and momentum to the FCTC process. A landmark in this regard was the publication by the World Bank of the 1999 report *Curbing the Epidemic* (Jha & Chaloupka, 1999), the dissemination of which has contributed greatly to recognition of the national economic benefits associated with effective tobacco control. This politically critical message has been reinforced by the more detailed exploration of economic issues surrounding tobacco use in developing countries (Jha & Chaloupka, 2000).

The FCTC process has aimed to encourage the participation of actors traditionally excluded from the state-centric politics of UN governance. Some indication of the breadth of engagement that has been facilitated is provided by the Public Hearings held in October 2000. This exercise, the first such ever hosted by WHO, provided an opportunity for interested groups to register their views before the start of intergovernmental negotiations. Over 500 written submissions were received, while 144 organisations provided testimony during the two-day hearings, encompassing TTCs, state tobacco companies and producer organisations as well as diverse public health agencies, womens' groups and academic institutions (WHO, 2001a).

[...]

A key element in the opening of participation sought by the FCTC process has been the attempt to find new ways of engaging with international NGOs that are active in tobacco control efforts. WHO has standard practices that govern the terms by which certain NGOs can participate in its proceedings. 'Official Relations' is a status achieved through a multi-year process by international health-related NGOs, usually international federations of national and regional professional NGOs. There are currently 193 NGOs in Official Relations with WHO, entitling them to observe proceedings and to 'make a statement of an expository nature' at the invitation of the chair (WHO, 2000d), generally restricted to a short period at the end of a session. NGOs that are not in Official Relations must find a sponsoring organisation to enter and observe a formal meeting, and are unable to make statements in the name of their organisation.

In order to contribute more fully to the FCTC process, NGOs have sought to ease the narrow parameters of participation enabled by Official Relations status, and to accelerate the protracted process by which this status has traditionally been conferred. Some member states have supported these aspirations to greater involvement, with Canada prominent in requesting greatly expanded NGO participation and the accreditation of expert national NGOs (WHO, 2001b). Following an open consultation held by Canada and Thailand, member states approved recommendations that the process of accreditation should be accelerated and that NGOs in Official Relations should have access to working groups. At the Second Session of the Intergovernmental Negotiating Body, it was reported that the Executive Board of the WHO had agreed to admit NGOs into provisional official relations with the WHO, a status that would be revised yearly throughout the FCTC process (WHO, 2001c). It should be noted that some public health NGOs have been cautious about seeking any radical change in the terms of access and participation, fearing that such expansion could serve to facilitate the entry of tobacco industry front groups into the negotiating process.

Perhaps more important than the formal terms of participation in the negotiating chamber is the scope facilitated by such access for NGOs to play a number of key supporting roles. Prominent among these has been an educative function, with NGOs organising seminars and preparing briefings for delegates on diverse technical aspects of the proposed convention. Lobbying activities have been extensive thanks to policy discussions with governments, letter-writing to delegates and heads of state, advocacy campaigns, press conferences before, during and after the meetings, and the publication of reports into tobacco industry practices and collusion in smuggling (Campaign for Tobacco Free Kids and ASH-UK, 2001; Campaign for Tobacco Free Kids, 2001). The NGOs have also been able to use such access to strengthen the effectiveness of their advocacy role, acting as the public health conscience during proceedings. Particularly important has been exposing the dangerous and obstructivist positions adopted by certain member states, with the negative role of the Bush administration leading to calls from some NGOs for the USA to withdraw from negotiations (ASH–UK, 2001; Bates, 2001). Additionally, prominent tobacco control advocates have occasionally participated in FCTC negotiations from within national delegations, examples including Jon Kapito, Margaretha Haglund and Luc Joossens for Malawi, Sweden and Belgium, respectively (WHO, 2000a). In each of these respects the public health NGOs can be seen as constituting a counterweight to the pressures exerted on national delegations by the tobacco industry (INFACT, 1999).

This pattern of NGO involvement does not preclude questions relating to legitimacy and barriers to entry. At the two working group meetings, in particular, participation was almost exclusively from high–income country NGOs and international health-based NGOs (WHO, 1999b; 2000c). For the subsequent INB meetings, high–income country NGOs and international NGOs have given some financial assistance to enable the participation of NGO representatives from developing countries, while there are hopes that some United Nations Fund money may reach low–income country NGOs for this purpose. The coherence of NGO activities and the scope for impact of developing country activists have, however, been significantly increased as a result of the formation of the Framework Convention Alliance. This grouping of over 60 NGOs was created to improve communication between those groups already engaged in the FCTC process and to address the need for a systematic outreach to smaller NGOs in developing countries (Wipfli *et al*, 2001).

Conclusion

The TTCs have long recognised that tobacco control issues are of supranational significance, transcending the national borders within which policies have primarily focused and disputes have largely been articulated. Such companies have recognised the scope for policy learning, and national regulation has frequently been resisted more through fears of a domino effect on other countries than for fear of direct impacts within the territorial limits of is application (Collin, forthcoming). As far back as 1986 Philip Morris International Corporate Affairs highlighted the essentially global nature of their contest with advocates of tobacco control, noting that 'the issues we face – taxation, marketing restrictions, environmental tobacco smoke (ETS) – are now literally world-wide problems, and the anti-smoking groups use sophisticated tactics to attack us on these issues throughout the world' (Whist, 1986).

The FCTC process constitutes an explicit attempt to counter the globalisation of the tobacco epidemic through a reconfiguration of health governance. It represents a necessary response to the extent to which the spread of a 'global bad for public health' has outstripped the capacity of existing modes of regulation (Taylor & Bettcher, 2001). As such, the tobacco epidemic demonstrates poignantly the limitations of national level health governance in a globalising world.

[...]

References

ASH-UK (2001) United States should pull out of tobacco treaty – EU needs new approach, 4 May, at http://www.fctc.org/press13.shtml, accessed 29 October 2001.

Bates, C (2001) Developing countries take the lead on WHO convention, *Tobacco Control*, 10(3), p 209.

Brundtland, GH (2000) Speech to WHO's International Conference on Global Tobacco Control Law: Towards a WHO Framework Convention on Tobacco Control, New Delhi, 7 January, at http://www. who.int/director-general / speeches/2000/20000107_new_delhi.html, accessed 29 October 2001.

Campaign for Tobacco Free Kids (2001) Illegal pathways to illegal profits: the big cigarette companies and international smuggling, April, at http://tobaccofreekids. org/campaign/global/framework/ docs/Smuggling.pdf, accessed 28 October 2001.

Campaign for Tobacco Free Kids and ASH-UK (2001) Trust us – we're the tobacco industry, April, at www.ash.org.uk/html/conduct/html/trustus.html, accessed 28 October 2001.

Chaloupka, F & Laixuthai, A (1996) *US Trade Policy and Cigarette Smoking in Asia*, Working Paper No 5543 (Cambridge, MA: National Bureau of Economic Research).

Chantornvong, S & McCargo, D (2000) Political economy of tobacco control in Thailand, in: JP Vaughan, J Collin & K Lee (eds) *Case Study Report: Global Analysis Project on the Political Economy of Tobacco Control in Low- and Middle-Income Countries* (London: London School of Hygiene & Tropical Medicine).

Collin, J (forthcoming) 'Think global, smoke local': transnational tobacco companies and cognitive globalisation, in K Lee (ed), *Globalization and Health: Case Studies* (London: Macmillan/St Martin's Press).

Dodgson, R., K Lee & N Drager (2001) Global health governance: a conceptual review, *Key Issues in Global Governance*, Discussion Paper No 1 (Geneva: WHO).

Doll, R & Hill, A (1950) Smoking and carcinoma of the lung: preliminary report, *British Medical Journal*, 143, pp 329–336.

Dollisson, J (1989) 2nd Revised Forecast Presentation – Corporate Affairs, 15 June, Bates Number: 2500101311-1323, at www.tobacco.org/Documents/dd/ ddpmbattleasia.html, accessed 28 August 2001.

INFACT (1999) *Mobilizing NGOs and the Media Behind the International Framework Convention on Tobacco Control*, FCTC Technical Briefing Series No 3, WHO/ NCD/TFI/99.3, at http://tobacco.who .int/en/fctc/papers/paper3.pdf, accessed 29 October 2001.

Jha, P & Chaloupka, F (eds) (2000) *Tobacco Control in Developing Countries* (Oxford: Oxford University Press).

Jha, P & Chaloupka, F (1999) *Curbing the Epidemic: Governments and the Economics of Tobacco Control* (Washington, DC: World Bank).

Levin, M, Golsdstein, H & Gerhardt, P (1950) Cancer and tobacco smoking: a preliminary report, *Journal of the American Medical Association*, 143, pp 336–338.

Saloojee, Y & Dagli, E (2000) Tobacco industry tactics for resisting public policy on health, *Bulletin of the World Health Organisation*, 78(7), pp 902–910.

Sheehy, P (1993) Speech to the Farmers President's Council Meeting, Guildford Depository, 8 June, Bates No: 601023526-3540 .

Taylor, A & Bettcher, D (2001) Sustainable health development: negotiation of the WHO Framework Convention on Tobacco Control, *Development Bulletin*, 54, pp 6–10.

Taylor, A, Chaloupka, F, Gundon, E & Corbett, M (2000) The impact of trade liberalization on tobacco consumption, in: P Jha & F Chaloupka (eds), *Tobacco Control in Developing Countries*, pp 343–364 (Oxford: Oxford University Press).

Vateesatokit, P, Hughes, B & Rittiphakdee, B (2000) Thailand: winning battles, but the war's far from over, *Tobacco Control*, 9, pp 122–127.

Whist, A (1986) Memo to Board of Directors: Subject – Philip Morris International Corporate Affairs, 17 December, Bates Number: 2025431401-1406, at www.pmdocs.com, accessed 12 October 2001.

WHO (1999) *World Health Report 1999* (Geneva: WHO).

WHO (2000a) Framework Convention on Tobacco Control: Introduction, at http://tobacco.who.int/ en/fctc/index.html, accessed 28 October 2001.

WHO (2000b) WHO Framework Convention on Tobacco Control: report by the Secretariat, Geneva, EB/107/30, 6 December.

WHO (2000c) List of participants, Intergovernmental Negotiating Body on the Framework Convention on Tobacco Control, Second session, A/FCTC/INB2/DIV/2 Rev.1.

WHO (2000d) Participation of nongovernmental organizations in the Intergovernmental Negotiating Body, Intergovernmental Negotiating Body on the Framework Convention on Tobacco Control, First session. A/FCTC/INB1/5 Paras 4, 6.

WHO (2001a) FCTC public hearings, at http://tobacco.who.int /en/fctc/publichearings.html, accessed 28 October 2001.

WHO (2001b) Intergovernmental Negotiating Body on the Framework Convention on Tobacco Control, First Session Part 1–2. Intergovernmental Negotiating Body on the Framework Convention on Tobacco Control, Second session, A/FCTC/INB2/3 Part 2, second session, Para 3.

WHO (2001c) Participation of nongovernmental organizations, Intergovernmental Negotiating Body on the Framework Convention on Tobacco Control, Second session, A/FCTC/INB2/6.

WHO & UNICEF (2001) Tobacco and the rights of the child, WHO/NMH/ TFI/01.3.

WHO Committee of Experts (2000) Tobacco company strategies to undermine tobacco control activities at the World Health Organisation, July, at http://filestore. who.int/~who/home/tobacco/tobacco.pdf, accessed 29 October 2001.

Wipfli, H, Bettcher, D, Subramaniam, C & Taylor, A (2001) Confronting the global tobacco epidemic: emerging mechanisms of global governance, in M McKee, P Garner & R Stott (eds), *International Co-operation and Health* (Oxford: Oxford University Press).

Woelk, G, Mtisi, S & Vaughan, JP (2000) Political economy of tobacco control in Zimbabwe, in: JP Vaughan, J Collin & K Lee (eds) *Case Study Report: Global Analysis Project on the Political Economy of Tobacco Control in Low- and Middle-Income Countries* (London: London School of Hygiene & Tropical Medicine).

World Health Assembly (1999) WHA Resolution 52.18 – Towards a WHO framework convention on tobacco control, at http://tobacco.who.int /en/fctc/ WHA52-18.html, accessed 28 October 2001.

Wynder, E & Graham, E (1950) Tobacco smoking as a possible etiologic factor in bronchogenic carcinoma, *Journal of the American Medical Association*, 143, pp 329–336.

Chapter 3.6

International Labour Organization (ILO) Philadelphia Declaration 1944

Preamble

Whereas universal and lasting peace can be established only if it is based upon social justice;

And whereas conditions of labour exist involving such injustice hardship and privation to large numbers of people as to produce unrest so great that the peace and harmony of the world are imperilled; and an improvement of those conditions is urgently required; as, for example, by the regulation of the hours of work including the establishment of a maximum working day and week, the regulation of the labour supply, the prevention of unemployment, the provision of an adequate living wage, the protection of the worker against sickness, disease and injury arising out of his employment the protection of children, young persons and women, provision for old age and injury, protection of the interests of workers when employed in countries other than their own, recognition of the principle of equal remuneration for work of equal value, recognition of the principle of freedom of association, the organization of vocational and technical education and other measures;

Whereas also the failure of any nation to adopt humane conditions of labour is an obstacle in the way of other nations which desire to improve the conditions in their own countries;

The High Contracting Parties, moved by sentiments of justice and humanity as well as by the desire to secure the permanent peace of the world, and with a view to attaining the objectives set forth in this Preamble, agree to the following Constitution of the International Labour Organization

[...]

Annex

Declaration concerning the aims and purpose of the International Labour Organization

The General Conference of the International Labour Organization meeting in its Twenty-sixth Session in Philadelphia, hereby adopts this tenth day of May in the year nineteen hundred and forty-four the present Declaration of the aims and purposes of the International Labour Organization and of the principles which should inspire the policy of its Members.

The Conference reaffirms the fundamental principles on which the Organization is based and, in particular, that –

(a)   labour is not a commodity;
(b)   freedom of expression and of association are essential to sustained progress;
(c)   poverty anywhere constitutes a danger to prosperity everywhere;
(d)   the war against want requires to be carried on with unrelenting vigor within each nation, and by continuous and concerted international effort in which the representatives of workers and employers, enjoying equal status with those of governments, join with them in free discussion and democratic decision with a view to the promotion of the common welfare.

Believing that experience has fully demonstrated the truth of the statement in the Constitution of the International Labour Organization that lasting peace can be established only if it is based on social justice, the Conference affirms that –

(a)   all human beings, irrespective of race, creed or sex, have the right to pursue both their material well-being and their spiritual development in conditions of freedom and dignity, of economic security and equal opportunity;
(b)   the attainment of the conditions in which this shall be possible must constitute the central aim of national and international policy;
(c)   all national and international policies and measures, in particular those of an economic and financial character, should be judged in this light and accepted only in so far as they may be held to promote and not to hinder the achievement of this fundamental objective;
(d)   it is a responsibility of the International Labour Organization to examine and consider all international economic and financial policies and measures in the light of this fundamental objective;
(e)   in discharging the tasks entrusted to it the International Labour Organization, having considered all relevant economic and financial factors, may include in its decisions and recommendations any provisions which it considers appropriate.

The Conference recognizes the solemn obligation of the International Labour Organization to further among the nations of the world programmes which will achieve –

(a) full employment and the raising of standards of living;
(b) the employment of workers in the occupations in which they can have the satisfaction of giving the fullest measure of their skill and attainments and make their greatest contribution to the common well-being;
(c) the provision, as a means to the attainment of this end and under adequate guarantees for all concerned, of facilities for training and the transfer of labour, including migration for employment and settlement;
(d) policies in regard to wages and earnings, hours and other conditions of work calculated to ensure a just share of the fruits of progress to all, and a minimum living wage to all employed and in need of such protection;
(e) the effective recognition of the right of collective bargaining, the cooperation of management and labour in the continuous improvement of productive efficiency, and the collaboration of workers and employers in the preparation and application of social and economic measures;
(f) the extension of social security measures to provide a basic income to all in need of such protection and comprehensive medical care;
(g) adequate protection for the life and health of workers in all occupations;
(h) provision for child welfare and maternity protection;
(i) the provision of adequate nutrition, housing and facilities for recreation and culture;
(j) the assurance of equality of educational and vocational opportunity.

Confident that the fuller and broader utilization of the world's productive resources necessary for the achievement of the objectives set forth in this Declaration can be secured by effective international and national action, including measures to expand production and consumption, to avoid severe economic fluctuations to promote the economic and social advancement of the less developed regions of the world, to assure greater stability in world prices of primary products, and to promote a high and steady volume of international trade, the Conference pledges the full cooperation of the International Labour Organization with such international bodies as may be entrusted with a share of the responsibility for this great task and for the promotion of the health, education and well-being of all peoples.

The conference affirms that the principles set forth in this Declaration are fully applicable to all peoples everywhere and that, while the manner of their application must be determined with due regard to the stage of social and economic development reached by each people, their progressive application to peoples who are still dependent, as well as to those who have already achieved self-government, is a matter of concern to the whole civilized world.

Chapter 3.7

Universal Declaration of Human Rights 1948

Preamble

Whereas recognition of the inherent dignity and of the equal and inalienable rights of all members of the human family is the foundation of freedom, justice and peace in the world,

Whereas disregard and contempt for human rights have resulted in barbarous acts which have outraged the conscience of mankind, and the advent of a world in which human beings shall enjoy freedom of speech and belief and freedom from fear and want has been proclaimed as the highest aspiration of the common people,

Whereas it is essential, if man is not to be compelled to have recourse, as a last resort, to rebellion against tyranny and oppression, that human rights should be protected by the rule of law,

Whereas it is essential to promote the development of friendly relations between nations,

Whereas the peoples of the United Nations have in the Charter reaffirmed their faith in fundamental human rights, in the dignity and worth of the human person and in the equal rights of men and women and have determined to promote social progress and better standards of life in larger freedom,

Whereas Member States have pledged themselves to achieve, in cooperation with the United Nations, the promotion of universal respect for and observance of human rights and fundamental freedoms,

Whereas a common understanding of these rights and freedoms is of the greatest importance for the full realization of this pledge,

Now, therefore,

The General Assembly,

Proclaims this Universal Declaration of Human Rights as a common standard of achievement for all peoples and all nations, to the end that every individual and every organ of society, keeping this Declaration constantly in mind, shall strive by teaching and education to promote respect for these rights and freedoms and by progressive measures, national and international, to secure their universal and effective recognition and observance, both among the peoples of Member States themselves and among the peoples of territories under their jurisdiction.

Article I

All human beings are born free and equal in dignity and rights. They are endowed with reason and conscience and should act towards one another in a spirit of brotherhood.

Article 2

Everyone is entitled to all the rights and freedoms set forth in this Declaration, without distinction of any kind, such as race, colour, sex, language, religion, political or other opinion, national or social origin, property, birth or other status.

Furthermore, no distinction shall be made on the basis of the political, jurisdictional or international status of the country or territory to which a person belongs, whether it be independent, trust, non-self-governing or under any other limitation of sovereignty.

Article 3

Everyone has the right to life, liberty and security of person.

Article 4

No one shall be held in slavery or servitude; slavery and the slave trade shall be prohibited in all their forms.

Article 5

No one shall be subjected to torture or to cruel, inhuman or degrading treatment or punishment.

Article 6

Everyone has the right to recognition everywhere as a person before the law.

Article 7

All are equal before the law and are entitled without any discrimination to equal protection of the law. All are entitled to equal protection against any discrimination in violation of this Declaration and against any incitement to such discrimination.

Article 8

Everyone has the right to an effective remedy by the competent national tribunals for acts violating the fundamental rights granted him by the constitution or by law.

Article 9

No one shall be subjected to arbitrary arrest, detention or exile.

Article 10

Everyone is entitled in full equality to a fair and public hearing by an independent and impartial tribunal, in the determination of his rights and obligations and of any criminal charge against him.

Article 11

1. Everyone charged with a penal offence has the right to be presumed innocent until proved guilty according to law in a public trial at which he has had all the guarantees necessary for his defence.

2. No one shall be held guilty of any penal offence on account of any act or omission which did not constitute a penal offence, under national or international law, at the time when it was committed. Nor shall a heavier penalty be imposed than the one that was applicable at the time the penal offence was committed.

Article 12

No one shall be subjected to arbitrary interference with his privacy, family, home or correspondence, nor to attacks upon his honour and reputation. Everyone has the right to the protection of the law against such interference or attacks.

Article 13

1. Everyone has the right to freedom of movement and residence within the borders of each State.

2. Everyone has the right to leave any country, including his own, and to return to his country.

Article 14

1. Everyone has the right to seek and to enjoy in other countries asylum from persecution.

2. This right may not be invoked in the case of prosecutions genuinely arising from non-political crimes or from acts contrary to the purposes and principles of the United Nations.

Article 15

1. Everyone has the right to a nationality.

2. No one shall be arbitrarily deprived of his nationality nor denied the right to change his nationality.

Article 16

1. Men and women of full age, without any limitation due to race, nationality or religion, have the right to marry and to found a family. They are entitled to equal rights as to marriage, during marriage and at its dissolution.

2. Marriage shall be entered into only with the free and full consent of the intending spouses.

3. The family is the natural and fundamental group unit of society and is entitled to protection by society and the State.

Article 17

1. Everyone has the right to own property alone as well as in association with others.

2. No one shall be arbitrarily deprived of his property.

Article 18

Everyone has the right to freedom of thought, conscience and religion; this right includes freedom to change his religion or belief, and freedom, either alone or in community with others and in public or private, to manifest his religion or belief in teaching, practice, worship and observance.

Article 19

Everyone has the right to freedom of opinion and expression; this right includes freedom to hold opinions without interference and to seek, receive and impart information and ideas through any media and regardless of frontiers.

Article 20

1. Everyone has the right to freedom of peaceful assembly and association.

2. No one may be compelled to belong to an association.

Article 21

1. Everyone has the right to take part in the government of his country, directly or through freely chosen representatives.

2. Everyone has the right to equal access to public service in his country.

3. The will of the people shall be the basis of the authority of government; this will shall be expressed in periodic and genuine elections which shall be by universal and equal suffrage and shall be held by secret vote or by equivalent free voting procedures.

Article 22

Everyone, as a member of society, has the right to social security and is entitled to realization, through national effort and international co-operation and in accordance with the organization and resources of each State, of the economic, social and cultural rights indispensable for his dignity and the free development of his personality.

Article 23

1. Everyone has the right to work, to free choice of employment, to just and favourable conditions of work and to protection against unemployment.

2. Everyone, without any discrimination, has the right to equal pay for equal work.

3. Everyone who works has the right to just and favourable remuneration ensuring for himself and his family an existence worthy of human dignity, and supplemented, if necessary, by other means of social protection.

4. Everyone has the right to form and to join trade unions for the protection of his interests.

Article 24

Everyone has the right to rest and leisure, including reasonable limitation of working hours and periodic holidays with pay.

Article 25

1. Everyone has the right to a standard of living adequate for the health and well-being of himself and of his family, including food, clothing, housing and medical care and necessary social services, and the right to security in the event of unemployment, sickness, disability, widowhood, old age or other lack of livelihood in circumstances beyond his control.

2. Motherhood and childhood are entitled to special care and assistance. All children, whether born in or out of wedlock, shall enjoy the same social protection.

Article 26

1. Everyone has the right to education. Education shall be free, at least in the elementary and fundamental stages. Elementary education shall be compulsory. Technical and professional education shall be made generally available and higher education shall be equally accessible to all on the basis of merit.

2. Education shall be directed to the full development of the human personality and to the strengthening of respect for human rights and fundamental freedoms. It shall promote understanding, tolerance and friendship among all nations, racial or religious groups, and shall further the activities of the United Nations for the maintenance of peace.

3. Parents have a prior right to choose the kind of education that shall be given to their children.

Article 27

1. Everyone has the right freely to participate in the cultural life of the community, to enjoy the arts and to share in scientific advancement and its benefits.

2. Everyone has the right to the protection of the moral and material interests resulting from any scientific, literary or artistic production of which he is the author.

Article 28

Everyone is entitled to a social and international order in which the rights and freedoms set forth in this Declaration can be fully realized.

Article 29

1. Everyone has duties to the community in which alone the free and full development of his personality is possible.

2. In the exercise of his rights and freedoms, everyone shall be subject only to such limitations as are determined by law solely for the purpose of securing due recognition and respect for the rights and freedoms of others and of meeting the just requirements of morality, public order and the general welfare in a democratic society.

3. These rights and freedoms may in no case be exercised contrary to the purposes and principles of the United Nations.

Article 30

Nothing in this Declaration may be interpreted as implying for any State, group or person any right to engage in any activity or to perform any act aimed at the destruction of any of the rights and freedoms set forth herein.

Chapter 3.8

Declaration of Alma-Ata: World Health Organization (WHO)/United Nations Children's Fund (UNICEF) International Conference on Primary Health Care (1978)

The International Conference on Primary Health Care, meeting in Alma-Ata this twelfth day of September in the year Nineteen hundred and seventy-eight, expressing the need for urgent action by all governments, all health and development workers, and the world community to protect and promote the health of all the people of the world, hereby makes the following Declaration:

I

The Conference strongly reaffirms that health, which is a state of complete physical, mental and social wellbeing, and not merely the absence of disease or infirmity, is a fundamental human right and that the attainment of the highest possible level of health is a most important worldwide social goal whose realization requires the action of many other social and economic sectors in addition to the health sector.

II

The existing gross inequality in the health status of the people particularly between developed and developing countries as well as within countries is politically, socially and economically unacceptable and is, therefore, of common concern to all countries.

III

Economic and social development, based on a New International Economic Order, is of basic importance to the fullest attainment of health for all and to the reduction of the gap between the health status of the developing and developed countries. The promotion and protection of the health of the people is essential to sustained economic and social development and contributes to a better quality of life and to world peace.

IV

The people have the right and duty to participate individually and collectively in the planning and implementation of their health care.

V

Governments have a responsibility for the health of their people which can be fulfilled only by the provision of adequate health and social measures. A main social target of governments, international organizations and the whole world community in the coming decades should be the attainment by all peoples of the world by the year 2000 of a level of health that will permit them to lead a socially and economically productive life. Primary health care is the key to attaining this target as part of development in the spirit of social justice.

VI

Primary health care is essential health care based on practical, scientifically sound and socially acceptable methods and technology made universally accessible to individuals and families in the community through their full participation and at a cost that the community and country can afford to maintain at every stage of their development in the spirit of self-reliance and self-determination. It forms an integral part both of the country's health system, of which it is the central function and main focus, and of the overall social and economic development of the community. It is the first level of contact of individuals, the family and community with the national health system bringing health care as close as possible to where people live and work, and constitutes the first element of a continuing health care process.

Primary health care:
1 reflects and evolves from the economic conditions and sociocultural and political characteristics of the country and its communities and is based on the application of the relevant results of social, biomedical and health services research and public health experience;
2 addresses the main health problems in the community, providing promotive, preventive, curative and rehabilitative services accordingly;
3 includes at least: education concerning prevailing health problems and the methods of preventing and controlling them; promotion of food supply and proper nutrition; an adequate supply of safe water and basic sanitation; maternal and child health care, including family planning; immunization against the major infectious diseases; prevention and control of locally endemic diseases; appropriate treatment of common diseases and injuries; and provision of essential drugs;
4 involves, in addition to the health sector, all related sectors and aspects of national and community development, in particular agriculture,

animal husbandry, food, industry, education, housing, public works, communications and other sectors; and demands the coordinated efforts of all those sectors;

5 requires and promotes maximum community and individual self–reliance and participation in the planning, organization, operation and control of primary health care, making fullest use of local, national and other available resources; and to this end develops through appropriate education the ability of communities to participate;

6 should be sustained by integrated, functional and mutually supportive referral systems, leading to the progressive improvement of comprehensive health care for all, and giving priority to those most in need;

7 relies, at local and referral levels, on health workers, including physicians, nurses, midwives, auxiliaries and community workers as applicable, as well as traditional practitioners as needed, suitably trained socially and technically to work as a health team and to respond to the expressed health needs of the community.

VIII

All governments should formulate national policies, strategies and plans of action to launch and sustain primary health care as part of a comprehensive national health system and in coordination with other sectors. To this end, it will be necessary to exercise political will, to mobilize the country's resources and to use available external resources rationally.

IX

All countries should cooperate in a spirit of partnership and service to ensure primary health care for all people since the attainment of health by people in any one country directly concerns and benefits every other country. In this context the joint WHO/UNICEF report on primary health care constitutes a solid basis for the further development and operation of primary health care throughout the world.

X

An acceptable level of health for all the people of the world by the year 2000 can be attained through a fuller and better use of the world's resources, a considerable part of which is now spent on armaments and military conflicts. A genuine policy of independence, peace, détente and disarmament could and should release additional resources that could well be devoted to peaceful aims and in particular to the acceleration of social and economic development of which primary health care, as an essential part, should be allotted its proper share.

The International Conference on Primary Health Care calls for urgent and effective national and international action to develop and implement primary health care throughout the world and particularly in developing countries in a spirit of technical cooperation and in keeping with a New International Economic Order. It urges governments, WHO and UNICEF, and other international organizations, as well as multilateral and bilateral agencies, nongovernmental organizations, funding agencies, all health workers and the whole world community to support national and international commitment to primary health care and to channel increased technical and financial support to it, particularly in developing countries. The Conference calls on all the aforementioned to collaborate in introducing, developing and maintaining primary health care in accordance with the spirit and content of this Declaration.

Chapter 3.9

Millennium Development Goals

Goal 1: Eradicate extreme poverty and hunger

Target 1:   Halve, between 1990 and 2015, the proportion of people whose income is less than $1 a day.

Target 2:   Achieve full and productive employment and decent work for all, including women and young people.

Target 3:   Halve, between 1990 and 2015, the proportion of people who suffer from hunger.

Goal 2: Achieve universal primary education

Target 1:   Ensure that, by 2015, children everywhere, boys and girls alike, will be able to complete a full course of primary education.

Goal 3: Promote gender equality and empower women

Target 1:   Eliminate gender disparity in primary and secondary education, preferably by 2005, and at all levels no later than 2015.

Goal 4: Reduce child mortality

Target 1:   Reduce by two thirds, between 1990 and 2015, the under-five mortality rate.

Goal 5: Improve maternal health

Target 1:   Reduce by three quarters the maternal mortality ratio.

Target 2:   Achieve universal access to reproductive health.

Goal 6: Combat HIV/AIDS, malaria and other diseases

Target 1:   Have halted by 2015 and begun to reverse the spread of HIV/AIDS.

Target 2:   Achieve by 2010, universal access to treatment for HIV/AIDS for all those who need it.

Target 3:   Have halted by 2015 and begun to reverse the incidence of malaria and other major diseases.

Goal 7: Ensure environmental sustainability

Target 1:   Integrate the principles of sustainable development into country policies and programmes and reverse the loss of environmental resources.

Target 2:   Reduce biodiversity loss, achieving, by 2010, a significant reduction in the rate of loss.

Target 3:   Halve, by 2015, the proportion of people without sustainable access to safe drinking water and basic sanitation.

Target 4:   By 2020, to have achieved a significant improvement in the lives of at least 100 million slum dwellers.

Goal 8: Develop a global partnership for development

Target 1:   Address the special needs of least developed countries, landlocked countries and small island developing states.

Target 2:   Develop further an open, rule-based, predictable, non-discriminatory trading and financial system.

Target 3:   Deal comprehensively with developing countries' debt.

Target 4:   In cooperation with pharmaceutical companies, provide access to affordable essential drugs in developing countries.

Target 5:   In cooperation with the private sector, make available benefits of new technologies, especially information and communications.

Section 4

Globalisations and welfare transformations

This section aims to provide an overview of debates about the impacts of globalisation processes on welfare formations and outcomes. We have divided the section into sub-sections that cover two overarching debates within the literature. The first is concerned with the disputed impacts of economic globalisation processes upon national welfare states, whilst the second addresses debates around the political influence of the 'Washington Consensus' on social policy, both nationally and globally.

4a: Impacts on national welfare states

One of the key, and perhaps most obvious, ways in which processes of globalisation may potentially transform welfare arrangements is through the impact of increasing global economic integration upon national welfare states. As social policy scholars began to engage with the growing awareness of globalisation processes in the 1990s, the argument was often advanced that 'globalisation', conceived of as some kind of homogeneous external force, was undermining the very foundations of the welfare state and/or placing constraints upon governments such that, whatever their political complexion, they were compelled to follow economic and social policies that were essentially neo-liberal. Such policies, it was often argued, involved cuts in taxation and social expenditure, privatisation, and labour market deregulation. In Section 1, the reading by Nicola Yeates summarises the arguments about the impact of globalisation on social policy that were being advanced by many scholars in the 1990s, and offers a useful early critique of those arguments. A vast literature has since developed which examines, critiques and refines these early arguments. In the first part of this section on welfare transformations, we include a small selection from this literature in order to illustrate the key arguments and counter-arguments that developed.

The first reading in this part of the section, by Ramesh Mishra, sums up this initial argument well by examining what he calls the 'logic of globalisation'. Mishra advances a number of propositions which encapsulate the argument that 'globalisation' pushes governments towards a neo-liberal policy agenda.

In the reading that follows, Colin Hay disputes this 'logic of globalisation' argument by questioning three of its core claims. First, he examines the claim that the welfare state has been undergoing a process of retrenchment, and finds that government expenditure as a share of Gross Domestic Product (GDP) has been more or less stable since 1980 rather than declining, although this apparent stability may mask a failure to keep up with demand for welfare services. Second, he examines the claim that changes in the level of world economic integration can appropriately be labelled 'globalisation', and argues that processes of world-regional integration have been much more important than genuinely global ones. Finally, he examines claims that the pressures for competitiveness brought about by these economic changes have constrained governments in the types of economic and social policies that they are able to pursue. He concludes that such arguments have been grossly exaggerated and that governments retain a much greater degree of policy autonomy than the 'logic of globalisation' thesis permits for.

The reading from Gosta Esping-Andersen discusses the apparent trade-off between egalitarian welfare state arrangements and high employment levels that arises as a result of the erosion of the 'Keynesian consensus' and the opening of economies. The way in which welfare states have experienced and responded to this dilemma has varied with their particular institutional arrangements, since whilst they pursued similar goals in the post-war period, they did so in different ways. Thus, Scandinavian countries pursued a strategy of expanding welfare state employment, Anglo-Saxon countries pursued neo-liberal policies of labour market deregulation and benefit retrenchment, and continental European countries sought to maintain existing levels of social security whilst reducing labour supply. Meanwhile, a number of 'emerging' economies are likely to build more comprehensive welfare arrangements in the future, and Esping-Andersen here provides an overview of their development up to the mid-1990s.

Esping-Andersen's work itself has been influential in more recent years in informing a trend in many countries towards supply-side approaches focused upon active labour market policies and the acquisition of the skills thought to be necessary to compete in world markets. The adoption of such pro-competitive supply-side approaches has been a feature of the 'competition state', outlined in the reading by Philip G. Cerny. The concept of the 'competition state' overcomes some of the simplistic notions of the crude 'logic of globalisation' thesis, by identifying states as active participants in the construction of 'globalisation'. As Cerny argues, in seeking to adapt to the set of complex processes labelled globalisation, states have not reduced, but paradoxically altered and expanded the forms of their intervention and regulation in order to facilitate international competitiveness and marketisation. Thus, whilst the welfare state (in the broad sense) of the post-Second World War era removed certain activities from the market, or 'decommodified' them, in order to allow the market to function effectively in other areas, the competition state actively pursues increased commodification, in order to ensure the international competitiveness of economic activities affecting national wealth production. Furthermore, different models of the competition state persist, although these are seen as 'feasible in the medium term only where they constitute relatively efficient alternative modes of adaptation to economic and political globalisation'. The competition state is thus conceived not simply as being constrained by globalisation, as it is in more simplistic accounts, but as an agent shaping global processes as well as adapting to them.

4b: From the Washington to Post-Washington Consensus?

The 'Washington Consensus' occupies a premier position in the analysis and practice of global social policy. The term 'Washington Consensus' is used to describe a set of neo-liberal economic policy prescriptions advanced by Washington DC–based institutions – the IMF, World Bank and US Treasury – through their lending and development measures. These prescriptions advance 'free' trade, market liberalisation and deregulation, privatisation, and residual social provision. There has been widespread debate about the nature, implementation and impacts on social policies around the world of this global policy doctrine, including about the nature of US influence on national sovereignty and policy autonomy. The four readings we include here identify a number of themes regarding the role and influence of the Washington Consensus (WC) on social policy formation, nationally and transnationally.

The first reading, by David Held, summarily rehearses the argument that the international community has failed to make substantial progress towards economic, social and environmental sustainability. He attributes this failure to a market-led model of economic globalisation, and specifically to the 'narrow scope and vision' of the WC orthodoxy. This, he argues, has 'failed to generate sustained economic growth, poverty reduction and fair outcomes', and has, through its pervasive influence on the orientation of the public domain to market-leading processes, undermined the capacity of public institutions to address common problems. But how does this relate to social policy specifically? This question is addressed at greater length in the readings by Paul Mosley, Santosh Mehrotra and Enrique Delamonica, and Bob Deacon.

One question concerns the effects of the WC on social policy formation. This is the subject of extensive debate and analysis, and the reading by Mehrotra and Delamonica, which discusses the effects of the Bretton Woods institutions' promotion of privatisation of social services, provides a flavour and an illustration of the kinds of concerns that have arisen. These authors argue that welfare pluralism, in particular the enhanced participation of the private commercial sector in these services, has been a core feature of the WC, and they argue that privatisation has been actively promoted by international financial institutions – in particular the World Bank and IMF – in each of the policy domains of education, health, and water and sanitation. This has had adverse effects on the quality, costs and effectiveness of these key social services. They point out that the use of public–private partnerships (PPPs) in the sanitation sector, for example, has generated significant tensions in the delivery of these services, and increased social conflict due to greater inequities in access to services as a result of privatisation. The interconnectedness of these three areas of social service provision is such that failure in one reduces the efficacy of measures in the others. They point to the severe limitations of increased reliance on the commercial sector to deliver comprehensive social provision and attain the Millennium Development Goals.

A second set of debates concerns the place of the Washington Consensus in global social policy formation. At the turn of the Millennium, in the aftermath of the 1997 'Asian' financial crisis, several commentators claimed to have detected a shift in these institutions' rhetoric, with some claiming that the Washington Consensus has been succeeded by a 'Post-Washington Consensus'. Emphasised here is how the 'new' global policy orthodoxy has come to emphasise the reform of the institutional economic architecture, including better regulation, institution- and capacity-building, civil society participation, good governance, transparency and 'smarter' conditionalities. But how has this shift impacted upon social policy? Both Mosley and Deacon, writing from the perspective of the early 2000s, address this question, cautiously outlining grounds for optimism. Mosley, for his part, argues that the World Bank's adoption of a more overt 'pro-poor' stance has involved recognising the limits of, and harms to, human security caused by market failure. While this has not entailed the World Bank renouncing market deregulation, it has accepted the value of certain market regulatory measures such as international capital controls. Deacon, too, also argues that the 'global tide' that is the Washington Consensus may be turning: he argues, on the basis of his reading of reports and publications from the World Bank as well as from various UN agencies, that 'the case is again put for finding ways of implementing universal public provisioning as part of an equitable social policy in developing countries'. At the same time, both authors highlight the need for caution in claims that the Washington Consensus has been consigned to history. Mosley points out that the World Bank retained its emphasis on 'rolling back' the frontiers of the state, while Deacon, referring to Mehrotra and Delamonica's article, reminds us that international pressure in favour of privatisation is intensifying as the World Bank and flanking agencies are identifying social services as new frontiers for privatisation.

As these readings suggest, the Washington Consensus has remained neither static nor insulated from wider political developments. Like social policy formation itself, it is the site of contestation and conflict. As David Held notes, the global economic orthodoxy at the heart of the Washington Consensus has been complicated by the development of a new orthodoxy, in the form of the post-2001 US security doctrine. This security doctrine's eschewal of a broad security agenda that would privilege wider development, welfare and human rights and address market-generated social disadvantage, in favour of a narrow one that focuses on threats to state security from 'terrorist' groups, not only compounds the existing failures of the WC but ultimately is likely to be confounded by it.

The theme of contestation and conflict in global social policy is also addressed by Bob Deacon, who argues that struggles at the level of global policy actors are essentially to 'define the nature of the social problems and effect their preferred societal visions in policies'. These struggles take place between institutions, such as between the societal visions of the UN and the World Bank. But they are also played out by competing factions within them. As Mosley makes clear, such struggles became expressed publicly in the drafting process of the World Bank's World Development Report, revealing 'the deep division within it over the extent to which adherence to a neo-liberal ideology best serves the interests of the poor'. Such struggles are evident not only in global organisations' discourses, as analysed by Mosley and Deacon, they are also manifested in policy implementation where Bretton Woods policies meet resistance and opposition. As Mehrotra and Delamonica point out, in the Latin American context government policies to pursue water privatisation, at the bequest of the World Bank, have released latent sources of social conflict, generating large-scale social protest. In Bolivia, this resulted in the company executives having to depart on advice from the state that it could no longer assure their safety, while in Peru and Brazil water privatisation plans 'had to be cancelled because of popular opposition'. Reinforcing themes in Section 1, which drew attention to the need to look outside the bureaux and boardrooms of global social policy formation, a final analysis of the extent to which the Washington Consensus, or indeed any other global policy doctrine, is deemed to have a hegemonic grip on global social policy needs to also take account of what happens across the entire global social policy process, from policy rhetoric to policy implementation. As the Mehrotra and Delamonica reading amply illustrates, an attempt to impose policy reforms that counter popular shared societal visions is likely sooner or later to run up against sustained opposition and become a reference point around and against which diverse intellectual and political forces worldwide advocating more progressive social policies mobilise.

Chapter 4a.1

The logic of globalization: the changing context of the welfare state

Ramesh Mishra

[...]

Decentring the nation state

The welfare state developed as and still remains very much a national enterprise. Historically the objectives of national integration and nation-building have been important in the development of collective social provision. In Europe at the turn of the century, acute national rivalries associated with imperialism provided a strong impetus to ruling elites to offer concessions to the lower classes. Reforms were intended to fashion a sense of national unity and national purpose demanded by economic and military competition. In Britain, for example, the national efficiency movement led to greater state involvement in promoting the education and health of the nation's children. After WW2 the full employment universal welfare state institutionalized the idea of 'one nation' by way of social citizenship. Moreover, tripartism and other similar arrangements were aimed at securing the cooperation of key economic players within the framework of the nation state in order to achieve national objectives.

In countries such as Canada, universal social programmes underpinned the sense of solidarity of a nation made up of diverse regions, two founding peoples and a sparse population spread across a vast land mass (Myles, 1996, p. 130; McBride and Shields, 1997). Indeed the idea of maintaining and consolidating the national community – economically, politically and socially – was the ideological underpinning par excellence of the welfare state.

As we approach the millennium the nation state seems to be in retreat. A resurgent globalization is increasingly blurring the economic boundaries of the nation state. Capital's freedom to move across the globe, the growth of multinational corporations and the transnational production of goods and services are marginalizing the nation as the site for economic organization and activity. As global sceptics have rightly argued, the idea that MNCs no longer have a national identity and interest is an exaggeration and it is more accurate to speak of greater internationalization rather than globalization of economies (Wade, 1996, p. 61; Hirst and Thompson, 1996, p. 16).

But there is little doubt that globalization has strengthened the hands of capital against the nation state. With growing free trade and the freedom to locate abroad, substantial sections of capital may have far less stake in the nation state. Neither domestic markets nor the domestic labour supply have the same significance as they had in the heyday of the welfare state. The weakening, if not decline of tripartism in European countries generally shows that in a globalizing economy, capital does not need labour's cooperation in part because for the former, the national economic framework is no longer the defining reality.

The return of unemployment, the decentralization of collective bargaining and the recommodification of labour markets are undermining the 'one nation' approach to economic and social issues which characterized the era of the welfare state. As often, the US shows in an extreme form a trend that may be growing, at least in Anglo-Saxon countries, if not more widely. In the US, apparently, economic elites no longer feel as connected with the rest of the nation as they once did. Affluent America is tending to withdraw into enclaves protected by private security guards and alarm systems with little concern for the fate of the rest of Americans (Reich, 1992, pp. 268-74; Rifkin, 1995, p. 212).

With globalization dividing societies increasingly into winners and losers, the concept of 'national interest' is becoming difficult to sustain and the concept of a national community is in danger of becoming 'increasingly empty' (Horsman and Marshall, 1995, p. 221). The question is whether, in the absence of a strong sense of a shared identity and interest in nationhood, the welfare state can survive as anything other than an institutional legacy of the past in the process of gradual decay.

The growth of regional economic associations such as the EU, NAFTA and others is yet another development weakening the sovereignty and autonomy of nation states. Whether these associations should be seen as an aspect of globalization, a regional response to it or an autonomous development is a debatable issue and will not be pursued here. What is not in doubt, however, is that these associations are here to stay and they restrict the sovereignty of nations with regard to fiscal, monetary and social policy. For example under the Maastricht Treaty the EU has laid down stringent conditions for membership in the European monetary union. These include keeping budget deficits within 3 per cent of GDP, accumulated national debts within 60% of GDP and inflation within certain specified limits. For many EU countries, reaching deficit targets has already meant a sizeable reduction in social expenditure since increased taxation is an unlikely option.

Major European countries such as France and Germany, in trying to meet the Maastricht criteria on deficits, have seen massive protests and demonstrations against policies of austerity and social retrenchment [...]. True, member states are free to pursue their own social policy and apart from the modest Social Charter, concerned with workers' rights and not legally binding as a whole, the EU has little by way of a common European social policy. On the other hand the economic policies of the EU are indirectly imposing significant constraints on the social policy of member countries.

NAFTA, with the US, Canada and Mexico as members, differs in many respects from the EU. For one thing the United States is the overwhelmingly dominant member and thus the most influential partner. For another, unlike the EU, NAFTA has no aspirations towards an economic and political union of member states. The network of social protection in the US is less well developed than in Canada, while Mexico has a much lower level of wages and social protection. There are no social policy provisions as such in NAFTA and member states are nominally free to follow their own social policies.

But this freedom is somewhat illusory. Economic provisions of NAFTA are meant to establish 'a level playing field' for competition in North America which includes the elimination of 'non-tariff' barriers. And although existing state services have been exempted, NAFTA places definite restrictions on the further development of social protection through the public sector. Measures judged to establish a monopoly in the supply of services or their subsidization are likely to be struck down. Moreover the influence of American neo-conservative ideology is strong and pervasive. Indirectly, therefore, NAFTA's free trade and competition policies restrict the sovereignty and autonomy of member countries to choose their own social and economic policies. Since NAFTA is meant to encourage competition, regulatory and interventionist policies suffer the most. The Chiapas uprising in Mexico is a poignant reminder of the social impact of NAFTA's economic policies. In Canada the influence of NAFTA seems to be towards social dumping and a strong pressure for the downward harmonization of social protection policies.

In sum the sovereignty and autonomy of nation states are being curtailed through globalization and the growth of regional economic associations. Although the latter – as can be seen in the case of the EU – have the potential to develop supranational social policy, this possibility seems to be rather limited. On the other hand the potential of regional associations for economic deregulation and downward pressure on standards of social protection of member states would seem to be greater (Leibfried and Pierson, 1995).

It is something of a paradox that we speak of the decline of the nation state at a time when in fact their numbers are multiplying. Moreover the desire for autonomy and nationhood on the part of linguistic and ethnic communities remains as strong as ever. Nonetheless globalization and regionalization are processes that are restricting the freedom of nations and sub-national units to pursue autonomous monetary, fiscal and social policies. At the same time, however, we also see national governments facilitating and promoting globalization (Cerny, 1997).

These are contradictory tendencies, but the contradiction is more apparent than real. Globalization and regionalization are limiting the range of choices available to nation states but only relatively, and then in respect of particular areas of policy. This still leaves nation states and other jurisdictions with a good deal of policy autonomy in respect of cultural, social and also many economic matters. Moreover, as we argued above, globalization must be seen as a form of transnational neoliberalism. It is the nation state that has to implement the agenda of liberalization and deregulation. Indeed neo-conservative regimes may be expected to go about this with considerable élan. And in this sense it would be correct to see national actors as facilitating and furthering globalization (Cerny, 1997, p. 251). It is also the case that the nation state as a linguistic, cultural and political community remains very much alive and real for the mass of the population which, after all, has no global identity. In this sense, again, nationhood and nationalism are not in decline.

However, and this is important for the welfare state, if the incentive for and the prospect of *nation-building* through collective social provision are weaker in today's world it is mainly because of globalization. Thus Japan in the 1970s and Korea in the 1980s seemed poised to develop more universalistic and encompassing social policies, somewhat along the lines of Western welfare states (Goodman and Peng, 1996, pp. 203-8; Pempel, 1989, pp. 153-4). However, a number of factors, including increasing international competition, economic volatility and neoconservative ascendancy in the West have inhibited this development. In general, then, nationhood and democracy are in conflict with the economic trends and tendencies privileged by globalization.

[...]

Social policy and the 'logic' of globalization

[...] Globalization, which must be understood as an economic as well as a political and ideological phenomenon, is without a doubt now the essential context of the welfare state.

In the following [...], we explore the relationship between globalization and social policy in some detail. The framework of this exploration is the 'logic' of globalization, i.e. given the nature of globalization as an economic process (albeit driven by politics and ideology), what are the likely consequences for the welfare state? The following propositions seek to spell out this logic in relation to social policy and social welfare.

1. Globalization undermines the ability of national governments to pursue the objectives of full employment and economic growth through

reflationary policies. 'Keynesianism in one country' ceases to be a viable option.

2. Globalization results in an increasing inequality in wages and working conditions through greater labour market flexibility, a differentiated 'post-Fordist' work-force and decentralized collective bargaining. Global competition and mobility of capital result in 'social dumping' and a downward shift in wages and working conditions.

3. Globalization exerts a downward pressure on systems of social protection and social expenditure by prioritizing the reduction of deficits and debt and the lowering of taxation as key objectives of state policy.

4. Globalization weakens the ideological underpinnings of social protection, especially that of a national minimum, by undermining national solidarity and legitimating inequality of rewards.

5. Globalization weakens the basis of social partnership and tripartism by shifting the balance of power away from labour and the state and towards capital.

6. Globalization constrains the policy options of nations by virtually excluding left-of-centre approaches. In this sense it spells the 'end of ideology' as far as welfare state policies are concerned.

7. The logic of globalization comes into conflict with the 'logic' of the national community and democratic politics. Social policy emerges as a major issue of contention between global capitalism and the democratic nation state.

[…]

References

Cerny, P.G. (1997) 'Paradoxes of the Competition State: The Dynamics of Political Globalization', *Government and Opposition,* 32(2).

Goodman, R. and Peng, I. (1996) 'The East Asian Welfare States', in Esping-Andersen, G. (ed.) *Welfare States in Transition*, London, Sage

Hirst, P. and Thompson, G. (1996) *Globalization in Question*, Cambridge, Polity.

Horsman, M. and Marshall, A. (1995) *After the Nation-State*, London, Harper-Collins.

Leibfried, S. and Pierson, P. (1995) 'Semi-sovereign Welfare States: Social Policy in a Multitiered Europe', in Leibfried, S. and Pierson, P. (eds) *European Social Policy*, Washington, DC, The Brookings Institution.

McBride, S. and Shields, J. (1997) *Dismantling a Nation*, Halifax, Fernwood Publishing.

Myles, J. (1996) 'When Markets Fail: Social Welfare in Canada and the United States', in Esping-Andersen, G. (ed.) *Welfare States in Transition*, London, Sage.

Pempel, T.J. (1989) 'Japan's Creative Conservatism', in Castles, E.G. (ed.) *The Comparative History of Public Policy*, New York, Oxford University Press.

Reich, R.B. (1992) *The Work of Nations*, New York, Vintage Books.

Rifkin, J. (1995) *The End of Work*, New York, G.P. Putnam's Sons.

Wade, R. (1996) 'Globalization and Its Limits', in Berger, S. and Dore, R. (eds) *National Diversity and Global Capitalism*, Ithaca and London, Cornell University Press.

Chapter 4a.2

Too important to leave to the economists? The political economy of welfare retrenchment

Colin Hay

Introduction

Perverse though this may seem, it is increasingly rare for welfare reform to be justified principally in terms of its social consequences – its contribution to the wellbeing of citizens. Welfare expenditure, it seems, can only be defended these days insofar as it is cast as an investment in economic performance, a down-payment on future competitiveness. Given the rhetoric of New Labour and the 'third way' more generally, this may sound like a peculiarly Anglo–centric comment – and at one time it would have been. Yet, as EU-level discourse on social reform since the Lisbon Summit of 2000 testifies, whether Anglophone in origin or not, the subordination of welfare reform to perceived economic imperatives is now a pan–European phenomenon. Indeed, it is probably no longer contentious to suggest that the welfare state is being exposed to a more extensive economic audit than at any point in its history. It is hardly surprising in this context that Philip G. Cerny's (1995, 1997) depiction of the process as the transition from the 'welfare state' to the 'competition state' has proved so popular.

The default assumption animating this reform agenda would seem to be that, whilst specific targeted social policies may have a series of discernible competitive-enhancing externalities (such as raising the stock of human capital), welfare provision *per se* is a net burden on competitiveness and hence a drain on economic performance. In short, unless a rigorous and exacting competitive audit reveals a demonstrative economic return on specific welfare 'investments', they should be scaled-back or eliminated altogether as a contribution to national competitiveness.

As this already serves to indicate, a series of often taken-for-granted economic assumptions serve to circumscribe the debate on the future trajectory, indeed the very viability, of the welfare state. Many of these, as we shall see, are intimately connected to debates about globalisation. No more powerful case can be made for the contemporary significance of the political economy of the welfare state. Yet this makes social policy analysis a more difficult task than once it was. For, in an era of putative globalisation, in which the logic of non-negotiable external economic constraint is frequently invoked, social policy analysts cannot but afford to have an opinion on the empirical content of such claims. The nature, severity and degree of negotiability of the external economic constraints that European welfare states are exposed to cannot be left to economists to adjudicate. Moreover, there is no substitute for engaging directly with the empirical evidence. Comforting though it might be to think so, there can be no reliance upon the crude, simplistic and never more than anecdotally empirical business school globalisation orthodoxy that so often informs our assumptions about contemporary economic imperatives.

In the all too brief discussion which follows I examine the recent comparative political economy of globalisation and regionalisation. The evidence that this body of literature assembles challenges, quite fundamentally, the view that globalisation is the proximate cause of welfare retrenchment in contemporary Europe and that high levels of welfare expenditure are incompatible with an open and competitive economy. It suggests, moreover, a consistent de-globalisation of European economies over the last 40 years, associated with the process, almost wholly absent from the existing debate, of European economic integration. It suggests, in short, that globalisation may have far less to do with the current trajectory of welfare reform than is often assumed, that the challenges European welfare states now face are perhaps rather closer to home than is often envisaged, and that national policy-makers retain far greater autonomy in matters of social policy than they would like to acknowledge. I turn first, however, to the question of retrenchment itself.

Retrenchment?

Given the default assumptions, which ostensibly inform the ongoing competitive audit of the welfare state, one might expect to see very clear evidence of welfare retrenchment in OECD countries in recent years. Yet if gauged in aggregate terms, the period of globalisation (conventionally the 1960s to the present day), does not seem to be associated with any systematic process of retrenchment.

Although state expenditure as a share of GDP peaked, in most cases, in the early to mid 1990s, in each and every case the size of the state has increased markedly since the 1960s. Moreover, these aggregate figures on state expenditure do not mask an underlying process of welfare retrenchment (at least in statistical terms) – with the share of public spending on subsidies and transfers rising significantly between 1980 and 1995 (Tanzi and Schuknecht, 2000; Wolf, 2004).

Yet we should be wary of inferring from aggregate data like these that there has been no process of welfare retrenchment in the states here considered. For this would be to assume that levels of need or demand for welfare have remained essentially static since the 1960s. This is far from being the case. A number of 'welfare-inflationary' factors might be identified. Amongst the most obvious are variations in the rate of unemployment, demographic change (an ageing population and an ever higher proportion of the population above or below working age), and the escalating unit costs of health care provision. Taken together, there are good reasons for thinking that, since the mid 1980s, relative stability in aggregate welfare state expenditure may mask an effective retrenchment in terms either of access to, or the quality of, provision – more likely, both. In short, whilst aggregate expenditure may have stabilised or even increased marginally in recent years, this is unlikely to have kept pace with the demonstrable growth in demand arising from rising numbers alone, far less that associated with the legitimate demand, by those reliant on state health care provision, for the latest therapies and drugs. At a time when costs are escalating and demand is growing any stabilisation in aggregate expenditure is likely to involve a loss of benefits and/or eligibility to (potential) welfare recipients.

It is nonetheless the case that the period of much-vaunted globalisation has witnessed the development of the largest welfare states the world has ever seen and, the above discussion notwithstanding, there is little evidence of this trend being reversed in any systematic way. This would certainly seem to imply that globalisation (if that is indeed what is occurring) is compatible with a far higher level of state expenditure than the prevailing wisdom on the subject invariably assumes. It certainly invites us to look once again at the evidence both for globalisation and for the constraints upon welfare state expenditure with which it is invariably associated. It is to these questions that we turn in the next section.

Globalisation?

Given the hold that globalisation seems to exert over policy-makers' and policy-analysts' imaginaries, it is chastening to review the contemporary comparative political economy of globalisation and regionalisation. For the most recent literature provides a powerful and now relatively exhaustive refutation of most if not all of the core assumptions and claims of the familiar globalisation thesis. The empirical evidence contains two major challenges to the thesis that globalisation is the proximate cause of welfare retrenchment in OECD countries and that high levels of welfare expenditure are incompatible with an open and competitive economy. The first relates to questions of whether globalisation is or is not occurring; the second to the extent to which existing patterns of economic integration (however labelled) exert the assumed downward pressure on welfare state expenditure. We consider each in turn.

The geographical character of economic integration

It is perhaps useful to begin by establishing what is not in dispute. However critical the new political economy of globalisation and regionalisation is about much of the conventional wisdom informing current welfare reform in Europe, it does not dispute the simple fact that European economies are, on average and in aggregate terms, more open than at any point since the early years of the twentieth century. In particular, the volume of cross-border economic transactions in which they are engaged has increased significantly since the 1960s. This, to reiterate, is not in dispute.

What is challenged is whether this process of economic integration is appropriately labelled globalisation – for the geographical character of such economic transactions has become ever more selective over time. In short, European economies (and the most recent evidence would suggest that Europe is by no means alone in this) have experienced not a globalisation of their economic relations over the past forty years, but a consistent and still accelerating de-globalisation. In short, they have regionalised (or, more particularly, EU-ised) rather than globalised.

Limits of space prevent all but the most cursory presentation of the empirical evidence (though, for a more detailed review, see Hay, 2005). But particularly notable here is the work of Jeffrey Frankel (1997, 1998). On the basis of a detailed examination of the empirical record he demonstrates that, within Europe as elsewhere and with respect to trade, any tendency to globalisation or even *inter*-regional economic integration has been swamped by the rapid growth in *intra*-regional integration. Intra-regional trade accounts for an ever-growing share of global economic activity, suggesting once again that globalisation is in fact an increasingly inaccurate characterisation of both the process of economic integration and the resulting pattern of economic interdependencies.

Such findings have been replicated for foreign direct investment flows to and from Europe (Kleinknecht and ter Wengel, 1998), and are further reinforced by the use of so-called gravity models to examine the geographical character of trade and foreign direct investment flows to and from European economies (Hay, 2004). In an era of globalisation, in which transportation costs have been diminished and many barriers to trade eliminated, we would expect to see the decreasing sensitivity of trade (and investment) to distance. Accordingly, a gravity model which assumes that trade decays exponentially with distance should become ever less effective in predicting patterns of trade (and investment). Yet far from showing a consistent pattern of globalisation since the 1960s, the gravity model becomes an ever better fit to the data. This demonstrates, once again, a pervasive regionalisation tendency in which trade and investment become more not less sensitive to geographical distance. European economies, it would seem, have experienced a consistent and ongoing process of de-globalisation since the 1960s, as the process of European economic integration has accelerated. Similar tendencies would appear to be underway in many, if perhaps not all, regions within the international economy. As this suggests, globalisation is a tendency that has, in the majority of cases, been swamped in recent decades by a regionalising counter-tendency.

With respect to European trade, in particular, such findings are not perhaps that surprising. For the process of European integration has clearly provided a major, and ongoing, boost to trade within the region; it is hardly surprising that this has had the net effect of reinforcing the regional character of European trade. So what are we to make of evidence like this? One thing is clear – proponents and defenders of the globalisation thesis are likely to protest that gravity models do not provide a fair test of the globalisation thesis, insisting as they do upon a rigid distinction between globalisation and regionalisation. If the ratio of intra- to inter-regional trade increases, this will be recorded as de-globalisation, even if there is a strong trend increase in inter-regional trade volumes (as a share of GDP). If globalisation is defined in less exacting terms – as, for instance, heightened economic integration between nations, regardless of the geographical character of that integration – then evidence like that assembled by the sceptics is by no means incompatible with the globalisation thesis.

This may seem like an appropriate response, and it certainly serves to establish the importance of semantics – whether globalisation is occurring or not depends, unremarkably, on what globalisation is taken to mean. But it is wrong in at least one significant respect. For, whilst the above evidence is certainly compatible with some (geographically-inexacting) definitions of globalisation, it is not compatible with the influential globalisation thesis. For this implies that European economies, for instance, are pitched into an increasingly intense competitive struggle with all other world economies by virtue of globalisation. If the trade and investment flows of such economies are, in fact, ever more regionally selective, then this is simply not the case – their economic performance is less and less dependent on their global competitiveness, whilst being more and more dependent on their regional competitiveness. Moreover, substitute other EU-European economies for all economies within the international system in a dynamic model of competition and the results will be very different – not least in terms of their implications for the viability of the welfare state.

As this suggests, as well as examining the geographical character of the economic exposure of European welfare states, it is perhaps equally important that we consider the extent to which existing patterns of economic integration (however labelled) exert the assumed downward pressure on welfare state expenditure. Once again the evidence is exceptionally difficult to reconcile with the prevailing orthodoxy.

The terms of competitiveness in an era of economic integration

It is one thing to show that European economies have been subject, if anything and in aggregate terms, to a process of de-globalisation rather than globalisation over the past few decades. Yet in and of itself this does little directly to challenge the pervasive argument that the characteristically over-regulated labour-markets and burdensome welfare regimes of Northern Europe are an unsustainable drain on competitiveness in an ever more closely integrated regional and/or global economy. It is to the direct evidence for this, then, that we must now turn (for further details see Hay, 2005). Again it is not comforting for the prevailing orthodoxy, which may be good news for European welfare states.

Much of the prevailing orthodoxy which predicts the competitive disadvantage of generous welfare states is premised on stylised assumptions about the preferences of mobile investors – that inward direct investors, for instance, favour deregulated labour-markets with lapse environmental standards, a non-unionised workforce and low levels of corporate taxation, whilst financial market actors favour rigid fiscal and monetary orthodoxy. Yet recent scholarship, which examines the *revealed* preferences of foreign direct investors and capital market participants as exhibited in actual investment decisions (rather than making *a priori* assumptions about such preferences), challenges this orthodoxy in important respects.

This recent scholarship makes two distinct contributions. The first examines the determinants of European inward foreign direct investment. This shows that after access and proximity to market are taken into account, educational attainment/skill level is the most critical factor in determining the attractiveness of a labour-market regime to mobile investors (see, especially, Cooke and Noble, 1998; Dunning, 1998; Swank, 2002; Traxler and Woitech, 2000). Low wages and labour-market flexibility are not positively correlated with inward FDI. Thus, for instance, in stark contrast to many of the assumptions informing public policy 'in matching the high labour skills requirements of operations located in high-skill-high-wage countries, US multinationals invest more in countries with both higher average education levels and higher hourly compensation costs' (Cooke and Noble, 1998: 596). Investors, it would seem, are perfectly prepared to pay the price of the highly trained and appropriately skilled workforce that (some) developed economies are capable of providing. As Cooke and Noble conclude their own study of US FDI, 'countries need not encourage ... wage restraint, since high hourly compensation costs do not reduce . . . foreign direct investment, provided these costs are matched by higher skills and productivity' (ibid.: 602).

The second body of recent work looks at the investment behaviour of financial market actors. Again, the prevailing orthodoxy is premised on stylised assumptions about such actors' behaviour; the recent literature, in contrast, examines revealed preferences and actual investment decisions. It changes the established picture significantly.

Though the liberalisation of financial markets has certainly increased the speed, severity and significance of investors' reactions to government policy, capital market participants appear far less discriminating or well-informed in their political risk assessment than is conventionally assumed. For advanced capitalist democracies, the range of government policies considered by market participants in making investment decisions is, in fact, extremely limited. As Layna Mosley explains:

> Governments are pressured strongly to satisfy financial market preferences in terms of overall inflation and government budget deficit levels but retain domestic policymaking latitude in other areas. The means by which governments achieve macropolicy outcomes, and the nature of government policies in other areas, do not concern financial market participants . . . [G]overnments retain a significant amount of policy autonomy and political accountability. If, for domestic reasons, they prefer to retain traditional social democratic policies, for instance, they are quite able to do so. (2003: 305)

Similar conclusions are reached by Duane Swank: 'rises in international capital openness, or exposure to international capital markets, do not exert significant downward pressure on the welfare state at moderate levels of budget imbalance [and] when budget deficits don't exist, some expansion of social protection is possible even in the context of international capital mobility' (2002: 94).

It would seem that the constraints imposed both by financial market integration and the presumed mobility of foreign direct investors upon domestic political autonomy have been grossly exaggerated.

Conclusions

As is now well-established, a powerful orthodoxy has engulfed debate in Europe as elsewhere on the need for the conjoined processes for labour-market and welfare reform in an era of globalisation. That orthodoxy is well expressed by John Gray in the following terms:

sovereign states are waging a war of competitive deregulation, forced on them by the global free market. A mechanism of downward harmonisation of market economies is already in operation. Every type of currently existing capitalism is thrown into the melting pot. In this contest the socially dislocated American free market possesses powerful advantages. (1998: 78)

Compelling though such a vision is, as I have sought to demonstrate in the preceding pages, the confidence with which an orthodoxy is expressed is no token of the strength of the evidential basis on which it is founded. Indeed, it is often something of a substitute for it. That would certainly seem to be [the] case here. For any review of the recent comparative political economy of globalisation and regionalisation can hardly fail to identify the disparity between the ideas which ostensibly inform policy-makers throughout Europe and the evidential basis for such ideas.

At minimum this suggests the urgent need to unpick the now conventional association between the conditions of competitiveness in an ever more open economy and the necessity of labour-market flexibilisation and welfare retrenchment. There is little evidence for such a link. It would seem somewhat perverse, then, to present globalisation as the proximate cause of welfare retrenchment in contemporary Europe when those economies have experienced neither a process of globalisation over the suggested time period nor a systematic process of retrenchment – at least if those terms are to mean anything specific. Moreover, even if we soften our definitional standards – describing recent developments as retrenchment and the increasing openness of European economies as globalisation – there is little or no evidence that such openness rewards flexible labour-markets and residual welfare states. High levels of welfare expenditure are simply not incompatible with an open and competitive economy.

Were labour-market flexibilisation and welfare retrenchment benign this might not be of such great import – but that is far from being the case. Labour-market flexibilisation, for instance, is not a costless reform to enact. Whilst it may well bring employment gains in the up phase of an economic cycle, as the British case demonstrates all to well, it exposes the economy to the perils of labour- and excess-capacity shedding on the down phase. [Thus] it is likely to prove strongly pro-cyclical, stretching peak-to-trough variations in unemployment and, indeed, economic growth rates. Such a reform trajectory should only be embarked upon if its competitive-enhancing consequences are unequivocal – and the available evidence demonstrates that this is simply not the case.

As this suggests, if we are keen to ensure that welfare reform contributes to the competitiveness of our economies and to good economic performance, we could do a lot worse than forgetting about competitiveness altogether.

The evidence reviewed in this paper would certainly seem to indicate that were welfare reform once again to be justified principally in terms of its contribution to the well-being of citizens and no longer seen as a down-payment on future economic performance, competitiveness would only be enhanced. Whether this is accepted or not, one thing is hopefully clear by now – such questions are far too important to be left to economists.

References

Bairoch, P. (1996), 'Globalisation myths and realities: one century of external trade and foreign investment', in R. Boyer and D. Drache (Eds.), *States Against Market: The Limits of Globalisation*, London: Routledge.

Cerny, P.G. (1995), 'Globalisation and the changing logic of collective action', *International Organization*, 49, 4, 595–625.

Cerny, P.G. (1997), 'Paradoxes of the competition state: the dynamics of political globalisation', *Government and Opposition*, 32, 2, 251–274.

Cooke, W.N. and Noble, D.S. (1998), 'Industrial relations systems and US foreign direct investment abroad', *British Journal of Industrial Relations*, 36, 4, 581–609.

Dunning, J.H. (1988), 'The eclectic paradigm of international production: an update and some possible extensions', *Journal of International Business Studies*, 19, 1, 1–32.

Frankel, J.A. (1997), *Regional Trading Blocs: In the World Economic System*, Washington, DC: Institute for International Economics.

Frankel, J.A. (Ed.) (1998), *The Regionalisation of the World Economy*, Cambridge, MA: National Bureau of Economic Research.

Gray, J. (1998), *False Dawn: The Delusions of Global Capitalism*, London: Granta Books.

Hay, C. (2004), 'Common trajectories, variable paces, divergent outcomes? Models of European capitalism under conditions of complex economic interdependence', *Review of International Political Economy*, 11, 2, 231–262.

Hay, C. (2005), 'Globalisation's impact on the state', in J. Ravenhill (Ed.), *Global Political Economy*, Oxford: Oxford University Press.

Hirst, P. and Thompson, G. (1999), *Globalisation in Question*, 2nd edition, Cambridge: Polity.

Kleinknecht, A. and ter Wengel, J. (1998), 'The myth of economic globalisation', *Cambridge Journal of Economics*, 22, 637–647.

Mosley, L. (2003), *Global Capital and National Governments*, Cambridge: Cambridge University Press.

Perraton, J., Goldblatt, D., Held, D., and McGrew, A. (1997), 'The globalisation of economic activity', *New Political Economy*, 2, 2, 257–278.

Swank, D. (2002), *Global Capital, Political Institutions and Policy Change in Developed Welfare States*, Cambridge: Cambridge University Press.

Tanzi, V. and Schuknecht, L. (2000), *Public Spending in the 20th Century: A Global Perspective*, Cambridge: Cambridge University Press.

Traxler, F. and Woitech, B. (2000), 'Transnational investment and national labour market regimes: a case of "regime shopping"?', *European Journal of Industrial Relations*, 6, 2, 141–159.

Wolf, M. (2004), *Why Globalisation Works: The Case for the Global Market Economy*, New Haven, CT: Yale University Press.

Chapter 4a.3

After the golden age? Welfare state dilemmas in a global economy

Gosta Esping-Andersen

According to T.H. Marshall (1950), modern citizenship is the fruition of a democratization that spans three centuries. In the eighteenth century the foundations were laid with the principle of legal-civil rights; political rights emerged in the nineteenth century; and, as a preliminary culmination of the democratic ideal, we see the consolidation of social citizenship in the twentieth century.

On the threshold of yet another century, legal and political rights appear firmly entrenched in most parts of the advanced, industrialized world. The same, however, cannot be said for social rights. Many believe that the welfare state has become incompatible with other cherished goals, such as economic development, full employment, and even personal liberties — that it is at odds with the fabric of advanced postindustrial capitalism.

The case for the inevitability of a third historical stage of social citizenship also seems circumspect when we broaden our analysis beyond the old, mature democracies. Despite what modernization theory believed some decades ago, the new emerging industrial democracies do not appear set to converge along the Western welfare state path. Was T.H. Marshall, then, wrong to assume that modern civilization is cumulative and irreversible? Or, put differently, what kind of welfare state is likely to emerge in the future?

The modern welfare state became an intrinsic part of capitalism's postwar 'Golden Age', an era in which prosperity, equality, and full employment seemed in perfect harmony. It cannot be for lack of prosperity that welfare states are in crisis. The dizzying levels of postwar economic growth are long gone, but nevertheless real gross national product in the rich OECD countries has increased by a respectable 45 per cent since the oil crisis in the mid 1970s. Public (and private) social outlays, of course, grew even faster but this trend was generally arrested in the 1980s. It is in the equality/full-employment nexus that the essence of the crisis must be found.

There seem to be as many diagnoses of the welfare state crisis as there are experts. Most can, nonetheless, be conveniently subsumed under three main headings. There is, firstly, the 'market-distortion' view which argues that the welfare state stifles the market and erodes incentives to work, save and invest. A second popular diagnosis focuses on the cataclysmic long-term effects of population ageing. And a third group of arguments focuses on the consequences of the new global economy, which mercilessly punishes profligate governments and uncompetitive economies.

Our study will not reject these arguments. We basically agree that a new, and quite fundamental, trade-off does exist between egalitarianism and employment; that global competition does narrow the field of domestic policy choice; and that ageing is a problem. At the same time, we feel that these standard accounts are exaggerated and risk being misleading. In part, the diversity of welfare state types speaks against too much generalization. In part, we must be very careful to distinguish what are chiefly exogenous and endogenous sources of the crisis. On the one hand, many of the difficulties that welfare states today face are caused by *market* failure: that is, badly functioning labour markets produce an overload on existing social programmes. Some, of course, insist that this is the fault of the welfare state itself. Thus, on the other hand, there is possibly also *welfare state* failure: that is, the edifice of social protection in many countries is 'frozen' in a past socio-economic order that no longer obtains, rendering it incapable of responding adequately to new risks and needs.

The malaise that now afflicts the advanced welfare states influences also strategic thinking on social security development within the emerging industrial democracies. Most pointedly, there no longer seems to be a Swedish 'middle way'. The neo-liberals suggest that the road to growth and prosperity is paved with flexibility and deregulation. Their recommendation for Latin America and East-Central Europe is therefore to emulate Chilean privatization rather than Swedish welfare statism. Critics hold that such a choice causes too much polarization and needless impoverishment, and that it may prove counter-productive for modernization. Comprehensive social security, they hold, is necessary because traditional familial, communal, or private market welfare arrangements are wholly inadequate. It is also necessary because stable democracy demands a level of social integration that only genuine social citizenship can inculcate.

Indeed, these were the very same issues that dominated in postwar Europe. Then, welfare state construction implied much more than a mere upgrading of existing social policies. In economic terms, the extension of income and employment security as a citizen's right meant a deliberate departure from the orthodoxies of the pure market. In moral terms, the welfare state promised a more universal, classless justice and solidarity of 'the people'; it was presented as a ray of hope to those who were asked to sacrifice for the common good in the war effort. The welfare state was therefore also a political project of nation-building: the affirmation of liberal democracy against the twin perils of fascism and bolshevism. Many countries became self-proclaimed welfare states, not so much to give a label to their social policies as to foster national social integration.

Such issues are of pressing concern in contemporary Asia, South America, and East Europe precisely because economic modernization tears apart the old institutions of social integration. Yet, policy makers in these nations also fear that such moral and political aims might jeopardize their comparative economic advantage (cheaper labour), traditional elite privileges (non-taxation of the rich in Latin America), or social culture (Confucianism in East Asia).

The advanced Western nations' welfare states were built to cater to an economy dominated by industrial mass production. In the era of the 'Keynesian consensus' there was no perceived trade-off between social security and economic growth, between equality and efficiency. This consensus has disappeared because the underlying assumptions no longer obtain. Non-inflationary demand-led growth within one country appears impossible; full employment today must be attained via services, given industrial decline; the conventional male breadwinner family is eroding, fertility is falling, and the life course is increasingly 'non-standard'.

Such structural shifts challenge traditional social policy thinking. In many respects the symptoms of crisis are similar across all nations. In others, there is notable divergence. Europe's single largest problem is chronically high unemployment, while in North America it is rising inequality and poverty. Both symptomize what many believe is a basic trade-off between employment growth and generous egalitarian social protection. Heavy social contributions and taxes, high and rigid wages, and extensive job rights make the hiring of additional workers prohibitively costly and the labour market too inflexible. The case in favour of deregulation seems validated in the North American 'job miracle' of the 1980s even if this occurred against the backdrop of greater inequalities.

Critics insist that the associated social costs of the American route are too high in terms of polarization and poverty. They suggest a 'social investment' strategy as an alternative. Rather than draconian roll-backs, the idea is to redirect social policy from its current bias in favour of passive income maintenance towards active labour market programmes that 'put people back to work', help households harmonize work and family obligations, and train the population in the kinds of skills that postindustrial society demands. The stress on human capital investment has, in the guise of 'productivist social policy', been official dogma in the Swedish model for decades. It is now also a leading theme in the Clinton administration, in the European Community, and also in East Asian countries (see European Community, 1993; Freeman, 1993).

The debate within the 'emerging' economies is quite parallel. Since their perceived advantage lies in competitive labour costs, there is a natural reluctance to build costly welfare state programmes. Many of these nations – particularly Japan – also face unusually rapid population ageing and the spectre of unpayable future pension burdens. They recognize, however, that as their wage cost advantage evaporates (there is always a cheaper economy waiting on the horizon), they will have to shift towards higher value-added production: hence, the East Asian governments' phenomenal stress on education.

What, then, are the prospects for the welfare state as we step into the twenty-first century? Will the advanced nations be forced to sacrifice some, or even most, of their welfare state principles? Will the new industrializing nations opt for a model without a welfare state or, alternatively, adopt some variant of Western style welfare states?

Overall trends, alas, give little comfort to those who adhere to the ideals of the welfare state, at least as it was traditionally conceived. The new conflict between equality and employment that the advanced nations confront is increasingly difficult to harmonize. The conditions that made the welfare state an essential part of economic development in the postwar Western nations may not apply to, say, contemporary Argentina, Poland, or South Korea. The causes of such pessimism are to be found in both international and domestic change.

The changing international environment

The harmonious coexistence of full employment and income equalization that defined the postwar epoch appears no longer possible. Many believe that North America's positive employment performance could only be achieved by deregulation and freed markets which, in turn, reward the winners and punish the losers: hence, rising wage and household income inequalities, growing poverty rates, and maybe even the re-emergence of an 'underclass' (Gottschalk, 1993; OECD, 1993; Jencks and Peterson, 1991; Room, 1990). Western Europe, with its much more comprehensive industrial relations systems, welfare states, and also powerful trade unions, has maintained equality and avoided growing poverty, but at the price of heavy (especially youth and long-term) unemployment, and swelling armies of welfare dependants, the combination of which overburdens social security finances. Demand-led, reflationary strategies are no longer an option, partly because unemployment is not merely cyclical, and partly because income growth leaks out of the economy to purchase imported goods.

The case for convergence: global integration

Integration in the world today almost automatically implies open economies. Sweden, Australia and New Zealand, Chile, and the ex-communist countries in Europe, are all shedding the protectionist measures that once upheld their respective welfare state arrangements.

Openness is said to sharply restrict nations' capacity to autonomously design their own political economy. Both Australia and Sweden illustrate the erosion of national options. As Castles shows [...] Australia could pursue what he calls the 'wage earners' welfare state' model of job security, full employment and high wages only as long as it adhered to protectionist measures. The price that Australia paid was lagging growth.

Sweden, as Stephens shows [...], could balance (over-)full employment with the world's most generous and egalitarian welfare state only as long as governments could control domestic credit and investments, and as long as the labour market partners could guarantee wage moderation consensually. Following liberalization in the early 1980s, the Swedish economy suffered heavy capital leakage abroad, thus undercutting domestic investment and job generation. At the same time, Sweden's tradition of centralized national social pacts eroded. Enhanced openness in both countries has compelled governments (both left and right) to cut back social expenditure. Is it, then, the case that openness inexorably drives welfare states towards a lowest common welfare denominator?

Much of Latin America and East–Central Europe is presently undergoing harsh liberal adjustment strategies. In the short run this tends to cause heavy unemployment, an often dramatic fall in incomes, and more inequalities. In the longer run – as the case of Chile since the mid 1980s suggests – it can improve nations' competitiveness, growth, and thus employment. The problem with radical liberalization is that its costs are unequally distributed and thus easily provoke organized resistance. The Chilean case is illustrative. Huber shows [...] that Chile's poverty rate rose from 17 per cent in 1970 to 38 per cent in 1986. In 1983, the unemployment rate reached a third of the labour force. In authoritarian Chile, organized resistance was effectively crushed. In liberal democracies, policy makers will have to rely on either persuasion or compensatory social guarantees. Persuasion assumes broad consensus, while compensation may strain governments' already fragile finances. In Latin America, as in East and Central Europe, the gap between social need and financial means is deepened by rising 'informalization' of employment. Employers and workers exit from the formal employment relationship to dodge taxation and job regulations.

If global wage competition is a major source of welfare state crisis in the advanced nations, convergence may paradoxically emerge from two opposite responses. Lowering wage costs in Europe and America may, at least in the interim, safeguard otherwise uncompetitive domestic firms. The offshoot, of course, is an implicit sanctioning of poor productivity performance. The other source of convergence would come from rising labour costs among the main global competitors, such as Japan, Korea or Taiwan. Their relative labour costs *have* been rising, and will do so even more if, as our study believes, these countries are hard put to stall major social security reforms in coming years.

The case for divergence: the role of institutions

There are additional reasons why we should not exaggerate the degree to which global forces overdetermine the fate of national welfare states. One of the most powerful conclusions in comparative research is that political and institutional mechanisms of interest representation and political consensus-building matter tremendously in terms of managing welfare, employment and growth objectives. The postwar European economies were able to maximize *both* welfare and efficiency owing to the capacity of encompassing interest organizations to promise wage restraint in return for full employment. For these reasons, a strong social safety net had no major negative effects on economies' adjustment capacities or, more generally, on growth (Calmfors and Driffill, 1988; Atkinson and Mogensen, 1993; Blank, 1993; 1994; Buechtemann, 1993).

But, countries with fragmented institutions will lack the capacity to negotiate binding agreements between contending interests. Opposed welfare, employment and efficiency goals more easily turn into zero-sum trade-offs, causing inflation and possibly an inferior capacity to adapt to change. Hence, a favourable institutional environment may be as capable as free markets of nurturing flexibility and efficiency. Thus, citing Ronald Dore, de Neubourg (1995: 6) points to the fallacy of wondering why, despite her rigid institutions, Japan manages to perform so well. Instead, the real question should be: 'which features make the Japanese institutional arrangements successful?' Strong consensus-building institutions in Sweden, as in Japan, helped avoid negative trade-offs for decades. It is arguably their erosion in the 1980s that best explains Sweden's dramatic recent slide.

These issues are clearly relevant for the new industrial democracies. For the ex-communist nations there is of course little doubt that the market transition requires sweeping privatization and institutional reconstruction. It is equally clear that Latin America's protectionist institutions have stifled growth. It may also be that the quite 'rigid' regulatory mechanisms that launched full employment growth in East Asia will erode. Japan's life-time employment guarantee, for example, is now threatened (Freeman, 1993; Freeman and Katz, 1994).

Our study documents the continued dominance of national institutional traditions. This comes out in two important respects. Firstly, while the postwar Western welfare states addressed fairly similar objectives, they differed both in terms of ambition and in terms of *how* they did it. Secondly, as these same welfare states today seek to adapt, they do so very differently. A major reason has to do with institutional legacies, inherited system characteristics, and the vested interests that these cultivate.

Challenges to Western welfare states

The contemporary advanced welfare state faces two sets of challenges, one specific to the welfare state itself, the other provoked by exogenous forces. In the former case, there is a growing disjuncture between existing social protection schemes and evolving needs and risks. This is due to changes in family structure (the rise of single-parent households, for example), in occupational structure (increased professionalization and differentiation), and in the life cycle (which is becoming less linear and standard). Hence, there is growing dissatisfaction with the welfare state's capacity to address emerging new demands.

In the second case, the welfare state crisis is spurred by changing economic conditions (slower growth and 'deindustrialization', for example) and demographic trends (especially population ageing), both of which threaten the future viability of present welfare state commitments.

[...]

The *economic* problems that confront the Western welfare states are typically identified in terms of the unemployment problem. The combination of high wage costs (due to mandatory social contributions) and rigidities (such as job tenure, costly termination payments, or generous social benefits) is widely regarded as a main impediment to job growth. Generous social benefits are also held to reduce the work incentive.

There is evidence that high marginal labour costs and stringent job rights prohibit job growth. However, privatization of social security may not offer a real solution. Firstly, as we know from the United States and, more recently, Chile, private plans depend on favourable tax concessions, that is on public subsidization. Secondly, experience from the United States shows that defined-benefit type occupational welfare plans may incur the exact same kinds of rigidities and cost burdens as social insurance. They tend to inhibit labour mobility because workers fear to lose benefits, and because of vesting requirements (the norm in the US is a five-year minimum); like social security, private plans also impose high fixed labour costs. Hence, public sector efforts to trim social security are paralleled in the private sector. In the United States, coverage under occupational plans has declined dramatically in the past decade: medical care coverage by 14 per cent, defined-benefit retirement coverage by 25 per cent. In its place have grown individual contribution plans.

Postindustrial employment trends are also potentially problematic. Since they favour professional and skilled occupations, demand for unqualified labour will depend mainly on low wages. They also seem to foster 'atypical', precarious jobs, such as in contingent work, involuntary part-time work, homework, or self-employment; the consequence may be greater polarization between a core and a periphery workforce (European Community, 1993; OECD, 1993). The United States enjoys comparatively low unemployment, but a disturbing rise in jobs that pay below-poverty wages. The level of many social benefits has followed suit, producing unprecedented levels of poverty.

Indeed, as we see in the United States, wage decline may easily produce a vicious downward spiral of social benefits too, since adequate social transfers in a low-wage environment are likely to nurture poverty traps. Hence, both unemployment insurance and social welfare have eroded noticeably. Poverty and polarization, in turn, may threaten the social order and thus burden the public sector on alternative expenditure accounts. The American male prison population is above one million (and is rising), pushing up spending on prisons, law and order. Security guards and law enforcement personnel are among the fastest growing occupations; the annual per-inmate cost of incarceration is almost twice that of tuition costs at Harvard University.

The 'endogenous' problems of the welfare state lie in the growing discrepancy between existing programme design and social demands. The contemporary welfare state addresses a past social order; its ideals of universalism and equality emerged with reference to a relatively homogeneous industrial working class. The much greater occupational and life cycle differentiation that characterizes 'postindustrial' society implies also more heterogeneous needs and expectations. With greater career uncertainty, demands for more flexible adjustment, and changing family arrangements, not to forget female employment, citizens also face more diverse risks.

Also the welfare state's erstwhile 'model family' is no longer pre-eminent. On the one hand, we see the rise of the two-earner, double-career unit; on the other, the rise of divorced, single-person, and single-parent households. The former are often privileged, but it is also clear that wives' labour supply is becoming the only means by which lower-income households can escape poverty or maintain accustomed living standards today. This is evident in the American case (Mishel and Bernstein, 1993). 'Atypical' families constitute a rapidly growing high-risk poverty clientele.

Welfare regime challenges in other regions

The ageing problem is, with the notable exception of Japan, less acute in other regions. However, an equally severe demographic problem is massive migration into urban industrial centres, a process which undermines traditional forms of social protection. In East Asia, this poses a dilemma between welfare state construction (in Japan and South Korea combined with corporate plans) and the Confucian tradition of familialism with its care obligations.

The main *economic* problems of the 'non–welfare states' depend on their position in the world economy, In Eastern Europe, the old communist welfare regime was characterized by three basic pillars: full and quasi-obligatory employment; broad and universalistic social insurance; and a highly developed, typically company-based, system of services and fringe benefits. In fact, very much as in Scandinavia, its employment-maximization strategy was the *sine qua non* of system equilibrium since it assured minimal social dependencies. The post-democracy reforms have eroded the first and third of these pillars. Instead of full employment has emerged mass unemployment; the collapsing (or privatized) state enterprises are decreasingly capable of furnishing accustomed services. As the viability of both is destroyed, existing income maintenance programmes face under-financing and over-burdening. The consequence, as Standing shows [...], is an alarming rise in poverty and mortality.

Where countries define their competitive edge in terms of favourable labour costs, they will be wary of major welfare state advances. This is, however, only partially the case. Following Japan, East Asia in general, and South Korea in particular, see their economic future in terms of an educated workforce – very much like Sweden did with her 'productivistic' welfare state design. This obviously implies growing commitments to edu-cation, health, and social services. A strong income maintenance system will probably be difficult to avoid in this scenario to the extent that (1) an increasingly educated, urbane, and professionalized labour force is likely to distance itself from the traditionalist principles of the Confucian culture; and (2) occupational company schemes are highly uneven in coverage, being rarely present or even viable in small or medium firms.

In contrast, Latin American development is to a much greater extent based on natural resources. As these countries abandon protectionist, import-substitution policies they clearly face the labour cost problem more acutely. It is in this light that Chile's vanguard attempt to shift social security from state to market must be understood.

Welfare state adaptation in the past decade

Simmering symptoms of crisis became increasingly evident in the past decade. Popular perceptions notwithstanding, the degree of welfare state roll-back, let alone significant change, has so far been modest. This is clear from the essentially stable levels of social expenditure [...]. Most nations, with the notable exception of Britain and New Zealand, have limited intervention to marginal adjustments, such as delayed benefit indexation, diminished income replacement rates and, most recently, a return to contribution-based (rather than earnings-based) pension benefit calculation. Still, marginal cuts today may have long-term cumulative effects of a quite radical nature. If social benefits gradually fall behind earnings, those who can seek compensation in private insurance will do so, thus weakening broad support for the welfare state. Among the 'new nations' the signs of system change are more evident: on the one hand, active privatization in Latin America and East-Central Europe; on the other hand, embryonic welfare state construction in East Asia.

Since the early 1970s, we can identify three distinct welfare state responses to economic and social change. Scandinavia followed until recently a strategy of welfare state employment expansion. The Anglo-Saxon countries, in particular North America, New Zealand, and Britain, have favoured a strategy of deregulating wages and the labour market, combined with a certain degree of welfare state erosion. And the continental European nations, like Germany, France and Italy, have induced labour supply reduction while basically maintaining existing social security standards. All three strategies were intimately related to the nature of their welfare states.

[...]

The emergence of new welfare states?

Are the nations of East-Central Europe, East Asia, or Latin America in the process of emulating the Western model, or are they following qualitatively new trajectories? If by 'new' we mean models that deviate markedly from existing welfare states, the answer is essentially no. Our survey suggests the makings of distinct trajectories that do not necessarily correspond to regional clusters.

One, comprising East-Central Europe, Chile, and Argentina, follows broadly a liberal strategy based on privatization of social insurance, a reduced public social safety net, a shift towards targeted means-tested assistance, and a free-market bias in labour market regulation. The market-driven strategy in Latin America must be seen against the backdrop of a highly status-segmented, quite clientelistic, and seriously underfunded social insurance tradition.

A second group of countries, exemplified by Brazil and Costa Rica, has so far shunned neo-liberalism and has in fact taken some steps towards strengthening their public social safety nets, in both cases adopting a fairly universalistic approach in terms of population coverage.

The third, East Asian, group is paradoxically both globally unique and a hybrid of existing welfare state characteristics. It shares with the continental European model an emphasis on familialism and an aversion to public social services. Its embryonic social insurance schemes tend to follow the European tradition of occupationally segmented plans, favouring in particular privileged groups such as the civil service, teachers or the military. In these countries, social security is far from comprehensive, nor does it aim to furnish income *maintenance*. By default more than design, the vacuum of social protection has spurred the rise of company sponsored occupational welfare, especially in Japan. As a consequence, a certain degree of 'Americanization' has evolved: the modesty of public welfare rests on the assumption that primary sector male workers will be covered under private plans.

[...]

Conclusions: major trends and policy dilemmas

In most countries what we see is not radical change, but rather a 'frozen' welfare state landscape. Resistance to change is to be expected: long-established policies become institutionalized, and cultivate vested interests in their perpetuation; major interest groups define their interests in terms of how the welfare state works. Thus, social security systems that are backed by powerful interest aggregations are less amenable to radical reform and, when reform is undertaken, it tends to be negotiated and consensual. Continental Europe is the clearest case of impasse, while Australia and Scandinavia represent change via negotiation. At the other extreme, in Chile and the ex-communist nations, whole scale change occurred against the backdrop of the collapse or destruction of the existing organizational structure. In between these poles are countries, like the United States or Britain, in which a more gradual erosion occurred in tandem with weakened trade unionism.

The decay of comprehensive and centralized consensus-building mechanisms over the past decade is one of the primary reasons for the difficulties that now also beset the famed Swedish model. Its long-standing capacity to reconcile ambitious and egalitarian welfare goals with full employment has seriously decayed.

There is a seemingly universal trade-off between equality and employment. Its roots may lie primarily in the new global order, but our study identifies significantly different national responses. Within the group of advanced welfare states, only a few have undertaken radical steps to roll back or deregulate the existing system. All, however, have sought to trim benefits at the margin or to introduce cautious measures of flexibilization. As we have seen, those following a more radical liberalization strategy do better in terms of employment but suffer a high cost in terms of inequality and poverty. In contrast, those resilient to change pay the price of high unemployment – continental Europe in particular.

A similar perception of a trade-off between equality and efficiency has always dominated social policy debates. In the postwar era it was widely accepted that the Keynesian welfare state provided a positive-sum solution. Today, there are few that are optimistic with regard to a viable 'third way'.

Still, many of the countries we have surveyed pursue strategies designed to mediate or soften the trade-off. One, represented by Australia and Canada, combines liberalization and a shift towards more selectivity and targeting with a concomitant rise in benefits to those most at risk. Their approach to selectivity is broad rather than narrow, aiming to guarantee against abject poverty and stark inequalities. Comparative income and poverty data suggest that the strategy is somewhat successful. These countries have enjoyed an employment performance that equals the American without alarming rates of impoverishment.

Another strategy, evident in Scandinavia, consists in shifting welfare state resources from passive income maintenance to employment and family promotion. The era of public employment growth has clearly ended and, instead, policy is directed to active labour market measures, such as training and mobility, and wage subsidies. Scandinavia appears now to have accepted that greater inequalities are unavoidable but seeks to build in guarantees against these being concentrated in any particular stratum, or becoming permanent across people's life courses. In this regard, the Nordic welfare states may be said to spearhead a 'social investment' strategy. They have clearly not escaped high unemployment, or the necessity for significant cuts in social benefit levels. Yet, their unemployment record must be gauged against the backdrop of record high activity rates and, contrary to continental Europe, very modest degrees of social marginalization, exclusion, and youth unemployment.

More generally, if a return to full employment will have to rely on greater earnings inequalities and a profusion of 'lousy' service jobs, active social investment policies should diminish the chance that certain groups become chronic losers. 'Lousy' jobs will constitute only a marginal welfare problem (and may even be beneficial) if they are merely stop-gap, or easy first-entry, jobs for school leavers or immigrant workers. They are a major problem if they become life cycle traps. We know that education and skills offer the best odds for people to move on to better jobs. Hence, a low wage-based employment strategy can be reconciled with equality if there exist guarantees of mobility and improvement.

Privatization is one of the most commonly advocated strategies in the current welfare state crisis. In fact, it is promoted for two distinct reasons: one, to diminish public spending burdens and encourage self-reliance; the other, to respond to the more differentiated and individualistic demands of 'postindustrial' society. In practice, there have as yet been very few substantial privatization reforms and the case of Chile remains therefore quite unique. However, a process of 'creeping' privatization may be under way in many countries, mostly because of gradual erosion of benefit or service levels.

If privatization entails a shift of welfare responsibilities to companies, it is very unlikely to become a panacea since corporate plans similarly inhibit flexibility and incur heavy fixed labour costs. Indeed, they are being rolled back in tandem with public programmes. In addition, such plans are hardly viable in a service-dominated employment structure where firms are smaller and the labour force less unionized. The alternative is defined contribution plans or individual insurance schemes (like the Chilean model, or the rapidly growing IRA or 401K type plans in America).

Individual plans do have positive aspects. Besides encouraging savings, they permit individuals to tailor their welfare package. However, if they are meant to substitute for, rather than merely supplement, public schemes, their capacity to furnish social security in any universal way is highly dubious. Besides, the growth of such schemes has everywhere been nourished by public subsidies, such as favourable tax treatment.

Parallel to privatization is a certain shift away from defined-benefit to contribution-based entitlements, particularly in pensions. This means essentially that welfare states (or companies) are withdrawing their commitment to benefit *adequacy* – one of the major welfare reforms of the 1960s and 1970s. In the Swedish case, this is less likely to generate major inequalities owing to the high levels of income security guaranteed by the basic, universal 'people's pension'. But this is not the case in systems, such as the Chilean, where individual contribution-based plans are the sole source of income maintenance – short of means-tested public assistance.

In many welfare states, income transfer programmes were perverted over the past decades, becoming an inducement *not* to work. In the continental European countries, this strategy has exacerbated rather than eased the underlying employment problem: adding to the burden of labour costs for the shrinking 'insider' labour force and thus raising the cost of entry for the 'outsiders', youth especially. It increases the family's dependence on the sole (usually male) breadwinner's job stability and pay.

It is, then, clear that one of the greatest challenges for the future welfare state is how to harmonize women's employment with family formation. Women demand employment and greater economic independence; the family is more likely to be flexible, and less likely to be poor, if it can rely on two earners; and the ageing burden will be lessened if fertility rises. The Scandinavian experience demonstrates that these demands can be harmonized with a comprehensive network of public services. However, the fiscal strains of contemporary welfare states generally prohibit such an expansion; high wage costs make it unlikely in the private sector.

To the extent that the trade-off between social security and jobs is induced by global wage competition, there is an alternative source of positive-sum outcomes since the main competitors to the advanced economies are likely to build more comprehensive social protection systems in the foreseeable future. It would, indeed, be a sad irony if the West engaged in welfare state dismantling in its drive to remain competitive if, at the same time, the main competition were to raise its labour costs.

On a final note, we should not forget that the initial impetus behind the postwar welfare state went beyond the narrower social policy concerns. As a mechanism for social integration, the eradication of class differences, and nation-building, the advanced welfare states have been hugely successful. Part of the welfare state crisis today may be simply a question of financial strain and rising unemployment. In part, it is clearly also related to less tangible needs for new modes of social integration, solidarity, and citizenship. The market may indeed be an efficient mechanism of allocation, but not of building solidarities. There is little doubt that these more intangible qualities constitute an important element in the embryonic welfare state evolution in the new industrial democracies of Asia, South America and Eastern Europe. The economic effects of the welfare state can certainly not be disregarded. Yet, we should not forget that the only credible rationale behind economic efficiency is that it will produce welfare. The idea of social citizenship may therefore extend also into the twenty-first century.

References

Atkinson, A.B. and Mogensen, G.V. (1993) *Welfare and Work Incentives*. Oxford: Clarendon Press.

Blank, R. (1993) 'Does a larger safety net mean less economic flexibility?', in R. Freeman (ed.), *Working under Different Rules*. New York: Russell Sage.

Blank, R. (ed.) (1994) *Social Protection Versus Economic Flexibility*. Chicago: University of Chicago Press.

Buechtemann, C. (1993) *Employment Security and Labor Market Behavior*. Ithaca, NY: ILR Press.

Calmfors, L. and Driffill, J. (1988) 'Bargaining structure, corporatism, and macroeconomic performance', *Economic Policy*, 6: 14-61.

de Neubourg, C. (1995) 'Switching to the policy mode: incentives by the OECD jobs study to change our mindset'. Unpublished paper, Faculty of Economics, University of Maastricht.

European Community (1993) *Green Paper on European Social Policy*. Bruxelles: DG5 (communication by Mr Flynn).

Freeman, R. (1993) 'How labor fares in different countries', in R. Freeman (ed.), *Working under Different Rules*. New York: Russell Sage. pp. 1-28.

Freeman, R. and Katz, L. (eds) (1994) *Differences and Changes in Wage Structure*. Chicago: University of Chicago Press.

Gottschalk, P. (1993) 'Changes in inequality of family income in seven industrialized countries', *American Economic Review*, 2: 136-42.

Jencks, C. and Peterson, P. (1991) *The Urban Underclass*. Washington, DC: Brookings Institution.

Marshall, T.H. (1950) *Citizenship and Social Class.* Oxford: Oxford University Press.

Mishel, L. and Bernstein, J. (1993) *The State of Working America, 1992-1993.* Armon, NY: M. E. Sharpe.

OECD (1993) *Employment Outlook.* Paris: OECD.

Room, G. (1990) *New Poverty in the European Community.* London: Macmillan.

Chapter 4a.4

Paradoxes of the competition state: the dynamics of political globalization

Philip G. Cerny

The transformation of the nation–state into a 'competition state' lies at the heart of political globalization. In seeking to adapt to a range of complex changes in cultural, institutional and market structures, both state and market actors are attempting to reinvent the state as a quasi-'enterprise association' in a wider world context, a process which involves three central paradoxes. The first paradox is that this process does not lead to a simple decline of the state but may be seen to necessitate the actual expansion of *de facto* state intervention and regulation in the name of competitiveness and marketization.

Furthermore, in a second paradox, closely intertwined with the first, state actors and institutions are themselves promoting new forms of complex globalization in the attempt to adapt state action to cope more effectively with what they see as global 'realities'. This interaction of economic transformation and state agency is leading to a restructuration of the state itself at a wide range of levels. Although embedded state forms, contrasting modes of state interventionism and differing state/society arrangements persist, such models are feasible in the medium term only where they constitute relatively efficient alternative modes of adaptation to economic and political globalization. At the same time, however, pressures for homogenization are likely to continue to erode these different models where they prove to be economically inefficient in world markets and therefore unattractive to state and market actors.

In this sense, a growing tension between economic globalization and embedded state/society practices increasingly constitutes the principal terrain of political conflict within, among, and across competition states. Thus a third and final paradox is that the development of this new political terrain in turn hinders the capacity of state institutions to embody the kind of communal solidarity or *Gemeinschaft* which gave the modern nation-state its deeper legitimacy, institutionalized power and social embeddedness. The combination of these three paradoxes means that the consolidation and expansion of the competition state is itself driving a process of political globalization which is increasingly relativizing the sovereignty of states and, indeed, forcing the pace of globalization in economic, social and cultural spheres too.

Competing explanations of globalization and the relativization of sovereignty

[...]

Globalization as a *political* phenomenon basically means that the shaping of the playing field of politics itself is increasingly determined not within insulated units, i.e. relatively autonomous and hierarchically organized structures called states; rather it derives from a complex congeries of multilevel games played on multilayered institutional playing fields, above and across, as well as within, state boundaries. These games are played out by *state actors*, as well as market actors and cultural actors. Thus globalization is a process of political *structuration*.[1] Political globalization involves reshaping political practices and institutional structures in order to adjust and adapt to the growing deficiencies of nation-states as perceived and *experienced* by such actors. Central to this experience is a deeply felt failure to achieve the kind of communal goals which have been the *raison d'être* of the Western state since the collapse of feudalism and especially since the national democratic and social revolutions of the eighteenth, nineteenth and twentieth centuries.

The modern world has seen only two truly internationalist political projects, liberalism and Marxism. But both were also assimilated into the confines and practices of the nation-state early in their historical trajectories, the first through the British, French and American revolutions, the second through the Russian and Chinese revolutions. Only then did they attain institutionalized power, for it was at the nation-state level that the most fundamental structures and institutions of society and politics had become embedded. The apparent history of the modern world was thus absorbed into a historiography of nation-states.

The concept of globalization in general challenges that prevailing framework in two ways. The first is through a rethinking of history. The emergence, consolidation and rise to structural pre-eminence of the nation-state itself is increasingly understood as having been the product of a global conjunction of events and longer-term structural developments, a quasi-accident reflecting the global situation of the late feudal period. The second challenge arises through the emergence of a new social-scientific discourse of globalization itself. This discourse challenges the significance of the nation-state as a paradigm of scholarly research,[2] suggesting that nation-state-based 'normal science' in history and the social sciences – sometimes referred to as 'methodological nationalism' – has been sufficiently undermined by new challenges and findings at a range of different analytical levels that its usefulness in constituting a *prima facie* scholarly agenda is rapidly being lost. A reshaping is taking place of the theoretical questions which have dominated 'modern' political philosophy and they are being reformulated in a more complex global context.[3]

Globalization in all its complexity, then, challenges what is most profoundly rooted in Western historiography, political science, sociology and economics. The nation–state superseded the kaleidoscope of overlapping and intertwined communities and authorities characteristic of the feudal era in a process which lasted until the latter half of the twentieth century. In turn, the conceptions of common interest and community which have legitimated the institutional authority of the nation–state over the past several centuries – however predatory in practice its origins and developmental trajectory[4] – have given the politics of the state an essential character well beyond pragmatism and 'interest' in the narrow meaning of that term. They involve attributing to the state a holistic character, a sense of organic solidarity which is more than any simple social contract or set of pragmatic affiliations – what Ferdinand Tonnies called *Gemeinschaft*.[5] If there is an increasingly paradigmatic crisis of the state today, it concerns the erosion of this posited underlying bond, and the demotion of the state to a mere pragmatic association for common ends – what Tonnies called *Gesellschaft* and Michael Oakeshott called an 'enterprise association'.[6] So long as the welfare of the people in a capitalist society was secured at least minimally by the state and protected from the full commodification of the market by national politics (the welfare state, or social state, in the broadest sense of those terms) – then the image of a national *Gemeinschaft* as the route to the common good could persist, even strengthen and expand, over the entire globe. The latent crisis of the nation–state today involves the erosion of that *Gemeinschaft* and the fragmenting of the political bond from both above and below.

Globalization itself is an elusive concept.[7] To some observers it is both bounded and well-defined, with a simple, sometimes even unidimensional, core or driving force (e.g., the convergence of interest rates or stock market prices, or the information technology revolution); therefore globalization has all too frequently been assumed to be a process of convergence, a homogenizing force. Increasingly, however, analysts are arguing that globalization is fundamentally complex and 'heterogenizing' – even polarizing – in its nature and consequences.[8] Complexity means the presence of many intricate component parts. It can mean a sophisticated and elegantly coordinated structure, but it can also mean that the different parts mesh poorly, leading to friction and even entropy. A globalizing world is intricately structured at many levels, developing within an already complex social, economic and political context. Many varied dimensions of convergence and divergence can and do coexist. Different markets, firms and economic sectors are organized in distinct ways. Owners of capital 'arbitrage' across these categories precisely because they are differently structured – and provide different rates of return. Even more problematic are the subnational, transnational and supranational ethnic cleavages, tribalism and other revived or *invented* identities and traditions – from local groups to the European Union – which abound in the wake of the uneven erosion of national identities, national economies and national state policy capacity characteristic of the 'global era'. Globalization can just as well be seen as the harbinger not simply of a 'new world order' but of a new world *disorder*, even a 'new medievalism' of overlapping and competing authorities, multiple loyalties and identities, prismatic notions of space and belief, and so on.[9]

Globalization cannot simply be verified empirically according to measurable criteria such as the convergence (or not) of corporate forms or social structures. Perhaps its most crucial feature is that it constitutes a *discourse* – and, increasingly, a hegemonic discourse which cuts across and gives meaning to the kinds of categories suggested above. In this sense, the spread of the discourse itself alters the *a priori* ideas and perceptions which people have of the empirical phenomena which they encounter; in so doing, it engenders strategies *and* tactics which in turn may restructure the game itself. With the erosion of old axioms, the concept of globalization is coming increasingly to shape the terms of the debate.

Analysts who emphasize 'interdependence' or 'internationalization', as supposedly distinct from globalization, by and large posit that the international *political* playing field is still essentially one constituted by the interaction of states concerned with their relative power positions (whether military or economic power, or both). Patterns of collective action *by and among states* in the international system, shaped by complex (mainly economic) interdependence, is thus seen as leading to the formation of both informal and formal international structures and institutions which can take on an autonomy of their own at the international level. Indeed, interdependence is said by John Ruggie and others to be leading to a 'new multilateralism', this time rooted in socio-economic behavioural imperatives rather than in idealist-type legal or constitutional structures.[10] The traditional distinction between domestic and international levels of analysis – embodied in 'two-level games' – is blurred, but not fundamentally undermined.[11] In contrast, the notion of globalization is an inherently more complex and heterogeneous phenomenon economically, socially and politically, involving at least three-level games.

Globalization is not part of a march to a higher – or indeed lower – form of civilization. It is a path-dependent process, rooted in real historical decisions, non-decisions and conjunctural turning-points. Social, economic and political institutions emerge in an environment where there is not one simple pathway or end point; there are in economic terminology 'multiple equilibrium points' available. However, once social relationships are established and power structures set in place in particular conjunctural settings, institutions tend to become 'locked in' and to resist fundamental restructuring.[12] As the globalization process takes shape, then, it does not involve some sort of linear process of the withering away of the state as a bureaucratic power structure; indeed, paradoxically, in a globalizing world states play a crucial role as stabilizers and enforcers of the rules and practices of global society. Furthermore, states and state actors are probably the most important single category of agent in the globalization process. As new forms of political organization surrounding, cutting across and coexisting with – and fostered by – the state crystallize, states and state actors are the primary source of the state's own transformation into a residual enterprise association.

From the welfare state to the competition state

State actors have acted and reacted in feedback loop fashion to the more complex structure of constraints and opportunities characteristic of the new environment. The outcome of the institutional selection process – the ultimate choice as to which equilibrium is eventually reached (if any) in attempting to cope with new pressures – depends upon the way agents react in real time in the real world. As international and transnational constraints limit the things that state and market actors believe the state can do, this shift is leading to a potential crisis of liberal democracy as we have known it – and therefore of the things people can expect from even the best-run government. In this context, for example, a new and potentially undemocratic role is emerging for the state as the enforcer of decisions and/or outcomes which emerge from world markets, transnational 'private interest governments', and international quango-like regimes.[13]

The essence of the post-war national welfare state lay in the capacity which state actors and institutions had gained, especially since the Great Depression, to insulate certain key elements of economic life from market forces while at the same time promoting other aspects of the market. These mechanisms did not merely mean protecting the poor and helpless from poverty and pursuing welfare goals like full employment or public health, but also regulating business in the public interest, 'fine tuning' business cycles to promote economic growth, nurturing 'strategic industries' and 'national champions', integrating labour movements into corporatist processes to promote wage stability and labour discipline, reducing barriers to international trade, imposing controls on 'speculative' international movements of capital, and the like. The expansion of the economic and social functions of the state was seen to be a crucial part of the process of social, economic and political 'modernization' for any 'developed' country.

But this compromise of domestic regulation and international opening – what John Ruggie famously called 'embedded liberalism'[14] – was eroded by increasing domestic structural costs (the 'fiscal crisis of the state')[15] as well as the structural consequences of growing external trade and, perhaps most important, of international financial transactions.[16] The crisis of the welfare states lay in their decreasing capacity to insulate national economies from the global economy, and the combination of stagnation and inflation which resulted when they tried. The world since then has seen the emergence of a quite different beast, the competition state. Rather than attempt to take certain economic activities *out* of the market, to 'decommodify' them as the welfare state was organized to do, the competition state has pursued *increased* marketization in order to make economic activities located within the national territory, or which otherwise contribute to national wealth, more competitive in international and transnational terms. The main features of this process have included attempts to reduce government spending in order to minimize the 'crowding out' of private investment by state consumption, and the deregulation of economic activities, especially financial markets. The result has been the rise of a new discourse and practice of 'embedded financial orthodoxy',[17] which is in turn shaping the parameters of political action everywhere.

Transnational factors and three-level games have forced four specific types of policy change to the top of the political agenda: (1) a shift from macroeconomic to microeconomic interventionism, as reflected in both deregulation and industrial policy; (2) a shift in the focus of that interventionism from the development and maintenance of a range *of* 'strategic' or 'basic' economic activities in order to retain minimal economic self-sufficiency in key sectors to one of flexible response to competitive conditions in a range of diversified and rapidly evolving international marketplaces, i.e. the pursuit *of* 'competitive advantage' as distinct from 'comparative advantage';[18] (3) an emphasis on the control of inflation and general neoliberal monetarism – supposedly translating into non-inflationary growth – as the touchstone of state economic management and interventionism; and (4) a shift in the focal point of party and governmental politics away from the general maximization of welfare within a nation (full employment, redistributive transfer payments and social service provision) to the promotion of enterprise, innovation and profitability in both private and public sectors.

[...]

[T]he challenge for state actors today, as viewed through the contemporary discourse of globalization, is to confront the perceived limitations of the state – mainly to attempt to combine a significant measure of austerity with the retention of a minimal welfare net to sustain sufficient consensus, while at the same time promoting structural reform at the mesoeconomic and microeconomic levels in order to improve international competitiveness. In the industrial world generally, major changes in government policy have resulted, changes which have serious consequences for the welfare state model – especially a shift in the focus of economic policy away from macroeconomic demand management towards more targeted mesoeconomic and microeconomic policies.

Divergences and convergences: competing forms of the competition state

Despite the vulnerability of the welfare state model, however, national policy-makers have a range of potential responses, old and new, with which to work. The challenge of the competition state is said to be one of getting the state to do both *more* and *less* at the same time. Getting more for less has been the core concept, for example, of the 'reinventing government' movement which is a major manifestation and dimension of the competition state approach.[19] The competition state involves both a transformation of the policy roles of the state and a multiplication of specific responses to change. In terms of policy transformation, several levels of government activity are affected. Among more traditional measures is, of course, trade policy. The core issue in the trade issue–area is to avoid reinforcing through protection the existing rigidity of the industrial sector or sectors in question, while at the same time fostering or even imposing adaptation to global competitive conditions in return for temporary protection. Transnational constraints are growing rapidly in trade policy, however, as can be seen in the establishment of the North Atlantic Free Trade Area, the Asia-Pacific Economic Cooperation group, and the World Trade Organization. Two other traditional categories, monetary and fiscal policy, are perhaps even more crucial today, and the key change is that relative priorities between the two have been reversed; tighter monetary policy (although with mixed results) is pursued alongside looser fiscal policy through tax cuts. And exchange rate policy, difficult to manage in the era of floating exchange rates and massive international capital flows, is nonetheless still essential, as the British devaluation of 1992 and the American devaluation of 1985–87 have shown.[20]

Potentially more innovative, combining old and new measures, is the area of industrial policy and related strategic trade policy. By targeting particular sectors, supporting the development of both more flexible manufacturing systems and transnationally viable economies of scale, and assuming certain costs of adjustment, governments can alter some of the conditions which determine competitive advantage: encouraging mergers and restructuring; promoting research and development; encouraging private investment and venture capital, while providing or guaranteeing credit-based investment where capital markets fail, often through joint public/private ventures;

developing new forms of infrastructure; pursuing a more active labour market policy while removing barriers to mobility, and the like. The examples of Japanese, Swedish and Austrian industrial policy have been widely analysed in this context.

A third category of measures, and potentially the most explosive, is, of course, deregulation. The deregulation approach is based partly on the assumption that national regulations, especially the traditional sort of regulations designed to protect national market actors from market failure, are insufficiently flexible to take into account the rapid shifts in transnational competitive conditions characteristic of the interpenetrated world economy of the late twentieth century. However, deregulation must not be seen just as the lifting of old regulations, but also as the formulation of new regulatory structures which are designed to cope with, and even to anticipate, shifts in competitive advantage. Furthermore, these new regulatory structures are often designed to *enforce* global market-rational economic and political behaviour on rigid and inflexible private sector actors as well as on state actors and agencies. The institutions and practices of the state itself are increasingly marketized or 'commodified', and the state becomes the spearhead of structural transformation to market norms both at home and abroad.

Although each of these processes can be observed across a wide range of states, however, there are significant variations in how different competition states cope with the pressures of adaptation and transformation. There is a dialectic of divergence and convergence at work, rather than a single road to competitiveness. The original model of the competition state was the strategic or developmental state which writers like John Zysman and Chalmers Johnson associated with France and Japan.[21] This perspective, which identifies the competition state with strong-state technocratic *dirigisme*, lives on in the analysis of newly industrializing countries (NICs) in Asia and other parts of the Third World. However, the difficulty with this approach has been that the scope of control which the technocratic patron-state and its client firms can exercise over market outcomes diminishes as the integration of these economies into global markets and the complexities of third-level games proceeds.

And as more firms and sectors become linked into new patterns of production, financing and market access, often moving operations offshore, their willingness to follow the script declines. However, there are distinctions even here. Within this category, for example, Japanese administrative guidance and the ties of the *keiretsu* system have remained relatively strong despite a certain amount of liberalization, deregulation and privatization, whereas in France the forces of neoliberalism have penetrated a range of significant bastions from the main political parties to major sectors of the bureaucracy itself.

In contrast, the orthodox model of the competition state today is not the strategic state but the neoliberal state (in the European sense, i.e. orthodox free-market economic liberalism, or what is called 'nineteenth-century liberalism' in the United States). Thatcherism and Reaganism in the 1980s provided both a political rationale and a power base for the renaissance of free-market ideology generally – not just in the United Kingdom and the United States but throughout the world. The flexibility and openness of British and US capital markets, the experience of Anglo-American elites with international and transnational business and their willingness to go multinational, the corporate structure of American and British firms and their (relative) concern with profitability and shareholder returns rather than traditional relationships and market share, the enthusiasm with which American managers have embraced lean management and downsizing, and the relative flexibility of the US and UK labour forces, combined with an arm's-length state tradition in both countries, are widely thought to have fought off the strategic state challenge and to have eventually emerged more competitive today.

Nevertheless, liberalization, deregulation and privatization have not reduced the role of state intervention overall, just shifted it from decommodifying bureaucracies to marketizing ones. 'Reinventing government', for example, means the replacement of bureaucracies which directly produce public services by ones which closely monitor and supervise contracted-out and privatized services according to complex financial criteria and performance indicators. And industrial policy is alive and well too, secreted in the interstices of a decentralized, patchwork bureaucracy which is the American tradition and the new British obsession.

Throughout the debate between the Japanese model and the Anglo-American model, however, the European neocorporatist model, rooted in the post-war settlement and given another (if problematic) dimension through the consolidation of the European Community (now the European Union), has been presented by many European commentators as a middle way. In bringing labour into institutionalized settings, not only for wage bargaining but for other aspects of the social market, in doggedly pursuing conservative monetary policies, in promoting extensive training policies, and in possessing a universal banking system which nurtured and stabilized industry without strategic state interventionism, the European neocorporatist approach (as practised in varying ways in Germany, Austria and Sweden in particular) has seemed to its proponents to embody the best aspects of both the Japanese and the Anglo-American models. However, despite the completion of the single market and the signing of the Maastricht Treaty, the signs of what in the early 1980s was called 'Eurosclerosis' have reappeared; the European Monetary Union project is widely regarded as deflationary in a context where costs are unevenly spread; and the liberalizing, deregulatory option is increasingly on the political cards again (as it was, for a while, in the 1980s), especially in the context of rapidly rising German unemployment. The competition state, then, comes in myriad forms. 'National developments' – i.e., differences in models of state/economy relations or state/societal arrangements – as Zysman writes, 'have, then, driven changes in the global economy.'[22]

At another level, of course, states and state actors seek to convince, or pressure, other states – and transnational actors such as multinational corporations or international institutions – to adopt measures which shift the balance of competitive advantage. Such pressure will generally combine elements of neo-mercantilistic self-interest, limited reciprocity, and multilateral hard bargaining – whether to limit trade in sensitive sectors such as textiles, automobiles or semiconductors, to develop new regional initiatives such as the European single market, to expand multilateral trade regimes in agriculture or services, or to reach agreements in areas such as exchange rate policy. The search for competitive advantage in a relatively open world adds further layers and cross-cutting cleavages to the world economy which may undermine pure multilateralism, but which increase the complexity and density of networks of interdependence and interpenetration. Finally, transnational pressures can develop – whether from multinational corporations or from nationally or locally based firms and other interests (such as trade unions) caught in the crossfire of the search for international competitiveness – for the establishment or expansion of transnational regimes, transnational neocorporatist structures of policy bargaining, transgovernmental linkages between bureaucrats, policy-makers and policy communities, and the like.

In all of these settings, the state is no longer able to act as a decommodifying hierarchy (i.e., taking economic activities out of the market). It must act more and more as a collective commodifying agent – i.e., putting activities *into* the market) – and even as *a market actor itself.* It is financier, middleman, advocate, and even entrepreneur, in a complex economic web where not only do the frontiers between state and market become blurred, but also where their cross-cutting structures become closely intertwined and their behavioural modes become less and less easy to distinguish. National differences therefore do not so much concern the possibility of resisting globalizing trends *per se*, but are best seen instead as representing different modes of managing a complex transition in which emerging political and economic structures are thought to be closely interwined but not yet terribly clear, and the possibilities for alternative equilibria are fluid.

Today the state remains the central focus for consensus, loyalty, and social discipline – the 'collective capitalist' maintaining the social fabric while fractions of capital compete. But this role puts the state into an increasingly contradictory location in political economy terms. Not only is the 'collective capitalist' role one which has to be exercised in a more and more complex field comprising both other states and transnational economic and social actors, but states are also increasingly quasi-market actors and commodifying agents themselves. In such complex conditions, the state is sometimes structurally fragmented, sometimes capable of strategic action. Despite elements of convergence, significant divergences remain, for different states have different sets of advantages and disadvantages in the search for international competitiveness. They differ in endogenous structural capacity for strategic action both domestically and internationally. They differ in the extent to which their existing economic structures, with or without government intervention, can easily adapt to international conditions. And they differ in their vulnerability to international and transnational trends and pressures.

The scope and limits of the competition state

The 'competition state', then, is a complex actor in a complex 'structured action field',[23] compelled to wear different hats at different times and in differently structured situations. State actors and market actors intermingle in changing international and transnational conditions. This complexity is nowhere more evident than in such fields as, for example, financial market regulation and environmental protection. On the one hand, financial market deregulation is of particular significance for understanding the nature of the new, more complex regulatory structures characteristic of a more integrated global financial marketplace.[24] On the other hand, environmental protection has gone through cycles of both regulation on a national level and deregulation or regulatory restructuring in the more freewheeling pro-market atmosphere of the early-to-mid-1980s; at the beginning of the 1990s, however, with environmental protection coming to be seen as not only a cross-border issue but also as representing a truly transnational public good, the dynamic of reregulation is once again at the forefront.

But the rapid rise of the competition state has given rise to a further paradox. As states and state actors have attempted to promote competitiveness in this way, they have – seemingly voluntarily – given up a range of crucial policy instruments. The debate rages over whether, for example, capital controls can be reintroduced or whether states are still able to choose to pursue more inflationary policies without disastrous consequences.[25] The 'genie is out of the bottle' – David Andrews has called it *hysteresis*[26] – and states are seeing their policy capacity and political autonomy eroding in ways which may not be recuperable. Political and social development is not merely a question of frictionless rational choices and cost-benefit analyses, but is inherently path-dependent and 'sticky', a process where conjunctural shifts can have structural consequences.

The nation-state, of course, is not dead, but its role has changed. In the first place, citizens will probably have to live more and more without the kind of public services and many of the redistributive arrangements characteristic of the national welfare states. The 'new public management' seeks not only to reorganize the state along the lines of private industry,[27] but also to replace public provision with private provision (pensions, prisons, etc.) and to replace direct payments for unemployment compensation, income support for the poor, etc., with time-limited, increasingly means-tested or work-related measures (or none at all). In the second place, the principal goal of state actors is increasingly one of minimizing inflation, in order to maintain the confidence of the international business and financial community. Central bankers have always played this role but are doing so to an ever-increasing extent.

In this context, states are less and less able to act as 'strategic' or 'developmental' states, and are more and more 'splintered states'.[28] State actors and different agencies are increasingly intertwined with 'transgovernmental networks' – systematic linkages between state actors and agencies overseeing particular jurisdictions and sectors, but cutting across different countries and including a heterogeneous collection of private actors and groups in interlocking policy communities. Furthermore, some of these linkages specifically involve the exchange of ideas rather than authoritative decision-making or power-broking – what have been called 'epistemic communities'.[29] The functions of the state, although central in structural terms, are increasingly residual in terms of the range of policy instruments and outcomes which they entail.

In international terms, states in pursuing the goal of competitiveness are increasingly involved in what John Stopford and Susan Strange have called 'triangular diplomacy', consisting of the complex interaction of state–state, state–firm, and firm–firm negotiations.[30] But this concept must be widened further. Interdependence analysis has focused too exclusively on two-level games and the state as a Janus-faced institutional structure. Although this is an oversimplification, I argue that complex globalization has to be seen as a structure involving (at least) three-level games, with third-level – transnational – games including not only 'firm–firm diplomacy' but also transgovernmental networks and policy communities, internationalized market structures, transnational cause groups and many other linked and interpenetrated markets, hierarchies and networks. As states and state actors get drawn more and more into the minutiae of cross-cutting and transnational economic relations, their activities become further constrained by the less manageable intricacies of complex situations.

[...]

Conclusion: globalization and the competition state as paradoxes

The central paradox of globalization is that rather than creating one big economy or one big polity, it also divides, fragments and polarizes. Convergence and divergence are two sides of the same coin. Globalization is not even a single discourse, but a contested concept giving rise to several distinct but intricately intertwined discourses, while national and regional differences belie the homogeneous vision as well.

Indeed, the power of globalization itself as process, practice and discourse – and thus as a paradigm – lies in this very complexity. Whatever direction the future takes, however, it will be a path-dependent one where hard political choices will have to be made and the very complexities of globalization will increasingly shape both the problematic and the understanding of potential solutions. The state is no longer the overarching institutional structure it once seemed to be, and the 'nation' as it has been known in the West is also succumbing to *Gemeinschaft* fatigue in the face of the democratic deficit, the challenge of transnational pressures, and the political and ideological forces of religious revival and new tribalisms. Political strategies and projects, therefore, will increasingly become multilayered and globally oriented – whether on the Right ('globalization' in the sense of pursuing economic efficiency in a liberalized world marketplace) or on the Left (a regeneration of genuinely internationalist socialism?).

Although state apparatuses are becoming bureaucratically more powerful and more intrusive in terms of monitoring economic activity, they have become residual in terms of the pursuit of some more profound form of common good. Social bonds are being reformulated around and through other structures and processes, and new types of embeddedness are crystallizing – in international finance, in ethnic groups both subnational and, indeed, transnational, in the world of international communications and the media, in strategic alliances among firms, in the mindset of international investors, in transgovernmental policy networks and transnational pressure groups, and in the discourse and practices of state actors themselves. In this context, different national models of state/economy relations or state/societal arrangements will at one level continue to shape developments in the global economy precisely because of the interaction of their differences; at the same time, however, that very interaction will generate new political pressures for convergence. The post-modern irony of the state is that rather than simply being undermined by inexorable forces of globalization, the competition state is becoming increasingly both the engine room and the steering mechanism of political globalization itself.

Notes

[1] On structures and political structuration, see P.G. Cerny, *The Changing Architecture of Politics: Structure, Agency and the Future of the State,* London and Thousand Oaks, Sage, 1990, chs 1-4.

[2] See Thomas Kuhn, *The Structure of Scientific Revolutions*, Chicago, Chicago University Press, 1962, for the notion of paradigms.

[3] P.G. Cerny, 'Globalization and Other Stories: The Search for a New Paradigm for International Relations', *International Journal*, Vol. LI, No. 4, Autumn 1996, pp. 617-637.

[4] Margaret Levi, 'The Predatory Theory of Rule', *Politics & 'Society*, Vol. 10, No. 4, Autumn 1981, pp. 431-65.

[5] Ferdinand Tonnies, *Community and Association*, East Lansing, MI, Michigan State University Press, 1957 (originally published as *Gemeinschaft und Gesellschaft*, 1887).

[6] See Josiah Lee Auspitz, 'Individuality, Civility, and Theory: The Philosophical Imagination of Michael Oakeshott', *Political Theory*, Vol 4, no. 3, August 1976, pp. 361-352; also Michael Oakeshott, 'On Misunderstanding Human Conduct: A Reply to my Critics', in ibid., pp. 353-67.

[7] Paul Hirst and Grahame Thompson, *Globalization in Question: The International Political Economy and the Possibilities of Governance*, Cambridge, Polity Press, 1995; Robert Boyer and Daniel Drache, (eds), *States Against Markets: The Limits of Globalization*, London, Routledge, 1996; John Zysman, 'The Myth of a "Global" Economy: Enduring National Foundations and Emerging Regional Realities', *New Political Economy*, Vol. 1, No. 1, Summer 1996, pp. 157-84.

[8] Hugo Radice, 'The Question of Globalization: A Review of Hint and Thompson', presented at the annual meeting of the Conference of Socialist Economists, Newcastle-upon-Tyne, 12-14 July 1996.

[9] Alain Minc, *Le nouveau Moyen Âge,* Paris, Gallimard, 1993; Robert D. Kaplan, 'The Coming Anarchy', *TheAtlantic Monthly*, February 1994, pp. 44-76; Bruce Cronin and Joseph Lepgold, 'A New Medievalism? Conflicting International Authorities and Competing Loyalties in the Twenty-First Century', paper presented to the annual meeting of the International Studies Association, Chicago, 23-27 February 1995; Stephen Kobrin, 'Back to the Future: Neomedievalism and the Post-Modern

World Economy', paper presented to the annual meeting of the International Studies Association, San Diego, CA, 17-21 April 1996.

[10] John Gerard Ruggie, James A. Caporaso, Steve Weber and Miles Kahler, *Symposium: Multilatmalism,* special section in *International Organization,* Vol. 46, No. 3, Summer 1992, pp. 561-708.

[11] Robert O. Keohane and Helen Milner, (eds), *Internationalization and Domestic Politics,* Cambridge, Cambridge University Press, 1996.

[12] Mark Granovetter, 'Economic Action and Social Structure: The Problem of Embeddedness', *American Journal of Sociology,* Vol. 91, No. 4, November 1985, pp. 50-82; Granovetter, 'Economic Institutions as Social Constructions: A Framework for Analysis', *Acta Sociologica,* No. 35, 1992, pp. 3-11.

[13] A 'quango', or quasi-autonomous non-governmental organization, is an authoritative body licensed by the state to carry out public regulatory functions but made up of appointed representatives of private sector interests. It is probably best considered to be a variant of state corporatism.

[14] John Gerard Ruggie, 'International Regimes, Transactions, and Change: Embedded Liberalism in the Post-War Order', *International Organization,* Vol. 36, No. 4, Autumn 1982, pp. 379-415; Ruggie here also uses the word 'liberalism' in its American meaning.

[15] James O'Connor, *The Fiscal Crisis of the State,* New York, St Martin's Press, 1973.

[16] Fred L. Block, *The Origins of International Economic Disorder: A Study of United States Monetary Policy from World War II to the Present,* Berkeley and Los Angeles, University of California Press, 1977; Susan Strange, *Casino Capitalism,* Oxford, Blackwell, 1986.

[17] P. G. Cerny, 'The Infrastructure of the Infrastructure? Toward "Embedded Financial Orthodoxy" in the International Political Economy', in Ronen P. Palan and Barry Gills, (eds), *Transcending the State-Global Divide: A Neostructuralist Agenda in International Relations,* Boulder, Co., Lynne Reinner, 1994, pp. 223-49.

[18] The distinction between comparative advantage and competitive advantage is a central theme of John Zysman and Laura and Andrea Tyson, (eds), *American Industry in International Competition,* Ithaca, NY, Cornell University Press, 1983.

[19] David Osborne and Ted Gaebler, *Reinventing Government: How the Entrepreneurial Spirit is Transforming the Public Sector, From Schoolhouse to Statehouse, City Hall to the Pentagon*, Reading, Mass., Addison-Wesley, 1992.

[20] Jeffry A. Frieden, 'Invested Interests: The Politics of National Economic Policies in a World of Global Finance', *International Organization*, Vol. 45, No. 4, Autumn 1991, pp. 425-51.

[21] John Zysman, Ithaca, NY, Cornell University Press, 1983; Chalmers Johnson, *M.I.T.I. and the Japanese Miracle: The Growth of Industrial Policy, 1925-1975*, Stanford, Cal., Stanford University Press, 1982.

[22] John Zysman, 'The Myth of the "Global" Economy': Enduring National Foundations and Emerging Regional Realities', *New Political Economy*, Vol. 1, No. 1, Summer 1996, pp. 157-84.

[23] Michel Crozier and Erhard Friedberg, *L'acteur et le système: les contraintes de l'action collective*, Paris, Editions du Seuil, 1977.

[24] P.G. Cerny, 'The Dynamics of Financial Globalization: Technology, Market Structure, and Policy Response', *Policy Sciences*, Vol. 27, No. 4, November 1994, pp. 319-42.

[25] John B. Goodman and Louis W. Pauly, 'The Obsolescence of Capital Controls? Economic Management in an Age of Global Markets', *World Politics*, Vol. 46, No. 4, October 1993, pp. 50-82; Ethan B. Kaplan, *Governing the Global Economy: International Finance and the State*, Cambridge, Mass., Harvard University Press, 1994; Eric N. Helleiner, 'Post-Globalization: Is the Financial Liberalization Trend Likely to be Reversed?', in Robert Boyer and Daniel Drache (eds), *States Against Markets: The Limits of Globalization*, London, Routledge, 1996; P. G. Cerny, 'International Finance and the Erosion of State Policy Capacity', in Philip Gummett (ed.), *Globalization and Public Policy*, Cheltenham, Glos., and Brookfield, VT, Elgar, 1996, pp. 83-104.

[26] David M. Andrews, 'Capital Mobility and State Autonomy: Toward a Structural Theory of International Monetary Relations', *International Studies Quarterly*, Vol. 38, No. 2, June 1994, pp. 193-218.

[27] Patrick Dunleavy, 'The Globalization of Public Services Production: Can Government Be "Best in World"?', *Public Policy and Administration*, Vol. 9, No. 1, Summer 1994, pp. 36-64.

[28] Howard Machin and Vincent Wright (eds), *Economic Policy and Policy-Making Under the Mitterrand Presidency, 1981-84*, London, Pinter, 1985.

[29] Peter Haas (ed.) *Knowledge, Power, and International Policy Coordination,* special issue of *International Organization,* Vol. 46, No. 1, Winter 1992; cf. Diane Stone, *Capturing the Political Imagination: Think-Tanks and the Policy Process,* London, Frank Cass, 1996.

[30] John Stopford and Susan Strange, *Rival States, Rival Firm: Competition for World Market Shares,* Cambridge, Cambridge University Press, 1991.

Chapter 4b.1

At the global crossroads (Part A): the end of the Washington Consensus?

David Held

[...]

Interconnectedness, integration and justice

The world we are in is highly interconnected, but it is far from integrated or just. By this I mean that the economic, political, social and environmental fortunes of countries are increasingly enmeshed, but that all too many nations do not share values or a commitment to remedying the position of the least well-off, most impoverished and most at risk.

The interconnectedness of countries can readily be measured by mapping the ways in which trade, communication, pollutants, violence, among many other factors, flow across borders and lock the well-being of countries into common patterns. Social integration can be measured by the extent to which countries share frameworks not just of communications but of cultural ideas, symbols and values. While the latter frequently diverge, the twentieth century gave rise to a grand meta-framework of values – those embodied in the international human rights regime. For the first time in history this provided a sense of the proper limits of the diversity of human associations. Yet, obviously enough, it is far from fully subscribed to and far from fully embedded in many parts of the world. By contrast, a global commitment to justice might be indicated by a sustained concern to ameliorate the radical asymmetries of life chances that pervade the world and by addressing the harm inflicted by these on people against their will and without their consent. However, we see no systematic and effective effort in this direction. The failure of the international community to get anywhere close to achieving the [Millennium Development Goals] is a case in point. In short, while there is a high degree of interconnectedness in the world, social integration is shallower and a commitment to social justice pitifully thin.

Why? Two reasons above all others will be focused on here: the old Washington Consensus, and the new Washington security agenda. These two hugely powerful policy programmes have profoundly shaped our age – and have profoundly weakened our public institutions, nationally and globally.

Only by understanding their failures and limitations can we move beyond them to recover a democratic, responsive politics at all levels of public life.

Economics

The Washington Consensus

The Washington Consensus can be defined in relation to an economic agenda which is focused typically on free trade, capital market liberalization, flexible exchange rates, market-determined interest rates, the deregulation of markets, the transfer of assets from the public to the private sector, the tight focus of public expenditure on well-directed social targets, balanced budgets, tax reform, secure property rights and the protection of intellectual property rights (see Table 4.5.1). It has been the economic orthodoxy for a significant period of the last 20 years in leading OECD countries, and in the international financial institutions. It has been prescribed, in particular, by the IMF and World Bank as the policy basis for developing countries.

The 'Washington Consensus' was first set out authoritatively by John Williamson (1990). While Williamson (see 2003) endorsed most of the policies listed above, he did not advocate free capital mobility. Williamson's original formulation drew together a policy agenda which he thought most people in the late 1980s and early 1990s in the policy making circles of Washington DC – the treasury, the World Bank and the IMF – would agree were appropriate for developing countries. Subsequently, the term acquired a very particular right-wing connotation as it became linked to the economic agenda of Ronald Reagan and Margaret Thatcher, with their emphasis on free capital movements, monetarism and a minimal state that accepts no responsibility for correcting income inequalities or managing serious externalities. There were important overlaps between the original Williamson programme and the neoliberal agenda, including macroeconomic discipline, a free market economy, privatization and free trade. Today Williamson distances himself from the neoliberal sense of the Washington Consensus, although he accepts that this version of the Consensus, with its endorsement of capital account liberalization, did become the dominant orthodoxy in the 1990s. I use the term Washington Consensus in this latter sense.

Critics charge that the measures of the Washington Consensus are bound up with US geopolitics, that all too often they are preached by the US to the rest of the world but not practised by it, and that they are deeply destructive of the social cohesion of the poorest countries. Interestingly, Williamson holds that while aspects of this may be true about the neoliberal version, his policy recommendations are sensible principles of economic practice whoever recommends and deploys them, and that they leave open the question of the progressivity of the tax system (see Williamson, 1993;

Table 4b.1.1: The original and augmented Washington Consensus

The original Washington Consensus
Fiscal discipline
Reorientation of public expenditures
Tax reform
Financial liberalization
Unified and competitive exchange rates
Trade liberalization
Openness to DFI
Privatization
Deregulation
Secure property rights
The augmented Washington Consensus: the original list plus:
Legal/political reform
Regulatory institutions
Anti-corruption
Labour market flexibility
WTO agreements
Financial codes and standards
'Prudent' capital-account opening
Non-intermediate exchange rate regimes
Social safety nets
Poverty reduction

Source: Rodrik (2001), p. 51.

2003). Two points will be at issue here. First, while some of the policies of the Washington Consensus may be reasonable in their own terms, others are not and, taken together, they represent too narrow a set of policies to help create sustained growth and equitable development. Second, the Washington Consensus underplays the role of government, a strong public sector, and the development of multilateral governance, with serious consequences for the capacity of public institutions to solve critical problems, national and global.

The Washington Consensus and development

The relationships between the Washington Consensus, economic liberalization and development has been extensively examined (see, for example, Mosley, 2000; Chang, 2002). The focus has been on the way the Washington Consensus has been implemented through loans (and debt rescheduling) that require developing countries to undergo 'structural adjustment' – the alignment of their economies to the requirements of the core policies – and on the subsequent results. In this context, some very serious issues have arisen which need to be confronted. They have been summarized pithily by Branko Milanovic (2003, p. 679) in the form of three questions:

1 how to explain why after sustained involvement and many structural adjustment loans, and as many IMF Stand-bys, African GDP per capita has not budged from its level of 20 years ago. Moreover, in 24 African countries, GDP per capita is less than in 1975, and in 12 countries even below its 1960s level;
2 how to explain the recurrence of Latin crises, in countries such as Argentina, that months prior to the outbreak of the crisis are being praised as model reformers;
3 how to explain that ...'pupils' among the transition countries (Moldova, Georgia, Kyrghyz Republic, Armenia), after setting out in 1991 with no debt at all, and following all the prescriptions of the IFIs, find themselves 10 years later with their GDPs halved and in need of debt-forgiveness.

Something is clearly awry. The dominant economic orthodoxies have not succeeded in many parts of the developing world; they have failed to generate sustained economic growth, poverty reduction and fair outcomes.

The Washington Consensus prescriptions can be misleading and damaging. It has been found that one of the key global factors impacting on the capacity of the poorest countries to develop is not tariff liberalization, but capital liberalization (see Garrett, forthcoming). The neoliberal Washington Consensus recommends both. Tariff liberalization has been broadly beneficial for low income countries. By contrast, rapid capital liberalization can be a recipe, in the absence of prudential regulation and sound domestic capital markets, 'for volatility, unpredictability and booms and busts in capital flows' (ibid.). Countries that have rapidly opened their capital accounts have performed significantly less well (in terms of economic growth and income inequality) than countries that have maintained tight control on capital movements and cut tariffs (see Bhagwati, 2004).

Both the crises in East Asia in the late 1990s and the recent recessions in Latin America show, Joseph Stiglitz (2004, p. 25) affirms, that 'premature capital market liberalisation can result in economic volatility, increasing poverty, and the destruction of the middle classes'. And a recent study by economists at the IMF itself finds that 'there is no strong, robust and uniform support for the theoretical argument that financial globalization per se delivers a higher rate of economic growth' and, more troubling, that 'countries in the early stages of financial integration have been exposed to significant risks in terms of higher volatility of both output and consumption' (2003, pp. 6, 7). Yet the Bush administration is still leading the way in demanding a tough form of such liberalization through international financial institutions and bilateral trade agreements. The governing capacities of developing countries can be seriously eroded as a result.

Moreover, the experience of China and India – along with Japan, South Korea and Taiwan in earlier times – shows that countries do not have to adopt, first and foremost, liberal trade and/or capital policies in order to benefit from enhanced trade, to grow faster, and to develop an industrial infrastructure able to produce an increasing proportion of national consumption. All these countries, as Robert Wade (2003) has recently noted, have experienced relatively fast growth behind protective barriers, growth which fuelled rapid trade expansion, focused on capital and intermediate goods. As each of these countries has become richer, it has tended to liberalize its trade policy.

Accordingly, it is a misunderstanding to say that trade liberalization per se has fuelled economic growth in China and India; rather, it is the case that these countries developed relatively quickly behind protective barriers, before they liberalized their trade. If it is the case that these countries, and others like them, did not straightforwardly develop as a result of trade liberalization, and if it is the case that some of the poorest countries of the world are worse off as a result of an excessive haste with respect to global capital market integration, then the case is strengthened for applying the precautionary principle to global economic integration and resisting the developmental agenda of the Washington Consensus.

Internal and external economic integration

While economic protectionism should be rejected as a general strategy (with its attendant risks of creating a vicious circle of trade disputes and economic conflicts), there is much evidence to suggest that a country's *internal* economic integration – the development of its human capital, of its economic infrastructure and robust national market institutions, and the replacement of imports with national production where feasible – needs to be stimulated initially by state-led economic and industrial policy. The evidence indicates that higher internal economic integration can help generate the conditions in which a country can benefit from higher external integration (Wade, 2003). The development of state regulatory capacity, a sound public domain and the ability to focus investment on job creating sectors in competitive and productive areas is more important than the single-minded pursuit of integration into world markets. This finding should not come as a surprise since nearly all of today's developed countries initiated their growth behind tariff barriers, and only lowered these once their economies were relatively robust. They did not begin their development by rapidly opening their economies to foreign trade, capital flows and investment, as recommended by the Washington Consensus.

The argument above should not be taken as a simple endorsement of state-centric development and of the progressive nature of state interventionism, just because the latter runs counter to the Washington Consensus. Rather, the argument here is that the Washington Consensus has eroded the ability to formulate and implement sound public policy and has damaged political capacity. Moreover, public-sector objectives can be delivered by a diversity of actors, public and private. The wider development of civil society – trade unions, citizen groups, NGOs and so on – is indispensable to a robust programme of national development, although there can, of course, be conflicts between economic development and the strengthening of civil society. All societies need significant measures of autonomy to work out their own ways of managing this conflict.

There is, in fact, no single route or set of policy prescriptions to economic development; knowledge of local conditions, experimentation with suitable domestic institutions and agencies and the nurturing of internal economic integration need to be combined with sound macroeconomic policy and some elements of external market integration. The most successful recent cases of development – East Asia, China, India – have managed to find ways of taking advantage of the opportunities offered by world markets – cheaper products, exports, technology and capital – while entrenching domestic incentives for investment and institution building. As Dani Rodrik (2001, p. 22) has succinctly put it:

> Market incentives, macroeconomic stability, and sound institutions are key to economic development. But these requirements can be generated in a number of different ways – by making the best use of existing capabilities in light of resources and other constraints. There is no single model of a successful transition to a high growth path. Each country has to figure out its own investment strategy.

Asymmetries of global market access are a pressing development problem, including selective protectionism, tariff barriers in the developed and developing world, European and American subsidies in agriculture and textiles and so on. But an exclusive focus on these can distort development strategies. Development thinking has to shift from a dogged focus on 'market access' to a more complex mindset (see Rodrik, 2001). Developing nations need policy space to exercise institutional innovations that depart from the old orthodoxies of the World Bank, IMF and WTO. Concomitantly, organizations like the WTO need to move their agenda away from a narrow set of policies concerned with market creation and supervision to a broader range of policies which encourage different national economic systems to flourish within a fair and equitable rule-based global market order.

The Washington Consensus and the limits of the public domain

The thrust of the Washington Consensus is to enhance economic liberalization, develop a neoliberal form of economic globalization and to adapt the public domain – local, national and global – to market leading institutions and processes. It thus bears a heavy burden of responsibility for the common political resistance or unwillingness to address significant areas of market failure, including:

- the problem of externalities, for example the environmental degradation caused by current forms of economic growth;
- the inadequate development of non-market social factors, which alone can provide an effective balance between 'competition' and 'cooperation', and thus ensure an adequate supply of essential 'public goods' such as education, effective transportation and sound health;
- the tendency towards the 'concentration' and 'centralization' of economic life, marked by patterns of oligopoly and monopoly;
- the propensity to 'short-termism' in investment strategy as fund holders and investment bankers operate policies aimed at maximizing immediate income return and dividend results;
- and the underemployment or unemployment of productive resources in the context of the demonstrable existence of urgent and unmet need.

Leaving markets to resolve alone problems of resource generation and allocation misses the deep roots of many economic and political difficulties; for instance, the vast asymmetries of life chances within and between nation-states which are a source of considerable conflict; the erosion of the economic fortune of some countries in sectors like agriculture and textiles while these sectors enjoy protection and assistance in others; the emergence of global financial flows which can rapidly destabilize national economies; and the development of serious transnational problems involving the global commons. Moreover, to the extent that pushing back the boundaries of state action or weakening governing capacities means increasing the scope of market forces, and cutting back on services which have offered protection to the vulnerable, the difficulties faced by the poorest and the least powerful – north, south, east and west – are exacerbated. The rise of 'security' issues to the top of the political agenda reflects, in part, the need to contain the outcomes which such policies provoke.

The Washington Consensus has, in sum, weakened the ability to govern – locally, nationally and globally – and it has eroded the capacity to provide urgent public goods. Economic freedom is championed at the expense of social justice and environmental sustainability, with long-term damage to both. And it has confused economic freedom and economic effectiveness.

Amending the Washington Consensus

The Washington Consensus has come under assault from many sides in recent years, from special domestic lobbies demanding protection for certain economic sectors (agriculture, textiles, steel) to the anti-globalization, environmental and social justice movements. The poor results and performance of the Washington Consensus itself have invoked deep unease and criticism. Disappointing economic growth and increasing insecurity in many parts of Latin America, economic stagnation or decline in many sub-Saharan countries, the Asian financial crisis and the stark difficulties experienced in some of the transition economies has led to a call to replace or broaden the policy range of the Washington Consensus. Within the IMF, World Bank and other leading international organizations there has been an attempt to respond to criticism by broadening the Consensus to encompass a concern with state capacity, poverty reduction and social safety nets. As a result, attention has slowly shifted from an exclusive emphasis on liberalization and privatization to a preoccupation with the institutional underpinnings of successful market activity (see Table 4.5.1). The new agenda still champions large parts of the old agenda, but adds governance and anti-corruption measures, legal and administrative reform, financial regulation, labour market flexibility and the importance of social safety nets.

To the extent that a country's public institutions are a crucial determinant of its long term development – and they are clearly very important – the new emphasis is helpful and welcome. But, as Rodrik (2001, p. 12) has emphasized, 'the institutional basis for a market economy is not uniquely determined. There is no single mapping between a well-functioning market and the *form* of non-market institutions required to sustain it.' The new agenda gives excessive weight to Anglo-American conceptions of the proper type of economic and political institutions such as flexible labour markets and financial regulation. In addition, the whole agenda is shaped by what is thought of as the necessary institutions to ensure external economic integration, e.g. the introduction of WTO rules and standards. Moreover, the new agenda provides no clear guidance on how to prioritize institutional change and gives little recognition to the length of time it has taken to create such developments in countries where it is well advanced. After all, nearly all the industrial countries which have nurtured these reforms did so over very substantial time periods (Chang, 2002).

[...]

Security

9/11, the War in Iraq and the further attack on multilateralism

If 9/11 was not a defining moment in human history, it certainly was for today's generations. The terrorist attack on the World Trade Center and the Pentagon was an atrocity of extraordinary proportions. Yet, after 9/11, the US and its major allies could have decided that the most important things to do were to strengthen international law in the face of global terrorist threats, and to enhance the role of multilateral institutions. They could have decided it was important that no single power or group should act as judge, jury and executioner. They could have decided that global hotspots like the Middle East which feed global terrorism should be the main priority. They could have decided that the disjuncture between economic globalization and social justice needed more urgent attention. And they could have decided to be tough on terrorism and tough on the conditions which lead people to imagine that Al-Qaeda and similar groups are agents of justice in the modern world. But they have systematically failed to decide any of these things. In general, the world after 9/11 has become more polarized and international law weaker. The systematic political weaknesses of the Washington Consensus have been compounded by the new Washington security doctrines.

The rush to war against Iraq in 2003 gave priority to a narrow security agenda which is at the heart of the new American security doctrine of unilateral and pre-emptive war. This agenda contradicts most of the core tenets of international politics and international agreements since 1945 (Ikenberry, 2002). It throws aside respect for open political negotiations among states, as it does the core doctrine of deterrence and stable relations among major powers (the balance of power). We have to come to terms not only with the reality that a single country enjoys military supremacy to an unprecedented extent in world history, but also with the fact that it can use that supremacy to respond unilaterally to perceived threats (which may be neither actual nor imminent), and that it will brook no rival.

The new doctrine has many serious implications (Hoffmann, 2003). Among these are a return to an old realist understanding of international relations as, in the last analysis, a 'war of all against all', in which states rightly pursue their national interests unencumbered by attempts to establish internationally recognized limits (self-defence, collective security) on their ambitions. But if this 'freedom' is (dangerously) granted to the US, why not also to Russia, China, India, Pakistan, North Korea and so on? It cannot be consistently argued that all states bar one should accept limits on their self-defined goals. The flaws of international law and the UN Charter can either be addressed, or taken as an excuse for further weakening international institutions and legal arrangements.

Narrow vs. Broad security agendas

Since 9/11 there has been a growing divergence between the American-led security agenda, on the one side, and the development, welfare and human rights agenda, on the other. The difference can be put simply by adapting Tony Blair's famous slogan on crime: 'tough on crime and tough on the causes of crime'. In global political terms this means being tough on security threats and tough on the conditions which breed them. This broader agenda requires three things of governments and international institutions – all currently missing (Held & Kaldor, 2001).

First, there must be a commitment to the rule of law and the development of multilateral institutions – not the prosecution of war on its own. Civilians of all faiths and nationalities need protection. Terrorists and all those who systematically violate the sanctity of life and human rights must be brought before an international criminal court that commands cross-national support. This does not preclude internationally sanctioned military action to arrest suspects, dismantle terrorist networks and deal with aggressive rogue states – far from it. But such action should always be understood as a robust form of international law enforcement, above all as a way, as Mary Kaldor (1998) has most clearly put it, of protecting civilians and bringing suspects to trial. In short, if justice is to be dispensed impartially, no power can act as judge, jury and executioner. What is needed is momentum towards global, not American or Russian or Chinese or British or French, justice. We must act together to sustain and strengthen a world based on common rules (Solana, 2003).

Second, a sustained effort has to be undertaken to generate new forms of global political legitimacy for international institutions involved in security and peace-making. This must include the condemnation of systematic human rights violations wherever they occur, and the establishment of new forms of political and economic accountability. This cannot be equated with an occasional or one-off effort to create a new momentum for peace and the protection of human rights, as is all too typical.

And, finally, there must be a head-on acknowledgement that the ethical and justice issues posed by the global polarization of wealth, income and power, and with them the huge asymmetries of life chances, cannot be left to markets to resolve, as already argued. Those who are poorest and most vulnerable, linked into geopolitical situations where their economic and political claims have been neglected for generations, may provide fertile ground for terrorist recruiters. The project of economic globalization has to be connected to manifest principles of social justice; the latter need to frame global market activity. Global social democracy must replace, in sum, the Washington Consensus.

[...]

References

Bhagwati, J. (2004) *In Defense of Globalisation* (Oxford: Oxford University Press).

Chang, H.-J. (2002) *Kicking Away the Ladder: Development Strategy in Historical Perspective* (London: Anthem).

Garrett, G. (forthcoming) *Globalization and inequality, Perspectives on Politics.*

Held, D. and Kaldor, M. (2001) What hope for the future? Available at http://www.lse.ac.u/depts/global/maryheld.htm.

Hoffmann, S. (2003) America goes backward, *New York Review of Books*, 12 June.

Ikenberry, G. J. (2002) America's imperial ambition, *Foreign Affairs*, September–October.

Kaldor, M. (1998) *New and Old Wars* (Cambridge: Polity).

Milanovic, B. (2003) Two faces of globalization: against globalization as we know it, *World Development*, 31(4).

Mosley, P. (2000) Globalisation, economic policy and convergence, *World Economy*, 23(5).

Rodrik, D. (2001) The global governance of trade as if development really mattered. Available at http://www.undp.org/bdp.

Solana, J. (2003) The future of transatlantic relations, *Progressive Politics*, 2(2).

Stiglitz, J. (2004) Distant voices, *The Guardian*, 12 March.

Wade, R. (2003) The disturbing rise in poverty and inequality, in D. Held & M. Koenig-Archibugi (Eds) *Taming Globalization* (Cambridge: Polity).

Williamson, J. (1990) *Latin American Adjustment: How Much has Happened?* (Washington, DC: Institute for International Economics).

Williamson, J. (1993) Democracy and the 'Washington consensus', *World Development*, 21(8).

Williamson, J. (2003) The Washington consensus and beyond, *Economic and Political Weekly*, 38(15).

Chapter 4b.2

Attacking Poverty and the 'Post-Washington Consensus'

Paul Mosley

[It is not the case] that the developing world as a whole enjoyed rapid growth as a result of reforms in the 1980s and 1990s. Indeed, growth in the developing world has been disappointing, with the typical country registering negative growth. [However], this disappointing growth should not be ascribed to the failure of reforms. [In addition] the macroeconomic evidence suggests a pattern in which all income groups benefit equally from reforms. Even among the countries of the former socialist bloc, where reforms have gone awry, inequality increased least in countries that successfully increased reforms. It increased most in countries which introduced reforms only partially or not at all. On the whole (the costs of reform) do not negate the benefits of the reforms discussed above. But they do point to the importance of social policies to ease the burdens which reforms impose. (World Bank, 2000b, p. 66).

Of all the reforms implemented, financial liberalisation stands out for having caused serious disruptions in economic performance. The combination of open capital accounts, weak regulation of the financial sector, and the volatility of short-term capital flows lie behind the major macroeconomic crises in the 1990s ... During the height of the 'reform rush' the prevailing view was that reforms should be introduced as quickly as possible in order to take advantage of the 'window of opportunity' provided by reform-friendly governments. This view is now changing. The financial crashes of the late 1990s in particular revealed the importance of creating adequate institutions (rules and organisations) and codes of behaviour, or 'social capital' (voluntary compliance with established laws, trust, cooperative behaviour, and basic codes of conduct) before market-oriented reforms are adopted. (World Bank 2000a, paragraphs 8.12/8.13).

Has the World Bank changed, and in the process dropped the 'Washington consensus' approach to liberalization and economic reform? The two quotations above from the *2000 World Development Report* suggest contradictory answers to this question: no and yes respectively. And this paper will indeed argue that 'yes and no' is the only possible answer to the question posed. Our initial evidence for the proposition is something of a cheat, as it juxtaposes a passage from the *final* draft of the *2000 World Development Report* with a passage from the *penultimate* (January 2000a) version, which was watered down in the final draft.[1] But this is necessary in order to demonstrate a fact which the Bank's new transparency has revealed, namely that there is deep division within it over the extent to which adherence to a neo–liberal ideology best serves the interests of the poor; and this division is best understood by reference to a larger debate concerning the positioning of the Bank within the global marketplace in the twenty-first century,

Table 4b.2.1: 1990 and 2000/01 World Development Reports: Themes and associated policy recommendations

1990		2000/01	
'Pillars'	Associated policies	'Pillars'	Associated policies
Labour-intensity	Small-scale industry; special employment measures; promotion of green revolution in small-farm agriculture		
Investment in the human capital of the poor	Promotion of primary health and education, especially amongst females; microfinance	Opportunity	Microfinance; land reform and other asset redistribution policies; fiscal etc. measures to reduce inequality; 'pro-poor' public expenditure patterns
Social safety-nets	Food subsidies; social funds; support for community-based redistribution	Security	'Tailor-made' social protection measures; measures to support asset diversification; insurance; 'international public good' defences against economic crisis, e.g. financial regulation; conflict prevention
		Empowerment	Democratisation, decentralisation, measures to build 'social capital'

which has been going on at least since the crisis of the early 1980s but was accentuated by the global financial crisis of 1997–98.

As is well known, the World Bank's second poverty report of 2000/01, like its first of 1990, employs a three-part diagnosis and prescription for global poverty (Table 4.6.1), with the original 'three-legged stool' of labour-intensity, investment in the human capital of the poor and social safety nets having been supplanted by the three new pillars of opportunity, empowerment and security.

As illustrated by Table 4.6.1, security and opportunity are the lineal descendants of 'social safety nets' and 'investment in the human capital of the poor' respectively, whereas empowerment is a completely new add-on to the approach of the 1990 report, which was often portrayed as excessively top-down and more guided by the internal voices of the Bank than the voices of the poor. The real battleground, however, is the security theme, which (depending on interpretation) can be used either to defend, to reform or to destroy the 'Washington Consensus'. We shall illustrate with reference to both international and domestic policy issues.

The concept of security adopted by the *World Development Report* is an extremely broad one, linking material and psychological security in a new definition of poverty to sit alongside the orthodox ones and at the same time linking the security of the individual household to the security of the nation-state and of the global economy. At the time of writing the *Report* the security of the global economy – and of many poor people – had been seriously shaken by the world financial crisis of 1997–99, and much that is in the *Report* can be seen as a reaction to this trauma, in particular the protectionist sentiments expressed in the second quotation at the head of this article. As early as January 1998, at the outset of the crisis, Joseph Stiglitz, at the time the Bank's chief economist, had insisted on the need for a new 'Post-Washington Consensus' (Stiglitz, 1998), permitting the search for 'broader goals' with the use of 'more instruments', among them competition policy, anti-corruption legislation and instruments of financial regulation. Although the possibility of supplementing these instruments of financial regulation with direct controls was not mentioned in Stiglitz's paper, it was only a short step from there to the advocacy of capital inflow controls à la Chile and even capital outflow controls à la Malaysia in the first draft of the *World Development Report* – and thus, on one interpretation, to the abandonment of the World Bank's laissez-faire position.

Of key importance to the position which the Bank chose to take were the positions already taken by Southern governments and by the other international financial institutions, in particular the IMF. The 'Washington Consensus', according to its original exponent (Williamson, 1993) was a consensus between at least these three groups of actors in favour of liberalism in the economic sphere and democracy in the political – a consensus whose spontaneity was open to question, and which was held together, through the 1980s, by severe doses of paternalism and conditionality from the Bank and the Fund. But whereas the Bank of the 1980s had been happy to forget the fact that some of its programmes were not 'owned' by what it saw as unenlightened or partisan Southern voices, the Bank of the 1990s could not; and least of all could this be done by the Bank of 2000 which saw it as its mission to give speech to the 'voices of the poor'. So if the voices of the South by then were insisting on the demise of the old Washington consensus in favour of pragmatic developmentalism (Gore, 2000), and in particular on suspension of financial liberalisation in support of global financial security, that was fine by (most of) the Bank – the more so since the Fund was still insisting on the opposite position.

The Fund, of course, had itself moved many miles from its pre-1980 role, in particular through its progressively increased involvement in micro issues such as public enterprise pricing, tax and tariff policy, the composition of public expenditure, and latterly even antipoverty strategy – as symbolized by the recent renaming of its Enhanced Structural Adjustment Facility, in 1999, as a Poverty Reduction and Growth Facility. As the Fund went more micro under the stress of the 1980s crisis, so the Bank through its simultaneously-established Structural Adjustment Lending went macro, and this muddying of the clean and simple division of labour set up by the Bretton Woods founding fathers was to lead to some harsh disputes between the Bank and the Fund of that time (Mosley *et al*, 1995, ch 2). Somewhat papered over during the boom of the early 1990s, these demarcation disputes resurfaced, as disputes do, during the time of adversity and insecurity at the end of the decade. During that crisis the Fund held firm (e.g. IMF, 1999) to the principle that capital movements should remain free and 'security' not be sought through direct controls, which could easily become competitive and cumulative as in the 1930s; the Bank chose this moment to break ranks, to align with the 'voices of the poor' and thus to disrupt the Washington Consensus in its own way. In the process, of course, it was hoping to reclaim from the Fund the anti-poverty policy territory to which M. Camdessus had impertinently laid claim.[2] The East Asian trauma stimulated a range of proposals for protecting the security of the global financial order early in the new millennium, several of which (e.g. Summers, 1999; Wolf, 1999; Meltzer, 2000) supported the Bank's insistence on being allowed to focus on concessional anti-poverty operations while the Fund concentrated on short-term financial rescue operations. Thus the 'Washington Consensus' could be converted, as under the original 1945 articles of agreement, into a 'Washington Division of Labour' in which the Bretton Woods partners would not need to agree, because they were doing different jobs.

The concept of 'security' therefore, has in the international sphere led the Bank, or part of the Bank at least, away from laisser-faire. There are impeccable reasons why this should occur, since markets do not deliver security and in a world of insecurity (read uncertainty) all the standard theorems which prove the optimality of a regime of free competition no longer hold. But at the same time any movement away from the espousal of free trade cannot but cause unease to the Bank, since it was the chaos caused by a collective movement away from free trade and investment during the interwar period which caused the Bank, indeed the entire Bretton Woods system, to be brought into being.

But this is just the international sphere, and that only occupies two of the *World Development Report's* eleven chapters. Most of the *Report's* analysis is occupied with the domestic dimension of poverty, and here the treatment of the security theme is very different. On the one hand, the report movingly illustrates how the market simply cannot function for many poor people since 'forces of circular and cumulative causation' as they were known in the 1950s (Myrdal, 1957), simply exclude them from participation:

> Extreme poverty deprives people of almost all means of managing risk by themselves. With few or no assets, self-insurance is impossible. With poor health and bad nutrition, working more or sending more household members to work is difficult. And with high default risks, group insurance mechanisms are often closed off. The poorest households thus face extremely unfavourable tradeoffs. When a shock occurs, they must obtain immediate increases in income or cut spending, but in so doing they incur a long-term cost by jeopardising their economic and human development prospects. These are the situations that lead to child labour and malnourishment, with lasting damage to children, and the breakdown of families (World Bank 2000, p. 146).

Some of the elements in this characterization are open to question – in particular, there is a lively debate within the Bank about whether and where child labour causes 'lasting damage to children' (e.g. Ravallion and Wodon, 2000). What is probably not open to question is that at the microeconomic level many of the key markets for assets and for access to them are simply not open to the poor; indeed the market for security itself – i.e. insurance – is described by the Bank, with poetic licence, as non-existent in developing countries.[3] In such an environment, liberalization and privatization are not so much right or wrong as irrelevant: [so that] the issue becomes how to bring markets into existence rather than how to 'unleash' them, to quote a phrase of the Bank's from a more macho era.

On this issue, the Bank is somewhat agnostic. It unveils, as its Table 8.3, a panorama of 'mechanisms' for managing the risks which poor people face, some of which such as microfinance are presented as private (and definitely market-based), some of which such as pensions and employment schemes are generally public, and some of which operate at the individual and community level, such as migration, management of common property resources and asset diversification. However, having emphasized at a formal level how large a range of non-state options is available for executing the traditionally public function of risk management and poverty reduction, the authors of the *World Development Report* abstain from any serious recommendation to shift public functions into the private domain, or indeed the other way about. They do say that 'if trust in the state is low, few people will put their faith in the government system' (World Bank, 2000b, p. 148) – and many of us are familiar with environments, from Kenya to Zambia to Bangladesh, where the state is gradually ceding poverty-reduction functions to NGOs as a consequence. But this is a tautology, and it is very different from the strident advocacy of the merits of private management over public which characterised the Bank position as recently as its report on *Adjustment in Africa* (World Bank, 1994). It is different even, in its emphasis on community action and social capital-building, from the 'Post-Washington Consensus' as articulated by Stiglitz (1998). But on how social capital should be built up in environments where it is missing, we again encounter agnosticism. One element is certainly peace, which takes us back to the security theme in the broad sense; and the provision of national security is cited in many textbooks as the primordial public-sector function. But, in developing countries at least, it no longer is; and security of this kind, from Rwanda to Ethiopia to Kosovo, is now pursued not by the state alone but by an 'emerging development-security complex' (Duffield, 2000) of recipient government, NGOs and aid donors.

One aspect, then, of the Bank's retreat from liberalization is a simple change in expository style: from aggressive advocacy of specific policies to a much more agnostic posture, just as the majority of development NGOs have been moving in the opposite direction. Nowhere is this more apparent than in the discussion of aid policy, where we are bluntly told that 'conditionality fails' (p. 193). 'Recipients do not see the conditions as binding', the *WDR* continues, 'and most donors are reluctant to stop giving aid when conditions are not met. As a result, compliance with conditions tends to be low, while the release rate of loan tranches remains high.' All this is of course the polar opposite of the position on conditionality articulated by the Bank during the age of adjustment in the 1980s, and indeed during the period immediately after the publication of the Bank's first poverty *World Development Report* in 1990, when conditionality was used by the Bank in order to try and make recipient countries adopt a more pro-poor pattern of policy. In place of conditionality donors are urged to adopt 'selectivity':

> If all aid money were allocated on the basis of high poverty rates and reasonably effective policies and institutions, a recent study estimates, even today's small aid flows could lift 19 million people out of poverty each year – almost twice the estimated 10 million now being helped (World Bank, 2000b, p. 196).

The 'recent study' in question is, of course, Collier and Dollar (2000), which has moved rapidly on from the very free-market definition of 'reasonably effective policies and institutions' adopted by Burnside and Dollar (2000) and instead advocates the basing of country-selectivity on a much broader list of criteria, including alongside the standard indicators of openness and fiscal stringency such indicators as 'environmental policies and regulations', 'poverty monitoring and analysis', 'pro–poor targeting and programmes', 'safety nets', efficiency *and equity* of resource mobilisation', 'efficiency *and equity* of public expenditures' (Collier and Dollar, 2000, p. 33, emphases added). It goes without saying that several of these selectivity criteria do not fit comfortably within the standard or even the (Stiglitz-)expanded 'Washington Consensus'. Whether they can and will be implemented any better than the earlier conditionality criteria is an issue for another paper. What is important here is the dilution of the Washington Consensus which they symbolize.

Our answer to the question of whether the World Bank has abandoned the preference of the Washington Consensus for free over controlled markets is, therefore, 'yes and no': no in the sense that the old agenda remains, yes in the sense that it has been supplemented by elements going beyond even Stiglitz's 'post-Washington Consensus', and yes and no in the sense that the weight put on the different criteria by different members and departments of the World Bank varies enormously; as it always has done, but these days in a more transparent way. Of the themes enunciated by the *2000/01 World Development Report*, we see the security theme as particularly antithetical to the free-market approach, because security in both a personal, a national and a global sense is not a characteristic which markets are well attuned to providing, least of all to the poor people who are the focus of the *Report*.

Our other main point has been that the Bank's approach and definition of its mission, both in this *Report* and elsewhere, should not be seen as an independent variable but rather by its own desire to position itself within the global market place – i.e. to survive, like the billion poor people with whom it so vividly empathises in the *Report*. The Bank, of course, has lost large chunks of its market over the years, first in the high–income and now in the middle–income countries: which may be a measure of its success but has moved it gradually out of the infrastructural finance business into a number of other core businesses in low–income countries, including social protection, knowledge creation and various global governance functions.

As it has moved down-market to countries where markets work less well or not at all, it has trimmed its advocacy of the market mechanism – driven by the triple pressure of adaptation to its new environment, the spirit of the age and not least a desire to differentiate its product in face of competition from its old rival the Fund. What matters in the end is not how these shifts are labelled but how much they reduce poverty – and that too is a matter for another paper, which cannot be written yet. But one competition the Bank has already won. This is beyond doubt the most visually beautiful in nearly a quarter-century of *World Development Reports*. No international financial organisation should dare to decorate its front cover with a map of the world ever again.

[...]

Notes

[1] The final version reads:

> Recognising (that there is a possibility of recurrence of international financial crisis), developing countries may wish to implement short-term safeguards to limit their exposure. These safeguards are of two types: controls on capital flows and measures to enhance liquidity. Controls on capital – including Chilean type taxes on inflows, quantitative controls on the banking sector's international short-term liabilities, and restrictions on capital outflows – have their problems, ranging from evasion to implementation difficulties and opportunistic imposition. They can also restrict a country's access to much needed capital. But each type of control can be effective in some situations in dampening the volatility of capital flows, thus helping to prevent crises. (World Bank, 2000b, p. 181).

[2] Through its creation of the Structural Adjustment Facility (subsequently Enhanced Structural Adjustment Facility, subsequently Poverty Reduction and Growth Facility); and through its various pro-poor declarations, notably M Camdessus's insistence at the UNCTAD conference (Bangkok, 13 February, 2000) that the Fund should be seen as the 'best friend of the poor'. For a published attack on the Fund's competence in poverty reduction policy by a Bank staff member, see the essay by Collier and Gunning (1999).

[3] The actual words are: 'In practice, there are almost no insurance markets in developing countries because of problems of contract enforcement and asymmetric information. People, especially poor people, have to rely largely on self-insurance and informal insurance instead.' (World Bank, 2000, p. 143).

References

Burnside C, Dollar D. 2000. Aid, policies and growth. *American Economic Review*, September 2000.

Collier P, Dollar D. 2000. Aid allocation and poverty reduction. Unpublished paper, World Bank.

Collier P, Gunning JW. 1999. The IMF's role in structural adjustment. *Economic Journal* 109   F634–F652.

Duffield M. 2000. 'The emerging development–security complex'. Talk at University of Sheffield, 29 November.

Gore C. 2000. The rise and fall of the Washington consensus as a paradigm for developing countries. *World Development* 28: 789–804.

International Monetary Fund. 1999. *World Economic Outlook* ch. IV. 'Financial Crises: characteristics and indicators of vulnerability', Washington DC: IMF.

Meltzer A. 2000. *Report of the International Financial Institution AdvisoryCommission* ('Meltzer Report'). US Department of the Treasury: Washington DC.

Mosley P, Harrigan J, Toye J. 1995. *Aid and Power* (2 vols). Routledge: London.

Myrdal G. 1957. *Economic Theory and Underdeveloped Regions* George Allen and Unwin: London.

Ravallion M, Wodon Q. 2000. 'Does child labour displace schooling? Evidence on behavioural responses to an employment subsidy', *Economic Journal* 110: C158–C175.

Stiglitz JE. 1998. *More instruments and broader goals: moving toward the post-Washington consensus.* WIDER Annual Lectures 2. Helsinki: World Institute for Development Economics Research.

Summers L. 1999. Speech at London Business School, *Financial Times* 15 December 1999. (The full text of the speech is reported at www.lbs.ac.uk.)

Williamson J. 1993. Democracy and the Washington Consensus. *World Development* 21: 1329–1336.

Wolf M. 1999. A new mandate for the IMF. *Financial Times*, 15 December.

World Bank. 1990. *World Development Report 1990: Poverty.* World Bank: Washington DC.

World Bank. 1994. *Adjustment in Africa.* Oxford University Press: New York.

World Bank. 2000a. *World Development Report 2000/01: Attacking Poverty.* First draft, 15 January.

World Bank. 2000b. *World Development Report 2000/01: Attacking Poverty.* Publication draft, September.

Chapter 4b.3

The private sector and privatization in social services: is the Washington Consensus 'dead'?

Santosh Mehrotra and Enrique Delamonica

Introduction

In the last two decades of the 20th century there have been reversals from the policies of universal provision of basic services by the state. These reversals have been characterized by efforts in social policies to expand the use of market mechanisms such as insurance, private pensions and user charges. This process has also been accompanied, at least in developing countries, by greater acceptance of the role of the private sector (as well as civil society and community organizations) as elements of a formal system of welfare provision.

This welfare pluralism (i.e. the idea that the state should not be the only, or even the primary, financier and provider of basic social services) was born out of the conservative tide of attacks on the welfare state in industrialized countries and the structural adjustment programmes in developing countries. This welfare pluralism takes the clock back to an earlier historical era when social advances and capabilities enhancement proceeded at a much slower pace than during the decades of state-led welfare provision.

In much of Europe, private providers dominated health, education and water services in the first half of the 19th century. But these services were limited. In the second half of the 19th century public financing and provision became predominant. Indeed, only when governments intervened did these services, especially health insurance and compulsory schooling, become universal in Western Europe and the northern USA – in the last quarter of the 19th and first half of the 20th century. After World War II, and especially after decolonization in Africa and Asia, similar (albeit much more limited) social policies were implemented. Industrialized countries, since 1980, started to experiment with more targeted interventions to reach the unreached, and then public–private partnerships to serve different markets – depending upon the nature of services in different sectors. However, there is no reason to believe that developing countries should embark on a path of extensive privatization in social services, especially as large parts of their populations are still not covered by the most basic education and health services.

The case for universalism in the provision of basic services in developing countries has already been agreed in multiple summits of governments over the last decade and a half. Who will provide these basic services? According to the Washington Consensus the answer is clear: the role of the state should be kept delimited.[1] The question is whether this advice from the Washington Consensus is still relevant. [...] In this article we address this question from the point of view of social policy and more specifically the provision of basic social services. This topic, of course is important in its own right as well as because of the impact of these policies on reaching the Millennium Development Goals (MDGs). The World Development Report 2004 was devoted to this issue. The latter explicitly rejuvenated the Washington Consensus by constraining state involvement in the social sectors through an '8 sizes fit all' model which based on 'scientific and technical analysis' determines which services should be provided by the state (very few) and which ones through market type mechanisms (most of them). Even immunization and public health campaigns are said to be left out of the states' purview.[2]

[...]

Why has private provision increased?

Three factors seem to have driven the private sector's growing role in health and education, and the push to privatize water and hospital services: lack of government resources, low-quality public provision and pressure to liberalize the economy. In other words, compulsions of various kinds have tended to drive the growing role of the private sector in social services in developing countries, rather than any particular merits that flow intrinsically from private provision of social services.

One of the reasons why governments have been unable to provide social services effectively or fund large investments in infrastructure is their budget deficits. They grew so large as the developmental state expanded its role excessively in the economy, especially its productive sectors, that many governments were forced to adopt structural adjustment programmes, based on International Monetary Fund (IMF) and/or World Bank lending.

In some cases, such as domestic water and sanitation (and irrigation and energy) the problem of limited government funds has been compounded by distorted tariff structures. State-owned enterprises often charge tariffs that are too low to recoup costs, and user failures (especially well-connected or ordinary middle-class users) to pay tariffs are often overlooked. This approach is the hallmark of inequity as it subsidizes the non-poor at the expense of the poor, as it is the latter that lack access. [...] Everyone is a loser – as water services decline in quantity and quality in middle-class neighbourhoods, and at the same time fail to reach new poor neighbourhoods.

Second, the lack of resources is linked to a weak record of public provision in many countries. According to Kremer et al. (2004), in India, Bangladesh, Papua New Guinea, Indonesia, Peru, Ecuador, Zambia and Uganda teacher absence ranges from 13% to 26% of teachers. Poorly paid public sector doctors often supplement their incomes by selling drugs intended for free distribution (Van Lerberghe et al., 2002). As a result poor (and non-poor) people are forced to use private providers, because such providers are more accessible and often dispense drugs as part of their consultations [...]. To access water, poor people often have to pay exorbitant prices for it from private tankers run by small vendors. Most residents of South Asian cities receive water through the municipal pipes for only a couple [of] hours at a time, and not every day (Leipziger and Foster, 2003).

The third source of encouragement to private provision and privatization came from the international financial institutions and from donors. The social services are seen as 'frontier areas' in privatization [...].

However, a very important reason for government financing and provision is that it may be difficult to trigger the synergies among health, family planning, water and sanitation, nutrition and education inputs and outcomes without simultaneous investment in each. Interventions in basic social services (health, nutrition, water and sanitation, education) complement each other. Each intervention has ramifications that lie outside its 'sector'. This is different from the existence of an externality, although they are of course present. Unlike the traditional treatment of externalities, which are usually exceptions and consequently can be dealt with (at least theoretically) by (re)specifying property rights, these interactions are pervasive. Moreover, they do not just affect another sector, they all impinge on each other, resulting in a mesh of interactions. In other words, it is a multidimensional synergetic system. Hence the need for the public sector to step in and finance these services.

If the investment is left to the private sector, there is much greater risk of coordination failure and lower efficiency than if the state was to provide the services, instead of merely financing them. This is not to say that private provision (and financing) should not play a complementary role in some non-essential services; we are only making the case here for a lead role for the state.

In this context, it is important to distinguish government financing from government provision. Additional reasons for the latter include:

- Economies of scale, e.g. water supply is in many ways a natural monopoly and provision by more than one agency (public or private) would result in higher unit costs. Thus, a single provider makes more sense. That the single provider should cover total costs may be crucial;[3] that it should earn profits is not so obvious.

- Practical contracting problems are particularly severe. As there is asymmetric information between the government (the financier) and the private party (the provider), the society-wide goals may be difficult to achieve. For instance, if reducing inter-regional inequalities was a goal of government, the state would have to supply these services in rural areas; contracts with private providers would be difficult to establish and even thornier to monitor and enforce.
- Basic social services are human rights, as defined by the Convention on the Rights of the Child and the Covenant on Economic, Social and Cultural Rights. If the private sector is unwilling or unable to provide these services, the rights of citizens imply a corresponding obligation on the part of the state to fill the gap. However, a 'provider of last resort' could be underfunded and suffer from high unit costs or low quality – thus universal provision is more efficient.

[...]

Education

[...]

A multitude of scholars who have examined the rise of schooling in the advanced capitalist countries agree on the predominant role of the state in ensuring universal schooling (Fishlow, 1966; Green, 1990; Sanderson, 1983; Stephens, 1998).

[...]

The source of some of the private supply was philanthropic or ecclesiastical, but it was the state that subsidized education [...]. More important, it was where local government ensured tax-financed public schooling that mass schooling became possible. What is also clear is that there was no crowding out effects of the increase in public education spending on private schooling. In other words, the rise of tax-based public schooling did not displace private schooling.

[...] It is not as though the industrialized countries were unusual in that the state played a predominant role in universalizing primary education. A similar pattern prevailed in high-achiever developing countries as well, where primary education became universal early in their development process when incomes were still low.

This policy of state support in the so-called high achievers was not restricted to basic education but extended to all basic social services; in other words, these states did not rely upon a trickle-down of the benefits of growth or a policy of 'unaimed opulence' (to borrow a term from Dreze and Sen, 1989). These countries, belonging to opposite ends of the political–economic spectrum in terms of macro-economic policies, made early public investments in basic social services when incomes were still low (Mehrotra and Jolly, 1997). In other words, they anchored their education policy on social integration, equality and lower unit costs through state provision [...].

The recent thrust in favour of multiple providers in the area of social provisioning (deriving partly from new institutional economics)[4] has tended to ignore the historical experience of industrialized countries in the 19th century, as well as the more recent experience of the high-achievers among developing countries. It has relied rather on other kinds of arguments to press the case for a greater role for private providers in education.

A first argument for private expansion made since the mid-1980s, relies on the scarcity of public funds. As budget deficits got out of hand in many African and Latin American countries in the 1980s, the IFIs in particular started making the case for private sector expansion in the school system. However, given the fiscal squeeze on government education budgets, the balance between elementary and secondary education in public expenditure allocation will have to respond to prevailing conditions. If primary schooling has not been universalized (e.g. India), then allocating a high share of public spending to secondary education may be inefficient and inequitable. But as primary education gets universalized, the balance of public education spending is bound to – and in fact must – shift in favour of the secondary level. A study by the United Nations Educational, Scientific and Cultural Organization (UNESCO) Institute of Statistics/OECD of 16 developing countries shows that the countries with the highest share of *private* upper secondary enrolment are also those with the lowest overall enrolment rates (India, Indonesia, Zimbabwe). But in China, Malaysia, Jamaica, Thailand – all with relatively high total secondary enrolment rates – more than 90% of direct expenditure on education reaches the public schools.

At the same time, a resource-constrained state cannot subsidize elementary education (i.e. grades 1–8) in the private sector, while the public sector is starved of funds. However, as Mehrotra et al. (2005) point out, that is exactly what is happening in India. In India, the private-aided (i.e. managed privately but receiving significant government funding) schools' share in enrolment tends to rise with the level of education: it is lowest at the primary level, rises sharply at the upper primary level, and is the highest at the secondary/higher secondary level. In fact, more than half of children at secondary/higher secondary level are in private (aided and un-aided) schools. This kind of subsidy to private schools tends to squeeze the funds available for public elementary schools.

A second argument for greater private provision in schooling is based on the better cognitive achievement (as manifested in language and math tests) of children in private schools compared with that of those in public schools, as indicated in several country studies. A number of papers emerged, largely from the World Bank, reporting a significant private school advantage in terms of cognitive achievement. Cox and Jimenez (1991), Jimenez, Lockheed, Luna et al. (1991) and Jimenez, Lockheed and Paqueo (1991) studied Colombia, the Dominican Republic, the Philippines, Tanzania and Thailand, and found that the private school advantage (on math scores) is in the range of 13% in Colombia to 47% in the Dominican Republic. In the same countries, Jimenez and Lockheed (1995) found that per pupil cost is lower in private schools. In any case this argument has been subjected to some methodological criticism and is not conclusive.

Bashir (1997) notes that these studies using single-level models seemed to show that private schools were more effective. These models tell us more about the possible variables that influence cognitive test achievement than the private–public comparison. There is such a variety in the possible variables influencing achievement that different studies come up with (including the ones cited), and yet very few variables that can be called 'school policy' variables have been shown to explain the variation in school outcomes. Colclough (1997) provides similar conclusions.

Thus the case for multiple providers, although it cannot be easily brushed aside, loses much of its force from empirical realities. Besides, the studies cited more often than not relate to the secondary level of education. In any case, the private sector is likely to grow regardless of whether the government subsidizes it or not, as incomes grow. Therefore, at all levels – elementary, secondary and tertiary – there is a need for much better regulation of the private sector.

[...]

[T]here is no question that there is a case for growth of private supply of secondary school and tertiary school places [...]; thus complementarity between the private and public sectors can be encouraged by letting the private sector concentrate on higher secondary and tertiary education, and if public resources are scarce, the public sector could focus on the primary and junior secondary levels. This is the path adopted by one of the early high-achievers, South Korea (Mason et al., 1980). Of course, this does not imply that free, public universities should be avoided. On the contrary, they play a fundamental role in expanding opportunities for poorer and lower middle-income households to see their children improve their chances for obtaining better jobs in dynamic occupations. The balance needs to be struck in a way that public universities can be financed without short-changing elementary education because in that case, the poorest children cannot arrive at the secondary schooling they need to proceed to the university and only the richest families enjoy the colleges and universities.

Health

[...]

As in the education sector, the World Bank has been encouraging welfare pluralism, especially in the delivery of health services. This is despite the historical evidence that the role of the public sector in the latter half of the 19th and early 20th century in Europe in both clinical services as well as areas of public health was predominant, notwithstanding the welfare pluralism. In fact, to date, in northern and southern Europe government finance provides access to health services for the majority of the population. In Switzerland and the USA it is mainly private insurance, and in Germany and the Netherlands social insurance prevails (Normand, 1997).

The experience from the high-achieving developing countries, which managed to improve their health indicators early in their development process relative to other countries in their region, is not dissimilar. They provided universally available health services to all, paid out of government revenues. In many of those countries the relatively well-off opted out by taking private health insurance (e.g. South Korea, Costa Rica), or where private insurance services were not available (e.g. Sri Lanka, Kerala) by making direct payment to private providers. But for the vast majority of the population a universally available and affordable system, financed out of government revenues, functional at the lowest level, made effective by allocating resources at the lower end of the health system pyramid – these were the keys to high health status (Mehrotra, 1997).

Nevertheless, since the mid–1980s many countries that had very limited or entirely banned for-profit practice (e.g. Malawi, Tanzania and Mozambique) have been encouraging private providers by regulatory liberalization and fiscal incentives (not necessarily privatization of public hospitals). Besides, many low- and middle-income countries already have a substantial and thriving private sector – in Latin America, South Asia, South-east Asia, and to a much lesser degree in Sub-Saharan Africa. Correspondingly, a very significant proportion of health expenditure in all regions is private. Not surprisingly, South Asia and Sub-Saharan Africa have among the worst health indicators of any developing region of the world.

More than any other regions, Latin America has experienced in the 1990s an unprecedented transnationalization of its health sector – with what results is worth examining (as we do later). There has been an increase in the export of managed care from the USA, and its adoption in Latin America. Several multinational corporations (e.g. Aetna, CIGNA, AIG and Prudential) have entered insurance and health services, and they intend to assume administrative responsibilities for state institutions and to secure access to medical social security funds. About 270m people in Latin America, 60%

of the population, receive cash benefits and health care services paid for by, and often delivered by the employees of, social security funds. [...]

One reason this transnationalization of the health sector has occurred is because it has been encouraged by the IFIs. World Bank advocacy for the private sector began with its 1987 publication, *Financing Health Services in Developing Countries*, which proposed four steps: (1) increase the amount patients pay for their own health care, (2) develop private health insurance mechanisms, (3) expand the participation of the private sector in health care, and (4) decentralize governmental health care services (World Bank, 1987). However, while a strategy of this kind ensures that government spending is focused on the most cost-effective interventions, it might still fail to ensure that the sector as a whole will operate in the most efficient manner, given the state's inability and often its unwillingness to perform appropriate regulatory functions. Later the Bank advocated public sector financing, and possibly provision, for a package of basic preventive and curative services, while more complex services are left to the private sector (as argued in World Bank, 1993).

The 1993 World Development Report (on health) states:

> In most circumstances ... the primary objective of public policy should be to promote competition among providers – including the public and private sectors ... Competition should increase consumer choice and satisfaction and drive down costs by increasing efficiency. Government supply in a competitive setting may improve quality or control costs, but non-competitive public provision of health services is likely to be inefficient or of low quality. (World Bank, 1993)

Where appropriate sectoral policies are adopted (e.g. as in the high-achiever countries) problems of quality and efficiency in the public provision of basic services [have] not proven insuperable. There are plenty of examples of 'highly efficient public health centres and district hospitals' (World Bank, 1993). Indeed, there is also increasing evidence that efficiency and effectiveness is closely tied to governance issues, and deep democratic decentralization has successfully addressed those problems in many locations. What evidence there is in respect of the claims the neoliberals make on behalf of the private sector in health, we examine briefly here.

The evidence on the standards of efficiency and quality in the private sector relative to the public sector is inconclusive (Bennett, 1997; Mills, 1997). First of all, the evidence is that there is very significant market segmentation between public and private sectors that makes it necessary that case-mix and severity of disease is the same across services before they can be compared. If the public sector is treating rather different types of cases from the private sector, comparisons will be invalidated. Evidence is lacking in developing countries that make these kinds of controls.

Second, there is plenty of evidence of market failure where health services are largely in the private sector. A significant proportion of the hospitals and health facilities are in the hands of the private sector in Asia, Latin America, and increasingly in Africa as well, though preventive measures are largely the responsibility of the public sector (Berman and Rose, 1996). Bennett and Tangcharoensathien (1994) found that in India, South Africa, Thailand and Zimbabwe private sector providers rely on relatively untrained staff with limited supervision from physicians. Studies also point out that over-servicing is a major problem in the private sector. In Brazil there was a high rate of caesarean sections in private maternity patients, explained by the financial pay-off for providers for operating rather than permitting a normal delivery (Barros et al., 1986). Similarly, Uplekar (1989, cited in Bennett, 1997) found that in a slum area of Mumbai drug prescriptions did not match WHO recommended practices, and a larger number of more costly items was prescribed.

Third, there is increasing evidence in many countries where private provision is extensive, both low- and middle-income, of rising costs and accumulation of technology. In 1993 drugs accounted for 52% of China's health spending, compared with 15–40% in most developing countries – contributing to unnecessarily high medical costs. In Korea and Thailand the availability of certain high technology equipment is the same or greater than that in most European countries, even though the level of per capita income is much lower (Nittayaramphong and Tangcharoensathien, 1994; Yang, 1993). Where in Latin America managed care organizations have taken over the administration of public institutions, increased administrative costs have diverted funds from clinical services. To attract patients with private insurance and social security plans, Buenos Aires public hospitals hired management firms that receive a fixed percentage of billings, increasing administrative costs. Administrative and promotional costs account for 19% of Chilean managed care (ISAPRE) annual expenditures (Iriart et al., 2001).

Fourth, it is often claimed that an expanding private sector will reduce pressure on an overextended public sector, thereby freeing up capacity and resources in the system as a whole. The International Finance Corporation (IFC; the arm of the World Bank group promoting private sector investment in developing countries), outlining its future strategic priorities, considered education and health as targets for the promotion of the private sector on precisely these grounds (IFC, 2002a). In fact, the IFC established a separate Health and Education Department in September 2001 (IFC, 2002b). However, as Bennett (1997) argues, there are no longitudinal studies examining changes in total funding levels in response to increased private sector funding. In fact, the IFC itself admits as such: 'By producing extra capacity in the sector as a whole, the public sector will be able to redirect its scarce resources to those most in need ... However, it [this argument] is undermined by a lack of any real evidence.' If anything, private sector growth may lead to a withdrawal of inputs from the public to the private sector. Thus the growth of the private sector in Thailand in the 1980s and 1990s saw a drain of personnel away from an already stretched public sector.

Finally, the effect of privatization of health services and the reliance on out-of-pocket financing is to worsen equity in health care. The most serious effect is that services are refused on account of inability to pay and illness goes untreated. Thus, the concerns about managed care in Latin America are about restricted access for vulnerable groups, and reduced spending for clinical services as opposed to administration and return to investors. In Chile, about 24% of patients covered under the new managed care organizations receive services annually in public clinics and hospitals because they cannot afford co-payments (required under the managed care programme). Public hospitals in Argentina that have not yet converted to managed care principles are facing an influx of patients covered by privatized social security funds. Self-management in Brazil and Argentina's public hospitals requires competition for capitation payments from social security funds and private insurance, as well as co-payments. To apply for free care at public institutions, poor patients now must undergo lengthy means testing, with rejection rates averaging 30–40% in some hospitals (Iriart et al., 2001). Meanwhile, those public hospitals in Argentina that have not yet converted to managed care principles face an influx of patients covered by privatized social security funds; they had earlier faced barriers to access due to co-payments and private practitioners' refusal to see them because of non-payment by the social security fund. Also, Latin American managed care organizations have also attracted healthier patients while sicker patients shift to the public sector – undercutting the very notion of pooling of health risk and undermining any possibility of cross-subsidy from the healthier to the more vulnerable.

The results for health equity of privatization of health services and private sector growth in health care are not dissimilar in the transition economies as in other developing countries. Thus, the impact of the transition to a 'socialist market economy' in China has been that the cost of health care increased rapidly due to health worker salary increases, growth in drug spending, and an increasing use of expensive technology (at least in richer areas). Meanwhile, government spending on health trailed behind the salary increases, and the public health services started deriving an increasing share of their budgets from [the] sale of drugs and user fees (Bloom, 1997). In household surveys in rural China, 35–40% of people who reported that they had an illness did not seek health care for financial reasons (Hao et al., 1997). In the Kyrgyz Republic, more than half the patients referred to hospital were not admitted, as they could not afford hospital costs. In Vietnam, the average cost of hospital admission is the same as two months' wages, resulting in loans and debts. Thus, in rural north Vietnam, 60% of poor households were in debt, with a third citing payment for health care as the main reason (Whitehead et al., 2001).

An increase in private medical practice and a huge growth in private pharmacies in developing countries is a further source of inequity in health. This arises from the irrational use of drugs, which raises costs and leads to drug resistance. In developing countries, drugs now account for 30–50% of total health care expenditure, while in industrialized countries it accounts for only 15% (Velasquez et al., 1998). Those who cannot afford professional services are essentially catered for by pharmacies, which often do not follow prescribing regulations. This is especially the case in South Asia, China and parts of Africa. In India, 52% of out-of-pocket health expenditure and 71% of in-patient expenditure goes to medicines and fees (Iyer and Sen, 2000). Pharmacies have a financial incentive to over-prescribe and sell drugs, which leads to unnecessary drug use, and the development of resistance to drugs. Vietnam has a high frequency of antibiotic resistance resulting from irrational drug consumption; two-thirds of those who reported illness in the previous four weeks had obtained medicines without consulting a medical practitioner (Tornqvist et al., 2000). In a poor region of Mexico, three-quarters of health care visits led to inadequate treatment, particularly from traditional healers or drug retailers. If poor patients have overspent on unnecessary drugs, they may not be able to continue a regimen of drugs (e.g. for malaria or tuberculosis). Then the ingestion of these drugs would become infructuous, and the drug resistance can threaten a whole community. In the developing world there is widespread over-prescription of antibiotics for cases of diarrhoea. In six Latin American countries a quarter of drugs bought from pharmacies required a prescription (as they needed medical follow-up), but were sold without one (Whitehead et al., 2001).

This evidence suggests that there is great need for regulation of the private sector in health services (as in education), for reasons of protecting consumers as well as containing costs. However, in most developing countries the government's health ministry normally has an extremely weak information system about the private sector (or for that matter about the public sector), underlining their inability (or unwillingness perhaps) to regulate the private sector. [...]

Water and sanitation

The water and sanitation sector is quite unique among the sectors discussed in this article. The proportion of the population of the world still lacking safe water and sanitary means of excreta disposal by far exceeds those lacking health or education services. There is little doubt that government provision of the 'merit good' of water, sanitation and public health has not been achieved in low- and middle-income countries. In the 1990s there has been a significant increase in the provision of urban water services in developing countries by the private sector.

This section begins with a review of the growth of private–public partnerships (PPP) internationally, goes on to examine some specific cases of PPP in low- and middle-income countries, and concludes with the possible way forward. The focus of this analysis is, by definition, on ensuring services to the poor and to those without services – rather than with promoting any particular form of ownership or management of the water and sanitation sector. This must take into account the fact that the vast majority of the poor in low-income countries live in rural areas. In middle-income countries, however, the majority of the population lives in urban areas [...].

It is remarkable that of the 715 reported PPPs since 1989 by region in water and sanitation, 60% are located in the most urbanized parts of the world – Western Europe (16%), North America (12%), Central/East Europe/CIS (6%), and most significantly Latin America and the Caribbean (26%) (Franceys, 2001).

[...] [T]he distribution of the remaining 40% of PPPs in the world is as follows: East Asia and the Pacific 16% (39% population urbanized), South Asia 10% (29%), Sub-Saharan Africa 10% (38%), and Middle East and North Africa 4% (62%). This is despite the fact that a much smaller proportion of the population is urbanized. In any case, world-wide, the present population reported served by PPPs in middle- and low-income countries probably represents less than 5% of the total urban population in these countries. In fact, in the 433 cities with a population larger than 750,000, 90 cities (or 20%) are currently served by PPPs (Franceys, 2001); however, there are around 40,000 smaller cities and towns.[5] The main concern, hence, remains the estimated 25% of the citizens of developing country cities that use water vendors purchasing water at significantly higher prices than piped water (Water and Environmental Health at London and Loughborough [WELL], 1999). The result of this growth in PPPs in water and sanitation in the 1990s has been that many governments now accept that the private sector can share a greater responsibility for the water and sanitation sector than before, and the approach is somewhat different from that for other utility monopolies, electricity and gas. Since there also seems to be increasing consensus among international donors (especially the World Bank and the IFC) to promote PPPs in urban and peri-urban areas, it is necessary to look at the experience of PPPs in both industrialized and developing countries.

[...]

Given the growing role of PPPs in the urban areas, what has been the experience with them? PPP contracts in the water and sanitation sector with increasing degrees of private participation, start from cooperatives, moving on to service contracts, management contracts, lease contracts, BOT (Build, Operate, Transfer) contracts and their variations, concession contracts, and finally divestiture implying full private ownership under a regulatory regime.[6] The last has mainly happened in industrialized countries (e.g. England and Wales, though not in Scotland and Northern Ireland) while the rest have been implemented in a variety of low- and middle-income countries. In France, the government owns the fixed assets and one of the three major private companies takes full responsibility to operate the systems, as in a lease contract. In the industrialized countries there is strong evidence that with PPP the prices have increased significantly, e.g. in France prices are higher in communes with PPP than those without, but there is no information as to what extent standards are correspondingly higher (Franceys, 2001). It is the French pattern that is now being promoted around the world, though the process was started in the UK in [the] early 1980s (where private company profits have been high).

Services contracts and management contracts together account for 45% of all PPP contracts by number (in operation until November 2000) in low- and middle-income countries. BOT accounts for another 23%, and concession contracts for 18%. The latter tend to be more complex contracts, while services contracts could be seen as an opportunity for developing country governments to build up expertise in the sector before taking on the more demanding role of managing a concession. Thus the more complex PPPs are mainly found in middle-income countries in regions such as Latin America, East Europe and South-east Asia. Among the low-income countries, only francophone West Africa has an established record in complex PPP – one reason for which may well be that the international companies most globally active are French ones. Initiatives are being pursued actively in Southern and Eastern Africa and also South Asia, with support from donors (Webster and Sansom, 1999).

By and large, so far, the term PPP in the water and sanitation sector really implies involvement with a foreign partner. Seventy percent of the operating PPPs requiring capital expenditure involve international contractors. Two-thirds of those contractors originate from France – the country with the longest domestic history of PPP (over 100 years). Contractors' share of low-and middle-income country market by reported capital expenditure shows that the French Lyonnaise des Eaux (50%) and Vivendi Water (17%) have two-thirds of the market. By number of reported PPPs the same two companies have [a] 55% share in the overall international market; the British companies have a quarter share but they have focused on safer markets in Europe and North America. The fact of foreign involvement indicates that privatization also involves about 1% (by staff numbers) of expensive expatriates (US$250,000 per annum) to deliver a so-called 'world class' water supply. As Franceys (2001) notes, this clearly puts a limit to the size of the city that can be served by a foreign PPP.

Evidence on whether the PPPs that have grown from almost nil at the beginning of the 1990s to over 2350 have been effective is mixed. One of the main claims for privatization was that it delivers the required new capital to the sector; that is the reason why PPPs are being discussed under the heading of mobilizing additional resources for basic services. It is unclear whether any significant new money is coming into the water and sanitation sector, as most PPPs have only a small equity contribution. At the same time, PPP is based on the assumption that in the end the customer pays. PPP has made this fact more obvious though that is not always government intention.

Sources of conflict in PPPs

There remain a number of sources of tension between the public and private partner in PPPs, some of which will become clearer in the specific cases in Latin America (e.g. Bolivia, Chile) and Africa (e.g. South Africa) that are discussed. First, there is usually a sharp difference between what private companies see as the minimal return necessary to sign a contract in a risky country and what governments view as an acceptable level of profit (Cowen and Penelope, 1997).

Second, management contracts can be good at improving services for those who already have water connections, but typically do not help those without connections, who are also less politically influential.

Third, given the few international companies in the business, as we saw above, competition is limited to begin with. The company winning the management contract for a limited period will start with an advantage for later contracts, and in the light of this fact, other bidders may not be attracted. Thus, in either case, competition is likely to be limited or absent during the shift to a more complex contract. In other words, despite all the theoretical arguments marshalled by new institutional economics in favour of competition, privatization need not necessarily result in competition, not even in the bidding process.

Fourth, countries have limited regulatory and administrative capacity to manage such contracts. The political importance of the sector makes bidders nervous about whether governments will maintain a favourable operating environment and tariff yielding a reasonable rate of return. Management contracts in turn require clear performance indicators and a monitoring agency with the skills, budget and autonomy to perform the task. However, many of the normal indicators of water utilities' performance may only partially be controlled by the private management contractor. For example, as Cowen and Penelope (1997) rightly note, water loss reduction in physical terms may depend upon government investing in rehabilitating pipes. Improved revenue collections may depend upon government users paying their own bills and state support for a policy of disconnection for nonpayment. Reduction in operating cost may depend on laying off workers.

Fifth, an initial contract in a PPP is often based on quite incomplete information about many factors, e.g. the condition of underground assets, or future investment requirements. Hence provision must be made in contracts to deal with unforeseen events over the life of a contract. International arbitration is often suggested in countries with little history of judicial or regulatory independence. Yet such arbitration is expensive, and for most disputes and for many smaller contracts it may not be realistic.

Case studies of PPPs

Many of these issues have arisen in two cases that are discussed here. Since 1984 the Bolivian government has been hailed by the IFIs as an 'early adjuster', and like Argentina had carefully followed the neoliberal policy package. However, as in much of Latin America, poverty had not declined. In 1999 the Bolivian government conducted an auction of the water system of the old Andean city of Cochacamba (Finnegan, 2002). The auction drew only one bidder: a consortium called Aguas del Tunari, the controlling partner in which was International Water, a British engineering firm then wholly owned by the Bechtel Corporation of USA. The government, regardless of its weak bargaining position, still proceeded. The terms of the US$2.5bn, 40-year contract reflected the lack of competition for the contract. Aguas would take over the municipal water network and all the smaller systems – industrial, agricultural and residential – in the metropolitan area, and would have exclusive rights to all the water in the district, even in the aquifer. The contract guaranteed the company a minimum 15% annual return on its investment, which would be adjusted annually to the consumer price index in the USA. On cooperative wells Aguas could install meters and begin charging for water. Residents would also be charged for the installation of meters. These expropriations were legal under a new water law that had been rushed through the Bolivian parliament.

The terms of the contract for water privatization were immediately questioned by engineers, environmentalists, a federation of peasant farmers who rely on irrigation, neighbourhood associations and water cooperatives. In January 2000 surprised business owners and middle-class householders joined the protest, as some bills had doubled, and ordinary workers had water bills that amounted to a quarter of their monthly income. The response of Aguas was simply that if people did not pay their water bills their water would be turned off.

The consortium had agreed in its contract to expand the city's water system, which was going to require large-scale repairs of the deteriorating existing system. The company claimed that they had to reflect in the tariff increase all the increases that had never been implemented before. The consortium had also agreed to finish a stalled dam project, Misicuni, which would pipe water through the mountains. Although plans for the dam had been around for decades, World Bank studies had pronounced Misicuni as uneconomic; nevertheless, the dam was included in the contract with Aguas.

The conflict sharpened, protests mounted, the government sent in troops from La Paz. In April 2000 the national government declared a national state of siege or martial law and it allowed mass arrests. The company's executives were told that the police could no longer guarantee their safety and they departed. The Mayor distanced himself from the company. The government informed the company that because the company had abandoned its concession, its contract was revoked. A new national water law was passed, 'written from below' as water-rights campaigners say. The management of Cochacamba's water system was returned to the old public utility (SEMAPA). In late 2001 the consortium filed a complaint against the Bolivian government. The claim is being made under a bilateral investment treaty between Bolivia and the Netherlands (after Bechtel moved its registration to Amsterdam). Bechtel and its partners are demanding at least US$25m in compensation for the broken contract.

One can see here several of the latent sources of conflict we mentioned earlier between the three parties involved: the people, the government and the company. There was hardly any competition during the bidding stage, and the company obtained terms that were part of the problem. Second, tariffs had presumably been low in the years in the run up to privatization, and the company's attempts to raise tariffs suddenly, rather than in a gradual manner, brought on massive protests, worsened by attempts to cut off water to those unable to pay. Third, the local and national government could have acted in a more participatory manner, consulting with the affected people, before taking decisions – but did not, with serious consequences. Fourth, the dispute has finally gone to arbitration abroad, rather than within Bolivia, which could prove rather expensive for the government.

As in Bolivia, water privatizations have caused large-scale protests in many parts of Latin America. Thus, in Panama popular discontent about an attempted privatization cost the President his bid for re-election. Vivendi, the French water transnational, had its 30-year water contract with the Argentine province of Tucuman terminated after two years because of alleged poor performance. There was a 100% increase in water rates after Vivendi was granted a 30-year concession to supply Tucuman province. Major water privatizations in Lima (Peru) and Rio de Janeiro (Brazil) have had to be cancelled because of popular opposition. Trinidad recently allowed a management contract with a British water company to expire. Protests against water privatization have also occurred in Indonesia, Pakistan, India, Poland, Hungary and South Africa (Finnegan, 2002).

It is not that there have not been some successes with the privatization of water services.[7] However, the most exhaustive review of the international literature lists the following likely problems with PPPs: 'corruption in the tendering and drawing up of contracts, particularly in the US; monopoly in the privatized service; higher user charges; inflated director's fees, share options, and management salaries; widespread retrenchments; and anti-union policies' (Hemson, 1997, cited in WELL, 1999).

In fact, the international water companies are themselves recognizing the risks and pulling back. Thames Water had run its Shanghai sewerage plant for four years before China's government ruled in 2002 that the agreed rate of return was illegally high. Thames pulled out in July 2004. Despite this pull out, China is the only country where the international water majors are staying. Veolia added a contract in December 2003 to seven already there.

A major reason for the majors pulling out is that in most contracts the rate of return is guaranteed in foreign currency, but the national currency often undergoes devaluation. In Jakarta, in Manila, in Argentina, in country after country where water services were privatized, there has been devaluation. The companies are happy enough while the national currency is stable, but when, for example, the Argentine peso (long tied to the dollar) collapsed in 2002, troubles started. Suez's debt was mainly in dollars, but its charges to consumers were in pesos, and it was denied permission to raise them accordingly. Unlike the currency of other developing countries where the majors have invested, China's is, if anything, likely to rise – and so in China the water majors are staying for now.

[...]

The private sector: full speed ahead?

[...] [T]here has been international pressure for PPPs and privatization in social services. In fact, recent developments in multilateral bodies – the World Bank, the IFC, World Trade Organization (WTO) – as well as bilateral policies are likely to force the pace of privatization and private sector development in health, education and water, and sanitation now. We discuss in turn the World Bank–IMF's Poverty Reduction Strategy Papers, the World Bank's new Private Sector Development Strategy, [and] the IFC's new strategic priorities [...].

Since 1999 the World Bank and IMF have required all Heavily Indebted Poor Countries (HIPCs) and all countries applying to the Poverty Reduction and Growth Facility (PRGF; or the erstwhile Extended

Structural Adjustment Facility [ESAF]) – or concessional lending facility
– to prepare a Poverty Reduction Strategy Paper (PRSP). PRSPs are also
required to obtain debt relief under the HIPC Initiative. The PRSP is merely
a renamed Policy Framework Paper, and the conditions are the same [...].
In fact, the PRSP Source-book of the Bank advocates 'establishing policies
that encourage competitive and efficient services sectors, such as allowing
entry where possible and encouraging foreign direct investment'.[8] In other
words, as a matter of policy, PRSPs will promote private sector participation
in basic services.

Similarly, the World Bank's Private Sector Development Strategy (2002)
plans to increase support to the private sector and its participation in the
provision of basic services. In addition, it will support a series of regular
surveys of the investment climate in developing countries, which will form
an essential element in the Bank's approval of PRSPs. In fact, the private
sector strategy paper calls for more effective coordination between its private
sector window, the IFC, and its soft loan window, IDA, which only lends to
78 low-income countries. The aim of the coordination is to involve private
sector participation in up to 40% of IDA operations. In other words, through
HIPC debt relief conditionality (via PRSP approval) and through regular
IDA conditionality for non-HIPCs – rather than through any national
ownership of policies – private sector participation is to be encouraged in
low-income countries.

That there is an interlocking set of conditionalities – between IDA, IFC
and the IMF – in respect of private sector participation in basic services is
clear from the above, as well as IFC's own paper setting out new strategic
priorities (IFC, 2002a). The IFC, according to this strategy, will now focus
on frontier areas where there is at present little available capital and frontier
countries that receive limited private capital from abroad. With this in view,
in September 2001, the IFC established a separate Health and Education
Department. The IFC will promote private sector health involvement in
India and Pakistan in South Asia; in the Philippines and China in East
Asia; in Kazakhstan, Poland, Romania and Russia in Central/East Europe
(CEE)/CIS; in Cote d'Ivoire, Kenya, Nigeria, South Africa in Sub-Saharan
Africa; in Egypt and Turkey in the Middle East; and, in Brazil, Colombia
and Mexico in Latin America. This is despite the common knowledge that
IFC investments in the past have responded to existing patterns of demand
from the affluent sections of the population in any country.[9]

Conclusions

In summary, despite the mixed experience with the private sector in school
education, the definitely harmful experience with privatization and with
private sector growth in health services, and the controversial developments

in private–public partnerships in the water and sanitation sectors in low- and middle-income countries, there is relentless pressure from all international agencies – through interlocking conditionalities and other means – to promote the growth of the private sector in basic social services, and where possible privatization of public services. This pressure, which signals that the Washington Consensus is alive and rejuvenated, tends to ignore the historical experience of industrialized countries as well as that of high-achiever developing countries in education, health and water/sanitation.

There are indeed circumstances where the private sector's role in education can be complementary to that of the public sector. Allowing private schools can help in certain circumstances – particularly if governments have trouble, on account of fiscal constraints, meeting the full costs (building schools, paying teacher salaries) required to achieve universal primary schooling. It is imperative, in these cases, to ensure that children from poor families unable to pay school fees are able to attend private schools. Thus in this manner there is scope for promoting complementarity between the public and private sectors. However, the evidence provided above does not support the view that private schools are more efficient or of higher quality.

There has been a deliberate effort to promote privatization in health services. But the evidence on the private sector in health services can be summarized thus. On efficiency/quality, the evidence on standards in the private sector relative to the public sector is inconclusive. At the same time, imperfect information on the part of patients may lead to severe market failures in health care services. On increased resources for health, government commitment to maintaining existing public finance levels is essential if total health resources are to increase with greater private sector entry. Private provision has also tended to raise costs. Finally, while consumer choice increases as a result of private provision, the implications for consumer welfare are ambiguous.

In the water and sanitation sector, while there is no question that public services in water supply, water treatment, waste water treatment and sewerage could not continue in the manner that they have been traditionally run, the evidence does not suggest that wholesale privatization has been very successful at achieving the social and economic objectives. In other words, the experience also suggests that while financial sustainability is important, financial profitability is not necessarily the only or main goal of water and sanitation services.

Where local institutions and the local private sector are weak, public sector provision of water and sanitation services will remain important. In the role of provider, the government is best able to ensure equity, wide coverage, economies of scale, and multisectoral coordination (synergies). At the same time, the role of the community in management will need to be recognized if sustainability of service is to be achieved. Governments can also play a role in strengthening decentralization and facilitating the interface between service providers and service users. In addition, the adoption of appropriate technology is vital for programmes to go to scale in a cost-effective manner. Technology transfer is best accomplished through collaboration between government and the private sector.

It should be noticed that these elements are not included in the simplistic approach of the World Development Report which basically looks at the public provision of basic services as a principal agent problem, and consequently focuses on ease of monitoring and type of contract, eschewing other considerations based on equity and distributional issues, inclusiveness of social policy, and synergies across sectors. [...] [B]oth the actual policy advice of the IFIs as well as its rhetoric show that in the basic social services arena the Washington Consensus still needs to be dethroned.

Notes

[1] Even Social Safety Nets, which are at best charity and at worst clientelistic, are supposed to be 'prevented from expanding' (see for example Cornia, 2001; Olivier et al., 2004; Tendler, 2002).

[2] World Bank (World Development Report, 2004: 16).

[3] This does not imply that users have to pay the full cost, as the revenue could come from general taxation. In that case fairness, ease of management, and political compromise may indicate that basic services should be free to all, including those who could pay. In this case, progressivity should be achieved through taxation.

[4] See the World Bank's (1997) World Development Report (on the role of the state), and the World Bank's (2000–1) World Development Report (on attacking poverty).

[5] Many of these – 2350 of them – have operating PPPs, according to Franceys (2001).

[6] For a detailed analysis of the various types of private participation in the provision of water services, see Lee and Jouravlev (1997).

[7] For evidence, see a series of reports, examining the pros and cons of various privatizations from around the world in the water sector (http://www.icij.org).

[8] A number of PRSPs already announce government plans for promoting private sector involvement in public service provision in Honduras, Mozambique, Nicaragua and Uganda. The PRSP in Burkina Faso is committed to eliminating monopolies

in public utilities, and Nicaragua and Kenya have agreed to increase private sector involvement in water delivery (Marcus and Wilkinson, 2002; Save the Children, 2002).

[9] For example, in Malawi, IFC has an 18% share in a 64-bed hospital, Blantyre, which has been a failure in both financial and health care terms. Thus, as Save the Children (2002) states: '...the private hospital has been unable to achieve even a 20 per cent utilisation rate' (p. 30).

References

Barros, F.C., Vaughan, J.P. and Victora, C. (1986) 'Why so many Caesarean Sections?: The Need for Further Policy Change in Brazil', *Health, Policy and Planning* 1(1): 19–29.

Bashir, S. (1997) 'The Cost Effectiveness of Public and Private Schools: Knowledge Gaps, New Research Methodologies, and an Application in India', in C. Colclough (ed.) *Marketizing Education and Health Developing Countries*. Oxford: Clarendon Press.

Bennett, S. (1997) 'Private Health Care and Public Policy Objectives', in C. Colclough (ed.) *Marketizing Education and Health Developing Countries*. Oxford: Clarendon Press.

Bennett, S. and Tangcharoensathien, V. (1994) 'A Shrinking State: Politics, Economics and Private Health Care in Thailand', *Public Administration and Development* 14(1): 1–17.

Berman, P. and Rose, L. (1996) 'The Role of Private Providers in Maternal and Child Health and Family Planning Services in Developing Countries', *Health Policy and Planning* 11(2): 142–55.

Bloom, G. (1997) 'Financing Rural Health Services: Lessons from China', in C. Colclough (ed.) *Marketizing Education and Health Developing Countries*. Oxford: Clarendon Press.

Colclough, C. (1997) *Marketizing Education and Health in Developing Countries: Miracle or Mirage?* Oxford: Clarendon Press.

Cornia, G.A. (2001) 'Social Funds in Stabilization and Adjustment: A Critique', *Development and Change* 32(1): 1–32.

Cowen, B. and Penelope, J. (1997) 'Getting the Private Sector Involved in Water: What to Do in the Poorest of Countries', Viewpoint Note No. 102, World Bank – Finance Private Sector and Infrastructure Network, http://www.worldbank.org/ html/fpd/notes/102/102summary.html

Cox, D. and Jimenez, E. (1991) 'The Relative Effectiveness of Private and Public Schools: Evidence from Two Developing Countries', *Journal of Development Economics* 34(1): 99–121.

Dreze, J. and Sen, A. (eds) (1989) *Hunger and Public Action*. Oxford: Clarendon Press.

Finnegan, W. (2002) 'Leasing the Rain: The World is Running out of Fresh Water, and the Fight to Control it has Begun', letter from Bolivia, The Conde Nast Publications, Inc., *The New Yorker* (8 April).

Fishlow, A. (1966) 'Levels of Nineteenth Century American Investment in Education', *Journal of Economic History* 26(4): 418–36.

Franceys, R. (2001) 'Patterns of Public Private Partnerships', paper presented at the Regional Conference on The Reform of the Water Supply and Sanitation Sector in Africa: Enhancing Public–Private Partnership in the Context of the Africa Vision for Water (2025), Kampala, Uganda, 26–8 February.

Green, A. (1990) *Education and State Formation, the Rise of Education Systems in England, France and in the USA*. New York: St Martins Press.

Hao, Y., Suhua, C. and Lucas, H. (1997) 'Equity in the Utilization of Medical Services: A Survey in Poor Rural China', *IDS BULLETIN*: 28(1).

International Finance Corporation (IFC) (2002a) *IFC Strategic Directions*. Washington, DC: IFC.

International Finance Corporation (IFC) (2002b) *Investing in Private Health Care: Strategic Directions for IFC*. Washington, DC: IFC.

Iriart, C., Elias, E.M. and Waitzkin, H. (2001) 'Managed Care in Latin America: The New Common Sense in Health Policy Reform', *Social Science & Medicine* 52(8): 1243.

Iyer, A. and Sen, G. (2000) 'Health Sector Changes and Health Equity in the 1990s in India', in S. Roghuram (ed.) *Health and Equity: Technical Report Series 1.8*. Bangalore, India: HIVOS.

Jimenez, E. and Lockheed, M. (1995) 'Public and Private Secondary Education in Developing Countries: A Comparative Study', World Bank Discussion Paper No. 309. Washington, DC: World Bank.

Jimenez, E., Lockheed, M., Luna, E. and Paqueo, V. (1991a) 'School Effects and Costs for Private and Public Schools in the Dominican Republic', *International Journal of Educational Research* 15 (special issue): 393–410.

Jimenez, E., Lockheed, E., and Paqueo, V. (1991b) 'The Relative Efficiency of Private and Public Schools in Developing Countries', *World Bank Research Observer* 6: 205–18.

Kremer, M., Muralidharan, K., Chaudhury, N., Hammer, J. and Rogers, H. (2004) 'Teacher Absence in India', Working Draft, World Bank, Washington, DC, accessed 1 September 2004, http://www.worldbank.org

Lee, T.R. and Jouravlev, A. (1997) 'Private participation in the provision of water services', (LC/L. 1024), Medio Ambiente y Desarrollo#2. Santiago de Chile: ECLAC.

Leipziger, D. and Foster, V. (2003) 'Is Privatisation Good for the Poor', International Finance Corporation, Washington, DC, http://www.ifc.org/publications

Marcus, R. and Wilkinson, J. (2002) *Whose Poverty Matters? Vulnerability, Social Protection and PRSPs*. London: Childhood Poverty Research and Policy Centre.

Mason, E., Kim M.J., Perkins, D., Kim, K.S., and Cole, D. (1980) *The Economic and Social Modernization of the Republic of Korea*. Cambridge, MA: Harvard University Press.

Mehrotra, S. (1997) 'Health and Education Policies in High-Achieving Countries: Some Lessons', in S. Mehrotra and R. Jolly (eds) *Development with a Human Face. Experiences in Social Achievement and Economic Growth* (pp. 63–110). Oxford: Clarendon Press.

Mehrotra, S. and Jolly, R. (eds) (1997) *Development with a Human Face: Experiences in Social Achievement and Economic Growth*. Oxford: Clarendon Press.

Mehrotra, S., Panchamukhi, P.R., Srivastava, R. and Srivastava, R. (2005) *Financing Elementary Education in India: Uncaging the Tiger Economy*. New Delhi: Oxford University Press.

Mills, A. (1997) 'Improving the Efficiency of Public Sector Health Services in Developing Countries: Bureaucratic versus Market Approaches', in C. Colclough (ed.) *Marketizing Education and Health in Developing Countries*. Oxford: Clarendon Press.

Nittayaramphong, S. and Tangcharoensathien, V. (1994) 'Thailand: Private Health Care Out of Control?', *Health Policy and Planning* 9(1): 31–40.

Normand, C. (1997) 'Health Insurance: A Solution to the Financing Gap?', in C. Colclough (ed.) *Marketizing Education and Health in Developing Countries*.

Olivier, M., Fourie, E. and Nyenti, M. (2004) 'Law as a Tool in Addressing Poverty: Social Protection Perspectives, with Particular Reference to Sub-Saharan Africa', Background Document, Workshop on Law and Poverty IV, CROP and Center for International and Comparative Labour and Social Security Law. Johannesburg, South Africa.

Sanderson, M. (1983) *Education, Economic Change and Society in England, 1780–1870*. London: Macmillan.

Save the Children (2002) *Globalisation and Children's Rights: What Role for the Private Sector?* London: Save the Children.

Stephens, W.B. (1998) *Education in Britain, 1750–1914*. New York: St Martin's Press.

Tendler, J. (2002) 'Why Social Policy is Condemned to a Residual Category of Safety Nets and What to Do about It', mimeo. Geneva: UNRISD.

Tornqvist, N., Wenngren, B., Nguyen, T.K.C. et al. (2000) 'Antibiotic Resistance in Vietnam: An Epidemiological Indicator of Inefficent and Inequitable Use of Health Resources', in P. M. Hung, I.H. Minas, Y. Liu, G. Dalgren and W.C. Hsiao (eds) *Efficient Equity-Oriented Strategies for Health: International Perspectives – Focus on Vietnam*. Centre for International Mental Health, University of Melbourne.

Van Lerberghe, W., Coneceicao, C., Van Damme, W. and Ferrinho, P. (2002) 'When Staff is Underpaid: Dealing with Individual Coping Strategies of Health Personnel', *Bulletin of the World Health Organization* 80(7): 581–4.

Velasquez, G., Madrid, Y. and Quick, J. (1998) 'Health Reform and Drug Financing: Selected Topic – Health Economics and Drugs', DAP Series No. 6, WHO/DAP/ 98.3. Geneva: World Health Organization.

Water and Environmental Health at London and Loughborough (WELL) (1999) 'Study, "Public–Private Partnership and the Poor: An Initial Review'", Task No. 164 (M. Webster and K. Samsom, eds), March, Loughborough University, UK, http://www.lboro.ac.uk/well/

Webster, M. and Sansom, K. (1999) 'Public–Private Partnership and the Poor: An Initial Review', WELL Study, Loughborough University, UK, URL (consulted 10 December 2004): http://www.lboro. ac.uk/well/

Whitehead, M., Dahlgren, G. and Evans, T. (2001) 'Equity and Health Sector Reforms: Can Low-Income Countries Escape the Medical Poverty Trap?', *The Lancet* 358(9284): 833–6.

World Bank (1987) *Financing Health Services in Developing Countries: An Agenda for Reform*. A World Bank Policy Study: Washington, DC.

World Bank (1993) *World Development Report: Investing in Health*. Oxford: Oxford University Press.

World Bank (1997) *World Development Report*. Oxford: Oxford University Press.

World Bank (2001) *World Development Report: Attacking Poverty*. Oxford: Oxford University Press.

World Bank (2002) *Private Sector Development Strategy*. Washington, DC.

World Development Report (2004) *Making Services Work for Poor People*. Washington DC: World Bank and Oxford University Press.

Yang, B.M. (1993) 'Medical Technology and Inequity in Health Care: The Case of Korea', *Health Policy and Planning* 8(4): 385–93.

Chapter 4b.4

From 'safety nets' back to 'universal social provision': is the global tide turning?

Bob Deacon

[...]

Preamble

Ideas articulated by epistemic communities within and around international organizations about what constitutes desirable national and international social policy are every bit as important in influencing national and international social policy as the perceived constraints of a deregulated global economy. Globalization and social policies appropriate to it at the national and international level are not so much determined economically but shaped politically. States make globalization every bit as much as globalization makes states (Yeates, 2001). Boas and McNeill (2004) have recently discussed the relationship between institutional power and the power of ideas in social development and argue that 'powerful states (notably the USA), powerful organizations (such as the IMF) and even, perhaps, powerful disciplines (economics) exercise their power by "framing" [the terms of the policy debate] which serves to limit the power of potentially radical ideas to achieve change' (Boas and McNeill, 2004: 1). Within a matrix of state and global institutional power ideas have a part to play in both sustaining those relations of power and in challenging them even if radical or socially progressive ideas have had a hard time of it in the last decades.

In terms of theoretical reference points for this short article we need then to include the work of Haas (1992) on epistemic communities. Focusing on national states he concluded that 'epistemic communities [networks of knowledge based experts] play a part in . . . helping states identify their interests, forming the issues for debate, proposing specific policies, identifying points for negotiation' (Haas, 1992). The same can be said about international epistemic communities, their associated think tanks and invisible colleges and the shaping of an international social policy agenda (Stone, 2004). That is not to say that trans-national social classes and the associated international class struggle that is identified within this framework by Sklair (2001) and others play no part in policy formation. If national welfare state formation was in part the outcome of class and gender and ethnic struggle (Williams, 1987, 1995) and the resultant formation of cross–class (and gender and ethnic) alliances so will be any trans–national social policy. Epistemic communities operate within this power contest matrix. The case study in this article illustrates the contest of ideas within the epistemic communities of economic and social policy scholars operating at a global level. [...] This article leads to the conclusion that the story told by Boas and McNeill needs to be revised. Their argument that the USA through the agency of multilateral financial institutions (MFIs) and with the language of economics shapes the international social policy debate needs to be revised and written in a more nuanced way to reflect the contending influence of other states using other agencies and other discourses.

The fall and rise of the concept of universalism in global discourse about national social policy

Both Peter Townsend (2004) and Judith Tendler (2004) have drawn attention recently to the domination of the concept of safety nets within global social policy discourse concerning desirable national social policies at the end of the last century. Townsend charts the post-Second World War rise of the Keynesian influence on social development policy and its subsequent demise and replacement by an era of the residualization of social policy. He goes on to argue the case for a reconsideration of a universal approach to social welfare development and for reforms in the global governance architecture that might bring this about. Judith Tendler asks why social policy has been condemned to a residual category of safety nets and suggests this had to do among other reasons with the projectization of international aid and the large role played by non-governmental organizations (NGOs) in this activity. She suggests how the tide might be turned. These observations reinforce earlier concerns of my colleagues and I (Deacon et al., 1997) when we researched the impact of international organizations on the making of post-communist social policy. Indeed only recently I restated the case that globalization represented a threat to equitable social welfare provision in the context of development (Deacon, 2003). In this section I want to comment briefly upon why the idea of social policy geared to securing greater equity through processes of redistribution and in particular universal social provision got so lost in the context of the global discourse about desirable social policy. I will then examine and demonstrate its reassertion within global discourse.

Four reasons might be offered for the decline of the idea. Globalization as we have suggested in terms of the form it took in the 1980s and 1990s was primarily a neoliberal political project born at the height of the transatlantic

Thatcher–Reagan alliance. This flavoured the anti–public provision discourse about social policy within countries and contributed to a challenge to the idea of the EU's social policy agenda. The collapse of the communist project coinciding as it did with the height of neoliberalism gave a further push to the rise of the myth of the marketplace. Most importantly the perceived negative social consequences of globalization generated a new concern for the poor. In the name of meeting the needs of the poorest of the poor the 'premature' or 'partial' welfare states of Latin America, South Asia and Africa (that the International Labour Organisation [ILO] had been so influential in building) were challenged as serving only the interests of a small privileged workforce and elite state employees. A new alliance was to be struck between the Bank and the poor (see Deacon et al., 1997; Graham, 1994). The analysis of the privileged and exclusionary nature of these provisions made by the Bank was accurate. However by destroying the public state services for this middle class in the name of the poor the politics of solidarity which requires the middle class to have a self-interest in public provision which they fund was made more difficult. The beneficiary index measures of the Bank showing how tertiary education spending and urban hospital provision benefited the elite contributed in no small measure to this development. *The Bank's technical experts who were very able to measure who received public services were ill-informed about the political economy of welfare state building which requires cross-class alliances in defence of public expenditure.* Once again American exceptionalism (in this case in terms of its residual welfare state) was sold as the desirable norm. Finally in the late 1980s and 1990s the self-confidence of defenders of the social democratic and other equitable approaches to social policy was temporarily lost. The critics of neoliberal globalization came to believe their worst-case prognosis.

Are there signs of a shift in the global discourse leading to a reassertion of the politics of social solidarity and universalism? I am not here concerned with the debate within developed welfare states. Here the evidence is clear that universalistic welfare states have been largely sustained despite globalization (e.g. Castles, 2004; Swank, 2002). There are a number of developments reflected in recent reports and publications from international organizations that suggest that the case is again being put for finding ways of implementing universal public provisioning as part of an equitable social policy in developing countries. Among them are:

1 The United Nations Research Institute for Social Development (UNRISD) research programme on Social Policy in a Development Context under the leadership of Thandika Mkandawire has the stated objective to 'move [thinking] away from social policy as a safety net . . . towards a conception of active social policy as a powerful instrument for development working in tandem with economic policy'. Research within

this programme that draws attention to the early origins of universalistic Nordic welfare states should refute the argument that universalism is not incompatible with a lower level of economic development (Mkandawire, 2004).

2   The rethinking presently being undertaken within the ILO concerning the sustainability of its traditional labourist approach to social protection. In particular is to be noted the ILO Socio-Economic Security Programme is researching new forms of universalistic social protection such as categorical (by age) cash benefits or universal school attendance allowances or even basic income entitlements to complement the very limited coverage in the Global South of work based social security schemes. Good practices being revealed within this programme could inform developing country social policy making (ILO, 2004).

3   The report of the UN Secretary-General (E/CN.5/2001/2) on 'Enhancing Social Protection and Reducing Vulnerability in a Globalizing World' prepared for the February 2001 Commission for Social Development almost became an important milestone in articulating a progressive UN social policy. Among the positive features of the report were (a) the fact that it was the first comprehensive UN statement on social protection, (b) the thrust of its argument was that social protection measures serve both an equity-enhancing and an investment function and such measures need to be a high priority of governments and regions, (c) it argued that social protection 'should not [serve only] as a residual function of assuring the welfare of the poorest but as a foundation ... for promoting social justice and social cohesion'. It has to be said however that discussion on even this paper became bogged down at the Commission and was never approved. It remains a non-paper. While the EU were supportive the G7 wished to link it to issues of global financing and global governance arrangements (Langmore, 2001). The north–south impasse on global social standards stemming from the labour standards and global social policy principles stand-offs bedevilled the Commission's work.

4. The more recent meeting of the Commission on Social Development (47th Session on 4–13 February 2004) seems to have managed to avoid this pitfall in terms of its discussion of the issue of Improving Public Sector Effectiveness. However, the Report of the Secretary General on this topic (E/CN.5/2004/5) did contain among its recommendations the sentiment that international cooperation should 'include the elaboration of norms and guidelines ... on the respective roles and responsibilities of the public and private sector' (para. 59a) but such an idea did not find expression in the (advanced unedited version) of the agreed conclusions now published on the United Nations Department of Economic and Social Affairs (UNDESA) web-pages. These agreed conclusions rather stress 'that each government has primary responsibility for its own

economic and social development, and the role of national policies and development strategies cannot be overemphasised' (para. 7). On the more central question of the issue of universalism versus targeting and the balance of public and private provision the agreed conclusions are very much in favour of universalism and equity. 'The Commission emphasise the crucial role of the public sector in, inter alia, the provision of equitable, adequate and accessible social services for all so as to meet the needs of the entire population' (para. 1) and again in the context of assessing the choice between public and private provision the Commission notes that while services can be provided by private entities it also 'reaffirms that any reform of public service delivery should aim at promoting and attaining the goals of universal and equitable access to those services by all' (para. 12). A review of this report is to be found in Scholvinck (2004).

5. Perhaps it is within attempts to steer developing countries towards the meeting of the Millennium Development Goals that are after all focused on *basic* education and *basic* health and *basic* sanitation and water services that we should look to see if these would lead to targeted residualism rather than universalism. Certainly the United Nations Development Programme (UNDP) Human Development report (UNDP, 2003) which focuses on these goals balances in an interesting way its focus on basic services for the poor with a concern for equity. In general terms it firstly reasserts some of the lessons of high human development achieving countries. In high achievers such as Botswana, Kerala in India and Cuba 'Public finance was adequate and equitable. In high-achieving countries political commitment is reflected not just in allocations of public spending to health and education but also in their equity' (UNDP, 2003: 87). Recognizing the concern of the Bank and others that none-the-less public spending on health and education can be 'captured' by the better off it strikes a balance between the need to maintain public expenditure for all social groups while also giving priority to the poor. In education it asserts the need to increase expenditure on primary education (to benefit the poor) but at the same time argues 'Still, additional resources are needed for higher education as well if countries are to build capacity to compete in the global economy – but not at the cost of primary education. Entire education budgets need to increase' (UNDP, 2003: 94). Within health policy the balancing of the concern with equity with a pro poor focus is handled by arguing for rationing and regulatory measures that ensure some health service workers are directed to work for the benefit of the poor. Thus for example countries could 'use service contracts to require medical personnel to spend a certain number of years in public service' (UNDP, 2003: 101). The report notes that in some regions for example Latin America there has been a massive push to private health provision because of pressures to liberalize combined with low public sector health

budgets. Here it is concerned that 'Because managed care organizations attract healthier patients, sicker patients are being shifted to the public sector. This two-tier system undercuts the pooling of risks and undermines cross-subsidies between healthier and more vulnerable groups' (UNDP, 2003: 113). It will be important to track this issue of reaching the poor while maintaining equity through the work of the Millennium Project through which the UN hopes to meet the Development Goals.

6. While attempts to restore the case for an equitable approach to social policy may not be unsurprising coming from UN agencies a more important indicator as to whether the global ideological tide is shifting would be what the World Bank is saying. A Nordic evaluation of the 2000/2001 World Bank Development Report on Poverty concluded that (Braathen, 2000) although the Bank at least at the discursive level had shifted from its 1990 focus of social paternalism to a 2000 focus on social liberalism and even social corporatism within which the poor are to be given a voice, it still did not embrace in any significant way the social radicalism approach which would involve redistributive policies except perhaps in the sphere of land reform. The latest World Bank's (2004) World Development Report that is focused on making services work for poor people suggests that there might be some movement. There is a tension within the text and probably among the authors between those who stay with the line that much public spending by developing countries benefits the rich and is therefore to be refocused on the poor (e.g. World Bank, 2003: 4, Figure 2) and those who would appear now to have accepted and argue the point that 'cross class alliances' between the poor and non-poor are needed to pressure governments to 'strengthen public sector foundations for service delivery' (World Bank, 2003: 180, Figure 10.1). Most striking is the assertion that 'In most instances making services work for poor people means making services work for everybody – while ensuring poor people have access to those services. Required is a coalition that includes poor people and significant elements of the non-poor. There is unlikely to be progress without substantial "middle class buy-in" to proposed reforms' (World Bank, 2003: 60). This section of the report goes on to quote the words of Wilbur Cohen, US Secretary of Health, Education and Welfare under President Lyndon Johnson in the 1960s: 'Programmes for Poor People are Poor Programmes'. Remarkable! The report itself is extraordinarily complicated in its recommendations and prescriptions and concludes with a rejection of the one size fits all approach which the Bank used to be accused of when it tried to sell Chile to the world. Instead it adopts an eight sizes fits all model. Which model is to be applied depends on the capacity of government, its openness to influence by the poor, the degree of homogeneity of the country, etc. At

least two of the models involve a strong emphasis on government being the major provider at either national or local level.

Progress in this direction in the Bank's World Development Report may in part be due to the fact that a lead author was a Finnish economist. Finland together with other Nordic countries has been undertaking a considerable amount of quiet influence by the placement of experts within the World Bank and some Regional Development Banks while also funding alternative UN research. Indeed at a seminar to evaluate interim progress with the large Nordic Trust Fund for Environmentally and Socially Sustainable Development (TFESSD) Desmond McNeill, Head of the Fund's Reference Group asserted that the fund had encouraged new ideas within the Bank and was influencing policy inside the Bank on social development and social protection. Whether this was impacting upon countries was another matter (McNeill, 2004).

It has to be said however that other World Bank reports have given prime emphasis to service privatization. In 2000 it published a report on its Private Sector Development Strategy where social services were highlighted as a focus for private development. Moreover the International Finance Corporation (IFC) Strategy Paper for 2002 highlights health and education as frontier areas for privatization (Mehrotra, 2004).

My conclusion is that the intellectual tide is turning against the neoliberal social policy prescriptions arguing everywhere at a *national* level for targeted benefits only for the poor. The restoration of the case for good quality public services universally available with additional measures to ensure they are accessed by the poor is once again being made.

Conclusions

This case study suggests that what is to be observed is not so much a global hegemony whereby the USA via the IMF and the language of economics shapes alone the terms of the debate about social policy. What we have instead is a war of positions within which intellectuals in and around the international organizations are engaged in a contest of paradigms and ideologies sometimes informed by empirical research. How influential particular organizations become at a particular time in history is probably a reflection of international power relations, the differential financing of the contending international organizations and intellectual and organizational effort on the part of key policy entrepreneurs associated with them.

From my normative standpoint there is room for some cautious optimism. Perhaps the US Treasury does not have total grip anymore? Perhaps the next edition of Boas and McNeill's book will conclude that powerful states (notably the USA) contend with other powerful states (notably Europe, and, given the fact the tectonic plates of the global economy are shifting even China, Brazil and India), powerful organizations (such as the World Bank) contend with other powerful organizations (such as the ILO) and powerful disciplines (notably economics) contend with other disciplines (notably social and political science) to wage a war of positions as to how the terms of debate about globalization and global and national social policy should be framed. To the extent that this is the case the role of intellectuals and their ideas struggling in and against the international organizations will have been important but not decisive. The shift in influence of contending ideas will reflect a shift in the balance of power both between countries and within and across borders whereby global social movements from below will have had an impact upon national governments and international actors and the relative power of contending international ideas.

References

Boas, M. and McNeill, D. (eds) (2004) *Global Institutions and Development: Framing the World*. London: Routledge.

Braathen, E. (2000) Commentary on World Development Report 2000–2001, accessed 1 December 2002, http://www.crop.org

Castles, F. (2004) *The Future of the Welfare State: Crisis Myths and Crisis Realities*. Oxford: Oxford University Press.

Deacon, B. (2003) 'The Prospects for Equitable Access to Social Provision in a Globalizing World', in Krizsan, A. and Zentai, V. (eds) *Reshaping Globalization: Multilateral Dialogues and New Policy Initiatives* (pp. 75–93). Budapest: Central European University Press.

Deacon, B. with Hulse, M. and Stubbs, P. (1997) *Global Social Policy: International Organizations and the Future of Welfare*. London: Sage.

Graham, C. (1994) *Safety Nets, Politics and the Poor*. Washington, DC: Brooking Institute.

Haas, P. (1992) 'Epistemic Communities and International Policy Co-ordination', *International Organizations* 46.

International Labour Organisation (2004) *Economic Security for a Better World*. Geneva: Socio-Economic Security Programme, ILO.

Langmore, J. (2001) 'The UN Commission for Social Development, February 2001: An Opportunity for International Political Evolution', *Global Social Policy* 1(3): 277–80.

McNeill, D. (2004) 'A Review of the Operations of the Fund: Aims and Achievements', paper presented at the TFESSD Annual Seminar, Helsinki, Finland, 10 June.

Mehrotra, S. (2004) 'The MDGs: Targeting Basic Services for the Poor or Ensuring Universal Access?', *Social Development Review* 8(2): 12–13.

Mkandawire, T. (ed.) (2004) *Social Policy in a Development Context*. Basingstoke: Palgrave.

Scholvinck, J. (2004) 'Improving Public Service Effectiveness: The Commission on Social Developments's Conclusions', *Social Development Review* 8(2): 22–5.

Sklair, L. (2001) *The Trans-National Capitalist Class.* Oxford: Blackwell.

Stone, D. (2004) 'Transfer Agents and Global Networks in the "Transnationalization" of Policy', *Journal of European Public Policy* 11(3): 545–66.

Swank, D. (2002) *Global Capital, Political Institutions and Policy Change in Developed Welfare States.* Cambridge: Cambridge University Press.

Tendler, J. (2004) 'Why Social Policy is Condemned to a Residual Category of Safety Nets and What to Do About It', in T. Mkandawire (ed.) *Social Policy in a Development Context* (pp. 119–42). Basingstoke: Palgrave.

Townsend, P. (2004) 'From Universalism to Safety Nets: The Rise and Fall of Keynesian Influence on Social Development', in T. Mkandawire (ed.) *Social Policy in a Development Context* (pp. 37–62). Basingstoke: Palgrave.

UNDP (United Nations Development Programme) (2003) *Human Development Report*, Geneva: UNDP.

Williams, F. (1987) *Social Policy: A Critical Introduction.* London: Sage.

Williams, F. (1995) 'Race/Ethnicity, Gender and Class in Welfare States: A Framework for Comparative Analysis', *Social Politics: International Studies in Gender, State, and Society* 2(2): 127.

World Bank (2003) *World Development Report 2004. Making Services Work for Poor People.* Washington, DC: World Bank.

Yeates, N. (2001) *Globalization and Social Policy.* London: Sage.

Section 5

Global social policy futures

Global social policy is at a crossroads. The Washington Consensus (WC) experiment has evidently failed to produce economic growth, economic security and social equity, and criticisms of the WC have widened to call into question not only the efficacy but the legitimacy of those institutions through which that policy doctrine has been promulgated. Various demands and proposals for reform have been advanced from across the political spectrum, from policy scholars, makers and activists, with the vibrancy of debates about what should succeed the WC reflecting the depth of the failings of the doctrine itself. Even before the latest crisis of globalisation, originating in the US financial sector and spreading around the world, the progressive unravelling of the WC and its collapse has been regarded by many as inevitable and necessary. But what should succeed that global policy regime? What are the desirable values and priorities of global social justice policies? This takes us boldly into the realm of successors to the current system of global governance itself; that is, questions about what should succeed market fundamentalism are inextricably linked to questions about alternatives to the global institutional and political order that gave rise to that fundamentalism.

The section opens with readings that propose institutional contours of a new global social policy founded on modern democratic values and principles. The first of these, by Patomäki and Teivainen, argues for the globalisation of democracy as a necessary precursor to, and an integral element of, a more socially just world. They set out a range of concrete proposals, ranging from the reform of existing institutions (e.g. strengthening ECOSOC to effectively coordinate global economic and social policy) to the establishment of new global institutions (e.g. UN People's Assembly and ultimately the creation of an elected World Parliament). They identify global power imbalances that play out in global policy-making (even in ostensibly more democratic, consensual-based systems such as the WTO), and US power in particular within the UN and Bretton Woods institutions, as key obstacles to the democratisation of global institutions. Interestingly, they accord especial significance to the World Social Forum (WSF) in global politics and policy-making. The WSF is 'the first serious attempt to create a shared platform for the bulk of global civil society' and is prefigurative of future forms of political organisation, a new way of doing politics, a process rather than an institution. That is, it aims to show by example alternative forms of global democratic organisation and practice and to advance the democratisation agenda everywhere. Although the WSF constitution (reading 2) prohibits any person or group to speak on behalf of the WSF, Patomäki and Teivainen suggest, controversially, that the WSF could develop ways of empowering some to speak from within the internal bodies of the WSF on matters of 'strategic importance'. Potentially, such matters could include global social policy, and such an arrangement might be one avenue for a more radical politics of global social policy to emerge.

If Patomäki and Teivainen's concerns lie squarely with the globalisation of democracy, those of David Held lie more specifically with the globalisation of *social democracy*. In the two readings by him in this section, he argues that global social democracy is *the* effective and credible alternative to neo-liberal globalisation and expounds on the values of cosmopolitanism underpinning global social democracy. In the first of these two extracts, he advocates a number of concrete measures: a Global Covenant that brings linked human security and human rights agendas into a coherent framework of law; a reformed UN system which has a coherent institutional locus of coordinated socio-economic security policies; a new global agency (World Environment Organisation) whose job it would be to ensure that international trade and finance are compatible with the sustainable use of resources; and independent funding streams in the form of new financial facilities and tax revenues. In the second of the two readings, he identifies eight cosmopolitan principles on which the new global order premised on social justice should be based.

Both Patomäki and Teivainen and Held point to the importance of financing in achieving a socially just global order. The former, for example, focus on debt, which has been a significant problem for developing countries in particular, and they argue for debt arbitration mechanisms to renegotiate 'developing' country debt and reduce debt dependency. They, together with Held, also argue in favour of instituting a global levy to raise additional revenue, and reduce state dependency on Bretton Woods institutions and the UN system on donor governments for financial resources. The fifth reading, by Bob Deacon, sets out in more detail how the funds generated by such a levy might be spent and how decisions about that expenditure might be determined. Importantly, he draws on actually existing examples of what are to date modest experiments in this area, such as the ILO's Global Social Trust Network in the realm of social protection, to demonstrate efforts that are already under way and which can provide a basis on which to progress this work in the future.

The question of how to address the problem of unregulated international economic competition that has been a key driving force in the 'race to the bottom' and the dismantlement of social protection in recent years is addressed by Ramesh Mishra. He argues that in order for social welfare considerations to regain their meaning and place in development a concept of social welfare that is based on *social standards* is needed. Social standards, rather than social rights, would afford the possibility of creating a 'social escalator': as economic standards rise so would social standards, with governments making upward adjustments to social investment accordingly. Noting the failure of the global campaign to insert a social clause into international trade agreements of the World Trade Organization, he advocates a strategy to develop a consensus around such 'escalators' such that social regulation becomes part of the 'game' of international competition – a socially-regulated globalisation. This would be underpinned by an international agreement. There are already nascent examples of such an agreement at world-regional level, in the form of the European Social Charter. Globalising this, he raises the possibility of a Multilateral Agreement on Social Standards (MASS) that agrees on basic minimum standards. Although he does not elaborate on it in detail (e.g. whether it would be voluntary or enforceable), such an agreement would, he argues, 'preserve the integrity of local and national communities', providing stability and continuity in a context of rapid global economic competition and technological change.

If, as Mishra suggests, in an age of globalisation social welfare needs to be linked to economic standards, so too global social governance reforms need to connect with global economic governance reforms. Despite the differences between the proposals advanced by these contributors, each of them is concerned with how to enhance the governance of economic globalisation by instituting a universally shared set of political rules based on agreed principles. Thus, for global social democrats, reformism is the best way of instituting globalisation with a 'human face' and developing a properly regulated globalisation in which economic globalisation proceeds but is subject to a commonly agreed set of social standards or minima that all governments sign up to and follow. But questions as to *what kind of* and *how much* global governance reform are contested. Proposals such as these have come in for criticism from some scholar-activists in 'developing' and 'developed' countries alike, who have argued that a more radical societal vision and a complete overhaul of global governance institutions is needed.

The seventh reading in this section, by Walden Bello, is illustrative of such an approach. His concerns similarly lie with the failings of global institutions but he argues that global governance reform must start from another place, and with a different objective: deglobalising the economy. Instead of the 'adjustment agendas' of global social democrats that take as a given economic globalisation and seek simply to regulate it better and institute alleviative social measures, he proposes a deconstruction agenda that aims to dismantle and abolish the current institutions along with their (Northern-dominated) global trade, aid and development agendas. A parallel reconstruction agenda oriented towards deglobalising the economy, reconstructing local economies in which production is geared towards meeting social needs and establishing an 'alternative system of global governance' supportive of these economic and social systems should be the priority, he argues. Such an economy would have no room for export-oriented production, or 'aid' policies that ensure funds return to donor countries, or transnational corporations however well they are socially regulated. The political values underpinning such alternative global governance arrangements are respect for economic diversity, policy autonomy and social equity. Thus, national programmes of social redistribution of income and wealth oriented towards equality and poverty reduction would feature alongside devolution and subsidiarity in the economic policy sphere.

An advocate of a radical Southern global social policy agenda, Bello essentially outlines a devolved system of global economic and social governance, in which policy autonomy is restored to nations. In this system, there is still a role for transnational policy coordination: the role of international organisations would be 'to express and protect local and national cultures by embodying and sheltering their distinctive practices' (John Gray, 2002, cited in Bello), while regional groups of nations would play a much greater role. The general proposition that there should be an enhanced role for world-regional groupings in global social governance is explored further in the eighth reading, by Nicola Yeates and Bob Deacon. They explore how political actors, both governmental and non-governmental, are increasingly looking to these transnational regional groupings as a way of strengthening global social regulation, redistribution and provision. They also examine the social policies these formations are instituting, and discuss what financial, political and other measures might be usefully deployed to build on these for the purpose of developing a comprehensive global social policy.

Global social policy is an area of vibrant and dynamic political practice and in recent years a number of Global Commissions have been set up to examine the failings of existing governance systems and policies as well as to identify and recommend reform options. We therefore include synopses of the recommendations of three such Commissions, one on the social dimensions of globalisation, a second on health and a third on international migration. These summarise the Commissions' overarching sets of principles, recommendations and plans of action for a global order based on social justice. Together they give a useful flavour of the kinds of debates in those global fora as to the kinds of global institutional and policy reforms deemed necessary to bring about a more coherent and effective global social policy.

Collectively, the readings in this final section illustrate diverse perspectives and recommended courses of action for future global social policy development; above all they demonstrate the dynamic nature of debate in this area. In keeping with the subject, the style and tone is overtly prescriptive and normative, with contributors setting out competing social, indeed societal, policy visions. While these different proposals emanate from different analyses as to what is wrong with the present system and what should succeed it, at the heart of these there is common agreement that a global vision of social justice, an effective system of global governance and coherent national and transnational (global) social policies to realise and maintain it are the most desirable and viable options for the future.

Chapter 5.1

A possible world: democratic transformation of global institutions

Heikki Patomäki and Teivo Teivainen

Conservative vs transformative proposals

The difference between conservative and transformative proposals is in principle simple. Are we stuck in the current framework of imaginative preconceptions and institutional arrangements? Or is it politically possible and feasible to change also parts of the background context of global political action? The case for a transformative approach is based on the idea that by changing relevant parts of the background context, at least some of the established identities and interests will be redefined. Institutional innovations may overcome the politics of compromise between narrow and short-sighted group interests. New alliances of partially redefined actors would facilitate new ties of solidarity and the opening up of new world political possibilities.

In order to develop a strategy for a global democratic change, we will first summarize the existing proposals and their relations to the contemporary institutional and world historical context, including social relations in the systems of finance and trade. Obviously, the line between conservative and transformative proposals is not categorical. If the relevant contexts are specified in sufficient detail, most global democracy initiatives, if implemented, would imply some transformations. Moreover, the difference, say, between a UN reform and the establishment of a world parliament may be small. Rather than categorical differences, we are talking about shades and degrees. Also by combining proposals into a systematic strategy, their transformative potential may increase and be reinforced by other simultaneous or subsequent reforms.

The key notion [...] is that a strategy of global democratic change requires a systematic analysis of the preconceptions and possible democratic improvements of different proposals. Tables 5.1.1 to 5.1.4 summarize the main points [of the strategy]. Who are supposed to have a franchise in different proposals and models? What is the scope of the proposed institutional arrangements? What would be the degree of authenticity of democratic will-formation? How are the proposed changes justified? Is there relevant political support, actual or potential, for that kind of change? Is it politically possible to make the proposal real? Is the suggested institutional arrangement feasible? And last but not least, what are the transformative implications of different proposals?

Tables 5.1.1 and 5.1.2 review the main proposals concerning reforms of existing international organizations. Table 5.1.1 sums up the four main areas of UN reform: the Security Council (UNSC); the General Assembly (UNGA); the People's Assembly (UNPA); and the Economic and Social Council (ECOSOC). Table 5.1.2 explicates the possible reforms of the Bretton Woods institutions, the WTO and the international courts. Tables 5.1.3 and 5.1.4 bring up proposed new institutional arrangements. Table 5.1.3 summarizes initiatives to empower global civil society through the World Social Forum as well as proposals to establish a global truth commission, world parliament or global referenda. Finally, Table 5.1.4 tackles schemes of debt arbitration mechanisms and global taxes, particularly the currency transaction tax and the global greenhouse tax.

All reviews or amendments of the UN Charter depend on the will of the permanent members of the Security Council (SC). They have a veto right also on any changes of the UN Charter. Therefore, abolition or gradual phasing away of their veto power could release the possibility of other UN reforms. Proposals to democratize the SC are justified in terms of immanent critique (democracy is the accepted principle of most member–states and in accordance with the spirit of the Charter); epistemological considerations (impartiality requires that the positions of the permanent members can also be criticized); and instrumentalist reasons (democratic reforms are necessary for an efficient and legitimate UN to tackle the salient problems of our times). None of the reform proposals would change the scope of the SC, but some would submit aspects of the SC's work under the scrutiny of the General Assembly.

The aim of most of the SC reforms would be to establish the principle of formal equality of sovereign states. Most of the explicit support for these reform proposals have thus far come from a few Third World states – although many of them appear obedient or silent – and, in particular, global civil society. The problem is that a real SC reform would seem to be possible only if all veto-powers gave up their privileges. The main problem is the dominance of the US. Also Russia and China may be unlikely to relinquish their veto right in the foreseeable future. It could be time- and energy-consuming to convince the governments of the UK and France that their seats are a mere relic from the past.

The General Assembly has been marginalized. In principle, within the confines of the existing Charter, it would be possible to strengthen the position of the GA by activating Article 13, which gives it powers to initiate processes concerning any matter related to peace, security or welfare.

Table 5.1.1: United Nations reforms

	Franchise	Scope	Authenticity	Justification	Political support	Politically possible/feasible	Conservative or transformative
UNSC (abolition of veto and supervision by GA)	States (FE)	Issues of peace and security; binding decisions and sanctions possible	Reforms would reduce the extent to which agenda and discussions are determined by great power politics	Immanent critique plus epistemological and instrumental justification	Mostly Southern states and global civil society	No, unless all veto-powers would give up their privileges	Could release the possibility of other UN reforms
UNGA (enhancing the role of GA and/or a change in principles of representation)	States (FE); there is a distant possibility of voting weights in terms of population	Recommendations, checks and initiatives, potentially as defined by Articles 12–14	Reforms would make the UN system more open to the full and effective participation of all states	As UNSC	As UNSC	No, unless changes in US policy or world context (and Charter revisions next to impossible)	If Charter revisions not possible, transformative effects will be fairly limited
UNPA (People's Assembly)	World citizenry	World opinion-making; perhaps framework-setting rules	Possibly only symbolic control; possibly steps towards WP	As UNSC but more straightforwardly in universalist terms	Global civil society	As UNGA plus non-democratic states would resist (re feasibility; see also WP)	If a step towards WP, transformative implications; otherwise no
ECOSOC (giving it the Charter-powers and proper infrastructure	States (FE) and civic actors	Central coordination of global economic and social institutions	Opinion-making and making the UN organs and BWIs more accountable	Instrumental	Some Northern and Southern states and civil society	Difficult, opposed by the US, BWIs and other neo-liberal forces	Potentially some transformative implications

Notes: FE = formal equality; WP = World Parliament; BWIs = Bretton Woods institutions

Table 5.1.2: IMF, World Bank, WTO and international courts

	Franchise	Scope	Authenticity	Justification	Political support	Politically possible/feasible	Conservative or transformative
IMF (revising decision-making and reducing or revising powers and scope)	States, principle of one dollar/one vote; reforms would allow more effective participation of all states and a few civic actors	Monetary adjustments, but in practice control of economic policies of 60–80 states and influence over many others	Reforms would increase the chance of non-orthodox interpretations; more authentic political will-formation	Epistemological and instrumental; right to self-determination	Many Southern states and global civil society; potentially many other states	Not likely, unless the US and allies unexpectedly change their policies; proposals should include a monetary system	Many proposals are conservative, but revising scope and powers could enhance transformative possibilities
World Bank (like the IMF)	As the IMF	Developmental projects and policies, in practice also like the IMF	As the IMF; reforms could make also non-economistic views possible	As the IMF	As the IMF	As the IMF	As the IMF
WTO (revising practices and procedures and introducing exit options and pluralism)	States, from FE towards pluralism and fair participation; participation of civic actors	Now anything can be defined as 'free trade'-related; scope to be drastically reduced	Reforms would create more space for different opinions and democratic will-formation	As the IMF	As the IMF	Because of one country/one vote principle, more open to changes than the BWIs	Procedural reforms relatively conservative, but reducing scope transformative
International courts (enhancing the role of the ICJ and ICC)	No democratic franchise per se, but rights to states and individuals	Legal interpretation and enforcement of global rules and principles	More impartial forum for legal discussions and decisions; would increase authenticity	Epistemological and principles of fairness and justice	Most Northern and Southern states and most parts of civil society	The US would like to retain the right to interpret and apply international law by itself	Mostly conservative; but facilitates democratic activities and practices

Notes: FE = formal equality; WP = world parliament; BWIs = Bretton Woods institutions

Table 5.1.3: The World Parliament, referenda, truth commission and civil society

	Franchise	Scope	Authenticity	Justification	Political support	Politically possible/feasible	Conservative or transformative
Transnational civil society organizations	Local, national and transnational and civic actors	Open space for any discussion or initiative, defined in terms of civic/social	Authenticity real but fragile; no voice in any process of global governance	Ethico-political plus instrumental (facilitates connections and other initiatives)	Wide support; civil society and some states North and South; locally contested	Yes, easy to back further developments	Potential indirect transformative implications
Global truth Commission	Unclear	Depends on specification, from human rights to justice and world history	Depends on the organization of franchise and access to global public domain	Instrumental? ('The 'truth' is expected to lead to reconciliation or compensations)	Parts of civil society, potentially many states	Yes, possible to realize; but if irrelevant because only symbolic, may not be feasible	If leaves existing institutional arrangements intact – conservative
World Parliament (WP)	World citizens	World opinion-making on any matter; or framework-setting rules; or limited or full legislative powers	Possibly only symbolic control; possibly real powers, but rarely well-specified	Moral universalism and equality of human beings and applying these globally (also domestic analogy)	Parts of civil society	If linked to the UN, may presuppose UNGA reform, and UNPA; however, no conditions for a world federation	Depending on the powers given to WP, potentially transformative; but if not feasible becomes not transformative
World referenda	As WP	Anything can, in principle, be subjected to a referendum	Probably advisory powers only, authenticity would depend on background conditions	As WP plus epistemological (ambiguous, if no authentic will-formation)	Parts of civil society plus some international organizations; potentially many states	As advisory 'opinion polls' possible to start now, may be extended	Depending on scope and authenticity, possibly transformative

Notes   WP = World Parliament

Table 5.1.4: Debt arbitration and global taxes

	Franchise	Scope	Authenticity	Justification	Political support	Politically possible/feasible	Conservative or transformative
Debt arbitration	States given the same rights as public agencies in domestic law	Procedures of insolvency and bankruptcy, implying far-reaching debt reductions and rearrangements	By building new impartial rules and mechanisms, there would be an increase in authenticity (now creditors can dictate the terms)	Standards of 'civilization', impartiality and justice (domestic analogy); also emancipation from debt dependency	Large-scale transnational movements; some states, also from the North; possibly but ambiguously also Washington	Yes, possible to realize by a grouping of states; IMF/US-based attempts also possible, but unlikely to democratize	Reasonably transformative and perhaps, by reducing debt-dependency, could contribute to transformations
Currency transactions tax (CTT)	National governments and parliaments, in proportion to their population; and civic actors given decision-making rights	Taxation and also regulation of a part of global financial markets (forex)	Authenticity implied by the creation of a new pluralist public domain, with control over substantial funds and regulation	Political, epistemological and instrumental	Main aim of global civil society plus support from an increasing number of states and international organizations	Yes, possible to realize, at first in a global but non-universal manner by a grouping of states	Reasonably transformative and could co-contribute to other transformations
Carbon dioxide tax	Semi-equal states, in consultation with civil society (unless new proposals are put forward)	Controlling climatic change (possibly also finance for development)	Organization of collective action against a serious global problem, but democratic control uncertain	Instrumental (tackling the root cause of the problem of greenhouse effect; finance for development)	As the CTT (the EU has advocated a tax instead of an emission trading system)	As the CTT plus the terms of Kyoto Agreement would have to be renegotiated	Conservative in itself, but if global funds used for democratization, potentially transformative

Notes   WP = World Parliament; BW = Bretton Woods

According to the Article the Security Council, however, is not obligated to obey the GA's decisions. The legal potential for the General Assembly to take a more active role will in any case remain unused until it has better resources and the majority of member-states have more self-confidence to challenge the dual hegemony of the US and neoliberalism. The world historical context has to change first.

Any changes that require amending the UN Charter appear highly unlikely. The most immediately 'realistic' reform is to incorporate non-state actors into the work of the GA. This means democratization only on the condition that authentic NGOs and trade unions and/or democratic parliaments are playing the main role. Including business-initiated non-governmental actors would only strengthen the one dollar/one vote principle. In any case, the transformative effects of a General Assembly reform appear fairly limited, especially if civil society actors would not take part in defining the agenda or real decision-making.

Under these circumstances, the proposals to establish a UN People's Assembly are bold. In most proposals, the People's Assembly would reflect the demographic realities of different countries; in some cases the non-governmental organizations would have a key role. In the most straightforward initiatives, however, the representatives of the UNPA would be chosen in direct global elections, as democratic parliaments are elected within countries. Franchise would thus be directly based on world citizenship. Usually the tasks and powers of UNPA are assumed to be limited, but possibly expanding. At first, it would be an opinion-making body, perhaps taking steps towards a world parliament proper. The UNPA is justified in universalist terms and supported mostly by some civic actors and movements only.

Establishing a UN People's Assembly appears more difficult to make true than any of the major GA reforms, also because non-democratic countries may not find the idea of an UNPA acceptable (particularly in its more ambitious and universalist forms). Its establishment would also require an amendment of the UN Charter. If the purpose was to establish a world parliament in the longer run, it might have more profound – but contingent and possibly ambiguous – transformative implications. Otherwise, the transformative effects would seem to be fairly limited.

Originally, ECOSOC was supposed to be the core of the UN governance of the world's social and economic affairs. It has, however, remained in the margins of the UN system. Most reform proposals concern making good the promises of the UN Charter. If ECOSOC assumed its role as the main coordinator of social and economic institutions, it could actually help to make the BWIs more accountable, for instance. The justifications for reforms are usually rather instrumental, the ECOSOC being a body that could help to establish certain social, economic and possibly democratic aims elsewhere.

There is some support for this idea among the states and in the global civil society, but even as a topic of reform it has remained relatively marginal. The US, the Bretton Woods institutions and other neoliberal forces would also oppose reforms. Although they cannot block changes in the same way as in the case of many other UN reforms, any change would seem to have an external impetus. In a more favourable world historical context, and in the connection of other global democratic reforms, however, ECOSOC reforms might well have some transformative implications.

The prospects for democratic UN reforms do not look good. On the contrary, since the mid-1980s at the latest, the UN system has been domesticated by the US. Its institutions have been downsized, neoliberalized and demoralized. Most of the UN reforms of the recent past – or under consideration – have little to do with democracy, the only minor exception being attempts to incorporate NGOs in the working of various UN bodies.

The democratic aspects of the UN, which were from the beginning a compromise between the great power interests and the principle of interstate equality, have been under attack and partially corroded. The key to many of the recent de-democratizing transformations has been money. The US in particular has used open financial blackmail to get its will through. Moreover, although the prosperity and rapid growth of the bureaucracies of the Bretton Woods institutions indicates that there is a double morality at play, the ethico-political justification for impoverishing the UN system has been based on the representation of the UN as an excessively big money-waster. In fact, the UN is smaller than the World Bank, and none of the two employs more people than, say, a middle-sized Northern European town. The essence of the neoliberal reforms has been to make the UN system more accountable to the main financial contributors, i.e. to accord more with the one dollar/one vote principle.

This, however, suggests that a new basis for the funding of the UN system might open up a way forward. A two-thirds majority of the General Assembly could decide to establish a ceiling of e.g. 10 per cent on any country's contribution to the UN budget. This is difficult to establish because of the resistance of the US, although in principle it is not as difficult as a UN Charter revision would be. The most promising path, however, is that of establishing new sources of funding, such as a UN lottery or credit card or, more ambitiously, global taxes. Some of this money could be fed into the UN system to empower the General Assembly, the ECOSOC and a number of UN organs and to relieve financial conditionality. This would also be likely to change the political situation within the UN system now paralysed by fear of reactions from Washington.

Table 5.1.2 explicates the possibilities of democratic reforms of the Bretton Woods institutions [BWIs] and the WTO. The BWIs are indeed twins in most regards. They have different tasks and bureaucracies, yet they tend to look the same. Although in principle the BWIs deal only with relatively modest volumes of lending for the purpose of monetary adjustments or development, together the BWIs control, to varying degrees, the economic and other policies of perhaps the majority of states in the East and the South. This control is based on debt-dependence and legitimized in terms of the doctrine of 'economic neutrality'.

The BWIs are perhaps the most utterly undemocratic part of global governance. Reform proposals can be reduced to two main categories. On the one hand, there are proposals that aim at restructuring the BWIs in order to make them function in a more fair, equitable and democratic way and, perhaps, to open up a pluralist discussion about their operational principles. On the other hand, there are proposals that try to reduce or redefine their scope and powers. But precisely because of their undemocratic structure, it is very difficult to reform the BWIs from the inside or outside. The one dollar/one vote principle, the *de facto* veto right of the US and other groupings, and the nature of their staff tend to make democratic reforms practically impossible. Only mere symbolic reforms, reminiscent of Orwellian manipulation of language, appear politically possible.

The Third World demands in the 1970s for a New International Economic Order were quickly defeated. Despite continuous revolts and worldwide mass campaigns against the BWIs since the early 1980s, and despite the systematic lobbying in Washington and elsewhere, the only minor change that has taken place is in the area of environmental policies, and to a lesser extent in gender issues, of the World Bank. In other words, the BWIs may be open towards some pressures coming from the White House or the US Congress, but otherwise they are closed systems. Democratization of these organizations is thus unlikely. The best way forward would be to overcome states' dependency on them.

The World Trade Organization is a more interesting case. On the one hand, its new scope and powers are nearly all-encompassing. The successive expansion of the area of 'free trade' has constituted a movement from the classical international trade of material goods to far-reaching liberalization and deregulation and, subsequently, neoliberal restructuration of the economy. The WTO thus limits, almost constitutionally, the scope and authenticity of existing democratic systems. At the same time, the 'consensual' agenda-setting and decision-making within the WTO does not mean that the WTO processes would be democratic in any meaningful sense of the term.

What could be done to make the WTO member-states more equal and the system as a whole more transparent, equitable and democratic? Reform proposals concern transparency, the preparatory process, negoti-ations and decision-making procedures and the dispute settlement system. It is telling that at least some of these are being supported also by many of the major industrial countries. Because the states are formally more equal within the WTO than in the Bretton Woods institutions, it is easier to build pressure for democratization. Of course, although a number of OECD countries and the EU have been in favour of a reform of WTO practices and procedures, the main point may have been to enhance the legitimacy of the trade liberalization process. Hence they may not be in favour of returning to a GATT-type arrangement with the poorest countries; or of opt-out mechanisms; or of limiting and redefining the scope of the WTO. Nevertheless, since the WTO procedures also make majority voting possible, in principle a sufficiently large number of states could turn the tide in the WTO. The WTO is not such a closed system as the Bretton Woods institutions are.

The International Court of Justice and the International Criminal Court do not grant democratic franchise to vote or participate. Rather, these organizations aim at establishing a set of background rights to the states (ICJ) or individuals (ICC) and make these rights more impartially enforceable. The ICJ is already in place, the ICC began to function in 2002. The reform proposals deal with enhancing the powers of these institutions or encouraging all states to join the system of ICC. The former, in the case of the ICJ, is unlikely because of the required revision of the UN Charter. As far as the latter is concerned, the US in particular will not only stay outside the jurisdiction of the ICC but intends actively – even militarily – to prevent any legal cases against any US citizens. The analysis of political possibilities notwithstanding, attempts to build systems of legal enforcement may even contribute to de-democratization. It depends on the context. Enhancing law and order does not necessarily mean democratization.

Table 5.1.3 summarizes our conclusions regarding the world parliament, referenda, truth commissions and the civil society. The World Social Forum is the first serious attempt to create a shared platform for the bulk of global civil society. The WSF is built on an urge to develop initiatives and take active part in global agenda-setting. For one thing, it is an open space for any discussion or initiative defined in terms of 'civil' or 'social'. It empowers local, national and transnational civic actors to create new projects and alliances, possibly new identities as well. Thus far the WSF has not attempted to speak with a single voice. The WSF is thus generally not recognized as an actor by states or multilateral institutions, although it may be evolving into a transnational political organization. The will-formation within the WSF may have been relatively authentic, particularly as far as spontaneity is concerned, but it remains quite unorganized and *ad hoc*, and thus fragile.

There are two main justifications for the WSF. As a platform, it is an end in itself, creating a public space for democratic politics. There is also an instrumental justification. The WSF facilitates networking and building of alliances and thus empowers parts of the global civil society to act in a more organized and systematic way for transformative aims. It enjoys wide and intensive support, even if its idea and aims are locally and globally contested. Also many states, North and South, as well as multilateral organizations have expressed a lot of interest in it. Further development of the WSF is politically possible and may have far-reaching transformative implications. Its feasibility depends, at least in the short- to medium-term, on whether it will be able to build the necessary infrastructure also outside Brazil and Porto Alegre; and whether it will be able to address and resolve satisfactorily the problems of creating a democratic global organization.

A global truth commission is an initiative that has emerged from the global civil society. It is difficult to assess this initiative because it is in fact a cluster of (thus far) rather unspecified proposals. It is not clear what the issues would be; or who would be allowed to take part in discussions; and what the moral, political or legal consequences of these discussions are supposed to be. The main justification is perhaps instrumental, i.e. the 'truth' that will emerge in the discussions is expected to lead to reconciliation, sanctions or compensations (the aims of the main proponents may be contradictory, which is of course a good starting point for real debates).

This initiative has found support from civil society, but also many states could support a particular specification of the idea. It would seem possible to realize a global truth commission, or truth-commission-like institutions, in one form or another. The problem is that if it is seen as an irrelevant club for selective discussions, it may not be a feasible institutional innovation. Likewise, if the idea is to establish 'the truth' in order to establish a claim for massive North–South compensations, the initiative may be neither politically possible nor feasible (or even particularly democratic). So although this initiative should be politically possible if adequately specified, it may also turn out to be an ambiguous innovation. It might also be relatively conservative, assuming it would leave existing institutional arrangements intact.

The proposals for a world parliament or global referenda may – and often do – come down to a straightforward attempt to re-establish the institutions of liberal-democratic states on a worldwide scale. In their more ambitious forms, WP and global referenda would give universal suffrage to every adult human being. Thus they would in part presuppose but in part also create a world citizenry. These ideas are justified in terms of moral universalism and equality of human beings, as well as in terms of analogies to the development of national states and federations (domestic analogy). At the moment, basically, only some parts of global civil society support a WP.

There are also less ambitious WP proposals. In principle, there are two possibilities. The idea may be to start with a symbolic WP and extend its scope and powers gradually. The intended final outcome would be a legislative body, something akin to parliaments of sovereign states. However, it is also possible to try to redefine the role and nature of parliament. A world parliament could, for instance, be a 'framework-setting' institution, with carefully circumscribed powers. Unfortunately, these ideas are not usually specified in sufficient detail. A closer look tends to reveal a domestic analogy buried underneath the surface of the proposal.

Depending on the powers given to it, a WP could be a potentially transformative institution. The problem is that it may not be feasible. The social conditions for a world federation do not seem to exist (even a global pluralist security community is still unrealized). Besides, a world federation may not be desirable if it for instance implies homogenization and exclusions. Now, if this kind of WP is not feasible, an attempt to establish it will not mean global democratization. The solution might be to turn to, or to start with, less ambitious proposals. However, if the idea of a WP is linked to the UN, it may require an UNGA reform and imply the establishment of an UNPA. This is not likely to be possible any time soon. Then, the more symbolic the WP is made, the less it would have any kind of transformative effects, and the more likely it would be to lack widespread popular support – or even passive legitimacy. So whatever the variation, the proposal appears ambiguous.

It seems to us that one reasonable way forward could be to organize a test referendum on different WP proposals. Only a statistically representative sample of world citizens would have to vote at this stage. This would make the idea more concrete; suggest the potential of the proposal in terms of popular support, which is probably very unevenly distributed; and, perhaps, give time and an opportunity to develop more innovative approaches to the idea of world parliament.

Finally, Table 5.1.4 displays our conclusions regarding the potential of a debt arbitration mechanism and global taxes. A debt arbitration mechanism is not a system of democratic will-formation in itself. The point is rather to establish minimal rule of law in international financial relations. Widely accepted – and domestically self-evident – standards of impartiality, justice and 'civilization' would seem to necessitate this kind of reform. The establishment of a debt arbitration mechanism could, however, also have far-reaching democratizing effects. The supremacy of Bretton Woods institutions over the economic (and other) policies of a large number of states stems from debtdependency. A debt arbitration mechanism is a set of rules and procedures for solving insolvency. In some of the most feasible proposals, states would be given the same rights as public agencies – such as municipalities – in domestic law, nothing more, nothing less. Under contemporary global circumstances, however, this would lead to massive debt reductions and rearrangements.

The best part of the story about a debt arbitration mechanism is that it is possible to establish. It has widespread support from large-scale global movements and from many states, particularly from the South, but also from the North. Since debt arbitration would not mean total debt cancellation, the G7 countries might find it acceptable – under intensive pressure – to establish such a mechanism. They also know that other mechanisms, such as credit rating, would tend to enforce the same kinds of neoliberal principles of economic governance anyway. Indeed, in the absence of alternatives, even the Bretton Woods institutions and the US seem, at times, to have been taking proposals for a debt arbitration mechanism quite seriously.

Although only a partial reform, the establishment of a debt arbitration mechanism would seem to be reasonably transformative of the global context and perhaps, by reducing debt-dependency, could co-contribute to many other transformations. However, the US, with some major creditor countries, and the BWIs are likely to be interested in retaining control over the economic policies of the majority of Southern and many Eastern states. This would be prohibited by the well-established rules and practices of debt arbitration. Therefore it may be that the most realistic way forward is to proceed without the consent of the US and some other main creditors.

Global taxes have emerged as a pivotal issue. The currency transactions tax and the greenhouse gas taxes both would tackle salient global problems. Both would yield huge revenues that could be allocated to global funds. Subject to democratic decision-making, these global funds could for instance help to empower the UN system; to contribute to a further solution to the debt crisis; and to create alternative sources of financing for development. In other words, the establishment of global funds of this kind could also serve the purpose of overcoming the power of the BWIs.

Of these two possibilities for global taxes, the currency transaction tax seems more promising as a global democracy initiative. The representatives of the movement supporting it are already questioning orthodox economic theory and arguing for global democratization. The concerns of this movement and the logic of the CTT make it a more plausible candidate to play a key role in a strategy for global democratization. This is of course contingent on the way the CTT will be organized. The tax base has to be defined comprehensively; the system has to be global and open to all states to join; the bulk of the revenues originating in the OECD-based transactions have to be allocated to a global fund; and the CTTO (Currency Tranctions Tax Organisation) has to be organized democratically. On these conditions, the CTT would be very likely to have important transformative effects by controlling some aspects of the power of global finance and by creating new options for the states and other actors to develop their own models within the global political economy. The CTTO could also facilitate creating new interests and alliances for further democratic reforms.

Outline of a strategy for global democratic change

It is virtually impossible to democratize the UN system or, in particular, the Bretton Woods institutions. The international courts are best seen as elements in the wider background context. Although important from the point of view of establishing the rule of law globally, the democratizing effects of creating or strengthening international courts are dependent on other reforms. The WTO seems to be the existing multilateral arrangement that is most susceptible to democratic change. The one country/one vote principle on which it is in theory based makes changes possible, however difficult they may appear at the moment.

The WTO is central to the global project of locking-in orthodox economic policies. The scope and powers of the WTO have been rapidly expanding. In principle, almost anything can now be related to trade and can thus be covered by the process of WTO law-making. Ultimately, trade is absolutely and perfectly 'free' only in an idealized and globalized model of neoclassical free market capitalism. In practice, the WTO is also biased towards serving the particular commercial interests of the powerful. Democratic reforms of the WTO should thus focus, primarily, on reducing and redefining its scope and, secondly, on democratizing its preparatory process, decisionmaking procedures and dispute settlement mechanisms. For the poorest countries, a mere GATT-type trade regime would be quite enough. For the other member-states, there should be opt-out mechanisms and room for different economic and developmental policies. Regulation of trade in services should be clearly disconnected from the project of liberalization and privatization of services. TRIPs (trade-related aspects of intellectual property rights) should be revised to be more conducive to diffusion of technologies and free communication and also moved out of the WTO, possibly back to the UN. TRIMs (trade-related investment measures) should be replaced with a new investment regime holding foreign direct investors and transnational corporations accountable to democratically elected and accountable global authorities.

Of the possible new institutional arrangements, a global truth commission and world parliament are interesting but ambiguous possibilities. Both need time to evolve into mature initiatives, and the social conditions for a global parliament in the currently prevalent senses do not exist. The latter claim could, however, be partially tested by means of a global proto-referendum.

The establishment of a debt arbitration mechanism and global taxes – and the currency transaction tax in particular – emerge as the most prominent possibilities. Since many crucial mechanisms of power in the global political economy are based on financial dependency, both the creation of a debt arbitration mechanism and the CTT would make a major difference. They would relieve the dominance of global finance over states, and thereby enhance the rule of law and democratic politics. Simultaneously, they would create new and more useful sources for financing development and other priorities.

A key obstacle to most global reforms is the strong opposition and hard hegemonic will of the US. Depending on the context, a number of other countries also tend to have reasons to oppose democratic reforms. In the case of the CTT, for instance, a number of off-shore financial centres and tax havens are disposed to block reforms. The only way forward may thus be to proceed without some countries. Indeed, what has been common to successful global initiatives of the 1990s is that they have been based on the possibility that a grouping of countries can proceed, at first, without the consent of the others. This has been true in the cases of, for instance, the International Criminal Court and the Ottawa mine ban convention. This is also the only realistic way of materializing the currency transaction tax and greenhouse gas taxes in the early 2000s.

The debt arbitration mechanism might be an exception. Occasionally, it has seemed that the possibility of some kind of debt arbitration mechanism has been taken seriously also by the US and the Bretton Woods institutions. Yet it is quite evident that they would like to retain the power to control, effective to varying degrees, the economic policies of sixty to eighty Southern and Eastern states. Some kind of compromise might be possible, particularly in the longer run, given the inadequacy of HIPC I and II initiatives and the pressures to recognize the *de facto* insolvency of a large number of states struggling with the debt problem. It is not inconceivable that this component in a strategy for global democratization might thus be nearly universal, comprising all major states and perhaps also giving the civic actors and movements a right to speak. Most likely, however, the only way to realize a rule-of-law-based and democratically organized debt arbitration mechanism is to proceed without the US.

As depicted in Figure 5.1.1, financial reforms should come first in the strategy for global democratization. By tackling important aspects of the power of finance and by creating democratic fora and new public sources of finance, the world political context can change. Most importantly, by relieving the effects of debt and short-term finance on the policies of states, the debt arbitration mechanism and CTT would make a number of states also more autonomous in the WTO negotiations. Also, for instance, UN reforms will become more likely once new sources of funding the UN system have been institutionalized. Partial reforms will in this way create new opportunities for further transformations.

Both the financial and the WTO reforms will be uncertain and contingent on the process of building political and social support. The precondition for this strategy is thus the empowering of new political forces. There must be a

Figure 5.1.1: Strategy towards global democratization

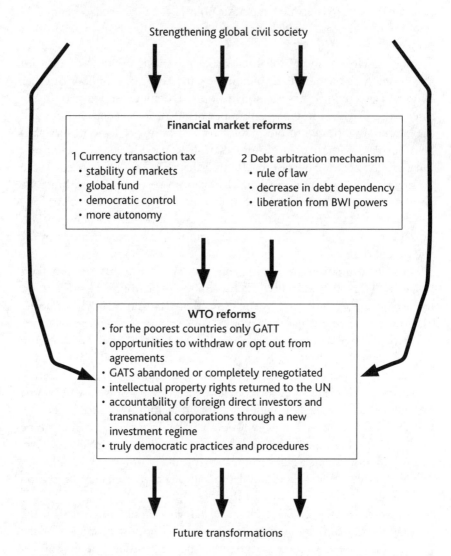

Strengthening global civil society

Financial market reforms

1 Currency transaction tax
- stability of markets
- global fund
- democratic control
- more autonomy

2 Debt arbitration mechanism
- rule of law
- decrease in debt dependency
- liberation from BWI powers

WTO reforms
- for the poorest countries only GATT
- opportunities to withdraw or opt out from agreements
- GATS abandoned or completely renegotiated
- intellectual property rights returned to the UN
- accountability of foreign direct investors and transnational corporations through a new investment regime
- truly democratic practices and procedures

Future transformations

strong transnational movement for global transformations. The World Social Forum process stands out as a new major space created by and for global civil society. It is noteworthy that the WSF process has been independent of any state (except for the support of the Brazilian state of Rio Grande do Sul). In a relatively short time, it has built the capacity to generate new projects and alliances. The further empowerment of the democratic elements of the global civil society, especially via the WSF process, would seem to be a fundamental component of a strategy for global democratization. More controversially, it is also possible that the WSF itself may emerge as a major political force.

The WSF is sometimes criticized for being a mere empty (and often rather chaotic) space for encounters. The original organizers of the WSF process have been reluctant to conceive the WSF as an entity with political goals. It is indeed important that the process retains and develops its openness and pluralistic and non-violent nature. New institutional developments are, however, needed to make the WSF more empowering and adequate. The International Council has become an increasingly important decision-making body within the WSF process, responsible for deciding upon the location of the main WSF events and various other key aspects. While most decisionmaking in the Council has until now been based on consensus, it would be useful to create transparent mechanisms for voting when needed.

The question of who should form part of the International Council has become an increasingly contested topic. In order to keep the Council open and democratically selected, its membership could be restricted for three or four years only, with the principle of rotation and possibly even lottery as the means to elect new members from among those qualified for, and interested in, membership. The need to maintain the institutional memory would be ensured by the fact that each year most members would continue.

One of the biggest challenges of the WSF is how to build into it mechanisms to further substantial projects, without giving in to the idea of a hierarchical and monological party of opinion. One possibility is that while the WSF itself continues to avoid taking stands on particular issues, it facilitates better the opportunities for its participants to find common ground for shared political action. To a certain extent, this has already taken place through the declarations of social movements that have gathered in the annual WSF events. A more controversial possibility is that some could be empowered to speak from within the internal bodies of the WSF, although no one would represent the WSF as a whole.

It is of course possible that the WSF may fail to take a key role in transformative civil society projects and other parts or (possibly already existing) projects of global civil society will assume a more dominant role in the future. Whatever form the strengthening of global civil society will take, it is important that concrete strategies of change emerge from within it. According to our analysis, the key is to tackle, first, the most immediate forms of financial dependency by establishing a debt arbitration mechanism and the currency transaction tax. Both can be created by a group of willing countries, supported by local, national and transnational civil society organizations. This would also empower a number of weak parties in the WTO to adopt more independent positions. Since the WTO allows for the possibility of majority decision-making (one country/one vote), this would open up the prospect for drastic but carefully prepared WTO reforms.

Rather than a closed model of global democracy, the proposed strategy is intended to constitute only the first steps in an open-ended process of global democratization. While we believe that this strategy has the potential to gain widespread support, it is also of the utmost importance that other strategic proposals emerge from within the WSF process and elsewhere.

Chapter 5.2

Charter of Principles of the World Social Forum, June 2001

1) The World Social Forum is an open meeting place for reflective thinking, democratic debate of ideas, formulation of proposals, free exchange of experiences and interlinking for effective action, by groups and movements of civil society that are opposed to neo-liberalism and to domination of the world by capital and any form of imperialism, and are committed to building a planetary society directed towards fruitful relationships among Mankind and between it and the Earth.

2) The World Social Forum at Porto Alegre was an event localized in time and place. From now on, in the certainty proclaimed at Porto Alegre that 'Another World Is Possible', it becomes a permanent process of seeking and building alternatives, which cannot be reduced to the events supporting it.

3) The World Social Forum is a world process. All the meetings that are held as part of this process have an international dimension.

4) The alternatives proposed at the World Social Forum stand in opposition to a process of globalization commanded by the large multinational corporations and by the governments and international institutions at the service of those corporations' interests, with the complicity of national governments. They are designed to ensure that globalization in solidarity will prevail as a new stage in world history. This will respect universal human rights, and those of all citizens – men and women – of all nations and the environment and will rest on democratic international systems and institutions at the service of social justice, equality and the sovereignty of peoples.

5) The World Social Forum brings together and interlinks only organizations and movements of civil society from all the countries in the world, but intends neither [sic] to be a body representing world civil society.

6) The meetings of the World Social Forum do not deliberate on behalf of the World Social Forum as a body. No one, therefore, will be authorized, on behalf of any of the editions of the Forum, to express positions claiming to be those of all its participants. The participants in the Forum shall not be called on to take decisions as a body, whether by vote or acclamation, on declarations or proposals for action that would commit all, or the majority,

of them and that propose to be taken as establishing positions of the Forum as a body. It thus does not constitute a locus of power to be disputed by the participants in its meetings, nor does it intend to constitute the only option for interrelation and action by the organizations and movements that participate in it.

7) Nonetheless, organizations or groups of organizations that participate in the Forum's meetings must be assured the right, during such meetings, to deliberate on declarations or actions they may decide on, whether singly or in coordination with other participants. The World Social Forum undertakes to circulate such decisions widely by the means at its disposal, without directing, hierarchizing, censuring or restricting them, but as deliberations of the organizations or groups of organizations that made the decisions.

8) The World Social Forum is a plural, diversified, non-confessional, non-governmental and non-party context that, in a decentralized fashion, interrelates organizations and movements engaged in concrete action at levels from the local to the international to build another world.

9) The World Social Forum will always be a forum open to pluralism and to the diversity of activities and ways of engaging of the organizations and movements that decide to participate in it, as well as the diversity of genders, ethnicities, cultures, generations and physical capacities, providing they abide by this Charter of Principles. Neither party representations nor military organizations shall participate in the Forum. Government leaders and members of legislatures who accept the commitments of this Charter may be invited to participate in a personal capacity.

10) The World Social Forum is opposed to all totalitarian and reductionist views of economy, development and history and to the use of violence as a means of social control by the State. It upholds respect for Human Rights, the practices of real democracy, participatory democracy, peaceful relations, in equality and solidarity, among people, ethnicities, genders and peoples, and condemns all forms of domination and all subjection of one person by another.

11) As a forum for debate the World Social Forum is a movement of ideas that prompts reflection, and the transparent circulation of the results of that reflection, on the mechanisms and instruments of domination by capital, on means and actions to resist and overcome that domination, and on the alternatives proposed to solve the problems of exclusion and social inequality that the process of capitalist globalization with its racist, sexist

and environmentally destructive dimensions is creating internationally and within countries.

12) As a framework for the exchange of experiences, the World Social Forum encourages understanding and mutual recognition amongst its participant organizations and movements, and places special value on the exchange among them, particularly on all that society is building to centre economic activity and political action on meeting the needs of people and respecting nature, in the present and for future generations.

13) As a context for interrelations, the World Social Forum seeks to strengthen and create new national and international links among organizations and movements of society, that, in both public and private life, will increase the capacity for non-violent social resistance to the process of dehumanisation the world is undergoing and to the violence used by the State, and reinforce the humanizing measures being taken by the action of these movements and organizations.

14) The World Social Forum is a process that encourages its participant organizations and movements to situate their actions, from the local level to the national level and seeking active participation in international contexts, as issues of planetary citizenship, and to introduce onto the global agenda the change-inducing practices that they are experimenting in building a new world in solidarity.

[...]

Chapter 5.3

At the global crossroads (Part B): the rise of global social democracy?

David Held

Introduction

Immanuel Kant wrote over two hundred years ago that we are 'unavoidably side by side'. A violent challenge to law and justice in one place has consequences for many other places and can be experienced everywhere. While he dwelt on these matters at length, he could not have known how profound his concerns would become.

Since Kant, our mutual interconnectedness and vulnerability have grown rapidly. We no longer live, if we ever did, in a world of discrete national communities. Instead, we live in a world of what I like to call 'overlapping communities of fate' where the trajectories of countries are deeply enmeshed with each other. In our world, it is not only the violent exception that links people together across borders; the very nature of everyday problems and processes joins people in multiple ways.

The story of our increasingly global order – 'globalization' – is not a singular one. Globalization is not just economic; for it also involves growing aspirations for international law and justice. From the United Nations to the European Union, from changes to the laws of war to the entrenchment of human rights, from the emergence of international environmental regimes to the foundation of the International Criminal Court, there is also another narrative being told – a narrative which seeks to reframe human activity and entrench it in law, rights and responsibilities.

Many of these developments were framed against the background of formidable threats to humankind – above all, Nazism, fascism and the Holocaust. Those involved in them affirmed the importance of universal principles, human rights and the rule of law in the face of strong temptations to simply put up the shutters and defend the position of only some countries and nations. They rejected the view of national and moral particularists that belonging to a given community limits and determines the moral worth of individuals and the nature of their freedom, and they defended the irreducible moral status of each and every person. The principles of equal respect, equal concern and the priority of the vital needs of all human beings are not principles for some remote utopia; they are at the centre of significant post-Second World War legal and political developments.

A clear moment of choice

The international community has reached a clear moment of choice. It is still possible to build on the achievements of the post-Second World War era. Alternatively, we can participate (actively or passively) in their erosion or dismantling. The signs are not good; for the postwar multilateral order is now threatened by the intersection of a number of crises. I shall emphasize four. Each one of these is a serious matter; taken together, they constitute the severest test.

First, the collapse of the trade talks at Cancún raised the possibility of a major challenge to the world trading system. At the same time, a large growth in bilateral trade arrangements and preferential trading agreements singled out some nation-states for favoured treatment by others. If the growth in bilateral agreements were to continue, there would be a real danger that the Doha trade round would collapse, or produce derisory results. Recent trade negotiations have made progress on phasing out agricultural subsidies, but there is no clear timetable attached to the implementation of many of the key points. There are many risks involved, but perhaps the most serious risk is to the world's poorest countries. They cannot alone overcome the handicaps of a world trading system marked by rigged rules and double standards. If the world's poorest countries (along with middle income nations) are to find a secure access point into the global economic order, they require a free and fair footing so to do. The slow progress of trade talks signals that they may not reach this point.

Second, little progress has been made towards achieving the millennium goals – the moral consciousness of the international community. The millennium goals set down minimum standards to be achieved in relation to poverty reduction, health, educational provision, the combating of HIV/AIDS, malaria and other diseases, environmental sustainability and so on. Progress towards these targets has been lamentably slow, and there is evidence that they will be missed by a very wide margin. In fact, there is evidence that there may have been no point in setting these targets at all, so far are we from attaining them in many parts of the world.

Third, little, if any, progress has been made in creating a sustainable framework for the management of global warming. The British chief scientist, Sir David King, has recently warned that 'climate change is the most serious problem we are facing today, more serious than the threat of terrorism'. Irrespective of whether one finds this characterization accurate, it is the case that global warming has the capacity to wreak havoc on the world's diverse species, biosystems, and socio-economic fabric. Violent storms will become more frequent, water access a battle ground, and the mass movement of desperate people more common. The overwhelming body of scientific opinion now maintains that global warming constitutes a serious threat not in the long term, but in the here and now. The failure of the international community to generate a sound framework for managing global warming is one of the most serious indications of the problems facing the multilateral order.

Fourth, the multilateral order has been weakened by the fall-out from the war in Iraq, as the report of Kofi Annan's High Level Panel clearly indicates. The value of the UN system has been called into question, the legitimacy of the Security Council has been challenged, and the working practices of multilateral institutions have been eroded. Post-Iraq, the weaknesses of the UN system have been exposed, the arrogance of the great powers has been dramatized, international law and legitimacy have been disorganized, and the prospects for combating global terrorism seem no better, if not worse.

[...]

Revitalizing social democracy

In contrast to the narrow scope and vision of the Washington Consensus, the nature and form of a free and fair global economy can, I believe, be articulated through the lens of social democratic concepts and values. Traditionally, social democrats have sought to deploy the democratic institutions of individual countries on behalf of a particular project; a compromise between the powers of capital, labour and the state which seeks to encourage the development of market institutions, private property and the pursuit of profit within a regulatory framework that guarantees not just the civil and political liberties of citizens, but also the social conditions necessary for people to enjoy their formal rights. Social democrats rightly accepted that markets are central to generating economic well-being, but recognized that in the absence of appropriate regulation they suffer serious flaws, especially the generation of unwanted risks for their citizens and an unequal distribution of those risks, and the creation of negative externalities and corrosive inequalities.

In the post-Second World War period, in particular, many Western countries sought to reconcile the efficiency of markets with the values of social community (which markets themselves presuppose) in order to develop and grow. The nature of the balance struck took different forms in different countries, reflecting different national political traditions: in the US, the New Deal, and in Europe, social democracy or the social market economy. Yet however this balance was exactly conceived, governments had a key role to play in enacting and managing this programme: moderating the volatility of transaction flows, managing demand levels and providing social investments, safety nets and adjustment assistance (see Ruggie, 2003).

Although for a few decades after the Second World War it seemed that a satisfactory balance could be achieved between self-government, social solidarity and international economic openness – at least for the majority of Western countries, and for the majority of their citizens – it now appears that this balance is much harder to sustain. The mobility of capital, goods, people, ideas and pollutants increasingly challenges the capacity of individual governments to sustain their own social and political compromises within delimited borders. New problems are posed by the increasing divergence between the extensive spatial reach of economic and social activity, and the traditional state-based mechanisms of political control. Moreover, these problems cannot be resolved within the framework of the Washington Consensus, old or new. Equipped with its policies, governance at all levels has too often been simply disarmed or naively reshaped.

While the values of social democracy – the rule of law, political equality, democratic politics, social justice, social solidarity and economic efficiency – are of enduring significance, the key challenge today is to elaborate their meaning, and to re-examine the conditions of their entrenchment, against the background of the changing global constellation of politics and economics. In the current era, social democracy must be defended and elaborated not just at the level of the nation-state, but at regional and global levels as well. The provision of public goods can no longer be equated with state-provided goods alone. Diverse state and non-state actors shape and contribute to their provision – and they need to do so if some of the most profound challenges of globalization are to be met. Moreover, some core public goods have to be provided regionally and globally if they are to be provided at all. From the establishment of fair trade rules and financial stability to the fight against hunger and environmental degradation, the emphasis is on finding durable modes of international and transnational cooperation and collaboration.

With this in mind, the project of social democracy has to be reconceived to include the promotion of the rule of law at the international level; greater transparency, accountability and democracy in global governance; a deeper commitment to social justice in the pursuit of a more equitable distribution of life chances; the protection and reinvention of community at diverse levels; and the regulation of the global economy through the public management of global trade and financial flows, and the engagement of leading stakeholders in corporate governance. These guiding orientations set the politics of what I call 'global social democracy' apart from the pursuit of the Washington Consensus – and, for that matter, from the aims of those pitched against globalization in all its forms.

Open markets and strong governance

If social democracy at the level of the nation-state means being tough in pursuit of free markets while insisting on a framework of shared values and common institutional practices, at the global level it means pursuing an economic agenda which calibrates the freeing of markets with poverty reduction programmes and the immediate protection of the vulnerable – north, south, east and west. This agenda must be pursued while ensuring that different countries have the freedom they need to experiment with their own investment strategies and resources.

Economic growth can provide a powerful impetus to the achievement of human development targets. But it does not necessarily achieve these targets; unregulated economic development which simply follows the existing rules and entrenched interests of the global economy falls short of managed economic change geared to the prosperity of all. Economic development needs to be conceived as a means to an end, not an end in itself. Understood accordingly, it should be recognized that while international trade has huge potential for helping the least well-off countries to lift themselves out of poverty, and for enhancing the welfare and wellbeing of all nation-states, the current rules of global trade are heavily structured to protect the interests of the well-off and are heavily structured against the interests of the poorest countries as well as middle income ones (see Oxfam, 2002; Moore, 2003; Wade, 2003).

Thus, while free trade is an admirable objective for progressives in principle, it cannot be pursued without attention to the power asymmetries of the global economy and to the poorest in the low and middle income countries who are extremely vulnerable to the initial phasing in of external market integration (especially of capital market liberalization), and who have few resources, if any, to fall back on during times of economic transformation (see Legrain, 2002; Garrett, forthcoming). A similar thing can be said, of course, for many people in wealthier societies. While they are not exposed to the unequal rules, double standards and inequalities of the global economic order in a parallel way to developing countries, if they lose their jobs or have to settle for lower wages they are also vulnerable in times of major economic shifts.

It is thus crucial to any social democratic agenda for free markets that it addresses simultaneously the needs of the vulnerable wherever they are. For the poorest countries this will mean that development policies must be directed to challenge the asymmetries of access to the global market, to ensure the sequencing of global market integration, particularly of capital markets, to ensure long-term investment in health care, human capital and physical infrastructure, to build a robust public sector, and to develop transparent, accountable political institutions. In developed countries this will mean the continued enhancement of strong, accountable political institutions to help mediate and manage the economic forces of globalization, and the provision of, among other things, high levels of social protection and generous safety nets, alongside sustained investment in lifelong learning and skills acquisition (cf. Swank, 2002). What follows here is complex and challenging for every country. But what is striking is that this range of policies has all too often not been pursued. This seems more a matter of psychology and political choice, and less a matter related to any fundamental obstacles in the nature of the economic organization of human affairs.

A more detailed social democratic agenda for economic globalization and global economic governance follows. Each element would make a significant contribution to the creation of a level playing field in the global economy; together, they would help reshape the economic system in a manner that is both free and fair. The agenda includes:

- salvaging the Doha trade round, and ensuring it is a development round that brings serious benefits to the world's poorest countries and to middle income ones
- reforming TRIPS to ensure it is compatible with public health and welfare and offers flexibility for poor countries to decide when, and in what sectors, they want to use patent protection;
- recognizing that for many developing countries phasing in their integration into global markets, and only pursuing this agenda after the necessary domestic political and economic reforms are in place, is far more important than the pursuit of open borders alone;
- building on organizations like the WTO legal advisory centre to expand the capacity of developing countries to engage productively in the institutions of governance of the world economy;
- setting a clear timetable for governments to reach the UN 0.7% GNP/overseas aid target, and raising it to 1% in due course, to ensure the minimum flow of resources for investment in the internal integration of the world's poorest countries;
- supporting further reductions in the international debt burden of heavily indebted poor countries, linking debt cancellation, for instance, to education and the provision of financial incentives for poor children to attend school;
- creating a fair international migration regime that can regulate flows of people in a way that is economically beneficial and socially sustainable for developing as well as developed countries;
- improving cooperation among international financial institutions and other international donors, thus consolidating the development and policy-making efforts of the international community within the UN;

- opening up international financial institutions to enhance developing countries' involvement by addressing their under-representation in existing governance structures, and expanding their role in, among other places, the Financial Stability Forum (FSF) and the Basel Committee;
- building global networks and institutions focused on poverty and welfare, to act as counterweights and countervailing powers to the market driving IGOs (the WTO, IMF and World Bank);
- instituting a substantial international review of the functioning of the Bretton Woods institutions, created more than 50 years ago and now operating in an economic context that has drastically changed.

Do we have the resources to put such a programme into effect? Concern has already been expressed about whether the political resources exist; the interlocking crises of the multilateral order are evidence of a lack of political will to confront some of the most pressing global threats. But at least it cannot be said, somewhat paradoxically, that we lack the economic resources for such a programme. A few telling examples make the point. The UN budget is $1.25 billion plus the necessary finance for peacekeeping per annum. Against this, US citizens spend over $8 billion per annum on cosmetics, $27 billion per annum on confectionery, $70 billion per annum on alcohol and over $560 billion per annum on cars. (All these figures are from the late 1990s and so are likely to be much higher now.) Further telling examples from the EU include $11 billion per annum spent on ice-cream, $150 billion per annum spent on cigarettes and alcohol and, from the EU and the US together, over $17 billion per annum on pet food. What do we require to make a substantial difference to the basic well-being of the world's poorest? Again, telling statistics are available. Required would be $6 billion per annum on basic education; $9 billion per annum for water and sanitation; $12 billion per annum for the reproductive health of women; and $13 billion per annum for basic health and nutrition. These figures are substantial but, when judged against major consumption expenditure in the US and EU, they are not excessive demands.

Moreover, if all the OECD agricultural subsidies were removed and spent on the world's poorest peoples this would release some $300 billion per annum. In addition, it can be noted that a half percentage point shift in the allocation of global GDP would release over $300 billion per annum. Clearly, it is not the right question to ask whether the economic resources exist to put in place reforms that might aid the world's poorest and least well-off. The question really is about how we allocate available resources, to whose benefit and to what end. It is not a question of whether there are adequate economic resources, it is a question of how we choose to spend them – whether we choose to meet the challenges of the social democratic agenda, summarized in Table 5.3.1.

[...]

Table 5.3.1: The social democratic agenda

Domestic
Sound macroeconomic policy
Nurturing of political/legal reform
Creation of robust public sector
State-led economic and investment strategy, enjoying sufficient development space to experiment with different policies
Sequencing of global market integration
Priority investment in human and social capital
Public capital expenditure on infrastructure
Poverty reduction and social safety nets
Strengthening civil society
Global
Salvaging Doha
Cancellation of unsustainable debt
Reform of TRIPS
Creation of fair regime for transnational migration
Expand negotiating capacity of developing countries at IFIs
Increase developing country participation in the running of IFIs
Establish new financial flows and facilities for investment in human capital and internal country integration
Reform of UN system to enhance accountability and effectiveness of poverty reduction, welfare and environmental programmes

[...]

What is to be done?

Clearly, agendas differ and are deeply contested. But there are a number of very pressing issues which need to be addressed if we are to salvage the achievements of the post-Holocaust world and build on them in a manner that provides not just security in the narrowest sense (protection from the immediate threat of coercive power and violence), but security in the broadest sense (protection for all those whose lives are vulnerable for whatever reason – economic, political, environmental and so on). Elsewhere, I have sought to set these out at length (Held, 2004). Here I will simply list some of the steps which could be taken to help implement a human security agenda at the heart of discussion in many parts of the world today ('old Europe', Latin America, Africa and Asia). These include:

- relinking the security and human rights agenda in international law – the two sides of international humanitarian law which, together, specify grave and systematic abuse of human security and well-being, and the minimum conditions required for the development of human agency;
- reforming UN Security Council procedures to improve the specification of, and legitimacy of, credible reasons for, credible threshold tests for, and credible promises in relation to, armed intervention in the affairs of a state – the objective being to link these directly to a set of conditions which would constitute a severe threat to peace, and/or a threat to the minimum conditions for the well-being of human agency, sufficient to justify the use of force;
- recognizing the necessity to dislodge and amend the now outmoded 1945 geopolitical settlement as the basis of decision-making in the Security Council, and to extend representation to all regions on a fair and equal footing;
- expanding the remit of the Security Council, or creating a parallel Social and Economic Security Council, to examine and, where necessary, intervene in the full gamut of human crises – physical, social, biological, environmental – which can threaten human agency;
- founding a World Environmental Organization to promote the implementation of existing environmental agreements and treaties, whose main mission would be to ensure that the development of world trading and financial systems are compatible with the sustainable use of the world's resources;
- understanding that 'representation' and 'taxation' presuppose each other; that is, that effective, transparent and accountable global governance requires reliable income streams, from aid to new financial facilities (as proposed by Gordon Brown) and, in due course, new tax revenues (for example, based on GNP, energy usage or financial market turnover).

In order to reconnect the security and human rights agenda and to bring them together into a coherent framework of law, it would be necessary to hold an international or global legal convention. Rather than set out a blueprint of what the results of such a convention should be, it is important to stress the significance of a legitimate process that reviews the security and human rights sides of international law and seeks to reconnect them in a global legal framework. One demonstrable result of such an initiative could be new procedures at the UN to specify the set of conditions which would constitute a threat to the peace and the well-being of humankind sufficient to justify the use of force. The question is often put in the form: do we need to amend the UN Charter to create new triggers for war or armed intervention in the affairs of another country?

Humanitarian armed intervention

A number of compelling accounts have emerged recently which seek to justify humanitarian armed intervention in exceptional circumstances. One prominent account comes from the Canadian-sponsored International Commission on Intervention and State Sovereignty (see Evans, 2003). The Commission's Report emphasizes the importance of a responsibility to protect people in the face of large-scale loss of life or ethnic cleansing. And it links this responsibility to additional principles which concern the use of proportional means in the face of a severe test to human well-being, the last resort use of military power, among other considerations. A second account has been offered by Anne-Marie Slaughter (2003). She focuses on three factors which, when present all at once, might justify armed humanitarian intervention: possession of weapons of mass destruction; grave and systematic human rights abuses; and aggressive intent with regard to other nations. Finally, Kenneth Roth of Human Rights Watch has recently argued that humanitarian intervention could be justified if it is an intervention of last resort; if it is motivated by humanitarian concerns; if it is guided by, and maximizes, compliance with international humanitarian law; if it is likely to achieve more good than bad; and if it can be legitimated via the UN Security Council (Roth, 2004).

Pressing additional questions arise when considering this matter and these include how one weighs the balance of the different factors involved, how one creates a framework that can be applied to all countries (and not just to those perceived as a threat by the West) and how one creates a new threshold test for legitimate use of force. All the positions which emerge in this regard need to be tested against the views and judgements of peoples from around the world – hence, a global legal convention – and not just against the views of those from the most powerful nation-states, if any new solution is to be durable and legitimate in the long run.

Moreover, we need to bear in mind that no modern theory of the nature and scope of the legitimate use of power within a state runs together the roles of judge, jury and executioner. Yet this is precisely what we have allowed to happen in the global order today. We need new bodies at the global level for weighing evidence, making recommendations, testing options and so on. These need to be separate and distinct bodies which embody a separation of powers at the global level. If one is in favour of the grounds that might legitimate humanitarian intervention one also needs to ask who is going to make these decisions and under what conditions. The weight of argument points in favour of taking seriously the necessity to protect peoples under extreme circumstances, and it also points in the direction of amending the institutional structures which pass judgement over these pressing matters. These structures need to be open, accountable and representative. Without suitable reform, our global institutions will be forever burdened by the mantle of partiality and illegitimacy. Table 5.3.2 summarizes the main reforms that are necessary if a new human security doctrine is to be achieved — and juxtaposes it with the Washington Security framework.

Table 5.3.2. The Washington and Human Security Doctrines

The Washington Security Doctrine
Hegemonic
Order through dominance
'Flexible multilateralism' or unilateralism where necessary
Pre-emptive and preventive use of force
Security focus: geopolitical and, secondarily, geoeconomic
Collective organization where pragmatic (UN, NATO), otherwise reliance on US military and political power
Leadership: the US and its allies
Aims: making world safe for freedom and democracy; globalizing American rules and justice
The Human Security Doctrine
Multilateralism and common rules
Order through law and social justice
Enhance multilateral, collective security
Last resort use of internationally sanctioned force to uphold international humanitarian law
Security focus: relinking security and human rights agendas; protecting all those facing threats to life, whether political, social, economic or environmental
Strengthen global governance: reform UN Security Council; create Economic and Social Security Council; democratize UN
Leadership: develop a worldwide dialogue to define new global covenant
Aims: making world safe for humanity; global justice and impartial rules

A new global covenant?

This agenda is not over-ambitious. The story of our increasingly global order is not a singular one. Globalization is not a one-dimensional phenomenon: it has helped generate vast new opportunities as well as risks. Moreover, the achievements of the post-Holocaust world — the consolidation of international law, multilateralism, the EU and other forms of supranational regionalism — can and need to be built upon.

A coalition could emerge to push this agenda further, comprising: European countries with strong liberal and social democratic traditions; liberal groups in the US polity which support multilateralism and the rule of law in international affairs; developing countries struggling for freer and fairer trade rules in the world economic order; non-governmental organizations, from Amnesty International to Oxfam, campaigning for a more just, democratic and equitable world order; transnational social movements contesting the nature and form of contemporary globalization; and those economic forces that desire a more stable and managed global economic order (Held & McGrew, 2002).

Europe could have a special role in advancing the cause of global social democracy (McGrew, 2002). As the home of both social democracy and an historic experiment in governance beyond the state, Europe has direct experience in considering the appropriate designs for more effective and accountable suprastate governance. It offers novel ways of thinking about governance beyond the state which encourage a (relatively) more democratic – as opposed to more neoliberal – vision of global governance. Of course, this is not to suggest that the EU should broker a crude anti–US coalition of transnational and international forces. On the contrary, it is crucial to recognize the complexity of US domestic politics and the existence of progressive social, political and economic forces seeking to advance a rather different kind of world order from that championed by the administrations of George W. Bush and by the Republican right of the political spectrum more broadly (Nye, 2002). Any European political strategy to promote a broad-based coalition for a new global covenant must seek to enlist the support of these progressive forces within the US polity, while it must resist within its own camp the voices calling for the exclusive re-emergence of national identities, ethnic purity and protectionism. An extended struggle will be required to create a new global covenant, a struggle that will last long after the unilateral mistakes of Bush – in trade, aid, the environment and security – are put right.

References

Evans, G. (2003) The responsibility to protect: when it's right to fight, *Progressive Politics*, 2(2).

Garrett, G. (forthcoming) Globalization and inequality, *Perspectives on Politics*.

Held, D. & McGrew, A. (2002) *Globalization/Anti-Globalization* (Cambridge: Polity).

Held, D. (2004) *Global Covenant: The Social Democratic Alternative to the Washington Consensus* (Cambridge: Polity).

Legrain, P. (2002) *The Open World* (London: Abacus).

McGrew, A. (2002) Between two worlds: Europe in a globalizing era, *Government and Opposition*, 37(3).

Moore, M. (2003) *A World without Walls* (Cambridge: Cambridge University Press).

Nye, J. (2002) *The Paradox of American Power* (Oxford: Oxford University Press).

Oxfam (2002) *Rigged Rules and Double Standards* (Oxford: Oxfam).

Roth, K. (2004) What price military intervention?, *Global Agenda*, January 2004.

Ruggie, J. (2003) Taking embedded liberalism global: the corporate connection, in pp. 93–129 D. Held & M. Koenig-Archibugi (Eds) *Taming Globalization* (Cambridge: Polity).

Slaughter, A.-M. (2003) A chance to reshape the UN, *Washington Post*, 13 April.

Swank, D. (2002) *Global Capital, Political Institutions, and Policy Change in Developed Welfare States* (Cambridge: Cambridge University Press).

Wade, R. (2003) What strategies are viable for developing countries today? The WTO and the shrinkage of development space, *Review of International Political Economy*, 10(4), pp. 18–46.

Chapter 5.4

The basis of a new internationalism: cosmopolitan principles

David Held

Clues as to what internationalism should mean today can be found in the emergent cosmopolitan values and standards [...] that characterize some leading elements of the multilateral political and legal order. What does cosmopolitan mean in this context? In the first instance, cosmopolitanism refers to those basic values that set down standards or boundaries which no agent, whether a representative of a global body, state or civil association, should be able to violate. Focused on the claims of each person as an individual or as a member of humanity as a whole, these values espouse the idea that human beings are in a fundamental sense equal, and that they deserve equal political treatment; that is, treatment based on the equal care and consideration of their agency, irrespective of the community in which they were born or brought up. After over two hundred years of nationalism and sustained nation-state formation, such values could be thought of as out of place. But such values are already enshrined in the law of war, human rights law and the statute of the ICC, among many other international rules and legal arrangements.

Second, cosmopolitanism can be taken to refer to those forms of political regulation and lawmaking that create powers, rights and constraints which go beyond the claims of nation-states and which have far-reaching consequences, in principle, for the nature and form of political power. These regulatory forms can be found in the domain between national law and international law and regulation – the space between domestic law which regulates the relations between a state and its citizens, and traditional international law which applies primarily to states and interstate relations (Eleftheriadis, 2000). This space is already filled by a plethora of legal regulation, from the legal instruments of the EU, and the international human rights regime as a global framework for promoting rights, to the diverse agreements of the arms control system and environmental regimes. Cosmopolitanism is not made up of political ideals for another age, but embedded in rule systems and institutions which have already transformed state sovereignty in distinct ways.

Yet the precise sense in which these developments constitute a form of 'cosmopolitanism' remains to be clarified, especially given that the ideas of cosmopolitanism have a long and complex history. For my purposes here, cosmopolitanism can be taken as the moral and political outlook which builds on the strengths of the liberal multilateral order, particularly its commitment to universal standards, human rights and democratic values, and which seeks to specify general principles on which all could act. These are principles which can be universally shared, and can form the basis for the protection and nurturing of each person's equal interest in the determination of the institutions which govern their lives.

Cosmopolitan values can be expressed formally, in the interests of clarification, in terms of a set of principles (see Held, 2002). Eight principles are paramount. They are the principles of:

1 equal worth and dignity;
2 active agency;
3 personal responsibility and accountability;
4 consent;
5 collective decision-making about public matters through voting procedures;
6 inclusiveness and subsidiarity;
7 avoidance of serious harm;
8 sustainability.

The meaning of these principles needs unpacking in order that their implications can be clarified for the nature and form of public life. While eight principles may seem like a daunting number, they are interrelated and together form the basis of a new internationalist orientation.

The first is that the ultimate units of moral concern are individual people, not states or other particular forms of human association. Humankind belongs to a single moral realm in which each person is equally worthy of respect and consideration (Beitz, 1994; Pogge, 1994). This notion can be referred to as the principle of individualist moral egalitarianism or, simply, egalitarian individualism. To think of people as having equal moral value is to make a general claim about the basic units of the world comprising persons as free and equal beings (Kuper, 2000). This is not to deny the significance of cultural diversity and difference – not at all – but it is to affirm that there are limits to the moral validity of particular communities – limits which recognize, and demand, that we must treat with equal respect the dignity of reason and moral choice in every human being (Nussbaum, 1996, pp. 42–3).

The second principle recognizes that, if principle 1 is to be universally recognized and accepted, then human agency cannot be understood as the mere expression of tradition or fortune; rather, human agency must be conceived as the ability to act otherwise – the ability not just to accept but to shape human community in the context of the choices of others. Active agency connotes the capacity of human beings to reason self-consciously, to be self-reflective and to be self-determining.[1] It bestows both opportunities and duties – opportunities to act (or not as the case may be), and duties to ensure that independent action does not curtail and infringe upon the life chances and opportunities of others (unless, of course, sanctioned by negotiation or consent: see below). Active agency is a capacity both to make and pursue claims and to have such claims made and pursued in relation to oneself. Each person has an equal interest in active agency or self-determination.

Principles 1 and 2 cannot be grasped fully unless supplemented by principle 3: the principle of personal responsibility and accountability. At its most basic, this principle can be understood to mean that it is inevitable that people will choose different cultural, social and economic projects and that such differences need to be recognized. People develop their skills and talents differently, and enjoy different forms of ability and specialized competency. That they fare differently, and that many of these differences arise from a voluntary choice on their part, should be welcomed and accepted (see Barry, 1998, pp. 147–9). These *prima facie* legitimate differences of choice and outcome have to be distinguished from unacceptable structures of difference reflecting conditions which prevent, or partially prevent, some from pursuing their vital needs. Actors have to be aware of, and accountable for, the consequences of actions, direct or indirect, intended or unintended, which may radically restrict or delimit the choices of others. Individuals have both personal responsibility-rights as well as personal responsibility-obligations.[2]

The fourth principle, the principle of consent, recognizes that a commitment to equal worth and equal moral value, along with active agency and personal responsibility, requires a non-coercive political process in and through which people can negotiate and pursue their public interconnections, interdependencies and life chances. Interlocking lives, projects and communities require forms of deliberation and decision-making which take account of each person's equal standing in such processes. The principle of consent constitutes the basis of non-coercive collective agreement and governance.

Principles 4 and 5 must be interpreted together. For principle 5 acknowledges that while a legitimate public decision is one that results from consent, this needs to be linked with voting at the decisive stage of collective decision-making and with the procedures and mechanisms of majority rule. The consent of all is too strong a requirement of collective decision-making and would mean that minorities (even of one) could block or forestall public responses to key issues (see Held, 2002, pp. 26–7). Principle 5 recognizes the importance of inclusiveness in the process of granting consent, while interpreting this to mean that an inclusive process of participation and debate can coalesce with a decision-making procedure which allows outcomes which accrue the greatest support (Dahl, 1989).[3]

The sixth principle, which I [refer] to as the principle of inclusiveness and subsidiarity [...], seeks to clarify the fundamental criterion for drawing proper boundaries around units of collective decision-making. At its simplest, it connotes that those significantly affected by public decisions, issues or processes, should, *ceteris paribus*, have an equal opportunity, directly or indirectly through elected representatives, to influence and shape them. By significantly affected, I mean, as noted previously, that people are enmeshed in decisions and forces that have an impact on their capacity to fulfil their vital needs. According to principle 6, collective decision-making is best located when it is closest to and involves those whose life expectancy and life chances are determined by significant social processes and forces. On the other hand, this principle also recognizes that if the decisions at issue are translocal, transnational or transregional, then political associations need not only to be locally based but also to have a wider scope and framework of operation.

The seventh principle is a leading principle of social justice: the principle of the avoidance of harm and the remedying of urgent need. This is a principle for allocating priority to the most vital cases of need and, where possible, trumping other, less urgent public priorities until such a time as all human beings, de facto and de jure, are covered by the first six principles; that is to say, until they enjoy the status of equal moral value and active agency and have the means to participate in their respective political communities and in the overlapping communities of fate which shape their needs and welfare. A social provision which falls short of the potential for active agency can be referred to as a situation of manifest harm in that the participatory potential of individuals and groups will not have been achieved; that is to say, people would not have adequate access to effectively resourced capacities which they might make use of in their particular circumstances (Sen, 1999). But even this significant shortfall in the realization of human potential should be distinguished from situations of the most pressing levels of vulnerability, defined by the most urgent need. The harm that follows from a failure to meet such needs can be denoted, as mentioned previously, as serious harm, marked as it often is by immediate, life-and-death consequences. Accordingly, if the requirements specified by the principle of avoidance of serious harm are to be met, public policy ought to be focused, in the first instance, on the prevention of such conditions; that is, on the eradication of severe harm inflicted on people 'against their will' and 'without their consent' (Barry, 1998, pp. 231, 207).

The eighth and final principle is the principle of sustainability, which specifies that all economic and social development must be consistent with the stewardship of the world's core resources – by which I mean resources which are irreplaceable and non-substitutable (Goodin, 1992, pp. 62–5, 72). Such a principle discriminates against social and economic change which disrupts global ecological balances and unnecessarily damages the choices of future generations. Sustainable development is best understood as a guiding principle, as opposed to a precise formula, since we do not know, for example, what impact future technological innovation will have on resource provision and utilization. Yet, without reference to such a principle, public policy would be made without taking account of the finite quality of many of the world's resources and the equally valid claims of future generations to well-being. Because the contemporary economic and military age is the first age to be able to take decisions not just for itself but for all future epochs, its choices must be particularly careful not to pre-empt the equal worth and active agency of future generations.

The eight principles can best be thought of as falling into three clusters. The first cluster (principles 1–3) set down the fundamental organizational features of the cosmopolitan moral universe. Its crux is that each person is a subject of equal moral concern; that each person is capable of acting autonomously with respect to the range of choices before them; and that, in deciding how to act or which institutions to create, the claims of each person affected should be taken equally into account. Personal responsibility means in this context that actors and agents have to be aware of, and accountable for, consequences of their actions, direct or indirect, intended or unintended, that may substantially restrict and delimit the opportunities of others. The second cluster (principles 4–6) forms the basis of translating individually initiated activity, or privately determined activities more broadly, into collectively agreed or collectively sanctioned frameworks of action or regulatory regimes. Public power at all levels can be conceived as legitimate to the degree to which principles 4, 5 and 6 are upheld. The final principles (7 and 8) lay down a framework for prioritizing urgent need and resource conservation. By distinguishing vital from non-vital needs, principle 7 creates an unambiguous starting point and guiding orientation for public decisions. While this 'prioritizing commitment' does not, of course, create a decision procedure to resolve all clashes of priority in politics, it clearly creates a moral framework for focusing public policy on those who are most vulnerable. By contrast, principle 8 seeks to set down a prudential orientation to help ensure that public policy is consistent with global ecological balances and that it does not destroy irreplaceable and non-substitutable resources.

These principles are not just Western principles. Certain of their elements originated in the early modern period in the West, but their validity extends much further. For these principles are the foundation of a fair, humane and decent society, of whatever religion or cultural tradition. To paraphrase the legal theorist Bruce Ackerman, there is no nation without a woman who yearns for equal rights, no society without a man who denies the need for deference, and no developing country without a person who does not wish for the minimum means of subsistence so that they may go about their everyday lives (1994, pp. 382–3). The principles are building blocks for articulating and entrenching the equal liberty of all human beings, wherever they were born or brought up. They are the basis of underwriting the autonomy of others, not of obliterating it. Their concern is with the irreducible moral status of each and every person – the acknowledgement of which links directly to the possibility of self-determination and the capacity to make independent choices.[4]

It has to be acknowledged that there is now a fundamental fissure in the Muslim world between those who want to uphold universal standards, including the standards of democracy and human rights, and reform their societies, dislodging the deep connection between religion, culture and politics, and those who are threatened by this and wish to retain and/or restore power on behalf of those who represent 'fundamentalist' ideals. The political, economic and cultural challenges posed by the globalization of (for want of a better label) 'modernity' now face the counterforce of the globalization of radical Islam. This poses many important questions, but one in particular should be stressed; that is, how far and to what extent Islam – and, of course, parts of the resurgent fundamentalist West (for instance, the religious right of the US) – has the capacity to confront its own ideologies, double standards and limitations.

It would be a mistake to think that this is simply an outsider's challenge to Islam. Islam, like the other great world religions, has incorporated a diverse body of thought and practice. In addition, it has contributed, and accommodated itself, to ideas of religious tolerance, secular political power and human rights. It is particularly in the contemporary period that radical Islamic movements have turned their back on these important historical developments and sought to deny Islam's contribution both to the Enlightenment and the formulation of universal ethical codes. There are many good reasons for doubting the often expressed Western belief that thoughts about justice and democracy have flourished only in the West (Sen, 1996). Islam is not a unitary or explanatory category (see Halliday, 1996). Hence, the call for cosmopolitan principles speaks to a vital strain within Islam that affirms the importance of autonomy, rights and justice.

The cosmopolitan principles set out above can be thought of as the guiding ethical basis of global social democracy. They lay down some of the universal or organizing principles which delimit and govern the range of diversity and difference that ought to be found in public life. And they disclose the proper framework for the pursuit of argument, discussion and negotiation about particular spheres of value, spheres in which local, national and regional affiliations will inevitably be weighed. These are principles for an era in which political communities and states matter, but not only and exclusively. In a world where the trajectories of each and every country are tightly entwined, the partiality, one-sidedness and limitedness of 'reasons of state' need to be recognized. States are hugely important vehicles to aid the delivery of effective public regulation, equal liberty and social justice, but they should not be thought of as ontologically privileged. They can be judged by how far they deliver these public goods and how far they fail; for the history of states is, of course, marked not just by phases of corruption and bad leadership but also by the most brutal episodes. An internationalism relevant to our global age must take this as a starting point, and build an ethically sound and politically robust conception of the proper basis of political community, and of the relations among communities. Global social democracy, guided by cosmopolitan principles, would constitute a major step in this direction.

Notes

[1] The principle of active agency does not make any assumption about the extent of self-knowledge or reflexivity. Clearly, this varies and can be shaped by both unacknowledged conditions and unintended consequences of action (see Giddens, 1984). It does, however, assume that the course of agency is a course that includes choice and that agency itself is, in essence, defined by the capacity to act otherwise.

[2] The obligations taken on in this context cannot, of course, all be fulfilled with the same types of initiative (personal, social or political) or at the same level (local, national or global). But whatever their mode of realization, all such efforts can be related to one common denominator: the concern to discharge obligations we take on by virtue of the claims we make for the recognition of personal responsibility-rights (cf. Raz, 1986, chs 14–15).

[3] Minorities clearly need to be protected in this process. The rights and obligations entailed by principles 4 and 5 have to be compatible with the protection of each person's equal interest in principles 1, 2 and 3 – an interest which follows from each person's recognition as being of equal worth, with an equal capacity to act and to account for their actions. Majorities ought not to be able to impose themselves arbitrarily upon others. Principles 4 and 5 have to be understood against the background specified by the first three principles; the latter frame the basis of their operation.

[4] It is frequently alleged that democracy itself is a Western imposition on many developing countries. Yet, as George Monbiot has recently pointed out, 'the majority of those who live in parliamentary democracies, flawed as some of them may be,

live in the poor world' (2003, p. 109). Democracy has deep roots in many parts of the world; it is not an exclusively Western ideal or institution.

References

Ackerman, B. (1994) 'Political liberalism', *Journal of Philosophy*, 91.

Barry, B. (1998) 'International society from a cosmopolitan perspective', in D. Mapel and T. Nardin (eds) *International Society: Diverse Ethical Perspectives*, Princeton: Princeton University Press.

Beitz, C. (1994) 'Cosmopolitan liberalism and the states system', in C. Brown (ed) *Political Restructuring in Europe: Ethical Perspectives*, London: Routledge.

Dahl, R.A. (1989) *Democracy and its Critics*, New Haven: Yale University Press.

Eleftheriadis, P. (2000) 'The European constitution and cosmopolitan ideals', *Columbia Journal of European Law*, 7.

Giddens, A. (1984) *The Constitution of Society*, Cambridge: Polity.

Goodin, R. (1992) *Green Political Theory*, Cambridge: Polity.

Halliday, F. (1996) *Islam and the Myth of Confrontation*, London: I.B. Tauris.

Held, D. (2002) 'Law of states, law of peoples: three models of sovereignty', *Legal Theory*, 8(1).

Kuper, A. (2000) 'Rawlsian global justice: beyond *The Law of Peoples* to a cosmopolitan law of persons', *Political Theory*, 28.

Monibot, G. (2003) *The Age of Consent*, London: Flamingo.

Nussbaum, M.C. (1996) 'Kant and cosmopolitanism', in J. Bonham and M. Lutz-Bachmann (eds) *Perpetual Peace: Essays on Kant's Cosmopolitan Ideal*, Cambridge, Mass: MIT Press.

Pogge, T.W. (1994) 'Cosmopolitanism and sovereignty', in C. Brown (ed) *Political Restructuring in Europe: Ethical Perspectives*, London: Routledge.

Raz, J. (1986) *The Morality of Freedom*, Oxford: Oxford University Press.

Sen, A. (1996) 'Humanity and citizenship', in J. Cohen (ed) *For Love of Country: Debating the Limits of Patriotism*, Boston: Beacon.

Sen, A. (1999) *Development as Freedom*, Oxford: Oxford University Press.

Chapter 5.5

Allocating a global levy

Bob Deacon

A progressive approach to globalisation will be distinct from neoliberal globalisation in developing a global social policy to complement and modify global economic policy. Social policy within one country embodies the three dimensions of social redistribution (from richer to poorer, from those at work to those not able to work, from one region to another), social regulation (to ensure that business activity does not contradict human needs) and social rights (to enable 'citizens' to access a reasonable degree of economic and social resources). Social policy within the most developed example of regional governance (the European Union) also provides for cross-border redistribution, cross-border social regulation and a cross-border declaration of social rights. Global social policy within the framework of a progressive globalisation will therefore aim to develop mechanisms for redistribution, regulation and the enhancement of social rights. [...] This chapter is concerned with global social redistribution within the framework of established international declarations concerned with social rights.

There has been considerable debate in recent years about the possibility of a global levy to fund an international programme of poverty alleviation and to augment or replace the problematic aid system. Most notably, a fully-fledged global campaign has now developed around the Tobin Tax, which would levy funds as a small percentage of international currency exchange transactions. Other ideas also exist, such as a tax on carbon emissions or as a simple percentage of GDP to be collected and provided by national governments. However, little thought has been given to how this new money might be spent or how international social transfers could take place. Even less thought has been given to what mechanisms for global resource allocation might be developed, who would decide, and on what criteria allocations would be made. Some initial answers to these questions are suggested below. How far these are developed in practice will be the outcome of a period of international and supranational debate and consensus building.

It is likely that steps towards a formal system of global redistribution that might eventually involve a Global Tax Authority and a Global Social Affairs Ministry will build upon, first, existing *ad hoc* mechanisms and, second, proposals for such mechanisms that are already within the global policy debate. Among existing mechanisms for international redistribution are the ones used by the Global Fund to Fight AIDS, TB and Malaria (www. theglobalfund.org). This fund uses a combination of criteria and mechanisms to allocate its resources where they are needed most in the world. Using the World Bank's categorisation of countries into low- and middle-income, the fund distinguishes between low-income countries who are fully eligible for monies and lower-middle-income countries who must match international funds with national funds and focus activities on the poor and vulnerable, aiming to be self-sufficient over time. A few upper-middle-income countries are also eligible in much the same way as lower-middle-income countries if they have exceptional need based on disease burden indicators.

The procedure used by this fund for allocating funds within the constraints above is based on a competition between bids from Country Coordinating Mechanisms (CCMs) within each eligible country. A partnership is aimed at between the global fund and national political effort that also embraces through the CCMs national partners drawn from the private sector, the professions and user groups. Where governments are non-functioning the applications can include non-governmental organisations. A board of internationally appointed technical experts adjudicate between competing applications using the following list of criteria: epidemiological and socioeconomic indices, political commitment (of recipient governments), complementarity (to national effort), absorptive capacity (of governance mechanisms), soundness of project approach, feasibility, potential for sustainability, and whether or not there is a suitable evaluation and analysis mechanism. There are arguments for and against this responsive mode of resource allocation. Such an approach might miss the most needy, who are unable to bid, but it does involve a partnership between national and global effort. At the same time there is room for debate about the implicit conditionality built into the allocation mechanism. Good national governance is likely to be rewarded (except where it is recognised that no effective government exists). On the other hand a global fund that simply poured money into the coffers of a corrupt national government is likely to be criticised. All of the above criteria in various combinations are eminently suitable for decision making about the allocation of monies arising from our proposed global levy. They might be used either in response to bids or in the context of a top-down planning/allocation system. Details could vary depending on whether the monies were to be used for health, education or social protection purposes.

An idea on the drawing board and ready to be experimented with is that of the Global Social Trust Network.[1] It builds on the idea and practice, in many richer countries, of social partnerships within one country that fund social protection, and it seeks to extend this to develop international social partnerships between people in richer countries and those needing social protection in poorer countries. This global fund will be derived from resources voluntarily committed (at the suggested level of €5 a month or 0.2 per cent of monthly income) by individuals in OECD countries via the agency of social partner organisations such as trade unions or national social security funds. National Social Trust Organisations would then be established in both donor and recipient countries, and transfers would be organised through a global board with technical assistance provided in this case by the International Labour Organisation (ILO). Monies would then be spent by the National Social Trust Organisations in poorer countries, working through embryonic social protection mechanisms at local level. One suggestion is that the Global Social Trust Network would finance universal pensions at the level of one dollar a day. Pensions are recognised as being a very good cash benefit that actually meets the needs of whole families within extended family networks in poorer countries. The director of the Social Protection Network of the World Bank has commented favourably upon the ideas so long as the payments are linked to its Poverty Reduction Strategy Papers process.[2] This ensures that countries do not receive cheap loans from the Bank or have debt written off unless a public and transparent policy process has been established within the recipient country to reduce poverty. There is room for discussion as to whether the priority for international social protection expenditure should be old age pensions or, as favoured by Townsend,[3] universal child benefits. Any global levy could usefully provide additional resources to put into this Global Social Trust and thereby build upon the eloquent idea of the international social partnership embodied in it. The levy could also supplement incomes already being collected for other global funds such as those for cheap drugs or those for a World Water Contract.[4]

In addition to building on the practice of and complementing the emerging global funds discussed above, which seek to supplement national resources, a global levy would also make a major contribution to the realisation of the provision of global public goods and the prevention of global public bads. Sustained intellectual work being undertaken under the umbrella of the United Nations Development Programme (UNDP) by Inge Kaul and her colleagues[5] is now shaping a conception of global public goods that goes beyond the mere formal economist's criteria of goods that are technically non-excludable and non-rival in their consumption (world peace, for example) to embrace goods such as basic education and health care that are (or should be) 'socially determined public goods', which might be considered rival and excludable, but which by political decision could be regarded as non-exclusive. Political decisions about this could reflect the list of global social rights embodied within the 1967 UN Covenant on Economic, Cultural and Social Rights. Another approach would be to regard as socially determined global public goods those goods listed among the internationally agreed Millennium Development Goals being pursued by the UN Millennium Project Task Force. In other words, those things that benefit us all but no individual entrepreneur has an interest in providing – such as education and health in poor countries – should be considered as global public goods and an international effort should ensure their provision either by public service or privately in ways and with access criteria that enable all to benefit. A global levy could be used for such purposes.

Kaul and her colleagues make a useful distinction between development assistance, whereby richer countries donate monies to enable poorer countries to catch up in the development stakes, and global public goods.[6] Development assistance might continue in the context of progressive globalisation and could be provided with additional funds from the global levy. Additionally, mechanisms need to be set up to manage the provision of genuinely global public goods and diminish the existence of global public bads. Kaul and her colleagues envisage the establishment over time by each country of 'global issue ambassadors' located within international development departments. These ambassadors would work for policy coherence towards global issues across ministries such as trade and aid. There would be ambassadors for climate stability, food safety, international drug running, etcetera. National ambassadors would liaise with each other and develop international policy under the guidance of a global chief executive (for food safety, for example). Such a CEO would be advised by a global board drawn from relevant international organisations and be responsive to global civil society and global business interests.

This approach effectively adopts the networking and partnership form of global policy development and practice shifting, which involves collaboration between stakeholders in the international organisations, the global corporate sector, international NGOs and civil society organisations. Such a shift in the locus and substance of global policy making and practice has received support recently from commentators coming from very different intellectual positions. Rischard, the World Bank's vice-president for Europe, argues in *High Noon: 20 Global Issues and 20 Years to Solve Them*[7] that global multilateral institutions are not able to handle global issues on their own, that treaties and conventions are too slow for burning issues, that intergovernmental conferences do not have adequate follow-up mechanisms, and that the G7/G8 groupings are too exclusive.

Instead what is needed are global issues networks (GINs) involving governments, civil society and business, and facilitated by a multilateral organisation. GINs create a rough consensus about the problem to be solved and the goal to be achieved, establish norms and practice recommendations, and report on failing governments and encourage good practice through knowledge exchange and a global observatory to back a name-and-shame approach. Charlotte Streck in *Global Environmental Governance: Options and*

Opportunities argues for global public policy networks (GPPNs)[8] which bring together governments, the private sector and civil society organisations. She insists that recent trends in international governance indicate that the focus has shifted from intergovernmental activity to multi-sectoral initiatives, from a largely formal legalistic approach to a less formal participatory and integrated approach. Such GPPNs can set agendas and standards, generate and disseminate knowledge, and bolster institutional effectiveness. Streck is building here on the work of Reinicke and Bennet, who argued that international organisations could play a particular role in GPPNs as conveners, platforms, networkers and sometimes partial financiers (see also www.gppi.net). If for now global policy making is likely to take this form, with global public goods being provided and global public bads being reduced through these mechanisms, then the global levy will provide useful additional revenues to this end.

In the long term, however, it is the aim of the progressive approach to globalisation to build support for a more systematic approach to global governance, especially in the social sphere. Those who argue for this[9] and those who only go along with the idea to a degree, and recognise that there are missing global institutions such as a tax authority,[10] all envisage either the creation within the UN system of an Economic and Social Security Council or a reformed Economic and Social Committee (ECOSOC) that will then assume responsibility for the steering of global social policy through the several UN agencies such as the World Health Organisation (WHO), the ILO, and the United Nations Educational, Social and Cultural Organisation (UNESCO), in collaboration with any residual functions still retained by the World Bank. In this future scenario the global levy will provide an additional and independent source of funding for all UN activity and the activity of its social agencies. In this case it is to be expected that several of the experimental global funds, such as those discussed earlier, and the several global issues networks reviewed above will be more firmly rooted within the UN system and be managed by a global council of ministers responsive to a global elected assembly.

There is one footnote to these proposals for spending a global levy that requires serious consideration. It is conceivable that, because of the opposition by the world superpower to any kind of global levy and any strengthening of the UN system, an alternative route to more systematic global governance might need to be considered in the concept of a strengthened 'regionalism with a social dimension'.[11] Within this scenario the EU would be joined by ASEAN, the Southern African Development Community (SADC), Mercosur, the South Asian Association for Regional Co-operation (SAARC) and new regions in a global federation of regions linked to, say, the Group of Twenty (G20) international governance mechanism. In this case a global levy would be allocated on socio-economic criteria of need to some regions, who would then decide to allocate it to activities and projects within the region using mechanisms already established by the EU or new mechanisms such as those under consideration by the Global Fund to Fight AIDS/TB/Malaria.

Notes

[1] Cichon, M. *et al.* (2003) *A Global Social Trust Network: a New Tool to Combat Poverty Through Social Protection*, Geneva: International Labour Organisation.

[2] Holzmann, R. (2002) 'Interview' reported in Cichon *et al.*, *A Global Social Trust Network*, Geneva: International Labour Organisation.

[3] Townsend, P. and D. Gordon (2002) *World Poverty: New Policies to Defeat an Old Enemy*, Bristol: Policy Press.

[4] Petrella, R. (2001) *The Water Manifesto: Arguments for a World Water Contract*, London: Zed Books.

[5] Kaul, I. *et al.* (1999) *Global Public Goods: International Cooperation in the Twenty-first Century*, Oxford: Oxford University Press.

[6] Kaul, I. *et al.* (2003) *Global Public Goods: Managing Globalisation*, Oxford: Oxford University Press, p. 358.

[7] Rischard, J. F. (2002) *High Noon: 20 Global Problems, 20 Years to Solve Them*, Oxford: Perseus Books.

[8] Streck, C. (2002) 'Global Public Policy Networks as Coalitions for Change', in D. Esty and M. H. Ivanova (eds.), *Global Environmental Governance: Options and Opportunities*, Yale: Yale University Press.

[9] Held, D. and A. McGrew (2002) *Governing Globalisation: Power, Authority and Global Governance*, Cambridge: Polity Press; Patomaki, H. (1999) Democratising Globalisation: the Leverage of the Tobin Tax, London: Zed Books; Deacon, B. *et al.* (2003) *Global Social Governance: Themes and Prospects*, Helsinki: Finnish Ministry of Foreign Affairs.

[10] Nayyer, D. (2002) *Governing Globalisation: Issues and Institutions*, Oxford: Oxford University Press.

[11] Deacon, B. (2001) *The Social Dimension of Regionalism*, Helsinki: Stakes (www. gaspp.org).

Chapter 5.6

Towards a global social policy

Ramesh Mishra

[...]

[G]lobal *laissez-faire*, entrenched welfare states and electoral democracy are an unstable combination which could prove to be explosive. If ultranationalism and protectionism, as a backlash against unregulated globalization, are to be avoided, then some form of international action on social protection – even symbolic action at this point by say the G7 nations could be significant – is needed to complement and so to 'save' economic internationalization. National responses need to be supplemented with action at the transnational level to establish and safeguard social standards. What are the problems and prospects of developing such standards at a supranational level?

Globalization and social standards: bringing the 'social' back in

Our starting point must be the growing dissociation between economic and social standards in a globalizing economy. The neoliberal thrust of globalization spearheaded by American capitalism is to strengthen market forces and the economic realm at the cost of the institutions of social protection – institutions which appear as so many impediments to profit maximization. As we witness the gradual impoverishment of the 'social' in Anglo-Saxon countries, let us remind ourselves of the great achievement of the golden age of welfare capitalism represented by the welfare state and the mixed economy. It was to recognize the importance of the social dimension and to bring the social and economic sectors together in a mutually supportive, positive-sum relationship.

This harks back to a fundamental problem of the market society and market relationships with which social thinkers such as Marx, Durkheim, Toennies, Polanyi and others wrestled. Essentially it had to do with the dire consequences of the ascendancy of the 'economic' and the attenuation of the 'social' in the market-oriented societies which emerged in Europe in the 19th century. The different prognoses and remedies proposed by these theorists need not concern us here. Rather we would like to note that the long reprise of the social which began with factory legislation in Britain and continued through the development of social insurance in Germany was followed by other measures leading up to the relatively balanced social order of the post-WW2 welfare state. The latter managed to reintegrate the economic and the social within the framework of the nation state. Late 20th-century globalization is dissolving the nexus between the economic and the social as it once more exalts the economic and downgrades the 'social', seeking to relegate the latter to the private sphere.

The process of downgrading the social began with the ascendancy of neoliberalism at the nation-state level in the late 1970s. Globalization has carried the process forward by empowering and privileging neoliberal economics as a transnational force beyond the control of nation states and governments. What economic globalizers fail to acknowledge, however, is that whereas economies can go global, people cannot. While money and capital have been set free to move across the globe, labour remains locked into the nation state, for example by strict control on immigration. By and large people have to live and survive locally. Indeed human communities are defined above all by language and culture and are thus rooted in a place – a geographical location. Economies have gone global but societies and communities remain national. The result is a growing hiatus between the needs of the economic realm, e.g. for cost-cutting and profit maximization, and those of the social realm for stability, security and a sense of belongingness and cohesion. In short the logic of economic *laissez-faire* is to destroy communities and social life altogether. Hence the problem of controlling the economic in order to save the social is back on the agenda. It is necessary to affirm once again the importance of the social and to make it an integral component – alongside the economic – of development and progress.

From social rights to social standards: a conceptual reorientation

The conceptual underpinning of the post-WW2 welfare state has been that of social rights of citizenship in a modern democratic state. Although it was the social democratic welfare state, developed most fully in Scandinavian countries, that went furthest in making social citizenship the basis of social policy, it is important to note that in virtually all Western welfare states the idea of state welfare as a 'right' or entitlement (as opposed to a form of stigmatizing charity) and as a more or less universal provision to include all citizens has been the key element which distinguishes modern from pre-war social policy. True, there were important differences among post-war welfare state regimes. But these cross-national variations have to be seen within the larger epochal shift in the conception of social policy from the pre-war to the post-war world.

Shorn of complexities, the basic shift can be summed up as that from a residual to an institutional conception of state welfare, although the latter conception found expression in a variety of sub-types, e.g. the social democratic, the conservative corporatist or Bismarckian, and the Anglo-Saxon liberal (Esping-Andersen, 1990). Be that as it may the theoretical underpinning and the normative justification of the institutional model has been the conception of social welfare as an essential institution of the modern state – expressing one of the rights of citizenship, namely social, alongside civil and political rights. In this perspective of modernization which we owe to T.H. Marshall (1950), social rights appeared in the wake of the establishment of civil and political rights, rounding off the development of citizenship in the modern democratic state. The last two decades have seen a burgeoning literature on citizenship and social rights (see for example Turner, 1986; Barbalet, 1988; Andrews, 1991; Roche, 1992). The critique, the refinements and the qualifications brought to bear on the idea of social rights in its various aspects need not concern us here. Rather the point to make is that social rights looked secure and well established during the golden age – a time when they appeared to be in a positive-sum relationship with economic and political rights. The welfare state appeared as positively beneficial for the economy and a major contributor to political stability and national integration. It was easy to see social rights as a part of the broader conception of human rights in a modem society.

Since the late 1970s, however, social rights have taken a beating, both ideologically and in practice, at least in Anglo-Saxon countries. The basic weakness of social rights as a concept is that it is not at par with the other two rights, i.e. civil and political. Whereas these two are essentially *procedural* and can be institutionalized as universal human rights, social rights are *substantive* in nature (Barry, 1990, pp. 78-81; Plant et al., 1980, pp. 71-82). They raise issues of mobilizing and redistributing material resources.[1] The bottom line is that the granting of social rights comes into conflict with economic or property rights, one of the basic rights in liberal capitalist societies. The substantive rather than procedural status of social rights meant that when Western economies ran into serious problems after the mid-1970s, it was economic or property rights that received priority. Social rights, which were seen as encroaching upon property rights, were downgraded. As a result while civil and political rights of citizenship are not a matter of contention and are being extended world-wide, social rights are on the defensive, if not in decline. Their future looks decidedly uncertain (Esping-Andersen, 1996a, p. 1).

A further problem with the concept of social welfare as a 'right' is its individual-centred nature. To claim that individuals have a right, say to an adequate income which must be granted to them from resources to which others have a duty to contribute, raises the question of individual merit, i.e. whether individuals are deserving or not and whether they have contributed in ways which entitle them to their 'right'. In short, the source of these *substantive* claims of individuals upon resources remains problematic.

Social rights are also problematic in that as substantive rights to a standard of life, they imply a *minimum* rather than an optimum standard. Yet mainstream social programmes such as pensions and health care go well beyond minimum standards and often aim at an optimum. As a result they are vulnerable to the argument that they should be reduced to a minimum (Barry, 1990, p. 80; Espada, 1996, pp. 121-3, 186-7).

Finally, the language of 'rights', especially the notion of individual rights, is largely *Western* in origin. In non-Western countries, e.g. the newly industrializing countries of East Asia, 'social rights of citizenship' mean very little. Thus the key concept of Western social welfare remains largely alien to the non-Western world (Goodman and Peng, 1996, pp. 215, 218 n.29; Jones, 1993, pp. 202, 209, 214). Yet what is valuable in the idea of social rights of welfare – and here T.H. Marshall's contribution is seminal – is the emphasis on the social or the community dimension of modern societies besides the economic and political dimensions. But the *form* in which it appears, i.e. as an *individual* right analogous to civil and political rights, is virtually unknown outside the Western tradition. In any case, faced with the challenge of property and market rights, social rights are in retreat as a normative concept. Indeed with the resurgence of the market principle and the privileging of the economic realm, the idea of social citizenship is losing credibility. True, systems of social protection still remain in place in most Western countries, but increasingly find themselves on the defensive. They survive primarily as a legacy of the past, defended by the citizenry and vested interests, but lacking a clear rationale and meaning in the new order of things. In sum the concept of social welfare needs revision – both from an ideological and theoretical standpoint and also in order to clarify the rationale of the institutions of social protection.

The first step in the renewal of the concept of social welfare is to restate its meaning and place in the development of modern industrial societies. We would argue that the 'social' dimension identified by Marshall must be seen as a universal category similar to those of the 'economic' or 'political' in modern society. The economic order is concerned with the efficient production of goods and services and the market is the key institution. The political is concerned with the mechanism of decision-making and the distribution and exercise of power. The democratic polity is the key institution. The social is concerned with the maintenance of community and social solidarity, and universal social provision is the key institution. Thus the 'community' emerges as a societal category similar to the economy and the polity. In other words we need to think in terms of *community standards* rather than *individual rights*, for it is the community as a collective that must have some social standards or norms, which entail both rights and obligations.

The concept of community, like democracy and other normative concepts, is a contested one (Plant et al., 1980). But it can be argued that membership in a national community which entails reciprocity, interdependence and solidarity presupposes basic rather than minimum standards. It is the role of the polity to guarantee or uphold these basic social standards.

The notion of a community or social collective has a far wider applicability and meaning than individual 'rights' – a concept of Western provenance. Social welfare as an expression of the basic social *standards* of a community and its concern for its members can thus be universalized across different cultures and societies (Doyal and Gough, 1991, p. 223). Secondly, social standards can be linked more logically to the economic standards and capacities of nations than the more abstract and procedural notion of *rights*. The idea of a standard commensurate with the economic development of nations could help overcome the vexed problem of developed societies demanding a level of social protection and labour standards from less developed societies, which appears arbitrary and which the latter can ill afford to provide (Doyal and Gough, 1991, pp. 230-31). Finally, the idea of a social standard commensurate with economic development could help overcome the problem faced by the International Labour Organization (ILO), the United Nations (UN) and other agencies in trying to apply social rights universally across countries of differing economic standards, which results in a wide credibility gap between rhetoric and good intentions on the one hand and reality on the other (Doyal and Gough, 1991, p. 240, Chapter 11 *passim*).

In a globalizing world, then, the way to institutionalize social welfare as an aspect of development would be to express it as a social standard in relation to the economic standard and capacity of nations, e.g. measured by per capita income. Such standards could become something like a social charter for nations albeit adapted to economic capacity. The link with the economic standard would provide an automatic 'social escalator', in that as societies develop economically, their social standard of living rises in tandem. This would make for an upward harmonization in social standards instead of the slide to the bottom that we are witnessing with unregulated globalization today.

We turn next to the question of how these social standards are to be worked out in relation to the economic capacity of nations. Who will formulate these standards and what validity or legitimacy would the latter have? These are important questions and one needs to be able to move from broad principles to the specifics of social protection. We believe that in the last analysis it is social consensus that must indicate appropriate standards. However, other factors, e.g. the experience of other countries and expert opinion, are also relevant. Here the developing countries have an advantage in that they can learn – both positive and negative lessons – from the experience of more developed countries. Moreover the expertise and experience of agencies of the UN, the ILO and the plethora of non-governmental organizations (NGOs) involved with social development constitute a rich resource (Deacon et al., 1997; Doyal and Gough, 1991).

Let us, however, outline a possible approach to formulating the social standards of nations. The WB classifies countries into three broad groups: high, medium and low, in terms of per capita income. The middle income group is further divided into an upper and a lower tier (World Bank, 1997, pp. 206-7). These economic classifications provide a basis for formulating social standards. At the top end of the classification we have rich industrial ized countries, most of which already have sizeable welfare states. In such countries universal health care and educational provision, adequate income maintenance programmes to ensure a low to zero level of poverty, universal day care for pre-school children and adequate elder care constitute some of the elements of basic social standards. A basic social standard of this nature would, of course, require welfare 'laggards' such as the US to raise their standards while more advanced welfare states would simply need to maintain their current level of social provision.

At the other end of the scale in the WB's classification we have the very poor countries of Asia and sub-Saharan Africa. At this level of development primary health care, sanitation, safe drinking water, adequate nutrition and the like may constitute basic social standards.[2] Countries at a level of development between these extremes would have commensurate social standards. Although affordability and the feasibility of instituting social programmes would depend on the economic level of nations, there would naturally be some variation around the basic standard, with some countries preferring a higher social standard than the basic. Moreover, aid to economically disadvantaged countries could boost their resources and help them reach or exceed basic standards. At any rate, the aim here is not to work out a neat formula but to arrive at a standard which takes into account expert opinion, public opinion and the level of economic development.

It is important to note that public opinion on state welfare in Western industrial societies both reveals the significance of the social dimension and provides a basis for building social standards. [...] [O]ne of the remarkable facts about Western industrialized countries is the continuing popularity of social programmes with strong support for universal programmes such as health care and pensions. These attitudes are common to all Western nations and show remarkable persistence over time (Borre and Scarbrough, 1995; Cook and Barrett, 1992; Taylor-Gooby, 1994). Clearly here is a rock-solid case as well as a benchmark for the formulation of social standards. Indeed, it is no secret that citizens in general and interest groups in particular have been dogged in their defence of existing programmes and standards (Pierson, 1994; Esping-Andersen, 1996b). Some analysts see this as merely a selfish defence of entrenched interests that blocks necessary reform (Esping-Andersen, 1996b, pp. 265-7). There is some truth to this allegation, but to see nothing else in this phenomenon is to miss a vital point.

We would argue that widespread popular support for welfare state institutions and their defence points to something deeper and more fundamental which has not been sufficiently appreciated. It is an attempt on the part of the people to preserve communitarian institutions, i.e. institutions which provide a measure of social security, stability and solidarity and thus sustain a sense of a national community. It is a plea to retain and strengthen the 'social' alongside the economic and political aspects of national life.

But this popular preference for social standards is being set aside by governments on the grounds that the 'social' is unaffordable. Affordability refers to the fact that in a globalized economy, governments must be lean and mean. The competition to become more competitive, in short competitive austerity, means a downward slide in standards of social protection. What seems to be emerging as a result is a double deficit. First, there is a *democratic* deficit in that the popular will is being thwarted as national governments bow to the dictates of a global market place. There is also a loss of democratic control in that what is happening to social standards as a result of global competition is not what national governments, e.g. of the Left, necessarily want. Secondly, there is an emerging *social* deficit which is leading to social degradation and the loss of community. Clearly a principled and supranational defence of social standards is necessary as a complement to the national defence of social programmes. The redefinition of the social and the articulation of basic social standards for nations, sketched in outline above, could be the theoretical underpinning of such a defence. It could be helpful in a number of ways.

First, linking social standards broadly to economic standards could create a level playing field for economic competition and thus leave less scope for social dumping. Secondly, it could provide a 'social escalator', i.e. a built-in mechanism for upward harmonization of social standards. Thirdly, in so far as consensus already exists over social programmes in the population at large in industrialized countries, a social charter for rich countries can perhaps be drawn up without too much difficulty. And if accepted and implemented – or even endorsed with a plan of gradual implementation – it could greatly strengthen the case, as well as the moral argument, for demanding labour rights and other minimum standards (commensurate with the level of economic development) from less developed countries. Finally, the most immediate benefit could be to halt the downward slide of social standards in advanced industrial countries.

One of the issues raised by the idea of basic social standards is that of financing, in short, taxation. In the early 1990s taxes and contributions taken together accounted for just over 38 per cent of GDP (OECD, 1997, pp. 467) and social protection expenditure for around 22 per cent of GDP (OECD, 1994, pp. 58-61, Tables 1a, 1b, 1c) for the member countries of OECD as a whole. There is no reason why something close to these figures should not be an acceptable level of taxation and expenditure, respectively, in rich coun-tries. Indeed if rich nations are committed to maintaining social standards, then it is likely that they will also converge in their levels of taxation, thus creating tax harmonization and preventing a race to the bottom in taxation. In any case basic social standards leave the question of how the social welfare sector is to be organized and financed entirely open. So long as there is a commitment to maintaining basic standards, each country would be free to devise the means best suited for the purpose. These could, for example, range from direct state provision of benefits and services at one end to private provision mandated by the state at the other.

To sum up: the basic social standards approach would send the message that by all means, let nations, corporations and others compete in the global market place. But let them do so on the basis of an agreed set of social standards. These social standards must not be allowed to become a part of the competitive game but must form a part of the *rules* of the game. In other words if we must globalize, let it be in the form of a *regulated* rather than an *unregulated* globalization.

Supranational action on social policy

It is one thing to argue, in principle, the case for basic social standards for nations. It is quite another to be able to demonstrate its feasibility. Clearly the latter belongs to the political economy of transnational social welfare [...] [G]iven the absence of a global government or regulating authority, what are the prospects of basic social standards becoming a reality? In order to help to answer this question, it might be useful to survey briefly the current approaches and agencies involved – directly or indirectly – in the making of supranational social policy.

[...]

The residual approach to social policy

The exercise of economic surveillance and the power to grant loans and arrange financial assistance for developing countries give the IMF and the WB a great deal of influence over the economic and social policies of these countries. The structural adjustment programmes initiated in the 1980s, to which many developing countries have been subjected, are a prime example of this influence (Cornia et al., 1987). More recently, the former communist countries have been faced with similar conditionalities attached to the granting of loans and other economic assistance by these institutions (Deacon et al., 1997, pp. 101, 107). However, in the case of Western industrial nations it is largely by way of policy prescription, expert advice and general economic surveillance that global institutions such as the IMF and OECD influence social policy. Their policy prescriptions which require governments to reduce national debts and deficits mainly through slashing social expenditure and privatizing social welfare amount to the supranational steering of social policy in a neoliberal direction. The same could be said about the insistence that labour markets be made more 'flexible' by, inter alia, weakening the measures of social protection, e.g. unemployment benefits.

Policy advice, the dissemination of research reports and studies, and ministerial conferences form a part of the ideological persuasion involved in such a process. This transnational steering of policy weakens further the autonomy of nation states to chart their own course. By adding to the pressures emanating from financial and capital markets, these global institutions insulate national governments further from the demands of their electorate for social protection.

Yet these IGOs are not directly representative of or accountable to any elected authority. It is no secret that agencies such as the IMF and the WB are largely under the sway of the US, the leading economic power and financial contributor. This is not surprising, given that voting strength in these Bretton Woods institutions is based on the financial status and contribution of member states (Tester, 1992, pp. 137–8). The OECD too represents, by and large, the neoliberal economic orientation associated with the US. True, these agencies differ somewhat in their approach to social policy, e.g. the IMF tends to be the most hard-line neoliberal, the WB is less so, while the OECD shows a greater appreciation of the usefulness of European-style social welfare institutions (Deacon et al., 1997, p. 72, Chapter 3 *passim*). Overall, however, it is fair to say that these IGOs tend to see the institutions of social protection largely as a 'burden' – an impediment to economic development and the free functioning of market forces. Given their economistic approach – focused on deregulation and the extension of the market as the road to prosperity and growth – these IGOs see social policy largely in residual terms, i.e. as an adjunct to economic policies and objectives and one which should provide only a basic social safety net.

Social policy as human rights

The UN and its agencies and affiliates such as the ILO are involved in the formulation of transnational social policy from the standpoint of human rights. While the UN is concerned with the whole gamut of economic and social rights, the ILO focuses on the social protection of workers and the promotion of workers' rights.

The UN's International Covenant on Economic, Social and Cultural Rights (ICESCR), adopted in 1966, includes a comprehensive set of rights such as 'the right to work ... the right to an adequate standard of living ... the right to social security including social insurance ... [and the] right to just and favourable conditions of work', each of which is spelled out in considerable detail (Buergenthal, 1988, pp. 2-3). By the early 1990s over 100 countries had ratified the Covenant (Bilder, 1992, p. 10). Although ratification creates a legal obligation for states to comply, they are expected to implement these rights 'progressively' and 'to the maximum of [their] available resources' (Buergenthal, 1988, p. 44). These caveats turn the Covenant largely into a statement of principles and objectives endorsed by a ratifying country rather than a set of standards to be developed within a specified time-frame.

Significantly, the UN's approach to civil and political rights differs markedly from its approach to economic and social rights. Covenants concerned with the former have no exceptions or caveats. Signatories are expected to implement these rights to the full since they are essentially procedural in nature and do not entail the mobilization of material resources (Buergenthal, 1988, pp. 44-5). Implementation of economic and social rights on the other hand requires the mobilization and redistribution of material resources. Since member states differ widely in respect of economic capacity and other relevant circumstances, compliance with the ICESCR becomes difficult to monitor. Not surprisingly, member states are required to do little more than report on progress from time to time.

Despite its impressive scope, then, the ICESCR remains largely ineffective as an instrument for promoting social rights. First, signing of the Covenant is purely voluntary. Secondly, signing imposes few obligations on nations regarding implementation. Thirdly, while the UN recognizes that the *standards* (as distinct from the *principles*) of social protection which are entailed by economic and social rights cannot be universal and must depend on the level of economic development of a nation, it has not tried to articulate this relationship systematically. This is the problem which we have tried to address through the idea of basic social standards linked to the economic development and capacity of nations.

Among international agencies, the ILO is distinctive in its tripartite composition which represents governments, employers and workers. Membership of ILO is voluntary, although most countries belong. The ILO is concerned with protecting workers' rights and with improving the conditions of labour, interpreted somewhat widely (Swepston, 1992; Deacon et al., 1997, pp. 73-4). At its annual conferences Recommendations and Conventions are adopted on a wide variety of issues. For example by 1992 the ILO had more than 172 Conventions on its books with 5500 ratifications. It is concerned with such matters as workers' rights to organize, the prohibition of child labour, the health and safety of workplaces and social security, including pensions and medical care (Swepston, 1992, p. 100). Ratification of an ILO Convention by a member state makes it legally binding and members are expected to report regularly on compliance. Although the process is slow and cumbersome, the ILO does monitor the implementation of its Conventions. Through a complaint procedure and a machinery of investigation and reporting, it has achieved some success in securing compliance with ratified Conventions (ibid., pp. 100-108).

However, in common with the ICESCR of the UN, ILO Conventions are universal in form and come up against the fact that member states differ greatly in their level of economic, social and cultural development. The ILO has tried to deal with the problem of diversity through flexibility, e.g. by taking such differences into account in the implementation of the Conventions. For example the Social Security (Minimum Standards) Convention specifies that a ratifying state need adopt only three out of nine types of social security provision contained in it. The Convention also allows temporary exemptions for countries with 'insufficiently developed' economic and other resources (Otting, 1993, pp. 166-7).

Although the ILO does rather better than the UN in securing compliance with its Conventions, it suffers from similar limitations as an agency of international social protection. First, ratification of Conventions is voluntary. Second, although the complaint procedure and the possibility of investigation gives some teeth to ILO Conventions, in the last analysis compliance remains voluntary and thus largely a matter of persuasion. In principle the ILO can recommend sanctions against a recalcitrant member. However, in practice this has never happened. Third, as in the case of the UN's ICESCR, the ILO has recognized the problem of the differing economic capacity of nation states but has not attempted to link labour standards in any systematic way with levels of economic development. Finally, the ILO's remit, unlike that of the UN, is limited to employment-related matters and does not extend to problems of social protection of the population as a whole.

Trading regimes and social policy

Trade Unions in Western countries, notably in the US, have long sought to have a social clause concerned with minimal labour and human rights included in trading agreements with developing countries (Hansson, 1983, pp. 24-8). The principal motivation for the unions' demands for minimum labour rights from these countries has been to limit unfair competition and social dumping and thus to protect industries, jobs and standards in developed countries. This is not to deny that other concerns, notably promoting labour and social rights in developing countries, have also played a part. However the protectionist – and therefore self-serving – aspect of these labour clauses have made them a contentious and divisive issue between the North and

South (Deacon et al., 1997, pp. 77-8). The irony of American workers demanding labour and trade union rights for workers in the developing world at the very moment when they themselves are being denied these rights in their own country has not been lost on many commentators (for example Singh, 1988). Moreover critics have drawn attention to the silence of American unions on issues such as the structural adjustment policies of the World Bank and low commodity prices – policies backed by the US – which have had a devastating impact on living standards in many developing countries (ibid., p. 262).

A major limitation of the social clause approach is that it is largely concerned with the basic rights of workers, e.g. the right to organize and to bargain collectively, within the developing world. It has little to say about conditions in industrialized countries. In recent years American workers have succeeded in having a social clause included in some of the trade agreements between the US and developing countries, e.g. the Caribbean Basin Initiative. But the effectiveness of such measures remains unclear since much depends on their implementation and monitoring procedures (see Charnovitz, 1987, pp. 565, 572-4). Attempts to insert a social clause as a part of GATT (now WTO) agreements, and therefore to be applicable more widely, have not been successful so far, chiefly because of the opposition of developing countries.

The Free Trade Agreement signed by the US and Canada and later extended to Mexico through NAFTA provided an opportunity to complement the economic common market in North America with minimum social standards. However, the social dimension was virtually ignored. Later, pressure from labour and other groups opposed to NAFTA resulted in the signing of the North American Agreement on Labour Co-operation, which requires each member country to enforce its own labour laws and other social legislation. These so-called side deals have thus far proven rather ineffective. Moreover they do not create any supranational social or labour standards (Stanford et al., 1993, pp. 56-63). On the other hand NAFTA's deregulatory economic and trading clauses and its notion of a level playing field for competition are heavily weighted against the superior social provision of countries like Canada (see for example, Sanger, 1993; Sinclair, 1993). Indeed in Canada the downward harmonization of social provision has already begun. Given the lower levels of economic and social standards in the rest of the Americas, the prospect of a steep decline in Canada's system of social welfare remains very real.

The Social Charter (The Charter of the Fundamental Social Rights of Workers of the European Union) represents the only attempt so far to develop a set of supranational social standards within a regional economic association. The Charter was drawn up by the European Commission in 1989 in preparation for closer economic integration of member countries but also in response to demands for minimum social standards by European trade unions (Silvia, 1991; Rhodes, 1995, p. 96). Opposition on the part of employers and by one of the member states led to the watering down of the original proposals. The Charter, concerned with conditions of work and the social protection of workers is a 'solemn declaration' and not a legally binding instrument. Only some of its provisions, such as those concerned with health and safety and maternity leave (an aspect of gender equity within the work force) have so far been included in binding legislation based on a majority vote rather than unanimous agreement of member states (Ross, 1993, pp. 50-4).

Overall, the status of the Charter as a non-binding document – a declaration of principles and objectives only – came as a great disappointment for European labour and others concerned with social rights (Rhodes, 1995, pp. 96-7). Moreover, one of the principles endorsed by the Maastricht Treaty – a treaty for the monetary union of EU countries – is that of 'subsidiarity', i.e. wherever possible, social and other issues should be dealt with at the local or national rather than the community level. This leaves social policy largely within the scope of the nation state (Ross, 1993, p. 61; Rhodes, 1992, p. 35). On the other hand the principles of solidarity and social citizenship within the European Community have found much less acceptance (Streeck, 1995; Rhodes, 1995, p. 97) [...]. Moreover, globalization is tending to privilege 'flexibility' and deregulation of the labour market in Europe. Compared with NAFTA's meagre concern with labour standards, the European Social Charter looks impressive. In fact it is a relatively modest measure for the protection of workers. The prospect that it might develop into a wider network of social protection does not look very bright (Streeck, 1996; Pierson and Leibfried, 1995).

[...] [T]he Maastricht Treaty on European monetary union emphasizes the importance of reducing debt and deficit and controlling inflation. Nations must meet strict targets in respect of these in order to qualify for monetary union. It appears that of the two conflicting tendencies within Europe, namely liberalism and social collectivism, it is the former that is winning out for the moment (Streeck, 1996; Ross, 1995). True, there are other institutions and provisions in place in Europe, e.g. for the protection of human rights and for the reduction of regional economic and social disparity. Together with the Social Chapter of the Maastricht Treaty these amount to a social dimension in the European Union which is by no means insignificant (Deacon et al., 1997, pp. 80-84). It is important to note, however, that unlike NAFTA, the EU is much more than a trading bloc. It has been inspired by the vision of political as well as economic integration. The development of a stronger social dimension within Europe in the future cannot be ruled out although it looks unlikely at the moment.

Conclusions

Clearly progress toward the development of supranational social standards has been somewhat limited and uneven, more impressive in rhetoric and symbolism than in reality. The influence of the IGOs which have been steering social policy in a residual direction, i.e. towards deregulation and weakening of social protection, has so far been much stronger than that of those seeking to establish social rights. However, the UN, the ILO and the EU, each in its own way has made some progress in formulating, and implementing, labour and social rights across nations. Moreover the UN and its affiliates continue to provide a forum for global discourse on social and humanitarian issues and to help focus attention on problems of poverty, social protection and social justice from a supranational perspective. In recent years special conferences or 'summits' have been held on a variety of issues, e.g. Children (1990), Development (1992), Population (1994), Social Development (1995) and Women (1996). Deliberations and debates on these issues have been followed by proposals for global action.

Despite these and other initiatives discussed earlier, social policy has remained essentially a national concern. The main reasons for limited progress in developing effective transnational social protection are two-fold: first, the absence of global institutions of governance with the authority to formulate binding standards and to ensure their implementation. The second and a related point is that although the important difference between civil and political rights on the one hand and economic and social rights on the other has been recognized, the implications of this difference have not been worked out. As we have argued above, to be viable social rights (or as we have argued, social standards) must be formulated in relation to the level of economic development. Otherwise they are likely to remain abstract principles with little purchase on socio-economic reality.

Although the task of spelling out the link between social standards and economic development is not easy, it is essential for making progress in developing basic social standards applicable globally. However, the first and by far the most difficult problem still remains. In the absence of an international government with democratic authority and accountability, social standards have to rely on voluntary compliance. But voluntarism is likely to be even less effective than in the past because of globalization. The Covenants and Conventions we reviewed above were developed at a time when it was almost conventional wisdom that social standards of nations must rise alongside economic growth. The relation between the two was seen as positive.

We are now in a situation where the economic growth of nations is seen as predicated upon lowering rather than raising social standards. The benign assumptions underlying the long-term, evolutionary perspective of an upward harmonization of standards have little validity today. Social standards in advanced industrial countries are sliding downwards and international action is needed to stop the process.

But what form might it take? And what are its chances of succeeding? The main problem here is that those conditions and social forces which made *national* welfare states possible, e.g. the existence of a state with legitimate authority for rule-making and rule-enforcement, electoral competition and representative government, strong industrial action and protest movements threatening the economic and social stability of nations, nationalism and nation-building imperatives, are unavailable at the international level. Moreover, globalization is disempowering citizens within the nation state as far as social rights are concerned without providing them with any leverage globally. At the same time transnational corporations and the global market place have been empowered hugely through financial deregulation and capital mobility.

In these circumstances prospects for global action on social protection do not look very encouraging. However, in a rudimentary form some of the elements which made the development of social standards possible nationally, are also present at the international level. These could form a nucleus around which further action in support of basic social standards might develop. Let us look at them briefly.

First, movement towards global governance and towards the reform of existing IGOs – including the Bretton Woods institutions – has been slowly gathering momentum (Commission on Global Governance, 1995; Deacon et al., 1997, pp. 89, 205-9). The need to make IGOs more representative, democratic, accountable and efficient is beginning to be recognized. Second, the division of policy-making into economic (Bretton Woods) and non-economic IGOs (UN, ILO) with little co-ordination between the two is acknowledged to be unsatisfactory and in need of reform (Deacon et al., 1997, pp. 207-8). Agencies such as the WB and even the IMF are beginning to acknowledge the importance of the 'social' dimension in development (Deacon et al., 1997, pp. 64, 68-70). Third, and more important, as globalization drives more and more nations into adopting policies of 'competitive austerity', national protest movements against cutbacks and social retrenchment are springing up in many countries. It is not too fanciful to suggest that they might coalesce into an international protest movement in defence of social programmes and standards, for example in OECD countries. Fourth, the 'global civil society' – made up of a wide variety of NGOs, churches and social movements is emerging as a player closely involved with global issues of the environment, development and social justice (ibid., pp. 211-12; Commission on Global Governance, 1995, pp. 253-60). Although somewhat amorphous and lacking in power, global civil society is contributing to a global discourse on social and environmental issues and seems to be growing in influence.

Finally, as Marx, Polanyi and other thinkers have emphasized, sooner or later an unregulated market economy wreaks economic and social havoc. We noted earlier that the unrestricted flow of money around the world has started destabilizing economies and is threatening to plunge the world into a severe recession. Other disequilibria and contradictions of global capitalism, e.g. lack of consumer demand, social unrest, and the weakening of democracy could intensify and compel global regulation. The question is whether we will wait for disaster to strike or forestall such possibilities through appropriate economic and social regulation. The basic belief underlying the argument for international action advanced here is that lessons of history should not be forgotten and that if we deregulate at the national level we could complement that with reregulation at the supranational level. For example a Multinational Agreement on Social Standards (MASS) could parallel the proposed Multinational Agreement on Investment (MAI).[3]

In sum, basic social standards could be an important focal point for regulating the global market economy. Their *raison d'être* would be to preserve the integrity of local and national communities and provide a level playing field for international competition. In this way it might be possible to preserve and/or build that integration between economic and social sectors which is perhaps the most important legacy of the post-WW2 welfare state. At any rate, basic social standards – applicable globally – are of the utmost importance today in that they can provide a degree of stability and continuity for human communities in the context of global economic competition and technological change.

Notes

[1] Procedural rights such as freedom of speech and association, and the right to due processes of law do not essentially require the mobilization or distribution of material resources. They rely on procedural action on the part of the state or other agents, e.g. forbearance. Substantive rights such as the right to an adequate income in retirement or the right to medical care on the other hand require the mobilization and/or redistribution of resources.

[2] An example of linking health goals with levels of economic development is provided by World Health Organization. See Doyal and Gough (1991, p. 240).

[3] The MAI has been shelved as a result of international mobilization against it and the failure of OECD countries to reach agreement on a number of key issues. Broadly similar objectives are now being pursued through the Transatlantic Economic Partnership (TEP) and the Millennium Round of the WTO.

References

Andrews, G. (ed.) (1991) *Citizenship*, London, Lawrence and Wishart.

Barbalet, J.M. (1988) *Citizenship*, Milton Keynes, Open University Press.

Barry, B. (1990) *Welfare*, Milton Keynes, Open University Press.

Bilder, B. (1992) 'Overview of International Human Rights Law', in Hannum, H. (ed.) *Guide to International Human Rights*, 2nd edn, Philadelphia, University of Philadelphia Press.

Borre, O. and Scarborough, E. (eds.) (1995) *The Scope of Government*, New York, Oxford University Press.

Buergenthal, T. (1988) *International Human Rights in a Nutshell*, St Paul, MN, West Publishing.

Charnovitz, S. (1987) 'The Influence of International Labour Standards on the World Trading Regime: a Historical Overview', *International Labour Review*, 126(5).

Commission on Global Governance (1995) *Our Global Neighbourhood*, Oxford, Oxford University Press.

Cook, F.L. and Barrett, E.J. (1992) *Support for the American Welfare State*, New York, Columbia University Press.

Cornia, G.A. et al. (1987) *Adjustment with a Human Face*, 2 vols, Oxford, Clarendon Press.

Deacon, B. et al. (1997) *Global Social Policy*, London, Sage.

Doyal, L. and Gough, I. (1991) *A Theory of Human Need*, London, Macmillan.

Espada, J.C. (1996) *Social Citizenship Rights: A Critique of F.A. Hayek and Raymond Plant*, London, Macmillan.

Esping-Andersen, G. (1996a) 'After the Golden Age? Welfare State Dilemmas in a Global Economy', in Esping-Andersen, G. (ed.) *Welfare States in Transition*, London, Sage.

Esping-Andersen, G. (1996b) 'Positive-Sum Solutions in a World of Tradeoffs?' in Esping-Andersen, G. (ed.) *Welfare States in Transition*, London, Sage.

Goodman, R. and Peng, I. (1996) 'The East Asian Welfare States', in Esping-Andersen, G. (ed.) *Welfare States in Transition*, London, Sage.

Hansson, G. (1983) *Social Clauses and International Trade*, Beckenham, Croom Helm.

Jones, C. (1993) 'The Pacific Challenge: Confucian Welfare States' in Jones, C. (ed.) *New Perspectives on the Welfare State in Europe*, London, Routledge.

Marshall, T.H. (1950) *Citizenship and Social Class and other Essays*, Cambridge, Cambridge University Press.

Midgley, J. (1997) *Social Welfare in Global Context*, Thousand Oaks, CA, Sage.

Mishra, R. (1977) *Society and Social Policy*, London, Macmillan.

OECD (1994) *Social Policy Studies No. 2: New Orientations for Social Policy*, Paris.

OECD (1997) 'OECD in Figures' (Supplement to *The OECD Observer*, 206).

Otting, A. (1993) 'International labour standards: a framework for social security', *International Labour Review*, 132(2).

Pierson, P. (1994) *Dismantling the Welfare State?* Cambridge, Cambridge University Press.

Pierson, P. and Leibfried, S. (1995) 'The Dynamics of Social Policy Integration', in Leibfried, S. and Pierson, P. (eds) *European Social Policy*, Washington DC, The Brookings Institution.

Plant, R., Lesser, H., and Taylor-Gooby, P. (1980) *Political Philosophy and Social Welfare*, London, Routledge.

Rhodes, M. (1992) 'The Future of the "social dimension" labour market regulations in post-1992 Europe', *Journal of Common Market Studies*, 30(1).

Rhodes, M. (1995) 'A regulatory conundrum: industrial relations and the social dimension' in Leibfried, S. and Pierson, P. (eds) *European Social Policy*, Washington DC, The Brookings Institution.

Roche, M. (1992) *Rethinking Citizenship*, Cambridge, Polity.

Ross, G. (1993) 'Social Policy in the New Europe', *Studies in Political Economy*, 40.

Ross, G. (1995) 'Assessing the Delors Era and Social Policy' in Leibfried, S. and Pierson, P. (eds.) *European Social Policy*, Washington, DC, The Brookings Institution.

Sanger, M. (1993) 'Public Services' in Cameron, D. and Watkins, M. (eds) *Canada Under Free Trade*, Toronto, James Lorimer.

Silvia, S.J. (1991) 'The Social Charter of the European Community: A Defeat for European Labour', *Industrial and Labour Relations Review*, 44(4).

Sinclair, S. (1993) 'Provincial Powers' in Cameron, D. and Watkins, M. (eds) *Canada Under Free Trade*, Toronto, James Lorimer.

Singh, A. (1988) 'Southern Competition, Labour Standards and Industrial Development in the North and South' in Herzenberg, S. and Perez-Lopez, J.F. (eds.) *Labour Standards and Development in the Global Economy*, Washington, DC, US Department of Labor, Bureau of International Affairs.

Stanford, J. et al. (1993) *Social Dumping under North American Free Trade*, Ottawa, Centre for Policy Alternatives.

Streeck, W. (1995) 'From Market Making to State Building? Reflections on the Political Economy of European Social Policy', in Leibfried, S. and Pierson, P. (eds) *European Social Policy*, Washington, DC, The Brookings Institution.

Streeck, W. (1996) 'Public Power Beyond the Nation-State', in Boyer, R. and Drache, D. (eds) *States against Markets*, London, Routledge.

Swepston, L. (1992) 'Human Rights Complaint Procedures of the International Labour Organization' in Hannum, H. (ed.) *Guide to International Human Rights*, 2nd edn, Philadelphia, University of Philadelphia Press.

Taylor-Gooby, P. (1994) 'Taxing Time', *New Statesman and Society*, 2 December.

Tester, F.J. (1992) 'The Disenchanted Democracy: Canada in the Global Economy of the 1990's', *Canadian Review of Social Policy*, 29(30).

Turner, B.S. (1986) *Citizenship and Capitalism*, London, Allen and Unwin.

World Bank (1997) *World Development Report*, New York, Oxford University Press.

Chapter 5.7

Deglobalization: ideas for a new world economy

Walden Bello

The crisis that is wrenching the current system of global economic governance is a systemic one. It is not one that can be addressed by mere adjustments within the system, for these would be merely marginal in their impact or they might merely postpone a bigger crisis. [...]

[...] Breaking with the past is a far more complicated affair when it comes to global economic governance. In social change, new systems cannot really be effectively constructed without weakening the hold of old systems, which do not take fundamental challenges to their hegemony lightly. A crisis of legitimacy is critical in weakening current structures, but it is not enough. A vision of a new world may be entrancing, but it will remain a vision without a hard strategy for realizing it, and part of that strategy is the deliberate dismantling of the old.

Thus a strategy of *deconstruction* must necessarily proceed alongside one of *reconstruction*.

Deconstruction

The big anti-corporate globalization demonstrations of the last few years have been right in bringing up the strategic demand of dismantling the WTO and the Bretton Woods institutions. Advancing this demand and getting more and more people behind it has been central in creating the crisis of legitimacy of these institutions.

Tactically, however, it would be important to try to bring coalitions together on more broadly acceptable goals, the achievement of which can nevertheless have a big impact in terms of drastically reducing the power of these institutions or effectively neutering them. In the case of the IMF, for instance, a demand that has potential to unite a broad front of people is that of converting it into a research agency with no policy powers but one tasked with the job of monitoring global capital and exchange rate movements – in other words turning it into an advisory and research institution along the lines of the Organisation for Economic Co-operation and Development (OECD).

In the case of the World Bank, uniting with the demand to end its loan-making capacity and devolving its grant activities to appropriate regional institutions marked by participatory processes (which would eliminate the Asian Development and other existing regional development banks as alternatives) could serve as a point of unity for diverse political forces and be a major step to effectively disempowering it. These initiatives could be coordinated with campaigns to boycott World Bank bonds, deny new appropriations for the International Development Association (IDA), and oppose calls for quota increases for the IMF. Unlike the Soros approach, the thrust of this multi-dimensional effort would be not one of reforming but drastically shrinking the power and jurisdiction of the Bretton Woods institutions.

Given its centrality and unique characteristics as a global institution, however, it is the WTO that must be the main target of the deconstruction enterprise. It is especially critical in the period leading up to the Fifth Ministerial Meeting of this most powerful of the multilateral agencies of global governance.

The strategy of the deconstruction enterprise must respond to the needs of the moment in the struggle against corporate-driven globalization. This can be derived only by identifying the strategic objective, accurately assessing the global context or conjuncture, and elaborating an effective strategy and tactical repertoire that responds to the particularities of the conjuncture.

For the movement against corporate-driven globalization, it seems fairly clear that the strategic goal must be halting or reversing WTO-mandated liberalization in trade and trade-related areas. The context or 'conjuncture' is characterized by a fragile victory on the part of the free trade globalizers at the Fourth Ministerial at Doha, where they bludgeoned developing countries into agreeing to a limited round of trade talks for more liberalization on agriculture, services and industrial tariffs. The conjuncture is marked by the globalizers' effort to build momentum so as to have the Fifth Ministerial in Mexico launch negotiations for liberalization in the so-called trade-related areas of investment, competition policy, government procurement and trade facilitation. *Their aim is to have the Fifth Ministerial expand the limited set of negotiations they extracted at Doha into a comprehensive round of negotiations that would rival the Uruguay Round.*

This expansion of the free trade mandate and the expansion of the power and jurisdiction of the WTO, which is now the most powerful multilateral instrument of the global corporations, is a mortal threat to development, social justice and equity, and the environment. And it is the goal that we must thwart at all costs, for we might as well kiss goodbye to sustainable development, social justice, equity and the environment if the big trading powers and their corporate elites have their way and launch another global round for liberalization during the WTO's Fifth Ministerial Assembly in Mexico in 2003.

Given the strategic goal of stopping and reversing trade liberalization, the campaign objective on which the movement against corporate-driven globalization must focus its efforts and energies is simple and stark: derailing the drive for free trade at the Fifth Ministerial, which will serve as the key global mechanism for advancing free trade.

[...] [T]he free trade partisan C. Fred Bergsten, head of the Institute of International Economics (IIE), has compared free trade and the WTO to a bicycle: they collapse if they do not move forward. Which is why Seattle was such a mortal threat to the WTO and why the globalizers were so determined to extract a mandate for liberalization at Doha. Had they failed at Doha, the likely prospect was not simply a stalemate but a retreat from free trade. For the movement against corporate-driven globalization, derailing the Fifth Ministerial or preventing agreement on the launching of a new comprehensive round would mean not only fighting the WTO and free trade to a standstill. It would mean creating momentum for a rollback of free trade and a reduction of the power of the WTO. This is well understood by, among others, *The Economist*, which warned its corporate readers that 'globalization is reversible'.

If derailing the drive for free trade at the 5th Ministerial is indeed the goal, then the main tactical focus of the strategy becomes clear: *consensus decision-making is the Achilles' heel of the WTO, and it is the emergence of consensus that we must prevent at all costs from emerging.*

Before the Fifth Ministerial, the anti-corporate globalization movement must focus its energy on ensuring that countries do not come into agreement in any of the areas now being negotiated or about to be negotiated, that is, agriculture, services and industrial tariffs; and at the Ministerial itself, preventing any consensus from emerging on negotiating the new issues of government procurement, competition policy, investment and trade facilitation. The aim must be, as in Seattle, to have the delegates go to the Ministerial with a 'heavily bracketed' declaration – that is, one where there is no consensus on the key issues – and at the Ministerial itself, to prevent consensus via last-minute horse-trading. *As in Seattle, the end goal must be to have the Ministerial end in disagreement and lack of consensus.*

If the goal is unhinging the game plan for greater free trade at the Fifth Ministerial, then the anti-corporate globalization movement has its work cut out for it. We must unfold a multi-pronged strategy whose components must include:

- unravelling the alliance between US Trade Representative Robert Zoellick and EU Trade Commissioner Pascal Lamy by exacerbating the US–EU conflict on Europe's agricultural subsidies, the Bush administration's failure to obtain unrestricted fast-track authority to negotiate from the USA's Senate, Washington's imposition of protective tariffs on steel and its resurgent trade unilateralism, and the US export of hormone-treated beef and genetically modified organisms (GMOs);

• intensifying our efforts to assist developing country delegations in Geneva to master the WTO process and formulate effective strategies to block the emergence of consensus on the areas prioritized by the trading powers and reassert the priority of implementation issues;

• working with national movements, such as peasant movements for food sovereignty in the South and citizens' movements in the North, to build massive pressure on their governments not to agree to further liberalization in agriculture, services, and other areas being negotiated;

• skilfully co-ordinating global protests, mass street action at the site of the ministerial, and lobby work in Geneva to create a global critical mass with momentum in the lead-up to the ministerial.

The task is immense and we have so little time. But we have no choice. The trading powers and the WTO learned from Seattle, and they brought the bicycle of the WTO back on its wheels in Doha. Likewise, we must learn from Doha so that we can wrestle the bicycle back to the ground in Mexico. And among the key lessons we need to absorb is that our coalition must have a co-ordinated strategy that brings our work on many different fronts, levels and dimensions to bear on one goal: unhinging the drive for free trade at the Fifth Ministerial.

Deglobalizing in a pluralist world

Hand in hand with the deconstruction campaign must unfold the reconstruction process or the enterprise to set up an alternative system of global governance.

There is a crying need for an alternative system of global governance. The idea is floating around that thinking about an alternative system of global governance is a task that for the most part is still in a primeval state. In fact, many or most of the basic or broad principles for an alternative order have already been articulated, *and it is really a question of specifying these broad principles to concrete societies in ways that respect the diversity of societies.*

Work on alternatives has been a collective past and present effort, one to which many in the North and South have contributed. The key points of this collective effort might be synthesized as a double movement of 'deglobalization' of the national economy and the construction of a 'pluralist system of global economic governance'.

The context for the discussion of deglobalization is the increasing evidence not only of the poverty, inequality and stagnation that have accompanied the spread of globalized systems of production but also of their unsustainability and fragility. The International Forum on Globalization (IFG) points out, for instance, that

> the average plate of food eaten in western industrial food-importing nations is likely to have travelled 2,000 miles from source to plate. Each one of those miles contributes to the environmental and social crises of our times. Shortening the distance between producer and consumer has to be one of the crucial reform goals of any transition away from industrial agriculture.[1]

Or as Barry Lynn has asserted, so much industrial production has been outsourced to a few areas such as Taiwan, that, had the earthquake of September 21, 1999 experienced by that island been 'a few tenths of a point stronger, or centered a few miles closer to the vital Hsinchu industrial park, great swaths of the world economy could have been paralyzed for months'.[2]

What is deglobalization? While the following proposal is derived principally from the experience of societies in the South, it has relevance as well to the economies of the North.

Deglobalization is not about withdrawing from the international economy. It is about reorienting economies from the emphasis on production for export to production for the local market.

- drawing most of a country's financial resources for development from within rather than becoming dependent on foreign investment and foreign financial markets;
- carrying out the long-postponed measures of income redistribution and land redistribution to create a vibrant internal market that would be the anchor of the economy and create the financial resources for investment;
- de-emphasizing growth and maximizing equity in order radically to reduce environmental disequilibrium;
- not leaving strategic economic decisions to the market but making them subject to democratic choice;
- subjecting the private sector and the state to constant monitoring by civil society;
- creating a new production and exchange complex that includes community co-operatives, private enterprises and state enterprises, and excludes TNCs;
- enshrining the principle of subsidiarity in economic life by encouraging production of goods to take place at the community and national level if it can be done at reasonable cost in order to preserve community.

This is, moreover, about an approach that consciously subordinates the logic of the market, the pursuit of cost efficiency, to the values of security, equity and social solidarity. This is, to use the language of the great social democratic scholar Karl Polanyi, about re-embedding the economy in society, rather than having society driven by the economy.[3]

True, efficiency in the narrow terms of constant reduction of unit costs may well suffer, but what will be gained – or perhaps the most appropriate term is regained – are the conditions for the development of integrity, solidarity, community, greater and more democracy, and sustainability.

It is these principles that today drive many bold enterprises that have achieved some success, mainly at a local, community level. As Kevin Danaher of Global Exchange has pointed out, the list includes fair trade arrangements between Southern farmers and Northern consumers in coffee and other commodities, micro-credit schemes such as the Grameen Bank, community currency systems delinking exchange from global and national monetary systems and linking it to local production and consumption, participatory budgeting as in Porto Alegre, and sustainable eco-communities such as Gaviotas in Colombia.[4]

The reigning god, however, is a jealous one that will not take lightly challenges to its hegemony. Even the smallest experiment must either be smashed or emasculated, as the imperious Bank of Thailand did when it told several villages in the Kud Chum district in Thailand's Northeast region to abandon their local currency system. Peaceful co-existence between different systems is, unfortunately, ultimately not an option.

Thus deglobalization or the re-empowerment of the local and national, however, can only succeed if it takes place within an alternative system of global economic governance. The emergence of such a system is, of course, dependent on greatly reducing the power of the Western corporations that are the main drivers of globalization and the political and military hegemony of the states – particularly the United States – that protect them. But even as we devise strategies to erode the power of the corporations and the dominant states, we need to envision and already lay the groundwork for an alternative system of global economic governance.

What are the contours of such a world economic order? The answer to this is suggested by our critique of the Bretton Woods-cum-WTO system as a monolithic system of universal rules imposed by highly centralized institutions to further the interests of corporations – and, in particular, US corporations. To try to supplant this with another centralized global system of rules and institutions, although these may be premised on different principles, is likely to reproduce the same Jurassic trap that ensnared organizations as different as IBM, the IMF and the Soviet state, and this is the inability to tolerate and profit from diversity. Incidentally, the idea that the need for one central set of global rules is unquestionable and that the challenge is to replace the neoliberal rules with social democratic ones is a remnant of a techno–optimist variant of Marxism that infuses both the Social Democratic and Leninist visions of the world, producing what Indian author Arundhati Roy calls the predilection for 'gigantism'.

Today's need is not another centralized global institution but the deconcentration and decentralization of institutional power and the creation of a pluralistic system of institutions and organizations interacting with one another, guided by broad and flexible agreements and understandings.

This is not something completely new. For it was under such a more pluralistic system of global economic governance, where hegemonic power was still far from institutionalized in a set of all-encompassing and powerful multilateral organizations and institutions, that a number of Latin American and Asian countries were able to achieve a modicum of industrial development in the period from 1950 to 1970. It was under such a pluralistic system, under a General Agreement on Tariffs and Trade (GATT) that was limited in its power, flexible and more sympathetic to the special status of developing countries, that the East and South-east Asian countries were able to become newly industrializing countries through activist state trade and industrial policies that departed significantly from the free market biases enshrined in the WTO.

Of course, economic relations among countries prior to the attempt to institutionalize one global free market system beginning in the early 1980s were not ideal, nor were the Third World economies that resulted ideal. They failed to address a number of needs illuminated by recent advances in feminist, ecological and post-post-development economics. What is simply being pointed out is that the pre-1994 situation underlines the fact that the alternative to an economic Pax Romana built around the World Bank–IMF–WTO system is not a Hobbesian state of nature. The reality of international relations in a world marked by a multiplicity of international and regional institutions that check one another is a far cry from the propaganda image of a 'nasty' and 'brutish' world the partisans of the WTO evoked in order to stampede the developing country governments to ratify the WTO in 1994.

Of course, the threat of unilateral action by the powerful is ever present in such a system, but it is one that even the most powerful hesitate to take for fear of its consequences on their legitimacy as well as the reaction it would provoke in the form of opposing coalitions.

In other words, what developing countries and international civil society should aim at is not to reform the TNC-driven WTO and Bretton Woods institutions, but, through a combination of passive and active measures, to either a) decommission them; b) neuter them (e.g., converting the IMF into a pure research institution monitoring exchange rates of global capital flows); or c) radically reduce their powers and turn them into just another set of actors co-existing with and being checked by other international organizations, agreements and regional groupings. This strategy would include strengthening diverse actors and institutions such as UNCTAD, multilateral environmental agreements, the International Labor Organization and regional economic blocs.

Regional economic blocs in the South would be important actors in this process of economic devolution. But they would have to be developed beyond their current manifestations in the European Union, Mercosur in Latin America and ASEAN (Association of Southeast Asian Nations) in Southeast Asia.

A key aspect of 'strengthening', of course, is making sure these formations evolve in a people-oriented direction and cease to remain regional elite projects. Trade efficiency in neoclassical economic terms should be supplanted as the key criterion of union by 'capacity building'. That is, trade would have to be reoriented from its present dynamics of locking communities and countries into a division of labour that diminishes their capabilities in the name of 'comparative advantage' and 'interdependence'. It must be transformed into a process that enhances the capacities of communities, that ensures that initial cleavages that develop owing to initial division-of-labour agreements do not congeal into permanent cleavages, and which has mechanisms, including income, capital, and technology-sharing arrangements that prevent exploitative arrangements from developing among trading communities.

Needless to say, the formation of such regional blocs must actively involve not only government and business but also NGOs and people's organizations. Indeed, the agenda of people-oriented sustainable development can succeed only if it is evolved democratically rather than imposed from above by regional elites, as was the case with the European Union, Mercosur and ASEAN. Regional integration has increasingly become an essential condition for national development, but it can be effective only if it is carried out as a project of economic union from below.

Many of the elements of a pluralist system of global economic governance already exist, but there are undoubtedly others that need to be established. Here the emphasis must be on the formation of international and regional institutions that would be dedicated to creating and protecting the space for devolving the greater part of production, trade and economic decision-making to the regional, national and community level. One such institution is the establishment of an effective international organization for the preservation and strengthening of the economies of the hundreds of thousands of indigenous economies throughout the world.

Indeed, a central role of international organizations in a world where toleration of diversity is a central principle of economic organization would be, as the British philosopher John Gray puts it, 'to express and protect local and national cultures by embodying and sheltering their distinctive practices'.[5]

More space, more flexibility, more compromise – these should be the goals of the Southern agenda and the international civil society effort to build a new system of global economic governance. It is in such a more fluid, less structured, more pluralistic world, with multiple checks and balances, that the nations and communities of the South – and the North – will be able to carve out the space to develop based on their values, their rhythms, and the strategies of their choice.

Notes

[1] John Cavanagh et al., 'Alternatives to Economic Globalization', International Forum on Globalization, San Francisco.

[2] Barry Lynn, 'Unmade in America: The True Cost of a Global Assembly Line', *Harper's*, June 2002, p. 36.

[3] See Karl Polanyi, *The Great Transformation* (Boston: Beacon, 1957).

[4] Speech at the University of Montana, Missoula, Montana, June 16, 2002.

[5] John Gray, *Enlightenment's Wake* (London: Routledge, 1995), p. 181.

Chapter 5.8

Globalisation, regional integration and social policy

Nicola Yeates and Bob Deacon

This chapter establishes the case for strengthened regional social policy as a necessary element of effective global social governance. The discussion is organised around four main sections. First [...], we set out the context of a research and policy focus on regional social policy, rehearsing arguments about the possible impacts of existing forms of globalisation upon *national* social policy on the one hand and the difficulties of securing a *global* social contract with effective global social policies on the other. We then proceed to set out [...] the case in principle for a *regional* social policy; several advantages of regional social policy and regional social integration are identified. The next section [...] elaborates possible social policy mechanisms along the axes of regional social redistribution, regional social regulation and regional social rights and elaborates idealised examples of regional standard-setting, regional policy coordination and regional identity mobilisation. [The final section] considers some of the challenges and issues for advocates of regional social policy.

The limits of global social policy

The global system that has emerged in the opening years of the 21st century has generated a vigorous debate amongst scholars, policy-makers and activists about how to preserve existing, and develop new, policies that adequately provide for the social needs of populations. Much of the context and impetus for this debate stems from the Northern-driven neo-liberal social experiments of the 1980s and 1990s that supported increased global production, global trade and the global delivery of a wide range of goods and services to respond to the preferences and demands of an expanding global consumer market. This strategy encouraged increased commercialisation, informalisation and privatisation of welfare services to meet unmet social needs more cost-effectively, and involved lighter touch social regulation conducive to a more flexible economic environment. The dynamics unleashed by these policies are manifesting themselves in the welfare arena: national social contracts are being undermined by welfare states being set in competition with each other and the creation of global

467

health and welfare markets. Extant systems of public service provision are less able to respond to social needs, and the idea of comprehensive public services is under threat. Overall, it has been clear that the supposed opportunities that such experiments were designed to create have been unevenly distributed; furthermore, they have created new and widespread social risks for populations as a whole, increasing the incidence of poverty and exacerbating social inequality, polarisation and conflict.

Growing concerns with the negative and widespread social consequences of neo-liberal 'free' trade-driven globalisation is feeding alternative global social imaginaries. Increasingly, attention is turning to address the kinds of systems and policies necessary for a socially-just globalisation, one that maximises the satisfaction of human needs of everyone, irrespective of their country of origin or residence, or their social background and position. One response to a perceived threat to public social provision at the national level has been to argue for more coherent trans-national cooperation and coordination. One expression of trans-national social policy involves *global* redistribution, regulation and social rights, involving reformed global institutions with 'teeth' and capable of tackling global social problems. One version of this global social reform agenda involves a strengthened UN-based global social governance, giving more powers to the Economic and Social Council (ECOSOC), as a means of curtailing the global influence of the World Bank. Another version involves more extended inter-organisational co-operation and policy dialogue between the Bank and UN agencies, as advocated by the ILO-sponsored World Commission on the Social Dimension of Globalisation which reported in 2004 (Deacon, 2007). Yet another would build upon the G20 as a more representative gathering of countries and strengthen it with a permanent secretariat (ODI, 2009).

However, formidable obstacles are involved. Many governments and non-governmental bodies in the Global North and Global South alike are unsure about the appropriateness of a Northern-driven reformed globalisation strategy imposing 'inappropriate' global social and labour standards, while many actors in the South are reluctant to buy into even the more progressive forms of conditionality. For some in the Global South (Keet and Bello, 2004; Bello, 2004) the point is not so much to reform and strengthen extant 'global' institutions that are controlled by and operate in the interests of the North, but to undermine and outflank them by creating new countervailing and pluralistic sources of power properly serving the interests of the Global South:

> [W]hat developing countries and international civil society should aim at is not to reform the TNC-driven WTO and Bretton Woods institutions, but ... [a strategy that] would include strengthening diverse actors and institutions such as UNCTAD, multilateral

environmental agreements, the International Labour Organization and regional economic blocs. (Bello, 2004: 116-117)

As this quote suggests, it is here that the construction and strengthening of regional organisations of countries enter the picture. Rather than seeking to develop a case for a *global social policy of redistribution, regulation and rights* that would also imply a strengthening of Northern-based and -controlled institutions, or to seek to win the Bretton Woods institutions over to a European progressive perspective on social policy so that the World Bank and the UN concur on the advice to national governments about the best social policies, the point should be to liberate a policy space where Southern governments and civil society can make their own policy choices. Thus, the focus should perhaps be on building several *regionally-based social policies of redistribution, regulation and rights* as part of a more general strategy of global economic governance based on economic devolution (Bello, 2004: 117). Thus, reforming global social governance should perhaps imply building a world federation of regions, in which the role of international organisations is 'to express and protect local and national cultures by embodying and sheltering their distinctive practices' (John Gray, 2002, cited in Bello, 2004: 118).

International civil society and several emerging trading blocks and other regional associations in the South are showing signs of concretely engaging with this regionalist global governance reform agenda. They are confronting key policy questions such as: how to forge an appropriately balanced relationship between trade and social (labour, welfare, health) standards? How to maintain levels of taxation and progressive tax structures in the face of international competition to attract and maintain inward capital investment? And how to balance national risk- and resource-pooling systems and mechanisms with regional ones? In the next part of this chapter we turn our attention to the principles of and arguments in favour of forging a social policy dimension of regional integration.

The advantages of regional cooperation and social policy

There are several potential advantages to countries of building a social policy dimension to regional groupings of countries. In this section we first set out these advantages in principle and relate them to current examples. These include a) creating a stronger voice in international negotiations and agreements; b) stronger protection from global market forces; and c) international economies of scale and risk pooling. We then proceed to discuss some of the ways in which the case for strengthened regional social policy is being taken up by global commissions and agencies.

In terms of *a stronger voice in international negotiations* since regional formations often entail groups of countries with similar (or at least less diverse) cultural, legal and political characteristics and legacies, agreement on the scope and nature of collaboration may be more feasible and progress can potentially be made more quickly compared with global multilateral negotiations involving a wide diversity of countries. Because of this greater similarity, regional formations can offer countries access to a broader menu of policy alternatives (Yeates, 2005). For smaller and developing countries in particular, regional formations offer enhanced access to and influence over policy developments (Yeates, 2005). In the EU, for example, small countries can have a strong blocking effect on the development of social policy. These national influences on regional formations are not necessarily negative: more socially-developed countries can force upwards social standards in the poorer members of that formation. Regional formations offer further advantages to countries within global multilateral negotiations and fora: by having earlier consultations and building common positions, regional formations offer significant advantages to countries within global multilateral negotiations and fora, namely avoiding rushed decisions, amplifying their voicing of regional circumstances and positions. Finally, given the aforementioned difficulties involved in the forging of global multilateral standards, regional formations might give countries especially those in the South a stronger voice to advance their own social standards and at a faster rate than would be possible through global fora (Yeates, 2005).

In terms of *protection from global market forces* in addition to grouped countries having a louder voice in the global discourse on economic and social policy in UN and other fora, such an approach affords protection from global market forces that might erode national social entitlements. Regional formations also offer a means of 'locking in' internationalising flows of finance and production and labour on a regional basis. Regionalist trading strategies are an effective means of protecting, promoting and reshaping a regional division of labour, trade and production. Nurturing and protecting internationalising trade flows enables fiscal resources to be generated for national and regional social policy purposes. Too often global trade comes with tax exemptions for local and global companies that erode such fiscal resources. At the same time Southern regional formations can become a 'transmission belt' that receives increased Overseas Development Assistance (ODA) or revenue from projected global taxes. In this way the social policy conditions placed upon countries in receipt of such global funds can be managed and determined through peer review mechanisms of countries within the same region. The offer by the African Union to manage the increased flows of ODA to Africa is one such example. Such strengthened regional formations can also provide a career move for

Southern civil servants who might otherwise be lost to the World Bank or other Northern agencies.

In terms of *international economies of scale and risk pooling* a third main set of advantages to countries of a regionalist social policy strategy relates to economies of scale and risk pooling. On the first of these, in a context of pressing social needs and limited resources, there are benefits from developing economies of scale whenever possible. For instance, where not all countries can develop expensive high quality universities and research centres, there is a major argument for uniting forces across neighboring countries and agreeing to create regional training/research centers. Cross-border agreements on education and the mobility of educators, scholars and students can also foster regional identity.

Regional integration can also redress some of the limitations of national social policies and schemes. One of the reasons why agricultural insurance experiments have failed across the world is because of their small size, collapsing when a major catastrophe occurred (e.g. national drought, plant pest or cattle disease affecting the whole country); in these situations, the insurance fund was unable to cover for all losses. However, by pooling risks internationally, and by adequate reinsurance, schemes can work. During disasters of widespread proportion when a nation's finances are at a low ebb, other countries can share the burden (Ortiz, 2001). Apart from agricultural insurance, there is the more basic question of natural disasters. The precarious conditions under which poor populations live generate catastrophic human and economic losses when natural disasters occur (e.g. earthquakes, typhoons, floods, volcanic eruptions). Regional social policies offer the possibility of increased rapid response for disaster mitigation, management and preparedness (Deacon, Ortiz and Zelenev, 2007).

Many of these arguments have found expression in on-going debates at the level of global commissions. The report of the World Commission on the Social Dimension of Globalisation (2004) claimed that regional integration can contribute to a more equitable pattern of globalisation, but only if regional integration has a strong social dimension. According to the Commission, regional arrangements can achieve this by empowering people and countries to better manage global economic forces, by helping to build capabilities needed to take advantage of global opportunities, and by improving the conditions under which people connect to the global economy (WCSDG, 2004:71). The WCSDG refers to the regional governance level with respect to: (i) the need to build representative regional institutions and organize regional social dialogues, (ii) the importance of linking trade liberalization (at the global and regional level) to the respect for labour rights, (iii) the need to make investment rules more development-friendly, and (iv) the urgency to provide a more appropriate regulatory framework for migration.

In terms of *regional social dialogues* it argues that 'Representative bodies, such as regional parliaments, have an important role to play. We believe that regional integration should be advanced through social dialogue between representative organisations of workers and employers, and wider dialogue with other important social actors, on the basis of strong institutions for democratic and judicial accountability. The creation of tripartite or wider councils and forums at the regional level … provides an important institutional framework for such dialogue' (WCSDG, 2004:73).

In terms of *labour standards* as we noted earlier increasing openness to global competition has imposed costs on labour in industrial countries through downward pressure on wages, the erosion of social security systems, and the weakening of trade unions and labour standards. While the trade-labour linkage has been side-stepped at the multilateral level, labour standards are now increasingly incorporated into Regional Trade Agreements (RTAs) and bilateral FTAs, led by the United States and the EU [...].

In terms of *investment rules* regional collective action and rulemaking, as suggested by the Commission, could indeed reproduce a number of potential benefits of a multilateral investment regime (greater transparency and less incompatibilities leading to lower transaction costs, less rules, competition among capital-importing countries, …), while at the same time making progress on, for example, finding a new balance between domestic policy objectives and investment provisions and reaching more transparency and balance in dispute settlement. Collective renegotiation of bilateral investment treaties at the regional level might be an interesting option, although the economically and politically 'optimal size' of the regions remains to be established, as well as the legal bases for such collective action.

In terms of *the cross border movement of people*, migration patterns and issues (forced migration, remittances, etc.) may differ and evolve sensibly between regions. Regional specificities exist, related to the nature of migration in the different regions, as regards integration or return policies, or, more generally, immigration or emigration policies. Nonetheless, much more emphasis is now put, at this regional level, on the positive effects of cross-border movements of people such as migration compensating for the demographic deficit of industrialised aging countries. The current debate focuses on the means of reaping these benefits by managing migration orderly and efficiently. In its final report, acknowledging these changes in migration patterns and policies, the WCSDG recommends the development of a multilateral framework for 'orderly and managed' cross-border movements of people, a framework that could contribute to 'enhance global productivity' and 'eliminate exploitative practices' by 'complementing measures to achieve a more balanced strategy for global growth and full employment'. According to the World Commission, with a global framework based on more democratic rules and the respect of the human rights of migrants, the countries of origin and destination, as well as the migrants themselves, could maximize the benefits of migration and minimize the negative sides: this framework could 'provide uniform and transparent rules for cross-border movements of people' and 'balance the interests of both migrants themselves and of countries of origin and destination'. The WCSDG insisted further on the fact that 'the issues and problems associated with the movement of people across national borders cannot be addressed by single countries acting in isolation or on a unilateral basis'. Thus, this implies the development of effective cooperation arenas at the regional level (WCSDG, 2004: 94, 96-99).

Within the UN system too, such ideas about reinforcing the regional level in order to 'tame' globalisation are increasingly popular. In the July 2006 session of ECOSOC the UN Secretary-General declared that multi-stakeholder policy dialogues at the national and regional level have to be developed 'with the objective of building national and regional capacity to develop a multi-disciplinary approach to economic and social issues' (UNSG, 2006). This came on the back of on-going initiatives within other parts of the UN. In 2005 UNESCO organised a High-Level Symposium on the Social Policy Dimension of Regionalism in Montevideo in the context of the UNESCO International Social Sciences Policy Nexus Forum (Deacon, Yeates and Van Langenhove, 2006). The resulting Buenos Aires Declaration called upon 'the regional organisations such as MERCOSUR and the African Union, in association with social scientists and civil society, to further develop the social dimension of regional integration and [called] upon the UN to facilitate inter-regional dialogues'. Since then, arguments for strengthened regional dimensions of their social policies have continued to gather pace. The UN Department of Economic and Social Affairs commissioned a working paper arguing the case for regional social polices as a contribution to poverty alleviation (Deacon, Ortiz and Zelenev 2007), while the proposals of the High Level Panel on UN Reform calling for *'One-UN'* at national level call also for the regional UN Economic Commissions and the UN social agencies to rationalise their regional structures and better target their efforts on actually existing regional associations of countries (UN, 2006). There is some evidence that donors are taking up these ideas too. The *New Consensus on Comprehensive Social Policies for Development* (Wiman, Voipio and Ylönne, 2007) arising out of a meeting of donors paid significant attention to the case for regional as well as national and global social policies.

The content and mechanisms of regional social policy

In principle therefore, through intergovernmental agreements, regionalism would make possible the development of regional social policy mechanisms of cross-border redistribution, regulation and rights as well as facilitating a number of other cross border cooperation mechanisms. In this section we outline the form that such mechanisms could take. This discussion refers both to idealised forms as well as actually-existing ones.

- Regional social *redistribution* mechanisms
  These can take several forms ranging from regionally-financed funds to target particularly depressed localities or to tackle particularly significant health or food shortage issues or to stimulate cross-border cooperation. Capacity-building of weaker governments by stronger ones is another approach. If such mechanisms are in place then North-South transfers either funded by ODA or global taxes could be transmitted to specific localities via the regional structure.

- Regional social, health and labour *regulations*
  These can include standardised regulations to combat an intra-regional 'race to the bottom'. Such regulations are commonly thought of as relating to health and safety, labour and social protection, and agreements on the equal treatment of men and women, majority and minority (including indigenous) groups, but they could also extend to a range of other areas including food production and handling standards and utilities. Regional formations may also in principle be in a stronger position in relation to private suppliers to set, monitor and enforce cross-border rules regarding, for example, access rights to commercial services.

- Regional mechanisms that give citizens a voice to challenge their governments in terms of social *rights*
  Principles of social policy and levels of social provision could be articulated and used as benchmarks for countries to aspire to. In the long term the EU's European Court of Justice or the Council of Europe's Court of Human Rights could serve as useful models of mechanisms by which citizens can be empowered to challenge the perceived failures to fulfil such rights.

- Regional *intergovernmental co-operation*
  Governments within a region could cooperate in social policy in terms of regional health specialization, regional education cooperation, regional food and livelihood cooperation and regional recognition of social security entitlements.
  The possibilities for the sharing of specialist health services are numerous. Cross border agreements on education mobility can foster regional identity. Cross border labour mobility issues can be managed more effectively and with greater justice if there are social security mobility rights. Regional cooperation can also create an opportunity

to learn from good practices that have worked at national level through intergovernmental policy dialogue.

There are a range of different mechanisms and methods of regional social policy to bring about redistribution, regulation and rights and cross border cooperation and sharing including standard-setting, policy coordination, legislation and regional identity mobilisation. The UNDESA working paper – *Regional Social Policy* (Deacon, Ortiz and Zelenev 2007) focuses primarily on developing countries and listed some possible policies in different sectors of social policy. The following is based upon part of the recommendations of that working paper.

Employment and decent work

Creating decent employment is a result of employment-sensitive economic policies, combined with adequate labour market interventions at the national level. However, this can be fast-tracked with regional support. The European Union (EU) offers a good example of how harmonization of labour regulations under the EU *acquis communautaire* and EU regional funds can promote employment and decent work at the local level. For developing countries, the two critical priorities are to ensure that policy-makers understand the links between economic and social policies, and that regional funds are created to promote employment in poorer areas that otherwise could not be supported by national administrations. Among specific policies in this policy domain are: enhanced inter-ministerial cooperation (economic and social sectors) to ensure that economic policies are employment-generating; sharing of experiences and best practices in the areas of employment, sustainable livelihoods and labour standards; establish regional funds for programmes for employment generation and for promoting formalization of informal work (promoting small and medium enterprises, cooperatives, wage subsidies, public works, guaranteed job schemes, and special employment programmes for women, youth, and persons with disabilities); and skills development programmes (training and retraining of labour to enhance employability and productivity).

Health

The cross-border spread of diseases (e.g. HIV/AIDS, SARS, Tuberculosis, Malaria, Avian Flu, etc) must be prevented and collaborative efforts between governments strengthened. Extending coverage of health is a priority in most countries and international co-operation on the development of accessible and affordable quality health care can effectively support national health systems. Additionally, there are also benefits from economies of scale in the regional production of cheaper generic drugs. A good example can be found in South America's MERCOSUR harmonization of pharmaceutical legislation and regulations to facilitate economies of scale among Argentina, Brazil, Paraguay, Uruguay and Venezuela. Regional policies could include regional Early Warning Systems of epidemics coupled to the regional coordination of specialists for rapid deployment to affected areas; bolstering of the ability of border controls to monitor the movement of persons from and into affected areas; establishing effective procedures for disinfecting people, livestock and vehicles; facilitating regional access of citizens to specialized health care facilities through partnerships; coordination of regional procurement and production of pharmaceuticals and benefit from economies of scale; investigating the viability of mobile medical and health care units to ensure that remote rural communities have access to diagnosis and treatment; and coordinating approaches to global health funds.

Social protection

Social protection instruments, particularly social security systems, social pensions and social assistance, are priority instruments to expedite poverty reduction. If well designed, social protection instruments are highly redistributive and important to raise incomes and initiate a positive spiral of aggregate demand in domestic markets. Like employment, social protection is mostly a national issue; however, there are benefits from regional cooperation. An example can be found in the Andean Community (Bolivia, Colombia, Ecuador and Peru) decision to strengthen and harmonize their social security systems (2004) and create an Andean Social Humanitarian Fund and an Integral Plan for Social Development (2005), to unite efforts to fight poverty, exclusion and inequality. Potential regional programmes include: cross-border social protection programmes to address remote communities development needs (e.g. distant areas near borders, ethnic minorities, etc); regional funds to ensure transfers to vulnerable populations like children (child benefits), older and disabled persons in rural areas (social pensions) and development of cross-border cooperation policies in social security and social protection policies that included policies for low-skilled and casual economic migrants as well as the highly skilled mobile labourers, including portability of benefits.

Higher education and research

The erosion of public expenditures on higher education in many developing countries due to structural adjustment combined with the brain drain of the few highly trained experts into the aid industry has led to the reduction of research capacity in the field of social policy. Addressing lack of funding is an urgent priority. Given resource limitations, there are major advantages from a regional division of labour in research and education; not all countries need to develop expensive high-quality research, advantages are to be found in regional cooperation, creating regional centres with higher quality research addressing local topics. Potential regional programmes include: funds for regional academic fellowships to build research capacity in national and regional institutions; support for regional tertiary education, and academic networks.

Regional social policy: challenges and issues

The opportunities for, and practices of, developing a regional social policy are not without their difficulties and challenges. These are discussed under four headings: origins and orientations of regional formations; emergence of open and bilateral trading arrangements; financing; and long-term policy learning.

Elite origins and orientations of regional formations

There has been little popular demand for regionalist projects, and such formations have tended to originate in discussions and negotiations within restricted policy-making circles involving trade and finance Ministers and economists. This problem of extant regional formations originating as regional elite projects does not deny or curtail the possibilities for subsequent involvement by labour organisations, development agencies and wider civil society actors in regionalist political processes, or the fact that such organisations and agencies can use these processes to demand a stronger social dimension to national and regional policies. However, it has meant that these formations mostly exist primarily as trade (or political) agreements of various kinds; their purpose is neither primarily a social developmental one nor are they conceived of as being a social union (Yeates, 2005). Even in the EU, which has by world standards an advanced regional social policy and relatively extensive involvement by non-state actors in policy-making, the difficulties of forging a comprehensive regional social policy have been significant. Here, the absence of a vision for a regional social union in the founding articles and treaties has been apparent in the inhibited development of social integration processes (Threlfall, 2003). The conception of regional integration as an elite project means, moreover, that most regional formations exist purely as inter-governmental trade agreements or semi-institutionalised regional fora and consequently have limited or no supranational-level political authority or set of institutions that many argue is necessary for a coherent, binding and effective regional social policy (Yeates, 2005).

Competition from trans-continental open and bilateral trading arrangements

The rise of free trade agendas within US-led mega-regional formations, such as the attempted Free Trade Association of the Americas (FTAA) and Asia Pacific Economic Cooperation (APEC) is also a concern for those in favour of regional social policies. To what extent are relatively 'closed' regions that currently have, or which might develop, a social dimension cut across by relatively 'open' regions that exist essentially as global trading blocs which downplay these social equity and social policy dimensions? Mercosur provides one illustration of this issue. The question was whether its social dimension could have survived the creation of the mega-regionalist free trade project of the FTAA. While both Mercosur and the FTAA aimed to promote international trade, the model of economic integration underpinning these formations was quite different (Yeates, 2005). Thus, whereas Mercosur aims at the free movement of production factors, the FTAA was concerned with market access (goods, services and investment) and sought to internationalise the NAFTA model across the Americas (Vaz, cited in Yeates, 2005). [...] The FTAA's absence of a social agenda did not go unchallenged. Indeed, the FTAA process generated the mobilisation of social forces nationally and trans-nationally to oppose the FTAA [...]. The derailment of the FTAA in favour of a Latin American only trading bloc hinged on the ability of these forces to forge 'multilateralism from below'. Recent developments within Latin America [...] indicate the increased awareness of the limitations of pursuing free trade policies through such mega-regionalist mechanisms. Indeed, there has been a strategic resurgence of affiliation with existing regional groupings (Mercosur combining with the Andean Community) as a means through which to pursue regionalist internationalisation (including social policy) strategies.

Bilateral trade agreements generate similar pressures on regional policies. For example there is a concern that the separate trade deal between South Africa and the EU might undermine regional solidarity within SADC. The USA's Africa Opportunity Act encouraging bilateral deals between African countries and the USA may have such an effect too. Additionally, bilateral trade agreements benefit wealthy countries more than developing countries (UNDESA, 2005). The use of bilateral trade agreements to undermine regional agreements, and attempts to insert free trade clauses into them, also cuts across and potentially undermines attempts to develop social policy on a regional basis. [...]

Overall, the multiplicity of bilateral trade agreements and mega-regional associations cuts in a bewildering way across systematic attempts to develop a strong social dimension to regional formations – and can potentially undermine achievements made at regional level. In a major review of

Southern Regionalism Page (2000: 290) concluded that: 'So far … regions have moved more in the direction of extending their liberalization to the rest of the world than finding ways of discriminating more tightly'. At issue here is the overall coherence of the multi-level strategies that governments pursue, and the possible tensions arising from this multiplicity.

Financing

Financing is a major challenge to regional social policies. Developing countries are starved of capital, so regional policies should not displace necessary expenditures for national social development. Developing regional policies and programmes requires funding. Funding may originate at the regional level, if some regional countries are prepared to cover the costs of regional integration. This has been the case for Germany and other wealthier northern European countries, which accepted the role of supporting the lesser developed countries of the EU periphery in view of the common public interest. This is also the case of oil-rich Venezuela, supporting the development of less prosperous ALBA countries, and the Gulf States with their neighbour Arab countries. However, other regional groupings do not have the benefit of having one or more wealthy financier partners (Deacon, Ortiz and Zelenev, 2007).

The paper commissioned by UNDESA (ibid, 2008) outlines two main financing sources for regional social policies: international funds and intra-regional transfers. In what follows we highlight key points of that discussion. In terms of international funds, the official channel for international redistribution is ODA. Given the limited magnitude of ODA, aid has focused on national interventions, and regional policies have not been a priority. Generally bilateral donors have been reluctant to finance multi-country programmes given the lack of a single interlocutor that can be held accountable. This could be overcome by forming accountable implementing institutions, as they have been created in post-war Europe (to disburse Marshall Aid) and in Africa (NEPAD).

Since the mid-1990s more innovative international financing mechanisms have emerged, mostly a variety of public-private partnerships in the area of health. Such is the case of the Global Health Program of the Gates Foundation (started 1994), the Global TB Vaccine Foundation (1997) or the Drugs for Neglected Diseases Initiative (2003), among others. These institutions are a potential source of funds for selected cross-border social policies in specific areas. New international sources of development finance have been proposed (Atkinson, 2005), mainly taxing luxury activities or activities with negative social/environmental externalities. If operative, these could become sources of funding for global and regional social policies.

Intra-regional transfers are another source of finance for regional social policies. This requires, of course, the existence of at least one higher income country in the regional association, as well as willingness to pay for regional solidarity. Such is the case of the EU, ALBA and the League of Arab States (LAS). In Europe, intra-regional redistribution has emerged from a policy to develop the EU internal market. The EU set a range of policy instruments, known collectively as Structural Funds, to direct transfers from wealthy to poor regions, designed to assist lagging areas to build infrastructure, human capital, and jobs. Thus intra-European redistribution is a central element of the EU's policies. Regional solidarity appears also to be a component in Chavez's vision for the Latin American ALBA. Although ALBA lacks as yet any accountable democratic regional institutions, oil-rich Venezuela has been funding a number of social policies among ALBA member countries (literacy and health programmes, emergency relief). Gulf States have also redistributed wealth among members of the League of Arab States, funding mosques and educational services. The main issue for ALBA and LAS is sustainability. ALBA and LAS redistributive policies depend on the price of oil. Diversification of regional contributions and lesser dependency on a single resource is advised to ensure sustainability. Financing regional social policies will require adequate institutional arrangements and good-governance to attract either international or intra-regional funding. The degree of institutional complexity will change case to case; however, what is essential is that sound management practices and controls must be put in place to ensure prudent and efficient use of resources.

Long-term policy-making

Regional policies are based on the political will of governments to jointly commit to a common interest. Interstate cooperation on social policy is a voluntary accession to policies and codes that does not challenge the principle of sovereignty in a fundamental sense, but styles of leadership, entrepreneurial cultures, stereotypes, rivalries and mistrust, may hinder negotiations.

A great obstacle to regional social policies comes in the short-term goals of policy-makers. Democratic systems have many benefits, but one of the pitfalls is that administrations focus on short-term policies, that is, policies that provide results within the four or five years of mandate. Regional social policies require a long-term vision to which not all administrations are prepared to adhere. Leadership for longer term issues is not common. Anti-imperialism and 'affirmative regionalism' can play an important role, as in the case of the Venezuelan led ALBA, or in a rather more muted style in the EU. Ideologies such as pan-Arabism or pan-Africanism could consolidate regional social policies in these world regions (Deacon, Ortiz and Zelenev, 2007).

[...]

References

Atkinson, A.B. (2005) *New Sources of Development Finance*, Oxford, OUP.

Bello, W. (2004) *Deglobalization: Ideas for a New World Economy*, London: Zed.

Deacon, B. 2007. *Global Social Policy and Governance*, London: Sage

Deacon, B, Ortiz, I and Zelenev S. (2007) 'Regional Social Policy', *UN DESA Working Papers Number 37*, New York, UN DESA.

Deacon, B., Yeates, N. and Van Langenhove, L. (2006) *Social Dimensions of Regional Integration – A High Level Symposium: Conclusions*, UNU-CRIS Working Paper O-2006/13, Online. Avaulable http://www.cris.unu.edu/fileadmin/workingpapers/20060607105556.O-2006-13.pdf

Keet, D. and W. Bello (2004). *Linking Alternative Regionalisms for Equitable and Sustainable Development*. Amsterdam, Transnational Institute.

ODI (Overseas Development Institute) (2009) *G20 – A Development Agenda*, London. ODI.

Ortiz, I. (ed) (2001) *Social Protection in Asia and the Pacific*. ADB, Manila.

Page, S (2000) *Regionalism among Developing Countries*, Basingstoke, Macmillan-ODI.

Threlfall, M. (2003) 'European social integration: harmonization, convergence and single social areas', *Journal of European Social Policy*, 13(2): 121-139.

UN (2006) *Delivering as One: Report of the Secretary-General's High Level Panel*, New York: UN.

UNDESA (2005) *Report on the World Social Situation: The Inequality Predicament*. New York: UN Division for Social Policy and Development.

UNSG (2006) *Report of the Secretary General on the Themes of the 2006 ECOSOC Coordination Segment*, New York: UN.

Wiman, R., Voipio, T. and Ylönne, M. (2007) *Comprehensive Social Policies for Development in a Globalising World*, Helsinki, Ministry for Foreign Affairs. (Also at www.stakes.fi/social-policies-for-development)

WCSDG (World Commission on the Social Dimensions of Globalization) (2004) *A Fair Globalization: Creating Opportunities for All*. Geneva: International Labour Office – World Commission on the Social Dimension of Globalisation.

Yeates, N. (2005) *Globalisation and Social Policy in a Development Context: Regional Responses*, Social Policy and Development Programme Paper, Number 18, United Nations Research Institute for Social Development: Geneva.

Yeates, N. and Deacon, B. (2006) *Globalism, Regionalism and Social Policy: Framing the Debate*, United Nations University Centre for Comparative Regional Integration Studies (UNU-CRIS) Working Paper 0-2006/6, April 2006, Bruges, Belgium.

Chapter 5.9

A fair globalization: creating opportunities for all

World Commission on the Social Dimensions of Globalization 2004

Introduction

Our remit, the Social Dimension of Globalization, is a vast and complex one. As a Commission we were broadly representative of the diverse and contending actors and interests that exist in the real world. Co-chaired by two serving Heads of State, a woman and a man, from North and South, we came from countries in different parts of the world and at all stages of development. Our affiliations were equally diverse: government, politics, parliaments, business and multinational corporations, organized labour, academia and civil society.

Yet, through a spirit of common purpose, we arrived at the shared understandings that are before you. As a collective document it is quite different from alternative reports each one of us would have written individually. But our experience has demonstrated the value and power of dialogue as an instrument for change. Through listening patiently and respectfully to diverse views and interests we found common ground.

We were spurred on by the realization that action to build a fair and inclusive process of globalization was urgent. This could only happen in the future through forging agreements among a broad spectrum of actors on the course for action. We are convinced that our experience can and should be replicated on a larger and wider scale, expanding the space for dialogue aimed at building consensus for action.

A vision for change

Public debate on globalization is at an impasse. Opinion is frozen in the ideological certainties of entrenched positions and fragmented in a variety of special interests. The will for consensus is weak. Key international negotiations are deadlocked and international development commitments go largely unfulfilled.

The report [...] offers no miraculous or simple solutions, for there are none. But it is an attempt to help break the current impasse by focusing on the concerns and aspirations of people and on the ways to better harness the potential of globalization itself.

Ours is a critical but positive message for changing the current path of globalization. We believe the benefits of globalization can be extended to more people and better shared between and within countries, with many more voices having an influence on its course. The resources and the means are at hand. Our proposals are ambitious but feasible. We are certain that a better world is possible.

We seek a process of globalization with a strong social dimension based on universally shared values, and respect for human rights and individual dignity; one that is fair, inclusive, democratically governed and provides opportunities and tangible benefits for all countries and people.

To this end we call for:

- *A focus on people.* The cornerstone of a fairer globalization lies in meeting the demands of all people for: respect for their rights, cultural identity and autonomy; decent work; and the empowerment of the local communities they live in. Gender equality is essential.
- *A democratic and effective State.* The State must have the capability to manage integration into the global economy, and provide social and economic opportunity and security.
- *Sustainable development.* The quest for a fair globalization must be underpinned by the interdependent and mutually reinforcing pillars of economic development, social development and environmental protection at the local, national, regional and global levels.
- *Productive and equitable markets.* This requires sound institutions to promote opportunity and enterprise in a well-functioning market economy.
- *Fair rules.* The rules of the global economy must offer equitable opportunity and access for all countries and recognize the diversity in national capacities and developmental needs.
- *Globalization with solidarity.* There is a shared responsibility to assist countries and people excluded from or disadvantaged by globalization. Globalization must help to overcome inequality both within and between countries and contribute to the elimination of poverty.
- *Greater accountability to people.* Public and private actors at all levels with power to influence the outcomes of globalization must be democratically accountable for the policies they pursue and the actions they take. They must deliver on their commitments and use their power with respect for others.
- *Deeper partnerships.* Many actors are engaged in the realization of global social and economic goals – international organizations, governments

and parliaments, business, labour, civil society and many others. Dialogue and partnership among them is an essential democratic instrument to create a better world.

- *An effective United Nations.* A stronger and more efficient multilateral system is the key instrument to create a democratic, legitimate and coherent framework for globalization.

Globalization and its impact

Globalization has set in motion a process of far-reaching change that is affecting everyone. New technology, supported by more open policies, has created a world more interconnected than ever before. This spans not only growing interdependence in economic relations – trade, investment, finance and the organization of production globally – but also social and political interaction among organizations and individuals across the world.

The potential for good is immense. The growing interconnectivity among people across the world is nurturing the realization that we are all part of a global community. This nascent sense of interdependence, commitment to shared universal values, and solidarity among peoples across the world can be channelled to build enlightened and democratic global governance in the interests of all. The global market economy has demonstrated great productive capacity. Wisely managed, it can deliver unprecedented material progress, generate more productive and better jobs for all, and contribute significantly to reducing world poverty.

But we also see how far short we still are from realizing this potential. The current process of globalization is generating unbalanced outcomes, both between and within countries. Wealth is being created, but too many countries and people are not sharing in its benefits. They also have little or no voice in shaping the process. Seen through the eyes of the vast majority of women and men, globalization has not met their simple and legitimate aspirations for decent jobs and a better future for their children. Many of them live in the limbo of the informal economy without formal rights and in a swathe of poor countries that subsist precariously on the margins of the global economy. Even in economically successful countries some workers and communities have been adversely affected by globalization. Meanwhile the revolution in global communications heightens awareness of these disparities.

A strategy for change

These global imbalances are morally unacceptable and politically unsustainable. What is required to change this is not the realization of a Utopian blueprint in one swoop. Rather it is a series of coordinated changes across a broad front, ranging from reform of parts of the global economic system to strengthening governance at the local level. All this should and can be achieved in the context of open economies and open societies. Though interests diverge, we believe that there is increasing convergence of opinion throughout the world on the need for a fair and inclusive process of globalization.

We have formulated a wide-ranging set of recommendations to realize this. Given the necessary political will, immediate action is feasible on some trade and financial issues that have been the subject of protracted multilateral negotiations and discussion in policy circles. On these issues, the required course of action is clear but the urgent need for change has not yet dawned on some major players. Here continued advocacy and a stronger public opinion is essential to carry the proposals forward. Advocacy to prepare the ground for the consideration of new issues will also be important. But on these newer issues, such as the development of a multilateral framework for the cross-border movement of people or the accountability of international organizations, the prime lever for the decision to act is broad-based dialogue among State and non-State actors. Through this, consensus and resolve can be forged on what needs to be done, how, and by whom.

The governance of globalization

We judge that the problems we have identified are not due to globalization as such but to deficiencies in its governance. Global markets have grown rapidly without the parallel development of economic and social institutions necessary for their smooth and equitable functioning. At the same time, there is concern about the unfairness of key global rules on trade and finance and their asymmetric effects on rich and poor countries.

An additional concern is the failure of current international policies to respond adequately to the challenges posed by globalization. Market opening measures and financial and economic considerations predominate over social ones. Official Development Assistance (ODA) falls far short of the minimum amounts required even for achieving the Millennium Development Goals (MDGs) and tackling growing global problems. The multilateral system responsible for designing and implementing international policies is also under-performing. It lacks policy coherence as a whole and is not sufficiently democratic, transparent and accountable.

These rules and policies are the outcome of a system of global governance largely shaped by powerful countries and powerful players. There is a serious democratic deficit at the heart of the system. Most developing countries still have very limited influence in global negotiations on rules and in determining the policies of key financial and economic institutions. Similarly, workers and the poor have little or no voice in this governance process.

Beginning at home

There is thus a wide range of issues to be addressed at the global level. But this alone will not suffice. Global governance is not a lofty, disembodied sphere. It is merely the apex of a web of governance that stretches from the local level upwards. The behaviour of nation States as global actors is the essential determinant of the quality of global governance. Their degree of commitment to multilateralism, universal values and common goals, the extent of their sensitivity to the cross-border impact of their policies, and the weight they attach to global solidarity are all vital determinants of the quality of global governance. At the same time, how they manage their internal affairs influences the extent to which people will benefit from globalization and be protected from its negative effects. In this important sense the response to globalization can be said to begin at home. This reflects the simple but crucial fact that people live locally within nations.

We therefore anchor our analysis at the national level. We do not, of course, presume to make specific recommendations for all the greatly diverse countries of the world. Rather, we set out the broad goals and principles that can guide policy to deal more effectively with the social dimension of globalization, fully recognizing that their implementation must respond to the needs and specific conditions of each country. From this perspective it is clear that national governance needs to be improved in all countries, albeit more radically in some than in others. There is wide international agreement on the essentials which we must all urgently strive for:

- good political governance based on a democratic political system, respect for human rights, the rule of law and social equity.
- an effective State that ensures high and stable economic growth, provides public goods and social protection, raises the capabilities of people through universal access to education and other social services, and promotes gender equity.
- a vibrant civil society, empowered by freedom of association and expression, that reflects and voices the full diversity of views and interests. Organizations representing public interests, the poor and other disadvantaged groups are also essential for ensuring participatory and socially just governance.
- strong representative organizations of workers and employers are essential for fruitful social dialogue.

The highest priority must be given to policies to meet the central aspiration of women and men for decent work; to raise the productivity of the informal economy and to integrate it into the economic mainstream; and to enhance the competitiveness of enterprises and economies.

Policy must focus squarely on meeting peoples' needs where they live and work. It is thus essential to nurture local communities through the devolution of power and resources and through strengthening local economic capabilities, cultural identity, and respecting the rights of indigenous and tribal peoples.

Nation States should also strengthen regional and sub-regional cooperation as a major instrument for development and for a stronger voice in the governance of globalization. They should reinforce the social dimension of regional integration.

Reform at the global level

At the global level, we have more specific recommendations to make. Some key ones are highlighted below.

Global rules and policies on trade and finance must allow more space for policy autonomy in developing countries. This is essential for developing policies and institutional arrangements best suited to their level of development and specific circumstances. Existing rules that unduly restrict their policy options for accelerating agricultural growth and industrialization and for maintaining financial and economic stability need to be reviewed. New rules must also respect this requirement. The policies of international organizations and donor countries must also shift more decisively away from external conditionality to national ownership of policies. Affirmative action provisions in favour of countries that do not have the same capabilities as those who developed earlier need to be strengthened.

Fair rules for trade and capital flows need to be complemented by fair rules for the cross-border movement of people. International migratory pressures have increased and problems such as trafficking in people and the exploitation of migrant workers have intensified. Steps have to be taken to build a multilateral framework that provides uniform and transparent rules for the cross-border movement of people and balances the interests of both migrants themselves and of countries of origin and destination. All countries stand to benefit from an orderly and managed process of international migration that can enhance global productivity and eliminate exploitative practices.

Global production systems have proliferated, generating the need for new rules on Foreign Direct Investment (FDI) and on competition. A balanced and development-friendly multilateral framework for FDI, negotiated in a generally accepted forum, will benefit all countries by promoting increased direct investment flows while limiting the problems of incentive competition which reduce the benefits from these flows. Such a framework should balance private, workers' and public interests, as well as their rights and responsibilities. Cooperation on cross-border competition policy will make global markets more transparent and competitive.

Core labour standards as defined by the ILO provide a minimum set of global rules for labour in the global economy and respect for them should be strengthened in all countries. Stronger action is required to ensure respect for core labour standards in Export Processing Zones (EPZs) and, more generally, in global production systems. All relevant international institutions should assume their part in promoting these standards and ensure that no aspect of their policies and programmes impedes implementation of these rights.

The multilateral trading system should substantially reduce unfair barriers to market access for goods in which developing countries have comparative advantage, especially textiles and garments and agricultural products. In doing so, the interests of the Least Developed Countries (LDCs) should be safeguarded through special and differential treatment to nurture their export potential.

A minimum level of social protection for individuals and families needs to be accepted and undisputed as part of the socio-economic 'floor' of the global economy, including adjustment assistance to displaced workers. Donors and financial institutions should contribute to the strengthening of social protection systems in developing countries.

Greater market access is not a panacea. A more balanced strategy for sustainable global growth and full employment, including an equitable sharing among countries of the responsibility for maintaining high levels of effective demand in the global economy, is essential. Enhanced coordination of macroeconomic policies among countries to this end is a key requirement. A successful global growth strategy will ease economic tensions among countries and make market access for developing countries easier to achieve.

Decent Work for all should be made a global goal and be pursued through coherent policies within the multilateral system. This would respond to a major political demand in all countries and demonstrate the capacity of the multilateral system to find creative solutions to this critical problem.

The international financial system should be made more supportive of sustainable global growth. Cross-border financial flows have grown massively but the system is unstable, prone to crises and largely bypasses poor and capital scarce countries. Gains in the spheres of trade and FDI cannot be fully reaped unless the international financial system is reformed to achieve greater stability. In this context developing countries should be permitted to adopt a cautious and gradual approach to capital account liberalization and more socially sensitive sequencing of adjustment measures in response to crises.

A greater effort is required to mobilize more international resources to attain key global goals, particularly the MDGs. The 0.7 per cent target for

ODA must be met and new sources for funding over and above this target should be actively explored and developed.

The implementation of reforms in international economic and social policy will require worldwide political support, the commitment of key global actors, and the strengthening of global institutions. The UN multilateral system constitutes the core of global governance and is uniquely equipped to spearhead the process of reform. For it to cope with the current and emerging challenges of globalization it has to enhance its effectiveness and improve the quality of its governance, especially with respect to democratic representation and decision-making, accountability to people, and policy coherence.

We call on developed countries to reconsider their decision to maintain zero nominal growth in their mandated contributions to the UN system. It is essential that the international community agree to increase financial contributions to the multilateral system and reverse the trend towards raising voluntary contributions at the expense of mandatory ones.

Heads of State and Government should ensure that the policies pursued by their countries in international fora are coherent and focus on the well-being of people.

Parliamentary oversight of the multilateral system at the global level should be progressively expanded. We propose the creation of a Parliamentary Group concerned with the coherence and consistency between global economic, social and environmental policies, which should develop an integrated oversight of major international organizations.

A critical requirement for better global governance is that all organizations, including UN agencies, should become more accountable to the public at large for the policies they pursue. National parliaments should contribute to this process by regularly reviewing decisions taken by their countries' representatives to these organizations.

Developing countries should have increased representation in the decision-making bodies of the Bretton Woods Institutions, while the working methods in the World Trade Organization (WTO) should provide for their full and effective participation in its negotiations.

Greater voice should be given to non-State actors, especially representative organizations of the poor.

The contributions of business, organized labour, civil society organizations (CSOs), and of knowledge and advocacy networks to the social dimension of globalization should be strengthened.

Responsible media can play a central role in facilitating a movement towards a fairer and more inclusive globalization. Well-informed public opinion on issues raised in this Report is essential to underpin change. Policies everywhere therefore need to emphasize the importance of diversity in information and communication flows.

Mobilizing action for change

We believe that broad-based dialogue on our recommendations, especially on issues that are not currently being negotiated on the global agenda, is the essential first step in mobilizing action for change. It is of primary importance that such dialogue begins at the national level in order to construct the foundations of the necessary consensus and political will.

At the same time the multilateral system has to play a pivotal role in carrying forward reforms at the global level. We propose a new operational tool for upgrading the quality of policy coordination between international organizations on issues in which the implementation of their mandates intersect and their policies interact. Policy Coherence Initiatives should be launched by the relevant international organizations to develop more balanced policies for achieving a fair and inclusive globalization. The objective would be to progressively develop integrated policy proposals that appropriately balance economic, social, and environmental concerns on specific issues. The first initiative should address the question of global growth, investment, and employment creation and involve relevant UN bodies, the World Bank, the International Monetary Fund (IMF), the WTO, and the ILO. Priority areas for other such initiatives include gender equality and the empowerment of women; education; health; food security; and human settlements.

A series of multi-stakeholder Policy Development Dialogues should also be organized by relevant international organizations to further consider and develop key policy proposals – such as a multilateral framework for the cross-border movement of people, a development framework for FDI, the strengthening of social protection in the global economy, and new forms of accountability of international organizations.

A Globalization Policy Forum should be organized by the UN and its specialized agencies to review on a regular and systematic basis the social impact of globalization. Participating organizations could produce a periodic 'State of Globalization Report'.

Our proposals call for a wider and more democratic participation of people and countries in the making of policies that affect them. And they also require those with the capacity and power to decide – governments, parliaments, business, labour, civil society and international organizations – to assume their common responsibility to promote a free, equitable and productive global community.

Chapter 5.10

Migration in an interconnected world: new directions for action

Global Commission on International Migration 2005

Principles for Action and Recommendations

I. A world of work: Migrants in a globalizing labour market

Principle – Migrating out of choice: Migration and the global economy

Women, men and children should be able to realize their potential, meet their needs, exercise their human rights and fulfil their aspirations in their country of origin, and hence migrate out of choice, rather than necessity. Those women and men who migrate and enter the global labour market should be able to do so in a safe and authorized manner, and because they and their skills are valued and needed by the states and societies that receive them.

Recommendations

1 The number of people seeking to migrate from one country and continent to another will increase in the years to come, due to developmental and demographic disparities, as well as differences in the quality of governance. States and other stakeholders must take due account of this trend in the formulation of migration policies.

2 States and other stakeholders should pursue more realistic and flexible approaches to international migration, based on a recognition of the potential for migrant workers to fill specific gaps in the global labour market.

3 States and the private sector should consider the option of introducing carefully designed temporary migration programmes as a means of addressing the economic needs of both countries of origin and destination.

4 The GATS Mode 4 negotiations on the movement of service providers should be brought to a successful conclusion. Given the linkage

between international trade and international migration, greater efforts should be made to foster a dialogue between officials and experts dealing with the two issues.

5   Governments and employers should jointly review current barriers to the mobility of highly educated professionals, with a view to removing those which are unnecessarily hindering economic competitiveness.

6   Greater efforts should be made to create jobs and sustainable livelihoods in developing countries, so that the citizens of such states do not feel compelled to migrate. Developing countries and the industrialized states should pursue economic policies and implement existing commitments that enable this objective to be achieved.

II. Migration and development: Realizing the potential of human mobility

Principle – Reinforcing economic and developmental impact

The role that migrants play in promoting development and poverty reduction in countries of origin, as well as the contribution they make towards the prosperity of destination countries, should be recognized and reinforced. International migration should become an integral part of national, regional and global strategies for economic growth, in both the developing and developed world.

Recommendations

7   Cooperative relationships between labour-rich and labour-poor countries are required to promote human capital formation and the development of a global pool of professionals. Providing appropriate pay, working conditions and career prospects in order to retain key personnel must be an integral component of such strategies.

8   Remittances are private money and should not be appropriated by states. Governments and financial institutions should make it easier and cheaper to transfer remittances and thus encourage migrants to remit through formal transfer systems.

9   Measures to encourage the transfer and investment of remittances must be combined with macro-economic policies in countries of origin that are conducive to economic growth and competitiveness.

10   Diasporas should be encouraged to promote development by saving and investing in their countries of origin and participating in transnational knowledge networks.

11   States and international organizations should formulate policies and programmes that maximize the developmental impact of return and circular migration.

III. The challenge of irregular migration: State sovereignty and human security

Principle – Addressing irregular migration

States, exercising their sovereign right to determine who enters and remains on their territory, should fulfil their responsibility and obligation to protect the rights of migrants and to re-admit those citizens who wish or who are obliged to return to their country of origin. In stemming irregular migration, states should actively cooperate with one another, ensuring that their efforts do not jeopardize human rights, including the right of refugees to seek asylum. Governments should consult with employers, trade unions and civil society on this issue.

Recommendations

12   States and other stakeholders should engage in an objective debate about the negative consequences of irregular migration and its prevention.

13   Border control policies should form part of a long-term approach to the issue of irregular migration that addresses the socio-economic, governance and human rights deficits that prompt people to leave their own country. This approach must be based on interstate dialogue and cooperation.

14   States should address the conditions that promote irregular migration by providing additional opportunities for regular migration and by taking action against employers who engage migrants with irregular status.

15   States should resolve the situation of migrants with irregular status by means of return or regularization.

16   States must strengthen their efforts to combat the distinct criminal phenomena of migrant smuggling and human trafficking. In both cases, perpetrators must be prosecuted, the demand for exploitative services eradicated and appropriate protection and assistance provided to victims.

17   In their efforts to stem irregular migration, states must respect their existing obligations under international law towards the human rights

of migrants, the institution of asylum and the principles of refugee protection.

IV. Diversity and cohesion: Migrants in society

Principle – Strengthening social cohesion through integration

Migrants and citizens of destination countries should respect their legal obligations and benefit from a mutual process of adaptation and integration that accommodates cultural diversity and fosters social cohesion. The integration process should be actively supported by local and national authorities, employers and members of civil society, and should be based on a commitment to non-discrimination and gender equity. It should also be informed by an objective public, political and media discourse on international migration.

Recommendations

18 While recognizing the right of states to determine their own policies in relation to the situation of migrants in society, all migrants must be are able to exercise their fundamental human rights and benefit from minimum labour standards.

19 Authorized and long-term migrants should be fully integrated in society. The integration process should value social diversity, foster social cohesion and avert the marginalization of migrant communities.

20 Local and national authorities, employers and members of civil society should work in active partnership with migrants and their associations to promote the integration process. Migrants should be properly informed of their rights and obligations and encouraged to become active citizens in the country to which they have moved.

21 Particular attention should be given to the empowerment and protection of migrant women, as well as ensuring that they are actively involved in the formulation and implementation of integration policies and programmes. The rights, welfare and educational needs of migrant children should also be fully respected.

22 While temporary migrants and migrants with irregular status are not usually granted the right to integrate in the society where they are living, their rights should be fully respected and they should be protected against exploitation and abuse.

23   Those individuals and organizations that have an influence on public opinion must address the issue of international migration in an objective and responsible manner.

V. A principled approach: Laws, norms and human rights

Principle – Protecting the rights of migrants

The legal and normative framework affecting international migrants should be strengthened, implemented more effectively and applied in a non-discriminatory manner, so as to protect the human rights and labour standards that should be enjoyed by all migrant women and men. Respecting the provisions of this legal and normative framework, states and other stakeholders must address migration issues in a more consistent and coherent manner.

Recommendations

24   States must protect the rights of migrants by strengthening the normative human rights framework affecting international migrants and by ensuring that its provisions are applied in a non-discriminatory manner.

25   All states must ensure that the principle of state responsibility to protect those on their territory is put into practice, so as to reduce the pressures that induce people to migrate, protect migrants who are in transit and safeguard the human rights of those in destination countries.

26   Governments and employers must ensure that all migrants are able to benefit from decent work as defined by the ILO and are protected from exploitation and abuse. Special efforts must be made to safeguard the situation of migrant women domestic workers and migrant children.

27   The human rights component of the UN system should be used more effectively as a means of strengthening the legal and normative framework of international migration and ensuring the protection of migrant rights.

VI. Creating coherence: The governance of international migration

Principle – Enhancing governance: Coherence, capacity and cooperation

The governance of international migration should be enhanced by improved coherence and strengthened capacity at the national level; greater consultation and cooperation between states at the regional level, and more effective dialogue and cooperation among governments and between international organizations at the global level. Such efforts must be based on a better appreciation of the close linkages that exist between international migration and development and other key policy issues, including trade, aid, state security, human security and human rights.

Recommendations

28   All states should establish coherent national migration policies that are based on agreed objectives, take account of related policy issues and are consistent with international treaty law, including human rights law. Governance at the national level should be effectively coordinated among all concerned ministries and should also involve consultation with non-state actors.

29   The international community should support the efforts of states to formulate and implement national migration policies through the contribution of resources, appropriate expertise and training.

30   Bilateral agreements are a valuable means of addressing migration issues that affect two states. They must always respect the normative framework affecting international migrants and thereby safeguard migrant rights.

31   Additional efforts are required to ensure that regional consultative processes on migration have worldwide coverage, engage civil society and the private sector, and are not focused solely on migration control. Greater interaction between the different processes is essential given the global nature of migration.

32   The new willingness of a range of states, institutions and non-governmental stakeholders to take global initiatives on international migration is welcome. The UN General Assembly High-Level Dialogue provides an opportunity for greater interaction and coherence between these initiatives, and to ensure that their momentum is maintained. The ongoing UN reform process provides a window of opportunity

to realize this momentum through a revision of current institutional arrangements.

33 The Commission proposes to the UN Secretary-General the immediate establishment of a high-level inter-institutional group to define the functions and modalities of, and pave the way for, an Interagency Global Migration Facility. This Facility should ensure a more coherent and effective institutional response to the opportunities and challenges presented by international migration.

Chapter 5.11

Closing the gap

Global Commission on the Social Determinants of Health

The Commission's overarching recommendations

1 Improve daily living conditions

Improve the well-being of girls and women and the circumstances in which their children are born, put major emphasis on early child development and education for girls and boys, improve living and working conditions and create social protection policy supportive of all, and create conditions for a flourishing older life. Policies to achieve these goals will involve civil society, governments, and global institutions.

2 Tackle the inequitable distribution of power, money, and resources

In order to address health inequities, and inequitable conditions of daily living, it is necessary to address inequities – such as those between men and women – in the way society is organized. This requires a strong public sector that is committed, capable, and adequately financed. To achieve that requires more than strengthened government – it requires strengthened governance: legitimacy, space, and support for civil society, for an accountable private sector, and for people across society to agree public interests and reinvest in the value of collective action. In a globalized world, the need for governance dedicated to equity applies equally from the community level to global institutions.

3 Measure and understand the problem and assess the impact of action

Acknowledging that there is a problem, and ensuring that health inequity is measured – within countries and globally – is a vital platform for action. National governments and international organizations, supported by WHO, should set up national and global health equity surveillance systems for routine monitoring of health inequity and the social determinants of health and should evaluate the health equity impact of policy and action. Creating

501

the organizational space and capacity to act effectively on health inequity requires investment in training of policy-makers and health practitioners and public understanding of social determinants of health. It also requires a stronger focus on social determinants in public health research.

Three principles of action

1 Improve the conditions of daily life – the circumstances in which people are born, grow, live, work, and age.
2 Tackle the inequitable distribution of power, money, and resources – the structural drivers of those conditions of daily life – globally, nationally, and locally.
3 Measure the problem, evaluate action, expand the knowledge base, develop a workforce that is trained in the social determinants of health, and raise public awareness about the social determinants of health.

These three principles of action are embodied in the three overarching recommendations above.

[...]

Actors

Here, we describe those on whom effective action depends. The role of governments through public sector action is fundamental to health equity. But the role is not government's alone. Rather, it is through the democratic processes of civil society participation and public policy-making, supported at the regional and global levels, backed by the research on what works for health equity, and with the collaboration of private actors, that real action for health equity is possible.

Multilateral agencies

An overarching Commission recommendation is the need for intersectoral coherence – in policy-making and action – to enhance effective action on the social determinants of health and achieve improvements in health equity. Multilateral specialist and financing agencies can do much to strengthen their collective impact on the social determinants of health and health equity, including:

• *Coherence in global monitoring and action:* Adopt health equity as a fundamental shared goal, and use a common global framework of indicators to monitor development progress; and collaborate in multi-agency thematic working groups for coherent social determinants of health action.

- *Coherent and accountable financing:* Ensure that increases in aid and debt relief support coherent social determinants of health policy-making and action among recipient governments, using health equity and social determinants of health performance indicators as core conditions of recipient accountability.
- *Improved participation of UN Member States in global governance:* Support equitable participation of Member States and other stakeholders in global policy-making fora.

WHO

WHO is the mandated leader in global health. It is time to enhance WHO's leadership role through the agenda for action on the social determinants of health and global health equity. This involves a range of actions, including:

- *Policy coherence globally and nationally:* Adopt a stewardship role supporting social determinants of health capacity-building and policy coherence across partner agencies in the multilateral system; strengthen technical capacity globally and among Member States for representation of public health in all major multilateral fora; and support Member States in developing mechanisms for coherent policy and intersectoral action for social determinants of health.
- *Measurement and evaluation:* Support goal-setting on health equity and monitoring progress on health equity between and within countries as a core developmental objective; support the establishment of national health equity surveillance systems in Member States, and build necessary technical capacities in countries; support Member States in development and use of health equity impact assessment tools and other health equity-related tools such as a national equity gauge; and convene a regular global meeting as part of a periodic review of the global situation.
- *Enhancing WHO capacity:* Build internal social determinants of health capacity across the WHO, from headquarters, through the Regional Offices, to Country Programmes.

National and local government

Underpinning action on the social determinants of health and health equity is an empowered public sector, based on principles of justice, participation, and intersectoral collaboration. This will require strengthening of the core functions of government and public institutions, nationally and sub-nationally, particularly in relation to policy coherence, participatory governance, planning, regulation development and enforcement, and standard-setting. It also depends on strong leadership and stewardship from the ministry of health, supported by WHO. Government actions include:

- *Policy coherence across government:* Place responsibility for action on health and health equity at the highest level of government, and ensure its coherent consideration across all ministerial and departmental policy-making. Ministers of health can help bring about global change – they will be pivotal in helping to create buy-in by the head of state and from other ministries.
- *Strengthening action for equity:* Commit to progressive building of universal health-care services; establish a central gender unit to promote gender equity across government policy-making; improve rural livelihoods, infrastructure investment, and services; upgrade slums and strengthen locally participatory health urban planning; invest in full employment and decent labour policy and programmes; invest in early childhood development; build towards universal provision in vital social determinants of health services and programmes regardless of ability to pay, supported by a universal programme of social protection; and establish a national framework for regulatory control over health-damaging commodities.
- *Finance:* Streamline incoming international finance (aid, debt relief) through a social determinants of health action framework, with transparent accountability; strengthen revenue through improved progressive domestic taxation; and collaborate with other Member States in the development of regional and/or global proposals for new sources of international public finance.
- *Measurement, evaluation, and training:* Build towards universal birth registration; set cross-government performance indicators for health equity through the establishment of a national health equity surveillance system; build capacity to use health equity impact assessment as a standard protocol in all major policy-making; ensure training of practitioners and policy-makers on the social determinants of health; and raise public awareness of the social determinants of health.

Civil society

Being included in the society in which one lives is vital to the material, psychosocial, and political aspects of empowerment that underpin social well-being and equitable health. As community members, grassroots advocates, service and programme providers, and performance monitors, civil society actors from the global to the local level constitute a vital bridge between policies and plans and the reality of change and improvement in the lives of all. Helping to organize and promote diverse voices across different communities, civil society can be a powerful champion of health equity. Many of the actions listed above will be, at least in part, the result of pressure and encouragement from civil society; many of the milestones towards health equity in a generation will be marked – achieved or missed – by the attentive observation of civil society actors. Civil society can play an important role in actions on the social determinants of health through:

- *Participation in policy, planning, programmes, and evaluation:* Participate in social determinants of health policy-making, planning, programme delivery, and evaluation from the global level, through national intersectoral fora, to the local level of needs assessments, service delivery, and support; and monitor service quality, equity, and impact.
- *Monitoring performance:* Monitor, and report and campaign on, specific social determinants of health, such as upgrading of and services in slums, formal and non-formal employment conditions, child labour, indigenous rights, gender equity, health and education services, corporate activities, trade agreements, and environmental protection.

Private sector

The private sector has a profound impact on health and wellbeing. Where the Commission reasserts the vital role of public sector leadership in acting for health equity, this does not imply a relegation of the importance of private sector activities. It does, though, imply the need for recognition of potentially adverse impacts, and the need for responsibility in regulation with regard to those impacts. Alongside controlling undesirable effects on health and health equity, the vitality of the private sector has much to offer that could enhance health and wellbeing. Actions include:

- *Strengthening accountability:* Recognize and respond accountably to international agreements, standards, and codes of employment practice; ensure employment and working conditions are fair for men and women; reduce and eradicate child labour, and ensure compliance with occupational health and safety standards; support educational and vocational training opportunities as part of employment conditions, with special emphasis on opportunities for women; and ensure private sector activities and services (such as production and patenting of life-saving medicines, provision of health insurance schemes) contribute to and do not undermine health equity.
- *Investing in research:* Commit to research and development in treatment for neglected diseases and diseases of poverty, and share knowledge in areas (such as pharmaceuticals patents) with life-saving potential.

Research institutions

Knowledge – of what the health situation is, globally, regionally, nationally, and locally; of what can be done about that situation; and of what works effectively to alter health inequity through the social determinants of health – is at the heart of the Commission and underpins all its recommendations. Research is needed. But more than simply academic exercises, research is needed to generate new understanding and to disseminate that understanding in practical accessible ways to all the partners listed above. Research on and knowledge of the social determinants of health and ways to act for health equity will rely on continuing commitments among academics and practitioners, but it will rely on new methodologies too – recognizing and utilizing a range of types of evidence, recognizing gender bias in research processes, and recognizing the added value of globally expanded Knowledge Networks and communities. Actions in this field of actors include:

• *Generating and disseminating social determinants of health knowledge:* Ensure research funding is allocated to social determinants of health work; support the global health observatory and multilateral, national, and local cross-sectoral working through development and testing of social determinants of health indicators and intervention impact evaluation; establish and expand virtual networks and clearing houses organized on the principles of open access, managed to enhance accessibility from sites in all high-, middle-, and low-income settings; contribute to reversal of the brain drain from low- and middle-income countries; and address and remove gender biases in research teams, proposals, designs, practices, and reports.

Index